How Milton Works

STANLEY FISH

How

Milton

Works

The Belknap Press of Harvard University Press

CAMBRIDGE, MASSACHUSETTS, AND LONDON, ENGLAND / 2001

Library of Congress Cataloging-in-Publication Data

Fish, Stanley Eugene.

How Milton works / Stanley Fish.

p. cm.

Includes bibliographical references and index.

ISBN 0-674-00465-5 (alk. paper)

1. Milton, John, 1608–1674—Criticism and interpretation.

I. Title.

PR3588 .F57 2001

821'.4—dc21   00-052977

To the memory of

Clyde de Loach Ryals and David Yanis

"Henceforth thou art the Genius of the shore."

—*Lycidas*

ACKNOWLEDGMENTS

I began writing this book in 1973 as I was teaching a Milton seminar at the University of Southern California. The first analysis I worked out was of "At a Solemn Music," and everything followed from that and continues to do so. It may seem strange to acknowledge that one's thoughts have not changed much in more than a quarter-century, but since one of my theses is that Milton himself changed very little, except to offer slight variations on a few obsessions that were his from the very beginning, I am comfortable with the notion that I keep discovering the same patterns and meanings over and over again.

Like all critics, I have more debts than I can record, but a principal one is surely to my students at the University of Southern California, Johns Hopkins, Duke, and the School of Criticism and Theory, with which I have had a strong association for more than twenty years. I owe a debt of a different but equally important kind to those who have helped with the preparation of the manuscript: Maria Ascher, Sara Connell, Ben Saunders, Laura Sell, David Urban, Lindsay Waters, and Tracy Wise. And finally I am grateful to the National Humanities Center for giving me the space and leisure to write the introductory chapter in the spring of 1998.

CONTENTS

How Milton Works

Introduction

In a famous passage from *Beyond the Pleasure Principle,* Freud invites us to "suppose . . . that all the organic instincts are conservative, are acquired historically and tend toward the restoration of an earlier state of things."[1] As Freud soon makes clear, the historical acquisition of organic movement is not (at least in the view he is now entertaining) a good thing. Rather, it is the product of a disturbance from the outside of an original condition of rest and stasis: "the phenomena of organic development must be attributed to external . . . and diverting influences." What these influences divert *from,* Freud goes on to say, is an "elementary" or "beginning" point, where "elementary" is to be understood in its root sense of a fundamental constituent part not reducible to anything else, and "beginning" is to be understood not as the first stage in a journey toward something better or more complete, but as a first stage so complete that nothing either need or should succeed it. "The elementary living entity would from its very beginning have had no wish to change." And, indeed, if it remained always what it originally was, every moment (a spatial not a temporal concept) would be a repetition of every other: "it [the elementary living entity] would do no more than constantly repeat the same course of life." Moreover, says Freud (and this is the heart of this speculative paragraph), this remains the goal of those wayward energies that have acquired a historical (i.e., temporal) existence: despite the appearance of forward direction, what they really seek to do is go back. It may seem as if they are "forces tending towards change and progress"; in fact "they are merely seeking to reach an ancient goal." Not a new goal "which had never been attained," but an "*old* state of things, an initial state from which the living entity has . . . departed and to which it is striving to return by the circuitous paths along which its development leads." "Development" might be better put as "de-development"; for what the striving aspires to is an end to striving, an end to the accidental variations that mark its regrettable busyness, an end to the departure from a still center that remains the only true source of life. The organic entity, in short, wishes to undo its separateness, to cease its movement, to cease to be; and once we understand this, Freud concludes, "we shall be compelled to say that '*the aim of all life is death.*'"

Although Freud certainly didn't intend it as such, this is, I believe, a perfect description of Milton's thought and work. All we need do is substitute for Freud's organicist vocabulary the vocabulary of theology, and for his materialist story the story of creation, sin, redemption, and reunion. In the beginning (and before the beginning) was God and the creation by God of creatures at one with Him and dedicated (these are their only actions) to praising him and doing his will. Some of those creatures, however, have wills of their own, given by that same God, and one of the things those wills are free to do is to depart from him, or at least think to depart from him ("impiously they thought / Thee

2

to diminish, and from thee withdraw").[2] One such endowed-with-free-will creature decides to do just that, "breaks union" (*PL*, V, 612), and with his action inaugurates this "mortal world," a world of risk, design, ambition, projects, purposes, successes, failures, beginnings, middles, and ends. This entire landscape, with its ups and downs, highs and lows, opportunities and obstacles—the landscape, in short, of history—is the equivalent of Freud's "circuitous paths along which [the living entity's] development leads."

At this point, however, we must leave the analogy with Freud behind, because for Milton the issues at stake are theological ones and the circuitous paths are the vehicles either of redemption or damnation. Where a path leads to depends on whether those who are on it believe that they are striking out in new and adventurous directions (going boldly where no man has gone before) or whether, like Dorothy in *The Wizard of Oz*, they are trying to get back home—that is, to a place where their strivings are unnecessary because the goals toward which they move (completeness, satisfaction without surfeit, the height of happiness) are achieved in the perfect dependence of union with the center of all being. Those who set out in the spirit of independence and adventure ("Let us . . . / . . . seek / Our own good from ourselves" [*PL*, II, 249, 252–253]) only assure that they will forever be displaced wanderers, consumed in "eternal restless change."[3] Those who seek to find rest in service to the deity ("Bright-harness'd Angels sit in order serviceable")[4] act independently in the hope that they may one day cease to do so because their labors and their voices will have been reabsorbed into the rhythms and harmony of eternity:

> O may we soon again renew that Song,
> And keep in tune with Heav'n, till God ere long
> To his celestial consort us unite,
> To live with him, and sing in endless morn of light.[5]

It is in this sense that the aim of life, rightly lived, is death; what dies in the vision of these lines (and in similar visions in *Paradise Lost* and *Lycidas*) is the self with a separate existence, the self born (as Satan is born at line 666, book V, of *Paradise Lost*) at the moment of disobedience and movement *away;* what lives is the self glorified by subordination to the highest, the self unconcerned with the figure it cuts in the world, the self that, like Abdiel, "gladly" mixes (*PL, VI,* 21) and has no desire whatsoever to stand out.

Two questions present themselves immediately. How do you know whether or not you are such a non-self-regarding self, a self whose exertions only appear to be aimed at measurable effects in the world but are really aimed at getting back in tune with heaven? And how do you know whether others are as you are (if, that is, you really are what you hope yourself to be)? The answer to both questions is that you cannot know, and the answer follows from the event (the fact that there ever was one is the trouble) that brought "circuitous paths" into the world in the first place. If the act of disobedience is a breaking away from the center, one result of disobedience is that the center is no longer easily identifiable, for the link between it and the disobeying actor is precisely what has been removed by what he or she has done. In the prelapsarian condition—in Freud's terms the condition before historical development—a link with the center was provided physically and symbolically by the interdicted tree: refrain from eating from it and the link is maintained; eat of it and the link is broken. The moral life is thus concentrated in this one choice, and other choices, while they may be more or less advisable, are not fatal. This clarity (a clarity that can, however, be obscured and missed by the same free will whose arena of trial it presents) stands in marked (or, rather, unmarked) contrast to the postlapsarian condition, which is burdened by two related difficulties: the true path is no longer so conveniently illuminated by a single focused context, and the vision of those who would rediscover it is irremediably darkened, so that a person's conviction that he is on it and that others (his enemies?) are not can never be supported by independent evidence and can always become a matter of doubt. When he married Dalila, Milton's Samson was sure that he was acting in accordance with God's will; when the marriage turns out badly, he begins to suspect (what his father had said in the first place) that he had confused God's will with his own desires. The young Jesus, according to his own self-report in *Paradise Regained*, contemplated all sorts of heroic political and social actions before realizing that they were vainglorious and resolving to work in quieter, more internal ways. The poet of the *Nativity Ode* confuses service with personal honor when he begins to write ("Have thou the honor first, thy Lord to greet" [26]), but ends by labeling his song "tedious" (belated) in a way that brings him closer to the bright harnessed angels who sit in order serviceable.

In each of these instances, interior motives, which because they are interior are not available to inspection, give a moral or immoral coloring to an action, and the actor, as well as those who observe him, is left to make his way without knowing for certain that it is the right one and not its "false resemblance."[6] Notice that the uncertainty attaches not to the identification of the imperative—do God's will—but to the identification of the stance or course of action that is its local fulfillment. Milton criticism sometimes offers us the choice between an absolutist poet with a focused vision and a single overriding message and a more tentative, provisional poet alert to the ambiguities and dilemmas of the moral life. The truth is that Milton is both, and is so without either contradiction or tension. He never wavers in his conviction that obedience to God is the prime and trumping value in every situation. But because in his antinomian theology the roadway of obedience is an internal one not available to external confirmation or disconfirmation, the taking of any path is fraught with the danger that it may be the path of self-aggrandizement rather than the path of faith. In the midst of resolving to love the Lord thy God with all thy soul and with all thy might, you could end up embracing and enacting a form of the self-love you think to have renounced. By freeing you from external constraints, the doctrine of Christian liberty (see *Christian Doctrine*, I, chapter 27) delivers you to a freedom whose exercise puts you on a high wire without a safety net.

This is as true of Milton as it is of everyone. Expert at portraying those moments when agents mistake a base gesture for a noble one (as when Adam makes Eve the vehicle of his idolatry in the name of the "Bond of Nature" [*PL*, IX, 956]), he may himself be exhibiting the same failing—a possibility he (inadvertently?) acknowledges when he more than once raises, and then loudly rejects, the suggestion that he writes in order to satisfy personal ambitions. It cannot be an accident that temptations of glory and fame are his constant theme or that he spends so much time giving all the credit to his muse, making great claims only in *her* name, or that again and again he identifies as the most subtle error (even the archangel Michael commits it) the error of thinking that one can resolve things, put them right with a single stroke, be it the stroke of a sword or the stroke of a pen. The aggressive assertion of humility ("I conceav'd my selfe to be now not as mine own person, but as a member incorporate into that truth wherof I was perswaded"), the insistence (in *An Apology against a Pamphlet*) that he speaks of himself only for the sake of his religious cause lest it be besmirched by association, the announcement in *The Reason of Church Government* that he is only (who would not want to be such an "only"?) God's mouthpiece—by their very excessiveness these declarations speak to a fear that what Milton (quite literally) demonizes and pushes away may be what he desires: that is, to be first, preeminent, outstanding, independent, new, separate. He wants at once to celebrate humility and to be celebrated as the celebrator of humility. He is the poet of submission and corporate identity ("Mee hung'ring . . . to do my Father's will" [PR, II, 259]) and he is also the poet who would write something the world will not willingly let die. He calls men to the glorious antiglory of self-abnegation, of individual silence as a member of a universal chorus, and he resists his own call with verse that demands attention to itself and its artisan, and a voice so distinctive that no one could mistake it and everyone tries (and fails) to imitate it. He longs to be absorbed by a power greater than he, and he experiences absorption as a threat (see the invocation to *Paradise Lost,* book VII) to his very being.

If this is the structure of his consciousness (as I think it is), it is also the structure of his prose and poetry. As I describe them, Milton's tracts and poems are always engaged in an act of containment. Centrifugal forces—named, variously, Satan, Comus, Chaos, Chance, the Prelates, the Confuter, Belial, Mammon, Moloch, Beelzebub, Sin, Death, Dalila, Adam, Eve, and, sometimes, Milton—are struggling to get out, to set up their own shop, to nominate their own values, to establish their own empire, to write their own literature, to draft their own laws, to go their own way, to have their own circuitous paths; and always they are reined in, as an omniscient and pervasive power either routs them (as in book VI of *Paradise Lost*), or expels them to a place he has prepared (and therefore a place that is his and not a world elsewhere), or reveals their plans to be a subset of his, or turns their designs against them ("Who seeks / To lessen thee, against his purpose serves / To manifest the more thy might" [PL, VII, 613–615]), or works out a path of redemption they negotiate only by his permission and guidance ("Yet not of will in him, but grace in me" [III, 174]). "Who can impair thee, mighty King, or bound / Thy Empire?" (VII, 608–609), ask the loyal angels, and the answer to the rhetorical question is obvious: no one, nothing can impair God in either of the two senses of "impair"—take something away from him, make him less, or make a pair with him, a rival power and therefore a rival deity.

Much of what goes on in the prose and poetry is the story of the many who try, by building tall structures, or inventing gunpowder, or setting up elaborate rituals, or proclaiming themselves God's viceroy, or assembling a rout of monsters, or seducing angels, or seducing men and women, or fashioning vast philosophical systems, or engaging in virtuoso exercises of rationalization, or writing majestic verse, or composing enchanting music. It is the energy of these always doomed attempts to match or overgo or evade God that fills up the space of Milton's work. Typically he gives these attempts full reign, allowing their elaboration to capture the eye and ear, before a reinvocation of the Truth they must contrive to forget or miss—that God is God and no one or nothing else is—brings all the "magic structures" that have been "rear'd so high" (*Comus, 798*) tumbling down. A nicely illustrative moment occurs in book X of *Paradise Lost*. Called to account for his disobedience, Adam spends twenty lines explaining that he would like to take the entire responsibility for what happened, but knows (a) that he could not bear the "insupportable" (134) punishment, and (b) that God would see through him anyway, and, besides, it was God, wasn't it, who gave Eve to him, and made her so attractive that (a) he could not suspect her of an ill deed, and (b) her perfection, again God-given, seemed to justify it, so, after all, (c) what could I do, right? To this mixture of historical analysis, moral casuistry, self-extenuation, and accusation of deity, the Son replies with devastating brevity, "Was shee thy God, that her thou didst obey / Before his voice?" (145–146). The Son does not bother to reply point by point to Adam's disquisition because in the light of the truth he recalls him to (God, not she, is God), his points are not only wrong but unreal. That is, if the issue is obedience or disobedience to God, the virtues, attractions, capacities, and origin of the person or thing in whose name disobedience is contemplated are irrelevant; although Eve and Satan are certainly different creatures with whom one might and should have different relationships (of trust, affection, regard), as sources for reasons to disobey they are perfectly equivalent. Disobedience to God is not wrong when the countervailing value is base (sell me your soul and I'll give you riches) and kind of okay when the countervailing value is a higher one (she's my wife, and I love her, and I have to be there for her); disobedience to God is just plain wrong, and any value that seems to urge it is, at least in this moment of choice, base.

You may have noticed that my gloss on "Was shee thy God?" is almost as long and convoluted as the speech of Adam's that provoked it. It is so because I was aware how easy it is, amid the panorama of goods, values, and meanings thrown up by the world, simply to lose sight of the master good or highest value or overriding meaning in relation to which all the others enjoy their legitimate being. While "Was shee thy God?" is definitive, it does not settle everything for everyone; there will still be some (Milton critics among them) who will say "Yes, but" and immediately reinstate the reasons (she's his wife, he has a duty to her, etc.) the Son has just exploded—some, that is, who will respond to the spirit of Comus' "This is mere moral babble" (807) or share Satan's exasperation when he asks Jesus, "What dost thou in this World?" (PR, IV, 372) or wonder with the speaker in Lycidas why anyone should continue to meditate the thankless muse. Food, wine, women, family, country, glory, fame, great literature, civil conversation, social justice—these are the things one should appreciate and enhance; and must we devalue them and set them aside for an abstraction?

This question (or some version of it) impels an important strain in Milton criticism; as old as Blake and as new as the New Historicism and Cultural Materialism, it points to realities in the world, in our world, and refuses to grant either power or legitimacy to what seems to be the mere "brute assertion" (the phrase is Leavis' in an essay now sixty-five years old) of an omniscient God whose will must be obeyed. The force of this line of argument (which, like Antaeus, is thrown down only to rise again re-invigorated) is augmented by its sheer bulk in relation to the argument it dismisses. One can go on forever about the pleasures and complexities of domestic, social, political, military, aesthetic, and intellectual life, but there is little to say for and about the perspective of obedience and worship except to issue one-line reminders like "Was shee thy God?" or "they themselves ordain'd thir fall" (*PL*, III, 128) or "Think'st thou such force in Bread?" (*PR*, I, 347). Moreover, not only is there little to say; there is nothing you can cite to support the little that you do say, no evidentiary procedure or authoritative document or revered wise-man. This is not a defect in the perspective, but a reassertion of it: if it looked for confirming support to someone or some text or some system of thought, that one or text or system would be in a position of precedence to it, would be the equivalent of God. If God is God, and not merely the name seized by some politically ambitious agent (this is how he is thought of always by the Satanic host), then there is nothing much to be said about him, if only because he cannot be the object of a consciousness he enables.

What this means is that affirming God is not something you do on the basis of evidence; it is something you do against the evidence provided by forms of life considered apart from his creative and sustaining power, forms of life that appear real and compelling in their attraction but that are finally (and always) unreal and therefore without any claims on us at all. For the agent who performs the act of faith called for in every one of Milton's poems, that evidence will simply fade away (like the vaunted power of the pagan gods in the *Nativity Ode* and the spectral shapes that threaten the Lady in *Comus*), but it will still have weight and seem very substantial to those who refuse the affirmation or see no reason to make it. In fact, there is no reason— no external reason, that is—to make it, and the enormous number of reasons on the other side (or other sides; the plurality of values is the chief assertion of those who would go their own way) assures that at almost any moment in a Milton poem, except for the moments when paradigmatic figures make either mysterious (you could never understand the sage and serious doctrine of virginity) or starkly authoritative ("Was shee thy God?") statements, nearly everything in the foreground, everything one might, in the ordinary sense, see, points away from the perspective to which the poet would bring us. What I have called the centrifugal forces are in constant motion and vie for our attention, yet the official morality of the poem or tract periodically asks us to affirm against them. That is why, as I have already said, the poems and much of the prose are engaged in an act of containment, in the forcible undoing and dispelling of energies (of thought, action, language) that are protean in their resourcefulness even though they are finally illusory and without substance.

Or, to be more precise (and the qualification is an important one), are without substance as independent entities that have independent value. Milton is not a poet of rejection, although it is easy to misunderstand his insistence on the priority and sustaining power of an originary power that cannot be identified with or captured by any of its material creations as an assertion that materiality and its pleasures are to be shunned in favor of some abstract colorless world of neoplatonic essences. (And I must acknowledge that at times both Milton's pronouncements and my account of them encourage such a misunderstanding.) But in fact Milton asks us not to shun the world of mortal experience but to appreciate it for the right (Augustinian) reason—for the reason that it is, in all its variety, a testimony to the goodness of its cre-

11

ator. If this reason is the content of your apprehension and appreciation, then delight in the created world is not only allowable but is, as Uriel tells the disguised Satan, an obligation:

> thy desire which tends to know
> The works of God, thereby to glorify
> The great Work-Master, leads to no excess
> That reaches blame, but rather merits praise
> The more it seems excess. (PL, III, 694–698)

Satan himself exhibits the alternate and wrong reasoning when he sits like a cormorant in the Tree of Life so that he might have a better view of the Paradise he is about to pollute:

> nor on the virtue thought
> Of that life-giving Plant, but only us'd
> For prospect, what well us'd had been the pledge
> Of immortality. (IV, 198–201)

The Lady reads the same lesson to Comus when she responds to his celebration of the consumption of nature's bounties by saying that only if one enjoys those bounties in the context of a praise "due paid" (776) to the bestower does one avoid the sins of blasphemy and idolatry. And in *Paradise Regained,* Jesus spends four books patiently refusing to ally himself with human goods and projects so long as they are offered to him either as substitutes for an alliance with God or as the *necessary* vehicles of achieving that alliance—although as the local habitation and expression of that alliance, those same goods can be welcomed and employed.

If this is Milton's view of the matter (as I certainly believe it to be), it is wrong to regard his poetry as the site of conflicting loyalties and impulses or as the reflection of a tension in him between the absolute demands of a monist theology and the multiform appeal of a variegated nature. Indeed the great error, at once anatomized in his work and made available as a possibility of performance for those who read it, is the error of thinking that such a conflict or tension could ultimately exist—of thinking, for example, that you might be asked to choose between God and your wife or between obedience and freedom or between truth and pleasure or between the clarity of moral thought and the experience of intense emotion. Such choices would be possible—would be real—only if the alternatives proffered were independent of one another and thus could be cleanly opposed: on this side God, on that Eve; on this side obedience to God, on that a life of freedom; on this side the truth about the world, on that the pleasures it affords. But it is precisely Milton's thesis that the persons, things, and values that form one pole of this opposition are without coherence and shape if severed from that to which they are the supposed alternatives. An Eve cut off from God's informing spirit is no longer the last best gift Adam cherishes. A freedom without a center in relation to which its exercise is meaningful is merely directionless movement. What is true about the world is that God created it, and to enjoy its fruits as if they created or sustained themselves is to join Satan in chewing "bitter Ashes" (*PL*, X, 566). A joy taken in ephemeral things—in things that will pass away—is a "short joy" (*PL*, XI, 628), sure to be followed both by satiety and ever-renewed hunger (an expense of spirit in a waste of shame). Milton's God demands no such choices and requires no such abstinences and refrainings; rather, he demands and requires that you engage with his created fertility *as his*, that you say yes to persons, experiences, and projects because you see them as manifestations and vehicles of the loyalty you continue to affirm and not as entities valuable in and of themselves. There are not two landscapes but only one in Milton's poetry, and not two values but only one in his thought. The presence and appeal of what Comus calls "another meaning" (754) emerge only when an agent (either in the poem or outside it) takes his or her eye off the object and surrenders to the claims of the secondary, and specifically to the claim of the secondary to have its own franchise, to be "self-begot, self-rais'd" (*PL*, V, 860).

In short, and as I shall argue below in Chapter 1, conflict, ambivalence, and open-endedness—the watchwords of a criticism that would make Milton into the Romantic liberal some of his readers want him to be—are not constitutive features of the poetry but products of a systematic misreading of it, a misreading performed *in* the poetry by Comus and Satan, a misreading *of* the poetry as old as Blake and Shelley and as new as Lucy Newlyn when she celebrates the "doubleness" of an art in which "a valuation of the fallen world conflicts with the poem's moral design,"[7] or David Mikics when he complains that "Fish reads only one half of Protestant poetics" by "preferring the drive to escape from life's mutability into an otherworldly stasis."[8] In these and related statements, Newlyn and Mikics (along with Catherine Belsey, John Rogers, and a host of others) reinstate and reinvoke the dualism Milton so often rejects; for it is only if the first principle of Milton's thought—that God is God and not one of a number of contending forces—is denied or forgotten that his poetry can be seen as conflicted or tragic or inconclusive or polysemous or paradoxical, words that name literary qualities most of us have been taught to admire. They are not, I will argue, qualities Milton admires; and while their absence in his work might properly be a reason for declining to read it, it should not be a reason for rewriting it in the name of values he everywhere rejects when they are offered as alternatives to the single but complex life— faith, obedience, chastity of mind and deed—he everywhere celebrates.

Then why, one might ask, is the poetry so full of what it finally asks us to affirm against? The answer is that the lesson he would teach us—that we must forsake the letter for the spirit— can be taught only in the discursive forms the letter provides. Those forms are at once the vehicles of our instruction and the habitation of temptation—that is, of the temptation to take them seriously for themselves rather than as instruments of a supreme pedagogical intention, Milton's intention and, as he believes (see the second book of *The Reason of Church Government*), the intention of his God. There is, then, a double game going on in the poetry and the prose, but it is a doubleness impelled by the desire for its own erasure.[9]

Such at least is the story I will tell in the following chapters. It begins in Part I with a somewhat stark presentation of what I call the Miltonic paradigm, with its rigorous internalization of value and collapsing of all values (and decisions) into one. Part II considers the pressures that beset the paradigm even as it is articulated, pressures Milton came more and more to acknowledge. Part III catalogues and explores the counter-paradigms (really only one) ceaselessly elaborated by Milton's villains and imperfect heroes and heroines. And Part IV reaffirms the argument of Part I, with a few qualifications and almost no concessions. An epilogue comes full circle and returns us to the concerns of this introduction.

Before entering into the main body of the argument, I must take up a question not explicitly considered in the following chapters: the authorship of *De Doctrina Christiana,* or the *Christian Doctrine.* Thomas Burgess, bishop of Salisbury, was the first to question Milton's authorship of the treatise not long after it was discovered in 1823 in a bundle together with a collection of transcriptions of Milton's State Papers, and in 1991 Burgess' argument was revived and amplified by William B. Hunter in a series of articles culminating in 1998 in a monograph, *Visitation Unimplor'd: Milton and the Authorship of "De Doctrina Christiana."*[10] As Hunter acknowledges, he shares with Burgess the desire to rescue Milton from the charge of heresy and to reaffirm the poet's orthodoxy. (It is no small irony that in order to champion

Milton's orthodoxy, Hunter must himself become a heretic in the community of Milton scholars.) His strategy has two prongs: (1) to show that there is no conclusive evidence of Milton's authorship, no "smoking gun," and (2) to point out doctrinal inconsistencies between the treatise and the undoubtedly canonical poetry and prose. The first strategy is of course also inconclusive in the other direction: we cannot know that Milton did *not* write the *Christian Doctrine,* and Hunter does not have another candidate to offer, although he does conjecture that the true author might have been one of Milton's students, who perhaps "composed, at his direction, a summary of faith based on Wolleb and Ames" (151). It is important to note the ways in which Hunter's skepticism is qualified. He does not deny that the manuscript was in Milton's possession: "There is no doubt that when Milton died in November 1674 he had in his possession the copy of *DDC* that survives today in London's Public Record Office" (149). He does not deny that Milton may well have used "the treatise as a convenient concordance for quotations and perhaps for ideas" (97). He does not deny that Milton was probably involved in alterations to the manuscript, perhaps in collaboration with its "original author" (39), especially in the period 1658–1660. He does not deny that, when for some reason the original author "could no longer work on his great projected religious treatise" (33), Milton "carefully preserved [the] manuscript and dictated over the years a considerable number of what he regarded as minor improvements." He does not deny that the evidence suggests strongly that Milton had a hand in the composition of at least one chapter—the tenth of the first book—and used its wording in *Paradise Lost* (50). And he does not deny that the evidence (of detailed stylistic analysis) also suggests strongly that Milton was the author of the treatise's preface, which does seem to merit the designation "Miltonic" (156).

The question naturally arises: If it is necessary to posit an "originary author" lost to history in order at once to deny Milton's authorship of the treatise and yet acknowledge the evidence of his association and involvement with it, why not apply Occam's razor and come to the simple and economical conclusion that Milton wrote it? The authors of "The Provenance of *De Doctrina Christiana*"[11] pose the same question: "The document may have been passed by its author to friends. . . . The document may have come into Milton's possession in this way, and he may have chosen to retain it, having comments inserted by a series of casual amanuenses. . . . But if it were not Milton's, why, given how important it seems to have been to its author, did Milton retain it?" (97). "The best reply to this question," declare Stephen Dobranski and John Rumrich, is "that it belonged to him."[12] He retained it because it was his, and all of the positive evidence, as opposed to the conjuring up of ghostly first begetters, supports that identification, which has been assumed by almost everyone (including Hunter in an earlier incarnation) since 1823. Stephen Fallon agrees: "The case for Milton's authorship mounted in response to Hunter [by Maurice Kelley, John Shawcross, Barbara Lewalski, Christopher Hill, and others] strikes me as insurmountable."[13] Dobranski and Rumrich are even firmer: "By ordinary standards of attribution—which none of the participants in the controversy has challenged—Milton's authorship is indisputable" (7). By this they do not mean that he wrote every word of the treatise, a requirement more in keeping with modern post-Romantic standards of authorship than with "seventeenth-century practices" (9), which saw persons putting their names to compilations and gatherings they did not originate. Milton's *Artis Logicae*, Dobranski and Rumrich point out, is the product of just such a process. No one doubts it to be Milton's, and critics regularly look to it for evidence of Milton's views. So much less, say Dobranski and Rumrich, should anyone doubt the authorship of the *Christian Doctrine*, for it "expresses Milton's thought and convictions more fully and centrally than the tract on logic, more fully and centrally than any other single work in the accepted canon of his writings" (10).

But of course that is precisely the question. Is the *Christian Doctrine* compatible with the Milton we know from the canonical poetry and prose? It is because he would answer no that Hunter is moved to separate Milton from the tract in the first place; for, given its obvious heterodoxy, the tract is an embarrassment to the Milton he finds in *Paradise Lost* and elsewhere: "So many of Milton's genuine ideas are at odds with those in *DDC* that he could not have been its author unless he were the most incoherent thinker in history" (153). But in Rumrich and Dobranski's view (and in mine too), Milton's "genuine ideas," as found in the epics and the polemical prose, are precisely congruent with the ideas in the *Christian Doctrine*. The incoherence argument will not have any force for those who see no incoherence—those who, for example, are not discomfited, as Hunter is, by those places in the treatise where the author "downplays scriptural authority in favor of the illumination that the 'Spirit' can provide" (63), because they see the same downplaying in the climactic moment of *Paradise Regained,* in the "rousing motions" of *Samson Agonistes,* in the radical internalization of authority proclaimed over and over again in *An Apology against a Pamphlet*. The question of authorship cannot be settled either by demonstrating a harmony between the theological treatise and the other works or by demonstrating its opposite, for either demonstration will rest (in a circular but not vicious relationship) on a conclusion already reached about the kind of person and thinker Milton is. That leaves only the evidence already rehearsed and the facts we know: the manuscript was certainly on Milton's desk; it corresponds in size and content to a work he was known to have been preparing; there are undoubted verbal echoes that link it to passages in the poetry; it was found together with others of his writings and copied in part by the same hand; his name and initials were affixed to it, probably in the nineteenth century; it was represented as his by Daniel Skinner, who came into possession of it after the poet's death. Although the evidence falls short of an identification beyond challenge, it is at least as weighty as the evidence that warrants our believing that Marvell was the author of the poems we attribute to him. At any rate, given what we do know and what we don't know, I come to the conclusion that the answer to the question "Who wrote Milton's *Christian Doctrine?*" is "Milton." To be sure, the fact that I have come to that conclusion will not settle the matter, but it does settle it for the purposes of this book.

PART I

The
Miltonic
Paradigm

CHAPTER ONE

How Milton Works

Unsightly

Milton works from the inside out. (From an inside to an outside or from an inside that *is* an outside? The answer is both, but that will come later in the story.) In saying that I mean several things.

1. The priority of the inside over the outside is thematized obsessively in Milton's prose and poetry. Indeed, "priority" is at once too weak and misleading, since often outsides will either be declared nonexistent and illusory or found to be indistinguishable from the insides of which they are the local manifestation.

2. In Milton's prose and poetry, the direction of knowledge is from the inside out. In the world as he conceives it to be, truth and certainty are achieved not by moving from evidence gathered in discrete bits to general conclusions, but by putting in place

general conclusions in the light of which evidence will then appear. Rather than confirming or disconfirming belief, the external landscape, in all of its detail, will be a function of belief.

3. When one interprets Milton, the language should be allowed to generate questions of philosophy, theology, history, and politics rather than the other way around. Even the first-time reader who has little knowledge of dualism, monism, republicanism, free will, or the doctrine of the Fortunate Fall will be led to the issues named by these abstractions if he or she is responsive to the demands of the verse and prose.

I shall call these three points the *thematic thesis,* the *epistemological thesis,* and the *interpretive thesis,* answerable to the questions, "What is Milton about?," "What is Milton's account of knowing and perception?," and "How is Milton to be read?"

In the form I have put them, both these questions and my answers remain somewhat abstract and await the examples that might flesh them out and clarify the nature of my claims. Let me begin, therefore, with a small example, one that centers on a single word. The word is "unsightly" and it appears in this passage from *Comus:*

> Amongst the rest a small unsightly root,
> But of divine effect, he cull'd me out;
> The leaf was darkish, and had prickles on it,
> But in another Country, as he said,
> Bore a bright golden flow'r, but not in this soil:
> Unknown, and like esteem'd, and the dull swain
> Treads on it daily with his clouted shoon.[1]

On the most obvious level "unsightly" means "unattractive," but it also bears the secondary (and for Milton, finally, primary) meaning of "not available to sight" (as when Truth is said in the *Areopagitica* to be "unsightly" in its "first appearance to our eyes")—at least, that is, to some sights. The dull swain cannot see the true—inner—value of the root, but the "certain Shepherd Lad" (619) who has culled it for Thyrsis can see it, as can, presumably, virtue's "true Servants" (10) who, even though confined to the "dim spot, / Which men call Earth" (5–6), "aspire / To lay their just hands on that Golden Key / That opes the Palace of Eternity" (12–14). What makes this sequence typically Miltonic is the way in which the double meaning of "unsightly" at once generates and is glossed by the oppositions that fill the following lines—earthly / divine, this country / another country, darkish / bright, prickles / flower, unknown / known, dull / clear-eyed. The root is ignored or undervalued by those whose vision is (quite literally) superficial, those who know nothing of any "other Country," those whose limitation of sight—they too are "unsightly" in still another sense, lacking the ability truly to see—restricts what is for them a possible sight. In effect, the pun flowers into an essay on epistemology in which the field of perception—of what appears or does not appear to you—is a function of a prior inner orientation: what you can see depends radically on what you believe you can see.

The Attendant Spirit makes the point baldly when he declares that "unbelief is blind" (519). That is, if something or someone or some concept is not already affirmed in the deepest recesses of your being—if you don't believe in it—you will be blind to it; it will not appear for or to you. The reader or viewer has already seen a dramatic illustration of this lesson when the Lady comes to a place where she finds "nought but single darkness" (204). The very emptiness of the space causes her to populate it with the creatures of her anxiety—"calling shapes and beck'ning shadows dire" (207)—until, in a supreme effort of the will, she reminds (a nice word) herself of the true source of her security—a "virtuous mind" (211)—and immediately the dire shapes and shadows disappear and are replaced by the personages presupposed in the structure of her renewed (self-)confidence:

> O welcome pure-ey'd Faith, white-handed Hope,
> Thou hov'ring Angel girt with golden wings,
> And thou unblemish't form of Chastity,
> I see ye visibly, and now believe. (213–216)

What the Lady welcomes when she addresses these abstractions is nothing more (or less) than herself, newly re-collected. Faith, Hope, and Chastity are not what she sees but what she sees *with* (or within); they are the content of her consciousness, and when that consciousness turns outward it "discovers" its own presuppositions—that is, it discovers the world as it *must be,* given the preunderstanding that structures it. The Lady sees threatening shapes and shadows because for a moment she grants an independent agency (and power) to external forces; but once she affirms the superior and controlling agency of "the Supreme good, t' whom all things ill / Are but as slavish officers of vengeance" (217–218), that inward affirmation generates the visible evidence that can then be cited as its support. The entire small sequence is a gloss on and is glossed by the great definition of faith that opens Hebrews 11: "Faith is the substance of things hoped for, the evidence of things not seen." The "silver lining" (224) that dispels the single darkness of the night is an outward projection of the Lady's inner faith. By the force of that faith, and on no other basis, she transforms what is apparently unsightly into a sight of comfort and assurance.

Not only is the scene a lesson in faith; it is a lesson in writing. The single darkness of the Lady's physical situation is a blackboard waiting for inscription, and the question is who or what will inscribe it. For the moment that she describes herself as "startled" (210)—taken from her purpose, turned out of her way—the Lady allows her story to be written by forces outside her, and it is these forces that imprint "shapes," "shadows," and "syllables" on the black tablet. But when she recalls herself to her center (faith in the Supreme Good) and projects her calm outward, it is her pen, wielded from the inside, that draws the gold and silver lines of her present and future story.

Nor is this solipsism. The Lady is not a seventeenth-century precursor of Wallace Stevens' solitary singer of whom it is said, "There never was a world for her / Except the one she sang and, singing, made."[2] She is not "the single artificer of the world in which she sang." Rather, it is her knowledge (based on faith) of the real Artificer and of his attributes (omniscience and benevolence) that stabilizes and gives form both to her interior landscape and the landscape in which her physical body moves. What anchors and enlivens her (she refers at the moment of recovered equilibrium to her "new-enliv'n'd spirits" [*Comus*, 228]) is not her own power but the superior power trust in whom is the core of her very being. When she looks inside, what she finds written on the fleshly tables of her heart is *His* message; and when she speaks, it is that message that issues from her. What sounds like self-assertion is an assertion of radical dependence on an internalized other.

Even Comus recognizes this, albeit involuntarily. In response to hearing the Lady's song—the aural expression of her inner harmony—he exclaims, "Sure something holy lodges in that breast, / And with these raptures moves the vocal air / To testify his hidd'n residence" (246–248). As usual, Comus doesn't quite get it right; he imagines a kind of ventriloquism or ghost in the machine, a form of demonic possession. What he can't imagine (for the same reason that he can only hear the invocation of "the sage / And serious doctrine of Virginity" [786–787] as "mere moral babble" [807]) is a being infused with spirit to the extent that "his" residence and "her" agency are indistinguishable. Nevertheless, he is right to say that the resident spirit is "hidden," not available on the surface and therefore not accessible to those (like him) for whom surfaces—outsides—are everything.

With "hidden" and its contrast with surface, we are right back to "unsightly," the two meanings of which we have never left. The holy is "hidden" only to those whose perception is not answerable to it—to those, like the dull swain, who find its manifestations unattractive. To those in whose breast it lodges, the holy is everywhere evident as the first principle of both seeing and doing. If you regard the world as God's book before you ever take a particular look at it, any look you take will reveal, even as it generates, traces of his presence. If, on the other hand, the reality and omnipresence of God is not a basic premise of your consciousness, nothing you see will point to it and no amount of evidence will add up to it. You will miss it entirely, as Mammon does when all he can see in the soil and minerals of hell is material for a home-improvement project, one that will make up for the loss of heaven: "Nor want we skill or art, from whence to raise / Magnificence; and what can Heav'n show more?"[3] He's not kidding; he really means it. As far as he can see (a colloquialism I want to take very seriously), there is nothing more to see than the phenomena his art and skill will be able to produce; and those phenomena will bring heaven back to him because he never knew what it was in the first place (he has earlier been described as someone who walked around heaven admiring its physical riches detached from any sense of their source in deity [I, 679–684]). Had he truly known heaven, he could not have moved away from it, for it would have been "a heaven within" (as it is for Abdiel, whose physical removal to the North leaves him unchanged in his essence); and were he now to know it by realizing what he had lost and could not replace by feats of construction, he would no longer have lost it, for its reality would be animating him even in exile and he would be in the position the Elder Brother imagines for his virtuous sister: "He that has light within his own clear breast / May sit i'th' center, and enjoy bright day" (Comus, 381–382).

This state of never having to seek your treasure elsewhere because you carry it within (where it is hidden from those who seek their good in external forms) is recognized, again involuntarily, by Comus when he contrasts the Lady's song with the songs of his mother Circe and her attendant Sirens:

> Who as they sung, would take the prison'd soul,
> And lap it in *Elysium* . . .
> Yet they in pleasing slumber lull'd the sense,
> And in sweet madness robb'd it of itself,
> But such a sacred and home-felt delight,
> Such sober certainty of waking bliss,
> I never heard till now. I'll speak to her
> And she shall be my Queen. (256–257a; 260–265a)

The distinction is clear: one song is like a drug and induces self-forgetfulness; its "pleasing" effect lasts only for a short time, after which the self is returned to the fears and anxieties it wished to escape. The other song issues from a self that is already one with the object of its desire. What others seek (with a feverish restlessness that can never be satisfied) this self has already internalized; its good is never further away than its own heart and mind. That is what "home-felt" means: a "delight" that is inseparable from a certain state of being, the state of knowing (not from a distance but in every pore and molecule) exactly who one is—a servant and client of a greater power—and where one is—always moving in the safe and sanctified sphere (coterminous with the universe) created by and presided over by that power. (In strict terms she is always in her "Father's residence" [947], if only because that residence is her breast in which the "something holy" [246] lodges.)

But even as Comus gives voice to the relevant distinction and accurately names the "home-felt delight" breathed by the Lady's song, he betrays his inability to understand what the distinction and the appellation mean. The last thing a being centered by a total commitment to another needs is to become anyone's queen, let alone the queen of an itinerant master of revels. In fact, such a being doesn't need *anything*—brothers, light, physical security, mobility—in order to feel completely at home. She is wholly self-sufficient, not in the prideful sense Comus attributes to her when he calls her a Stoic (707), but in the sense of having pledged and attached herself to a power whose sufficiency is boundless. (In George Herbert's words, she has "imped her wing on his.")[4] This is the content both of her chastity (she belongs to him and to no other) and her confidence (it is confidence in *him* and in his regard for her), and it is what Comus can never understand, as she herself declares:

> Thou hast nor Ear nor Soul to apprehend
> The sublime notion and high mystery
> That must be utter'd to unfold the sage
> And serious doctrine of Virginity . . .
> Thou art not fit to hear thyself convinc't. (784–787; 792)

Conviction is usually thought to follow upon the marshaling of evidence: pile up enough evidence and conviction will at some point occur. Yet in the Lady's epistemology (which is also Milton's), conviction is not an event mechanically produced but a capacity that depends on the prior state of one's settled beliefs. If Comus' understanding does not already contain the notion of virginity—if the joy of selflessly pledging oneself to another without reservation or thought of gain is alien to his way of thinking—no amount of explanation could convey it to him. And indeed the very fact that it would have to be conveyed—that it was not inscribed in his being—assures that it never will be. You can only be convinced of what has already convinced you. Unbelief is blind, and what you can't see—what will be for you unsightly—will always appear to you as unsightly, as something with "prickles," or if it is a verbal form, as something unintelligible, as "mere moral babble" (807).

Another Meaning

I trust that the foregoing paragraphs will have made my triple thesis clear. If you attend with a certain intensity to Milton's language—that is, if you lean on words like "unsightly" or phrases like "home-felt delight," or assertions like "unbelief is blind"—they will display a double meaning and structure that correspond to the distinction between inner and outer, the distinction between a deep truth always present and always governing and the appearances and surfaces that seem to be, or seek to be, divorced from it. It will be the claim of the surface form—Circe's song, Comus' cup, the "precious gems" (719) he celebrates—to teach you something (where true value resides) or take you somewhere (to ease, happiness, pleasure, power). The rightly oriented soul—the soul possessed by a sober certainty of waking bliss—will respond by declaring that it already knows all it is necessary to know ("he who receives / Light from above . . . / No other doctrine needs")[5] and that it already enjoys everything that might possibly be offered ("secure / Of surfeit where full measure only bounds / Excess" [PL, V, 638–640]), and therefore that it need not go anywhere or seek anything, but merely continue to be what it already is, unencumbered either by desire or fear ("Fool . . . , / Thou canst not touch the freedom of my mind" [Comus, 662b–663]). The surface form will always say: Look over here or out there for meaning, salvation, illumination, truth. The settled and certain soul will decline the invitation and look within for the perspective in the light of which what is over here or out there is correctly and truly configured.

This lesson—the priority in every way of the inside over the outside—can be embodied in an extended scene, or an entire work, or even a single word. When the Attendant Spirit speaks of those who "aspire / To lay their just hands on that Golden Key / That opes the Palace of Eternity" (12–14), we are asked to attend to the pun in "aspire." In context, "aspire" means to move from where you are to a place, and an existence, that is better; but the Latin root of the word—*aspirare*, "to breathe"—tells us (what the mask will tell us again and again) that the goal of aspiration is the internalization of what you seek, to the extent that you express and exhale it with your every breath; you aspire in order to achieve the state in which aspiration signifies not a lack but a sufficiency. This is the state the Lady has already achieved (as has the Son of *Paradise Regained*), which is why, despite the Attendant Spirit's prologue, we do not see her aspiring—looking for love in all the wrong places—but see her aspiring, breathing out, at every moment and in circumstances that are physically very different, the same meaning, the same loyalty, the same sober certainty, the same home-felt delight, the same faith. Again, even Comus recognizes this about her (although, as his subsequent actions show, he doesn't understand it) when he asks in amazement, "Can any mortal mixture of Earth's mold / *Breathe* such Divine enchanting ravishment?" (244–245, my emphasis). That is, can any mortal be so wholly at peace and ease that nothing in her surroundings could either add to or disturb a perfect inner equilibrium?

Merely to describe the Lady's nonprogress and nonaspiring in this way is to surface (pardon the pun) the obvious objection to this account of *Comus* in particular and Milton's work and thought in general. It is so terribly static. The objection should not be refuted but embraced, for it points to another of the implications and consequences of Milton's working from the inside out. The inside to which he gives priority is the location of first principles, of beliefs (about God, good and evil, right action, and so on) so basic that they are constitutive of consciousness, and, because they are constitutive of consciousness, determinative of what the agent sees and thinks to do. For someone settled in his or her beliefs, as the Lady is (even though she can be startled and misled by "vizor'd falsehood" [698]), it is never a question of altering one's sense of obligation or changing one's loyalty in the light of circumstances, but rather a question of figuring out, in situations that may never have been encountered before (as the Lady has not before encountered a beguiling sorcerer), how an abiding obligation, defined by an unshakable loyalty, can be once again affirmed. This is what passes for a "plot" in Milton's poetry: the tension (sometimes barely registered by a protagonist like the Lady or the Son of *Paradise Regained,* but always felt by readers) between the protean possibilities of interpretation and action apparently offered by the world and the single-mindedness of agents who see the world as a space or tablet on which only one interpretation—known in advance and hewed to—can and should be inscribed.

That is why there is always a contrast between the busy energy of Milton's tempters (Satan, Comus, Dalila), as they move here and there pointing out many things, and the stillness of the Miltonic hero, for whom movement—departure from an already achieved state of knowledge and illumination—is a temptation. And that is also why plot—the linear vehicle of the unfolding and emergence of meaning—is never where the true action is in a Milton poem. The true action resides in the effort (sometimes so habitual as to seem effortless) of the person who is already in possession of, and possessed by, the meaning—there is only one—to find it amid the welter of particulars that do not in and of themselves point to it. Indeed, that is precisely the temptation: to think that particulars have an existence in and of themselves. When Comus says to the Lady about her eyes and hair and lips, "There was another meaning in these gifts, / Think what" (754–755), he advises her to look at the physical properties of a part of the world and allow them to tell her what she is ("you are but young yet" [755]) and what she should do. He advises her, in short, to be an empiricist. But she does not have to look at her gifts (or at anything else) to determine their meaning; she knows that what she has she has from heaven, and that the meaning of what she has is that it comes from heaven, and that the way to lose what she has is to find "another meaning" in it, for another meaning would always imply another bestower and another obligation.

That is just what Comus implies (too weak a word) when he tells the Lady that Nature's profusion (she "pour[s] her bounties forth / With such a full and unwithdrawing hand" [710–711]) argues for the necessity of consumption, lest the earth "be quite surcharg'd with her own weight, / And strangl'd with her waste fertility" (728–729). She replies by distinguishing between a female Nature and the male "giver" (775) who is the source of the nourishment she offers. What He requires is "praise due paid," and one can hardly pay due praise if one is focused so obsessively on the bounty that no thought is left for its provider:

> for swinish gluttony
> Ne'er looks to Heav'n amidst his gorgeous feast,
> But with besotted base ingratitude
> Crams, and blasphemes his feeder. (776–779)

"Advis'd" (755) to look for another meaning in the facts and features of the world, the Lady responds by reasserting the meaning already inscribed in her heart (all things come from him and testify to his goodness and glory) and using it to refute Comus' account of natural processes. The force of his account—and this is what makes it a temptation—is to give natural processes an independent status to which one must be responsive. This is what he means by "another meaning"; and she rejects it because she knows that another meaning means another God, and she knows, and continues to remember, that there is only one.

Not all of the characters in Milton's poetry perform so well. When Adam, faced with an Eve who has already transgressed the single prohibition, exclaims (to himself), "I feel / The Link of Nature draw me" (*PL*, IX, 913–914), he does exactly what Comus urges the Lady to do: he detaches a piece of nature from its sustaining source and then imagines for himself the choice (and dilemma) of opting for one or the other. Had he remembered that all value proceeds from God, he would have seen that the only hope for Eve is the remaking of the connection between her and deity, and he would have known that he could best help her by interceding for her restoration to favor, a role ultimately taken up by the Son. Instead he decides, disastrously, "to incur / Divine displeasure for her sake" (992–993), forgetting that there is no "her"—at least as a positive value—if the link between her and the Divine has been broken. Eve in her turn has already displayed an even more egregious version of Adam's error when, after eating the apple, she does obeisance to a tree—"O Sovran, virtuous, precious" (795)—at once granting it an independent existence and deifying it (to do one is to do the other). The speaker of *Lycidas* makes the same error in the opposite direction, attributing to natural processes not the power of salvation but the power of destruction. How has it happened, he asks, that a young man of such virtue and promise has died before his prime? It must be because of the "Felon winds"[6] or the "sounding Seas" (154) or the "stormy *Hebrides*" (156) or the "whelming tide" (157), or, most desperately, the "eclipse" (101) in which the "fatal and perfidious Bark" (100) was rigged. Wind, tide, sea, and planets are endowed with a malignant purpose that is pursued independently of any providential design or oversight. This is the world of empirical accident, where anything can happen and disaster is only a moment away. It is only when the swain replaces that world with one overseen by providence that the same forces, now seen as agents of a divine benevolence, are recharacterized as the vehicles of a great gift:

So *Lycidas,* sunk low, but mounted high,

. . . . .

With Nectar pure his oozy Locks he laves,
And hears the unexpressive nuptial Song,
In the blest Kingdoms meek of joy and love. (172, 175–177)

Until he is able to say this, the swain repeats Adam's mistake of detaching parts of nature from the larger framework that gives them meaning, just as Samson does when he speaks of his strength as if it were a renegade force neither he nor anyone else can control—"strength is my bane, / And . . . the source of all my miseries" (*Samson Agonistes,* 63–64). But neither misery nor joy follows from the mere fact of physical energy; it is what is done with that energy—the service to which it is put, the spirit in which it is exercised—that determines its value, as Samson later realizes when he rededicates his strength to the service of the God by whom he had thought himself abandoned.

What You Believe Is What You See Is What You Are Is What You Do

In each of these instances (and many others could be adduced) a surface or material form—food, gems, Eve, trees, seas, strength—is granted an independent identity, and regarded as if it were either an alternative deity ("another meaning") or a malignant rival to deity (often, in the poems, called "fate" or "chance"—i.e., wild-card exceptions to providential design). And while each instance is an instance of error—always the same error, the failure to identify and cling to the true object of devotion and fear—it is a creative error. For once particulars are separated from the larger context that stabilized their identities, value, and meaning, there opens up the possibility of assigning (or claiming) other identities, inventing plural values, and discovering many (perhaps conflicting) meanings; there opens up, in short, a space or a gap in which one can search for what has been lost or missed, a search that would be unnecessary had the initial error—the breaking of union, the worship of false gods, the desire to be God, the substitution of plural meanings for God's meaning—never been made. Indeed, it would not be too much to say that from error comes everything of interest—everything that is complex (almost a technical word)—in Milton's work. This may sound like a reformulation of a familiar account in which Milton is of the devil's party with or without knowing it and is most animated when he releases the energies his orthodoxy condemns, but that is not at all what I mean. What I mean is that the usual sources of interest in life and in narrative—the clash of competing but legitimate values, the attempt to discern intelligibility and design amid the apparently random details of experience, the struggle to achieve self-authenticity as one acts on life's many stages, the suspense of waiting to see how things turn out, the excitement of not knowing what comes next, the conception and execution (or failure) of long-term projects—become available to the agent only when he or she has wandered away from, lost sight of, ceased to be filled with, that home-felt delight and sober certainty of waking bliss that make for total sufficiency, for that condition in which joy is "secure / Of surfeit" (*PL*, V, 638–639) because it is known in a measure so "full" (639) that neither lack nor "Excess" (640) attend it.

One who inhabits that condition can be said to have nothing to do, nowhere to go, no goal to achieve; and, indeed, the idea of a "new" enterprise or an alternative destination or an enhanced position (as in "you shall be my Queen" or "ye shall be as Gods") constitutes a temptation. It is the temptation offered by Satan to the Son of *Paradise Regained* in as many forms as the archfiend can devise—money, women, authority, power, philosophy, poetry, even charity—and in response the Son does nothing, or at least nothing positive; he simply says, no, I don't need that, and he says it so consistently that Satan finally asks in exasperation, "What dost thou in this World?" (IV, 372), to which the answer (not given explicitly) is, I continue to be what I am. What Satan's exasperation registers is the radical absence of drama, of visible movement, in the Son's posture. Satan wants (what many readers also want) something to happen; what the Son says (by saying very little) is that everything has already happened, and that all one need do is continue to "Quaff immortality" (*PL*, V, 638) and praise its bestower.

Satan scorns such nonactivity and names those who engage in it "the Minstrelsy of Heav'n" (VI, 168), those who spend all their time chanting hymns or performing pointless tasks in response to arbitrary commands. Such beings have no real *project,* and it is a project—something to accomplish, a road to travel, an injustice to redress—that Satan gives himself when he uses the occasion of the exaltation of the Son to generate a world of lack and injury: "Here I am, a long-time loyal son now rewarded by seeing an undeserving newcomer promoted over me. Something must be done about this." At once the story is set in motion, and genuine (as opposed to ritual) action is for the first time available, bringing along with it suspense, crisis, strategy, plots, alliances, victory, defeat—all that we know as drama, all that we know as interest.

These forms of interest, however, are (as I have already said) unreal, at least from the perspective of those who celebrate the joy of total dependence; these forms of interest emerge and become available as experiences in the wake of a mistake. And although they are surely felt to be substantial by those who have made the mistake, they are finally without weight, illusions no more substantial than those the Lady dispels by a simple and (for those who perform it) easy act of the will. Among the illusions generated by the mistake of misidentifying the source of meaning and value are (1) the illusion that there could be an opposition between loyalty to God and loyalty to some part of his creation, an illusion possible only if you forget (and it is just as easy to forget as it is not to forget) that the object of alternative loyalty is precisely that—*God's* creation—as Adam does when he "chooses" Eve (if making her the vehicle of his idolatry can be regarded as choosing her); (2) the illusion that particulars could point in more than one direction and therefore constitute a puzzle, as the dove which descends on the Son's head constitutes a puzzle to Satan, who is in doubt as to "whate'er it meant" (*PR*, I, 83), a doubt that will never be removed by the empirical inquiries he has long since begun, a doubt (and a puzzle) he never would have experienced had he not been seeing with the eyes of doubt rather than with the eyes of faith; (3) the illusion that the self has an independent status and independent powers, that it can be the source rather than the beneficiary of creation, as Satan claims to be when he offers the invention of cannon and shot as a prosthetic device capable of erasing the difference between the rebels and God, or as Mammon claims to be when he urges his cohorts to "seek / Our own good from ourselves" (*PL*, II, 252–253) and thus gives voice to the impulse behind, and the (apparent) achievement of, Pandemonium.

It is above all this third illusion—of a self that can originate its own projects and make its own world—that impels the forward action in Milton's poetry, as opposed to the more static action (if "action" is the word) of those who find their happiness in service. The angels who occupy the last line of the *Nativity Ode* can serve as examples of the latter: "Bright-harness'd Angels sit in order serviceable."[7] The line at once describes and mimes Milton's constant theme of constancy. Rather than moving forward to make its point (though it does that too), it makes it with every word. The angels wear their harness as a sign of their service; service is what they do. That is why they sit rather than stand or run; theirs is a posture of waiting, and what they wait for is the command of their Lord. They sit in order—not randomly or singly positioned—to indicate their corporate, soldierly identity. And in this they are precisely serviceable, capable of rendering service and of rendering service at this moment because they are content merely to be ready and do not require heroic fields of valor on which to prove themselves. They prove themselves by not needing to.[8]

Another, and shorter, way to put this is to say that they are unified—that is, without division. There is no division between their desires and the will of God; their desire *is* to do the will of God (like the Son of *Paradise Regained,* who describes himself as "hung'ring . . . to do my Father's will [II, 259]). There is no division between their head and heart, between their thoughts and their feelings; what they feel is the urgency and joy of service, and service is what they think about. There is no division between their insides and their outsides. The brightness of their harness is a perfect emblem and reflection of the inward discipline that defines the characteristic and repeated form of their actions; that discipline is what will be expressed no matter what those forms happen to be—sitting, fighting, praying, singing, reading, sleeping, waking. The variety of postures is a superficial phenomenon; what shines through the variety is always the same. Like the "starry Sphere / Of Planets," they are "regular / . . . when most irregular they seem" (*PL,* V, 620–621; 623–624).

Satan recognizes (or at least says he does) the same radical unity in the Son:

> I see thou know'st what is of use to know,
> What best to say canst say, to do canst do;
> Thy actions to thy words accord, thy words
> To thy large heart give utterance due, thy heart
> Contains of good, wise, just, the perfect shape. (*PR,* III, 7–11)

Like the morning prayer Adam and Eve send up in book V, this description can be read backward or forward or from point to point, since what is being declared is a system of equivalences, of nested boxes. You can start with knowledge (line 7) or with the shape of the heart (10–11); it doesn't matter, because the referent will be the same—an inner orientation so total, so saturating, that it is the content of what is known (if the reality of the one thing needful possesses you, it is what you will know), of what is said (testimony to your basic allegiance will be the burden of your songs, however apparently various), and of what is done (if you believe there is only one mission, one obligation, your every step will be taken in its name). In short, for such a unified being, *what you believe is what you are is what you know is what you say is what you do.*[9] And conversely if you don't believe, if your heart does not contain—does not have written on its fleshly tables—the shape of goodness, wisdom, and justice, you will know nothing of goodness, wisdom, and justice, and you will be able to say nothing about goodness, wisdom, and justice, and you will be incapable of enacting goodness, wisdom, and justice. And if you are a poet, wisdom, goodness, and justice can be your themes only if they are (already) your life: "he who would not be frustrate of his hope to write well hereafter in laudable things, ought him selfe to bee a true Poem, that is a composition, and patterne of the best and honourablest things; not presuming to sing high praises of heroick men, or famous Cities, unlesse he have in himself the experience of all that which is praise-worthy."[10]

It would be difficult to overestimate how radical a sense of being this is; for the equivalences it declares (between believing, knowing, saying, doing) are usually regarded as distinct modalities more often than not in tension with one another. (That again is where the *interest* is thought to lie.) The distinction between knowledge and belief is a given for a post-Cartesian world in which the inner realm of subjectivity (now first invented) has been severed from, and put in an ever-problematical relation to, external reality. A subject thus separated from the real has no direct way to apprehend or confirm the truth about things and must have recourse to impersonal mechanisms (mathematics, scientific experiment) devised to neutralize and/or bypass its partiality. Such a subject can never be sure of anything, and, like the Satan of *Paradise Regained,* must always be in search of more knowledge (there will never be enough) in order to shore up its faith. Since that same subject is (as a condition of its existence) cut off from the truth, it will be guided by its own desires and passions, which will intersect with duty and obligation only accidentally or as a result of discipline externally applied. Such a subject—autonomous and, because autonomous, adrift—will always be torn between the directions of its impulses (sexual, material, political) and the direction a rule or a sovereign or a God would enjoin. And even when such a subject has come to "know" (by report, rumor, "sacred" text) of something larger and more abiding than it, it will turn away from that knowledge to the safety of its own circuit of habits and opinions; it will know one thing and *do* another. And because it will sometimes give voice to what it knows but declines to follow, it will *say* one thing and do another. And, finally, because such a subject wants to think well of itself and hide from itself its (inevitable) self-centeredness, it will sometimes say one thing—I love you, I am telling the truth, I will be here for you—and *mean* another, although even in duplicity, in the doubleness of word and will, it will continue to think itself sincere.

This is the subject of modernity, and along with it comes the modern world—mysterious, available to any number of descriptions, possessed of its own shape, value, and significance but yielding knowledge of them only to the most rigorous and *impersonal* methods. Two large zones of independence, the self and the world of objects and action with which it would connect but from which it is ever distant unless a bridge or a microscope or a telescope or a spaceship is available to convey it. For the modern subject, the world is always a puzzle, and much of the work to be performed and enjoyed is the work of solving the puzzle, of figuring out what something is made of or what it means or how it might be improved or overcome. Adam flirts with this stance when he proposes a doubt about the operations of the heavens, which he finds inefficient. Raphael replies not by giving him a larger telescope or instructing him in Copernican cosmology (although Copernican cosmology is put to rhetorical use when it is at once introduced and deauthorized), but by telling him that he's reasoning in the wrong direction, from particular observations to general conclusions. He should begin with a general conclusion—with a first principle of faith—and if he sees within its light the particulars will fall into place, without strain or involved calculations. Just remember, Raphael advises, who set this all up and what kind of person He is and what kind of creature you are, and all will become clear:

> for the Heav'n's wide Circuit, let it speak
> The Maker's high magnificence, who built
> So spacious, and his Line stretcht out so far;
> That Man may know he dwells not in his own;
> An Edifice too large for him to fill. (*PL*, VIII, 100–104)

From this perspective the world is anything but a puzzle, because it immediately yields the meanings you know it to have; and you know that not at the end of a sequence, of an experiment, of an investigation, but *in the first place,* which is the place you never leave (home-felt delight is also home-felt knowledge, of everything) yet continually inhabit and continually discover wherever you go or wherever you look. In short, there is no division, no doubleness, either in you—your head and your heart, your faith and reason, your belief and knowledge, your words and your commitments, are not at odds but perfectly in tune—or between you and reality; for, having internalized the real, all the motions of your perception, intellection, and action repeatedly disclose it and breathe it out.

None But Good Men Can Give Good Things

Much of the drama of Milton's poetry consists of confrontations between these two ways of being in the world (or these two ways of being *and* the world): one that regards every situation as a space of new possibilities and new meanings, the other that regards every situation as a space to be filled with certainties already known and inscribed with the single meaning everything always displays; one that looks to the world and to the unfolding of events for guidance, the other that looks with a guidance already in place and sees in every event an opportunity to reaffirm its imperative. When Comus offers the Lady a "cordial Julep" (672) he endows it with attractive and restorative properties— "This will restore all soon" (690)—but her reply pays no attention to the drink and focuses instead on the character of the giver:

> Were it a draught for *Juno,* when she banquets,
> I would not taste thy treasonous offer; none
> But such as are good men can give good things,
> And that which is not good, is not delicious
> To a well-govern'd and wise appetite. (701–705)

"None but good men can give good things." What this does is identify the properties of the object with the intention or spirit in which it is either offered or accepted. That is to say, you can't read the world by attending to its surface features and then attempting to derive from them the proper way of proceeding. You must already be *in* the proper way of proceeding, already moving in a committed direction, and from the perspective of that direction—in the light of its imperatives—the features of the world will plainly reveal themselves. The Lady is committed to the something holy that lodges in her breast. Comus has revealed himself to be a liar ("false traitor" [690]) and therefore someone who would turn her from her path; there is nothing he could do or offer that would not be tainted by his foul inside. He has shown himself to be the wrong kind of person, and everything he touches—physically, verbally, cognitively—is polluted and off limits to "a well-govern'd and wise appetite." Again, it is not the properties of the "fragrant Syrups mixt" (674) that are harmful, but the moral context that envelops them. Strictly speaking, the syrups have no properties (just as the apple Adam and Eve are forbidden to eat has no properties) until they are either well or ill used. Had another, more benign agent proffered the glass, there would have been no danger or sin in taking it (as the Son partakes of the repast offered by a fiery globe of angels in *Paradise Regained*).

It is important to note what the Lady is *not* saying here. She is not saying: yes, this quite likely tastes good, but I will myself to resist and refuse it. That would make her a divided being, one whose "natural" desires are at odds with her higher commitments. No, she is saying: it won't taste good (she needn't even try it to know), because goodness does not inhere in the agent who offers it. We are accustomed to think that the taste of something is a function of its chemical makeup; it is a physical matter. But the Lady is insisting that the physical aspects of experience follow from or are determined by one's moral orientation. Nothing that is not good in the sense of not issuing from a benevolent motive will taste good to one such as she. Even sense data have no existence independent of the inner state of those who either provide it or experience it.

The same holds for aesthetic data. When Satan recommends

the glories of Greek and Roman literature ("the secret power / Of harmony in tones and numbers hit" [*PR, IV,* 254–255]), the Son responds with a famously troubling dismissal—"Remove their swelling Epithets thick laid / As varnish on a Harlot's cheek, the rest, / Thin sown with aught of profit or delight" (343–345)— and declares the superiority of the psalms ("*Sion's* songs"), which, "In thir majestic unaffected style" (359), will be judged by "all true tastes" to be "excelling" (347). The question one might ask is: What's the difference between a majestic unaffected style and a majestic affected style? The answer could not be found in a sty- listic comparison of the usual kind, in which the presence or absence of certain formal or figurative marks (metaphor, apos- trophe, personification, epic simile) forms the basis of a classifica- tion, for both styles are "majestic" in the sense that their formal features would be conformable to the description of the "high style" one might find in any manual of rhetoric and poetics. The difference, then, must reside in the opposition of affected to *unaf- fected*. That is, it must be located in the different spirits within which two formally indistinguishable pieces of verse or prose are produced; the difference is a difference in sincerity. One kind of author lays the figures of speech on with a trowel, and the result is a kind of appliqué work ("varnish on a Harlot's cheek"); the other produces gloriously figurative language spontaneously as an outward expression of an inward majesty.

But if this is the case, the difference will be undetectable to the naked eye or ear—it will be a *secret* difference, one that transpires on the inside. And it is a difference that can only be told (in both the passive and active senses; if you can tell the difference, you will at the same time be telling—declaring, extending—it) by someone whose inside is perfectly congruent with the inside of the truly inspired author, by someone, that is, of "true taste." Whether it is the taste of a brimming glass or the taste of a po- etic line, the success and quality of the transaction depend not on the properties of the object, be it liquid or verbal, but on the connection (amounting almost to a likeness) between two persons informed by the same understanding of what is true and real. In short, in the matter of recognizing either true nourishment or true poetry, it takes one to know one, or it takes one to hear one, or it takes one to taste one, or (remember the "unsightly root") it takes one to see one.

The negative side of this interior circuit of knowledge and communication is that you can't really know or value something you haven't internalized. Only the villains in Milton's poetry believe that knowledge is a matter of outward (empirical) inspection. It is the belief Satan declares in *Paradise Regained* when he says, "Most men admire / Virtue, who follow not her lore" (I, 482–483). That is to say, most men are able to recognize and value virtue even though they swerve from her dictates. The flaw in this assertion is captured by the double meaning of "admire"— to esteem and to wonder or marvel at. The one meaning—"esteem"—contains Satan's claim: he is capable of properly evaluating virtue. The other meaning—"marvel at"—undoes the claim: "wondering at" is something one does from a *distance;* its object is by definition strange and alien to the wonderer; and it is alienation that marks Satan's relationship to the virtue he does not follow. If he really knew virtue he would not wonder at it, because its shape would be as familiar to him as the interior motion of his heart; it would *be* the interior motion of his heart; and it would be impossible for him *not* to follow her lesson ("lore") because that lesson would be imprinted on every fiber of his being and would be enacted with his every step or breath. Then it could be said of him what Milton says of the worshiper who has no need of set prayers because, from his "sincere heart," "free and unimpos'd expression . . . unbidden come into the outward gesture."[11] A sincere heart is a heart wholly made of one thing and not a mixture, and it is because his heart is not sincere that Satan can present himself as a divided being, one who can, like a connoisseur of fine wines or rare birds, appreciate virtue (oh, there's a fine instance of it; how interesting!), yet follow another path.

Earlier he attempted the same self-presentation in terms that even more obviously undermine it:

> Though I have lost
> Much luster of my native brightness, lost
> To be belov'd of God, I have not lost
> To love, at least contémplate and admire
> What I see excellent in good, or fair,
> Or virtuous; I should so have lost all sense. (PR, I, 377–382)

This is a virtual dissertation on the idea of loss and on Satan's inability to comprehend it. He does know that he has lost brightness, the physical manifestation of his inward probity; but he doesn't know what that means, because the loss of his connection to God—a connection made through loyalty and obedience—is also a loss of any understanding of what that loss actually is. He seems to display some dim awareness of this when he retreats from the claim to still love goodness (as if love were a form of aesthetic appreciation) and substitutes the softer and distance-acknowledging vocabulary of contemplation and admiration. The more ambitious claim returns in the assertion that he can *see* what is excellent in goodness and virtue, but the syntax—"What I see excellent"—allows us to turn the assertion into a question. Does what *he* sees as excellent correspond to what actually *is* excellent? The answer is surely no, an answer that points us to the ambiguity of "I should so have lost all sense." The sense he hasn't lost is the sense of the senses; he knows that he's not as bright and shiny as he once was. The sense he has lost is sense in the sense of understanding, and that loss is registered in his every word, a loss mimed in the verse by the *traductio* on "lost." Lost, lost, lost, lost—that is the sound that traverses this passage and provides an undermining counterpoint to its boasts of even a partial sufficiency.

It is no accident that Satan's description of himself as a conflicted agent, still half in love with the thing he has rejected and compelled to catalogue its attractions, is so suffused with pathos; presenting oneself as a divided being is not only an admission (I'd like to be a certain way, but I just can't manage it), it is an *appeal* (look how torn I am and because I am torn how interesting I am). Of course it isn't true. Satan is not conflicted; he plays at being conflicted, just as at the beginning of book IV of *Paradise Lost* he plays at being repentant. He has the capacity to philosophize about repentance or about loving and being beloved by God, but he can't *do* either because he can't know either. That is what being Satan or any other agent cut off from God means: there is no longer anything in you that corresponds to the virtues you claim to admire or the knowledge from which you have turned away. All you can do is mime the one and discourse about the other, as Satan discourses about "submission" in both books I and IV but can understand it only as an unthinkable (I, 661) act of self-diminishment ("*Disdain* forbids me" [IV, 82]) rather than as the act of self-enhancement the loyalists know it (without reflection) to be when they gladly defer to the authority of the Son at the end of book VI.

Another way to say this is that Satan theatricalizes inner conflict and makes its vocabulary a rhetorical ploy. Perhaps the clearest instance of this occurs in the third book of *Paradise Regained* when he cries "worst is my Port" (209) and tells the Son that he "would be at the worst" if only to find his "ultimate repose" (209–210) and respite from his "evil state" (218). The moment and its expression are poignant, but in the next moment the sentiments are revealed to be stage effects preliminary to one more attempt to tempt: "If I then to the worst can be haste, / Why move thy feet so slow to what is best" (223–224)? At the beginning of the passage Satan is said to be "inly rackt" (203), but here we learn (what we should have known anyway) that it is all put on, the artificial production of an inner life by a being whose defining characteristic is that he has none.

The Temptation of Being Conflicted

In the previous paragraphs, I have been making two points: first, that conflict in Milton's universe is the mark of a divided being because an integrated being, someone like the Lady or the Son (or even in his way Satan), breathes out in word and action the allegiances and commitments that constitute him; and second, that, given Milton's refusal to compartmentalize belief, cognition, and action—given his insistence that outsides are generated by in-sides—there can be no divided beings, no beings who believe one thing and do another. This is not to say, of course, that the condi-tion of being divided is not presented or paraded in Milton's work (Satan enacts it on many stages; Adam and Eve invoke it as a justification of their sin; Dalila claims it in several forms); only that when it appears it is either a pose, as it is when Satan pre-tends to anguish, or a mistake, as it is when the backsliders in *The Tenure of Kings and Magistrates* recoil from punishing the king for whose removal they had clamored. The mistake is one that has proved particularly attractive to literary critics because it allows them to find in Milton's work those kinds of literary interest usu-ally associated with tragedy and lyric poetry: passions pulling in different directions, forward movement arrested by indecision be-fore equally attractive alternatives, accidents and contingencies that settle the fates of agents who are ignorant of them, emo-tions at war with the intellect, love in tension with duty. For many, discovering those interests at play in Milton's poetry is to demonstrate that he is interesting and to rescue him from the charge that he is monolithic, achromatic, authoritarian, patriarchal, insufficiently attuned to difference, and always the same.[12] What I want to say is that the rescue is performed at the expense of what is really interesting in Milton's work: a sustained and incredibly focused effort to explore the relationship between an imperative to be single-minded—to affirm one thing, one truth, one meaning, one God, one obligation—and a world (his world and our world) that seems to offer many paths and to invite us, with Comus, to search for other meanings.

As an example of the attempt to provide Milton with the interest modernists think he should have if he is to merit his place in the canon, let me cite a judgment made by John Reichert in his analysis of Adam's fall: "I see no way to do justice to the complexity of Adam's act, and of its consequences, other than with the aid of paradox: Adam does the wrong thing for good reasons."[13] This statement would make coherent sense only if the universe were made up of discrete realms of value in each of which a context-specific obligation formed the baseline in relation to which a reason might be said to be good. In that case, one might experience a clash of obligations and be faced with a choice between competing sets of good reasons, as in: on the one hand it is good to cleave to my wife, but on the other it is good to obey the command of God, so whatever I do I'll be doing a wrong thing (abandoning my wife or disobeying God) for a good reason. But Milton's universe is not so structured. If God is God and not merely the name of some regional warlord whose surveillance one might hope to evade—if God is the creator and sustainer of life and value—the obligation to obey him, to testify always to his centrality, is overriding and is not to be relaxed in favor of some other value that presents itself as competing. That is to say, the wrongness of disobedience is not a relative wrongness to be balanced against the relative rightness of the form an act of disobedience might take; the wrongness of disobedience is simply, and without any qualifications, wrong, and no reason for engaging in disobedience can be good. It can *appear* good, and one can surround that appearance with reasons, as when Adam declares, "I feel / The Link of Nature draw me" (*PL*, IX, 913–914), but that only means that he has forgotten what spirit and force animates nature's links and is the source of the worth of any one of them. Were he to remember that, he would say, "I feel the Link of Nature draw me" and mean not Eve but God, and then he would do the right thing for the only reason that could possibly be a good one. The supposed tension between good reasons and things good to do can be experienced only if the category of "good" reasons is filled up independently of any consideration of what is in fact, and ultimately, good. That is, only if giving reasons is an activity separate from the identification of the good, if it is a skill like writing limericks or playing tennis, can one be good at it and give good (as opposed to sloppy, unsupported-by-evidence) reasons even when they lead to a bad moral outcome.

It is Milton's view, however, that one's conviction as to what is good and true and moral comes first, and that the reasons one might have for acting flow from—and are given their status as "good" by—that prior conviction. If a man begins, as Adam does, with the conviction that he owes everything to "some great Maker . . . / In goodness and power pre-eminent" (VIII, 278–279), and that his life's work is to know that maker and "adore" (280) Him, no "reason" that takes him away from that path and sets him another can be good. Not only does Reichert's statement—Adam does the wrong thing for good reasons—betray a failure to understand how morality and action work in Milton's universe; it is internally incoherent. Reichert can't mean "good reasons" unless good is a merely technical approbation—a compliment paid to someone displaying a certain mental agility—and he can't mean "wrong thing" unless the wrongness in question is an infraction of some inessential and dispensable convention, like spelling or taking off your hat in the presence of a lady, and not the infraction of a moral *law.* It is only if he doesn't take the words "good" and "wrong" seriously—as really meaning something—that he can sever them and put them at odds with each other in the structure of some poignant paradox.

To be sure, Reichert is not alone in distinguishing the goodness of reasons from an orientation to goodness. It is a distinction that comes along with the modern moment, in which a world informed by a single value gives way to a world of multiple values with no "sure and foregoing" way of choosing between them. In that world, choices are complex and persons are always pulled this way and that by equally compelling values, and reason, as a technical faculty, becomes one of the tools you have recourse to in the face of moral ambiguity. In Milton's world, however, there are no moral ambiguities, because there are no equally compelling values. There is only one value—the value of obedience—and not only is it a mistake to grant independence to values other than the value of obedience, it is a temptation. Indeed, it is *the* temptation—the temptation to seek a separate, self-sustaining existence—that Milton obsessively explores.

It is the temptation Satan repeatedly presents to the Son in *Paradise Regained* in the form of various courses of action (feeding the hungry, removing a tyrant, gaining a kingdom) that are said to be necessary to the fulfilling of his destiny ("Great acts require great means" [II, 412]). The Son makes only one reply: all I need is the aid and love of the living God. "Why dost thou then suggest to me distrust?" (I, 355). He would evidence distrust if he accepted any of the actions Satan urges as paramount; for he knows, and it is a knowledge he will not swerve from, that what is paramount—not in this or that situation or occasionally, but at every moment without exception—is the obligation to do God's will. Being faithful to that obligation may or may not involve the means (wealth, power, eloquence) to which Satan would bind him. When, however, those means are urged not as auxiliaries to the doing of God's will but as substitutes for it or as vehicles it uniquely requires, they must be rejected, not because they are bad in and of themselves ("in and of themselves" is not a category in Milton's universe), but because as Satan presents them they occupy the position of idolatry, and invite the twin mistakes of idolatry: the mistake of preferring the created thing (or agent) to the creator, and the mistake of thinking that without the created thing the creator's will cannot be done. The *locus classicus* of this point is the first book of Augustine's *On Christian Doctrine*, where he distinguishes between using a thing to move toward blessedness and enjoying it for its own sake; if you do the latter, the journey toward blessedness will be retarded and you will be "shackled by an inferior love."[14]

The basic distinctions are made concisely by the final lines of *Paradise Regained*, book II: "Riches are needless then, both for themselves, / And for thy reason why they should be sought, / To gain a Scepter, oftest better miss't" (484–486). Note the precision with which riches are pushed away but not condemned altogether. They are not to be sought "for themselves," as a supreme value, because he who possesses them is possessed by them and they become for him a "cumbrance if not snare" (454). If they are sought, however, for a good reason—the possibility of there being one is left open by "thy," which, if strongly emphasized, suggests the existence of a reason that would be acceptable—the act of accumulating them is blameless, since the goodness of the reason baptizes them and takes away the taint of idolatry (they are being used, not enjoyed). But Satan's reason—gaining a crown—is not good, and for the same reason that riches worshiped for themselves are not good: rather than happiness and a sober certainty of waking bliss, a crown "Brings dangers, troubles, cares, and sleepless nights" (460). Satan has attempted to establish a hierarchy in which a crown is a higher goal than mere wealth. What the Son tells him is that anything sought for itself is a false God and that the reason for seeking it—whether it be material comfort, political power, social welfare, or even love—is always a bad reason.

What reason would then be good? Only a reason indistinguishable from the desire to obey God. If riches or a crown or glory or eloquence happens to accrue to you in the course of your efforts to do his will, nothing compels you to reject them because you are in no way bound to them. In short, and here we return to Reichert, there is only one good reason for positively valuing created things: as either a manifestation of the creator's goodness and glory or as part of a response to the creator's goodness and glory. Any other reason is a bad reason—an idolatrous reason—and when another reason takes the form of disobedience, as in "I will disobey God for the reason that I love my wife," it is not, and could not be, a good reason. Adam could not possibly have done the wrong thing for a good reason. If the reason was good—and remember, the only good reason is one consonant with the obligation to obey—the thing would have been good; since the thing was (as Reichert acknowledges) wrong, the reason for doing it is necessarily bad. An Eve who has become the occasion for disobeying God cannot occupy the place of a "good reason" and instead occupies the place of idolatry. This is precisely what the Son means when he says to an Adam full of reasons, "Was shee thy God?" (PL, X, 145)—by which he means not that obedience to God is a better reason but that it is the only reason.

I have no doubt that this analysis is correct, and I also have no doubt that many of my fellow Miltonists will resist it, if only because it flies in the face of what they believe as good post-Enlightenment liberals. Liberals believe that knowledge of an object (be it a piece of data, a person, a concept) is one thing and evaluation of it is another, so that it makes perfect sense to say, as Satan does, I know what the good is—I just choose another path (as if knowledge and inclination could be severed from each other and opposed). Liberals believe that facts (of history, justice, science) are independent of the knower, and that it is the knower's obligation to approach the task of knowing with as few preconceptions as possible so that the understanding he finally achieves is impersonal rather than a reflection of his antecedently held views and preferences; one must come to any situation calling for a decision (about what to think or what to say or what to do) with an open mind, a mind prepared to jettison its most cherished convictions should the evidence tell against them. Liberals believe that evidence lies about in the world waiting to be gathered and then arranged in patterns it itself suggests. Liberals believe that if we are sufficiently careful in our gathering of evidence (careful, that is, to keep ourselves and our desires out of the process) the truth will finally emerge in a form everyone (whose mind is open) will acknowledge. Liberals believe that when the truth to be determined is the meaning (political, moral, legal) of an action, the previous history of the actor—whether he has in the past been a good or bad man—is largely irrelevant and that we should look only to the shape of the present circumstances when assessing him. And because liberals believe in all of the above, they believe in the efficacy of procedures—scientific, parliamentary, judicial—designed to protect us from the overhasty judgments we make when we allow our commitments and allegiances to blind us. Liberals believe that the most important of these procedures is the machinery of rationality, of those laws of logic attached to no agenda or vision, but sufficiently general in their scope as to provide a normative perspective from the vantage point of which any agenda or vision can be assessed and, if necessary, corrected. Liberals believe that communication and persuasion take place (or should take place) in the context of that rationality and that it is possible to bring anyone—except, perhaps, the mentally impaired—to a clear understanding, so long as he or she is willing to set aside or bracket all biases and preconceptions.

Milton believes none of these things. He believes that all the evidence is in and that it points to a single conclusion—we must discern the will of God and do it—that should form the basis of our thought and action in any and all situations. He believes that there is a great divide between those who have reached that conclusion and those who have reached some other, and that communication between the two groups is impossible, because their respective members start from diametrically opposed positions of belief (or nonbelief) and see with different eyes and hear with different ears. (That is why the antiprelatical tracts end not with a call to understanding, but with a prayer and a curse: a prayer in praise of those regenerates who already agree with Milton, and a curse against those unregenerates who don't.) He believes that the gap between these groups cannot be bridged by pointing to evidence, because their opposition extends to the interpretation of evidence and even to the issue of what the evidence is. (The opposition is dramatized in that wonderful moment when Satan replies to Michael's characterization of the War in Heaven as "evil" by declaring, "The strife which thou call'st evil . . . wee style / The strife of Glory" [PL, VI, 289–290].) He believes that the most important thing to do when dealing with someone is to identify his party—where and with whom he stands—and that one's obligation to others differs according to their moral status. (Thus, when the Son discerns Satan to be other than he seems [PR, I, 348], he receives everything the archfiend says as already tainted. Samson hears Dalila's various justifications of her actions in the same way.) He believes that rationality is a perfectly good tool for everyday purposes, but he knows, with Augustine, that rational entailments are only as good as the presuppositions on which they build and that whenever one thinks to subject those presuppositions (God is good, Christ redeemed our sins) to the test of rationality, one has inverted the hierarchy of first and second and made rationality into an idol. (Eve says as much in book IX: "of this Tree we may not taste nor touch; / God so commanded, and left that Command / Sole Daughter of his voice; the rest, we live / Law to ourselves, our Reason is our Law" [*PL*, 651–654].) He believes that reasons sort themselves into good and bad quite readily, and without presenting puzzles, by the degree to which they do or do not comport with the presuppositions that are the content of true knowing, true thinking, true saying, true seeing, true acting, true being. He believes that once those presuppositions, and no other, fill your mind, every thought you think and every step you take will extend and reaffirm them, and that so long as you do not relax your attachment to them—so long as you do not look for "another meaning" and thereby raise the possibility of another obligation—no one of your thoughts and actions can be in conflict with any other.

Secret Knowledge

The moments when this vision of Milton's is most stringently asserted are those moments that produce discomfort in so many readers—when God lays out the inexorable logic by which Adam and Eve are declared guilty with no mitigating circumstances, when the Epic Voice condemns both Adam's act and his reasons, when the Son in *Paradise Regained* turns his back on hungry people, enslaved tribes, tyrant-ridden populations, and the life of the mind, when Samson responds to Dalila's pleas by threatening to tear her apart, when Comus' celebration of Nature's fertility is met with a dissertation on his inability to understand, when Milton answers the criticism of the regicide by declaring himself sure that the execution of Charles I makes a most pleasing savor in the nostrils of God, or tells those who preach against divorce that they are "senseless trunks" mired in the carnality of flesh. What links these moments is the peremptory assertion of a viewpoint in the company of a contemptuous dismissal of alternative viewpoints and an immediate moral condemnation of those who hold them. These "others" are, typically, not given a hearing, but told that they are blind, have no ear, lack judgment, couldn't possibly understand, are not fit to be convinced. Moreover, they look for meaning and direction in the wrong places—in empirical data, in tradition, in custom, in biblical commentaries, in the proclamations of authorities—and they do this because there is inside them no light by which they might see, no (pre)understanding by which they might hear.[15] As a result, everything important is hidden from them—a secret—and no amount of explanation (short of conversion, which must come *first*) will make the secret theirs.

This last allows us to see another difference between Milton and post-Enlightenment thought: he does not privilege public knowledge. The requirement, standard since Kant, that laws and rules be promulgated in a form that would be understood and accepted by all those to whom they might apply is not one he recognizes, because in both his epistemology and his politics the circuit of communication goes from one regenerate heart to another and the law that counts is written on the fleshly tablets of those regenerate hearts and not on the tablets of others. What this means is that typically in Milton's poetry the important thing is either never said or said in a manner addressed only to initiates (as when the Lady declines to explain the "sage and serious doctrine of virginity"); the climactic act either occurs offstage (as in *Samson Agonistes*) or in silence (as in all of the things the Son *doesn't* say in *Paradise Regained*) or in a declaration that remains mysterious in relation to everything that precedes it (as when the speaker in *Lycidas* declares, "Henceforth thou art the Genius of the shore" [183]).

The doctrine underlying this determined reticence is given in *Lycidas* at the point where the speaker's complaint that fame eludes the good man who dies young is countered by the dramatic (and wholly unprepared-for) intervention of Phoebus:

> *Fame* is no plant that grows on mortal soil,
> Nor in the glistering foil
> Set off to th'world, nor in broad rumor lies,
> But lives and spreds aloft by those pure eyes,
> And perfect witness of all-judging *Jove;*
> As he pronounces lastly on each deed,
> Of so much fame in Heav'n expect thy meed. (78–84)

Note first that fame, or rather true fame, is in exactly the same (double) position as the unsightly root in *Comus:* it takes no necessary worldly form (battles won, books published, ecclesiastical preferment) and is therefore missed by the worldly-limited eye, to which it is invisible. Of course the very notion of an invisible fame seems paradoxical, since visibility is the chief reason fame is sought and valued. Milton does not ignore the paradox but drives it home in the negative construction of "Nor in the glistering foil / Set off to th'world." What a foil does is set off by contrast; it is in the light of *its* glister or glitter that the set-off action is seen. Independently of the foil that frames it, the action would have no shape and therefore no fame; its distinctiveness, that which makes it what it is in the eyes of beholders, is a function of that which it is not, of a border that brings it into relief and therefore into visibility.

What is true of actions grown in mortal soil (they borrow what they are from what they are not) is true also for mortal moments, moments which because they are *in* time—and that is what mortality is, the condition of being bound by temporality—are experienced not in their own fullness (whatever that would mean) but as transitions between a past that hollows them out and a future toward which they lean. When Satan, in *Paradise Regained,* urges the Son to act *now,* "now" is valued for what may follow upon it—success, happiness, fulfillment—rather than for what it "now" is. The Son resists the appeal to the "now" of temporal urgency because in his "now"—the "now" of obedience and loyalty—fulfillment, the sober certainty of waking bliss, is always and already achieved, and is complete in itself without reference either to a past less full or to a future more full.

Fullness and completeness name the condition of not being framed, of not being set off, of not being mortal, and therefore the condition of not being visible in a public scene where there are objects and actions viewed by observers whose responsibility it is to form judgments from a distance. In the scene of fullness and completeness, there is no distance. The observer (exactly the wrong word) resonates to a value and a vision that already constitute him and there is no need for the marks of public recognition, since recognition (on the order of "Yea, brother") has already occurred and is always occurring. The field of fame is entirely internal to a network of self-recognizers, and that is why the agency of true fame is not a report or a citation or a parade of triumph, but the eye of someone who knows a kindred soul when he sees one. It is *by* such an eye—it at once notes, verifies, and "spreds"— that one's fame is broadcast to others whose eyes constitute the network and remains unnoticed (again like the "unsightly root") by those whose eyes are dependent on external (frame or foil-like) structures of distinction and evaluation. God, or someone wholly allied to God, is a "perfect" witness to the good you have done because the act of witnessing takes place instantaneously and without the need for intermediary documentation.

The perfection of the witnessing is precisely its noncoincidence (except in contingent moments not sought for) with the kind of witnessing that takes the form of applause or heraldic titles or monuments of stone and marble. This perfect (independent of any worldly notice) witnessing is dramatized and glossed when God commends Abdiel at the beginning of the War in Heaven: "Servant of God, well done . . . / . . . for this was all thy care / To stand approv'd in the sight of God, though Worlds / Judg'd thee perverse" (*PL*, VI, 29, 35–37). The moment is at once exemplary and anomalous. It is exemplary because it illustrates the doctrine Phoebus declares in *Lycidas:* the mark of true note is one that only the initiate (and God) can see. It is anomalous because in the usual course of things God isn't going to come down and tell you that even if no one else has taken the measure of your worth, he has. Rather, you will be left to supply for yourself the alternative to the world's judgment, to assert against every sign a reality that cannot be confirmed by the only kind of evidence—external, empirical evidence—the unregenerate can recognize. Unbelief is blind.

If what I have termed Milton's "determined reticence" is the deepest feature of his work, it is not surprising to find that work repeatedly thematizing and enacting its own illegibility. This happens in ways large and small. When Adam walks out to meet Raphael, he is described as "without more train / Accompanied than with his own complete / Perfections; in himself was all his state" (*PL*, V, 351–353). What this tells us is, first, that no signs of his dignity surround Adam as he moves forward; second, that such signs would be superfluous because the perfections they would be signs of—majesty, greatness of mind, largeness of spirit—already signify themselves in his naked (in several senses) person; and, third, that because these perfections are attributes of his soul they have no publicly accessible visible form (the "in" in "in himself was all his state" means "inside")—they cannot be listed and need not be listed, at least for those capable of recognizing them. A similar compliment—the compliment of needing no complement—is paid to Eve when she is described—or, more correctly, not described—as "Undeckt, save with herself" (380).

That is, nothing external to her proclaims her worth or adorns her, but, nevertheless, she is her own adornment. This is of course a conventional and clichéd honorific, but Milton means it in an unconventional way: as a statement of the impossibility of assessing (or even knowing) her by referencing something not her. If you want to know what she's like, he is saying, she's not like—comparable to and therefore known in relation to—anything. Like Sabrina in *Comus,* she is her own foil, set off only by herself, and thus unavailable to a system of description—a public system—that operates by contrast. In both these small instances, there is a flourish, a gesture promising identification and revelation, followed by a withdrawal (into the interior) of what has been announced as forthcoming.

This is true on a poem-length scale of *Paradise Regained,* which begins with the first-person narrator's declaration that in what follows he will "tell of deeds / Above Heroic, though in secret done, / And unrecorded left through many an Age, / Worthy t' have not remain'd so long unsung" (I, 14–17). Here the promise is the bringing to public light of what has long remained hidden, and narrative surprise is forgone when we are told in advance that the end of this story will see Christ confirmed "By proof th' undoubted Son of God" (11). This suggests, at the least, the marshaling and documenting of evidence of such public weight that no reasonable person could miss its significance. But the first discerning of significance presented in the poem is of quite another kind. When the Son comes to the river Jordan in response to John the Baptist's general call, he comes "obscure, / Unmarkt, unknown" (24–25); nevertheless, despite the absence of any outward identification, "him the Baptist soon / Descried, divinely warn'd" (25–26). One might think that a divine warning is more than a sufficient substitute for external markings, but the device of warning—"and in likeness of a Dove / The Spirit descended" (30–31)—is no more self-declaring than the true (secret) identity of the Son. After all, Satan, along with everyone else, sees the dove, but doesn't know what to make of it: "I saw . . . / A perfect Dove descend, whate'er it meant" (79, 83). The Baptist knows what to make of it not because his eyesight is better, or because he has more information than those who don't (everyone has the same information), but because he sees within the structure of a faith that confers the right meaning on everything, immediately and without the need of further confirmation. When the Son recalls the same event, he is explicit about his own interpretive processes: "I as all others to his Baptism came, / Which I believ'd was from above" (273–274). His belief is not supported by evidence, but constitutes evidence; he does not come and then believe; he believes and then he comes. Like the Baptist, and in contrast to Satan, the Son experiences no hermeneutical difficulties. What is hidden (and remains so) to Satan is perfectly perspicuous to them; in their eyes the "secret"—who the Son really is, what the dove means—is always and already out in the open.

The poem, then, enacts a paradox: everything is secret, and everything is fully known; although no proof (of the kind apparently promised) will be forthcoming, no proof will be needed, because to those who have eyes to see—perfect witnesses—the proof is everywhere, right on the surface, which is not really a surface because it is suffused with the meaning of which it is the local embodiment. Although disguise, misdirection, rhetorical flourishes, theatrics, light shows, and displays of military might are everywhere in *Paradise Regained,* they are less than distractions to the Son, who sees right through them without even trying. The basic move—hardly a move, because it is so quiet and effortless—is on display in the very first confrontation, when, after listening to an "aged man in Rural weeds" (314), the Son says (in a parenthesis; it doesn't even merit independent assertion), "I discern thee other than thou seem'st" (348). It is important to realize what has *not* happened here. The Son has not displayed a superhuman capacity to penetrate disguises. He just hears a wrong note, and knows that a wrong note comes from a wrong person—not a particular wrong person, but just a person who is wrong, and because wrong, not like him, not wired into the same network of vision and witnessing.

This is all the Son means when he says, "Knowing who I am, as I know who thou art" (356). What is remarkable about this difficultly simple line (just try to write one like it) is that although it declares everyone's knowledge of everything, it gives away nothing itself. That is, it does not say anything so flatfooted or specific as: I know that you are the Prince of Darkness, just as you know that I am the Messiah and the second person of the Trinity. If the Son had said this, the game and the poem would be over, not only because Satan would have succeeded in his stated mission— "Who this is we must learn" (91)—but because he would also have succeeded in winning the contest between them. It is one of the ironies of the poem that although Satan regards his efforts to get a "fix" on the Son as strategic—he will be better able to combat his adversary if he knows exactly who he is—the achievement of that goal would be not preliminary but final. Satan hopes that he is dealing with a mere man—impressive no doubt, yet no more impressive, perhaps, than Alexander or Scipio (196–200)—and at the same time is afraid that he may be dealing with divinity. But the revelation he fears—"Yes, I am the Son of God in a special way, so special that in effect I *am* God"—would, if it were to occur, be the revelation that gave him victory; for any such announcement would take away the exemplary status of the Son's performance, which would no longer be available as a model to those without supernatural powers. Neither of the possibilities Satan sees as exhaustive—he is a God, he is mere man— are ones the Son can embrace. The first makes what he does in response to the temptations too special; the second slights the special qualities of the man who is more than "mere," not because he *is* God (in the sense of that being his secret identity) but because he is pledged to God, trusts in Him, and relies on His power rather than on the exercise of his own ("Who brought me hither / Will bring me hence" [335–336]). It is the notion of a mode of being sustained by faith in another, and "On other surety none" (*PL*, V, 538), that escapes Satan; and the Son, in turn, escapes Satan's mousetrap devices by refusing either to claim godhead or to disclaim the special—not supernatural—abilities that attend perfect dependence.

One of those abilities is the ability to discern impious suggestions, suggestions that give too much to your own powers and too little to God's ("Why dost thou . . . suggest to me distrust?" [*PR*, I, 355]). When you hear such a suggestion you can say, "I discern thee other than thou seem'st," and mean only, "I see that you are one of those without a moral center," and you can also say, "Knowing who I am, as I know who thou art" and mean only, "Knowing as you and I both do that we are on opposite sides." To this last assertion, at once unequivocal and withholding, Satan responds by saying in effect, "I don't want to know what side you're on; I want to know who and what you are." But what the Son knows is that he *is* the side he is on (an account of identity exactly the opposite of the liberal one), and he knows too that his identity (knowledge of which Satan frantically seeks) is a function of an inward orientation that shows itself not in public acts of proof but in private acts of allegiance; and since the allegiance is precisely not to anything visible, it cannot be made visible in a way that will satisfy Satan's scrutiny. Indeed, to make the allegiance visible, to present it in terms Satan could comprehend, would be to default on it, to give palpable empirical form to that which must remain entirely internal. In order to continue to be what he is—a being on the side of spirit—the Son must refuse to go public, even though public proof is promised both by the epic narrator and by God: "*Gabriel,* this day by proof thou shalt behold" (130). No doubt Gabriel does behold, because unlike Satan he can see the inward action informing the refusal to act spectacularly (to turn stones into bread, or dethrone tyrants). What the Son does is no secret to him, even as it must be secret—undisclosed, hidden—to those (characters and readers) looking for the evidence of things seen.[16]

De-Authorizing Public Writing

But how does one write a poem that declines to yield its meaning, that withholds revelation, that resists saying anything in response to the questions (what's going on here? what's at stake? why did he do, or not do, that?) it provokes? What fills up the space of four books? The answer (worked out in *Of Prelaticall Episcopacy*, as we shall see in Chapter 5) is that *Paradise Regained* displays reticence, acts out its withdrawal from legibility, and makes a plot (of a curious kind) out of promising repeatedly to provide more than it ever delivers. The promise is particularly explicit when the epic narrator describes the Son as he moves into the desert:

> Meanwhile the Son of God, . . .
>
> . . . . .
>
> Musing and much revolving in his breast,
> How best the mighty work he might begin
> Of Savior to mankind, and which way first
> Publish his Godlike office now mature,
> One day forth walk'd alone, the Spirit leading,
> And his deep thoughts, the better to converse
> With solitude, till far from track of men,
> Thought following thought, and step by step led on,
> He enter'd now the bordering Desert wild,
> And with dark shades and rocks environ'd round,
> His holy Meditations thus pursu'd. (*PR*, I, 183, 185–195)

67

The opening lines of the passage provoke two expectations: first that the result of the Son's deliberation will be a plan with world-shaking consequences (some "mighty work"), and second that the plan will be made public—will be, as the verse says, published—so that both its beneficiaries and its targeted adversaries can know what is in store for them. The disappointing of this expectation is already under way when the action preliminary to the "mighty" action—the action of taking a walk in a particular landscape—loses its physical specificity as the landscape becomes entirely mental. The transformation is at first gradual: one can make conventional narrative sense out of the idea of a walk that is in some way led by a spirit; but the addition of "And . . . deep thoughts" as the co-subject of "leading" internalizes the animating force and by doing so confines the action taking place to the realm of thoughts, to the mind. The sense of isolation (the very antithesis of anything "public") is confirmed and intensified when we are told that the Son walks out so as to be able "better to converse / With solitude"—that is, so he can keep company with (*converso*) himself. "Far from track of men" is not only a flatfootedly literal description of the desert surroundings; it also declares the absence that makes this moment so typical of the poem—the absence of marks one could decipher, directions one could follow, signs one could point to.

In the next line the process of internalization is complete when "Thought following thought" precedes "step by step," and we know that the steps are steps of reflection and have no reference at all to actual physical movement. (Milton had already perfected this psychologizing of landscape as early as *Il Penseroso*, when the "pensive Nun" walks in a way so abstracted and abstract that she finally forgets herself to marble [42] and is "held in holy passion still" [41], where "still" has the triple meaning of quietly, without movement, and with duration.) When the object of "pursu'd," a word in the vocabulary of quest and drama, turns out to be "holy Meditations," no adjustment is required on our part as readers, for we have long since left behind any expectation that something will, in any crude sense, happen.

The pattern, in which the anticipation of measurable and publicly confirmable effects gives way to the referencing of effects that transpire in no particular place and are recorded on no page, is repeated when the Son rehearses the career of his "deep thoughts." He remembers when his "mind was set" to do "public good" (*PR*, I, 202, 204), perhaps by performing "victorious deeds" (215) and "heroic acts" (216); but at some point he abandons these spectacular projects for a project less visible in its (immediate) consequences, though more efficacious in the long run: "Yet held it more humane, more heavenly, first / By winning words to conquer willing hearts, / And make persuasion do the work of fear" (221–223). That work, it hardly need be said, will be "inside work," and it may or may not result in changes in the material world. That is, it may remain invisible, unrecorded, unsung, "in secret done," known to no one except to the "perfect witness of all-judging *Jove*" (*Lycidas*, 82). Although the Son continues to invoke the vocabulary of the public stage "Now . . . I no more should live obscure, / But openly begin, as best becomes / The Authority which I deriv'd from Heaven" (*PR*, I, 287–289)—obscurity, in the sense of giving away nothing, continues to be the (non)mark of his performance, and the only thing he does "openly" is refuse to open himself up to Satan's ceaseless attempts ("Still will be tempting him who foils him still, / And never cease, though to his shame the more" [IV, 13–14]) to bring him out into the open.

Nor is this merely a negative strategy—it corresponds perfectly to the nature of the Son's mission as he understands it:

> henceforth Oracles are ceast
>
> . . . . .

> God hath now sent his living Oracle
> Into the World to teach his final will,
> And sends his Spirit of Truth henceforth to dwell
> In pious Hearts, an inward Oracle
> To all truth requisite for men to know. (I, 456, 460–464)

The Son is a living oracle because the message ventriloquized by involuntary oracles like Satan is written on the fleshly tables of his heart, where it is accessible to, because it is also written in, other hearts similarly pious (in the sense of dedicated to deity). The appearance of the Son on earth inaugurates the end of writing understood as public marks forming a system of conventions and available for deciphering to all who have learned, at least at the mechanical level, to read, and substitutes a writing that has receded from public view.

This holds true even if the public writing is Scripture. Satan's last ploy, after he has taken the Son to the pinnacle of the temple's spire, is to invite him to cast himself down and to do so on Scripture's authority: "safely if Son of God: / For it is written, He will give command / Concerning thee to his Angels, in thir hands / They shall up lift thee" (IV, 555–558). The Son replies in the most disputed line-and-a-half in the poem:

> Also it is written,
> Tempt not the Lord thy God; he said and stood.
> But Satan smitten with amazement fell. (560–562)

What smites Satan is the ease with which the Son again repels his probing by producing an utterance that is at once authoritative and devoid of any claim that would amount to a revelation. He does not say, "I am the Lord thy God—don't tempt me," but, rather, "If I were to do what you urge, I would be making trial of God, as if he could be the object of my judgment." In saying this he stands, both in the sense of not falling from his "uneasy station" (584) and in the sense of not falling to the temptation to claim godhead. Yet the alternative reading in which the Son does in fact claim godhead is not entirely wrong; for by refusing to exert himself (either physically or verbally) in ways that would call into question the sufficiency of the power in whom he trusts, he attaches himself to that power and becomes its receptacle, its temple, its living oracle, the lodging of "something holy." As he does so, he turns words—scriptural words—that might in the mouth of another be the expression of pride into an expression of perfect dependence; and as he does that, he adds Scripture to the long list of objects (money, armies, books) and actions (feeding the hungry, freeing captive peoples) that in and of themselves bear no obvious significance, but acquire significance (and value) according to the person who avails himself of them. The Scriptures, what is written, are quite another thing when they issue from the Son than they are when they issue from Satan; the guidance they offer is only as good as the speaker who quotes them and the hearer who receives them. Their true meaning lies not on their surface, but in the secret hidden-from-view depths where those who can discern it already live.

This decentering of Scripture as a self-sufficient and publicly available source of authority in favor of the internal authority of rightly constituted hearts is perhaps the best, because most extreme, confirmation of my thesis that Milton works from the inside out. It is a confirmation Milton performs again and at length in the *Christian Doctrine*. We have, he says, "a double scripture. There is the external scripture of the written word and the internal scripture of the Holy Spirit which he, according to God's promise, has engraved upon the hearts of believers."[17] Although the external Scripture "is of very considerable importance," nonetheless the "pre-eminent and supreme authority . . . is the authority of the Spirit, which is internal." After all, Milton reminds us, the Scriptures, as we have them, have been transmitted by "a variety of hands, some more corrupt than others" (589), and needless to say the "visible church" has often suffered corruption of more than a textual kind. Therefore it is "the hearts of believers" and not the visible church "which, since Christ's ascension . . . , are the real *house and church of the living God,* I Tim. iii. 15" (589). Milton is aware of the irony involved in citing Scripture in order to de-authorize it, but he regards that as Scripture's best office; even "on the evidence of scripture itself, all things are eventually to be referred to the Spirit and the unwritten word" (590).

The unwritten word is not illegible; it's just that reading it is a matter not of parsing the written word but of hearing it within a certain spirit. Absent that spirit, the written word is an unreliable guide to the truth with which we would join, and it may be a positive impediment if we rest in it and mistake its apparent solidity for that which it cannot contain. If we must have writing, let it be writing that discourages such premature rest by provoking us to look beyond it, as do the "evangelick precepts" of Christ, which because they are "given us in proverbiall formes" work "to drive us from the letter, though we love ever to be sticking there."[18] We love to be sticking there because in the absence of the letter—of visible marks of direction, meaning, significance, value—there seems to be no way of determining with certainty what is true and false, real and unreal. There seems, in short, nothing to hang on to, which is why when the letter is taken away from someone who has always clung to it and has steered by its compass, he feels cast adrift, without moorings, confused, disoriented, abandoned, betrayed.

Becoming Parchment

This is exactly how the speaker of *Lycidas* feels when he hears the news of the death of a young and promising friend: it seems to him to be the end both of intelligibility and of a reason to persevere in his labors. After all, why go on ("What boots it with uncessant care?" [64]), if at any moment your efforts can be cut short long before their fruition, as "the blind *Fury* with th'abhorred shears / . . . slits the thin-spun life" (75–76)? It has long been obvious to commentators that the lament for Lycidas (Edward King) is a lament for the loss of confidence the speaker suffers when he applies the (apparent) lesson of his friend's fate to himself. He fears that he too may not live long enough to earn his place in the tradition of pastoral poetry, a tradition on which he is dependent for his own sense of dignity and worth. He responds to this fear with a double gesture: he will memorialize Lycidas in verse and thus make sure that the drowned youth does not disappear from the records of time; and by doing this he will insert into those same records evidence of his own abilities, even if that evidence is offered prematurely, and he must write with "forc'd fingers rude" (4)—that is, with fingers that force an early composition because they are themselves forced by unhappy (and despair-inducing) circumstances. He will make a mark for Lycidas and at the same time make his own mark and thus deprive the blind Fury of her victory.

Both the desperation of the effort and the multiple anxieties informing it are on display in three densely packed lines:

> He must not float upon his wat'ry bier
> Unwept, and welter to the parching wind,
> Without the meed of some melodious tear. (12–14)

What the speaker imagines is quite precise: a body tossed about on the surface of the water and exposed to the effects of the sun and wind. It is when we stay a moment on these lines that the deeper (beneath the surface) story they tell becomes legible. The key is the word "parching," which triggers a pun of the kind Milton particularly likes: a wind that parches (dries) a body turns that body into parchment, into a scraped and tightly stretched piece of skin made ready to receive writing, to bear marks. In the course of achieving (exactly the wrong word) that condition, the body's own marks, the distinguishing features of its physiognomy, the characters (inscribed lines and wrinkles) that give it character, are effaced, and other marks, made by forces wholly indifferent to its history and identity, have their way and make their imprint. The physical and metaphysical fears here are mirrors of one another: water will wear away the protuberances and declivities of the body and render it unrecognizable, a smooth and empty tablet indistinguishable from any other; time will wear away the memory of whatever one accomplishes, and as the accomplishments of others crowd the stage it will be as if one had never lived.

That is why Lycidas *must not* float upon his watery bier unwept, without some notice of his having been here. The "melodious tear" the speaker promises, the tear that is this poem, will quite literally remoisten the parched body and return to it some measure of what the wind and sun have taken away, some measure of distinctiveness; and that same tear, if it is sufficiently melodious, will display the poet's own distinctiveness, his own ability to "build the lofty rhyme" (11), and be evidence that his own juices have not run dry. (Milton here might well be alluding to, and playing against, the opening lines of Spenser's "Januarye" eclogue, where Colin Cloute laments the drying up of his procreative powers—"my lustfull leafe is drye and sere"—and resolves to break his pastoral pipe.)[19]

What is at stake in the poem is enormous, nothing less than the potency of separate agency, the capacity for inscribing in the registers of time some indication of one's existence, the hope of performing actions (physical and verbal) that will leave a mark and perhaps even generate fructifying effects—a lineage of some kind—after one has died. The horror occasioned by the possibility (augured by the example of Lycidas) that the case will be quite otherwise, that what awaits one is annihilation, effacement, and barrenness, finds expression in the many images of castration that haunt the poem—the abhorred shears of the Fury, the dismemberment of Orpheus with special attention to his severed head, the closing of the "remorseless [*remordere*, to bite again] deep" (50) over the head of Lycidas, the allusion to the story of Hyacinthus, a beautiful youth cut off in his prime by Apollo, the blind mouths that don't know how to hold a sheep hook, the two-handed engine ready to smite. All of these are figures (not at all shadowy) for the act of violence that prompts the poem, the act that not only hurls Lycidas into the oblivion of the remorseless deep (so deep that he will never be seen again) but tells the poet that his own oblivion is imminent. Will it be tomorrow, next week, next year? Who can know and, not knowing, who can inaugurate a design, build a rhyme, start a family, protect the sheep, reform the church? Who can do anything given the prospect of one's "own obliteration,"[20] the prospect of being made into parchment, into a surface on which many meanings will be written (by water, wind, rocks, shark's teeth) but never the meaning one originates, never the meaning that says "Here *I* am" or "*I* was here"?[21]

One thing the poet can do, or try to do, is mount an act of counter-violence by writing a poem that refuses to be reconciled to the fate awaiting all individual utterances. This is, I think, the significance of his doing without the conversation between shepherds that traditionally frames the pastoral elegy and marks its status as a conventional performance, something that has been done before and in a way which at once enables and constrains the present lyric moment. What the frame says is, "This expression of sorrow and pain is staged, and staged in conformity with a preexisting model. It's been said before and will be said again. There's nothing new under the sun." It is in response to the tradition's claim to be first and to have scripted in advance what he can say that the speaker simply bursts in and starts talking without so much as a by-your-leave. To be sure, he does acknowledge the breach of decorum—I'm "crude," I'm "rude," I'm speaking before my turn and without regard for your timetable, I'm shattering your leaves before the mellowing year—but the apology is also a boast: I *can* be crude, I *can* be distinctively unpolished, I *can* be out of sync with your rules and conventions, I *can* occupy a space of utterance not already preempted. Indeed (the lines declare), I can do more than that: I can clear you away, disperse your leaves, and bring my own to the fore. It's payback time; you've disturbed my season—I'm going to disturb yours. So there!

Of course the pretense to genuine (as opposed to conventional) resistance is undermined by its very expression, by its first words—"Yet once more"—at once a cry of exasperation ("There you go again, cutting short the lives of the wrong people, upsetting the best-laid plans") and an acknowledgment, however inadvertent, that there is not, nor could there be, anything original about this; it's happened to others, it's happening to Lycidas, it will happen to me. The acknowledgment is openly made in a few lines as the poet anticipates the day when "some gentle Muse" (19) will speak a few words over "my destin'd Urn" (20). This is as much to say, "Here I am," or, rather, "Here I am not, just one in a series, like all the others, with nothing to say for myself."

But if the speaker is unable to distance himself from the tradition that claims him as a mere item in its history, he can attempt to achieve distance in another way: by subjecting the events in that history to a cause/effect analysis that renders them less mysterious than they seem when they first occur. By coming to understand what has happened to Lycidas and may happen to him, the poet can in a sense master his fate even if he cannot escape it; for if an anomaly like the unmerited death of a young man can be explained by charting the convergence of physical forces (even if the convergence remains fortuitous and contingent), the explanation will perform the double service of taming the anomaly and putting off the day when one must confront the implications of living in a world in which God has removed his ways "from human sense" (*PL,* VIII, 119). Indeed, whenever a character in Milton's poetry seeks to avoid coming to terms with his or her creaturehood in order to claim a measure (however small) of independence, he or she will have recourse to empirical reasoning. Thus Satan says to Eve, "look on mee" (IX, 687), inviting her to substitute the observation of physical processes (in this case illusory) for the first principles she is pledged to maintain. Eve, in her turn, makes literal the substitution when she offers its logic (along with the apple) to Adam: "On my experience . . . freely taste" (988). Mammon performs the first physicalist reduction, designed specifically to exclude any recognition of deity and spirit, when he resolves to build a new heaven from the raw materials of hell, a resolution that makes sense to him because his conception of heaven is so relentlessly material: "what can Heav'n show more?" (II, 273). Satan shows him the way when with even more audacity he offers cannon and shot as devices for making the rebels equal, perhaps superior, to God. Adam flirts with the same impiety when he demands an account of heavenly movements that would satisfy the criteria of an efficiency expert. In *Samson Agonistes,* this form of thought is given a name—appointing heavenly disposition—and everyone, including the ruined hero, gets in on the game by offering tidy (if mutually exclusive) explanations of why God's favorite now sits eyeless in Gaza.

What informs each of these moments is a faith in the possibility of getting to the truth of things from the ground up, which is also the possibility of acquiring deep knowledge by extrapolating from surfaces, which is also the possibility of going from the outside (or from many outsides) to the inside. Although such reasoning is the very antithesis of the way of knowing that Milton

everywhere celebrates, it is entirely characteristic of him to catalogue and even caress its attractions on the way to rejecting
them. Nearly a quarter of *Lycidas* (88–131) is taken up by an investigation of the cause or causes of the fatal shipwreck. Was it
the waves? Was it the winds? Did Hippotades let a stray gust escape from his dungeon? The answers are all negative, and lead
only to further questions, first by Camus, spokesman for the
power of knowledge and civilization, who has no information to
offer and asks plaintively, "Who hath reft . . . my dearest pledge?"
(107), and then by Peter, who, rather than assuaging the poet's
outrage, amplifies it by dwelling on the manifest injustice and
loss to the world ("How well could I have spar'd" [113]) that attend Lycidas' "accident." The best that Peter can do is predict that
those unworthies who unaccountably flourish while Lycidas wel-
ters in the parching wind will get theirs too. Someday, the two-
handed engine, whatever it is, will smite and the ledger will be
balanced—that is, *everyone* will have suffered. Hardly comforting,
and of no help whatsoever to the anyone who is trying to understand. When Peter ends his diatribe, the first-person speaker has
gained nothing but a fuller knowledge of how much he doesn't
know. He doesn't know what happened. He doesn't know who
did it. He has no evidence, no body, no direction of inquiry. As
far as he can tell the event whose explanation he seeks couldn't
possibly have happened. After all, the air was calm and the waters
unperturbed (98). After rounding up all the suspects (including
the Nymphs, who for some reason were not on duty), putting
the relevant questions, taking depositions, he is reduced to the
manifest absurdity of blaming the boat ("It was that fatal and
perfidious Bark" [100]), and conjecturing—it is a conjecture of
desperation—that some unidentified and malign power has put a
curse on it for some unidentified and malign reason.

But this, Milton would say, is where empirical investigation always gets you: nowhere or (it is the same thing) anywhere. When

you look at particulars severed from any already-in-place assumption about what things mean generally, they tell you nothing or they tell you anything. The Satan of *Paradise Regained* spends four books finding this out, although he never accepts it and at the very last is still hoping that some alternative test or method of interrogation will yield what years of "narrower Scrutiny" (IV, 515) have failed to uncover. He was present at the Son's birth, perhaps in the form of a farm animal in the corner of the stable; he was watching even in the Son's private moments (perhaps a fly on the wall); he came to the baptism; he followed him around (as he has followed him into the desert); he has employed microscopes and telescopes; he has never "ceas'd to eye" (507) him; he has collected evidence and extrapolated from it his "best conjectures" (524)—and after all that, he still hasn't the slightest idea of "In what degree or meaning thou art call'd / The Son of God" (516–517), any more than the speaker in *Lycidas* has the slightest idea of what it means that his friend of so much promise has died young.[22]

At least Satan puts his finger on the problem when he observes that the phrase "Son of God" "bears no single sense" (517). Exactly! No particular, no fact, bears a single sense—declares a firm and unequivocal meaning—if it is viewed in isolation from the larger sense of which it is a manifestation. Strange as it may seem to the empiricist, you have to know what something means *before* you see it; and then, when you see it, the meaning you already know it to have will be perspicuous for you, without conjectures, collections, evidence gathering, narrower scrutinies, inquests, trials, methods, or tests. And, conversely, if you don't already know what something means, its meaning, when you see it, will be hidden from you. So long as he is looking out at the world's landscape and trying to deduce from its "shows" the significance of an item or an event (a young man's dying), the poet in *Lycidas* finds everything unintelligible, a puzzle, an impasse.

The impasse cannot be removed by collecting still more information, for in the absence of a prior specification of what it is information *about*, additional details will only deepen the mystery.

That is why, as so many have observed, the turn in *Lycidas* from lamentation to rejoicing occurs (as it also does in Spenser's "November" eclogue) without preparation. One moment we are caught up in a current of despair conveyed verbally by a concatenation of words beginning with *w*—"Whilst" (154), "Wash" (155), "Whether" (156), "Where" (157), "whether" (159), "Where" (161), "waft" (164)—and in the next moment the same consonant sweeps us up in celebration: "Weep no more, woeful Shepherds weep no more" (165). Nothing is changed and everything has changed. With no more evidence than he had before, and with Lycidas still "Sunk . . . beneath the wat'ry floor" (167), the poet nevertheless finds affirmation where he previously had found only doubt and darkness; the long-lost body is discovered in a new place, in a landscape radically disjunct ("other groves, and other streams" [174]) from the one whose barrenness he has been cataloguing, and in a position that more than redeems the fact of its physical death:

> Now *Lycidas*, the Shepherds weep no more;
> Henceforth thou art the Genius of the shore,
> In thy large recompense, and shalt be good
> To all that wander in that perilous flood. (182–185)

The strength of this declaration cannot be overestimated. "Henceforth" is practically a decree, and what it decrees is the undoubted and benign meaning of Lycidas' death. That meaning does not follow from the facts independently surveyed; it precedes and delivers the facts, and it delivers them not as the result of an act of calculation—a putting together of little bits of evidence so that they form a whole—but as the result of an act of transformation effected by a decision, and a willful decision, to see things one way rather than another. The confidence of "Henceforth" is independent of the evidence of things seen and is the projection outward of an inward vision unsupported by anything but itself. "I say, and by so saying bring it about, that henceforth thou art the genius of the shore."

On what authority? The answer has been given in line 173: "Through the dear might of him that walk'd the waves." That is, I proclaim Lycidas the genius of the shore not on my own authority, but on the authority of the Savior in whom I believe and of whose holiness I am the lodging. The "might" the Savior displays by walking on the waves is not the might of a supernatural being but, as the allusion to Matthew 14 makes clear, the might of one who does not doubt. Peter begins to sink because, like the Lady in *Comus* when the "single darkness" (204) threatens to unsettle her, he reasons from the physical situation ("when he saw the wind boisterous" [14:30]) to a loss of inner confidence ("he was afraid"). The Lady recovers herself, and by an act of the believing will transforms the external landscape into an emblem of the hope she carries within her. Peter does not recover himself, and is the recipient of Jesus' precise and just rebuke: "O thou of little faith, wherefore didst thou doubt?" (14:31).

For more than 160 lines, the poem's speaker has displayed little, if any, faith, looking for some boisterous wind that might render intelligible and (relatively) acceptable an event that has both startled and astounded him, in search of the very kind of evidence (of things seen) on which Peter—the same Peter who in lines 108–131 can offer only a narrative of retribution and damnation—so unhappily relies. That search fails, and at the moment when its promise has proved so empty that nothing could reanimate it, the poet abandons it and turns inward to the reservoir in him of the "might" his God both enacts (on the water, on the

Cross) and demands: the might of faith, the might of affirming in the absence of evidence or against evidence a bottom-line reality that, once affirmed, orders the world in its every detail. With that reality in place (in the speaker's heart), a new question is asked: not "How can we make sense of the senseless cutting short of a promising life?" but "Given a God who is all-powerful, benign, and ever regardful of the just and good (he is the 'perfect witness'), what does it mean that Lycidas has been taken?" The answer comes back immediately. It must mean—the "must" follows from the premise that it is this kind of God who presides over us—that Lycidas is being rewarded, and rewarded in a way that will redound not only to his benefit but to the benefit of us all ("and shalt be good / To *all*" [184–185]). Faith is so mighty that it makes sense not only of the present occasion but of occasions yet to come.

At this moment all the tensions and discordances in the poem are resolved. The fear that the speaker, like his drowned friend, may one day become parchment, a stretched surface from which the marks of individuation have been removed, a blank tablet ready for inscription by forces indifferent to its mortal career, is turned into a celebration by the invocation of a deity who voluntarily underwent just such a loss of power and agency. In preparation for his redemptive mission, the Son freely puts off his "glory" (*PL*, III, 240, 239) to become mere (or in his case not so mere) man. He empties himself of the glory and the form of his divinity (the doctrine is called *kenosis*)[23] and gives himself up to be marked by the tribulations and wounds of mortal life, even to the extent of having his body pierced by nails and a spear thrust. And as if this were not enough, he defaces and disfigures himself further by taking to himself the sins of countless others, allowing the marks of their pride to be written on his body. In response, those for whom he performed what Milton calls this "God-like act" (XII, 427) need only give themselves up to him and to the Holy Spirit, who will erase from their hearts the carnal and cupidinous messages naturally there and write on the expunged tablets the message of heavenly love.

In this vision, the prospect of having one's own features effaced (by water, by disease, by senility), of losing the distinctiveness of one's voice, of being written on rather than writing, is to be viewed not with horror but with joy, and it is joyfully that the poet imagines a Lycidas who is blessed *because* he has lost his identity:

> With *Nectar* pure his oozy Locks he laves,
> And hears the unexpressive nuptial Song,
> In the blest Kingdoms meek of joy and love. (175–177)

He hears the song because he is one of those knit in marriage by its harmonies. He is thus a component in the song, at once a producer and a consumer, existing not as a single entity but as a member of an ensemble of a "solemn troop" or "sweet society." And the fact that the song is "unexpressive"—not taking any material form—presents no difficulty; since it lives within him and makes him what he is (and what he isn't), it need not be audible in order to be heard. One (no longer *a* one) hears the music of one's own being, hears the inner music, *is* the inner music.

In the preceding paragraphs I have uncritically accepted the poem's conclusion as the triumph that finally arrives after so many false surmises and exploded fictions. But if we shake free of the mesmerizing power of these lines, another possible relationship between this moment and the earlier moments it supposedly transcends comes into view. It may mark not the leaving behind of the egoism and concern for achievement that give the poem its early power, but a sublimation of those self-regarding impulses into a register so rarefied that they are almost (but perhaps not quite) unrecognizable. The question, as Peter Sacks observes, is undecidable, for although the poem's last section surely "reflects back on Christ's power to effect a spiritual sunlike rise for man," at the moment of strong assertion ("Henceforth thou art") it is Milton who "has calmly assumed the power himself," it is Milton who "makes the uncouth swain rise" (*The English Elegy*, 116). What we may be seeing here, Sacks concludes, is "an internalizing counter-usurpation of totemic power" in which "the figure of the elegist" has been "substituted . . . for both the sun and God" (117). Sacks's speculation reopens what the poem (and my analysis of it) attempts to close: the question of what authorizes the poet's announcement of Lycidas' new job as genius of the shore. I have argued that the poem's crucial turn occurs when the speaker abandons the search (and the need) for an external authorization and looks inward for the authorization provided by his faith in him who walked the waves; but it is precisely because that authorization is internal and is confirmed by no outward public marks that it is vulnerable to the challenge of the unbeliever who says "Show me!" and who suspects that the speaker may too easily have conflated his own (merely asserted) authority with the authority of God. That is, if he ceases his prideful efforts to write Lycidas' story himself (as either the story of a young man badly treated by the fates or as the story of a mystery that resists explanation) and instead resolves to read (and proclaim) the story written in his heart by the Holy Spirit, how can he be sure—how can *we* be sure—that this new story is any less his than the stories it supplants? How can we be sure that the power (to understand, to master) the speaker has forsworn is not being reclaimed in a gesture of only apparent submission? How can you (or anyone) know that in the guise of offering yourself as parchment you are not once again inscribing (or at least trying to inscribe) your own meaning on the blank tablet of the world?

How can you know that what is presented as an act of faith (I do not say this, Christ does; not me, but my master in me) is not the hubris of someone who wants to have both the first and the last word and only pretends (the pretense may fool *him*) to defer to the word of another? How can you know whether what is being performed here is the triumphant assertion of the poetic will or the surrender of that will (and its pretensions) to the will of God? How can you be sure that "Henceforth" is not the most presumptuous word a poet has ever spoken?

Hardly To Be Discerned

There are no answers to these questions. Answers would be available only if the world's surfaces directed one (everyone; that's what *public* verification requires) to its true meaning, and it is precisely Milton's contention, as we have seen again and again, that the true meaning can be discerned only by the heart and mind already informed by it, and that therefore neither you nor anyone listening to you can be certain of the source (prideful or faithful) from which your utterances issue. This holds not only for the speaker in *Lycidas* but for all of Milton's speakers, and for Milton himself. When the Lady claims a power that would shake the earth and bring Comus' palace down around his ears, she claims it as a "rapt" (794) spirit, possessed by and speaking in the name of an agent greater than she. But how can she or we tell whether that is, in fact, the case, or whether, perhaps, she speaks from within a delusion of grandeur? When Samson feels "Some rousing motions"[24] and, impelled by them, pulls down the Philistine temple, killing two thousand people, does he act at the behest of his Lord or is he once again a "petty God" (529) who deceives himself into thinking that he is in the service of the real one? (These alternative readings continue to be played out in the criticism.) When Milton, or his epic voice, promises to "soar / Above th' *Aonian* Mount" (*PL*, I, 14–15) and quickly attributes his future success to the spirit that dwells in his "upright heart and pure" (18), can we take him at his word? After all, we have only his word that the word he is asking us to take is greater than his.

Catherine Belsey casts a cold deconstructive eye on such gestures of prideful humility, and argues in her *John Milton* that while the claim to be merely the vehicle of a deep and unmediated truth is made often by Milton's heroes and by Milton himself ("I conceav'd myself to be not now as mine own person, but as a member incorporate into that truth wherof I was perswaded" [*Apology*, I, 871]), that truth, and indeed any truth, is available only in a represented form, in the form of a signifier that is always at a remove from its signified. Truth with a capital *T*, says Belsey, is never ours; we have only its textual—and therefore debatable, challengeable, revisable—assertion. The mature Milton would not disagree, for from the time of the divorce tracts he proclaims at once the singleness of truth and the impossibility of knowing with certainty that one is in possession of it. Certainty would be achieved only in a world where disagreements could be referred to some authoritative and self-interpreting source—say, the Ten Commandments or Scripture in general. But in a world where authority is internalized and the true meaning of an act depends on the spirit that animates it—a spirit that is by definition removed from external inspection—you can never be completely secure in your judgments, and indeed security, in the root sense of being without care, is a danger: "he who thinks we are to pitch our tent here, and have attain'd the utmost prospect of reformation, that the mortall glasse wherein we contemplate, can shew us, till we come to *beatific* vision, that man by this very opinion declares, that he is yet farre short of Truth."[25] The proper relation to truth requires that you always be uneasy with respect to your present sense of it, always alert to the possibility that you may have failed to identify it or have identified it with the wrong receptacle; for truth is such that its "first appearance to our eyes blear'd and dimm'd with prejudice and custom, is more unsightly and unplausible than many errors, even as the person is of many a great man slight and contemptible to see to" (*Areopagitica*, 330). (Note the appearance of our old friend "unsightly," here accompanied by a gloss of the meaning Milton intends—an excellence that escapes the eye of the merely outward discerner.)

Nor is it easy for anyone to be a discerner of the unsightly, of what does not "show," for "the knowledge of good is so involv'd and interwoven with the knowledge of evil, and in so many cunning resemblances hardly to be discern'd, that those confused seeds which were imposed on *Psyche* as an incessant labour to cull out, and sort asunder, were not more intermixt" (287). "Hardly" means both "barely" and "with difficulty," and in this double sense the word names the epistemological and moral situation of those living in a world whose truths and meanings are "unsightly": one is always at risk of falling into error, of taking evil for good; moreover, there is no rule or benchmark or overarching calculus to which you could refer your judgments, should you be in doubt (as you always should be) as to their status. Danger surrounds us and comes in two chief forms: the danger of mistaking a fair outside for a fair inside (the mistake Raphael counsels Adam against and the one Milton fears he himself made when he married Mary Powell) and the danger of misreading our own motives, of mistaking our carnal desires for the desire to do God's will (this is the mistake Manoa accuses Samson of making and the mistake Samson thinks himself to have made in marrying Dalila: "I thought it lawful" [231]). There are only two acts one can perform in a world created and presided over by a God who is at once everywhere and nowhere: either an act that affirms his preeminence and claims nothing more (or less) than to be tracing out the meanings he has already inscribed on the face of things, or an act that affirms the self and claims the ability to generate one's own meanings and, through them, one's own world. The question one is always asking—whether as actor, observer, or reader—is "Which is it?" and the answer, at least as Milton gives it, is that the difference can hardly be discerned.

At times, however, the difference seems clearly marked, as it is in the contrast between God's writing of the world in book VII of *Paradise Lost* and Satan's efforts in book VI to rewrite it in his own image. The distinctive character of divine writing is established when the Son is given his charge by the Father: "And thou my Word, begotten Son, by thee / This I perform, speak thou, and be it done" (VII, 163–164). What this Word utters it effects immediately, just as when a judge pronounces sentence or says, "I declare you to be man and wife." The world, or the relevant part of it, conforms itself to the condition he announces: the defendant is now and henceforth an incarcerated felon; there exists now a new compound entity, a married couple. In speech act theory (as originated by J. L. Austin), this is what is known as a "declarative"—an utterance that brings into being the state it names, and does so by virtue of the unique authority of the speaker (when an umpire declares "You're out," you're out, but when a fan or a fellow player says it, he succeeds only in expressing his opinion). In this case the speaker's authority is truly unique, for as the founding agent of all creation—there is nothing before him and no thing he has not brought to life—the Real is a product of his speaking it: "speak thou, and be it done."

That is why this Word is called "Omnific" (217) and why the act of creation is an act of writing:

> He took the golden Compasses, prepar'd
> In God's Eternal store, to circumscribe
> This Universe, and all created things:

One foot he centred, and the other turn'd
Round through the vast profundity obscure,
And said, Thus far extend, thus far thy bounds,
This be thy just Circumference, O World. (225–231)

"Circumscribe" means literally "to make lines around," and normally we expect it to be a transitive verb—i.e., "to make lines around" *something; but* this act of circumscription creates that to which it simultaneously refers. There is nothing prior to it and therefore it is not a representation, is not secondary in relation to a preexisting object. (The world of "O World" is brought into being in the instant it is addressed.) Because it is not a representation or secondary, there is no gap—no area in which it might stray—between its performance and what it designates; and because there is no gap, there is no requirement of accuracy or verisimilitude it must meet. If you ask "How far is 'thus far'?" or "Exactly how is the justness of the circumference to be determined?" you miss the point; this is not an act performed according to a norm, but an act that constitutes a norm at the moment of declaring it. It is not a norm available to judgment but one that establishes the parameters of judgment, the parameters which succeeding circumscriptions must then respect. Only this original act of writing is free and independent; all others are constrained by it and must bow before it.

It is precisely this condition of constraint that Satan and all who follow him (his comrades, Adam and Eve, you, me, even Milton) find intolerable and wish, somehow, to escape. Typically, escape is sought in the formulation and articulation of another world whose story is written by the would-be-independent agent, the agent who (like the lyric voice in *Lycidas*) thinks to speak and circumscribe in a language indebted to no previous circumscription, a language that can begin anew and inaugurate creation,

89

and, with creation, fact, value, and meaning. Satan is already at it when we and his fellows first spy him in the "spacious North" (*PL*, V, 726):

> High on a Hill, far blazing, as a Mount
> Rais'd on a Mount, with Pyramids and Tow'rs
> From Diamond Quarries hewn, and Rocks of Gold,
> The Palace of great *Lucifer*, (so call
> That Structure in the Dialect of men
> Interpreted) which not long after, he
> Affecting all equality with God,
> In imitation of that Mount wheron
> *Messiah* was declar'd in sight of Heav'n,
> The Mountain of the Congregation call'd;
> For thither he assembl'd all his Train,
> Pretending so commanded to consult
> About the great reception of thir King,
> Thither to come, and with calumnious Art
> Of counterfeited truth thus held thir ears. (V, 757–771)

What we see here is the piling up of signs—lighting effects, tall structures made of diamond and gold—that strive to pass themselves off as signifieds, that present themselves not as the theater of glory but as the real thing. The lie to this confection is given in the line "Affecting all equality with God," where "affecting" bears the double meaning of "aspiring or longing after" and "pretending to the status of." The pathos of the performance, of the attempt to acquire value by putting on its trappings, is made clear in the subsequent line when it receives its proper name: imitation. By definition, an imitation cannot be equal to the original. No matter how careful and fastidious the artisan may be, there will always be a distance—a gap, a difference—between what he produces and what precedes him; and every effort to fill the gap (by adding more gold or building still higher) will not remove it but merely relocate it at the point where the imitation leaves off.

It is the gap between representation and the reality represented that provides the space for equivocation, doubleness, and insincerity. There is no such space when God or the agent wholly informed by him (the agent who is the repository, the lodging, of his authority) speaks or writes, because what he or she gives out is what lives within, and what lives within is not the simulacrum of spirit, but spirit—and meaning and truth—Itself. But when the agent intent on making his own way, on originating his own meanings, speaks and writes, what issues from him is a product and reflection of the unanchored state he has perversely sought. His words display the false freedom of irresponsibility—the freedom that comes with not being tethered to anything but the emptiness within, a freedom that is initially exhilarating because within its license you can go on forever just making it up, pretending, counterfeiting. But that is all you can do; and the more frantically you do it, the more fictions you proliferate, the greater the distance between you and what is real and true.

It is important for the agent "enjoying" this self-deluding freedom, the agent playing in the gap opened up by his apostasy, that neither he nor those who listen to him be reminded of what they are so eager to forget: that they are secondary, and can be authentic only by acknowledging and embracing their secondariness. Two strategies abet this forgetting. The first is the production of representations so alluring that they fill the imagination and deflect attention from anything they do not contain; the imitation of the Mount on which the Messiah was declared "in sight of Heav'n" (V, 765) must be so dazzling that the sight of Heaven and the recollection of its priority are driven from everyone's mind. The second strategy contradicts the first, but in this brave new world of self-creation and self-authorization, contradiction is merely one of the resources of self-deception; it is the strategy of bringing the one greater than you down to your level, the strategy of making him secondary too, so that any difference or conflict is simply the difference or conflict between rival manipulators of signs. Thus, Satan asks his followers if they are prepared to bow down to an "image" (784), to a mere "double" (783), to a late-born son of whom they are at least the equal; and further on, when Michael accuses him of bringing evil—the departure from truth and goodness—into the world, he replies with a sublime assertion of artistic potency, "The strife which thou call'st evil . . . wee style / The strife of Glory" (VI, 289–290). That is, you're just telling a different story from ours, and we prefer ours, thank you. Once storytelling is freed from any obligation of fidelity, once storytelling becomes the prime act, no one's story is better than anyone else's—and may the best fiction win.

Of course the elaborate structures of fiction, the empire of signs, can be made to collapse in an instant by the merest invocation of what they labor so hard to occlude. That is why Abdiel is met with such hostility when he dares to utter (what is for them) the abominable truth: "Shalt thou give Law to God . . . / . . . who made / Thee what thou art, and form'd the Power's of Heav'n / . . . and circumscrib'd thir being?" (V, 822–825). That is, how can you think of using your powers against him who is their source, against him whose initial act of circumscription—both a demarcation and a limitation—is responsible for whatever identity you have, an identity you will lose if you cut yourself off from him? Remember, in short, that you are a creature. This is precisely what Satan doesn't want to hear (indeed, can't hear; that's what makes him Satan), although he repeats it in derision: "we were form'd [circumscribed] . . . say'st thou? and the work / Of secondary hands?" (853–854).[26] The insult is double—first you say I was fashioned, sculpted, scripted by another, and then you say the task was assigned to a subordinate—but the reply, indignant though it is, provides support for the insult: "who saw / When this creation was? . . . / We know no time when we were not as now; / Know none before us, self-begot, self-rais'd /

. . . Our puissance is our own" (856–857, 859–860, 864). Or, in other words, since I don't remember anyone making me, I must have made myself. The assertion cannibalizes itself: if the "I" that comes to this conclusion did not exist at the moment of its claimed potency, then attributing "puissance" to it is obviously absurd. Satan, in short, is speaking nonsense (compare Adam's "how came I thus, how here? / Not of myself; by some great Maker then, / In goodness and in power preëminent" [VIII, 277–279]), although at one point his language speaks truer than he knows: he *is* "self-rais'd," not in the sense of self-formed but in the sense (on which Milton repeatedly plays in the poem) of self-razed or self-erased. By claiming to have authored, written, circumscribed himself, he "breaks union" (V, 612) with his true author; and self-deprived of heavenly support, of the support of one who is "preëminent," he is without center and without being. Abdiel says as much when he renames him "alienate from God" (877)—a literal description of his self-razing action—and declares him to be already lost and fallen.

Not Uninvented

Satan, of course, accepts no such verdict, and in the battle that follows he is busily reinflating his claim to original potency, to independence, to authorship. His finest moment occurs at the end of the first day, when Nisroch complains of this new experience of pain and calls for someone to "invent / With what more forcible we may offend / Our yet unwounded Enemies, or arm / Ourselves with like defense" (VI, 464–467). Satan's response is immediate: "Whereto with look compos'd *Satan* replied. / Not uninvented that, which thou aright / Believ'st so main to our success, I bring" (469–471). The "I bring" emerges triumphantly at the end of the statement in the manner of one (and this is an attribute of deity) who always has an answer and has *already* done what is being requested. Moreover, this already accomplished feat is given the name of "invention," a term that resounds in several registers. In the register of technology, an invention is the thinking up, the creation from scratch, of a new device (telescope, microscope, telephone, television, computer, spaceship) that extends the scope of agency. After an invention, agents can do things they were unable to do before, and it is characteristic of those who invent to believe that there is nothing they could not do if given enough time; technology typically recognizes no limit to its future successes. In another register, invention is the first and founding part of rhetoric; it is the devising of the matter or content that will later be organized, embellished, committed to memory, and delivered in the form of a polished oration. In a more narrowly literary register, invention is the creation, out of whole cloth and from the zodiac of one's own wit (the phrase is Sidney's) of a fable or a story or an allegory or a lyric. Obviously, not all of these senses of invention are equally honorific; the last invites the charge of fabrication and insubstantiality. Technological inventions are supposed to be real; if they don't work, they are accused of being the other kind of invention, of being just made up, of being fantasies, imaginary constructions.

Satan will present his invention as something very real and he will test it in the next day's battle, but his introduction of it is rhetorical and makes use of rhetorical terms. He is described as "with look compos'd" (469), which means at once that he has the demeanor of someone who has remained unruffled by the first day's events, and that this demeanor is one he has carefully put on, composed, affected. He has composed himself, and this composition (of a being supremely confident) is a component in the larger composition—writing, scripting—of the situation he and his host will inhabit. Nisroch has painted a bleak picture of that situation; Satan must now paint over it in brighter colors, and it is as a painter or inscriber that he sets himself before "the bright surface / Of this Ethereous mould" (472–473), the canvas for his invention.

In the lines that follow, the language of technological ingenuity is interwoven with the language of writing and composition and with the language of sexual procreation, different but related vehicles for the tenor of the irresistible force the rebels hope to wield and discharge. William Kolbrener has remarked on the extent to which Satan thinks of the battle as at once a military and a linguistic competition: "the satanic 'invention,' gunpowder, is deployed through 'hollow'd bodies made of Oak or Fir' [VI, 574], canons with a strange resemblance to pastoral pipes."[27] The same cannons, as Roy Flannagan notes,[28] bear more than a little resemblance to phalluses: they are hollow and filled with a frothy excrescence of subterranean materials that are "dark and crude" (PL, VI, 478); when they are chock-full of those materials, they dilate (swell, expand) and explode at the "touch of fire" (carnal heat), disgorging a "devilish glut" (an emission of surfeit matter or liquid) in all directions (485, 589). This glut, unlike semen, does not fructify but destroys, dashing "To pieces . . . whatever stands" in its way (489). In an aside to Adam and Eve, Raphael speculates that in future times some mortal "inspir'd / With dev'lish machination might devise / Like instrument to plague the Sons of men" (503–505), and a little later he describes the instrument as an engine of "missive ruin" (519), where "missive" means both missile (i.e., shot) and letter or official writing. "Missive ruin" is precisely what Satan visits on Eve when he inserts into her heart "words replete with guile" (IX, 733), an act of destruction presented in the same mix of linguistic, military, and sexual terms that attend the invention of gunpowder. It is with the pen—with words—as well as with weapons of material force that Satan does his deadly work, "By falsities and lies the greatest part / Of Mankind" corrupting (I, 367–368). As Linda Gregerson observes, "Satanic rhetoric is itself a 'devilish Enginry' (VI, 553) of manifold consequence."[29] It is as a phallic rhetorician, swelling with "passion" (IX, 667) and "to highth upgrown" (IX, 677), that Satan labors to dash to pieces the unity and clarity of God's words by endowing him with motives other than the one we know him to have if we know him to be God.

The interchangeability of military, sexual, and verbal aggression is made explicit in Satan's punning speeches. The first presents itself as an "overture" (VI, 562), often a term applied to the beginning of marriage negotiations. Overture also means "opening" or "hole": the devils present themselves as wide open and "ready to receive" (561), even as they hide the phallic instrument whose glut they will soon let loose. (Throughout the passage they play both the male and female roles, as when the "triple-mounted row of Pillars" [572] juts forward and up and is at the same time described as a "hideous orifice" gaping "wide" [577]—as obvious a threat of castration as one could wish or fear.) They promise to "discharge" (564; emit a mucous fluid) their "part" (565; a familiar euphemism for private part), but worry that those they woo may present the wrong orifice by turning back "perverse" (562)—that is, by turning the wrong way.

In the second speech, the sexual/military puns continue and are joined by puns that equate the force of shot and writing. Remarking the wild and extravagant dance (a strange mating ritual?) of the loyalists, Satan wonders at this odd response to the "propounded terms / Of composition" (612–613), where "composition" refers at once to the "concocted" (514) powder their cannons have discharged and to the rhetorical composition of the present performance. Belial, attempting to match his leader's verbal ingenuity, extends the punning, and in his near literalism glosses it: "Leader, the terms we sent were terms of weight, / Of hard contents, and full of force urg'd home" (621–622)—home into the body, home into the mind assaulted by this evidence of diabolic power, home into whatever orifice presents itself.

The puns do not merely assert diabolic force; they are evidence of it and of its malign effects. "Scoffing in ambiguous words" (568)—saying one thing and meaning another or several others—is at once an ability the devils have and a mode of performance to which they are doomed. The consequence of unmooring oneself from deity is that one loses the point of reference in relation to which entities can be stably defined, and which includes the entity—the independent self—in whose name the unmooring has been performed.[30] Rebelling in order to gain identity, the would-be-autonomous self is set adrift in a world where each chance collocation of atoms brings a new and temporary "order" ("To whom these most adhere, / Hee rules a moment" [II, 906–907]), and a new and temporary identity. Secondariness detached from the primary that anchors it can go nowhere or (it is the same thing) anywhere; it is in effect sterile and can reproduce nothing but its own sterility. As Gregerson puts it, "the sign, no longer bound by its referent, proliferates" (208). Representation freed from the responsibility of verisimilitude presides over its own unbounded empire, but it is an empire of waste and death, "A Universe of death, which God by curse / Created evil, for evil only good, / Where all life dies, death lives, and Nature breeds, / Perverse, all monstrous, all prodigious things" (PL, II, 622–625). This is exactly the work of "ambiguous words," words with no fixed meaning and therefore with as many meanings as there are kaleidoscopic changes in scene—endlessly to breed more words and more significances all equally (there is a terrible democracy in this scenario of de-authorization) remote from the truth that would, if acknowledged (as in "Shalt thou give law to God?"), arrest their play.

Ambiguous words, in short, are what inevitably follows once the creature pretends to set up its own kingdom. "Excessive self love"—love so strong that it cannot bear to acknowledge dependence—"spawns a progeny both monstrous and legion" (Gregerson, 206), a genealogy that is presented with schematic precision in Sin's account of her own birth. Sin is born as the result of Satan's copulating with himself (earlier, in plot time, he has conceived himself in the same manner [*PL*, V, 659–666]), and she is at first received with fear by the rebel host ("back they recoil'd afraid [II, 759]) who, in the same line, name her Sin and take her "for a Sign" (760). One might ask, "Sign of what?"—but what makes her so monstrous, so unnatural, is that she is a sign of nothing, a self-referring sign who has emerged full-blown from another entity that signifies nothing but itself. (This is Satan's wish, and to his endless detriment he gets it.) Sin *is* the state of being a signifier without a signified, an agency with no inborn direction, a secondary thing no longer connected with that which would give it meaning, an entity severed from the ground of its being and therefore wholly empty. Its only recourse (one mired in self-delusion) is to forget what it doesn't have—not to have it was the desire that eviscerated it—and pretend to be the originator of its own stability. This is done exactly as the rebels do it when they make their peace with Sin, now "familiar grown" (761). That is, they get used to her—which is easy, since what they are getting used to is their own condition, the condition of being unattached to anything but themselves; and getting used to her and themselves is the same as getting used to a representation (sign) that does without anything to represent. This is the first step in the linked careers of sin and sign, becoming comfortable ("familiar grown") with the horror or abyss of total self-referentiality, of being without ground; and once that step has been achieved (an achievement that makes real achievement impossible), sin and sign embark upon the endless effort to derive a ground—a source of true being and power—from themselves.

This is what Satan is doing in the battle: trying to supply out of himself (a self with nothing inside it) the deficiency that is the result of his breaking union. He is trying to bootstrap himself back up to deity by material and mechanistic means.[31] By conceiving his task in this way, he fails in it, and his failure is (as it must be; sin can breed nothing but sin) a repetition of his prior failure to understand what deity is, an order of being that is fundamentally different from, and infinitely superior to, one's own— a source not a rival. The failure of Satan's understanding is fully displayed when he imagines that, confronted by the newly invented cannon and shot, the loyalists will lose heart and "fear we have disarm'd / The Thunderer of his only dreaded bolt" (VI, 490–491). By "only dreaded bolt" Satan means that the only thing that separates the rebels from God, the only thing they might be afraid of, the only thing that makes the odds between them, is his possession of a superior weapon. The superiority is imagined as wholly technological—a matter not of what God *is* but of what he has in the way of prosthetic devices—and because it is technological it can be matched and perhaps overcome by a more sophisticated technology. All they need is a bigger weapon, a better invention. All they need too (by this reasoning) is a better invention in another sense: a better story.

When Satan says to Michael, The strife you call evil, "wee style / The strife of Glory" (289), he is claiming to be able to tell a more persuasive story (about heroism, resistance to tyranny, valor in the face of incredible odds) than the story told by the hymn-warbling loyalists; and he can cite as evidence the many who have followed him and who now have "boastful Argument[s]" (84), accounts of their heroic deeds, emblazoned on their shields. The fact that as yet they have performed no deeds— they have only yesterday formed themselves as a host—is not merely beside the point; it *is* the point. If you are a sufficiently skillful stylist, a wielder of a sufficiently supple stylus—an instrument for erasing previous markings and replacing them with your own—you can inscribe and establish whatever meanings suit your ambition and interests; you can give yourself a heraldry that is independent of any actual events (here again, the power of representation free of the demand to be truthful).[32] You can just as easily overcome an opponent with the stab of a pen as with the thrust of a sword; in both cases it is a question of having the bigger weapon. You can also have, or claim to have, a bigger penis. In the game Satan thinks himself to be playing (he cannot admit that he is being played *with*), the "boastful argument" is always "Mine is bigger than yours," and that is the argument he thinks he's making when he comes up with his invention: in devising an instrument more powerful than God's "only dreaded bolt" (491), he is also, he believes, displaying a greater ability to create, to generate entities in his own image, to unmake and make worlds.

Bigger thunderbolt, bigger pen, bigger penis, dashing enemies to pieces, replacing their stories and meaning with your own, giving birth to alternate universes. These are the means and actions Satan and his legions pin their hopes on in their effort to make up the gap between themselves and the God they regard as just one more rival warrior, one more rival artist, one more inscriber of worlds. Anything he can do, we can do better, they think; and, "highth'n'd in thir thoughts," they presume "eternal might / To match with thir inventions" (629–631). As it turns out, however, it is only in their thoughts—in the illusions and delusions that crowd their darkened minds—that the presumed efficacy of their inventions has any substance. As soon as the real thing—the real wielder of power, the real inscriber, the real generator of life— appears, the effects they seem to have achieved are reversed and revealed to have been mere fictions, allowed their half-life for heavenly purposes and now erased with a single stroke, with a single word. At the Son's voice, "the uprooted Hills retir'd / Each to his place, . . . and went / Obsequious, Heav'n his wonted face renew'd" (781–783). So much for the power of reinscription by agents not heavenly; the landscape they sought to rewrite and disorder has snapped back into its proper (originally given) shape; the rents caused by their weapons are instantly repaired; the expanse of Heaven is once again unperturbed by eruption; all Nature is "Obsequious"—that is, dutiful in response to the command of her true author.

None of this makes any impression at all on the rebels, who persist in their hopes, "Weening to prosper, and at length prevail/ Against God" (795–796). Only the brute physical force of the paternal chariot as it rolls over them ("since by strength / They measure all, of other excellence / Not emulous" [820–822]) serves to deflate them, and the description of their rout mocks the military, phallic, and literary ambitions that have sustained them. They are said to have lost "all courage" (839), which means simultaneously to have lost all inner animation, to have lost all purpose, to have lost valor, to have lost sexual vigor; their weapons drop (839)—that is, they are no longer erect; they can neither cut nor inscribe; they are "idle" (839)—that is, empty, void of meaning, not moving, without foundation, all of which were available contemporary meanings and all of which apply both to the weapons and to the hopes of those that wielded them; their strength is "wither'd" (850)—that is, shrunken, without vitality, dry (the image could not be more graphic); they have been "drain'd" (851), emptied of any inside; they are "Exhaust'd" (852)—that is, used up, empty; and they are "spiritless" (852), a word that in its related significances is the sum of all those that precede it—deprived of an animating principle, depressed, dejected, downcast, lacking ardor, destitute of energy or enterprise, flat and insipid (applied to literary productions), and, of course, lacking spiritual zeal.

This last alerts us to what we should already have seen: not only are the words describing the rebels' condition interchangeable (pretty much variations of one another); they refer to a condition that antedates the battle, the condition that brings them to

101

the battle in the first place—the condition of having broken the connection with deity. "Spiritless" is at once a word that names one of the effects of their defeat and reminds us of why they are (self-)defeated before the first blow is struck: aspiring to be independent of the spirit, to be self-begot and therefore self-proliferating, they succeed (simply *by* so aspiring) and are immediately spirit-less, then, now, always. Although the passage describes physical states in an apparent narrative sequence, each successive state is a reflection and repetition of the internal state the rebels occupy and *are;* what is being described and redescribed is the situation of being alienated from God.

This is certainly true of the last "event" in the story, the opening wide of a "spacious Gap" in the "Crystal wall of Heav'n" (861, 860) and the disclosure of a "wasteful Deep," a "monstrous sight" that strikes the rebels "with horror" and from which they recoil "backward" (862–863). This recalls the moment when they first see Sin—"back they recoil'd afraid" (II, 759). Indeed, it is the same moment with the same content: the sin they recoil from is the image of their own apostasy, the horror of which strikes them when it takes external form; they recoil from themselves (until they are to themselves "grown familiar"), and they do so here again when they recoil from the monstrous sight of the spacious (huge, unbridgeable) gap. The gap is not the space before them; it is the space (filled by nothing) within them—a vast interior vacuity emptied, in an act of willful and irrevocable choice, of any resources, of any way of connecting up again with the inspiriting vitality they have spurned. The monstrous sight is the castrating sight (made literal by their impotence in the face of the chariot) of the loss—of power, vigor, potency—they have inflicted upon themselves. It is the sight (avoidable until the literal force of the chariot "drives it home") of themselves, of what they have become, of what they are not, of what they are; and what they are is a zone of waste, literally "wasteful," and it is as waste matter that they are evacuated and purged by Heaven in what amounts to a large bowel movement.[33] What they are evacuated into is the pit of hell, which they also are ("myself am Hell; / And in the lowest deep a lower deep" [IV, 75–76]). The "bottomless pit" (VI, 866)—monstrous sight, gap, wasteful deep—they fall into and are always falling into and began by wanting to fall into is themselves: "themselves they threw / Down from the verge of Heav'n" (864–865), words apparently descriptive of an action newly taken, but more deeply descriptive of the original action—of breaking union—whose meaning and effects they act out over and over again even when it appears (especially to themselves) that they are doing something else.

Says Who?

Or so I say. The analysis of the preceding pages got started when I declared that the difference between God's and Satan's inscribings in books VI and VII seems clearly marked in contrast to other differences that are "hardly to be discerned" because no visible or formal configuration unambiguously declares them. But that can't be right if I am right about the larger point that Milton works from the inside out. It can't be that he works from the inside out sometimes and that at other times the outside is a "sure foregoing sign" (PR, IV, 483) of an inner significance; for if that were the case, one could begin with those sure signs and, using them as an anchoring center of reference and interpretive stability, map out the entire moral universe in a way that would provide every wayfaring pilgrim with a blueprint and a set of directions. The unavailability of any such signs is the first consequence of Milton's internalization of value, his unwillingness to grant authority to any external form, even one so hallowed and pedigreed as the Ten Commandments (see Christian Doctrine, II, i); and from this follows the extraordinary mixture of confidence and hazard—confidence in the reality of God's Truth and the hazard of identifying that truth in the absence of any (sure) external indication of its location—that makes the experience of Milton's world so arduous both for his characters and for his readers.

As one of those readers, I cannot claim an exemption from the general condition and say that the difference between God's writings or stylings and Satan's is obvious and perspicuous. If it were, then it would be perspicuous to Satan, and everything would be settled; that it is not is what gives Satan's "wee style [it] / The strife of Glory" (PL, VI, 289–290) such force, not because it is necessarily persuasive but because it has been persuasive to him, and to his followers, and to William Empson and to Catherine Belsey. In the absence of any formal mechanism by which to adjudicate interpretive alternatives—in the poem or about the poem—we are all in the same endless game, reading an inside which, rather than being confirmed by an outside, generates it.

The exchange between Abdiel and Satan at the beginning of the battle illustrates the process and its resistance to closure. Abdiel says to Satan: See, I told you so. Surely now

> thou seest
> All are not of thy Train; there be who Faith
> Prefer, and Piety to God, though then
> To thee not visible, when I alone
> Seem'd in thy World erroneous to dissent
> From all: my Sect thou seest, now learn too late
> How few sometimes may know, when thousands err. (VI, 142–148)

Abdiel thinks that Satan has been deceived by a tendency to draw general conclusions from limited visibilia; if only there had been more like him to stand up and challenge Satan's pronouncement, the meeting in the North might have gone another way. Now that innumerable loyalists stand before Satan, he will see (albeit belatedly) that the apparent dissenting position is really a majority one and that, rather than being a member of a sect (a word meant sarcastically), Abdiel stands firmly in the political and moral center.

A true sectarian, however, is not so easily dislodged from his position:

> Whom the grand Foe with scornful eye askance
> Thus answer'd. Ill for thee, but in wisht hour
> Of my revenge, first sought for thou return'st
> From flight, seditious Angel, to receive
> Thy merited reward, the first assay
> Of this right hand provok'd, since first that tongue
> Inspir'd with contradiction durst oppose
> A third part of the Gods, in Synod met
> Thir Deities to assert . . . (149–157)

Abdiel identifies Satan's "World" with its physical dimensions, including its (except for one) homogeneous population; but Satan knows that his world is underwritten by a way of thinking and conceiving which is flexible and capacious enough to turn anything into evidence of its rightness. If the numerical advantage now seems to belong to the loyalists, then this is merely proof of how few are up to the demands of freedom: "now / I see that most through sloth had rather serve" (165–166). It is all a matter of extending one's first assumptions into the landscape of fact, and it is no trick at all to characterize (inscribe) that landscape so that its phenomena speak those assumptions. Satan shows you how to do it when he calls Abdiel a "seditious Angel"—that is, someone who has rebelled against a duly constituted authority. To Abdiel's ears (presumably) this sounds insane, since he knows that the duly constituted authority is the one he continues to serve. That knowledge, however, flows not from particulars (like the size of one's party) but from the perspective, already in place and tenaciously adhered to, that gives particulars their meaning. Sedition is not a feature of the world waiting to be described but a tendentious assertion of a state of affairs, and the reality of that state of affairs, the extent to which it becomes a taken-for-granted matter of fact, will be a function of the strength of the assertion, of its capacity to become the standard story everyone tells and lives out.

It is, in short, a question not of seeing clearly (as Abdiel seems to believe) but of saying strongly, of declaring—on the model of the Omnific Word's "Thus far"—that things are this way rather than that. Satan is right when he accuses Abdiel of performing "contradiction," a saying against; for if meanings cannot be read off surfaces but must be read into surfaces by an interpretive act of the will ("On other surety none" [V, 538]), saying, affirming, testifying, will be the primary mode of action, and every saying will be a saying against, and what it will be against is another saying, another specification of what is, with no expectation that the world will stand up and say to one of the sayers that he or she has got it right. This is the mode, as Abdiel rightly observes, of faith (VI, 143), a form of action not supported by evidence but productive of it, a form of action marked by a freedom that is its own burden. The freedom is from prepackaged meanings, from ready-made and confining outsides; the burden is the burden of linking up with and adhering to an inside—the secret, hidden, saving truth—whose status either as the one thing needful or a piece of mere moral babble will always be open to doubt, to the possibility that, when you say "Henceforth thou art the Genius of the shore" (*Lycidas*, 183) you are celebrating your own power rather than God's, to the possibility that the content of your breast is not something holy but your old self-serving desires wearing the garment of holiness, to the possibility that when you decide "I with this Messenger will go along" (*Samson Agonistes*, 1384) and then tear down the temple, what moves you is not the hunger to do God's will but the thrill of exercising your own, to the possibility that however you style your strife—as the strife of glory, faith, love, goodness—its true significance (seen only by the perfect witness of all-judging Jove) may be quite other, to the possibility that when all is said and done and judged you will not hear a voice declare, "Well done, good and faithful servant!" In the climactic moment in every one of Milton's poems and in much of his prose, someone—sometimes Milton himself[34]—speaks from the inside out and stakes everything on an inner resolution supported by nothing but itself.

CHAPTER TWO

Milton's Aesthetic
of Testimony

Inbred Goodness

In the preceding chapter I described Milton's universe as a homogeneous structure of nested boxes (called aesthetics, politics, philosophy, value, knowledge, virtue) each of which, when opened, reveals the same content: an acknowledgment of, and a determination to serve, a benevolent and all-powerful deity. But I also observed that the homogeneity is not apparent to those whose hearts are filled with something else (envy, pride, ambition, self-worship), and that even for those whose hearts are the lodging of "something holy," the possibility of forgetting who they really are—dependent creatures—and thus of falling into difference and disunity is an ever-present danger against which they must always be vigilant. The radical oneness of all things is a stable feature of the universe and remains so even when some fail to apprehend it; but the home-felt conviction of that oneness and of its source in a hidden ("unsightly") power is an achievement—one must affirm it by resisting the appeal of the evidence of things seen—and as an achievement it is precarious. In later chapters I shall explore that precariousness and trace out its literary effects, but for now it is the homogeneity, the unity, that I wish to explicate, and I shall do so by looking closely at an early prose work that at once thematizes and enacts it.

Somewhat after the midpoint of that curious piece he calls *An Apology*, Milton pauses to perform an act of praise. He is quite self-conscious about interrupting his own discourse and, in what would seem to be the equivalent in rhetoric of a fair-labeling practice, he characterizes the pages to follow as "a digression from the ensuing matter."[1] Later I shall have the occasion to look more closely at this apparent scrupulosity on Milton's part and to consider exactly what is and is not a digression in this tract, but for the moment it is the act of praise itself that concerns me, for in its peculiarity it can serve as an illustration of Milton's strategy, here and elsewhere in his work.

The praise is for Parliament, then sitting to decide the very issues Milton is raising, and it is clear that in this passage he anticipates a strategy that will be writ larger in *Areopagitica*: the bestowing of praise on a person or persons in order to urge them to a particular course of action—that is, just and virtuous as you are, you cannot but choose to do the right thing. But Milton, I think, has another purpose here, and it is revealed in the indirection with which he approaches, and forces us to approach, his point. He begins in what seems a perfectly straightforward manner: "First therefore the most of them being either of ancient and high Nobility, or at least of known and well reputed ancestry, which is a great advantage towards vertue . . . " (922–923). This is reassuring in two ways: (1) it promises an order in which the reasons for praise will be related to one another in a logical fashion, and (2) it promises to justify the praise by producing a list of specifiable attributes and accomplishments. Neither promise is redeemed, however, since the sentence takes an unexpected turn with its very next words: "one way, but in respect of welth, ease, and flattery, which accompanies a nice and tender education, is as much a hindrance another way." Suddenly what had appeared to be advantages turn into disadvantages, as wealth, ease, and education, often cited in other contexts as aids to virtue, are termed its hindrances. The effect of this turn is to unsettle the sentence even before we arrive at its main clause (everything so far hanging in a suspended state of apposition), which follows immediately: "the good which lay before them they took." Although this clause resolves the syntax (at least momentarily), it only accentuates the irresolution of the argument; for it is not at all clear what is meant by "the good which lay before them," since what had seemed to be the good (nobility, family, ancestry) has been discredited. Nor is the point made clearer by the explanatory clause that follows—"in imitating the worthiest of their progenitors"— because the question of by what marks the worthiest are to be identified remains vexingly unanswered.

It is finally answered, but in a peculiar way, by the rest of the sentence: "and the evill which assaulted their younger yeares by the temptation of riches, high birth, and that usuall bringing up, perhaps too favourable and too remisse, through the strength of an inbred goodnesse, and with the helpe of divine grace, that had markt them out for no meane purposes, they nobly overcame." At first it seems that "evill" is the object (along with "the worthiest") of "imitating," and it is a moment or two before a reader realizes that the sentence is once again suspended in midair, waiting for a main clause. The correction of course is made, but the confusion has nevertheless occurred and done its part in once again unsettling the reader. When the sentence regathers itself, it is to reinforce its negative point by repeating the indictment of what had at its beginning been presented so positively: riches, high birth, a favorable bringing up. It is only then, when the vehicles of temptation are firmly and visibly in place, that we are at last introduced to the strength that will withstand them and to the object of Milton's praise: an "inbred goodnesse" which, with the help of grace, overcomes all obstacles.

Notice, however, that "inbred goodnesse," while it finally names the attribute for which Parliament is being praised, also removes it from sight. Unlike the nobility of birth or the accumulation of riches, "inbred goodnesse" is not something you can point to; and as a result the word "markt" becomes a comment on the promise it fails to redeem: rather than listing the marks by which the worthiest are known, the sentence ends by telling us that the markings they bear are interior and therefore invisible.

In a footnote the editor of the Yale edition of Milton's prose works is moved to comment, "A somewhat involved sentence." My point is that it is intentionally so, and that when Milton delivers us to the strong closing of "they nobly overcame," he means us to recall the beginning of the sentence and to realize that one of the things they nobly overcame was their (heraldic, external) nobility. The sentence is not only an act of praise but a lesson in what does and does not deserve praise, a lesson we readers learn on our pulses when we are allowed for a time to think that the reasons for praise are the usual ones.

In the event that we may have missed it, Milton gives us the lesson again, twice. As before, he begins with a participial clause that characterizes what would seem to be a praiseworthy and advantageous state: "for being train'd up in the knowledge of learning, and sent to those places which were intended to be the seed plots of piety and the Liberall Arts . . ." The reader who has experienced the first sentence may be alerted by the word "intended" to the impending turn in this one; it arrives right on schedule: "but were become the nursuries of superstition and empty speculation." Rather than the seed plots of piety, the universities are said to be the place of "abused studies and labours," labors against which the future members themselves had to labor, "correcting . . . the errors of their mis-instruction" by the "clearnesse of their owne judgement," a judgment that has specifically been detached from (because it has been opposed to) the process of their education. After nobility and education, the next conventional category of praise to be discredited is example. Here the prose is straightforward; we know from the first that the "lot" which situates them in "such times and . . . such places" as the contemporary scene affords will constitute an obstacle to their virtue, and we are not surprised to hear them praised for failing to be "misled by the single power of example, as their riper years were knowne to be unmov'd with the baits of preferment, and undaunted for any discouragement and terror which appear'd often to those that lov'd religion, and their native liberty."

Words like "unmov'd" and "undaunted," coming as they do at the end of this sequence, have more than a local descriptive force, for they at once specify the peculiar nature of the action for which Parliament is being praised and point us precisely to the reason why that praise is so self-consciously unconventional. The members of Parliament are worthy not because of what they do (in the sense that would allow one to list their accomplishments), but for what they refuse to do: they refuse to act in response to the pressures exerted by their birth, family, material advantages, upbringing, education, and example. In the face of these temptations they simply remain what they have always been—that is, they remain "unmov'd" and steadfastly cling to the clearness of their own judgment, a judgment that was not formed by a commerce with the world but that entered with them into the world and is maintained only by keeping aloof from the world. When Milton concludes that, "in the midst of all disadvantages and disrespects," the future members of Parliament nevertheless gave "proofe of themselves to be better made and fram'd by nature to the love and practise of vertue" (924), the only proof he has educed is the negative one of refraining from the practices that might have been expected of them, given their circumstances.

The self-consciousness of Milton's performance here is underlined by his reference at the beginning of this section to "that which is call'd *Decorum* in the writing of praise" (920). What he has in mind are the many rhetorical manuals in which the categories of praise are listed and discussed. These lists vary somewhat in their ordering of the categories, but the categories themselves are standard; and this list from the *Rhetorica ad Herennium* can be regarded as representative: "descent, education, wealth, kinds of power, titles to fame, citizenship, friendships, and the like."[2] When Milton pointedly declines to praise the members of Parliament for precisely these attributes, he is obviously calling up the traditional categories only in order to reject them.

It could be argued, however, that in so doing he is himself no less traditional. The theory of praise, of epideictic rhetoric, has always recognized a distinction between the praise of externals and the praise of character or mind, and preferred the latter to the former as a mode more in touch with the essential worth of the individual.[3] Milton, then, could be said to be simply following his models when he deemphasizes the attributes of fortune and birth in favor of the attributes of the spirit. (*Animus* is the all-purpose word for this category in the Latin treatises.) But when Milton follows models it is almost always to overgo them, to take their position further than they themselves had ever thought to go. In this case he departs from his predecessors by turning a taxonomic distinction into a judgment. For the rhetoricians, the external attributes of persons may be "comparatively unimportant" (Quintilian, *Institutio Oratoria,* III, vii, 12), but they are attributes nevertheless and deserve the title of virtues;[4] as Aristotle puts it, "good fathers are likely to have good sons, and good training is likely to produce good character."[5] But for Milton, these same attributes are obstacles and impediments. Their relationship to the formation of character virtue is entirely negative; they are what must be withstood or overcome if one is to remain virtuous. Moreover, in his account, the state of virtue is itself represented no less negatively; in place of the list of virtues and virtuous actions that fills out the traditional analysis of praise, he speaks only of the actions that have been avoided; we never see the members of Parliament doing anything except, as he describes them later in the passage, "sitting here in peace" (926).

Sitting is a curious posture in which to imagine the object of one's praise, especially since the supposed purpose of praise is quite literally to allow someone to stand out from the crowd. The recipients of Milton's praise do not stand out; they sit, and they sit *together* in "one globe" of "united excellence" (924). The image of a globe is one of a succession of images in Milton's poetry and prose—the "one great cube" of *The Reason of Church Government*,[6] the "celestial consort" of "At a Solemn Music," the "homogeneal" body of Truth in *Areopagitica*, the "one huge Christian personage" in "Of Reformation"—images in which the state of virtue is figured forth as corporate or communal. In such a state the individual is distinguished by not being distinguished, by being so identified with a large and transcendent truth that he is no more (or less) than an element of its structure. The globe of united excellence is made up not of individual excellences who happen to join in a common purpose, but of individuals (no longer individuals) whose excellence inheres precisely in their being englobed, in their being extensions of a forming and informing principle that not only speaks through them but speaks them, animating their every action and expression. Of course, if to be virtuous is to be thus englobed, then the condition of nonvirtue, of evil rather than excellence, will be the condition of being separate, of breaking ranks, of singing a discordant note, of being *outstanding*—the condition, in short, that would make one the proper object of praise as it is taught and exemplified in the rhetorics. In what can only be characterized as a tour de force of the genre, Milton ends by praising the members of Parliament for their not being available to praise.

True Eloquence and True Poems

Why does Milton make such a show of employing the conventions of praise only in order to undermine them? Answering that question will be the business of this chapter, and we can begin by juxtaposing this moment in *An Apology* with another in which the issues are superficially different but finally the same. The link between them is the topic of praise, which once again figures in a curiously negative way. In this case the praise is for Milton and it has been offered by the Modest Confuter, who expresses admiration for the poet's eloquence and declares that were it his own thoughts that were being expressed, *"he would never desire to have them better cloth'd"* (948). Milton responds to this compliment by rejecting it, by renouncing any claim to the artfulness with which he has been credited. Indeed, he renounces the very claims of art itself, and in a single remarkable sentence he lays down the principles of what can only be called an anti-aesthetic:

> For me, Readers, although I cannot say that I am utterly untrain'd in those rules which best Rhetoricians have giv'n, or unacquainted with those examples which the prime authors of eloquence have written in any learned tongu, yet true eloquence I find to be none but the serious and hearty love of truth: And that whose mind so ever is fully possest with a fervent desire to know good things and with the dearest charity to infuse the knowledge of them into others, when such a man would speak, his words (by what I can expresse) like so many nimble and airy servitors

115

trip about him at command, and in well order'd files, as he
would wish, fall aptly into their own places. (948–949)

The source of the extraordinary power of this sentence is
a tension between its performance and its message. Its performance is highly, even spectacularly, rhetorical; its message is that
the rules of rhetoric are irrelevant to true eloquence. Milton is in
effect having a dialogue with his own presentation as it unfolds,
and it is a dialogue that is already proceeding on an advanced
level in the very first clause: "although I cannot say that I am utterly untrain'd." On its face this is a simple instance of litotes, the
figure by which one says something by denying its contrary.
Puttenham calls it "the *Moderator*," emphasizing its usefulness as
a way of softening a statement of self-praise, and his illustration
could well have served as Milton's model: "if you would say, I
am not ignorant, for [i.e., in place of] I know well inough."[7] Milton's litotes, however, is more complicated than this example and
finally has a quite different effect. First of all, it is embedded in a
concessive clause; and this entirely changes the force of the negative statement. The difference, for example, between "I am not
ignorant" and "although I am not ignorant" is that the latter implies that he wishes he were. In Milton's sentence the difference is
even sharper, for he interposes between the concessive and the
negative assertion another clause—"I cannot say that"—which
makes it even clearer that what follows is what he would like to
be able to say; he would like to be able to say that he is untrained,
but he cannot. Like a conventional litotes, the sentence finally
claims something by denying its contrary—it claims training—
but the claim is made regretfully, and is in fact an apology for not
being able to not make it.

As complicated as this is (at least in the telling, if not in the experiencing), it is complicated further by the adverb "utterly,"
which has the effect of blurring the claim Milton is unable not to

make. That is, because of "utterly," we are not even sure of the extent of the training he would like to be unable to claim; to not be utterly untrained is, perhaps, to be partially trained or to be trained in an imperfect or inconsequential way. As a result, it remains perfectly (utterly) unclear as to what judgment, if any, is being made on "those rules which best Rhetoricians have giv'n"; indeed, one does not know exactly how to take "best," since it is an honorific offered by a speaker of whom it can only be said that he is not utterly untrained.

The resolute indeterminacy of the sentence is continued in the next clause, which further informs us as to what Milton cannot say: "or unacquainted with those examples which the prime authors of eloquence have written in any learned tongu." Here we meet with our previous questions in a slightly different form. What does it mean to not be utterly unacquainted? In the context of what standard are these authors said to be "prime"? What are we to understand by "authors of eloquence"? Is it authors who are judged eloquent, according to some external measure, or authors who generate, in the sense of giving birth to, eloquence? This last question touches on a familiar debate in rhetorical theory: Is eloquence achieved by following rules or by imitating the examples of eloquent men? And in back of this debate is an even more basic one, between those like Quintilian (*Institutio Oratoria*, II, 17) who believe that there is in fact an art of eloquence and those like Augustine (who follows Antonius in Cicero's *De Oratore*, I, xviii–xxi) who contend that eloquence is nothing more or less than the unsought-for effect of "natural genius"[8]—that is, of inspiration. To be sure, Milton does not pause to pronounce on these issues or even to raise them directly, but they are implicitly present in the contrast between rules and example, and therefore they form part of the context against which the sentence resonates.

That context keeps expanding until it seems to include almost the whole of rhetorical history, with all of its distinctions and disputes. Even the phrase "in any learned tongu" alludes, if only glancingly, to the dispute between those who insist that eloquence is possible only in the classical tongues and those who champion the strength and grace of the vernacular. On other occasions, Milton speaks out strongly for his native tongue, but that is not his purpose here. He does not recall the long and continuing history of rhetorical practice in order to insert himself into its controversies; rather, he makes his sentence thick with those controversies only in order to dismiss them, and with them the way of thinking of which they are a manifestation.

That dismissal is effected by a single word—"yet"—and it is followed by a redefinition of eloquence that detaches it from the validation of rule and example and identifies it with an interior moral state: "Yet true eloquence I find to be none, but the hearty and serious love of truth." Once again Milton has taken a familiar formulation and given it a twist that brings out its more extreme implications. Rather than asserting, as do Quintilian (*Institutio Oratoria*, II, xv) and others, that eloquence and character should go together or that the arts of eloquence are useless (or even worse) if they are disjoined from a commitment to truth, or that eloquence can be achieved only by a just man (Quintilian, II, xv, 28), Milton flatly says that eloquence and the love of truth *are* one and the same. In this definition, eloquence is disjoined from speech; it need have no visible form at all, no particular manifestation. It is instead an ever-present potential that may or may not flower in words, but remains, even in silence, what it always is.

Eloquence so characterized is the verbal or *a*verbal equivalent of Milton's conception of action, which he repeatedly equates not with any physical gesture but with an inner readiness that may issue (or not issue) in any gesture at all. Thus, for example, the last line of the *Nativity Ode* finds "Bright-harnass'd Angels" who "sit in order serviceable"[9]—that is, capable of performing services which they are not now performing, although in being so capable, so ready, they are in fact performing all the time. To be sure, it may be the case on some later occasion that they will be called to a specific action, just as it may be the case that the eloquence which exists independently of expression may issue in actual speech; and in the second half of his sentence, Milton describes and exemplifies in his description what will then happen. First he glosses "serious and hearty love of truth" in such a way as to prevent us from assuming that the love of truth is something someone can have as a possession. Rather, it is something by which one is "possest"; it is a "fervent desire to infuse" which has itself been infused, so that there is no distinction to be made between it as a psychological state and the will of the possessed individual. "Such a man" is in that most exalted of Miltonic conditions: so at one with truth that his every motion (or non-motion) breathes it out.

That condition is not only one that Milton here names; he also (implicitly) claims it in what is the most daring—indeed, breathtaking—moment in the sentence; for when he begins the downward sweep of the period by saying "when such a man would speak," he wants us to believe that such a man is now speaking. That is, the parenthetical "by what I can expresse" should be read "by what *I* can expresse." He is asking us for applause, for a recognition that he himself is eloquent in the way he has defined; and moreover, it is a recognition we can give only if we are ourselves "possest" by the same love that animates him. This is so because by the logic of the argument the sign of eloquence cannot be formal or conventional, recognizable by anyone who knows the rules; rather, eloquence is known by its relationship (of reflection or extension) to an inner state; and by the rules of Milton's game, the direction of validation must be from the inner to the outer, and not the other way around. What this means is that we cannot at the same time understand the sentence and admire

119

its artistry; that is, we are required (the word is not too strong) to realize that what seems to be its artistry is really the involuntary (nonplanned) effect of virtue. It is an emperor's-clothes strategy in reverse: Milton is asking that we see him as naked at the very moment when, as a rhetorician, he seems most adorned—the moment when his words perform exactly the action they are reporting, and "like so many nimble and airy servitors trip about him at command, and in well order'd files, as he would wish, fall aptly into their own places." We have not correctly read this sentence, and matched its testimony with our own, unless we know with a moral certainty that "well order'd files" refers to no order that any rhetoric could capture, but to the inner order of a rightly constituted soul.

One can see now that Milton rejects the praise of the Confuter for the same reason he feels compelled to bestow praise on Parliament; in both cases, praise has been conferred for the wrong (external) reasons by someone who is incapable of recognizing the right ones. In both cases, when praise is rightly conferred it is for actions—physical and verbal—that take no necessary visible form, and instead take whatever form (which can be no form at all) is demanded by an inner orientation, an "inbred goodnesse," a "serious and hearty love of truth." And finally, in both cases the act of praise is possible only if the praiser is himself informed (a word whose literalness should be stressed) by the same virtue to which his words bear witness.

Two apparently disparate moments in Milton's tract—one concerned with the deeds of Parliament, the other with the definition of eloquence—turn out to have exactly the same shape and the same components, and they in turn can be linked with a third moment, one of the more famous in Milton's prose, when he declares that "he who would not be frustrate of his hope to write well hereafter in laudable things ought himselfe to bee a true Poem, that is, a composition, and patterne of the best and honourablest things; not presuming to sing high praises of heroick men, or famous Cities, unlesse he have in himselfe the experience and the practice of all that which is praiseworthy" (890). The context is again praise and praising. Milton has been recalling his youthful reading of poetry and his discovery that the best poets accounted it "the chiefe glory of their wit . . . that they were ablest to judge, to praise, and by that could esteeme them-selves worthiest to love those high perfections which under one or other name they took to celebrate" (889). Notice that the name given to the perfection doesn't matter; what does matter is the perfect judgment that will be able to recognize the essence of perfection, irrespective of the name it happens to be wearing. The praiser of the worthy testifies to his own worthiness, and this circle of acknowledgment is extended to him who can praise the praisers of the worthy. As always, the circle is self-validat-ing—it seeks no external confirmation; the only evidence one can consult is the evidence within, and to consult it is already to have found it, as Milton finds it immediately: "I thought with my selfe by every instinct and presage of nature which is not wont to be false, that what imboldn'd them to this task might with such dili-gence as they us'd imbolden me, and that what judgement, wit or elegance was my share, would herin best appeare, and best value it selfe, by how much more wisely, and with more love of vertue I should choose (let rude eares be absent) the object of not unlike praises" (889–890).

As he relives the glorious moment of self-recognition, Milton is quite aware of the impression he may be making on those who stand outside the company he now joins. That is why the paren-thetical "let rude eares be absent" is more than a casual gesture or a bow to his Virgilian model; it is an acknowledgment that at least one-half of his audience is certain to misunderstand him by reading into his personal history an immodesty and self-aggran-dizement that are the reverse of what he intends. He knows also that no amount of evidence or persuasion will convince them otherwise, for rather than being informed by the spirit of truth and charity they are *"fill'd with their own devices"* (874)—that is, it is they, not Milton, who are proud and egocentric, and they demonstrate or testify to their obstinacy by "refusing divine instruction" (874). Of course such a charge in itself seems to be just the kind of claim (of divinity) to which his opponents presumably will object, but Milton anticipates and disarms the objection by making another claim, or rather by making a *dis*-claimer. I conceive myself, he says, "to be now not as mine own person, but as a member incorporate into that truth wherof I was perswaded" (871). By "perswaded" he does not mean compelled by reasons and arguments, but is referring, rather, to the inner persuasion that is the result of God's spirit working in him.[10] It is, in short, a persuasion of faith, as Milton makes clear when in the *Christian Doctrine* he glosses "saving faith" as "THE FIRM PERSUASION IMPLANTED IN US BY THE GIFT OF GOD BY VIRTUE OF WHICH WE BELIEVE."[11] Here, then, is the true rhetoric, as opposed to the carnal rhetoric of rules and examples, and one sign of its trueness is that the things it persuades to *are not seen*. Carnal rhetoricians, on the other hand (and "carnall textman" is one of the epithets Milton later hurls at the Confuter), are concerned only with surfaces; they believe only what they can see, because in the absence of a saving belief, they cannot see with the eyes of faith. Consequently, they are not "fit persons to be taught"; they are the "false Doctors of mens devices," and as such "be taught they will not; but discover'd and laid open they must be" (874).

What discovers them and lays them open (in the sense of exposing them) is their response to divine instruction, whether it take the form of the revealed word or the words of someone who speaks not in his own person, but as a member incorporate of the truth to which he has been persuaded. By thus characterizing in advance the negative reception he expects and even hopes for, Milton adds, if only implicitly, another layer or tier to the circle of those who are joined by a spiritual or inward sameness. Just as a true poem can be written only by him who is a true poem, so can such a poem be read only by a reader no less true, by a reader who will not presume to sing high praises of the singer of high praises "unlesse he have in himselfe the experience and practice of all that which is praiseworthy"; a reader who has something else inside him will only be able to give that something back, and his reproaches will be worn by the truly eloquent—that is, the truly good—as a badge of honor. Early in the tract Milton recalls the "reviles" he has already received from the mouth "of this Modest Confuter," and says that by them "I have gain'd a name bestuck," but immediately he corrects himself: "or, as I may say, bedeckt." That is, he will be better clothed by the opprobrium of his opponent than he would have been by his praises (praises he will later reject), and indeed that opprobrium "shall be to me neither strange, nor unwelcome; as that which could not come in a better time" (875).

From a Sincere Heart Unbidden

Now in one sense this is an obvious polemical strategy designed to neutralize criticism even before it appears; but it is a strategy that harbors its own danger, the danger that it may succeed too well and thus call into question the efficacy and point of the polemical effort itself. That is to say, if one-half of your audience is presumed to be incapable of being persuaded because it is made up of persons not fit to be taught, and the other half is already persuaded because it is made up of persons who, like you, are members incorporate of an indwelling truth, it is hard to see how your writing could possibly have any effect. There would seem to be a tension, perhaps even a contradiction, between Milton's conception of his project and his decision to prosecute it, and it is a tension he does not conceal but embraces. At several points he pauses to characterize his two audiences and their relationship to the tract they are reading. The first such characterization occurs on the second and third pages of the original edition, where Milton declares that in his dispute with the Confuter "I doubt not to be justifi'd" (871); the only thing that worries him is the possibility that those of his own party "will condemme me to have wasted time in throwing downe that which could not keepe it selfe up." For those readers, what he has to say will be obvious and necessary; as for the others, "who notwithstanding what I can allege have yet decreed to mis-interpret the intents of my reply, I suppose they would have found as many causes to have misconceav'd the reasons of my silence" (871). The key word here is "decreed": the reader of a certain sort, because he is of that sort, has already, before he even hears them, misconstrued Milton's arguments; and indeed, so firmly entrenched, so much a part of him, is his interpretive predisposition, that it will operate even in the absence of material or occasion. In the context of this conclusive demonstration of the futility of his enterprise, it is, to say the least, disconcerting when the very next words—words with which Milton opens a new paragraph—are "To, beginne therefore."

Somewhat later the same sequence is negotiated again. Milton has just completed the autobiographical digression for which the *Apology* is principally known, and he pauses, as he did before, to take rhetorical stock. Some of his readers, he knows, will already believe him "to be of life and purpose neither dishonest nor unchaste," and those same readers, he predicts, "will be easily induc't to thinke me sober both of wine and of word" (893); but on the other hand, those whom he has "already been successelesse in perswading" will hear all that he can "furder say" in "vaine," and "it will be better thrift to save two tedious labours, mine of excusing, and their of needlesse hearing." But it appears that the labors will not be saved, for once again Milton goes on to the next paragraph—which begins "Proceeding furder" (894), even though the pointlessness of proceeding further has just been acknowledged. From the very beginning Milton emphasizes the reluctance with which he has taken on this task, and his distaste for it is no less great at its conclusion. Of his opponents, he says for the last time what he has said so often before: "And if yee thinke that soundnesse of reason, or what force of argument soever, will bring them to an ingenuous silence, yee think that which will never be" (953). In short, there is no point in trying to persuade the Prelats; they are what they are, "possest" not by a serious and hearty love of truth but by a hunger of the belly, "which being well drain'd and taken downe, their great Oracle, which is only there, will soone be dumbe, and . . . forwith expiring, will put us no more to trouble with tedious antiquities and disputes." It is always with a shock that one realizes that the progress of the sentence charts the progress of waste matter as it moves through the intestinal tract and expires in wind. In a characteristically defiant gesture, Milton commits a final act of indecorum by reducing the words of his opponents to farts, and, as if that weren't enough, he allows his own words to fall under the same description, for as still another instance of a tedious dispute the *Apology* itself is finally no more than wind answering wind.

Of course this only raises, in the most urgent form, the obvious question: Why write? But it is a question that implies deliberation, planning, and above all choice, and it is choice that Milton repeatedly disclaims, both in explicit statements and in his various accounts of virtuous men in action. The first explicit statement is one I have already cited: when Milton declares himself to be speaking not in his own person but as a member incorporate of the truth to which he has been persuaded, he is also saying that the persuasion effected by that truth is so total that it leaves him incapable of doing anything but what it moves him to do.

That is what it means to be no longer his own person; as Milton puts it in *The Reason of Church Government,* someone so filled with the love of truth—as opposed to being *"fill'd with their own devices"*—"cannot but testify."[12] That is precisely the condition of those whom Milton praises—the parliamentarians who act not in response to family history or education or example but as they are compelled to act by an "inbred goodnesse," the truly eloquent man who neither calculates nor withholds his eloquence (as if it were something apart from him) but simply exudes it as a natural consequence of his "fervent desire to know good things," and the true poet who, because he is a "composition and patterne of the best and honourablest things," produces compositions of the same pattern whenever he opens his mouth to sing.

In another section of the *Apology* Milton expands the category of those whose actions are involuntary (because they simply do what they are) to all of those who have the gift of prayer. The subject is set forms, and the claim of those who urge set forms is that they conduce to *"the preserving of order, unity and piety"* (937). Milton replies by redefining "order" so that it refers not to any particular arrangement or structure, but to whatever configurations happen to form when an inwardly illuminated man prays. "For I Readers, shall alwayes be of this opinion, that obedience to the Spirit of God, rather than to the faire seeming pretences of men, is the best and most dutifull order that a Christian can observe" (937). To the imagined objection of the "formalist" who cries "What! no decency in Gods worship?" (941), Milton responds with a declaration that can serve as a gloss on each of the passages we have examined: "Certainly Readers, the worship of God singly in it selfe, the very act of prayer and thanksgiving with those free and unimpos'd expressions which from a sincere heart unbidden come into the outward gesture is the greatest decency that can be imagin'd. Which to dresse up and garnish with a devis'd bravery abolisht in the law and disclaim'd by the Gospell addes nothing but a deformed uglinesse" (941–942). The key word here is "unbidden," which means without premeditation or (in the usual sense) volition; along with "unimpos'd," "unbidden" carefully defines the mode of these expressions which are neither compelled from without by a set of mechanical rules or forms, nor willed from within by an agent who could have, if he wished, willed otherwise. They simply well up, and then out, into whatever "outward gesture" happens to be their momentary, not essential, form. What they are an expression of is the worship of God, the fervent and hearty desire to know good things, an "inbred goodnesse," the state of being a true poem, all of which are equivalent to one another and equivalent also to the abstractions whose shape Milton *refuses* to identify—decency, beauty, bravery, eloquence, order, virtue, goodness, and truth.

This very tract is just such an expression, one that comes unbidden into the outward gesture from a heart that is "possest" by a fervent love to which it cannot help giving voice. The answer to the question "Why write?" is that he is literally unable not to write, because the truth that animates him will not let him be silent. This, then, is the explanation of both the value and the fact of the *Apology*: it is not so much an argument as a breaking out of what cannot be kept within; and it is valuable not because of the readers it may persuade (indeed, by Milton's own account there could be no such readers) but because of its source in a spirit already persuaded—that is, a spirit filled with saving faith. It is, as Milton says (prophetically) of the *Areopagitica*, "not a Trophey," in the sense of being evidence of victory, but a "testimony,"[13] the verbal and visible sign of an "inward Sanctity."[14] It is not that Milton, as a private person, *wants* to say the disagreeable things he says in the antiprelatical tracts; it is just that "when God commands to take the trumpet and blow a dolorous or a jarring blast, it lies not in mans will what he shall say, or what he shall conceal."[15] The man so commanded speaks not primarily to either his friends or his foes but to an audience of one, who will remember on the Day of Judgment whether or not "he could heare thy voice among his zealous servants" (805). "Neither envy nor gall hath enterd me upon this controversy," Milton declares, "but the enforcement of conscience only" (806).

The word "enforcement" indicates the paradoxical condition of freedom and bondage that characterizes this aesthetic of testimony. Although he is free of the concerns that animate other writers—the concern that he be persuasive, that he be timely, that he be decorous—Milton is constrained by the very truth he serves to speak out, and to speak out even at those moments when the conditions for speaking seem least propitious. In 1642, when he first assumes this posture, the conditions seem more favorable than not, but in 1659 the conditions could hardly be worse: everything has changed—everything, that is, but Milton, who, on the eve of the Restoration, is still giving forth with unimpos'd and unbidden expressions independently of whether or not anyone, except God, is listening. In the final paragraph of *The Readie and Easie Way*, he says of what he has written: "Thus much I should perhaps have said though I were sure I should have spoken only to trees and stones; and had none to cry to, but with the Prophet, *O earth, earth, earth!*"[16] And in the last sentence of *The Likeliest Means*, he declares once again, at the end of his polemic career, the principle that has informed it from the very beginning: "If I be not heard nor beleevd, the event will bear me witnes to have spoken truth: and I in the mean while will have borne my witness not out of season to the church and to my countrey."[17]

Digressions and Main Paths

If bearing witness or giving testimony is what the *Apology* is, this is also what it is about, at every point. That is to say, no matter what topic has been taken up, the analysis of it has exactly the same shape: a standard or norm (of praise, action, style, eloquence, prayer, liturgy) is first invoked—usually by way of reference to the strictures of the Confuter—and then it is discarded in favor of a norm or standard that has no form except the form of faith.[18] (Milton's definition of "good works" in the *Christian Doctrine* is works that have the form of faith.) At the heart of every section of the tract we find the same figure in the same posture: be he a member of Parliament, or a poet, or a "competent discerner," or a truly eloquent man, he is always physically inactive, sitting not standing, able to write but not yet writing, full of eloquence but not yet speaking—except in imagined situations, when his words will trip about him like airy servitors. Yet what is predicated of him is an extraordinary power, a power that is all the more felt because it has not been exercised but instead exists in a state of readiness, of inward conviction and resolve; and even in that apparently quiescent state, it is capable of exerting more pressure than the most overt of physical actions. Thus it is said of Parliament that "With such a majesty had their wisdome begirt it selfe, that wheras others had levied warre to subdue a nation that sought for peace, they sitting here in peace could so many miles extend the force of their single words as to overawe the dissolute stoutnesse of an armed power" (925–926). In the sentences that follow this one, the members of Parliament are celebrated because, "notwithstanding" all the events that swirl around them (plots, rebellions, invasions), "they have not bin yet brought to change their constant resolution," and this resolution "hath gain'd them . . . an admiration from all good men," who see in their constancy a continual "testifying [of] their zeale and desire to spend themselves . . . upon the grievances and wrongs of their distressed Nation" (926).

If testifying is the action to which each of Milton's considerations leads, and also the action he himself is exemplifying, then the *Apology* is a radically unified tract, everywhere the same, even though it appears to be a loose collection of topics disparately handled. Of course the *Apology* enjoys no such reputation; it is thought of as fragmentary and discontinuous, a work to be quarried for its intermittent biographical interest, but in no important way a sustained and powerful performance. In part, this bad press can be attributed to the author himself, who takes delight, it would seem, in pointing out the many ways in which "the discourse is not continu'd but interrupt" (898). He elaborately announces each new subject and takes no pains at all to disguise the mechanical nature of his transitions. He simultaneously laments the necessity of his journey and monitors its halting progress, noting every turn, every way station, and above all every digression.

Now, a digression is, by definition, a swerve from the main path, and an author who announces his digressions, as Milton does, might be said to be advertising the extent to which his treatise is ill-structured. Milton's digressions, however, have the reverse effect because their occurrence is made so much of that they finally become a part of the tract's subject and therefore no digressions at all. Consider, for example, the digression with which this chapter began—the praise of Parliament, which Milton introduces with an elaborate apology (an apology within *An Apology*):

> Now although it be a digression from the ensuing matter, yet because it shall not be said I am apter to blame others than to make triall my selfe, and that I may after this harsh discord touch upon a smoother string, awhile to entertain my selfe and him that list, with some more pleasing fit, and not the lest to testifie the gratitude which I owe to those publick benefactors of their country, for the share I enjoy in the common peace and good by their incessant labours, I shall be so troublesome to this declamer for once, as to shew him what he might have better said in their

praise. Wherin I must mention only some few things of many, for more than that to a digression may not be granted. Although certainly their actions are worthy not thus to be spoken of by the way, yet if hereafter it befall me to attempt something more answerable to their great merits, I perceave how hopelesse it will be to reach the height of their prayses at the accomplishment of that expectation that weights upon their noble deeds, the unfinishing whereof already surpasses what others before them have left enacted with their utmost performance through many ages. (922)

First of all, this section (which goes on for five pages) is labeled not only as a digression but as an act of testimony ("and not the lest to testifie"), an opportunity for Milton to display a judgment and a capacity equal to the capacities he is about to celebrate. Moreover, those capacities are characterized in a way that links them with every other presentation of action in the tract: their labors are "incessant," less a matter of "noble deeds" that have been accomplished than of an expectation (the expectation one has of them is their true accomplishment) arising from the knowledge of what they are and therefore cannot but do. His labor (of praise) necessarily has the same form: it is as unfinished as are their deeds, and like those deeds it will be ongoing and never-ending. Obviously these thematic connections work against the ostentatious announcement of a digression, but that announcement itself has something of a self-consuming quality; it speaks of a "smoother string" that will now follow upon a "harsh discord," but smoothness is an attribute of a discourse that is not "interrupt," and discord, the disruption of harmony, is what occurs when a digression takes one away from the main path. The language calls into question the very distinction it is making: the digression would seem to be a recovery of the true road, of the "still time" free of "chiding" and "noises" (892) from which he has been taken by the swerve that is the tract itself.

Lest the point be missed, Milton makes it again at the conclusion of the digression in terms that are unmistakable: "Thus farre I have digrest, Readers, from my former subject; but into such a path, as I doubt not ye will agree with me, to be much fairer and more delightfull than the rode way I was in. And how to break off suddenly into those jarring notes, which this Confuter hath set me, I must be wary, unless I can provide against offending the eare, as some Musicians are wont skilfully to fall out of one key into another without breach of harmony" (928). By the "notes which this Confuter has set me," Milton means the numbered subdivisions of the Confuter's tract; these act as a form of external compulsion forcing Milton to just the kind of outward conformity against which he inveighs. The structure of the *Modest Confutation* is a "set forme," a "shew of order" to which Milton must submit if he is to perform the task he has, however unwillingly, accepted. At the moment he takes on that task, he is already on a "rode way" far removed from the "fairer path" of praise and thanksgiving. In relation to that "rode way," the lengthy encomium of Parliament is a digression; but in relation to the way he would prefer to be traveling, the digression is the fairer path itself. Similarly, although he falls out of key by turning from the task the Confuter has sent him, he falls back into the harmony of virtuous parliamentarians praised by the singer whose virtue is one with theirs and therefore in no way singular. Forced by his assignment to defend himself and highlight his accomplishments, Milton seems by this very performance to be adding to the discord he laments. Perhaps the better course would have been the one he had commended to himself before he began: "Silence, and Sufferance" (871).

That, however, would be far too simple a view of the matter. Although Milton throughout his career is obsessed with the notion of keeping tune, of not breaking union, of closing up the ranks, he is no less obsessed with the danger of too narrowly identifying the proper stance either with an action one must perform or with an action from which one must refrain. One keeps in tune not by doing this rather than that—remaining silent rather than speaking—but by doing whatever one does or doesn't do in response to the inner prompting of a saving faith, and the problem is to determine in any situation which of the possible courses of action or inaction is consonant with that prompting. (*Samson Agonistes* is about just this problem.) The faithful action can take any form—even a form that on some future occasion would constitute a temptation, or a form that at first sight seems disagreeable, and distracting.

It is this latter that is almost always the case in Milton's prose and poetry. The Miltonic hero typically finds himself burdened with a task that seems to be taking him away from "beholding the bright countenance of truth in the quiet and still air" (*Reason of Church Government*, 821–822), and consequently it is a task he is reluctant to perform. Thus, the Attendant Spirit in *Comus* is loath to leave "the starry threshold of *Jove's* Court / . . . where those immortal shapes / Of bright aërial Spirits live inspher'd" for "the smoke and stir of this dim spot, / Which men call Earth";[19] the speaker of *Lycidas* feels himself "bitterly constrained" by the demands of an occasion he neither sought nor ever hoped to see;[20] and the Milton of the prose tracts declares repeatedly his distaste for the arena of polemic and controversy and his unhappiness at being taken away from quieter and more lofty pursuits. The pattern is established as early as the seventh prolusion, when the poet complains of the "annoying task of speaking" which has "been imposed upon me entirely at the wrong time" (16).[21] Nothing, he laments, can be more irksome than these "frequent disturbances" that deprive one of the serenity of study and contemplation. But as it turns out—and as it always turns out—what had seemed to be an interruption, a digressing, a swerving, is, when properly seen, an opportunity to continue in the path from which he had thought himself diverted; and within a few sentences he is able to declare that "this speech is obviously not an interruption, for who would say he interrupts by praising and defending what he loves, what he admires, and what he wants to follow with all his heart?" (16).

The point is that the ways in which one follows and admires are various, and may involve the irksomeness of defense as well as the pleasure of praise; in fact, these two actions so dissimilar in what they require and in their rewards are indistinguishable as actions performed in the service of God. Anyone, says Milton, who "can distinguish learned pains from unlearned drudgery" can "imagin what pleasure or profoundnesse can be in this, or what honour to deal against such adversaries." "But," he adds immediately, "were it the meanest under-service, if God by his Secretary conscience injoyn it, it were sad for me if I should draw back."[22] Answering the Confuter section by section, point by point, is just such a mean under-service, but it is no less glorious *as* service than the more delightful refreshments which Milton gives himself and his readers when he digresses to praise Parliament or to recall the "course of my yeares and studies" (*Apology*, I, 888). These passages, then, although they are labeled digressions, are finally not digressions in two senses: first, because they portray and exemplify activities (of praise and thanksgiving) that are exactly to the point, and, second, because they have nothing to digress from, since even the jarring notes from which they are a fair departure are simply the sound of service in another key, and therefore no jarring notes at all. The answer to the question of what is and is not a digression in the *Apology* is that nothing is, because nothing could be: whatever posture the speaker assumes, whatever topic or dispute demands his intention, whether he is celebrating, impugning, attacking, or even reviling, he is in essence always doing the same thing—following with all his heart what he loves and admires—and therefore the tract, in all its variety, is always the same, its movements like the movements of the starry spheres, "Eccentric, intervolv'd, yet regular / Then most, when most irregular they seem: / And in thir motions harmony Divine."[23]

Sanctified Bitterness

It is significant that it is irregularity, and especially irregularity of style, of which Milton is accused by the Confuter. On his very first page, the Confuter recoils with horror from Milton's language, and asks how the claim of "Christian meeknesse" in a "religious cause" can be reconciled with "lewd profanations, scurrilous jests, slanderous and reproachfull calumnies."[24] Milton begins to answer this question even before he takes it up. In the early pages of the *Apology*, he attacks the Confuter as "one who makes sentences by the Statute, as if all above three inches long were confiscat" (873). The objection is not to sentences of three inches or any other length, but to sentences made by the statute—that is, made in accordance with some prefabricated rule or measure; for they are the exact opposite of "those free and unimpos'd expressions which from a sincere heart unbidden come into the outward gesture" (941). They might display a "shew of order," but are in fact the "greatest disorder" (937) because the decorum they achieve has nothing to do with the inner decorum of a heart wedded to the serious and hearty love of truth.

That decorum is not rhetorical or stylistic but religious, and when Milton turns to a justification of his own style, he begins by invoking just that distinction. It would be possible, he says, to make a defense as if the issue "were in oratory," for then he could cite various rhetorical authorities as to the propriety of a "vehement vein" directed upon an "object that merits it" (899); but "since the Religion of it is disputed, and not the art, I shall make use only of such autorities, as religion cannot except against."

That authority turns out to be "Our Saviour" himself, who as a teacher exercised "his indoctrinating power in what sort him best seem'd; sometimes by a milde and familiar converse, sometimes with plaine and impartiall home-speaking . . . otherwhiles with bitter and irefull rebukes" (899). The consistency of Christ's teaching inheres not in any surface fidelity to stylistic norms but in the "dearest charity" (949) that informs his every gesture and is the meaning of his every word, even when that word is, by conventional standards, "not so mannerly to use" (902), as when "God himselfe uses the phrase *I will cut off from Iereboam him that pisseth against the wall*" (902). Those who translate this verse so as to make it less offensive claim implicitly to be "of cleaner language than he who made the tongue" (903); they would be more pure than "god who is the author of purity and eloquence"; they "would teach men to read more decently than God thought good to write" (903). The true decency, the "greatest decency" (941), has its source in a zeal "whose substance is ethereal" (900)—that is, impalpable, not confined to any particular range of figures and devices, but free to take whatever form seems appropriate to its holy task, including the form of "derision and scorne." "Thus," declares Milton, "did the true Prophets of old combat with the false; thus Christ himselfe the fountain of meeknesse found acrimony anough to be still galling and vexing the Prelaticall Pharisees" (900–901).

With this last phrase, the poet makes explicit the connection between his present effort and scriptural example: Christ and the prophets speak with "a sanctifi'd bitternesse" (901) against the Prelatical Pharisees; he is now authorized to do the same against the Pharisaical Prelates. The authorization is claimed not from precedent or historical example but from a radical and internal kinship. Christ, the prophets, and Luther are cited not because they came before Milton but because they are like him, informed by the same commitment to the "dearest charity" and therefore released from the external decorums of which their styles are sometimes a violation. They may swerve from stylistic "good order," but they do so only as the digressions in the *Apology* swerve from the order set by the Confuter—that is, as servants (and members) of a truer order, to whose dictates they remain faithful whether they write in praise or in harsh condemnation. The true style, like the true poet, like the true poem, like the true prayer, goes wherever virtue demands; for not only do *"all those things for which men plough, build or saile, obey virtue,* but . . . all words . . . shall at some time in an unwonted manner wait upon her purposes" (903). Virtue's purposes legitimate any act performed in her name, including both the act of vituperation—"I take it to be manifest that, that indignation against . . . actions notoriously bad, hath leave and autority . . . to utter such words . . . as in common talke were not so mannerly to use" (903)—and the (even more suspect) act of self-celebration: "I thought it my duty, if not to my selfe, yet to the religious cause I had in hand, not to leave on my garment the least spot, or blemish in good name so long as God should give me to say that which might wipe it off" (871). That is, if I seem to be speaking too much of myself, it is only in relation to the duty enjoined on me by God and my religion; to those of "rude ears" my words may sound boastful, but the "competent discerner" will hear me as zealous not in my own cause but in the cause of truth and virtue.

It is at moments like this that one becomes aware of the audacity of Milton's performance. Standing on the principle "that obedience to the Spirit of God, rather than to the faire seeming pretences of men, is the best and most dutifull order that a Christian may observe" (937), he is able to justify anything he says or does by recasting it as an issue of obedience, and, conversely, anything said or done by his enemies, no matter how outwardly decorous or courteous, will be redescribed as the mere outside of a foul (because opposed to his) intention, as a "pretence." What we see here is the aesthetic component of Milton's antinomianism, his reserving to the godly (self or internally identified) the privilege of breaking laws others (not moved by the same heavenly prompter) are obliged to keep. Just as Jael is justified by her purpose even though she commits murder, so is Milton justified by the purity of his intention, even though the expression of that purity is, by ordinary standards, gross and vile.[25] It is by means of this magic solvent that obscenities are turned into sanctified bitterness, digressions turned into main paths and main paths into digressions, displays of eloquence turned into unbidden inner promptings, praise (by the wrong people) turned into insult and insult (by the same wrong people) into praise, advantages of breeding and education turned into liabilities, and—the biggest trick of all—57 pages of fragments, polemical outbursts, disparate topics, and stylistic instabilities—turned into a tract everywhere the same.[26]

Does it work? Well, the fact that I have had to work so hard to make it work tells its own story, and it is a story of strain: almost everything in the world appears to be going in one direction, but a single just man (like Abdiel and the solitary heroes who periodically turn up in the otherwise bleak narrative of books XI and XII of *Paradise Lost*) knows better, and loudly proclaims his better knowledge—all the while refusing to defend or support it by the usual evidentiary standards, refusing to measure himself "by other mens measures" (904–905). Nevertheless, it is other men's measures—measures of behavior, style, prayer, worship, composition—that fill up most of Milton's pages, in this tract, in others, and in the poetry; and as a result, the surface energies in his work are almost always attached to the perspective and forces he would have us repudiate. This is hardly a new insight; it has been ours ever since Blake and Shelley noted Satan's magnificence and speculated that Milton may have been of the devil's party with or without knowing it. What I would add is that, given the principles Milton everywhere proclaims, it could not be otherwise. If it is true, as he says again and again, that validation and legitimacy (of a prayer, of a poem, of a style, of a life) can be conferred only from the inside and can be discerned (read) only by those whose insides are similarly a composition of the best and honorablest things—if it takes one to know one—it follows that the values he celebrates cannot be shown, and, moreover, that to show them by reducing them to rules or decorums or set forms would be to forsake their spirit for a mere and momentary letter.

It is the letter (of the law, of aesthetics, of prayer, of right action) from which Milton, following the example of Christ, wishes to drive us,[27] yet it is only by means of the letter—of those material forms instinct with spirit but all too capable of being detached from spirit and made into idols—that living and writing can proceed. Called to write, yet fully aware of the dangers that writing, like any other materiality, carries, Milton does not avoid those dangers. Instead, he makes polemical and literary capital of them, cataloguing the ways of error (as he catalogues the arguments of the Confuter), and challenging readers to resist them in favor of a true way no one but the faithful can see.

CHAPTER THREE

Problem Solving in Comus

If *An Apology* is the discursive presentation of Milton's aesthetic of testimony, with its relentless privileging of the inner over the outer, *Comus*, or *A Mask Presented at Ludlow Castle,* is its early and full expression in the poetry. Not only are the two works, so dissimilar in every surface respect, concerned with exactly the same issues, but the figures of virtue at their centers are interchangeable even though one is a mature male polemicist and the other a young girl. (As we shall see, this difference in gender is less of a difference than it might appear to be.) Each is engaged in affirming a set of values—moral, political, aesthetic—for which there is no evidence in the external landscapes that offer themselves as guides and repositories of meaning; and each turns resolutely from the meanings proffered by the world to the meanings already residing within.

We can begin by noting that *Comus* criticism is preeminently a criticism of problems. Here, for example, is B. A. Rajan's report on just one of the disputes that has grown up around Milton's mask: "The confrontation between the Lady and Comus seems to be set in a dark wood of critical disagreement. The most popular view is that the Lady wins largely by refusing to lose and that Comus walks off with the forensic and poetic honours. Other suggestions are that the Lady is right but not the Elder Brother, that both the Lady and Comus are wrong and the epilogue right, that nobody and nothing is right except the whole poem and even that the whole poem seems to have gone wrong somewhere."[1]

The question here is: Who is right, the Lady or Comus? but it cannot be asked without asking a series of other questions. Is the Lady, as Comus claims, a stoic? In what sense, if any, are we obligated to nature? When does temperance become "lean and sallow Abstinence"?[2] What are the terms "By which all mortal frailty must subsist" (686)? What exactly is the "sage / And serious doctrine of Virginity" (786–787)? And if we turn to other parts of the mask, the questions multiply: Why do the brothers leave their sister? Why is the Lady taken in by Comus' disguise? Is she in any way tempted by what he offers? Is she safe, as the Elder Brother declares, or is she, as the Younger Brother insists, "single" and "helpless" (402), vulnerable to the "rash hand of bold Incontinence" (397)? What is Haemony? Who is Sabrina? Why are the brothers and the Attendant Spirit unable to free the Lady? Whose "glutinous heat" (917) besmears the seat on which she sits? With whom, if anyone, are we to identify Adonis, Venus, Cupid, Psyche? And as if these questions were not enough, the mask ends with an implied question:

> Mortals that would follow me,
> Love virtue, she alone is free,
> She can teach ye how to climb
> Higher than the Sphery chime;

> Or if Virtue feeble were,
> Heav'n itself would stoop to her. (1018–1023)

Well, is virtue feeble or is she not? The verse forces the question, but the poet, like Bacon's jesting Pilate, does not stay for an answer.

The critics, of course, have stayed, but the answers they give do not, on the whole, satisfy. I intend not to offer my own answers but rather to suggest that we pay more attention to the questions—that is, to the pattern of their asking and to the pattern of response their asking creates. For if the criticism proves anything, it is that questioning is the activity to which *Comus* moves us, and therefore it seems reasonable to regard the questions we are moved to ask as primary data, rather than as loose ends that are to be tied up as neatly and quickly as possible.

As a first step in that direction, let me point out that in addition to the questions posed directly and urgently by the events of the narrative, there are those that surface only for the moment it takes to read or listen to a word or a line. Consider, for example, the introductory speech by the Attendant Spirit:

> Before the starry threshold of *Jove's* Court
> My mansion is, where those immortal shapes
> Of bright aërial Spirits live inspher'd
> In Regions mild of calm and serene Air,
> Above the smoke and stir of this dim spot,
> Which men call Earth, and with low-thoughted care
> Confin'd and pester'd in this pinfold here,
> Strive to keep up a frail and Feverish being,
> Unmindful of the crown that Virtue gives
> After this mortal change, to her true Servants
> Amongst the enthron'd gods on Sainted seats.
> Yet some there be that by due steps aspire
> To lay their just hands on that Golden Key

142

That opes the Palace of Eternity:
To such my errand is, and but for such,
I would not soil these pure Ambrosial weeds
With the rank vapours of this Sin-worn mold. (1–17)

These seventeen lines firmly establish a two-tiered Platonic universe, and they also establish an opposition between the freedom and expansiveness of the higher tier and the closeness and constraint of the level to which the spirit descends. Earth is a "dim spot," a "pinfold" (enclosure for animals); its inhabitants are frail and feverish; they are confined and restricted, both in their physical circumstances and in their point of view; they are prisoners of a "Sin-worn" mold which the Attendant Spirit most uncharitably disdains to assume.

In the next line, however, the language and the system of value it reflects suddenly change (the Attendant Spirit is still speaking):

But to my task. *Neptune,* besides the sway
Of every salt Flood, and each ebbing Stream,
Took in by lot 'twixt high and nether *Jove*
Imperial rule of all the Sea-girt Isles
That like to rich and various gems inlay
The unadorned bosom of the Deep;
Which he to grace his tributary gods
By course commits to several government,
And gives them leave to wear their Sapphire crowns,
And wield their little tridents; but this Isle,
The greatest and the best of all the main,
He quarters to his blue-hair'd deities;
And all this tract that fronts the falling Sun
A noble Peer of mickle trust and power
Has in his charge, with temper'd awe to guide
An old and haughty Nation proud in Arms;

Where his fair offspring nurs't in Princely lore,
Are coming to attend their Father's state
And new-entrusted Scepter. (18–36)

The perspective is still one that looks downward from aery heights to spotlike enclosures, but the colors have changed from the gray and brown of smoke and mold to the richly various colors of sapphire and other gems inlaid in the blue bosom of the sea; and the inhabitants of these spots, one of whom is "greatest" and "best," are no longer low-thoughted or feverish or rank, but noble, powerful, tempered, and fair.

There is of course a simple explanation for this shift: presumably neither Milton nor Lawes would wish to insult the Earl of Bridgewater by suggesting that he and the members of his family were sinful, much less odorous;[3] obviously they are among those few that "by due steps aspire" to be free of their earthly prison. I do not want to belittle this explanation, but it would be difficult to extend it to the subsequent instances of the same pattern; for repeatedly the verse invites us to adopt an attitude toward some thing or person or action, only to turn in a few lines and apparently sanction exactly the opposite attitude. This is true even of those objects and places which, as Roger Wilkenfeld has shown, "establish the masque's concern with the varieties of restraint and confinement":[4] pinfolds, spots, prisons, dungeons, cells, caves, cages, caverns, grots, sties, snares, traps, vaults, sepulchers, graves, every kind of enclosure imaginable, including the verbal enclosures of "well-plac't words of glozing courtesy" (Comus, 161) and "false rules prankt in reason's garb" (759). Chief among these is the enclosure of "the drear wood" in whose "perplex't paths" the Lady and her brothers wander (37). This wood is "ominous" (61), thick with "black shades" where hidden dangers lurk "imbow'r'd" (62); it is a "wild Wood" (312), a "close dungeon" (349), a "surrounding waste" (403), a "dark sequester'd nook"

(500), a "hideous Wood" (520), the "haunt" of sorcerers who are "Immur'd in cypress shades" (521), a place of "inmost bow'rs" (536), where a monstrous rout like "stabl'd wolves" (534) can be heard howling. Yet at times these same woods wear a quite different face; if they are "ominous" when the Attendant Spirit speaks of them at line 61, they are friendly, or at least sympathetic, at line 86, when he recalls how they ceased their waving in response to the "soft Pipe and smooth-dittied Song" of Thyrsis. In one breath the Lady complains of her confinement in "the blind mazes of this tangl'd Wood" (181), and in the next she remembers how inviting these woods seemed only a short time ago, when "the spreading favor of these Pines" (184) offered lodging and shade. Even now, in the midst of her danger, she refers to the "kind hospitable Woods" (187) which provide berries and other cooling fruits. Of course the balance remains negative—the wood continues to be the prime symbol of the menace of enclosure; but then enclosures are themselves not always perceived as menacing. As the Younger Brother debates the degree of his sister's danger, he is conscious of the peril he himself confronts, lost and imprisoned in "this close dungeon of innumerous boughs" (349); but when he turns for solace to an image, it is of an enclosure no less confining than the one he would escape: "might we but hear / The folded flocks penn'd in their wattled cotes" (343–344). If danger is a dungeon, then safety, it would seem, is a cage, and when the Elder Brother asks "hath any ram / Slipt from the fold, or young Kid lost his dam, / Or straggling wether the pent flock forsook?" (497–499), safety is again strongly equated with confinement.

What are we to make of this? Are some enclosures good and others bad? Are the same enclosures now good, now bad? It is possible at times to read this pattern of "ambiguous valuing" as a reflection of the psychology of characters who wander uncertainly in a landscape whose exact configurations elude them.

When the Lady calls the wood "kind and hospitable," she does not display the vulnerability that will soon lead her to say to Comus, "Shepherd, I take thy word, / And trust thy honest offer'd courtesy" (321–322). To solve the problem in this way, however, is only to confront a larger one. Why is it that the good characters in the mask seem so much at a disadvantage? The Lady is the victim not only of Comus' rhetoric but of Milton's irony. She calls to Echo and asks for grace; she is heard by Comus and delivered up to the enemy. While her soon-to-be-tempter addresses her in a curious and suspect mixture of overcourtly and overpastoral diction, she responds with platitudes about the likely residence of true courtesy, and blithely cries, "Shepherd lead on" (330). Her brothers fare no better. Their lapse, excusable or not, leads directly to the crisis, and their performance in the climactic scene is no more happy, as the Attendant Spirit is quick to point out: "O ye mistook, ye should have snatcht his wand / And bound him fast; without his rod revers't, / And backward mutters of dissevering power, / We cannot free the Lady that sits here / In stony fetters fixt, and motionless" (815–819). Not that the Spirit himself is notably successful; he was dispatched, he tells us, for "defense and guard" (42), but he is always appearing a moment after the damage has been done, and whatever Haemony is, his possession of it does not enable him to free the Lady.

I am not suggesting that we are confused as to who is good and who is bad. Indeed, it is precisely because we are *not* confused that the unfolding of the mask presents us with a succession of problems; for given the certain knowledge that the Lady deserves our sympathy and admiration, while Comus does not, we are pressed in the course of reading or viewing to find textual confirmation of that certain knowledge. An older tradition of criticism[5] is surely right to insist that the theme of *Comus* is simply the superiority of virtue over vice; but in our experience of the mask that theme is apprehended negatively, because for so much of the time we are learning wherein the superiority of virtue does *not* reside. It does not reside in physical strength, or in invulnerability, or in infallibility; it does not even reside, as we discover, in a delicacy of perception. When the Lady appears on the scene, her first words are "This way the noise was, if mine ear be true" (170), and in fact her ear at that point *is* true, for she correctly assesses the nature of Comus' rites even though she has not, like us, had the advantage of seeing them. (This impressive performance should be a sufficient answer to those who see in this speech the fastidiousness of a prig.) If we are tempted, however, to generalize from this to an assertion of the superior trueness of virtuous ears, we are stopped short by the example of Comus himself, who in the very same scene displays an ear no less true: "Can any mortal mixture of Earth's mold / Breathe such Divine enchanting ravishment? / Sure something holy lodges in that breast" (244–246). Indeed, as it turns out Comus finally has the best of this comparison, as he does of others; for while he draws the correct conclusion from the Lady's voice, she is disastrously mistaken about his: "Shepherd, I take thy word." Of course Comus is disguised, the Lady is not, and as Rosemond Tuve points out, virtue does not enable one "to see through to the true nature of that which . . . simply says it is other than it is."[6] Here, then, is a firm point of difference between virtue and vice: one is open, the other works by guile. This distinction, however, holds up no better than the others. The Attendant Spirit (as Dr. Johnson complains) also works by guile; he too disguises himself as a shepherd, and the putting on of his disguise is the first action we see. Indeed, since they never appear on stage at the same time, the Attendant Spirit and Comus could be played by a single actor.

To this, one might object that while the Attendant Spirit and Comus perform identical actions, their intentions differ, and that difference is essential. Yes it is—but notice how we have come to that conclusion: by entertaining more immediately available points of difference and then discarding them because they prove to be *inessential*. This, I believe, is precisely what we are doing (or should be doing) when we read *Comus*: learning to perceive essential (and often hidden) differences in the context of apparent similarities. That is to say, reading (or viewing) the mask provokes us to cognitive acts of discrimination in the course of which we discover what something is by first discovering what it is not. We are prodded to this discovery by the apparent lack of fit between the characters (as they are labeled) and what they do or say; but this lack of fit exists only if value is thought to be a property of things or actions (that is, of words and disguises), and it is precisely that way of thinking which the mask is designed to change. In short, I am suggesting that the problems posed by the mask are heuristic; they are there not because we are to solve them, but because we are to be moved by them to engage in a certain kind of activity—the activity of discerning an inner truth beneath the surface of external representations.

This is precisely the activity in which the Elder and Younger Brothers are engaged, and indeed, their conversation should be seen as either a model or a parody of the dialogue taking place in our minds. The point of debate between them is exactly the point at issue in our experience as readers or viewers—not whether the Lady is virtuous (that is assumed), but the nature and shape of her virtue; and they proceed as we do, by progressively refining their idea of what is essential. They begin on the smaller (but related) issue of whether or not the Lady is in danger, and the Elder Brother weighs in immediately with a generalization: "Virtue could see to do what virtue would / By her own radiant light, though Sun and Moon / Were in the flat Sea sunk . . . / He that has light within his own clear breast / May sit i'th' center, and enjoy bright day" (373–375, 381–382). To this ringing declaration, the Younger Brother replies with a common-sense objection: "You may as well spread out the unsunn'd heaps / Of Miser's treasure by an outlaw's den, / And tell me it is safe, as bid me hope / Danger will wink on Opportunity, / And let a single helpless maiden pass" (398–402). It might appear at this point that the Elder Brother begins to give ground, but what he does is define more precisely the ground on which he continues to stand. That is, he uses his brothers' objections, much as we are to use the discontinuities we perceive, to make finer and finer discriminations. It is not, he declares, our sister's physical strength in which I have confidence, but "a hidden strength / Which you remember not" (415–416). And what is that, the Younger Brother obligingly asks (how like a philosophical dialogue this is), and he is immediately told: "'Tis chastity, my brother, chastity: / She that has that, is clad in complete steel, / . . . no evil thing that walks by night / . . . Hath hurtful power o'er true virginity" (420–421, 432, 437). This raises the question of what is meant by *true* virginity, a question that is answered when Thyrsis arrives with news of the Lady's capture. Since the audience already knows what has happened, much of his speech is redundant; but its function is less to give information than to generate pressure for the further zeroing-in on the subject. Again, the Younger Brother takes the role of foil or prod: "Is this the confidence / You gave me, Brother?" (583–584). And the reply is so sure that it begins on the half line, without missing a beat:

> Yes, and keep it still,
> Lean on it safely, not a period
> Shall be unsaid for me: against the threats
> Of malice or of sorcery, or that power
> Which erring men call Chance, this I hold firm;
> Virtue may be assail'd but never hurt,
> Surpris'd by unjust force, but not enthrall'd,
> Yea even that which mischief meant most harm
> Shall in the happy trial prove most glory. (584–592)

In this passage the process of refining is accelerated, every line contributing to the further specifying of the Elder Brother's position and therefore of the conceptions that support it. To the earlier distinction between external and internal strength, he now adds a series of distinctions: virtue may be attacked (this is, after all, a comment on the attacker), but the attack will prove unsuccessful; of course it may *appear* successful in some merely physical sense ("Surpris'd by unjust force"), but that appearance will ultimately serve only to make virtue's inevitable triumph more dramatically satisfying; for in the end "evil on itself shall back recoil, / And mix no more with goodness" (593–594).

I am aware that my summary of these lines is selective, but I believe that my selection is true to the rhythm of the exchange, which is dialectical, moving from a consideration of relative strength and weakness, to the redefining of strength as an interior rather than a physical quality, to the identification of that quality as chastity, to the redefining of chastity as something (not yet specified) that can survive a bodily assault, even if, in some superficial way, that assault is successful. In short, what the brothers do, in cooperation, not in conflict, is separate (outward, visible) accidents from (inner, invisible) essentials, and since that is what we have been doing all along, their activities parallel and interact with ours. It follows, then, that we are not on one side of an argument but on both sides of a process, exploring with the brothers the contrasting perspectives on their sister's situation. Thus, when the Younger Brother expresses fear that the Lady may be in real danger, we know that he is right, and for that moment at least, he is, in his questioning, our surrogate; yet when the Elder Brother declares that the truly virtuous are dear to Heaven and are therefore under the protection of angels, we know that *he* is right, because we have seen and heard the angel who protects his sister. This scene is sometimes read as if at the end of it we were to award the palm to one of the speakers, but this is to ignore its dialectical movement and the answering movement it draws from us. The brothers are not adversaries (except on local issues of interpretation) but partners, with each other and with us, and our common goal, at least in that part of the scene which has been called "philosophical," is the goal of every philosopher: to find out what really matters.

And meanwhile, what of the Lady? What is she doing while her brothers philosophize and we proceed with them toward an identification of essentials? She is not trying to find out what really matters, for this is a knowledge she already possesses and is possessed by. While her brothers labor for three hundred lines to understand the extent and limits of her danger, and while we exercise our minds no less strenuously (if less formally), she articulates the crucial distinction within moments of her first appearance. After acknowledging (1) that she is lost, (2) that she is possibly in danger, and (3) that she is surely in the neighborhood of evil spirits (these are precisely the points the Younger Brother will later make), she declares simply: "These thoughts may startle well, but not astound / The virtuous mind" (210–211). If I were to paraphrase this, I could do no better than the Elder Brother's statement of lines 588ff.: "this I hold firm; / Virtue may be assail'd but never hurt . . ." The point of course is that the Lady is holding firm from the very beginning, aware, as her brothers are, of the possibility that she may be "Surpris'd by unjust force"—that is, "startled"—but knowing before they do (or at least before they articulate it) that such an assault cannot shake an inner composure which is based on a faith in something more real than the accidents of physical circumstance. The virtuous mind, in short, may be temporarily put off balance by something totally unexpected, but it will always recover itself and refuse to be paralyzed (astounded). The fact that the Lady will later be literally paralyzed is only one more indication of the extent to which the meaning of events is not discernible in their observable configurations.

Meanwhile, however, we are still left with our question, more sharply focused: If the Lady is not in the process of finding out what really matters, what is she doing? The answer is that she is gradually being placed in a position where the basis of the confidence she here displays is plainly visible, because every other basis for it has been taken away. Even before she appears on the scene, she has been stripped of the support provided by her brothers; and in rapid succession she is stripped of all the supports that remain: the stars are, as she says, "close[d] up" (197), and no lamp is available "to give due light / To the misled and lonely Traveller" (199–200); she then turns to her ear, "My best guide now" (171), and for a while it serves her well as she discerns perfectly the quality of the sounds she hears; but then Comus appears with his well-placed words of glozing courtesy, and what had been her "best guide" now points her in exactly the wrong direction: "Shepherd, I take thy word, / And trust thy honest offer'd courtesy" (321–322). Friends, light, vision, hearing, direction—one by one they are taken from her, until in Comus' lair she is deprived even of her mobility and is left with nothing at all.

Yet, as it turns out, she is left with everything—*everything that matters*. This is what is meant when she says to Comus, "Thou canst not touch the freedom of my mind" (663), or, in other words, "All of this—my weakness, your strength, the entire situation as it seems to be—is beside the point. I may be imprisoned in every sense you can conceive, but in truth I am free." The force of this moment (if it is felt) inheres in the way it reverses yet maintains the opposition in the opening lines between the constraint of earthly pinfolds and the freedom of those who sit on sainted seats. The Lady is obviously one who "by due steps" (12) aspires to sainthood, yet she sits here a virtual emblem of the confinement associated by the Attendant Spirit with feverish worldly striving. Here, then, is another problem for the audience, but it is solved even as it is (literally) posed if we realize that a distinction originally made in terms of place is here redefined as a distinction of spirit: from the point of view of the physical circumstances, the Lady is helpless, defenseless, and "immanacl'd" (665); from a point of view that denies the primacy of the physical, she is formidable, protected, and free. It is this hierarchy of perspectives that the scene establishes, or rather asks us to establish by asking us to understand what the Lady says. The careers of the audience and the heroine are thus perfectly complementary: she begins with layers of support, but they gradually fall away, leaving her to rely on what is essential; we begin with an understanding of virtue, but it is gradually refined by our efforts, until at some point we identify what is essential. Her moment of trial (or, more properly, of self-exemplification) requires an affirmation, and we are required to comprehend it; the text for both is the same: "Thou canst not touch the freedom of my mind."

This, then, is the act (of understanding) for which the heuristic experience of the mask has been preparing us, and if we perform it, the problems that were the vehicle of that experience disappear, not because they are solved but because they have been made meaningful. That is, the distinction we are invited to make here, between a vantage point from which the Younger Brother's fears are justified and another from which they are irrelevant, operates retroactively to turn the questions that have led us to make it—Is the earth a pinfold or a gem? Are the woods ominous or kind? Are disguises good or bad?—into answers. The form of these questions is "either-or," but the answer in every case is "both-and": the earth is both a pinfold and a gem, depending on whether you are tied to it by "low-thoughted care" or live, at least in spirit, in "Regions mild of calm and serene Air" (6, 4); the woods are both ominous and kind, depending on whether Comus or some superior power is believed to be their proprietor; disguises are both good and bad, depending on the purpose for which they are put on; and of course the Lady is both secure and in danger, depending on whether one fears for her physical well-being or for the integrity of her mind and soul. Not one of the questions raised by the mask is to be answered unequivocally, although it is the search for unequivocal answers that brings us to this realization. The pattern of ambiguous valuing exerts a pressure for resolution and explanation, but when the explanation is found, it does not disambiguate. Rather, it gives significance to the pattern by establishing contexts in which the interpretive alternatives are simultaneously, but not indifferently, true. Once these contexts have been established, every event and image in the mask falls into place as a further exemplification of the only lesson it teaches: the lesson of the double perspective.

So powerful is this lesson that at a stroke it does away with the critical puzzles associated with *Comus,* not by making them disappear but by making them signify. Consider, for example, the puzzle (for which innumerable solutions have been proposed) of what exactly Haemony is. Temperance, reason, faith, knowledge, general grace, specific grace, prevenient grace, full grace, partial grace, anticipatory grace? The question has a literature of its own,[7] and I have no intention of adding to it, except to ask another question. What are we told about Haemony? Only that it is "a small unsightly root," the leaf "darkish" and "prickle[d]," but that in "another Country" it bears a "bright golden flow'r"—not, however, "in this soil," where it is "Unknown" and unesteemed and "the dull swain / Treads on it daily with his clouted shoon" (629–635). In short, Haemony is something that is weak and unimpressive from one point of view, but strong and glorious from another—precisely the distinction we have learned to make between virtue as it appears in earthly terms, and virtue as it is seen and valued in Heaven. I am not suggesting that Haemony is virtue, but that they both figure forth or fill out the double perspective which is at once the subject of the mask and the goal of our refined understandings. Those who assign a different significance to each of the mask's abstractions have the goal of arranging them in a linear pattern of cause and effect; but they exist in a relation of homology as successive manifestations of a single great image or controlling idea. The plot of *Comus* is not a series of crises (although several scenes have that appearance) but a series of transformations; and the pleasure we derive is, as Rosemond Tuve has said, "the pleasure of watching the central image unfold, display itself, dance before us. . . . The image which is the heart of this frail action slowly opens out one meaning after another, never disappearing, never standing still, looking at us with one face out of the long and leisurely speech of one stylized personage, with another face out of the songs and declarations of another, is seen in this position and in that" (154–155). Haemony, then, does not signify something *different* from the actions or symbols presented elsewhere in the mask; rather, it is one more face of the meaning that is continually exfoliating, the meaning I have identified as the double perspective, or the pattern of ambiguous valuing. The Lady's situation, fixed but free, is an emblem of that principle, Haemony, unsightly but beautiful, is another

The central temptation scene is another still; for the debate between Comus and the Lady is not to be watched with suspense (will she or won't she) or with a view toward judging the arguments, but as one more context for the unfolding of the points of view we have learned to distinguish. Thus, Comus' position is perfectly coherent given his assumption that man is bound to the processes of nature; for then the obligation he urges is indeed paramount and the Lady's abstinence is what he says it is, a self-glorying asceticism that would deny her involvement in the "condition / By which all mortal frailty must subsist" (685–686). The Lady, as many have observed (and complained), replies not by answering him but by *declaring* another position, one in which his offer and her behavior take on quite a different appearance: in her

155

vision, all mortal frailty subsists by virtue of the sustaining power of God, and Nature is only an intermediary bestower of that sustenance; therefore, to bind oneself to Nature in the manner Comus suggests is to set her up in place of God, and in fact to do her a disservice by placing her in a configuration of choice in which she is an idol. Temperance in this view is not the negative and constricting thing Comus takes it to be, but the sign of a refusal to be in bondage to natural processes and a declaration of dependence on a power that controls, and can at any time suspend, them. Temperance, then, is a positive and liberating action, and it takes its place with Haemony as something that signifies differently, depending on where you stand, just as Nature takes its place alongside earth, and the wood, and pinfolds, as something whose value is a function of your relationship to it—a prison if you allow yourself to be confined within its confines, a temple if, as you move within it, you continually look "to Heav'n" (777).

Together, the two positions in the debate form another instance in a continually exfoliating pattern of paired antitheses: the Lady's apparent situation is to her true situation as the unimpressive appearance of Haemony is to its true beauty and efficacy, as the superficial negativity of temperance is to its liberating intention, as the ominous woods are to the woods that are kind, as the disguise of Comus is to the disguise of the Attendant Spirit, as the enchanting song of Circe is to the holy song of the Lady's waking bliss, as the Nature that demands our worship is to the Nature that calls us to the worship of God. What makes these opposing pairs equivalent and even interchangeable is the larger opposition in which they participate and of which they are manifestations: on one hand a perspective that values on the basis of appearances, and on the other a perspective in which value is a function of an internalized hierarchy of loyalties. These perspectives are, as we have seen, present and distinguished in the opening lines, and the events of the plot serve only to confirm the previously chosen allegiances of the characters. Just as there is no progression in the action, so there is no advance in the level of insight displayed by the villain and heroine, who merely reaffirm and redefine the positions from which they always speak. For all its dramatic impact, the Lady's ringing "Thou canst not touch the freedom of my mind" is nothing more (or less) than a reformulation of her earlier declaration of a mind that can be startled but not astounded, and this in turn anticipates the Elder Brother's confident faith in a virtue that can be surprised but not enthralled. In each of these statements the interpretive center is shifted from the realm of physical accident to the realm of spiritual essence, and an ethic of intention is substituted for an ethic of observable effects.

That ethic receives yet another reformulation (and we receive yet another opportunity to understand) when the Lady refuses Comus' offer of a "cordial Julep" (672): "Were it a draught for *Juno* when she banquets, / I would not taste thy treasonous offer; none / But such as are good men can give good things" (701–703). This is the furthest (and inevitable) extension of the truth the mask continually presents. If virtue is a function of motives or loyalties, then it cannot be identified with things or actions, which are neither good nor bad in themselves but take on the moral coloration of those who use and perform them. The categories "good things" and "good actions" are determined by the spirit in which they are appropriated and executed. The Lady is not good because she does X; rather, X is good because *she* does it. And exactly the reverse is true of the actions and offers of Comus, which are intended (by Milton) less to persuade than to supply the other pole of the two worldviews the mask is always contrasting.[8]

Comus, then, is essentially static (a description that many have turned into a criticism) but its experience is not; for, as Tuve observes, although the "clearly opposed . . . positions do not conflict

157

in any stage personality, . . . we ourselves are that personality"
(121). What this means is that the events of the mask are always
serving a double purpose: they measure, from a variety of angles,
the distance between the two contrasting perspectives, and they
invite the audience to perceive that distance and to understand its
implications. Nowhere is the distance greater or the invitation
more pressing than when the Lady *declines* to expound "the sage
/ And serious doctrine of Virginity" (786–787):

> Fain would I something say, yet to what end?
> Thou hast nor Ear nor Soul to apprehend
> The sublime notion and high mystery
> That must be utter'd to unfold the sage
> And serious doctrine of Virginity. (783–787)

This too is a point of critical debate that has a literature of its
own, but, like Haemony, the sage and serious doctrine is a problem only if one wishes to assign it a separate meaning, for in fact
it is identical with the stable meaning every event and image
presents. The virginity celebrated here (even though it is unex-
pressed) is the virginity of the virtuous soul that refuses to ally itself with terrestrial values and is pledged instead to the higher
power of which all things terrestrial are evidences. It is this
pledge and self-betrothal (to something not seen) that Comus is
incapable of understanding, and the Lady proves *her* understanding (rather than her arrogance or ignorance) by not trying to explain it to him. What she leaves out, we are left to supply, performing an overt act that is precisely answerable to her act of
omission. "List mortals, if your ears be true," cries the Attendant
Spirit in the Epilogue (997); it is part of my thesis that *Comus* is a
device for the making true of its audience's ears, which are here
tested, as they have been tested before, by their ability to understand.

They are tested once more as the mask ends: "Mortals that

158

would follow me, / Love virtue, she alone is free, / She can teach ye how to climb / Higher than the Sphery chime, / Or if Virtue feeble were, / Heav'n itself would stoop to her" (1018–1023). You will recall this as one of the questions I posed at the beginning of this chapter. Is virtue feeble or is she not? It is hardly even necessary to answer, "She is and she isn't." She is, in the sense that external circumstances are beyond her control; she isn't, in the sense that the measure of her strength is the firmness of her will. That is why the appearance of Sabrina is only contingently related to the efforts of the brothers and the steadfastness of the Lady—not, as some have suggested, to protect the freedom of grace, but to underline the freedom of virtue, which is as independent (in its own sphere) of heavenly intervention as it is immovable before the lure of earthly temptations. Sabrina, the last of the problems for which criticism has sought a solution, is, like everything else in the mask, not an isolated value but a second term in a relationship that helps us to further refine our understanding of virtuous behavior. In a curious way, she is allied with Comus, for both function as foils to the Lady, who remains the center of an attention they serve to focus. It is as wrong to make the nymph the heroine of the action as it is to make a hero of the tempter. *Comus* is no more a celebration of grace than of nature. Rather, it is a celebration of human virtue, of her limited glory and glorious limitations.

Moreover, it is that everywhere, from the beginning, in the middle, at the end, with no progress at all in the level of understanding of insight presented to us by the text. The only movement in the action is the overdetermined movement of opposites reassuming their opposing positions in a variety of postures. There is (or should be), however, movement in the understandings of the spectators. As Stephen Orgel has observed, "It is not the Lady, but we ourselves who . . . come away with a lesson for our lives."[9] Learning that lesson (of the double perspective) is the activity to which the mask calls us; watching it repeated in a triumphant succession of exfoliations is the pleasure it offers. That pleasure is not transitory, for to enjoy it here is to have become capable of enjoying it when the performance is over and we move from the interpretive trials of art to the interpretive trials of living. The purpose of a mask, Orgel tells us (borrowing from Ben Jonson), is "to make the spectators understanders." In the course of understanding the Lady's virtue, we earn a share of it, becoming what we apprehend. The spirit that has been the key to every one of the mask's problems informs the reader or viewer who has learned to proceed in its light.

CHAPTER FOUR

Unblemished Form

Being Mindful

The Lady of course is already proceeding in the light, if only because it is a light she sheds. The questions noted and multiplied in the previous chapter are not questions for her. In her world everything is always (except for a single moment of being startled) quiet and serene, and the serenity, as we shall see in this chapter, is of a deep kind that knows neither bottom nor surface.

The first word in *Comus* is "Before," and one supposes that as a marker of place it will be part of a phrase identifying the location of the poem's scene; but the identification is made difficult, if not impossible, by the words that follow:

> Before the starry threshold of *Jove's* court
> My mansion is, where those immortal shapes
> Of bright aërial Spirits live inspher'd
> In Regions mild of calm and serene Air . . .[1]

161

The specific point of reference is Jove's court, but it is named as the place where the speaker is not; he lives elsewhere, *before* (spatially? temporally?), and we are not helped when elsewhere is described as the residence of immortal shapes. Later we shall learn what the word "immortal" should already be telling us: that shape itself is mortal, capable of change and therefore of death, and that therefore no shape, no specifiable configuration, can contain, capture, represent that which is "Before." We shall also learn that "inspher'd" spirits are precisely *not* enclosed or confined—that, like the angels of *Paradise Lost,* they "obstacle find none / Of membrane, joint, or limb, exclusive bars: / . . . Total they mix, Union of Pure with Pure."[2] That is, they are not bounded shapes, distinct, individual, unique, but rather intelligences composed of the same purity. That is why they live in regions "mild of calm and serene Air" (4): the regions are mild not only in that they avoid the atmospheric extremes of hot and cold; they are temperamentally mild, without the mental perturbations and eruptions that characterize mortal life. Immortal life is smooth in a way perfectly captured by the phrase "serene Air." "Serene," at once psychologically and physically descriptive, indicates an unruffled expanse, a surface that is perfectly even, without highs or lows, a surface whose every point is indistinguishable from every other point. With reference to it, one cannot pick out a particular spot, for it is everywhere the same.

The next five lines are ruled by another distancing mark of supposed reference, "Above":

> Above the smoke and stir of this dim spot,
> Which men call Earth, and with low-thoughted care
> Confin'd, and pester'd in this pinfold here,
> Strive to keep up a frail and Feverish being,
> Unmindful of the crown that Virtue gives . . . (5–9)

"Above" points us for a second time to the elsewhere the poem will never present, before descending (in several senses) to the sublunary world which is the unhappy opposite of the spirit's serene regions. It is spotted and therefore not everywhere of the same texture; and those who inhabit it both stir and strive. Rather than being perfectly at ease and still (meaning both quiet and always the same), they *move,* and move feverishly, not toward some goal that will allow them rest, but in response to a deep and undiagnosed malaise. (They are those who will later [596–597] be described as "in eternal restless change / Self-fed and self-consum'd.") They don't have their mind on the right thing and therefore miss the true goal, "the crown that Virtue gives."

In fact, it may be easy to miss because it is bestowed "After" (10). Here is the third key word that points us away from the presently available spatial and temporal coordinates to a beyond that never comes into view: it is always "Before," in front of wherever we are now, or "Above," not here but there, or "After," not now, but later. It is also removed from sensory apprehension. The mask abounds in references to phenomena (if that is the word) that cannot be seen or heard. "I must be viewless now" (92), the Attendant Spirit announces; that is, I must recede from anyone's view. This is precisely the status of Haemony, described punningly as an "unsightly root" (629). As we saw in Chapter 1, "unsightly" is a pun; at one level it means not good to look at, but on a deeper level it tells us that Haemony is not the kind of thing that yields itself to sight. It is a "root" in another nonhorticultural sense—the true source, the origin, the beginning—and as such it is precisely "unsightly," not seen, because it is within its unbounded boundaries that acts of perception and intellection occur. The cause and substance of everything visible, it is itself hidden, not because it is nowhere but because it is everywhere.

This may seem superficially to be a paradox: something that is hidden, yet pervasive; but it is finally no paradox, because it is hidden only to those who would find meaning and illumination in surfaces. Their shallow perception in effect creates the obstacles to clear seeing. They look around with carnal and empirical eyes and see only forms unanimated by any spirit; and when the claims of the spirit are pressed, they respond as Comus does, with bewilderment and exasperation: "This is mere moral babble" (807). Such persons display no consistency; they are changeable, living a life of ups and downs; they are continually agitated, never at rest, ever insecure and vulnerable to every shift in the panorama of the world's scenes.

Line 9 tells us as much, but its message is already given in the first word. "Unmindful" means what it literally says: not full of mind, but full of something else or of many things that jostle one another, creating discontinuities, depressions, elevations, agitation. It is a state the Second Brother imagines for his sister when he pictures her with "unpillow'd head fraught with sad fears" (355). The image is precise: her head will be full not of mind but of fears; it will be darkened, blotted, spotted, perturbed, not smooth, unruffled, serene. And as we know, there has been a moment when the Lady's equanimity (a word meant literally) is threatened by an invasion of foreign—not home bred—thoughts; a moment when, alone and surrounded by an unbroken "single darkness" (204), she is on the verge of panic: "a thousand fantasies / Begin to throng into my memory, / Of calling shapes, and beck'ning shadows dire, / And airy tongues that syllable men's names / On Sands and Shores and desert Wildernesses" (205–209). It is as if she were abstracted from the landscape of her consciousness and sees that in another instant its even surface will be marked by alien shadows and shapes. But then, in the nick of time, she dispels those shapes by declining to acknowledge them as her own; "thoughts" they may be, but they are thoughts from some outside agency, and as she refuses them they fade away (like the fleeing, sighing, pagan deities of the *Nativity Ode*) to be replaced by what was already there:

> These thoughts may startle well, but not astound
> The virtuous mind, that ever walks attended
> By a strong siding champion Conscience.—
> O welcome pure-ey'd Faith, white-handed Hope,
> Thou hov'ring Angel girt with golden wings,
> And thou unblemish't form of Chastity,
> I see ye visibly, and now believe. (210–216)

Threatened by variety, the Lady literally pulls herself together in the name of a single value, to which she gives different but equivalent names. The first name is "Conscience," that inner light which has its source in heavenly imperatives. The second name is Faith, the reliance not on the evidence of things seen, the world's evidence, but on the unseen (nonvisible, extrabodily) evidence of a promise whose substance, Hope (the lines rehearse the first verses of Hebrews 11), is in the future, but whose credibility, if it is accepted and, indeed, embraced, orders the present. The condition all of these abstractions point to—the condition of holding fast to faith despite the counter-evidence offered by the world, the condition of living on and for Hope—is Chastity. One who is chaste pledges herself to the highest possible service and rejects all other services as unworthy and idolatrous. The chaste person withholds herself from all but the one object of her commitment. She displays no divided loyalties, but is, in the literal sense, single-minded. There is only one thing (one desire, one affective orientation) in her mind, one thing her mind is full of.

The act of being mindful in this sense is entirely interior. One performs it not by bringing something from the external world back into the mind, but by clinging to something the mind already contains. One consults, in short, oneself. The "virtuous mind" is the mind that feeds on its own strength, disdaining the proffered strengths of circumstances and history. The act is not solipsistic or self-regarding (in the culpable sense), because what the mind finds in itself is the unchanging principle, the abiding commitment, the overriding loyalty, in relation to which temptations are resisted and fears allayed. The mind finds, that is, the sustaining Other that founds it and authorizes a self-sufficiency that is blameless because it is a sufficiency of perfect dependence. The mind that keeps its eye unerringly and continually on the value of which it is the repository repels foreign invasion without further effort, simply by being what it is. The Elder Brother's lines remain the best gloss on this "Virgin purity" (427): "Virtue could see to do what virtue would / By her own radiant light, though Sun and Moon / Were in the flat Sea sunk" (373–375); "He that has light within his own clear breast / May sit i'th' center, and enjoy bright day" (381–382). Just before these lines, the same brother affirms his confidence in the "constant mood" of his sister's "calm thoughts," and a calmness, he says, that no external threat could "stir" (371). The image is once again precise and familiar: an untroubled surface unmarred by any lines or disproportions, an evenness so steady (a word substituted for "constant" in the Trinity manuscript) and saturating that anyone gazing at it would see nothing—that is, no thing that stood out from any other in a way that would give it a separate identity.

But of course no one could gaze at it, because in order to "see" it one cannot stand in the relation of distance to it that gazing requires. One gazes *at* something from which one is necessarily (and fatally) distinct; but the light within the Lady's breast, the "something holy" (246) that lodges there, her virgin purity, her chastity, is not something she apprehends but something she moves within and therefore *is*. The point is brought home (an idiom intended quite literally) when, on the edge of surrendering to perturbation and in danger of becoming "stirred," she has recourse to herself, to the "hidden strength" (418) of her chastity.

The strength is hidden not because it must be kept from prying eyes, but because it is visible only to eyes already informed by it; to such eyes it is not hidden but visible and overwhelmingly visible, because the chaste vision sees everything in its own light and therefore sees only itself. When the Lady welcomes pure-eyed faith, white-handed (without color or spot) Hope, and her Champion, Conscience, she welcomes herself, and when she addresses herself to Chastity and says, "I see ye visibly" (216), she means, "I see *me* visibly; I see and affirm the lodestar of my being, and in so affirming I refuse to see—to be mindful of—anything else."

That is to say, the Lady sees chastity in the sense of declaring it or breathing it ("Can any mortal mixture of Earth's mold / Breathe such Divine enchanting ravishment?" [244–245]), and therefore there is no boundary between herself and what she sees; she sees chastity not against the background of something else but against its own background. Like the form of true fame in *Lycidas,* chastity is not a form set off by and from other forms; it is not known diacritically—conveyed by some medium, some system of differences anterior to it—but known directly. That is why it is characterized by the Lady as an "unblemish't form" (215). Not only is the form unblemished ("unspotted" in the Trinity manuscript), in the now familiar sense of without markings or varying textures; it is unblemished by any border, by any line that would mark a distinctness it must borrow from some defining other. Chastity is a figure that is its own ground; it is known only in relation to itself and therefore known only by those whose vision it constitutes and fills, by those from whom it is not separate. Others are in the position of Comus: "not fit to hear [themselves] convinc't" (792)—not fit because fitness depends on a conviction (state of belief) already in force. The trouble with Comus is not that he has too far to go, but that he has to go anywhere. He is not presently the residence of something holy that evidences itself (testifies) involuntarily in his every word and action. Comus is at a distance from the truth and would have to be conveyed to it; but to be conveyed is always to be in a state of mediation and therefore always at a distance from one's object. The only medium by which one can be properly conveyed is oneself, which means of course that one is not conveyed—moved, altered—at all, but is at every moment (in the words of an anti-Miltonist) "jumping up and down in one place."[3]

Echo and Narcissus

This motion that does not move but displays the same meanings in superficially different configurations is once again illustrated when the Lady sings a song to herself in the guise of singing to Echo, the maiden who, Ovid tells us, can respond to others only by giving back the words she hears from them ("auditaque verba reportat").[4] Moreover, the Lady invokes Echo in words that echo Comus' praise of her as the hidden residence of something holy: *"Sweet Echo, sweetest Nymph that liv'st unseen / Within thy airy shell"* (230–231). The homology is perfect: Echo's "airy shell" is to the Lady's earthly "mold" (244) as the "unseen" nymphly being is to the interior "raptures" that move "the vocal air" (247).

The pattern of things unseen but valuable is extended further when the Lady conjectures that her brothers may be "Hid . . . in some flow'ry Cave" (239), where they make a like pair with still another sequestered and secret beauty: *"a gentle Pair / That likest thy Narcissus are"* (236–237). Presumably the Lady intends only to celebrate the physical attractiveness of her brothers, but Narcissus is too highly charged a figure in classical mythology and its Renaissance moralizations to be thus confined. Once the name has been introduced, the judgment it usually implies seeks a location in the poem's foreground, and finds it, somewhat surprisingly, in the Lady, for she, more than her brothers, is likest Narcissus. The link between them is a devotion to self so exclusive that it repels all others. "Intoxicated with self-admiration," says George Sandys, Narcissists "sequester themselves from publique converse" lest they be distracted from the contemplation of their own virtues. The narcissist holds himself aloof from the polluting contact of inferiors, imitating the original, of whom it is said (in Sandys' translation of Ovid) "in his tender age his pride was such / That neither youth nor Mayden might him touch."[5] In the face of Echo's advances, Ovid's Narcissus cries, "I would rather die than be in your power" ("emoriar, quam tibi copia nostri," [*Metamorphoses,* 391]), a declaration uncannily doubled by the Lady's boast to Comus when he threatens to immobilize her: "Thou canst not touch the freedom of my mind" (*Comus,* 663). In her determined rejection of all external appeals and pressures, in her reliance on what she finds within her, the Lady would seem to be indistinguishable from the boy who "Is himself what he praises" ("qui probat, ipse probatur" [*Metamorphoses,* 425]).

This is certainly how Comus sees her. He characterizes her as one who scorns "the unexempt condition / By which all mortal frailty must subsist" (*Comus,* 685–686). She hoards (739) what nature would have us all pour forth (710). In the name of virginity, a cold and aloof virtue, she forsakes community—"mutual and partak'n bliss" (741)—and lives a solitary life that knows pleasure only "in th'enjoyment of itself" (742). Comus, in contrast, parades as the very type of generosity and public-spiritedness, urging the Lady to forsake the narcissism of self-absorption and seek fulfillment in a healthy commerce with nature's fertile word. He plays Sandys to her Narcissus, reminding her, in effect, that we ought not "overlove or admire our selves, which although hatefull in all ages, in youth is intollerable."[6] The Lady responds by redeclaring her independence of any and all of nature's forces, and goes so far as to claim an ability to control those forces should she choose to exercise it:

Thou art not fit to hear thyself convinc't;
Yet should I try, the uncontrolled worth
Of this pure cause would kindle my rapt spirits
To such a flame of sacred vehemence,
That dumb things would be mov'd to sympathize,
And the brute Earth would lend her nerves, and shake,
Till all thy magic structures rear'd so high,
Were shatter'd into heaps o'er thy false head. (792–799)

At this moment she seems to be displaying all the characteristics of what Freud calls narcissistic megalomania: "an over-estimation of the power of wishes and mental processes, the 'omnipotence of thoughts,' a belief in the magical power of words, and a method of dealing with the outer world . . . which appears to be a logical application of these grandiose premises."[7]

This is itself, however, a surface judgment, even if it is one Milton encourages. He does so in the hope that we will not rest in it but will remember, with Sandys, that one can be a narcissist in different, and differently valued, ways. Narcissus is condemned, says Sandys, not because he is self-centered but because he mistakes the part of himself that is worthy of such sustained attention. In his error, he does not consider "his proper essence or virtue, but pursues his shadow . . . that is, admireth bodily beauty, fraile and like the fluent water" (160). Fixated on his physical appearance, he is insufficiently attentive to the state of his soul. Self-involvement comes in two versions—one bad, because it fetishizes a mere "outside," and the other good, because it honors the spirit; and since the spirit is that which has been breathed into the person by another, by God, one who makes it the center of a continual attention is finally not self- but Other-regarding. Unlike the fallen angels, who "by reflecting upon themselves, and admiration of their owne excellency, forget their dependence on their creator,"[8] the virtuous narcissist is always affirming that dependence (as opposed to Comus, who "Ne'er looks to Heaven amidst his gorgeous feast" [*Comus*, 777]), reverencing not himself but the something holy that lodges in his breast. The virtuous narcissist is, without contradiction, Narcissus *and* Echo, at once self-absorbed and responsive, as Echo is, only to the voice of the Other.

A composite Echo-Narcissus is a perfect emblem of the "virtuous mind" that responds to crisis by turning inward to a strength that is at once its own and a gift of the superior power to whom it is loyal.[9] Although the Lady's two actions—summoning up her inner reserves in order to repel the invasion of foreign thoughts, and singing, Narcissus-like, to the unseen and hidden Echo—are consecutive and seem distinct, they are in fact the same (self-declaring) actions, glosses on each other and on a later moment (it is really the same moment) when the Elder Brother declares that his sister has "a hidden strength / Which if Heav'n gave it, may be term'd her own" (418–419) and then names it "chastity" (420). Thus defined, chastity is also a composite entity—at once a personal property and something bestowed and sustained by another—and as such is equivalent both to the being who is at the same time Narcissus and Echo and to the virtuous mind that "ever walks attended."

The Narcissus-Echo figure is composite in still another way: it is hermaphroditic, as is Narcissus himself, who displays a distinctively feminine beauty and attracts the passion of both nymphs and young men. (It is one of the latter group who, after being rejected, pronounces the fatal curse, "So may he himself love.")[10] His hermaphroditism is at once mirrored and reversed by the Lady: obviously female in appearance, she scorns her feminine beauty in favor of the interior worth of which it is a mere covering. This is precisely Comus' complaint about her in the great confrontation scene. Remember, he says, you're a woman (751ff.); "Think what" that means. No, she responds, I'm a mind —spirit, animus—and she might have added that by immobilizing her he has done her the service of framing the strength (hidden, inner, and masculine) that sustains her, a strength he cannot touch. In this and other scenes, the gender roles of the two central figures are reversed. It is Comus who argues for qualities Milton would have identified as female—fecundity, fluidity, movement, dispersal; also hermaphroditic, Comus is said to be "Much like his Father, but his Mother more" (57). True to this description, he says nothing of his father, but refers often to the mother from whom he has been separated (she presumably remains on her island); in contrast, the Lady is firmly oriented in the direction of the father to whose home she is journeying. The two represent different stages of psychic and sexual development: Comus wishes to unite with the mother and displace the father entirely; the Lady has internalized the father's authority and identifies with him so strongly that her feminine nature has been wholly subordinated. Mindful only of the father, she is full of him and only him. The asymmetry of surface gender roles and deep gender identity lends a comic, almost farcical, note to their meetings, as the one speaks words and utters sentiments that in the simpler models of their encounter belong to the other.

Venus and Aeneas

The chief model against which their exchanges resonate is the meeting, in book I of the *Aeneid,* of Aeneas and Venus. The parallel is announced when Comus hails the Lady as a "foreign wonder" (an epithet more accurate than he knows) and conjectures that she must be a goddess. Aeneas hazards the same identification ("o dea certe") and asks his disguised mother for guidance and direction.[11] Venus, on her part, represents herself as someone who has been separated from her sister; the Lady tells Comus that she is anxious to regain the "sever'd company" (274) of her brothers. The similarities are obvious and obviously intentional, but no less obvious than the systematic differences that make reading the scene an exercise in geometric cognition. The chief difference is that the Lady is at once Aeneas and the goddess, the wanderer in a dark wood *and* the divinity that points the way to the path of safety. She can play both roles for the reason we already noted at the end of the previous chapter: errant and vulnerable in earthly and physical terms, she is perfectly "sure" (Comus' word for her at 148 and 246) so long as she turns inward for guidance to the faith and hope of which she is the lodging. Later, when the Attendant Spirit promises to be her "faithful guide" and observes that "not many furlongs thence / Is your Father's residence" (944, 946–947), his aid is superfluous; faithful (full of faith) herself, she *is* her father's residence, the house (lodging) centered by his unquestioned authority. In a sense, then, she is the Father, the embodiment (despite her body, soon to be quiescent as the result of Comus' unintended gift) of the masculine principle of interior self-sufficiency, and therefore she is exactly the wrong object of Comus' desire. What Comus wants is that she be a substitute for his absent mother—"she shall be my Queen" (265), he cries in an embarrassingly obvious Oedipal ecstasy—but she is chaste in the same sense that Aeneas is *pius:* already pledged to *patria,* the father-land, the other country where the faithful always and already live.

With the Lady occupying all the available male positions, there is nothing for Comus to do but be more like his mother than ever, expressing his wish to join with her by doubling his feminine activities, offering the charming cup, urging surrender to "mortal frailty" (686), importuning the Lady to leave her self-willed fortress and "pour her bounties forth" (710). If she will not be Venus, he must assume the role (Sandys tells us that one of Circe's actions consists in "alluring some to inordinate *Venus*" [654]) and, like Virgil's goddess of Love, send Cupid (a role that he too plays; he is ever his mother's son) to enflame the heart of

Dido so that the hero will be kept from his destiny. But of course the coordinates are all wrong: there is no feminine heart to enflame except his own (he is his own Dido); only *his* family romance is replete with feminine desire, desire rooted in lack and imperfection; it is he who is not sufficiently "well stock't" (152), and must seek ever to piece out the defect of his being.

The Lady is embedded in quite another structure, allied not to the earthly but the Celestial Venus and to "Celestial *Cupid* her fam'd son" (1004). In this family there are finally no women at all, and no generation except by a line of male authority. The Celestial Venus is God's wisdom, begotten by Him before the heavens and earth were made and playing before him (nonerotically) in his presence (*Paradise Lost,* VII, 9–11). (In Plato's *Symposium,* she is identified with the male love of mind and opposed to the bodily love incited by women.) Celestial Cupid, her famed son, is of course Christ, God's only begotten son, begotten on his own Wisdom, and betrothed in a mystical marriage to a soul unencumbered with fleshly clogs—that is, to a soul defeminized. From God the Father, to Wisdom (the Celestial Venus), to Christ (the Celestial Cupid), to the chaste (not defiled by women) soul, the line is entirely male even when the outward form is female. (The Lady is at once an issue of this line and an emblem of its masculine self-sufficiency; even Comus recognizes that the something holy in her breast is masculine, and testifies to its—or rather his—hidden residence.)

This procreation that has no need of women and scorns their defiling touch is celebrated often in Milton's work. Adam, like the speaker in Marvell's "The Garden," wishes too late that Eden had been established "without Feminine": "this mischief had not then befall'n" (*PL,* X, 893, 895). In the *Areopagitica,* Milton declares England to be just such an Eden where male virtue (both goodness and power) reproduces merely by showing itself: "That our hearts are now more capacious," says Milton to the parliamentarians, "is the issue of your owne vertu propagated in us."[12] It is a virgin birth where all the virgins are male and practice the same celibacy celebrated in the *Apology,* when Milton praises that man who refuses to be deflowered by responding to something other than "the image and glory of God which is in himselfe."[13] No wonder Comus is unable to understand what the Lady means by the sage and serious doctrine of virginity: he can understand virginity only as a physical condition peculiar to women, whereas what the Lady proclaims and embodies is a virginity of the mind, the freedom of which Comus can't touch because it has nothing to do with the body and its organs. In every possible sense, Comus simply doesn't know whom or what he is talking to.

Nevertheless, he does get one thing right in a way that further deepens the link between the mask and the *Aeneid:* he recognizes the Lady by the way she walks: "Break off, break off, I feel the different pace, / Of some chaste footing near about this ground. / . . . Some Virgin sure" (*Comus,* 145–146, 148). If we miss the allusion here, we shall surely catch it when the Lady is hailed by Comus as a goddess. Perhaps the most famous moment in the meeting of Venus and Aeneas is when the son recognizes his mother by her step, her gait, her pace: "et vera incessu patuit dea" (I, 405). In a way, Comus' act of recognition is more impressive: he doesn't even see the Lady, but "knows" her from a distance by the feel of her "chaste footing." A chaste footing is, on one level, simply the footing of a virgin; but it is also a virginal footing, a footing that takes its direction from itself rather than from some external roadway to whose turnings it must conform. A chaste footing is, like virginity, self-contained; commerce with the outside does not enable but violates it. A chaste footing keeps itself aloof and requires nothing but itself to complete it; rather than following a path, it declares one; wherever it steps, and on whatever surface or nonsurface, is where the path is. This is the way a goddess walks, with no concern for where she treads—on the ground, in the air, on water; it is all the same. For the essential thing is not what she treads on but what she treads with, or, better still, within: she treads within the perfect confidence that the direction she takes is the right one simply because she takes it, and takes it without regard to the pressure exerted by anything outside her. It is the way the Lady walks once she stops worrying about the relationship between her "unacquainted feet" (180) and the "blind mazes of this tangl'd Wood" (181), and turns to the light cast by her own "virtuous mind" that "ever"—no matter what the physical constraints of her surroundings—"walks attended" (211) by Conscience, Faith, Hope, and of course Chastity.

The difference, then, between a chaste footing and a footing less pure is that the latter will depend for its confidence on the stability and visibility of the surface with which it must make contact in order even to become something so firm as a footing. The unchaste footing needs the reassurance and completion of something other than itself; it must achieve traction (since traction is not already constitutive of it), and therefore it treads heavily, anxious both to stabilize itself and to leave a mark it might then retrace. It is this heaviness that the Attendant Spirit responds to when he says, "I hear the tread / Of hateful steps" (91–92). What he hears is the dance of Comus' rabble in obedience to the sorcerer's call: "Come, knit hands, and *beat* the ground" (143, emphasis added). Such steps are hateful because they must do violence to the surface they meet, so that they can establish both mastery and identity—so that they can say, like Kilroy (dancing is a kind of writing), "We were here." Steps less anxious, steps already secure in a destination they reach merely by being, need not be heavy, and are the more chaste as they are the less visible or audible. The contrast is made again later, when the vulgar shepherds are told to step aside in favor of "lighter toes" (962) that are said "To triumph in victorious dance / O'er sensual Folly" (974–975). The dance is victorious because it is the reverse of sensual; it is lighter than air and is therefore scarcely apprehensible to anyone not participating in it—to anyone tied to the sensual, as is the "dull swain" who misrecognizes Haemony and "Treads on it daily with his clouted shoon" (634–635). In this antiphenomenal phenomenology of dance and movement, the chaste footing is a footing that does not leave a mark and is entirely internal to its own performance.

The Dance of Water

The great example of the pattern (if "example" and "pattern" can be predicated of the nonvisible) is Sabrina, who describes herself thus:

> By the rushy-fringed bank,
> Where grows the Willow and the Osier dank,
>   My sliding Chariot stays,
> Thick set with Agate and the azurn sheen
> Of Turquoise blue and Em'rald green
>   That in the channel strays;
> Whilst from off the waters fleet
> Thus I set my printless feet
> O'er the Cowslip's Velvet head,
>   That bends not as I tread. (890–899)

The pertinent observation was made long ago by Cleanth Brooks and J. E. Hardy: "Sabrina's sliding Chariot is simply the water and 'stayes,' waits for her beside the bank only in the paradoxical sense that there is always the flowing water there. The jewels that adorn it are only the names of gems applied to the colours of the water."[14] That is, Sabrina's chariot, the water, is adorned by itself; and since Sabrina *is* the water, the chariot that conveys her is her own substance. She is both what moves and the surface on which it moves, and that is why she can slide and stay at the same time. There can be no measurement of her progress, because in moving from one point to another she brings both points with her. There is nothing to measure her or her progress *against,* because there is no background in relation to which she can stand out as a figure. She is her own background, and thus the perfect emblem (and rescuer) of chastity, whose unblemished form is unblemished even to the extent of not being set off by some other form that gives it shape.

It makes perfect sense, then, that when this form whose measure is itself, whose points of reference are entirely internal, this form that rides on itself and is its own outside, treads, it makes no mark because what it is treading on (and with) and toward is itself. That is why its tread is "printless" in the double—but single—sense of leaving no imprint (leaving everything pure and unspotted), and of not constituting an inscription, a writing. The form whose object of knowledge is itself—whose obligation it is to continue to know what already resides within it—has no need of a vehicle of communication, no need of a chariot, other than the chariot (bearer of holiness) it already is, to convey it to a place where it already is. A chaste footing is a footing not characterized by incompletion, by a need to get somewhere—and therefore it is a footing that is always in the same place, where it forever traces out the same form: its own.

Once again we see how perfect is the homology between the figures and figurings that bear the positive values in the mask. The Lady, as someone always "mindful," moves indifferently in a landscape that is always the same because she is; when she walks, her eyes are turned inward to the faith that attends her and to which she attends; she is wholly self-involved, a moving vessel of "home-felt delight" (262), a kind of celestial Narcissus (allied with the Celestial Venus and her divine Son) whose tread, like Sabrina's, leaves no imprint, because the road she travels is wholly interior. The meaning that she need not seek is the meaning she declares with every breath, a meaning at once overwhelmingly

178

perspicuous (she sees it everywhere) and totally unapprehensible by someone not similarly informed. It is the meaning, dazzlingly obvious and maddeningly mysterious, of the "sage / And serious doctrine of Virginity" (786–787), itself one more figure for the "immortal shapes" (2) that the mask continually invokes but never quite presents. This virginity, which *Comus* could never understand because it has no visible manifestation, is entirely interior, an orientation of the mind that remains unaffected by any bodily assault. (Had the brothers and the Attendant Spirit not rushed in and the Lady been "forced"—raped—her virginity, in these terms, would have remained untouched.) It is mysterious in the sense of being hidden; it is, in the manner of Haemony, "unsightly" (629)—that is, not available to carnal vision and therefore unimpressive to carnal eyes. Like the chaste footing of those who exemplify it, this virginity leaves no mark, makes no *visible* difference; it does not offer itself for validation by others and seeks its affirmation only from itself ("Thou hast nor Ear nor Soul to apprehend / The sublime notion and high mystery" [784–785]); it is entirely self-sufficient, self-referring, with no distance at all between itself and that which it would apprehend, always and already at one with the meaning its every motion declares. It is an "unblemished form" in the strong sense of having no form, no shape that is differentially (as opposed to unmediatedly) apprehended.

Douglas Bush wonders, in the context of Brooks and Hardy's characterization of Sabrina as self-conveyed and self-adorned, "how this idea would be dramatically rendered."[15] The answer is given every time the mask refers to or presents the action that most characterizes the genre: dance. Dance is the one medium in which the signifying agent and the surface that is marked by the inscription are the same. One writes on a tablet or paper; one paints on a canvas; musical notes imprint the air (a fact noted twice in *Comus* in two remarkable similes). But in dance the medium, the message, and the enunciator of the message are one. Yeats's question goes in both directions: not only can you not tell the dancer from the dance; you cannot tell the dance from the dancer, figure from the background, form from substance, meaning from expression from expresser.

Dance is always, for Milton, a figure of the perfect union of matter and spirit. In "At a Solemn Music" (probably written within a year or two of *Comus*), prelapsarian creatures resonate "To their great Lord, whose love their motion sway'd / In perfect Diapason, whilst they stood / In first obedience and their state of good" (22–24). The point is made by the double reading of "whose love their motion sway'd." Does their motion sway, in the sense of persuading, their Lord to love them? Or are their motions—everything they think and do—swayed, in the sense of produced or informed, by their great Lord's love? The question is unanswerable, because it doesn't (and this should be heard quite literally) make any difference: their motions, his love, their actions, his meaning are indistinguishable. In the morning prayer Adam and Eve compose in book V of *Paradise Lost,* "all things" "Vary" in "ceaseless change," yet in their variation they declare only one thing: "his praise" (183–184, 199). In response to God's exaltation of the Son, the loyal angels spend the day "In song and dance about the sacred Hill, / Mystical dance" (V, 619–620), and their dance is an image and extension of the cosmic dance of planets, "mazes intricate, / Eccentric, intervolv'd, yet regular / . . . when most irregular they seem" (622–624) because their motions ceaselessly express a "harmony Divine" (625). Little wonder that it is a harmony to which "God's own ear / Listens delighted" (V, 626–627), since what he is listening to is himself.

The idea is not original: Milton would have found it in (among other places) John Davies' "Orchestra," where dancing is celebrated as "both love and harmony, / Where all agree and all in order move; / Dancing, the art that all arts do approve; / The fair character of the world's consent, / The heaven's true figure, and the earth's ornament."[16] Dance is the master art because it is at once ever diverse and ever the same, a perpetual movement at the center of which is a universal stillness:

> Concord's true picture shineth in this art,
> Where divers men and women rankèd be,
> And every one doth dance a several part,
> Yet all as one in measure do agree,
> Observing perfect uniformity. (338)

Not only do the dancers observe a perfect uniformity, but the observer who follows the dance becomes a part of it; for dance, in Ben Jonson's words, does not "perplex men unto gaze"—does not induce spectatorship, the state of being at a distance, of looking at, of being on the outside—but rather draws men into the perfection of its moving harmony. The men who are able to "Admire the wisdom of [the dancers'] feet" become the bearers of that wisdom, dancing out its shape in the exertions of their response:

> For dancing is an exercise
>   Not only shows the mover's wit,
> But maketh the beholder wise,
>   As he hath power to rise to it.[17]

The beholder becomes indistinguishable from what he beholds, tracing out in the motions of his mind the lineaments of that which he admires; at that moment he is no longer an admirer but a participant, no longer outside but inside. In dance as Milton and Jonson envision it, there is no inside or outside; nothing marks a boundary because nothing is left out or left over; no surface receives the imprint (tread) of the world's great dance, because every surface is itself in play and is therefore deeply and fully meaningful. The dance of "the world's consent" is the very definition of unblemished form, of a form coextensive with a significance that occupies all places and occupies them equally, evenly, with the same consistency through and through, a form that is not a form because it is suffused everywhere with content.

It is hardly necessary to say that this is also a definition of chastity (a loyalty unadulterated by even a recognition of alternative commitments), and of being mindful, of being ever at home no matter how superficially foreign the circumstances, of being at once Echo and Narcissus, all of which are homologous with and defining of the sage and serious doctrine of virginity. Not only does the mask celebrate a world in which what appears to be difference is always a repetition of the same; it *is* such a world, displaying at every point the deep serenity that is the reward of becoming one with its dance, a world without seams, where surface and depth are indistinguishable and everything is "In unsuperfluous even proportion" (772).

Bocking One's Bips

You will have recognized this last as a line from the Lady's great set piece, but the very fact that she feels compelled to utter it raises some disquieting questions (which I have been careful not to raise until now). If meaning and knowledge are equally and universally distributed, why should anyone need to *say* that they are? Why would there be anyone who needed to hear it? The Lady tells us that she speaks only because she cannot bear it "when vice can bolt her arguments, / And virtue has no tongue to check her pride" (760–761), but this justification of her performance has its own problems, not the least of which is the strain she places on her identity by casting herself as the male defender against a female threat. (Vice is egregiously feminized even though its Latin root—*vitum*—is ungendered, while the Lady claims for herself the name of virtue, from *virtus,* manly

strength.) Of course this is entirely consonant with the mask's repeated (non)presentation of a masculine interiority that is obscured by a female covering, by sensual sights and sounds that
distract the attention from its true, but hidden, object (chastity,
Haemony, virginity, spirit, mind, faith). But while the image is
glorious in the abstract, it is somewhat disturbing when we realize that as (self-)applied to the Lady, it places her in a relationship of opposition to her own skin. Again, this is merely one
more instantiation of a familiar Christian topos—the eternal soul
trapped in a mortal body—but the topos becomes uncomfortable
when it is literalized in the form of a woman who must continually suppress every impulse that might otherwise move her.

The effort is an extraordinary one and at the moments of high
crisis it appears to be successful, but we get a hint of the cost
when she begins her speech by saying, "I had not thought to have
unlockt my lips / In this unhallow'd air" (756–757). The gesture
offers itself as one of disdain (matching the disdain of the Attendant Spirit for his task)—"I find it distasteful even to be in
this neighborhood, never mind having to converse with its deni-
zens"—but in fact it is defensive. Locks perform a double function: they repel invasion—keep things out—and they prevent escape—keep things in. By keeping her lips locked, the Lady
protects herself against complementary dangers; her interior
strength—her virtue—will not be adulterated by foreign sub-
stances, nor will it lose its concentrated form in the dispersal that
might follow were the gates to be opened. The psychology here
is complicated and available to many characterizations: it is the
psychology of virginity, in which a treasure only is a treasure if it
remains untouched; it is the psychology of the anal character,
which hoards a currency of its own production; and it is the psychology of the fortress mentality, afraid that even the least breach
in the ramparts will bring disaster. The fierce strength of that
mentality, however, is also its weakness; it cannot be exerted

without acknowledging and even increasing the substantiality of what it fears. If so much effort must be expended to repel assaults on the one hand and to ward off depletion (perhaps defection) on the other, the zone of safety and supposed purity is obviously very small, and it becomes at least a question as to what is real and what is contingent, what is the norm and what is the aberration. After all, is it not counterintuitive to claim that although the entire world inclines in one direction, the true direction lies elsewhere, and in an elsewhere from which no visible or audible report ever emerges?

I realize that to say this is to come close to joining Comus when he cries, "This is mere moral babble" (807), but it is not my intention to endorse Comus' views. I wish only to point out that the power they acquire—a power confirmed by many readers and critics—is in large part a function of the vigor, bordering sometimes on desperation, with which they are combated. In *Comus,* Milton works out the implications of his Christian Neo-Platonism with a precision and rigor that extends to the smallest detail of the verse, but the energy he must deploy in order to shore up and support the structure whispers to us of its precariousness and of the extent to which the purity he celebrates is finally inseparable from the materiality he pushes away. It is a whisper he does not himself yet hear, but by the time of *Areopagitica* it will be the entire burden of his song.

PART II

The Paradigm under the Pressure of Time, Interpretation, and Death

CHAPTER FIVE

Driving from the Letter:
Truth and Indeterminacy in
Milton's Areopagitica

Banish All Objects of Lust

Some years ago, a very literate professor of law with more than a casual interest in the First Amendment confessed himself surprised when I reminded him that in the *Areopagitica* Milton excludes Catholics and some others from his plea for general toleration. He hadn't remembered it that way and had always thought of Milton as an exemplary spokesman for free speech and free expression. Of course, he isn't alone. As John Illo points out, Milton's tract has almost always been read as a classic liberal plea for "complete liberty." "The preponderance of English scholarship," Illo writes, "has drawn Milton into its own liberal centre, which claims a Western and ultimately an Attic heritage of universal freedom."[1] This is especially true in the modern day, when the *Areopagitica* (through an irony its author would have understood but not appreciated) has become a basic text supporting the ethic of disinterested inquiry, and Milton the revolutionary has become a man with the ability "to look at social issues without using the glasses of sectarian theology, which is . . . very rare in this passionate time."[2] The writer here is Harold Laski, one of many contributors to a volume marking the three hundredth anniversary of the publication of *Areopagitica* and titled, significantly, *Freedom of Expression*. In this volume, Milton is not only the apostle of unrestrained freedom (precisely the *accusation* leveled at him by his contemporaries), he is also and "above all, a Humanist—the greatest representative in England of that movement which had abandoned the dogmatism of the middle ages and was seeking for a natural or empirical basis for its beliefs" (125). The same encomiast declares of the *Areopagitica*, "there is no encroachment on 'the liberty to know, to utter and to argue freely' which it does not . . . oppose" (122), apparently forgetting the encroachments that the tract itself urges. And when Mulk Raj Arnand expresses the wish that the "great passage about the value of a book" be inscribed on the luggage labels of students in India, so that "the consciences of the Customs authorities at Bombay will be touched," he seems not to realize (or seems, again, to have forgotten) that in the sentence which introduces that very passage, Milton affirms the right of the Commonwealth to keep "a vigilant eye how Bookes demeane themselves" and "thereafter to confine, imprison, and do sharpest justice on them as malefactors."[3] Only the Dean of St. Paul's, W. R. Matthews, is apparently aware of the fact that "Milton's conception of the nature of tolerable books was limited." "It appears," he says gently, "that many who have not recently read his book have an exaggerated notion of what he urges as reasonable liberty" (78).

That "many," as Illo reminds us, would seem to include almost the whole body of Milton scholars. There have of course been exceptions: Illo himself, writing from the left, and Willmoore Kendall, writing from the right, have argued for a Milton less generous in his ecumenism, a Milton who is not above acts of exclusion and sharp judgment.[4] And Ernest Sirluck has given us a pragmatically political Milton who in the *Areopagitica* argues in several directions at once, hoping thereby to please the several constituencies whose support would be necessary for the revoking of the act of 1643.[5] But by and large, in the writings and minds of most men and women, the *Areopagitica* remains what it was for those who celebrated it in 1944, and one is not surprised to find this ringing statement at the conclusion of the entry for the tract in the *Milton Encyclopedia*: "*Areop.* has long been loved by learned and literate men . . . [for] its ability . . . to inspire almost all people to a sense of the sanctity of free expression."[6]

In what follows, I would like to continue in the direction indicated by the work of Illo and Kendall and advance a series of theses even more radical (at least in terms of received opinion) than theirs. Specifically, I will argue that Milton is finally, and in a profound way, not against licensing, and that he has almost no interest at all in the "freedom of the press" as an abstract or absolute good (and, indeed, does not unambiguously value freedom at all); and that his attitude toward books is informed by none of the reverence that presumably led the builders of the New York Public Library to have this sentence from the tract preside over their catalogue room: "A goode Booke is the precious life-blood of a master spirit, imbalm'd and treasur'd up on purpose to a life beyond life."

Let us begin with that sentence and with the famous paragraph from which it comes:

> I deny not, but that it is of greatest concernment in the Church and Commonwealth, to have a vigilant eye how Bookes demeane themselves, as well as men; and thereafter to confine, imprison, and do sharpest justice on them as malefactors: For Books are not absolutely dead things, but doe contain a potencie of life in them to be as active as that soule was whose progeny they are: nay they do preserve as in a violl the purest efficacy and

extraction of that living intellect that bred them. I know they are as lively, and as vigorously productive, as those fabulous Dragons teeth; and being sown up and down, may chance to spring up armed men. And yet on the other hand unlesse warinesse be us'd, as good almost kill a Man as kill a good Book; who kills a Man kills a reasonable creature, Gods Image; but hee who destroyes a good Booke, kills reason it selfe, kills the Image of God, as it were in the eye. Many a man lives a burden to the Earth; but a good Booke is the pretious life-blood of a master spirit, imbalm'd and treasur'd up on purpose to a life beyond life. 'Tis true, no age can restore a life, whereof perhaps there is no great losse; and revolutions of ages doe not oft recover the losse of a rejected truth, for the want of which whole Nations fare the worse. We should be wary therefore what persecution we raise against the living labours of publick men, how we spill that season'd life of man preserv'd and stor'd up in Books; since we see a kinde of homicide may be thus committed, sometimes a martyrdome, and if it extend to the whole impression, a kinde of massacre, whereof the execution ends not in the slaying of an elementall life, but strikes at that ethereall and fift essence, the breath of reason it selfe, slaies an immortality rather than a life. But lest I should be condemn'd of introducing licence, while I oppose Licencing, I refuse not the paines to be so much Historicall, as will serve to shew what hath been done by ancient and famous Commonwealths, against this disorder, till the very time that this project of licencing crept out of the *Inquisition,* was catcht up by our Prelates, and hath caught some of our Presbyters. (*Tract,* 271–272)

The first thing to say about this passage is that, detached from the literary idealism it apparently breathes, it is decidedly *un-*Miltonic; first because it locates value and truth in a physical object, and second because the reverence it apparently recommends toward that object is dangerously close to, if not absolutely identical with, worship. The passage seems, in a word, to encourage idolatry, and that is exactly the purpose to which it has been often put when it has been cited as a central "scripture" in the "religion" of the book (the religion, that is, of humanism). This, however, is not Milton's religion. The center of his theology is the doctrine of the inner light, and his entire career can be viewed as an exercise in vigilance in which he repeatedly detects in this or that political or social or ecclesiastical program one more attempt to substitute for the authority of the inner light the false authority of some external and imposed rule. In practical and operational terms, this means that he rejects the claim of any prefabricated or ready-made formulation to contain or identify what is true and valuable, and insists on referring all questions of truth and value to the standard written by the spirit of God in the fleshly tables of the regenerate heart.

It is in this spirit (a word precisely intended) that Milton makes a series of related arguments in the *Apology* (written only a year and a half before the *Areopagitica*). As I observed in Chapter 2, he rejects set prayers in favor of "those free and unimpos'd expressions which from a sincere heart unbidden come into the outward gesture"; he rejects the rules of rhetoric and composition in favor of the "true eloquence" that inheres naturally in the speech of one who is "possest with a fervent desire to know good things, and with the dearest charity to infuse the knowledge of them into others"; he rejects any criticism of his own style that would measure it by some external decorum, and claims as a justification for his bitter vituperative and even obscene words the spirit of zeal that moves him ("there may be a sanctifi'd bitternesse against the enemies of truth"); and he insists that a true poem can be written (and by implication read) only by one who is himself "a composition and pattern of the best and honourablest things; not presuming to sing high praises of heroic men . . . unless he have in himselfe the experience and the practice of all that which is praise-worthy."[7] We might be encouraged by this last assertion to assume that "that which is praise-worthy" or "best and honourablest" could be independently specified, but the phrase "in himselfe" insists on the internality both of those excellences and of the judgment authorized to identify them. In this and every other sentence in the *Apology*, Milton is continually alert to the danger of reifying some external form into the repository of truth and value; and it is the entire business of the tract to neutralize that danger, especially when the form it takes is superficially (another word precisely intended) attractive.

In the first edition of *The Doctrine and Discipline of Divorce* (published in 1643), the form of the danger is no less than the Bible itself. Milton's scorn in this tract is directed at those who believe that the essence of the law is to be found in its letter, in the actual words of the text; these he calls "extreme literalist[s]" and "letter bound" men: they display an "obstinate *literality*" and an "*alphabetical* servility," and have made the text into "a transcendent command" that is "above the worship of God and the good of man."[8] "Wee cannot," Milton thunders, "safely assent to any precept written in the Bible, but as charity commends it to us" (183), and charity is an attribute not of the text, which, like anything else, can be "congeal'd into a stony rigor" (145), but of the interpreter. "The way to get a sure undoubted knowledge of things" (183), Milton advises (following Saint Paul), is not to confine oneself to "textual restrictions" (189) but "to hold that for truth, which accords most with charity" (183); and it is with the rule of charity as an interpretive key that Milton proceeds to set aside the apparent meaning of Christ's words touching divorce in favor of the meaning dictated by a charity whose precepts he knows because they are written in his heart. This refusal to equate wisdom and truth with what is written in a book, even if the book is the Bible, will later lead him in the *Christian Doctrine* to reject the authority of the Ten Commandments because he follows the Pauline rule that "whatever is not in accordance with faith, is sin"—which is something quite different, he points out, from holding that "whatever is not in accordance with the ten commandments is sin."[9] And later still, this fierce anti-literalism turns into an even fiercer anti-literaryism as the Christ of *Paradise Regained* declares that the reading of books is "wearisome" and that he "who reads / Incessantly, and to his reading brings not / A spirit and judgment equal or superior, / (And what he brings, what needs he elsewhere seek), / Uncertain and unsettl'd still remains, / Deep verst in books and shallow in himself."[10]

If we return from this brief excursion into Milton's other writings (and additional examples could have easily been adduced) to the *Areopagitica*, the paragraph that offers so extravagant a praise of books looks very curious indeed. First of all, the notion that the essence of mind can be "stored up" in a "violl" sounds less like Milton than like Comus when he offers his magic potion to the Lady with the claim that "one sip of this / Will bathe the drooping spirits in delight / Beyond the bliss of dreams. Be wise and taste."[11] (The Lady, you will recall, is nourished by the "something holy" that "lodges in that breast" (246), something she carries within her and not in her hand, like a cup or a book.) It is also strange to hear Milton asserting that the spirit of a man can be abstracted from the conditions of its daily exercise, and that the truth which finds expression in varied and "unbidden" outward gestures can be so perfectly captured in one of those gestures that it can be "preserved" (in amber, as it were) between the covers of a book. And it is stranger still to find Milton displaying what he himself would describe as a papist idolatry of relics when he exalts the dead letter of a physical object ("imbalm'd" and "preserv'd" indeed) above the living labors of faithful men, and dismisses as "no great losse" the truth that perishes with a life, reserving for the loss of an "impression" or edition the vocabulary of homicide and massacre. It is almost as if he were writing an early draft of the sonnet on the Waldensians and had decided to begin that poem not with "Avenge O Lord thy slaughtered saints" but with "Avenge O Lord thy slaughtered books."

I do not, however, want to rest my case for the falseness of this passage on what Milton had previously written or on what he would later write. My best evidence comes from those places in the *Areopagitica* itself where Milton gives voice to sentiments that undermine (if they do not flatly contradict) any argument for the sanctity of books. Consider, for example, a sentence, some thirteen pages further on in the tract, that begins, "Banish all objects of lust." The phrase "objects of lust" is ambiguous between two readings; it can mean "banish all lustful objects"—that is, all objects that have, as a special property, the capacity to provoke lust; or it can mean banish all objects to which an already existing lust can attach itself. The attraction of the first reading is that it specifies a course of action that can be followed—"Let's get rid of these lust-provoking objects"—while in the second reading the recommended course of action is self-defeating because it would require the banishing of everything.

As it turns out, however, the second reading is the correct one: "Banish all objects of lust, shut up all youth into the severest discipline that can be exercis'd in any hermitage, ye cannot make them chaste that came not hither so" (297). That is to say, chastity is a property not of objects but of persons; and one can neither protect it nor promote it by removing objects from the world. Indeed, even if one went to the impossible lengths of removing all objects, the flourishing of lust and other sins would continue unabated, for, "Though ye take from a covetous man all his treasure, he has yet one jewell left, yet cannot bereave him of his covetousnesse"; and with that "covetousnesse" as the driving force of his very being, such a man will populate the world— even if it is only the inner world of his imagination—with the objects of his desire, with the objects of lust.

It is easy to see how this line of reasoning fits into the case against licensing: insofar as licensing is urged as a means of combating sin, it is, as Milton says, "far insufficient to the end which it intends" (297), because sin does not reside in the objects licensing would remove. But, curiously, if this is a strong argument against licensing (and it is so strong that Milton makes it at least six times), it is equally strong as an argument against the alternative to licensing, the free and unconstrained publishing of books. For it follows that if men and not books are the source of sin, then men and not books are the source of virtue; and if sin will not be diminished by removing its external occasion, then virtue will not be protected by preserving its external representation. If the banishing of books will not eradicate sin, then neither will it prevent the flourishing of virtue; for as conditions of the will rather than of the world, both sin and virtue are independent of the materials on which they happen to operate.

In short, the argument against licensing, which has always been read as an argument *for* books, is really an argument that renders books beside the point: books are no more going to save you than they are going to corrupt you; by denying their potency in one direction, Milton necessarily denies their potency in the other and undercuts the extravagant claims he himself makes in the passage with which we began. Whatever books are, they cannot be what he says they are in those ringing sentences—the preservers of truth, the life-blood of a master spirit, the image of God.

We Bring Impurity Much Rather

Why then does he say it? It will be the business of this chapter to answer that question, and we can begin by noting that at least on the local level he says it *in order* to move away from it. As the prose reaches the rapturous height of calling books an "ethereall and fift essence" and "the breath of reason itself," and seems about to take off into the empyrean, Milton suddenly applies the brakes: "But lest I should be condemn'd of introducing licence, while I oppose Licensing." As it turns out this rhetorical flourish looks forward to the historical digression of the succeeding paragraph, but for a moment it also refers backward to the license Milton has himself committed in transforming books—which are, after all, only objects—into the means and vehicle of grace. The moment passes quickly, almost before it has registered, but it is enough, I think, to cast the shadow of a qualification on what has just been said, a qualification we carry with us as we move into the brief history of "what hath been done by ancient and famous Commonwealths, against this disorder" (272).

By "this disorder," Milton means license, the supposed harm that follows from allowing books to be "as freely admitted into the World as any other birth" (281). It is this liberal practice, Milton tells us, that characterized the societies he is about to survey; and one would expect the point of the ensuing history to be that in these "ancient and famous Commonwealths" the absence of licensing would have as one of its effects the flourishing of virtue. Indeed, this is a directed expectation, given the praise of books as the privileged containers ("violls") of truth and reason, but it is an expectation that is disappointed by a history that never achieves so sharp a focus. Milton begins with what one would think would be his strongest example—the city of Athens, "where Books and wits were ever busier than in any other part of Greece" (273); but rather than celebrating the benefits of this "busyness," he turns immediately to the measures taken by the Athenians to curtail it, and finds "only two sorts of writings which the Magistrate car'd to take notice of; those either blasphemous . . . or Libellous." The tonal instability of this section is established immediately by "car'd to take notice of" which hesitates between an expression of approval for the magistrate's restraint and the suggestion that if he had been properly vigilant, he would have taken notice of *more*. That suggestion is given an additional half-life when Milton lists the "sects and opinions" (273–274) of which the magistrate "tooke no heed" (274) and characterizes them in ways that are strongly judgmental: they are in general "tending to voluptuousnesse" (274) and include "that libertine school of *Cyrene*" and "what the *Cynick* impudence ut- ter'd" and "*Aristophanes* the loosest of them all."

When the survey turns from Greece to Rome the double argu- ment continues, as Milton simultaneously reports on the restraint exercised by magistrates who decline to license and describes the fruits of that restraint (or, more precisely, absence of restraint) in terms that call into question its wisdom. Is it, after all, a good or a bad thing that the "naked plainness" of Lucilius and Catullus and the "wanton" poems of Ovid are allowed to do their work un- checked? This question is never asked in so many words, but Milton's judgmental vocabulary is continually implying it; and, moreover, there is nothing to counter the question on the other side, no instancing of books whose publication is casually related to a virtuous result. The only books Milton ever mentions are those that were allowed to appear despite the fact that they were impious or impudent or scurrilous or loose; it is this fact (estab- lished ever so casually but with a cumulative force) that domi- nates the history Milton surveys, a history which therefore makes the rather narrow and negative point that in a number of socie- ties—some good, some bad, some cultured, some brutish—the absence of prepublication licensing doesn't seem to have made very much difference at all.

Significantly, the lack of a difference goes in both directions: not only is it the case that what Milton will later call "promiscu- ous reading" did no particular harm; neither, at least on the evi- dence offered here, did it do any particular good. It seems in fact a "thing indifferent" not correlated in any observable way with the moral status of a commonwealth; and if licensing is thus indifferently related to the production or protection of virtue, so also are books, and the entire history becomes discontinuous with the encomium that introduces it. Rather than providing concrete instances of the extent to which truth and reason are preserved in books, this brief and rather ragged sketch says nothing at all of truth and reason and does not encourage us to draw any conclusion from the fact that until the Inquisition "Books were . . . freely admitted into the World" (281)—except the disturbing conclusion, implicit in Milton's judgmental asides, that if *he* had been in a position of authority, that freedom would have been severely restricted.

It is only after the history has been concluded that Milton takes up the question it might have been expected to answer: "what is to be thought in generall of reading Books, . . . and whether be more the benefit, or the harm that thence proceeds?" (283). Earlier, when it seemed that what was or was not *in* books was going to be the issue, this would have been just the right question, and one would have had every confidence that it would be answered by a demonstration that the benefit far outweighed the harm, especially since it is through books (or at least it is so asserted) that man has access to "reason itselfe" and the "Image of God." Now, however, in the wake of the inconclusive account of Greek and Roman practice, the question sounds oddly, as if it were posed by someone who hadn't yet realized that the agenda it assumes—the agenda of separating the bad from the good in books—has more or less been abandoned. Nevertheless, that someone pushes on, and offers as a first defense of books the political argument that "heathen learning" is necessary if Christians are to be able to defend themselves against the attack of their pagan enemies. If this sounds reasonable, it also sounds weak, at least in the context of the much stronger claims that have already been made. (It is also an argument with which Satan tempts Christ in *Paradise Regained*.) It is further weakened, at least as a straightforward defense, by the example that is adduced to support it: Jerome's dream of having been whipped by an angel for reading Cicero. Milton attributes the dream to the "politick drift" of "the Divell," who presumably wished to deprive Jerome of Cicero's wisdom; and he adds that "had an Angel bin his discipliner," Jerome would have been more properly chastised not for "grave *Cicero*" but "for scurill Plautus whome he confesses to have bin reading not long before" (284). But if the intention here is to defend the free reading of pagan books, it is hardly furthered by the phrase "scurill Plautus," which (like similar phrases in the history) suggests not freedom but the need for more restraints than are present in Jerome's dream, whoever was its inspirer. Once again the *Areopagitica* displays a curious inability to settle down and to pursue unambiguously the line of argument that was so strongly promised when books were the object of an apparently unqualified praise.

But then, almost before we know it, the tract takes a decisive turn and apparently stabilizes (at least for the moment) when Milton counters Jerome's dream with a vision reported by Dionysius Alexandrinus as he was debating with himself whether or not it was lawful to "venture . . . among" the "defiling volumes" of "hereticks." Milton identifies this second vision as one "sent from God," who speaks to Dionysius in these words: "Read any books what ever come to thy hands, for thou art sufficient both to judge aright, and to examine each matter" (285). This "revelation," as Milton terms it, decides the issue by dissolving it, by transferring the question of value from books, of whatever kind, to Dionysius, who is "sufficient" in the strong sense of *self*-sufficient, capable by virtue (literally) of what is already in him of turning all that he reads into good. Lest we miss the point, Milton drives it home by supplementing Dionysius' citation from Thessalonians ("Prove all things, hold fast that which is good") with "another remarkable saying of the same Author: To the pure all things are pure," which is then immediately and power-fully glossed: "not only meats and drinks, but all kinde of knowl-edge whether of good or evil; the knowledge cannot defile, nor consequently the books, if the will and conscience be not defil'd." In this declaration Dionysius' anxiety about "defiling volumes" is countered by simply denying that volumes defile; indeed, in this respect books are even more "things indifferent" than meats, for while "bad meats will scarce breed good nourishment in the healthiest concoction," bad books "to a . . . judicious Reader serve . . . to discover, to confute, to forwarn, and to illustrate" (285). Of course, by the end of this sentence, there are no bad books, in the sense of books that can in and of themselves do harm; for all books, once they enter into the heart of the judi-cious reader, become the occasion and means by which that judi-ciousness is exercised and extended. But by the same reasoning, neither are there any good books, in the sense of books that can in and of themselves produce wisdom; for as Milton says within a few pages, if "a wise man like a good refiner can gather gold out of the drossiest volume, . . . a fool will be a fool with the best book, yea or without book" (291–292). The logic of this is ines-capable and certainly supports the conclusion that licensing will bring no benefits, since the absence of what we keep from a fool "will be no hindrance to his folly" (292); but it also supports the corollary conclusion that whatever we make available to a wise man will not be essential to his wisdom, for he will be wise with any book, "yea or without book."

At this point the argument of the *Areopagitica* seems simply to have reversed itself. Where at first the question to be answered was whether the power in books will work for good or evil (a question directly related to the case for and against prepublica-tion licensing), by the time Milton declares that all things are pure to the pure the issue is no longer what is or is not in books, but what is or is not in persons; and consequently it has become a matter of indifference as to whether or not books are licensed, since, at least by the arguments that have so far been marshaled, the flourishing of *either* good or evil does not depend on books. From here, there is a straight line to the sentence that begins "banish all objects of lust" (a recommendation that makes sense only if books are the source either of lust or of virtue) and ends by asserting that "ye cannot make them chaste that came not hither so."

But if the new point of the *Areopagitica* is that men and not books are the repository of purity, then it is a point that barely survives its own introduction; for within a page of saying that all things are pure to the pure, Milton also says that "we bring not innocence into the world, we bring impurity much rather" (288), and by saying this he immediately problematizes what had for a moment seemed to be a resolution (or a dissolution) of the dilemma initially posed, to license or not to license. After all, it isn't much help to observe that purity is a condition of the heart and therefore independent of external pressures and stimuli, if all of our hearts enter the world in a condition of impurity. This impurity is one of the reasons licensing must be numbered among the "vain and impossible attempts" (291) ("how shall the licensers themselves be confided in unlesse we can confer upon them, or they assume to themselves above all others . . . the grace of infallibility and uncorruptednesse?"), but it is also a reason for something close to despair, since it leaves mysterious the process by which purity or even its near approximation can be achieved. If licensing is "far insufficient to the end which it intends," both because the "end" is not an external but an internal state and because we enter life *already* fallen from that state, then it would seem that licensing's insufficiency is general and that there is *nothing* we can do "to repair the ruins of our first parents."[12] If purity can be found neither in books, where it first seemed to reside, nor in naturally pure hearts, where the argument next seemed to place it, then it cannot be found anywhere.

That in fact turns out to be the right conclusion, but with a difference that redeems its negativity; for in the very same sentence that proclaims our congenital impurity Milton introduces us to its remedy: "Assuredly we bring not innocence into the world, we bring impurity much rather: that which purifies us is triall and triall is by what is contrary" (288). If virtue is not to be found anywhere—either in a book or in an object, or even in a heart—it is because it must be *made,* and it can be made only by sharpening it against the many whetstones provided by the world, by "what is contrary" (288). Not only does this give a positive direction to an argument that has for a while emphasized only what cannot be done and what will not succeed; it also reanimates the question of licensing and makes it once again weighty. For if the emergence of virtue depends on the availability of materials against which it can be exercised, then it follows that the more materials the better—which means, in turn, the more books there are, the better; and that is why, after the tract has unfolded almost half its length, Milton can finally offer a coherent and noncontradictory argument against licensing: anyone who thinks that he can "remove sin by removing the matter of sin" is mistaken, because sin is a feature not of the outer but of the inner landscape and can be removed (if that is the word) only when that landscape is transformed; and since that transformation can be accomplished only by a continual exercise of the faculty of judgment, it is crucial that the judgment be supplied with occasions for its exercise. Although licensing is offered as a way of promoting virtue, it will operate to eliminate the conditions of virtue's growth by removing the materials on which growth can feed: "look how much we thus expell of sin, so much we expell of vertue; for the matter of them is both the same"; we cannot, therefore, afford to abridge or scant "those means, which books freely permitted are, both to the triall of vertue and to the exercise of truth" (297). Once again, then, books are declared to be absolutely essential to the maintenance of truth and virtue—not, however, because truth and virtue reside in books (as they were said to so many paragraphs ago), but because it is by (the indifferent) means of books that men and women can make themselves into the simulacra of what no book could ever contain.

But this may seem a long way around the barn. If Milton had wanted to tell us (as he now tells us) that books are "necessary to the constituting of human vertue" (288)—as opposed to being the very essence of virtue—why didn't he just come right out and say so in the first place? Why go through the indirect route of first glorifying books excessively and then demonstrating that they cannot possibly be the repository of glory, but can only play an instrumental role in its emergence? The question is its own answer once one realizes that it amounts to asking: Why didn't he simply hand over the truth he wished us to have? To have done so, or rather to claim to have done so, would have been to claim for the *Areopagitica* the very capacity it denies to all other books: the capacity of being the repository of what no book can contain, because it can be written only in the fleshly tables of the heart. In short, if the *Areopagitica* is to be faithful to the lesson it teaches, it cannot teach that lesson directly; rather, it must offer itself as the occasion for the trial and exercise that are necessary to the constituting of human virtue. It must become an instrument in what Milton will later call "knowledge in the making" (321).

The tract performs this self-effacing office in two related ways. First it continually comments on its own inability to capture the truth that informs it.[13] In the very first paragraph, Milton reports that he is in the grip of a "power" within him that simply will not respect the decorums of the formal oration; and as a result he finds himself speaking with a "passion" (266) one does not usually find in a preface. A few pages later he makes a valiant attempt to monitor and control his discourse by "laying before" his readers the order of his arguments, but soon after he has concluded his inconclusive history he finds himself in danger of departing from that order and he catches himself up: "But I have first to finish, as was propounded" (283). He then gets himself back on track and is apparently proceeding according to plan, when suddenly he finds that he is already in the midst of making a point that was to have come later—finds, as he puts it, that the truth has prevented or anticipated him "by being clear already while thus much hath bin explaining" (292). In other words, he has been surprised by truth, and in response he exclaims, "See the ingenuity of Truth, who when she gets a free and willing hand, opens herself faster than the pace of method and discours can overtake her" (292).

The image here is one that will loom larger and larger: it is of a truth that is always running ahead of any attempt to apprehend it, a truth that repeatedly slips away from one's grasp, spills out of one's formulations, and escapes the nets that for a moment promise to catch it. Here that net is the tract itself, which is at this moment disqualifying itself as a vehicle of the truth it wants to convey; but at the same time and by the very same process, it is playing its part in the fashioning of another vehicle, one more able to bear the inscription of the Holy Ghost's pen. That vehicle is the heart of the reader, who is the direct beneficiary of the *Areopagitica*'s failure, or, to be more precise, of Milton's strategy. That strategy is one we have been tracking from the beginning of this chapter: it involves encouraging the reader to a premature act of concluding or understanding, which is then undone or upset by the introduction of a new and complicating perspective. As we have seen, this happens not once but repeatedly, as the reader is first allowed to assume that the point at issue is the purity or impurity to be found in books, and then is told that the content of books (or any other object) is a thing indifferent relative to the purity or impurity already in persons, and finally (or is it finally?) is reminded that all persons are congenitally impure ("we bring impurity much rather") and that therefore the problem must be entirely rethought. The result is, of course, disorienting, but it is also salutary, for in the process of being disoriented the reader is provoked to just the kind of labor and exercise that is necessary to the constitution of his or her own virtue. Thus, by continually defaulting on its promise—the promise of separating the true from the false—the *Areopagitica* offers itself as a means by which its readers can realize that promise in their very activities. In this way, the tract becomes at once an emblem and a casualty of the lesson it teaches: the lesson that truth is not the property of any external form, even of a form that proclaims this very truth.[14]

Pitching Our Tents Here

It is a strategy supremely pedagogical, and one that Milton both describes and names within the year in *Tetrachordon*, as he turns his attention to the manner of Christ's teaching. Milton is particularly struck by Christ's habit of breaking the external, written law in order to fulfill the law of charity; and he compares Christ's actions with the gnomic form of his precepts, and finds that both have the advantage of preventing his followers from too easily identifying the way of virtue with a portable and mechanical rule. "Therefore it is," says Milton, "that the most evangelick precepts are given us in proverbiall formes, to drive us from the letter, though we love ever to be sticking there."[15] By "letter" Milton means any prefabricated, external, and codified packaging of the truth, any identification of the truth with a piece of the world or a piece of behavior or a piece of language that may or may not be its local expression. The opposite of the letter is spirit; and it is the nature of spirit always to resist any attempt to circumscribe or delineate it. Spirit or the law of love is a disposition or orientation of the human heart, an orientation that can take many forms—of action, writing, thought—but cannot be equated with any one of them. To mistake a possible manifestation of the spirit for the spirit itself is to have literalized it and to have made that manifestation into an idol, just as Eve does when, in the first effect of the original sin, she worships a tree. Of course most versions of idolatry are less obviously absurd than Eve's, and since all idolatry presents the opportunity of substituting some easy formula (such as the Ten Commandments) for the strenuous life of following the spirit, it is a persuasive and powerful human temptation—which is why we love ever to be sticking to the letter, and why, too, we must always be driven from it.

In the *Areopagitica* we are continually being driven from the letter, first from the quite literal letter of books, and then from the letter as represented by the history of Athens and Rome, and then from the letter of a comforting, but finally too comforting, Scripture ("to the pure all things are pure"). Of course all of these letters, along with others that could be instanced, are provided by the *Areopagitica* itself, which also provides the arguments that make them momentarily attractive; so that one of the letters the tract is driving us from is itself, as we are not allowed the comfort and false security of sticking to or with any of the formulations it presents in what is finally a self-canceling sequence. By saying you won't find it there—in books, in history, in verses of Scripture—the *Areopagitica* is also saying you won't find it *here*—in the pages of this tract—and finally saying that you won't find it at all, because you can only become it, which is what the tract in its small and self-sacrificing way is helping you to do.

It is a help the need for which is self-replenishing. That is, driving from the letter is a strategy that can have no end, for each time it succeeds it generates the conditions that once again make it necessary: the very act of demonstrating that truth and virtue do not reside "here" will always have the side effect of suggesting that they will instead be found "there"; and at that moment, "there" becomes a new letter from which we must then be driven. The only positive lesson the *Areopagitica* teaches (a lesson it also exemplifies) is the lesson that we can never stop, and it receives a particularly powerful (although of course not definitive) formulation when Milton declares that "he who thinks we are to pitch our tents here and have attain'd the utmost prospect of reformation that the mortall glasse wherein we contemplate, can shew us, till we come to *beatific* vision, that man by this very opinion declares, that he is yet farre short of Truth" (316). By "here" Milton means both the present state of human knowledge and understanding and this particular moment in his own tract. Whatever place or object or condition holds out the possibility of rest and attainment has at that moment become a letter, the occasion for idolatry (and for self-worship, since the temptation is to be satisfied with what one can see by looking in the mirror of one's present opinion rather than to be drawn forward by the future prospect that is not so much disclosed as promised by another "mortall glass," the newly discovered telescope).[16]

As this sentence shows, one of those occasions can even be the Reformation, which for Milton is not a turning back of the clock to some prior state of apostolic purity, but a life-long response to an exhortation with which no one of us can ever comply: "be ye perfect." Although the letter of that exhortation can never be adhered to, one can adhere to its spirit by always looking beyond the prospect one has attained. Those who think of the Reformation as a finite program or agenda—as a series of steps at the end of which the job will have been done and the goal accom-

207

plished—make exactly the same mistake that is made by the proponents of licensing: they think that the issues of the moral life, of the attempt to align oneself with the will of God and with truth, can be settled once and for all by a single action (and the point holds even if the action has several steps). The would-be licensers think that the moral life will be perfected when the landscape has been cleared of all objects of lust; the reformers think that the moral life will be perfected when, in accordance with the precepts of Zwingli and Calvin, we have divested ourselves of some of the trappings of popery. In their different ways, both groups bring about "a dull ease and cessation of our knowledge" and "starch us" into as "stanch and solid peece of frame-work, as any January could freeze together" (312). The "laziness of a licensing Church" (314) is also the laziness of a church that is "ever staring on" the light given us by the early reformers, and does not receive that light as a beacon inviting us always "to discover onward things more remote from our [present] knowledge" (318). Licensing and the premature closure of a weak Reformation are alike forms of a single temptation: the temptation to substitute for the innumerable and inconclusive acts that make up the process by which the self is refined and purified some *external* form of purification that can be mechanically applied. It is a temptation felt by every one of Milton's heroes (even the young Jesus of *Paradise Regained*), and it is a temptation that Milton makes the readers of *Areopagitica* feel again and again as he beckons us forward in the name of a truth that always escapes his formulations and our straining apprehensions.

This pattern of seeking and *not* finding is most spectacularly displayed in those passages in which the nature of truth is the overt subject. As we first come upon it, the assertion that a "man may be the heretick in the truth" (310) seems available to a comfortable reading in which an independent truth can be held by a man in one of two ways: either with personal conviction or simply on the strength of what someone else—a pastor, a pope—had told him. Only the first kind of holding is authentic, and as for someone who does the other, "the very truth he holds becomes his heresie." But if the logic of this distinction is pursued, the very notion of a truth that one can hold either rightly or wrongly is problematized; for on the one hand a truth that has not been internalized is no longer the truth, and is merely an empty letter, while on the other a truth sincerely held cannot be given a literal form such that it can be said that someone else is not really holding "it." There is no "it" that is detachable from the holding or being held, and therefore no real sense can be given to the phrase "heretick in the truth." Insofar as it seems for a moment to have a sense, it is itself one more letter—one more invitation to premature closure—from which we must be driven.

We are driven from it again in a sequence that begins with a famous question: "Who ever knew Truth put to the wors in a free and open encounter?" (327). Here truth and falsehood are imagined as opposing armies—clearly distinguishable—that meet on a battlefield. But as the military image is developed, its configurations change; suddenly truth is no longer a property of one of the contending forces, but is rather what will emerge when the reasons of one adversary prove themselves superior to the reasons of the other. Rather than being a participant in the battle, truth is now the name of its outcome; the distinguishability of truth from falsehood is not something with which we begin, but something we must achieve by marching out "into the plain" and trying "the matter by dint of argument" (328).

Truth, in short, has receded from our view, but the rhetoric of the passage still allows us to assume that she will once again come into focus if only we allow "the wars of truth" to continue without prior restraint. The point is made by a comparison of truth with Proteus, the notorious shape shifter and emblem of deception. Proteus, Milton reminds us, would appear in his own shape only when he was bound; but in the case of truth it is exactly the reverse: if you bind or constrain her, "she turns herself into all shapes, except her own" (328). The moral is clear: "give her but room," allow those who claim to know her to contend in the field, and she will soon be discernible.

But that moral becomes unavailable with the very next sentence: "Yet is it not impossible that she may have more shapes than one." But if she has more shapes than one, then she has no shape and is exactly like Proteus—a figure who escapes every attempt to bind her, even when that attempt takes the form of a carefully staged battle at the end of which she is to emerge. The notion of a battle, which seemed at the beginning of this passage to promise an eventual cessation to our labors, now delivers the same inconclusiveness we have met so many times before; and when Milton concludes this sequence by declaring that "Truth may be on this side, or on the other, without being unlike her self," the reflexive pronoun is an almost mocking reminder that the object of our quest has never more escaped us than when we think to have it in view, and is *always* unlike herself.[17]

That object is held out as a lure and a temptation in still another passage, perhaps the most famous of all. It begins with a sad tale. Once upon a time, "Truth indeed came . . . into the world . . . and was a perfect shape, most glorious to look on"; but then "a wicked race of deceivers . . . hewd her lovely form into a thousand pieces" (316–317). One might say, then, that truth has receded from this story before it even begins; but all, it would seem, is not lost, for the dismemberment of truth has left us with a definite task—the task of "gathering up limb by limb," still as we can find them, the pieces of her body. "We have not yet found them all," says Milton, an observation that would seem preliminary to one more exhortation to continue in our search and not to pitch our tents here. But then he adds something much more devastating in its apparent finality: "nor ever shall doe, till her Masters second comming."

This is at once the low point and the high point of the tract for the readers who wish to derive from it an understanding of their situation and of the possibilities that situation offers for achieving genuine knowledge. It is a low point because it denies the possibility of ever achieving knowledge and thereby renders the search pointless, of no more efficacy than licensing; but it is the high point if we are able to apply the lesson the *Areopagitica* has repeatedly taught—the lesson that knowledge and truth are not measurable or containable entities, properties of this or that object, characteristics of this or that state, but *modes of being,* inward dispositions, conditions of a heart always yearning for new revelations. In the context of that lesson the fact that we will never succeed in finding every limb and member loses its poignancy; because in the very act of searching, of exercising our judgments and faculties in the manner the tract at once urges and provokes, we are in the process of transforming ourselves into that which we vainly seek. The search is futile only if we conceive of it as a search for something external to us, as a kind of giant jigsaw puzzle made up of precut and prefabricated pieces; but if we think of the search as the vehicle by means of which our knowledge is "in the making" (321) and our virtue is in the constituting, then it is always and already succeeding even when, as in this story, it is forever failing. We will indeed never find all the pieces of truth, but if we nevertheless persist in our efforts, when Christ finally does come to "bring together every joynt and member" (317) each of us shall be one of them.

The moral, then, is not "Seek and ye shall find," but "Seek and ye shall become." And what we shall become, in a curious Miltonic way, is a licenser, someone who is continually exercising a censorious judgment of the kind that Milton displays when he

211

casually stigmatizes much of Greek and Roman literature as loose or impious or scurrilous. This is the judgment not of one who is free of constraints but of one whose inner constraints are so powerful that they issue immediately and without reflection in acts of discrimination and censure.[18] Ironically it is only by permitting what licensing would banish—the continual flow of opinions, arguments, reasons, agendas—that the end of licensing—the fostering of truth—can be accomplished; accomplished not by the external means that licensing would provide, but by making ourselves into the repository of the very values that licensing misidentifies when it finds them in a world free of defiling books. Books are no more the subject of the *Areopagitica* than is free speech; both are subordinate to the process they make possible, the process of endless and proliferating interpretations whose goal is not the clarification of truth, but the making of us into members of her incorporate body so that we can be finally what the Christ of *Paradise Regained* is said already to be: a living oracle (*PR*, I, 460).

To be a living oracle is to be a totally unified being, one whose "heart / Contains of good, wise, just, the perfect shape" (*PR*, III, 10–11). This, however, is the condition only of Christ; all other men exist at a distance from that which would make them whole, exist in that state of seeking and searching which for Milton marks at once the deficiency and the glory of this vale of tears. Like the moment of mortality, the moment of the *Areopagitica* is situated between two absent unities, one always and already lost, the other to be realized only in the absorption of those consciousnesses that now yearn for it. Although truth "indeed came once into her divine Master and was a perfect shape most glorious to look on," she has long since withdrawn, leaving us to the delusive attraction of those many shapes that would compel us in her name; and although she shall one day be reassembled "into an immortall feature of loveliness and perfection" (318), that day is ever deferred and is only projected that much more into the future each time its dawning is prematurely proclaimed.

Meanwhile, man lives in the gap. Indeed, he *is* the gap, a being defined negatively by the union which perpetually escapes him, and which, once achieved, will mark the cessation of his separateness, his end, in two senses. The impurity we bring into the world is the impurity of difference, of not being one with God; yet it is because of that impurity that difference must not be denied or lamented but embraced; for given the condition in which we all labor—the condition of inevitable fallibility—any unity we might achieve would be a false unity, a conformity not with truth but with some temporally limited project that has solicited our idolatrous worship. The temptation of idolatry, of surrendering ourselves to the totalizing claims of some ephemeral agenda, can be resisted only by the relentless multiplication of that which signifies our lack, the relentless multiplication of difference. We will be "wise in spirituall architecture" (322) only if we build with dissimilar—disunified—materials: "there must be many schisms and many dissections made in the quarry and in the timber, ere the house of God can be built."

This allows us for a moment to assume that in time the house of God will in fact be built, but this is exactly like the assumption, so often encouraged, that the truth will finally emerge, and it is immediately disappointed: "And when every stone is laid artfully together, it cannot be united into a continuity, it can but be contiguous in this world" (322). The first half of this sentence increases the expectation that the second half will report an eventual triumph (when every stone is laid artfully together, the building will be complete), but the triumph is, as it has been so many times before, deferred, and we are left with more of the same— that is, with more difference, with side-by-side (in space and time) efforts which do not cohere except insofar as they signify, in a variety of ways, their own insufficiency and incompleteness. It is an incompleteness that must be at once lamented and protected; lamented because it is the sign of our distance from bliss, protected because as such a sign it is a perpetual reminder that bliss awaits us in a union we can achieve (precisely the wrong word) only when we are absorbed by another into a structure not made by human hands.

CHAPTER SIX

Wanting a Supplement:
The Question of Interpretation
in Milton's Early Prose

Only Able

You will have noticed that the Milton of the previous chapter begins with a conviction of general fallibility and, in the context of
that conviction, argues for a process in the course of which error—the mistaking of a stage of enlightenment for the final
"beatific vision"—must be detected and corrected, not once but
endlessly. This is not the Milton of *Comus* or *An Apology against a
Pamphlet;* for that Milton, as we have seen, there are but two categories of persons: the regenerate (inwardly illuminated) and the
unregenerate (bound to some false outside). In the early poetry
and prose, we meet the members of these two categories already
fully formed and forever alien to one another—the Lady and Milton on one side, Comus and the Modest Confuter on the other.
There is no sense of possible movement in either direction, and
consequently there is no genuine role for time, which is imagined
not as the vehicle of change but as a succession of spaces in

which agents already constituted (either in the truth or in its opposite) testify to what they are and what they are not. In *Areopagitica* it is all different. Virtue is not constituted but in the process of becoming; knowledge of the truth is provisional and always under revision; and time is the crucible of change and the generator of illuminations in which we are not allowed to rest.

What accounts for this transformation in Milton's sense of man's situation, and of the obligations and hazards it contains? Although I cannot answer this question definitively, I can at least deepen it by examining two texts that mark the transformation, even if they don't explain it.

Very little has been said about Milton's second antiprelatical tract, *Of Prelaticall Episcopacy,* in part because there is not very much to say about a tract that is determined to say nothing at all. It does, however, say one thing, loudly and often: that Scripture is "the onely Book left to us of *Divine* authority, and not in anything more Divine then in the all-sufficiency it hath to furnish us."[1] The important assertion here is not of Scripture's divinity—that, after all, goes without saying, and therefore in some sense to say it is to say nothing—but of Scripture's all-sufficiency; for this means not only that the Scriptures are all we need but that the Scriptures themselves do not need anything, and most certainly they don't need us. To think otherwise, to think that the Scriptures cannot convey their message without some intermediary aid, is to commit the impiety of thinking that "divine Scripture wanted a supplement, and were to be eek't out" (626). The impiety is captured in one of the meanings of "eke," "to make good a deficiency" *(OED):* if the Scriptures must be eked out, they are not all-sufficient, and if they are not all-sufficient, they are not divine. Indeed, the case is even worse than that: if the Scriptures are deficient, then they are not complete—are not, in some sense, themselves—until their deficiency is supplied by some addition or supplement; and since that supplement can be supplied only by human agents—by the very men and women whose needs the Scriptures supposedly furnish—the Scriptures turn out to be fashioned, made into what they are, by those who look to them as an independent (free-standing, objective, acontextual) source of authority. Rather than providing a transcendent and self-declaring guide to human activity, the Scriptures become the product of human activity and, in Milton's worst-case scenario, become indistinguishable from "the devices and imbellishings of mans imagination."[2]

The supplement, then, is at once unnecessary and dangerous; it is unnecessary because the Scripture is by definition sufficient and complete in and of itself, and it is dangerous because, as something added, a supplement may come to stand in place of, to overwhelm, that which it is brought in to assist. But while they are linked in Milton's argument, these two characterizations of the supplement finally strain against each other, for to insist on the danger of the supplement is finally to call into question the all-sufficiency and independence of that which can supposedly do without it. If the Scriptures can be threatened by a supplement, are they not more fragile and less secure in their identity—in their fullness—than Milton claims? And if they are "so perspicuous" (651) as to make any addition to them an "impiety" (651), why do so many go to such lengths (a phrase intended literally) to eke them out? Is there something about the Scriptures that provokes such efforts, and what could that something be except a deficiency that makes a supplement necessary? When Milton dismisses, as an obvious absurdity, the possibility that "the divine Scripture wanted a supplement," is he denying that the Scriptures are in *need* of a supplement, in which case he would be affirming their self-sufficiency, or is he denying that they lack a supplement, in which case he would be affirming their incompleteness by identifying them as the product of a supplement they already have?

These are not questions that Milton explicitly raises, although in our time they have been raised by Jacques Derrida, who in a series of texts has explored the long history in which the supplement has always been regarded as dangerous. In the story Derrida tells, "the supplement" or "supplementarity" is another word for what he calls "writing in general," not writing in the "vulgar" sense but writing as a name for the supposed exteriority of representation or signification in relation to the thing represented or signified. "Writing, the letter, the sensible inscription, has always been considered by Western tradition as the body . . . external to the spirit, to breath, to speech, and to the logos."[3] In that same tradition (the tradition of "logocentrism") writing is that specious outside or conveying which by engaging and capturing our attention turns us away from an interior reality; supposedly an aid to the presentation or commemoration of the real, it usurps the position of the real and seduces us into a forgetfulness of its own secondariness: "Writing, a mnemotechnic means, supplanting good memory, spontaneous memory, signifies forgetfulness" (37). What is forgotten or lost sight of is the origin or logos which "without writing . . . would remain in itself" (37). In its movement away from the full and immediate perception of the origin—of presence before mediation has removed it—writing is the "original sin" (35).

Writing, in short, is "that dangerous supplement" (the title, taken from Rousseau, of a chapter in Derrida's *Of Grammatology*), that "menacing aid," that "surplus" or extra or addition which pretends to be in the service of plenitude (although one might wonder why plenitude requires service) but, in fact, "adds only to replace" (145); and what it replaces is that which is entirely "other than it" (145). The supplement is that substitute "mediocre makeshift" which insinuates itself into the heart of the "self-sufficient"—of that which *ought* to lack nothing at all in itself," that which "does not have to be supplemented" because "it suffices" (145).

It is hardly necessary to note the similarity between Derrida's vocabulary and the vocabulary of Milton, but of course one notes the similarity only to remark on (what appears to be) the difference: while Milton endorses the distinction between the thing itself and the proposed supplement to it, Derrida rehearses it only to undermine it, or to reveal it undermining itself. His thesis is simple and, in its way, devastating: the condition of supplementarity—of an incompleteness that requires an addition to eke it out—is originary, and is itself the origin of that which is opposed to it in the name of purity and presence. The supplement or writing is not secondary, does not come after a plenitude it then threatens; rather it is "primordial" and names, and *thereby marks* the absence of, a plenitude that is not now and never was available in and of itself. The supplement does not offer itself as an addition to something already fully formed and complete; it "comes to *make up for* a deficiency . . . to compensate for a primordial nonself-presence."[4] That nonself-presence, that "so-called all- and self-sufficient fullness, "can be filled up *of itself* [can become what it is], can accomplish itself, only by allowing itself to be filled [pieced or eked out] through sign and proxy";[5] and if writing or the supplement "must necessarily be added . . . to complete the constitution of the ideal object," or presence, "it is because . . . 'presence' . . . had already from the start fallen short of itself."[6]

This does not mean, as Derrida hastens to add, that there is no such thing as presence, or the experience of presence, of immediacy, of total sufficiency, of ground; it is just that presence—whether it be of God or the world or the self—rather than occupying a realm independent of and prior to the articulations that strain to characterize it, is the product of those articulations, of systems of signification, of writing, of the dangerous supplement. Thus, while presence remains a category and an effect one can experience, it can no longer be posited as "the absolutely matrical form of being" but should be seen as a "determination" of that which is supposedly derivative of it.[7] And therefore in the strict sense—that is, in the sense in which these terms have always been sounded in the logocentric tradition— "there never has been and never will be a unique word, a master name."[8]

This last pronouncement returns us forcefully to Milton and *Of Prelaticall Episcopacy;* for it is in the (master) name of a self-sufficient and self-generating and unique word that Milton speaks. (Or does he speak? That, as we shall see, is the question.) The Scripture is, if anything is, the "transcendental signified . . . pure auto-affection . . . which does not borrow from outside itself . . . any accessory signifier, any substance of expression foreign to its own spontaneity."[9] On the very first page, Milton is insisting that the Scripture is "only able" by which he means both that among all things it only is able and that it is able "only," by itself without any aid; and twenty-three pages later he is still sounding the same note, urging us, as the tract ends, to give "our selves up to be taught by the pure and living precept of *God's* word onely, which without more additions, nay with a forbidding of them hath within it selfe the promise of eternall life, the end of all our wearisome labours" (652).

As an assertion and a claim, this statement would seem to be an obvious candidate for a deconstructive reading, an easy target for just the kind of analysis to which Derrida subjects Plato, Husserl, Saussure, Lévi-Strauss, Austin, and Rousseau. One can almost hear the questions: Isn't a discourse that argues for the self-sufficiency of an ideal object a disconfirmation of that very argument? Doesn't the very fact of the tract's existence, the fact that someone felt compelled to produce it, belie its own message? How can so many words be expended in the service of something that requires no aids? If additions to the pure and living precept of God's word are forbidden, what is the status of this very effort? Isn't *Of Prelaticall Episcopacy* an impiety of just the kind it condemns? Isn't it the very thing it thunders against? Isn't it a supplement?

In some readings of a deconstructive or postmodernist kind, these questions would mark not the beginning but the end of the matter, for they would indicate that once again a discourse has been shown to stand on its putative ground only by forgetting or repressing the intuition that would unsettle it, by concealing from itself "a certain exterior" that it cannot name or describe without undoing its constitutive rhetoric.[10] In this case the rhetoric is the rhetoric of scriptural self-sufficiency, and what the discourse conceals and represses is the "scandal" of its own existence, all the more easy to "overlook" because it is so obvious. But we cannot stop here, because rather than being blind to the "problematic" of his own activity, Milton foregrounds that problematic and makes it the basis of a strategy. I am not suggesting that Milton is a proto-poststructuralist; I am merely saying that in the context of the position he self-consciously espouses, he is inevitably aware of the difficulties and "troubles" on which poststructuralism feeds. That is, like many a modern author too much aware of the duplicity of his craft, he is uneasy about his performance, and for good reason. Given the fact of scripture, that performance is superfluous, and because it is superfluous, it is also, potentially at least, impious. If Scripture is fully able to satisfy us, there is no need to say anything else, and since the fullness of Scripture is the tract's first assertion, it is over before it begins.[11] At the same time that the opening sentences promise to adjudicate between the respective claims of Scripture and tradition, Scripture is declared to be the judge of the dispute, and almost immediately the tract finds itself all dressed up with nowhere to go. Indeed, going somewhere is precisely the error it wishes to avoid, as from the outset danger and impiety are associated with movement. Those who are "not contented with the plentifull and wholesom fountaines of the Gospell" (626) are described as failing to "hold fast to the grounds of the reformed Church" (624); instead they "run to that indigested heap . . . which they call Antiquity" (626); and when they are not running, they are "forraging" (627); they "stagger" and are "mislead" (627); they "gadde" (631), and "fondly straggle"; they "change" (632); they "fetch" (637); they "fall to searching" (639), they "truant" (642), they "creep by degrees" (650), they "labour" (652), they "deduce" (652).

"Deduce" may seem a strange word to bring up the rear of this list, but in fact it captures in a precise and abstract way what is wrong with movement: deduction begins from first axioms and then moves away from them toward a conclusion; but the first axiom to which Milton is committed—that the Scriptures are all-sufficient—contains its own conclusion and therefore expressly prohibits (nay, forbids) seeking for conclusions elsewhere. The act of deducing is a repeated target of scorn in the tract. It is by the degrees or steps of deduction that the prelates arrive at their claims of authority; "Episcopall men," Milton observes in accusation, "would cast a mist before us, to deduce their exalted *Episcopacy* from Apostolick times" (648). The (insubstantial) content of that mist is a "petty fog of witnesses" (648) and "testimonies" (649)—"witness" and "testimony" being two other words that reappear often and are always allied with deduction as the components of a suspect practice, a practice which leads men to seek in some external formula that which should reside within them. The practice is conceived of as a legalistic one, and in the course of it witnesses and testimonies are always found to be "grey," "bare," without "credit," "alleged," and "corrupt," inauthentic, broken, disfigured, and tainted. Implicitly opposed to this practice is another in which witness and testimony are (quite literally) redeemed because they have reference to an interior motion which is, in fact, no motion at all: you witness by holding fast to that with which you are already allied; and you testify to the residence within of the "something holy [that] lodges in [your] breast."[12] As Milton will soon put it in the *Apology*, "The testimony of what we believe in religion must be such as the conscience may rest on to be infallible, and incorruptible, which is only the word of God";[13] and since the word of God is inscribed on the fleshly tables of the heart, the circuit of testimony (and of witness) can (indeed must) be completed without moving an inch from the center of an illuminated self.

Significantly, this is exactly the circuit (or noncircuit) that Milton himself travels (by not traveling) when he speaks of what has "moved" him to the present occasion: "it came into my thoughts to perswade my selfe, setting all distances, and nice respects aside, that I could do Religion, and my Country no better service for the time then doing my utmost endeavor to recall the people of God from this vaine forraging after straw, and to reduce them to their firme stations under the standard of the Gospell" (627). At first it seems that the impulse to action (exactly the wrong word) is external—"it came into my thoughts"—but then it turns out that the phrase "it came" means no more than "it occurred to me"; the origin of the thought is internal, as is the activity it prompts, "to perswade my selfe." What is described is a psychological process that is wholly self-contained, a process that occurs without his ever taking a single step, and one that issues in a resolution to recall others from the steps they have taken imprudently, so that they can once again assume the posture Milton himself exemplifies, marching in place "under the standard of the Gospell."

I Will Not Stand to Argue

This, then, will be the business of the tract—to retard and reverse movement—but to say as much is once again to encounter the tract's problematic, the fact that it will itself necessarily move through time, in a succession of propositions; and characteristically Milton chooses to foreground that problematic by providing the reader with an advance plan of what he intends: he will recall the "vaine" foragers by "making appeare to them, first the insufficiency, next the inconvenience, and lastly the impiety of these gay testimonies, that their great Doctors would bring them to dote on" (627). "Making appeare" would seem to name a very strong action, one that could hardly be prosecuted without engaging in the very activities—of reasoning, deducing, proving—Milton rejects and indicts; but "making appeare" can also name a softer action in which the actor's contribution is limited to the clearing away of film and debris. Such an actor would not be guilty of adding to Scripture, of covering it with his own writing, for he would merely be removing the coverings and addition of others so that Scripture can do what it must be allowed to do—speak for itself.

Needless to say, this is a difficult strategy to execute, since it is always in danger of turning into the very thing it opposes, of turning into a supplement. The trick is to do as little as possible, to perform in a way so minimal that it is not a performance at all; and that is why the first thing Milton tells us as he approaches his task is what he will *not* do: "in performing this I shall not strive to be more exact in Methode, then as their citations lead me" (627). That is, his movements will be dictated by the "gay testimonies" of the "great Doctors," and therefore they will not be *his* movements; by being thus careless in his method, he will forsake method. Method, after all, is crucial only if the truth is not yet found; but for one whose truth is within, method is beside the point, because the point to which method would bring one is always and already achieved. Such a one "shall not strive," because he need not strive, and because he need not strive he should not strive.

Milton's (anti)method of (non)striving is on display in the very first sentence of the tract's main section: "First therefore concerning *Ignatius* shall be treated fully, when the Author shall come to insist upon some places in his Epistles" (627). "First therefore" promises a reasoned sequence of deductions based on evidence marshaled and considered; but the sequence never even gets started, because the evidence is withdrawn *before* it is placed on the table. Of course it is true that Ignatius' appearance is only postponed, but, as we shall see, even when he returns he will be treated no more "fully" than he is here. Meanwhile, Milton proceeds with a "Next" that has no proper reference, since the previous event has not yet occurred. What occurs now is the apparent citing of "one *Leontius Bishop* of *Magnesia*," but he too is dismissed before he can take the stand; for he is "but an obscure and single witness" who, for all we know, might be "factious and false" (628). And "how," asks Milton, "shall this testimony receive credit from his word, whose very name had scarce been thought on, but for this bare Testimony?" (628) That is, how can you accept as authoritative the word of someone whose authority is itself in question? Any reasoning based on such a bare testimony is obviously circular and self-vitiating.

Of course Milton's reasoning (if that is the word) is also circular, beginning and ending in a word; but that word is God's and the testimony is authoritative *because* it is bare, because it issues from an unimpeachable source that has no need of the external validation lacking to Leontius and others. It is because such validation is lacking that Leontius' testimony (whatever that might be) is never heard, and Milton returns him to the obscurity from which he has not been allowed to emerge, saying only, "I will not stand to argue" (628). This is more than a report on his present intention; it is a perfect description of his performance: he stands exactly in the position he had assumed in the beginning, and he has declined to move from that position by arguing, despite the appearance of phrases like "First therefore" and words like "Next."

In this sequence, which shall be repeated again, we see the whole of Milton's minimalist strategy: he will not so much consider evidence as consider considering it; and in every instance he will find, before the evidence is even brought to light, that it is inadmissible, first because it is itself corrupt and second because the foundations on which it may be said to rest are similarly corrupt. As a result, he will have managed the considerable nonfeat of remaining always in the same position, of not moving at all, because every time it appears that he is about to make a move it is aborted. To say that the strategy is negative is in fact to give it more positivity than Milton allows it to have. He doesn't discredit the evidence; he discredits the possibility of either crediting or discrediting the evidence, and thereby saves himself both the labor and the possible presumption that would inhere in even the slightest of actions. In ways that find many parallels in the poetry (see Chapters 9 and 11), *Of Prelaticall Episcopacy* is full of moments when action of some kind seems imminent, but never quite occurs.

As Milton leaves Leontius (without ever having encountered him), he takes a few Parthian shots at some other arguments that will likewise not be heard. One could say that "hee was a member of the Councell and that may deserve to gaine him credit with us," but such an argument will presume on the soundness of the councils, and as everyone knows, "nothing hath been more attempted, nor with more subtilty brought about . . . then to falsifie the Editions of the Councels, of which wee have none but from our Adversaries hand" (628–629). Not that Milton wishes to argue the point; he introduces the topic by dismissing it—"nor shall I neede to plead at this time, that . . . "—and he concludes it, without ever having raised it, by saying that he does not here "purpose to take advantage of" it, "for what availes it to wrangle about the corrupt editions of Councells" (629). "Much rather," he says, "should we attend to what *Eusebius* the ancientest writer extant of Church-history . . . confesses" (630–631). For a moment it seems that Milton is about to accept an authority other than the Bible and risk the danger of becoming a supplement to a supplementer; but then it turns out that what Eusebius confesses is that the distinction between bishops and presbyters is not one that is made clearly in the Scriptures. Eusebius is being invoked not so that he can give evidence but so that he can admit his inability to go beyond the evidence already available in the Bible. And if Eusebius, "a famous writer," is unable to find support for episcopacy, "much more may we think it difficult to *Leontius* an obscure Bishop" (631). The logic here simultaneously employs and eviscerates the standards by which tradition and history determine authority: as the more ancient and the most famous, Eusebius deserves a hearing, but he is heard only so that he can disqualify himself in favor of an authority that knows no time and transcends history: "Thus while we leave the Bible to gadde after these traditions of the ancients, we heare the ancients themselvs confessing, that what knowledge they had in this point was such as they had gather'd from the Bible" (631).

It is no surprise, then, when Ignatius, who had been sent away with the promise that he would later "be treated fully," returns to become the object of exactly the same treatment—that is, no treatment at all—he met with in the first place. Predictably, Ignatius' *Epistles* are disqualified before they can be examined; five of them, Milton points out, have been rejected as "spurious" (635) because they have been seen to contain "Heresies and trifles, which cannot agree in Chronologie with *Ignatius*" (635–636).

Once again the "proof" supposedly provided by patristic authority is discredited by the same standards by which that authority
would maintain itself—that is, the evidence is declared to be
doubtful in its own terms; and here doubt is cast not only on the
texts, known by even those who cite them to be "interlarded with
Corruptions," but also on the author, who, on the "evidence" of
those same corruptions, cannot be securely identified as Ignatius.

This line of reasoning allows Milton to come to his favorite
kind of conclusion, one that squeezes his opponent from opposite directions: either these epistles are not by Ignatius at all and
thereby lose the authority of his name, or else Ignatius is their
author but he is not the Ignatius of repute, not "a Martyr, but
most adulterate, and corrupt himselfe" (639). Ignatius, then, is
not himself; rather he exists only in pieces—in Milton's words,
"disfigur'd," "interrupted," "broken and disjoynted" (639)—and
he must therefore be put together by the very person who will
then cite him as authoritative. "How," Milton asks, can we credit
"such an Author, to whose very essence the Reader must be fain
to contribute his own understanding" (639)? With this question
Milton returns us to his opening paragraphs (which in fact we
have never left): Ignatius, both as a person and as a text (there is
finally no distinction), is not "all sufficient" and therefore cannot
furnish us with that which we must ourselves supply. Moreover,
the fact that there are some who are moved (a word whose spatial dimension should be stressed) to supply it indicates that they
are themselves no less deficient than he is, and in the same way:
they too have no "essence," no "all sufficiency" to which they are
united and of which they are an extension, and it is their incompleteness which sends them in search of supplementary aids, a
search which ends only in the discovery of bodies even more
"broken and disjoynted" than their own.

Later Milton (or at least his Adam) will decide that "single imperfection" can be remedied by joining in "Collateral love and . . .

amity" with others of like defectiveness (*Paradise Lost,* VIII, 423–426), but here in 1642 the mathematics are more severe; the union of imperfection begets only more imperfection. What is required is a union that need not be sought, because it is a mode of being in which we have so completely "given our selves up to be taught by the pure, and living precept of *Gods* word" (652) that we are, quite literally, animated by the word. At that point we will have become what Milton claims he already is in the *Apology*—"a member incorporate into that truth whereof I was perswaded" (871)—and what Christ declares himself to be in *Paradise Regained,* a "living Oracle" (I, 460). Rather than betaking our selves to the "scraps, and fragments of an unknown table," we should feed on the "Evangelick Manna" (639) that God has placed on the fleshly tables of our hearts. He who has been nourished by that manna will feel no need to seek elsewhere for something that is already his substance. Not "disjoynted" himself, but an incorporate member, he will immediately see the disjointed texts of Ignatius and others for what they are—"verminous, and polluted rags dropt . . . from the toyling shoulders of Time"—and will disdain those rags in favor of "the spotlesse, and undecaying robe of Truth" (639), a garment in which he is already clothed.

In this opposition between truth and time, the several components of Milton's position coalesce. Time is the medium of motion and process, of eking out, of adding, supplementing; it is, in a word, the medium of incompleteness, although its perpetual promise is that wholeness and illumination are only a step away. Truth, on the other hand, is what abides; it does not need the temporal dimension in order to emerge; like Milton's muse, it was present "Before the Hills appear'd, or Fountain flow'd" (*Paradise Lost,* VII, 8) and it remains fully present in every moment of what is no longer a succession of differences but an order of the same. As Milton puts it at the close of this amazing passage, "Truth" is "the daughter not of Time but of Heaven, only bred up . . . in Christian hearts" (639). This declaration not only displays Milton's deepest convictions, but explains, if it does not justify, the curious structure of a tract which, in Donald Davie's words (he directs them at *Paradise Lost*), declines to take advantage of the fact that it is "a shape cut in time,"[14] a tract which refuses to move forward or even to take a first step, a tract which never adds anything to its opening pronouncement (a pronouncement that announces its own superfluousness), a tract which in its determination to avoid burdening the world with one more "needlesse tract" (626) systematically withholds satisfaction of the needs felt by every reader of discursive prose, the needs for argument, evidence, testimony, deduction. These are the needs of the distracted "multitude" who have somehow wandered and must be recalled "from this vaine forraging after straw" and returned "to their firme stations under the standards of the Gospell" (627)—must be recalled, that is, to the security and self-sufficiency of their own Christian hearts, where everything they vainly seek is always and already found.

Don't Even Look

At this point it would seem that Milton surely could rest on his circular conclusion, but he has pledged himself to be led in his "methode" by the citations of his adversaries, and he proceeds doggedly, "jumping up and down in the same place."[15] Ignatius is followed by Irenaeus and Tertullian, who now take their turns— or rather, do not take their turns—as their authority and even their identities are impugned in what is by now a familiar manner. Irenaeus is dismissed twice, first because although he reports that he was present when *"Polycarpus was made Bishop of Smyrna by the Apostles,"* he was at the time, by his own confession, only a boy; and therefore, says Milton, we would be "rash to rely upon" his "young observation" (640, 641). But lest we think that his

230

youth is the only reason to distrust him, Eusebius is brought in to testify that in his maturity Irenaeus became "infected" with the errors of Papias, another eyewitness of the acts of the Apostles, but one who was known to be of "shallow wit" and incapable of understanding what he saw and heard. The infection Irenaeus receives is retroactive, casting further doubt on the accuracy of his youthful report and on eyewitness testimony in general. As a consequence, Polycarpus too is infected, since his Apostolic bishopric is attested to only by the now thoroughly discredited Irenaeus. Only Eusebius escapes, but he is relied on only to point out the unreliability of the tradition of testimony of which he is himself a part.

Indeed, the Apostles themselves are tainted, for although they are not directly attacked, there is a sustained attack on those who, like Irenaeus, Papias, and Polycarpus, attend to their persons rather than to what they had written (writing of course inspired by the Spirit). In a manner most un-Miltonic, Milton imagines the pilgrimages (error is once again always associated with movement) of those who would make a shrine of any place or spot to which the Apostles were known to have repaired: "O happy this house that harbour'd him, and that cold stone whereon he rested, this Village wherein he wrought such a miracle, and that pavement bedew'd with the warm effusion of his last blood, that sprouted up into eternall Roses to crowne his Martyrdome" (642). This lyrically suspect apostrophe is followed (as similar moments of "indulgence" will be in *Paradise Lost*) by a stringent and devastating indictment as idolatry of everything that might have seemed attractive in such scenes: "Thus while all their thoughts were pow'rd out upon circumstances, and the gazing after such men as had sate at table with the *Apostles* (many of which *Christ* hath profest, yea though they had cast out Divells in his name, he will not know at the last day) by this meanes they lost their time, and truanted in the fundamentall grounds of saving knowledge"

(642). The syntax here is double: "many of which" can refer either to "such men" or to the Apostles, and even though it is likely that we will settle on the former reading, the latter is available and even (given the juxtaposition of *"Apostles"* with the parenthesis) insistent. If only at a subterranean level, the Apostles too become "infected" with the same kind of waywardness or truancy that characterizes those who idolize them: they become "disjoynted" and "interrupt" from the truth and text of which they are incorporate members; and once again that truth and that text stand alone as the only authorities in a landscape from which all other authorities—Leontius, Ignatius, Irenaeus, Polycarpus, Papias, the Apostles themselves—have been cleared.

But no sooner has the ground been cleared than another of that "petty fog of witnesses" thrown up by tradition and custom threatens to befoul it. *"Tertullian,"* Milton announces, "accosts us next" (644), but he is turned away before he can speak because his testimony "is of no more force to deduce *Episcopacy,* then the two former" (644). In the paragraphs that follow, the words "testimony" and "deduce" appear with increasing frequency, emphasizing at once everything that is being declared suspect (because unnecessary) and everything that Milton is ostentatiously declining to do. The only testimony he will offer is the testimony of his unwillingness to consider any testimony; the only deduction he will make is that the deduction is superfluous and dangerous, since it involves a movement away from the truth that should already reside in "Christian hearts" (639). He has nowhere to go, nothing to do except "to prove the insufficiency of these . . . *Episcopall* Testimonies" and point out the "inconvenience" we fall into if we allow ourselves "to bee guided by these kind of Testimonies" (650). If the Fathers are read in this spirit, with the purpose of marking "how corruption, and *Apostasy* [have] crept in by degrees," they can do us no harm, and can by negative example provide us with materials with which to "stop the mouthes of our adversaries, and to bridle them with their own curb" (650). This is a precise description of what Milton has himself been doing (insofar as he has been doing anything), and the key terms of that description—"stop," "bridle," and "curb"—capture perfectly the determined nonmotion of a tract designed not to produce words but to stop their flow, not to generate conclusions but to block them, not to initiate movement but to bridle it, not to provide satisfaction—for that would be to arrogate to itself that which it denies to others—but to induce frustration and a longing for a Word that has no need of it or anything else.

That, at least, is Milton's thesis, the self-sufficiency of Scripture; and, as we have seen, it is a thesis that provides him with a justification for the minimalist strategy of dismissing extra-scriptural evidence even before it is examined. So successful is this strategy that it obscures the even more basic strategy that lies behind it: by foregrounding his efforts to prevent us from looking at texts other than Scripture, Milton averts our attention from the fact that we are at the same time being prevented from looking at Scripture itself. The effect is something very much like a sleight of hand: so intent are we on following the ways in which the Fathers and their texts are being dismissed that we never even notice that *Scripture is nowhere cited*. On one level this can be seen as an extension of Milton's point: even to look at Scripture is to be at a distance from that which should be the very content of one's heart and mind; to hold Scripture at arm's length as if it were merely an object is to be "interrupt" from it, and to be, like Ignatius, in a "broken and disjoynted plight" (639). But on another level, Milton's disinclination even to cite Scripture in a tract that everywhere asserts its self-sufficiency can be seen as an admission, probably inadvertent, that behind the assertion is a fear—a fear of what will happen if he allows himself or his readers the slightest of movements, even the movement of opening an eye and taking a look.

That fear is made explicit in the final paragraph, when Milton says of Scripture that "if one jot be alterable it is . . . possible that all should perish" (652). Although the reference here is to biblical passages that proclaim the power and imperishability of the Word (the word authorizes itself) the context suggests a Word so vulnerable that every motion toward it carries the threat of alteration. At this moment what becomes clear (although perhaps not to Milton) is that Scripture's very uniqueness is the source of the danger posed to it by something so small as the glances of men. Unlike any other "word," Scripture (or so the claim goes) is self-interpreting (this is just another characterization of its self-sufficiency), which means not only that it needs no interpretation but that it cannot survive interpretation; that is to say, as a self-reading text it cannot be read without being turned into something other than it is. Even to look at it is to mark it with the differentiating lines that are necessarily the content of any temporally bound vision. This is what Derrida means by "originary violence"[16]—a violence that does not occur after perception, but is another name for perception, for what happens when *within* a system of differences (and there is no perception apart from some or other system) an act of predication, an act of demarcating, takes place. The violence is originary because what becomes pick-outable or legible is the product of what points it out, of the differential system within which (to borrow George Herbert's words) "We say . . . This or that is."[17] The "this" or "that" which is thus constituted can never be grasped in its "pre-read" shape, in a shape that is entirely its own and has not yet been obscured or overlain by the fatal touch of representation.

The logic is at once inexorable and paradoxical: in order to preserve the sacred text, one must protect it from being read—protect it, that is, from the very condition of being a text, of being at once the object and the product of an act of interpretation.

Milton's entire enterprise depends on two related attempts to avoid textuality: he labors to prevent his own text from achieving a substance that would make it an addition, a supplement; and he avoids giving a textual substance to the interior Word, by averting his eyes from it. The assertion of the tract is that Scripture is complete in and of itself, but it is a completeness that is compromised by the slightest inspection, and indeed by any action more volitional than the unconditional surrender urged by Milton in his final paragraph. We must, he says, give "our selves up to be taught by the pure, and living precept of *Gods* word onely, which without more additions, nay with a forbidding of them hath within it selfe the promise of eternall life, the end of all our wearisome labours" (652). The statement is a complicated one, simultaneously a warning, a promise, and the expression of a fear. The warning is the same as the one with which the tract began: do not look to and/or become an addition. The promise is that by ending the presumptuous and unnecessary labors of adding or supplementing, we shall gain eternal life. And the fear is that if we persist in such labors, they will prove not only wearisome but fatal, since their effect will be to "open a broad passage for a multitude of Doctrines that have no ground in Scripture, to break in upon us" (651). In this sentence, which ends the penultimate paragraph, the fear is nakedly and pointedly expressed: once the Word has been subjected to even the slightest scrutiny, its bulwarks (the sense of a fortress under siege is unmistakable) will have been breached and all will be lost. The way to forestall this disaster is to remain closed up within the fortress we ourselves become so long as we do not stir or move in any way. The "ground" which supports us will simply crumble if we so much as glance at it. The warning in its conspicuous anxiety recalls the warnings given to Orpheus and to Lot, but it is even more severe: Not "Don't look back," but "Don't look at all."

Skillful and Laborious Gathering

It is therefore all the more extraordinary to realize that in less than two years Milton will aggressively violate every injunction he here lays down, and will not only look Scripture full in the face but will urge in the strongest possible terms the very activities he now forbids.[18] In *The Doctrine and Discipline of Divorce* (1643), Scripture is the object not only of direct scrutiny but of an interpretation so strenuous that even the word "manipulation" is too mild to describe it. Reading is not forbidden; instead it is commanded, and is to take exactly the form which in *Of Prelaticall Episcopacy* poses the greatest danger. In order to read Scripture correctly, Milton announces, one must be "a skillfull and laborious gatherer," and the reason this is required—an amazing reason given the antiprelatical tracts—is that in the Gospel Christ nowhere gives "full comments or continu'd discourses" but rather "scatters . . . the heavnly grain of his doctrin like pearle heer and there,"[19] a doctrine which must therefore be put together and made whole by an interpreter. In short, Scripture is neither complete nor self-sufficient but itself demands—that is, wants—a supplement. The reversal could not be more total: that which should supply our needs must be itself supplied by our labors. Milton has himself let loose the forces whose containment was so much the business of his earlier work. What has happened? What does this mean?[20]

One answer to this question would center around Milton's domestic situation, which had presumably led him "naturally" to the question of divorce. Arthur Barker maintains that even before Mary Powell deserted him, Milton had reached conclusions about the lawfulness of divorce, and that his personal problems served only to sharpen and focus arguments he had already prepared. As post-Freudians we may be properly skeptical of Barker's generosity, but we must certainly agree when he declares that

236

Milton "found it impossible to believe . . . that the opinion on divorce at which he had arrived could be contrary to the divine will."[21] This opinion can easily be shown to be continuous with his other opinions and especially with the insistence, from which he never wavers, on the primacy of conscience and internal illumination. In principle the argument for divorce—that it is a necessary relief from the merely formal bondage of a spiritual misyoking—is of a piece with many of the arguments Milton makes in the antiprelatical tracts for the primacy of conscience and the inner light. What is different is that the argument cannot make its way in the company of a strenuous literalism, because the chief support of the opposing argument is an apparently unequivocal verse from the Gospel of Matthew: "Whosoever shall put away his wife, except it be for fornication, and shall marry another, committeth adultery" (19:9). It is the fact of this verse and the impossibility of avoiding it that dictates Milton's strategy and makes unavailable to him the anti-interpretivism which informs *Of Prelaticall Episcopacy*. As Barker puts it, "Instead of opposing the plain truth of Scripture to custom, he had now to reinterpret the precept on which custom seemed firmly to base itself."

Indeed, the case is worse than that. What Milton must do is somehow show that a verse that seems to everyone else to disallow divorce except for one particular offense should be read as allowing divorce for any of the myriad offenses that might fall under the general and expandable rubric of incompatibility. He must show that when Christ *says* a man can put away his wife only for reason of fornication, he *means* that a man can put away his wife for any reason he likes. The logic of his position is clear: it is the logic employed by Paulus Emilius when he was asked "why he would put away his wife for no visible reason" and replied by pointing to his shoe and saying, *"This shoo . . . is a neat shoo, a new shoo, and yet none of yee know wher it wrings me"* (DDD, 348). His point is Milton's point: the reality of an internal lack of fit (between foot and shoe or man and wife) is independent of any external manifestation, any "visible reason"; it is a matter not of outward behavior but of the "inward man, which not any law but conscience only can evince"—where "evince" is a Miltonic joke, since the argument is precisely that what is essential is what does *not* show.

But as Milton himself points out, no matter how cogent his reasoning may be (and how much it follows from the general Puritan arguments against vestments and set forms), someone might still object that the cogency is worth nothing, "as the words of Christ are plainly against all divorce, except in the case of fornication" (281). By raising this objection himself, Milton highlights the interpretive issue and glances backward to the way his earlier work relies on the argument he is about to reject, the argument for the "plain, and unaffected stile of the Scriptures" which are forever "protesting their own plainnes, and perspicuity."[22] This is an early instance of what becomes a characteristic Miltonic strategy: to think through a problem by revisiting and complicating an earlier treatment of it. Milton is continually in dialogue with himself, responding not so much to the external challenges of ecclesiastical and parliamentary debate (although of course these things also figure in his thinking) as to the challenge represented by his former selves to the position he would now espouse. In *The Doctrine and Discipline of Divorce,* the two Miltons, the old and the new, meet in the single word that becomes their battlefield: "plainly" and all its cognates. The considerable tension in the tract derives from the fact that the claim of plainness is central both to the stance he abandons and the stance he proceeds to assume.

It is a tension Milton seems to exploit deliberately when he responds to his own devil's-advocate question ("What are all these reasonings worth . . . when as the words of Christ are plainly against . . . divorce?") by offering a theory of meaning in which the sense of an utterance cannot be construed independently of the conditions of its production. If we are to understand what Christ says, we must attend to "The occasion which induc't [him] to speak of divorce" (282). He did not speak in a vacuum but spoke *to* someone in a particular situation with its own structures and emphases. In this case he was speaking to the Pharisees, who had put to him a "tempting question"—a question designed to reveal him as lax with regard to the Law. It is in response to that question that he gives an answer more severe than he would have given to questioners of a more generous spirit:

> So heer he may be justly thought to have giv'n this rigid sentence against divorce, not to cut off all remedy from a good man who finds himself consuming away in a disconsolate and uninjoy'd matrimony, but to lay a bridle upon the bold abuses of those over-weening Rabbies; which he could not more effectually doe, then by a countersway of restraint, curbing their wild exorbitance almost into the other extreme; as when we bow things the contrary way, to make them come to thir natural straitnes. (283)

That is, since this stricture was meant only for those of pharisaical temper, the freedom of men who are not Pharisees—the freedom of "good" men—cannot properly be abrogated by invoking a prohibition that was not addressed to them. Therefore, while Christ might say to the Pharisees, "*You* can divorce only for reason of adultery," he says to us good men, "To *you* divorce is permitted if, in your judgment, your marriage is not a true spiritual union."

It is, to say the least, an ingenious argument, in the course of which Christ's plain decree is set aside in favor of a "laboriously gathered" interpretation; but no sooner has that interpretation been fashioned than it is proclaimed to be "most evident" (283)—that is, plain—and indeed it is introduced as something "we may plainly discover" (282). It is in these sentences that the text sets its own problem: How can plainness at once be dismissed as an "obstinate *literality*" and an "*alphabetical* servility" (279) and then in the very next instant be claimed for a reading that no one else had ever thought of? The solution to the problem lies in a distinction (itself finally a problem) between the entities of which plainness can be predicated. For a literalist of the kind Milton was such a short time ago, it is the text, more or less self-construing, that is plain; for Milton in his new role as active interpreter, it is the stance of the speaker in relation to a particular situation that is, or can be, plain. Once that stance has been determined, once it is clear from what angle a speaker makes his intervention, and with what purpose in mind, the words he produces acquire an obvious shape and can then be declared plain. That is why Milton can at once scorn plainness and claim it; he scorns it as a property of words and claims it as a property of the contextual conditions within which they are uttered. Indeed, he says as much at the end of this sequence: "And that this was the only intention of Christ was most evident" (283).

It is the word "intention" that formally announces Milton's new theory of interpretation,[23] for it names the place where meaning has been relocated now that it is said no longer to reside in words. But even as it names that place, the word presents us with a new problem: if words do not specify the intention with which they are produced but rather must be construed in the light of that intention, how is it that we determine what the intention is? How is *it* brought to light? The difficulty becomes apparent at the very moment when Milton declares his thesis: "That we are not to repose all upon the literall terms of so many words, many instances will teach us: Wherin we may plainly discover how Christ meant not to be tak'n word for word, but like a wise Physician, administring one excesse against another" (282–283). It is Christ's intention, says Milton, to be understood intentionally (within a specific purpose) and not word for word; but how do we know that intention? The immediate answer is that it will be known if we examine other "instances" of Christ's speech—we should attend, Milton advises, to "his own words . . . not many verses before." But presumably those words too are to be understood intentionally, and therefore the support they give as evidence of an intention must itself be supported by additional evidence that will in turn display the same deficiency (wanting a supplement). Once words have been dislodged as the repository of meaning in favor of intention, no amount of them will suffice to establish an intention, since the value they have will always depend on that which they presume to establish.

The same circularity is on display in an earlier moment when Milton considers the verse on which his entire case is based: *"It is not good . . . that man should be alone; I will make him a help meet for him.* From which words so plain, lesse cannot be concluded . . . that in Gods intention a meet and happy conversation is the chiefest and the noblest end of marriage" (245–246). Although the assertion is that interpretation proceeds from the words to the calculation of God's intention, the actual direction is the other way around; the language does not dictate Milton's reading, and it would be open to someone with a different view to argue (for example) that the remedy for loneliness is the interpenetrating oneness achievable only in the act of intercourse. In short, there is nothing plain about the *words;* what is plain, at least in the eyes of Milton, is the intention in relation to which the words could only have the meaning he stipulates for them. Still, the question remains: How is that intention determined? And finally the only answer Milton gives (by not giving it) is that intention is not determined but simply assumed, and that its assumption is supported by its own strength—the strength of belief—and by nothing else ("On Other Surety None"). That is to say, what is supposedly the end of the interpretive process—the specification of what a speaker means—is in Milton's "proce-dure" its beginning. He starts with a conviction that his God is of a certain temper and inclination; and therefore he knows, in ad-vance of the appearance of any of God's particular words, what they *must* mean.

Nowhere is this clearer than in those passages in which rival interpretations are dismissed because to accept them would be to accept the picture of a God who is cruel and deceptive.[24] Noting that a strict reading of the verse from Matthew would entail assuming that the latitude allowed to divorcers by Mosaic law amounted to the sanctioning of sin, Milton says that this is a doc-trine he will "ever disswade" himself from believing; for "Cer-tainly this is not the manner of God, whose pure eyes cannot be-hold, much lesse his perfect Laws dispence with such impurity" (303–304). "Can wee conceave without vile thoughts," he asks, "that the majesty and holiness of God could endure so many ages to gratifie a stubborn people in the practice of a foul pollut-ing sin?" (316). The "vile thoughts" would be the thoughts one would have to have about God, about the kind of person he was, in order to read *that* signification into his words. It is a matter, Milton says, of the "honour of God," which is "misreputed" if he is read as "dispencing legally with many ages of ratify'd adultery" (354–355). We repute him correctly only if we read him as grant-ing a permission that was never withdrawn (except in the very special case of the Pharisees), for only then will we "recover the misattended words of Christ to the sincerity of their true sense" (355).

This statement is supposedly made on behalf of the words, as if sense and sincerity were properties that have somehow been taken away from them and are now to be returned by the inter-preter's labors. But, in fact, sense and sincerity are what the inter-preter *lends* to the words by bypassing them in favor of some-thing that stands behind them, the immaterial (because inner) intention that, quite literally, informs them. It is by means of the intentional context that the interpreter is able to construct both sense and sincerity, but since that context is itself without visible form, it too must be constructed even as it is invoked as a support. It is hardly necessary to remark how different this is from the antiprelatical tracts, where, in a typical passage, Milton enumerates the "extrinsic" contexts from which the prelates derive their arguments and says, as he dismisses them in turn, "we shall tell them of Scripture,"[25] the same Scripture which in another place is exalted above the insubstantiality of "unwritt'n traditions."[26] In *The Doctrine and Discipline of Divorce,* the unwritten controls the written to the extent of rewriting it whenever its apparent sense is inconvenient. While in *Of Prelaticall Episcopacy* Milton dismisses with contempt the authority of an author "to whose very essence the Reader must be fain to contribute his own understanding" (I, 639), this is precisely what he does when he supplies the essence of God by specifying for him an intention for which there is no evidence save the persuasiveness of its assertion.

Restoring and Recovering

Of course, Milton would not assent to this description of his labors, for although he acknowledges that he is performing them, he continues to speak as if they made no contribution whatsoever to the text they elaborate. He speaks, in short, as if the minimalist strategy of the antiprelatical tracts were still in force, as if his incredibly manipulative exertions were nothing more than a bit of light housecleaning: "I trust, through the help of that illuminating Spirit which hath favor'd me, to have done no every daies work: in asserting after many ages the words of Christ with other Scriptures of great concernment from burdensom and remorsles obscurity, tangl'd with manifold repugnances to their native lustre and consent between each other" (*Complete Prose Works*, II, 340). The sentence proceeds in alternate fits of self-assertion and self-effacement. The fact that Milton does work is qualified in advance when it is attributed to the Spirit. The fact that the work is assertive is qualified when the asserting is said to be an action that removes rather than adds. What he asserts is nothing of his own but "the words of Christ," and simply by doing this (that is, by doing very little) he rescues Christ's words from the encrustations left by interpreters less circumspect than he. The effect is double and simultaneous and is captured in the syntax of "asserting *from*," which must be read as "asserting *away* from": by performing the minimal action of allowing Christ to speak for himself, Milton (or so is his claim) undoes the presumptuous and "burdensom" actions of others, replacing their layers of "obscurity" with the "native lustre" of a self-declaring text.

But it is a text that is allowed to appear only after Milton has carefully established the conditions within which it will be read. Had Milton introduced the key verse from Matthew at the beginning, it would have been heard within the nonstrategic interpretive context assumed by his opponents. It has been his entire effort to dislodge that context, not so that the verse can be shown in its "native lustre" but so that he can establish another context in relation to which the meaning he desires the verse to have will seem inescapable. Here, thirty-six pages into a forty-eight-page tract, he is betting that the new context has, in fact, been established, and therefore he risks displaying "the sentence it self that now follows." "Having thus unfoulded those ambiguous reasons, wherewith Christ, as his wont was, gave to the Pharises that came to sound him, such an answer as they deserv'd, it will not be uneasie to explain the sentence it self that now follows: *Whosoever shall put away his wife, except it be fornication, and shall marry another, committeth adultery*" (329). But of course the "sentence it self" is no longer the sentence *itself* (it never was) but is now the sentence as it is (must be) given the assumptions (about Christ's nature, God's intentions, and the proper way to respond to Pharisees) that Milton has so laboriously put into place. If the sentence is now "clear," as Milton asserts it to be in the same paragraph ("It being thus clear, that the words of Christ can be no kind of command, as they are vulgarly tak'n" [331]), its clarity is not really its own, but is the effect and property of the commentary with which he has surrounded it.

The tension between Milton's repeated disavowal of any interpretive activity (he wants merely to clear away the interpretive debris of his predecessors) and the interpretive work he is so spectacularly doing can be read back into the tract's title:

THE DOCTRINE AND DISCIPLINE OF DIVORCE:
RESTOR'D TO THE GOOD OF BOTH SEXES
FROM THE BONDAGE OF CANON LAW, AND OTHER MISTAKES,
TO CHRISTIAN FREEDOM, GUIDED BY THE RULE OF CHARITY.
WHERIN ALSO MANY PLACES OF SCRIPTURE, HAVE RECOVER'D
THEIR LONG-LOST MEANING

Here the words "restor'd" and "recover'd" bear the double senses that will play themselves out in the argument. On the one hand, to restore something is to return it to an original state of self-identity ("native lustre"). On the other, it is to make good a loss (to re-store) by putting something in place of what once was; and in the same way, something that has been "recover'd" has either been returned to open and unobstructed view or dressed in new clothes, covered *again*. I am not claiming that these double meanings appear in the text by design. Rather than effects of Milton's intention, these ambiguities are signs of the extent to which he is the site of impulses and desires that pull against one another. Clearly he hopes to bring about a loosening of the constraints on divorce, and it is in the service of this project that he employs the very interpretive skills he had earlier condemned. At the same

245

time, however, he is reluctant to acknowledge (even to himself) the constitutive power of those skills; for if he were to do so, he would have to relinquish the independence of the text—and relinquish too his claim to be faithful to it and nothing more. He wants simultaneously to let the genie out of the bottle and to control it. He wants at once to displace textual authority and to claim it. He wants to put the force of interpretation into play and to arrest that play the moment it produces the configuration he desires.

That is why in a tract that repeatedly proclaims the necessity of interpretation—"there is scarce any one saying in the Gospel, but must be read with limitations and distinctions, to be rightly understood" (II, 338)—he repeatedly attempts to shut it down. He attempts to shut it down first by identifying a verse—"I will make him a help meet for him" (246; Genesis 2:18)—that is somehow exempt from the general rule and can be the basis of the plainness he denies to every other saying; later he attributes that same plainness to God's intention, although the plainness of that intention is belied by the exertions required to establish it; and in the last section of the tract, plainness—always invoked as a stay against interpretation's incursions—is said to reside in the "all-interpreting rule" of charity. The rule of charity (really a version of the argument from intention) tells us that God would not require more of his creatures than they are able to perform, and therefore he would not require that they remain joined to unsuitable partners. But the rule fails as a constraint on interpretation in the same way that intention fails; for the question of what charity means is, like the question of God's intention, an interpretive one. There is nothing to prevent Milton's opponents either from defining charity differently—so that, for example, it would be charitable of God to enforce strict divorce laws because he would thus provoke men to more virtue than they would otherwise achieve—or from declaring that the "rule of charity" should not be extended to the issue of divorce, because, Milton notwithstanding, it is within the capacities of fallen natures to make something valuable out of a less-than-perfect choice. In short, the "all-interpreting rule" of charity must itself be interpreted in order to be applied, and if it is interpreted once, then it can always be interpreted again.

It is these further turns of the interpretive screw that Milton seeks to preclude by doing, or claiming to have done, the interpretive job once and for all. When he declares that he has "done no every daies work . . . in asserting . . . the words of Christ," the suggestion is that the work is now complete and need never be supplemented; but the suggestion is undermined by his very success (if, for the sake of argument, we grant it to him). For if *he* has been able to "assert" Christ's words by embedding them in a constructed context of intelligibility (the context of Christ's relationship to the Pharisees), then someone who comes after him will be able (like those who came before him) to re-embed the same words (which, of course, are never the same) and assert them just as "plainly," but differently. When Milton declares that the "sincerity" and "true sense" of Christ's words have been recovered with the key of charity, he seems not to realize that once that key has opened the door, it can't be shut.

It is because he does not or cannot see this that *The Doctrine and Discipline of Divorce* is at once so like and so unlike *Of Prelaticall Episcopacy.* In the earlier tract interpretation is closed down even before the (non)argument begins; the Scriptures are not exposed even to anything so glancing as a look. In the later piece interpretation is supposedly licensed, but the license is withdrawn whenever it threatens the meanings Milton would privilege. The look the Scriptures receive is long and full, but it is finally a gorgon's look—freezing, or attempting to freeze, what it sees so that

247

no one will ever be able to see it in any other way. Like so many interpreters before and after him, Milton wants to crown his efforts by declaring—in opposition to the evidence provided by those efforts—that interpretation stops here.

Women, Interpretation, Difference

It may seem that in turning *The Doctrine and Discipline of Divorce* into a tract about interpretation, I have slighted what are after all its major and explicit concerns, marriage and sexuality; but in fact the problematics of sex and interpretation, far from being disparate, are, at least in the context of Milton's concerns, one and the same. When he warns us in *Of Prelaticall Episcopacy* against admitting external authorities into our hearts and minds lest "we open a broad passage for a multitude of Doctrines that have no ground in Scripture, to break in upon us" (I, 651), the language is the same as that with which he urges the divorcing of an "Idolatresse . . . lest she should alienate his heart from the true worship of God."[27] In both instances an internal purity must be maintained by pushing away the defiling touch of something alien and unholy. In one case it is the touch of an impiously supplementing interpretation, in the other the touch of an "enticing" woman who "allures [her husband] from the faith"; but finally this is a distinction without a difference, for, as Milton points out, the important thing is that in the end "God . . . looses him a servant." In both tracts the central image is of a vessel already informed by or "dedicate"[28] to God, a self-sufficient text on the one hand, a person "full of praise and thanksgiving" on the other, and in both the integrity of the vessel is threatened by a force that would first breach its boundaries and then scatter its contents, thereby robbing it of its potency. In *Of Prelaticall Episcopacy* that force is called "supplementing" or "adding," while in

The Doctrine and Discipline of Divorce it is called, simply, woman; structurally, "woman" and "interpretation" are one and the same, alike secondary to a purity that will be compromised if they are admitted into its holy place. Once commentary invades the fortress of Scripture and mixes with its substance, that substance is hopelessly adulterated; once the fortress of the "dedicate" soul opens itself up to female enticements, its manly vigor is dissipated and the firmness of its faith may be lost forever.

In making this equation between the dangers of interpretation and of pollution by women, Milton does nothing new; he merely avails himself of various strains in an established misogynist tradition, one that has already appropriated and marked the very texts on which his argument depends. Howard Bloch cites Philo Judaeus on the designation of woman as a helpmeet made *after* and in the service of man: "The helper is a created one, for it says 'Let us make a helper for him'; and . . . is subsequent to him who is to be helped, for He had formed the mind before and is about to form its helper."[29] "Thus," Bloch concludes, "woman, created from man, is conceived from the beginning to be secondary, a supplement," and as a supplement she must be kept in her place and not be allowed to substitute her own authority for the higher authority to which she is naturally subservient. This is of course exactly the vocabulary in which Milton declares the superfluousness and impiety of "additions" to the "pure, and living precept of *Gods* word" (I, 652). "What ever is *plastered* on is the devil's work," thunders Tertullian. "To superinduce on a divine work Satan's ingenuities, how criminal it is!"[30] Whether the divine work be the pure word or the heart of a man wholly (purely) bent on serving God, the imperative is the same: that which is essential and prior must keep itself separate from that which is secondary and supplementary, or risk the loss of its identity.

The extent to which this "Nazarite" way of thinking informs

Milton can be seen in the following passage from *The Reason of Church Government*. The subject is the "reverence" men should bear "to their own persons":

> And if the love of God as a fire sent from Heaven to be kept ever alive upon the altar of our hearts, be the first principle of all godly and vertuous actions in men, this pious and just honouring of ourselves is the second, and may be thought as the radical moisture and fountain head, whence every laudable and worthy enterprize issues forth. And although I have giv'n it the name of a liquid thing, yet it is not incontinent to bound it self as humid things are, but hath in it a most restraining and powerfull abstinence to start back, and glob it self upward from the mixture of any ungenerous and unbeseeming motion, or any soile wherewith it may peril to stain it self. (I, 841–842)

The "liquid thing" of which Milton admits to speaking metaphorically is in fact a quite literal reference to sperm, which he identifies in the second edition of *The Doctrine and Discipline of Divorce* as "the best substance of [man's] body, and of his soul too," a substance that one must not improvidently "pay out" (II, 271). The man who "starts back" from mixture and refuses to spend the "radical moisture" of his "fountain head" remains in a "filiall relation with God" (I, 842), while the man who gives himself up to an "unbeseeming motion"—either by leaving the Bible to "gadde after" supplements or by allowing a woman to "delay [his] duty to religion" (II, 262–263)—exchanges that relation for marriage to an inferior, either in the form of a commentary that comes after or of a creature who is "subsequent." In *Of Prelaticall Episcopacy* the sign of one's fidelity to God is a virgin text, one that has not been opened up (and therefore emptied) by interpretation. In *The Doctrine and Discipline of Divorce*, the sign of one's fidelity to God is a virgin marriage or the marriage of a virgin— of a man who keeps the proper distance from a helpmeet who must be prevented from breaking up the (male) union of a man and his Creator.[31]

In the conflicted economy of *The Doctrine and Discipline of Divorce,* the notion of a helpmeet occupies the same structural (and ambiguous) position as does the notion of interpretation: both are at once valorized and resisted. The admission that Scripture must indeed be "eek't out" by interpretation is precisely paralleled by the acknowledgment that man is radically incomplete and requires the supplement of a helpmeet; the introduction of interpretation as an activity *constitutive* of authority is accompanied by—is indeed the same thing as—the introduction of woman as a piecing-up of male imperfection. But while this notion of a "unity defective" that requires the remedy of "Collateral love" is embraced by Milton in *Paradise Lost* (VIII, 425–426), here in the divorce tracts he draws back from it by repeatedly subordinating the helpmeet to a masculine interiority that is no less a closed fortress than the text he is supposedly opening up. But of course he is *not* opening it up; or rather, having opened it up (with the "helpmeet" verse as his wedge), he moves to close it down again by claiming that all he has done is let the (still self-sufficient) text speak for itself. In both contexts—the context of interpretive theory and the context of marital politics—the promise of liberation (from "obstinate literality" and pharisaical rigidity, respectively) is not redeemed, as Milton moves, despite his pronouncements to the contrary, to reimpose the authority he was on the verge of decentering.

The result is an argument that is everywhere divided against itself (in a state, one might say, of divorce), always moving in a direction from which it is at the same time recoiling; moving toward interpretive freedom, yet reserving that freedom to itself, urging a generous (charitable) flexibility in marital relationships, yet reserving that flexibility for only one of the partners so that he can better preserve his status as a separate and inviolate being.

("If they . . . seduce us from the worship of God," we must respond with nothing "lesse then a totall and finall separation" [II, 263].) And always the interpretive and sexual issues are indissolubly entwined. Interpretive fecundity is finally refused for the same reason that the helpmeet must be prevented from helping too much: in order to keep the lines of authority firmly in place. Milton is no more willing to share the interpretive franchise than he is willing to share the government of a household; rigid boundaries—of interpretive procedure and marital relations—are denounced only until they can be reestablished in a new form of patriarchy; the claims of the (female) body are acknowledged only so that, after being satisfied, the (masculine) mind will once again be free to exercise its sway. Again and again, on every level (of structure, theme, imagery, argument) a self-sufficient and self-propagating male unity—of person and text—is defended against the encroachments of difference, woman, sexuality, interpretation, all forces that Milton has himself set in motion, but forces he feels compelled to deny when their subversive threat comes too close to home.

Who Can Think Submission?

It has become a commonplace to note these contradictions in the divorce tracts and to attribute them to Milton's "deeply masculinist assumptions."[32] It is said (by Mary Nyquist, James Turner, Stephen Fallon, and others)[33] that these assumptions war with Milton's more radical sympathies, and that, at least in the case of the divorce tracts, radical sympathies lose out. There is more than a little to be said for this view of the matter, but I find it limited by its origins in a criticism that offers us the dispiriting alternative of either chastising Milton for his bourgeois-capitalist sins or praising him for having foregrounded the tensions and fissures in an ideology from which he was unable to extricate himself.

252

David Aers and Bob Hodge are, I think, closer to the truth when they observe that despite his gestures in the direction of mutuality and the decentering of authority and power, Milton "still deeply feared and resisted the dissolution of the ego."[34] (Big surprise!) Aers and Hodge term this a paradox, but if it is one it is hardly attached to a particular ideology or set of assumptions, masculinist or any other. The question is a perennial one and it is posed by Belial when he asks, "Who would lose, / Though full of pain, this intellectual being, / Those thoughts that wander through Eternity, / To perish rather, swallow'd up and lost?" (PL, II, 146–149).

One answer is that Milton would, at least at those times when he expresses a desire to lose himself in a union with deity: to join a heavenly choir in which no single voice is heard and one's identity (exactly the wrong word) is relational, conferred by the community (of saints) that defines the shape of action; to march in a perfect cube, in a configuration that prevents any one person from standing out, from being i-identified, except as a component of a structure that gives him a being he cannot claim as his own. "I conceived my selfe," he declares in An Apology, "to be now not as mine own person, but as a member incorporate into that truth whereof I was perswaded" (I, 871). It is a conception to which Milton returns often, but this very formulation of it betrays the difficulty he can never remove: "conceiving" is itself an action of the consciousness that seeks its own absorption, and therefore to conceive oneself as a member incorporate is to have measured and thereby reinstituted one's distance from the state (of nonappearance) so conceived. Milton wants two contradictory things: he wants (in Aers and Hodge's words) to dissolve his ego, and he wants to be the one (the ego) that announces and performs the dissolving; he at once seeks and resists dissolution—or rather, *in* seeking it, he is also (and necessarily) resisting it. "For who can think Submission?" asks Satan (PL, I, 661), a question that is precise in its articulation of a requirement that cannot be met. One can think *about* submission all day long, but with every thought about submission, submission itself will once again have been deferred. It is not possible to affirm the diacritical nature of one's being without betraying that affirmation in the very act of producing it.

This is the dilemma to which Milton's entire career is a response, a dilemma that informs and structures his consideration of every issue he confronts. One sees it in the *Nativity Ode*, when the wish to "join his voice unto the Angel Choir" (27) and thereby "lose . . . this intellectual being" (*PL*, II, 146–147) is accompanied by the need to be the "first" (26) to do so—that is, to do so preeminently. One sees it in *Paradise Lost*, when the prospect of merging in an undifferentiated union with a God who shall be "All in All" (III, 341) turns into the horror of a uni-verse in which all distinctions will have been effaced and the landscape will be reduced to a "Universal blanc" (III, 48). And one sees it here, in *Of Prelaticall Episcopacy* and *The Doctrine and Discipline of Divorce*, when the scattering touch of interpretation and woman is at once courted and pushed away.

In saying this, my intention is not to slight the historical nature of Milton's concerns, but merely to point out that they come to him already structured by habits of thought that persist through every vicissitude of his literary and political life. Surely the divorce tracts are about divorce, and surely in the early 1640s the issue of divorce is intimately related to debates about domestic and political authority that will lead in a few years to the execution of a king. But if one is interested, as I am, in the source of the energy that makes Milton's writing (on every subject) so powerful, that source will be found not in the historical particulars to which he responds—and responds in a way wholly committed—but in the abiding (though not transcendental) obsessions of which his various and occasional responses are the transformations. This is not to suggest that Milton's work is everywhere the same, only that the differences (some of which have been noted here) between his productions can perhaps be best understood as differences in the ways in which he manages, or avoids, or makes capital of, the anxieties to which his self-divided ambition—to lose his voice and to celebrate that loss ("my advent'rous Song, / That with no middle flight intends to soar / Above th' *Aonian* Mount" [*PL,* I, 13–15])—makes him subject, or rather makes of him the kind of subject he is, forever split between the desire for absorption into deity and the desire to experience (and record) that desire as no one before him ever has.

CHAPTER SEVEN

Lycidas:
A Poem Finally Anonymous

The Swain Speaks

The tension that emerges at the end of the preceding chapter—
between the desire to lose oneself in a union with deity, and the
desire either to defer the moment of union or to master it by in-
tellectualizing it—is a feature of the poetry as early as the *Nativity
Ode*. In *Lycidas*, it is a master theme; and once it is steadily seen as
such, it provides a vantage point from which we can make a kind
of narrative sense of the poem's many and surprising twists and
turns.

Much of *Lycidas* criticism is an extended answer to those who,
in the tradition of Dr. Johnson, see the poem as an "irreverent
combination" of "trifling fictions" and "sacred truths," or as a lament marred by intrusive and unassimilated digressions, or, more
sympathetically, as "an accumulation of magnificent fragments,"[1]
or simply (and rather notoriously) as a production more "willful
and illegal in form" than any other of its time.[2] This last judg-

ment—it is John Crowe Ransom's in his famous essay "A Poem Nearly Anonymous"—indicates the extent to which the poem has been brought before the bar. The indictment has included, among others, the following charges: the tenses are inconsistent and frustrate any attempt to trace a psychological progression; there are frequent and unsettling changes in style and diction; the structure is uncertain, hesitating between monologue, dialogue, and something that is not quite either; the speaker assumes a bewildering succession of poses; the lines on Fame are poorly integrated; the procession of mourners is perfunctory; the Pilot's speech is overlong and overharsh; the flower passage is merely decorative; the Christian consolation (beginning "Weep no more, woeful Shepherds")[3] is unconvincing and insufficiently prepared for; the shift to the third person in the final lines is disconcerting and without any persuasive justification. Together and individually, these characterizations constitute a challenge to the poem's unity, and it is as an assertion of unity that the case for the defense is always presented.

Typically, that defense proceeds by first acknowledging and then domesticating the discontinuities that provoke it. Thus, William Madsen observes that the voice that says "Weep no more, woeful Shepherds" at line 165 does not sound at all like the voice we have been listening to; but no sooner does he note this breach in the poem's logic than he mends it by assigning the line and what follows to the angel Michael,[4] although he fails to explain, as Donald Friedman points out, why among all the speakers in *Lycidas,* Michael is the only one who "is introduced without comment or identification."[5] Friedman himself is concerned with another moment of disruption, occasioned by the voice of Phoebus, whose unexpected appearance as a speaker in the past tense blurs the narrative line and creates "confusion about the nature of the utterance we are listening to" (13). That confusion, however, is only "momentary," at least in Friedman's argument, where it is soon brought into a relationship with "the coda in which Milton subsumes the entire experience of the swain" (13). That coda, of course, brings its own problem; for, as Stewart Baker observes, the appearance of a third-person narrator after 185 lines constitutes a "surprise." But after acknowledging the surprise in the opening sentence of his essay, Baker proceeds to accommodate it, and by the time he finishes, it has been removed, along with Saint Peter's dread voice, as a possible threat "to the unity of the poem."[6] Defending the poem's unity is also the concern of H. V. Ogden, who writes in part to refute G. W. Knight's early characterization of *Lycidas* "as an effort to bind and clamp together a universe trying to fly off into separate bits."[7] Ogden cannot but acknowledge that the poem abounds in "abrupt turns in new directions," but these turns are explained or explained away by invoking the seventeenth-century principle of "aesthetic variety," and one can almost hear Ogden's sigh of relief as he declares triumphantly that "*Lycidas* is a disciplined interweaving of contrasting passages into a unified whole."[8]

Examples could be multiplied, but the pattern is clear: whatever *Lycidas* is, *Lycidas* criticism is "an effort to bind and clamp together a universe trying to fly off into separate bits." It is, in short, an effort to put the poem together, and the form that effort almost always takes is the putting together of an integrated and consistent first-person voice. Indeed, it is the assumption that the poem is a dramatic lyric and hence the expression of a unified consciousness that generates the pressure to discover a continuity in the narrative. The unity in relation to which the felt discontinuities must be brought into line is therefore a *psychological* unity; the drama whose coherence everyone is in the business of demonstrating is mental. In the history of the criticism, that coherence has been achieved by conceiving of the speaker as an actor in one of several possible biographical dramas: he may be remembering a past experience from a position of relative tranquillity (the position of the last eight lines); or he may be performing a literary exercise in the course of which he creates a naive persona (the uncouth swain); or he may be in the process of breaking out of the conventional limitations imposed on him by a tradition; or he may be passing from a pagan to a Christian understanding of the world and the possibilities it offers him. These readings are written in opposition to one another, but in fact they all share an assumption that is made explicit by John Henry Raleigh when he declares that *Lycidas* is "an existential poem. . . . It is about 'becoming,' the emergence of the ego to its full power."[9] Given this assumption, the poem can only be read as one in which the first-person speaker is a seventeenth-century anticipation of a Romantic hero.

The notorious exception to this way of dealing with *Lycidas* is John Crowe Ransom, who explains the discontinuities in the poem as evidence of a failure to *suppress* the ego, a failure to realize the proper poetic intention of remaining "always anonymous" (66). In Ransom's account, the "logical difficulties of the work" (80), the shifts in tense, the changes in tone, the interpolations of different speakers, the roughness of the verse, are the intrusive self-advertisements of a poet who cannot keep himself out of his poem, who is "willful and illegal" so that "nobody will make the mistake of not remarking his personality" (80). In general the Milton establishment has not been impressed by Ransom's argument, which is now viewed as something of a curiosity. In what follows, I will attempt to revive it, but with a difference. Ransom is right, I believe, to see that the shifts and disruptions in the poem reflect a tension between anonymity and personality; but I do not think, as he seems to, that the personality in the poem is triumphant because it is irrepressible. Indeed, it will be my contention that the suppressing of the personal voice is the poem's achievement, and that the energy of the poem derives not from the presence of a controlling and self-contained individual, but from forces that undermine his individuality and challenge the fiction of his control. If the poem records a struggle of personality against anonymity, it is a struggle the first-person speaker loses, and indeed the triumph of the poem occurs when his voice can no longer be heard.

That voice, when we first encounter it, is heard complaining about the task to which it has been called by "sad occasion" (6). The complaint is all the more bitter because it takes the form of an apology. "I am sorry to have to do this to you," the speaker says to the apostrophized berries, but what he is really sorry about is something that has been done to him. The double sense of the lines is nicely captured in the ambiguity of "forc'd" in line 4 ("And with forc'd fingers rude"), which can be read either as a characterization of his own action, or as an indictment of that which has made the action necessary (he is forced to do the forcing). In the same way, "rude" is at once a deprecation of his poetic skills and an expression of anger at having to exercise them prematurely: his fingers are rude because they have been forced to an unready performance. The pretense of an apology is continued through line 5, where it is once again undermined by the phrase "the mellowing year." Thomas Warton objected to an "inaccuracy" here, because "the 'mellowing year' could not affect the leaves of the laurel, the myrtle, and the ivy . . . characterized before as 'never sere.'"[10] Just so. The "inaccuracy" is there to call ironic and mocking attention to the inappropriateness of the apology: the laurel, the myrtle, and the ivy have no "mellowing year" to shatter; what has been shattered, in different ways, are the mellowing years of Lycidas and the speaker; and it is in response to the violence (interruption) done to them that these lines are spoken. By the time we reach line 7, it is impossible to read "disturb your season due" as anything but a bitter joke. It is the speaker's season that has been disturbed and by a disturbance (the death of Lycidas) even more final; and it is with the greatest reluctance that he is compelled to give voice to this "melodious tear" (14).

This posture of reluctance is one often assumed by Milton's characters, most notably by the Attendant Spirit in *Comus,* who is more than a little loath to leave the "Regions mild of calm and serene Air"[11] for the "smoke and stir of this dim spot, / Which men call Earth" (5–6). It is also the posture in which Milton likes to present himself in the prose tracts, so that typically he will declare with what small willingness he leaves the "still time" of his studies to engage in "tedious antiquities and disputes,"[12] or announce that only in response to the "earnest entreaties and serious conjurements" of a friend has he been "induc't" to break off pursuits "which cannot but be a great furtherance . . . to the enlargement of truth."[13] The labor to which he is called in these tracts is always an *interruption,* something that comes between him and a preferred activity, a discontinuity that threatens the completion of his real work.

This is especially true of *The Reason of Church Government* where his situation, as he characterizes it, exactly parallels that of the speaker in *Lycidas.* He writes, he tells us, "out of mine own season, when I have neither yet compleated to my minde the full circle of my private studies."[14] "I should not," he says, "chuse this manner of writing wherin knowing my self inferior to my self . . . I have the use . . . but of my left hand" (808). He would rather be "soaring in the high region of his fancies with his garland and singing robes about him," where, in response to the "inward prompting" of thoughts that have long "possest" him, he "might perhaps leave something so written to aftertimes, as they should not willingly let it die" (810). It is from those exalted "intentions" that he has been "pluckt" by the "abortive and foredated discovery" (820) of the present occasion ("sad occasion dear"), and he knows that the reader will understand how reluctant he is "to interrupt the pursuit of no lesse hopes than these . . . to imbark in a troubl'd sea of noises and hoars disputes, put from beholding the bright countenance of truth in the quiet and still air of delightful studies" (821–822). In *Lycidas,* the still and quiet air of studies is punctuated by the "Oaten Flute" and by the song beloved of "old *Damaetas*" (33, 36); but as in *The Reason of Church Government,* this is a lost tranquillity now recollected from the vantage point of a present turmoil, of a "heavy change" (37). In both contexts the change is the occasion for premature activity, for the hazarding of skills that are not yet ready in the performance of a task that is unwelcome.

There is one great difference however. The Milton of *The Reason of Church Government,* like the Attendant Spirit in *Comus,* is soon reconciled to that task because he is able to see it not as an interruption but as an extension of the activity from which he has been called away. He may be "put from beholding the bright countenance of truth," but it is as a witness to the same truth that he takes up the labor forced upon him by the moment. All acts performed in response to the will of God are equally virtuous, and "when God commands to take the trumpet and blow a dolorous or a jarring blast, it lies not in mans will what he shall say" (803). Indeed, "were it the meanest under-service, if God by his Secretary conscience injoyn it" (822), then it is impossible for a man to draw back. It is the same reasoning that leads him in *Of Education* to accede to the entreaties of Hartlib, for although the reforming of education is not the pursuit to which the love of God was taking him, he is able to see the present assignment as one "sent hither by some good providence" (363) and therefore as an opportunity to manifest that same love. In *An Apology,* he has decided, even before he descends to the disagreeable business of replying to slanders and calumnies, that it is his duty to do so, lest the truth and "the religious cause" which he had "in hand" be rendered "odious." "I conceav'd my self," he declares, "to be not now as mine own person, but as a member incorporate into that truth whereof I was perswaded."[15]

This conception of himself as "not . . . mine own person" is essential to his ability to see the disrupting activity as an instance or manifestation of the activity from which he has been *unwillingly* torn. That is, the disruption looms large only from the perspective of his personal desires—he would rather be writing poetry, or reading the classics, or furthering some long-term project—but from the vantage point of the truth whereof he is but a member incorporate, there is no disruption at all, simply a continuity of duty and service. It is here that the point of contrast with the speaker in *Lycidas* is most obvious: he takes everything *personally,* and as a consequence whatever happens is seen only as it relates to the hopes he has for his own career. This, of course, is the great discovery of twentieth-century criticism— that in *Lycidas* Milton is "primarily taking account of the meaning of the experience to himself";[16] but for Milton to be *primarily* doing this is for him to be doing something very different from what he does in the prose tracts, where egocentric meanings are rejected as soon as they are identified. That is, the stance of the speaker in *Lycidas* is anomalous in the Milton canon; for rather than relinquishing the conception of himself as "his own person," he insists on it, and by insisting on it he resists incorporation into a body of which he is but an extending member.

Indeed, insofar as the poem can be said to have a plot, it consists of the speaker's efforts to resist assimilation. He does this in part by maintaining an ironic distance from the conventions he proceeds to invoke. As we have seen, that irony is compounded largely of bitterness, and it takes the form both of questioning the adequacy of the conventions to the occasion, and of claiming a knowledge superior to any the conventions are able to offer. Irony is itself a mode of superiority: the ironic voice always issues from a perspective of privilege and presents itself as having penetrated to meanings that have been missed by the naive and the innocent. The ironic voice, in short, always knows *more*.

In this case it knows more than the traditions of consolation; it knows that they are fictions, false surmises. The method in the opening sections is to let these fictions have their say, only so that the speaker can enter to expose their shallowness. "He must not float upon his wat'ry bier" (*Lycidas*, 12) seems, as we read it, to be the sentiment of someone who believes that there is something to be done, but this belief is dismissed and mocked by the first word of line 13, "Unwept." He will, in fact, continue to float on his watery bier, and the only thing that will be done is what the speaker is doing now—producing laments in the form of "some melodious tear" (14). This characterization of his own activity is slighting, but it does not mean that he is assuming a stance of modesty or self-deprecation; the criticism extends only to the means or tools, and not to the workman who finds them inadequate. It is their failure and not his that is culpable; and indeed, his recognition, even before he employs them, that they will not do the job validates the superiority of his perception.

Even when the pastoral conventions are invoked, they are invoked in such a way as to call into question their capacities. The elegy proper begins with an echo of Virgil's messianic eclogue: "Begin . . . and somewhat loudly sweep the string" (15, 17). That eclogue, however, specifically promises to transcend the genre, and therefore to invoke it is already to assume the insufficiency of the tradition in the very act of rehearsing its tropes. One of those tropes is the recollection of past delights, and it is given an extended, even lingering evocation in lines 25–36 (the lines to which Dr. Johnson so objected); but even as we listen, in the place of "old *Damaetas*," to this song, we are aware, with Douglas Bush, that it is "a picture of pastoral innocence, of carefree youth unconscious of the fact of death."[17] We therefore hear it with *con-*

descension and with an expectation that it will be succeeded by a perspective less naive. As a result, when the speaker breaks in with "But O the heavy change" (*Lycidas*, 37), the tone may be elegiac but the gesture is a triumphant one, made by someone who is able to present himself as "sadder, but wiser." What he is wiser than is the pastoral mode and all of the ways by which it attempts to render comfortable what is so obviously distressing. One of those ways is the doctrine of natural sympathy, which would tell us that in response to the death of Lycidas, "The Willows and the Hazel Copses green / Shall now no more be seen" (42–43); but that assertion is allowed to survive only for the moment, before the succeeding line at once completes the syntax and, in an ironic reversal, changes the meaning: "Shall now no more be seen, / Fanning their joyous Leaves to thy soft lays." The willows and the hazel copses green will in fact be seen, but they will be seen fanning their joyous leaves to someone else's soft lays, for it is Lycidas who will be "no more." This new meaning does not simply displace but mocks the old: "How foolish of any one to believe that nature takes notice of the misfortunes of man." Obviously, the speaker is not such a one, and, as always, the superimposition of his perspective on the perspective of the convention has the effect of establishing him in a removed and superior position. He maintains this position even when he appears to be turning on himself. "Ay me, I fondly dream" (56) has the form of a self-rebuke, but the fondness is displaced onto the tradition and its representative figures—the nymphs, the bards, the druids, the Muses, Orpheus, and even Universal Nature. It is their ineffectiveness that has led the speaker to break off his performance and to exclaim, "For what could that have done? / What could the Muse herself that *Orpheus* bore . . . ?" (57–58). What *he* can do, and very effectively, is to see and say just that and so disassociate himself from the failures he continues to expose.

I am aware that in other accounts of the poem this questioning of pastoral efficacy has received another reading, and is seen not as evidence of egocentricity but as a kind of heroism. B. A. Rajan, for example, reads the poem as the anguished discovery by the first-person voice that ritual and tradition are inadequate when confronted by the "assault of reality."[18] The poem is thus an attack on "its own assumptions" (56), an attack that is "mounted by the higher mood against the pastoral form" (54). In the struggle that ensues, "convention and elementality are the basic forces of contention" (54), and for "elementality" we may read the personal voice, characterized by Rajan, as the "cry out of the heart of experience" (62). His argument is more finely tuned than Raleigh's, but its point is the same: *Lycidas* is about becoming, the emergence of the ego to its full power; or in Rajan's more guarded vocabulary, "it is a voyage toward recognition" (63), a recognition that is won to some extent at the expense of the claims to adequacy of pastoral and other ritual or public forms.

For Rajan, then, the contest between the conventional and the real or personal is the story the poem tells; what I am suggesting is that it is a story the *speaker* tells, and that he tells it in an effort to situate himself in a place not already occupied by public and conventional meanings. It is less "a cry out of the heart of experience" than a *strategy*, a strategy designed to privilege experience, and especially *individual* experience, in relation to the impersonality of public and institutional structures. That is why the efficacy of the pastoral is called into question: so that the efficacy of the speaker, as someone who stands apart from conventions and is in a position to evaluate them, can be that much more firmly established. In other words, the characterization of the pastoral is deliberately low and feeble in order to display to advantage the authority and prescience of the speaker when he pronounces in his own voice, as he does at line 64: "Alas! What boots it with uncessant care . . . " Here, and in the lines that follow, the speaker is at the height of his powers, in the sense that he seems to have earned the questions he hurls at the world, questions whose force is in direct proportion to the claim (silently but effectively made) to sincerity. Here is no mediated pastoral voice, heard through a screen of tradition and ritual; here is the thing itself, the expression of a distinctive perspective on a problem that many have considered ("Yet once more" [1]), but never with such poignancy and perceptiveness. It is precisely what Rajan says it is, a cry out of the heart of experience, a cry which emerges from the wreckage of failed conventions to pose the ultimate question: In a world like this, what does one do?

The Swain Is Silenced

It is all the more startling, then, when that cry is interrupted by the voice of Apollo, a moment characterized by Ransom as "an incredible interpolation" and "a breach in the logic of composition." These are strong words, but they are in response to a very strong effect given the extent to which the speaker has, to this point, asserted his control over the poem and its progression. Here the control is taken from him in so complete a way that we as readers do not even know when it happens. The identification of Apollo's voice occurs at the beginning of line 77 (*"Phoebus* repli'd"), but the identification is after the fact, with the result that there is no way of determining who has been speaking. Many editors add punctuation so as to make it "clear" that Phoebus enters with "But not the praise" (76); yet as we read Milton's unpunctuated text, "But not the praise" seems to be part of a dialogue the first-person voice is having with himself on the nature of Fame and its relationship to effort ("uncessant care" [64]). The correction supplied by *"Phoebus* repli'd" does not result in a simple reassignment of the half-line, but blurs, retroactively, the assignment of the lines preceding. When does Phoebus begin to speak? Is this his first reply or has he begun to respond to the first-person complaint at line 70: *"Fame* is the spur"? The first person would then return in line 73—"But the fair Guerdon when we hope to find"—and *then* Phoebus would be heard to reply "But not the praise." My point is not to argue for this particular redistribution of the lines, but to demonstrate that it is possible; and because it is just one among other possibilities, and because the matter cannot be settled once and for all, the question of just who is in charge of the poem becomes a real one.

This is not the only question raised by Apollo's intervention. Because "repli'd" is in the past tense, what had presented itself as speech erupting in the present is suddenly revealed to be recollected or reported speech. As Ransom observes, "dramatic monologue has turned . . . into narrative" (79); and the result, in Friedman's words, is "a momentary confusion about the nature of the utterance we are listening to."[19] The confusion not only is generic (monologue or narrative), but extends to the kind of hearing we are to give to that utterance, for "if the memory of Phoebus' words is reported by the swain as part of the elegy, then what has happened to the pretense of spontaneity and present creation?" Friedman's question contains its own answer (although it is not the one he eventually gives): it is here that the spontaneity begins to be exposed precisely as a pretense, as a claim elaborately made by the speaker from his very first words: "Yet once more." Although these words acknowledge convention (by acknowledging that this has been done before), they are themselves unconventional, because they are not produced within the frame or stage setting that traditionally encloses the pastoral lament. From Theocritus to Spenser, elegiac song is introduced into a situation that proclaims its status as artifice, as a piece of currency in a social exchange (song for bowl), or as a performance offered in competition. In *Lycidas,* however, the frame is omitted, and what we hear, or are encouraged to hear, is an unpremeditated outpouring of grief and anger. When Apollo's reply is reported in the past tense, the pastoral frame is introduced retroactively, and the suggestion is that it has been there all the while. Immediately the spontaneity of the preceding lines is compromised, and compromised too are the claims of the speaker to independence. At the very moment he dismisses the pastoral, he is revealed to be a narrated pastoral figure, no longer the teller of his tale but told by it—identified and made intelligible, as it were, by the very tradition he scorns. Moreover, he is identified in such a way as to call into question his identity. When Apollo plucks his trembling ear, he repeats an action already performed in response to another poet who also has dreams of transcending the pastoral conventions: "When I tried a song of kings and battles, Phoebus / Plucked my ear and warned, 'A shepherd, Tityrus, / Should feed fat sheep, recite a fine-spun song.'"[20] Apollo, in short, puts Virgil in his place, and by doing so establishes a place (or commonplace) that is now occupied by the present speaker. That is, the desire of the poet to rise above the pastoral is itself a pastoral convention, and when the speaker of *Lycidas* gives voice to that desire, he succeeds only in demonstrating the extent to which his thoughts and actions are already inscribed in the tradition from which he would be separate. Not only are his ambitions checked by Apollo,[21] but they are not *his* ambitions, insofar as he is only playing out the role assigned him in a drama not of his making.

It is not too much to say, then, that the intervention of Apollo changes everything: the speaker loses control of his poem when another voice simply dislodges him from center stage (where he had been performing in splendid isolation), and, at the same time, the integrity of his own voice is compromised when this voice becomes indistinguishable from its Virgilian predecessor.

Apollo poses a threat to the speaker not only as a maker, as someone who is in the act of building the lofty rhyme, but as a self-contained consciousness, as a mind that is fully present to itself and responsible for its own perceptions. The speaker meets this twin threat by rewriting, or misreading, what has happened to him in such a way as to reinstate, at least for the moment, the fiction of his independence:

> O Fountain *Arethuse,* and thou honor'd flood,
> Smooth-sliding *Mincius;* crown'd with vocal reeds,
> That strain I heard was of a higher mood:
> But now my Oat proceeds . . . *(Lycidas,* 85–88)

The picture in these lines is of someone who has paused to listen, no doubt politely, to the opinion of another before proceeding resolutely on *his* way (the strong claim is in the *my* of "my Oat"). There is no acknowledgment at all of the violence of Apollo's entrance, of his brusque and dismissive challenge to the speaker's sentiments, of the peremptory and unceremonious manner in which he seizes the floor. Moreover, the action Apollo performs is misrepresented when it is reported as an action *against* the pastoral ("That strain . . . was of a higher mood"). In fact, it is an action against the speaker—a rebuke, as Mary Christopher Pecheux observes, to his "rebellious questioning."[22] If Apollo's words are higher, they are higher than the speaker's own; rather than supporting his denigration of the pastoral, they are precisely pastoral words, and mark the moment when the tradition interrupts the "bold discourse"[23] of one who scorns it and exposes the illusion of his control.

It is in order to maintain the illusion that the speaker sets Apollo against the pastoral, for he can then present himself as the judge of their respective assertions. But no sooner has he reclaimed the central and directing role ("But now my Oat proceeds") than it is once again taken from him: "But now my Oat proceeds, / And listens to the Herald of the Sea / That came in *Neptune's* plea" (88–90). Suddenly the voices competing for attention, and for the position of authority, multiply and become difficult to distinguish. Triton comes, but he comes in Neptune's plea, and therefore when we read of someone who "ask'd" the waves and felon winds (91) it is not clear whether that someone is Triton or Neptune, nor when it is that whoever it is speaks (it could be that Triton reports the investigative queries of Neptune—he "ask'd"—or that Triton *now* asks in the present of the narrative, but is reported as having done so in the present of the narrator, i.e., the voice that tells us Phoebus "repli'd"). The one thing that *is* clear is that the questioner is not the speaker, who is now reduced to the role of a listener while someone else conducts the investigation. Again, this someone else could be Triton or Neptune or the yet unknown third-person voice of whose existence we have had only hints; or, after line 96, it could be the "sage *Hippotades*" who brings someone's (it seems to be everyone's) unsatisfactory answers. By the time we reach the most unsatisfactory answer of all—"It was that fatal and perfidious Bark" (100)—there is absolutely no way of determining who delivers it. A poem that began as the focused utterance of a distinctive personal voice is by this point so diffused that it is spoken, quite literally, by everybody.

Not only is the original speaker now indistinguishable from a chorus, but he is not even the object of direct address, as he was when he listened to Apollo. Whoever it is that indicts the fatal and perfidious bark, he directs his remarks to Lycidas: "That sunk so low that sacred head of *thine*" (102; emphasis added). Moreover, the indictment and the entire investigation are once again proceeding in a narrated past. The fading of the speaker from the scene of his own poem coincides with the almost imperceptible

271

slide into the past tense, and both movements are complete when we hear (we have displaced the speaker, who is no longer even a prominent listener) that "Last came, and last did go / The Pilot of the *Galilean* lake" (108–109).

It would seem that with this figure the poem is once again dominated by a single controlling presence, but his identity (in two senses) is perhaps not so firm as we have been taught to think. Taking up a suggestion first made by R. E. Hone, Mary Pecheux has argued persuasively that the Pilot of the Galilean lake (who significantly is not named) is not Peter but a composite of Peter, Moses, and Christ. The speech thus dramatizes Milton's assertion in the *Christian Doctrine* that revelation was disclosed in various ages by Christ even though he was not always known under that name: "Under the name of Christ are also comprehended Moses and the Prophets, who were his forerunners, and the Apostles whom he sent."[24] This splitting of the "dread voice" has the advantage, as Pecheux points out, of being "consonant with the extraordinary richness and ambivalence" of the poem, with the sense one has "of having heard a multitude of overtones difficult to disentangle one from the other" (239). Again, the details of her argument are less important than the fact that it can be made, for this means that the question is an open one and that the Pilot's speech too proceeds from a source that is not *uniquely* identified.

That speech is also addressed to Lycidas ("How well could I have spar'd for thee, young swain" [113]), and its "stern" (112) message further shifts attention away from the first-person voice by replacing his very personal concerns with the concerns of the church as a whole. That is, the complaint one hears in these lines is quite different from the complaint that precedes Apollo's interruption: it is not an answer to the speaker's questions ("What boots it . . ." [64]) but a "higher" questioning in which the ambitions of any one shepherd or singer are absorbed into a more universal urgency, as rot and "foul contagion" spread (127). The focus of the Pilot's words is continually expanding, until it opens in the end on a perspective so wide that all of our attempts to name it are at once accurate and hopelessly inadequate. Whatever the two-handed engine is—and we shall never know—the action for which it stands ready will not be in response to any cry out of the heart of experience, and in this moment of apocalyptic prophecy the private lament that was, for a time, the poem's occasion is so much transcended that one can scarcely recall it.

This movement away from the personal is a structural component of Milton's work from the very beginning. It is seen as early as the *Nativity Ode,* where the poet begins by desiring to be first, to stand out ("Have thou the honor first, thy Lord to greet" [26]) and ends by being indistinguishable from the others (animals, angels, shepherds) who "all about the Courtly Stable, / . . . sit in order serviceable."[25] The glory he had hoped to win by being first is won when, in a sense, he no longer is, and is able to pronounce the glorious death of his own poetic ambitions ("Time is our tedious Song should here have ending" [239]). While the career of the speaker in *Lycidas* is parallel, it is also different because he does not relinquish his position voluntarily. He holds tenaciously to his own song and must be forcibly removed from the poem by voices that preempt him or displace him or simply ignore him, until at the end of the Pilot's speech he seems to have disappeared.

Indeed, so long has it been since he was last on stage (line 90) that when he suddenly pops up again he seems an interpolation more incredible than Apollo. He seems, in fact, a digression, a departure from what we have come to recognize as the poem's true concerns; and as a digression his gesture of reassertion is, in every sense, reactionary:

273

> Return *Alpheus,* the dread voice is past
> That shrunk thy streams; Return *Sicilian* Muse,
> And call the Vales, and bid them hither cast
> Their Bells and Flowrets of a thousand hues. (*Lycidas,* 132–135)

Once again the return of the speaker is marked by a rewriting that is a misrepresentation. He acts as if all had been proceeding under his direction, as if the voices in the poem require his permission to come and go—a permission he now extends to the pastoral, which is characterized as if it were a child that had been frightened by the sound of an adult voice. His strategy is two-pronged and it is familiar. He opposes the pastoral to the speech of the Galilean Pilot (as he had earlier opposed it to Apollo) and thus denies it the responsibility for documenting ecclesiastical abuses, a responsibility it was given in the Scriptures. In effect, it is he, not the Pilot, who shrinks, or attempts to shrink, the pastoral stream, and he does it, characteristically, in a denial of the extent to which his own stream has been shrunk in the course of the poem. It is a classic form of displacement in which he attempts, for the last time, to project a story in which he is a compelling and powerful figure.

It is as part of that story that he calls the role of flowers, a gesture intended not so much "to interpose a little ease" (152) but to set the stage for still another assertion of pastoral inadequacy: "Let our frail thoughts dally with false surmise" (153). As before, what is presented as self-deprecation is an act of self-promotion. The "frail thoughts" are detached from the speaker—he merely dallies with them—and identified with the failure of the convention; if, in some sense, he can do no better, at least he is able to recognize a false surmise when he sees one, and that ability in itself is evidence of a vision that is superior even if it is (realistically) dark: "Ay me! Whilst thee the shores and sounding Seas / Wash far away, where'er thy bones are hurl'd" (154–155). This is, of course, exactly what he has said before, when he breaks off his address to the nymphs to exclaim, "Ay me, I fondly dream" (56), and again, when his rehearsal of Orpheus' death (he also was hurled by shores and sounding seas) is followed by a bitter question: "Alas! What boots it with uncessant care?" (64). What is remarkable about the speaker is how little he is affected by those sections of the poem that unfold between his intermittent appearances. Higher moods and dread voices may come and go, but when he manages to regain the stage, it is to sing the same old song: Ay me, alas, what am I to do? What's the use? It's all so unfair. As the poem widens its perspective to include ever larger considerations (eternal fame, the fate of the church, the condition of the Christian community, the Last Judgment), the speaker remains within the perspective of his personal disappointment, remains very much "his own person," and therefore he becomes, as I have said, a digression in (what began as) his own poem. While he has been busily exposing the false surmises of pastoral consolation, the poem has been even more insistently exposing the surmise that enables him (or so he thinks) to do so—the surmise that his vision is both inclusive and conclusive, that he sees what there is to see and knows what there is to know.

What he sees is that there is no laureate hearse (only the "wat'ry bier" he saw at line 12), and what he knows is that there is neither justice nor meaning in the world. He seems to have heard in the Pilot's speech none of the resonances that have been reported by so many readers. His words remain determinedly bleak, and therefore they are all the more discontinuous with the call that is sounded at line 165: "Weep no more, woeful Shepherds, weep no more, / For *Lycidas* your sorrow is not dead." These are entirely new accents spoken by an entirely new voice. It is a voice that counsels rather than complains, that turns outward rather than inward, a voice whose confident affirmation of a universal benevolence could not be further from the dark and self-pitying questioning of the swain. Everything, in short, has been changed, and it has changed not even in a line but in the space between lines. It is at this point that the orthodox reading of the poem, in which "the troubled thought of the elegist" traces out a sequence of "rise, evolution, and resolution," founders.[26] There is no evolution here, simply a disjunction, a gap, and the seekers of unity are left with the problem of explaining it. In general, their explanations have taken one of two forms. Either the change is explained theologically as a "leap from nature to revelation"[27] and a "dramatization of the infusion of grace,"[28] or it is explained away by assigning the lines to another speaker. This is the solution of William Madsen, who notes the abrupt transition from the "plaintive" and "ineffectual" to the authoritative, and concludes that the consolation is spoken not by the swain but by Michael, who responds in a fuller measure than might have been expected to the speaker's appeal ("Look homeward Angel now, and melt with ruth" [*Lycidas*, 163]). Madsen offers his emendation as an alternative to the theological reading; but in fact there is very little difference between them, since in either reading this point marks the appearance in the poem of "a new voice." For Madsen that voice is Michael's; for Abrams and Friedman (among others) it is the voice of a regenerated (made new) swain. In either case, there is agreement that the voice we had been hearing is heard no more and that what takes its place is something wholly different. This is of course not the first time this has happened, and it is only because in Madsen's reading the event is unusual that he feels moved to assign the new voice a specific name (it is this assignment that has been objected to). In the reading that has been developed here, however, the appearance of new voices and the merging of old is occurring all the time; the speaker is repeatedly dislodged or overwhelmed or absorbed, and his disappearance at line 164 is just one in a series.

There is, however, a difference. This disappearance is the last; the speaker is never heard from again. Or if he is heard from again, it is not as his "own person" but as a "member incorporate" of a truth from which he is now indistinguishable. That is to say, Madsen is right to hear the voice as different, but he is wrong to hear it as anyone's in particular. The accents here, as Marjorie Nicolson long ago observed, are "choral" as "all voices combine in virtuous crescendo."[29] If the speaker is among them, he is literally unrecognizable, since what allowed him to stand out was the "dogged insistence"[30] with which he held on to the local perspective of his own ambitions. In the end he is not even distinguishable as an addressee: the choral voice responds not to one but to a mass of complaints; the consolation is for "woeful Shepherds," and the plural noun silently denies the speaker even the claim to have been uniquely grieving; the grief is as general as the consolation, and it simply doesn't leave room for anything personal. The distance that has been traveled is the distance from the melodious tear of line 14 to the "unexpressive nuptial Song" of line 176. The tear falls from a single eye; it is the poem as the product of one voice that demands to be heard, if only as an expression of inconsolability; but the nuptial song is produced by everyone and therefore *heard* by no one, in the sense that there is no one who is at a sufficient distance from it for there to be a question of hearing. That is why it is called "unexpressive," which means both inexpressible (can't be said) and inaudible (it can't be apprehended): both speaking and receiving assume a separation between communicating agents; but this song is not a communication at all—it is a testimony to a joy which, since it binds all, need not be transmitted to any. The mistake of the first-person voice has been his desire to speak, to proclaim from an analytic and judgmental distance a truth he only sees; but in the great vision of these soaring lines, the truth proclaims, because it

fills, its speakers, who are therefore not speakers at all but witnesses. They are in the happy condition for which Milton prays at
the end of "At a Solemn Music":

> O may we soon again renew that Song,
> And keep in tune with Heav'n, till God ere long
> To his celestial consort us unite,
> To live with him, and sing in endless morn of light. (25–28)

The wish that we may join that choir is the wish that we *not* be
heard as a distinctive and therefore alienated voice, the wish that
we might utter sounds in such a way as to remain silent (unexpressive). It is a wish that is here granted the would-be elegist,
whether he wants it or not, as finally he is no longer his own person but a member incorporate into that truth whereof he has
been persuaded.

I am aware that this might seem a backdoor way into the
usual reading of *Lycidas;* for just like any other critic, I have gotten the swain into heaven or at least into a position where a heavenly vision is available to him. But if he is now one of those who
sing and singing in their glory move, he could not be picked out
from among the other members of troops and societies, and
therefore his "triumph," if one can call it that, is not achieved in
terms that he would understand or welcome. As Friedman remarks, the speaker "fights *against* the knowledge" offered by the
poem's higher moods; his experience is "one of active struggle"
(5). My point is that it is a struggle he loses, and that the poem
achieves its victory first by preempting him and finally by silencing him. Rather than the three-part structure traditionally proposed for *Lycidas,* I am proposing a structure of two parts: a first
part (lines 1 through 75.5) where the first-person voice proceeds
under the illusion of independence and control, and a second,
longer part where that illusion is repeatedly exposed and finally
dispelled altogether. In place of an interior lyric punctuated by di-

gressive interpolations, we have a poem that begins in digression—the first-person voice is the digression—and regains the main path only when the lyric note is no longer sounded. We have, in short, a poem that relentlessly denies the privilege of the speaking subject, of the unitary and separate consciousness, and is finally, and triumphantly, anonymous.

It is anonymous twice. The last eight lines of *Lycidas* have always been perceived as problematic, because they insist on a narrative frame that was not apparent in the beginning, because the frame or coda is spoken by an unidentified third-person voice, and because that voice is so firmly impersonal. One advantage of the reading offered here is that these are not problems at all: if the introduction of a narrative perspective suggests that everything presented as spontaneous was in fact already spoken, this is no more than a confirmation of what has long since become obvious; if the new voice is unidentified, it is only the last in a series of unidentified voices or of voices whose single identities have long since been lost or blurred; and if the unidentified voice is impersonal it is merely a continuation of the mode the poem has finally achieved. In fact, the crucial thing about these lines is that there is no one to whom they can be plausibly assigned. They are certainly not the swain's, for he is what they describe, and they describe him significantly as someone who is "uncouth"—that is, unknown, someone who departs the poem with less of an identity than he displayed at its beginning; nor is there any compelling reason to assign them to any of the previous speakers, to the Pilot, or Hippotades, or Triton, or Neptune, or Cambridge, or Apollo. The only recourse, and it is one that has appealed to many, is to assign the lines to Milton; but of all the possibilities, this is the least persuasive. No voice in English poetry is more distinctive than Milton's, so much so that the characters he creates almost always sound just like him. But these lines do not sound like anyone; they are perfectly—that is, unrelievedly—conventional, and as such they are the perfect conclusion to a poem from which the personal has been systematically eliminated. Indeed, if these lines were written in accents characteristically Miltonic, they would constitute a claim exactly like that which is denied to the poem's first speaker: the claim to be able to pronounce, to sum up, to say it conclusively and once and for all. Instead Milton gives over the conclusion of the poem to a collection of pastoral commonplaces which are not even structured into a summary statement, but simply follow one another in a series that is unconstrained by any strong syntactic pressures. (The lines are markedly paratactic and conform to what Thomas Rosenmeyer has called the "disconnective decorum" of the pure pastoral.)[31] In short, Milton silences himself, just as the first-person voice is silenced, and performs (if that is the word) an act of humility comparable to that which allows him to call his *Nativity Ode* "tedious" at the very moment its intended recipient falls asleep. Rosemond Tuve once observed that in Herbert's career we can see a life-long effort to achieve the "immolation of the individual will." This has not usually been thought to be Milton's project, but the determined anonymity of *Lycidas* should remind us that the poet's fierce egoism is but one-half of his story.

CHAPTER EIGHT

With Mortal Voice:
Milton Defends against the Muse

There she was, for centuries, the big
broad with the luscious tits, the secret
smile, a toga of translucent silk, cool
hand on the shoulder of the suffering
poet—the tease who made him
squeeze those great words out. He
was the mirror and the lamp, she the torah
who burned with the blue butane of a pure
refusal, too good for mortal use, her breath
was cold as mountain streams, the chill
of the eternal—no hint of plaque
or any odor of decay. Ethereal as hell,
a spirit in chiffon, the mystery is
how she had got so rounded in the butt
and all her better parts as soft as butter,
why such a wraith should be so ample,
what her endowments had to do
with that for which she set example—
all this was surely Mystery, oh that elusive
object of desire, that "untouch'd bride
of quietness," that plump poetic dish
who lived on air but looked
as if she dined on pasta.

—ELEANOR WILNER, "The Muse"

Celestial Song

If the first-person voice of *Lycidas* struggles (unsuccessfully) to establish an identity independent of the tradition that claims him, the first-person voice of *Paradise Lost* engages with an even more powerful and relentless master agency: the agency of his muse. When Milton invokes his muse at the beginning of book VII of *Paradise Lost*, he does so with a hesitation that does not resolve itself in the following lines. The hesitation concerns the rightness of the name by which the muse is called: "Descend from Heav'n *Urania*, by that name / If rightly thou art call'd, whose Voice divine / Following, above th' *Olympian* Hill I soar."[1] These lines deliberately recall two earlier invocations—that of book I, in which the poet announces his intention "with no middle flight . . . to soar / Above th' *Aonian* Mount" (14–15), and that of book III, in which he rejoices at having "Escap't the *Stygian* Pool . . . while in my flight / Through utter and through middle darkness borne / With other notes than to th' *Orphean* Lyre / I sung of *Chaos* and *Eternal Night*" (14–18). All three invocations are addressed to the same person (?), and all three worry either the identity or the location of the addressee. Does the muse sit on the "secret top" (I, 6) of Oreb (in which case we still wouldn't be able to locate it, since the mount is secret), or on Sinai? Is the muse coexistent with "Light, offspring of Heav'n first born" (III, 1), or "hear'st thou rather pure Ethereal stream / Whose Fountain who shall tell" (7–8)? In these first two invocations, the question of the muse's gender is carefully avoided (although the phrase "Thou O Spirit" at I, 17, seems a reference to one of the persons of the Trinity and to the masculine noun for spirit, *animus; lumens,* "light," is neuter), but in the third the name given is unambiguously female. No sooner is it given, however, than it is qualified and even repudiated. I call, the poet says, not the name but the meaning; yet he doesn't tell us what the meaning is, except negatively: "for thou / Nor of the Muses nine, nor on the top / Of old *Olympus* dwell'st, but Heav'nly born" (VII, 5–7). That is, you are not one of those women, nor were you born of women, since "Heav'nly born" means precisely born of Heaven, of the Father, generated directly by him as were the Son and the Holy Spirit. Gender is admitted once again when the muse is said to converse "with Eternal Wisdom . . . / Wisdom thy Sister" (9–10), but the marking of Wisdom as female (and here Milton, as many have noted, follows Proverbs 8), tells us nothing about the muse who plays with Wisdom its sister but is not (or at least is not said to be) Wisdom's sister in turn. All we know is that both play "In presence of th' Almighty Father," who is "pleas'd / With thy Celestial Song" (11–12).

The introduction of the Almighty Father does not so much dispel the uncertainties of gender and person as render them less urgent; for the Father, precisely because he is almighty, grounds and centers a play that is anything but free, a play circumscribed by his "presence," by the fact of his unique status as the creator, as the *first,* derivative of nothing. The precedence of the Father, with respect to his creatures, is mimed in the verse when his presence counters the adverb that introduces them: "Before" (8). For a moment it seems that the adverb is truly theirs, that they exist before (prior to) anything; but then they are revealed to be "before" in another, lesser sense: they play before—on the stage of, in the prior sight of—the Father. No wonder he is pleased with the muse's celestial song; the song is his in the sense that its singers define themselves in relation to his generative and authorizing power—he is present, they are derivative— and therefore whatever their song, its content will be an acknowledgment and celebration of that same power: they please him because the desire to please him is constitutive of their very being.

None of this is said directly—all we have is the phrase "Celes-

tial Song"; but the phrase is enough in any of its several meanings: the most perfect, the song above all others. As a word indicating the matter of the song, "Celestial" tells us that its single
subject is the heavens, the realm of deity; and in its most literal
sense, "Celestial" names the instrument or medium of the song:
the heavens *produce* the song; its movements *are* the song. I call
this meaning "literal" because the putative singer of the song is
Urania, the muse of astronomy, and I refer to her as the "putative" singer because she is not the originating agent of the song
but a figure (in several senses) for its true agency, the machinery
of the heavens, or, in the more familiar designation, the music of
the spheres. It is this music, the operating sound of the universe
he everywhere informs (that is, after all, what "universe" means),
that pleases God; he is listening to his work or to his own works
working, as everything that issues from him (and, in the context
of Milton's materialist monism, the category of "issuing from
him" is all-inclusive) breathes back to him the spirit he first infused.

There are many descriptions of this universal choir in Milton's
work. In book IV, responding to Eve's wondering why the stars
shine even when the pair is asleep, Adam reminds her that the
business of the stars is not to provide light to humankind but to
offer "ceaseless praise" (679) to the creator:

> how often from the steep
> Of echoing Hill or Thicket have we heard
> Celestial voices to the midnight air,
> Sole, or responsive each to other's note
> Singing thir great Creator. (680–684)

"Echoing" is not a causal or formulaic word here, for it points to
the chief characteristic of this song: it has only one note—a note
that has been sounding long before any particular singer takes it

up; everyone is in the position of Ovid's Echo, always giving back the words of another ("auditaque verba reportat").[2] It doesn't matter, therefore, whether the singer is "sole, or responsive each to other's note," for the song is always *corporately* sung even when the singer is apparently single. And since this is a song that everyone sings, it is a song that no *one* sings; and, moreover, it is a song sung *to* no one, since there isn't anyone not already singing it. In the ordinary sense of "communication," the speaker offers listeners something (a message, insight, pleasure) that they do not yet have; but this is a scene not of communication—of distance between parties in different zones of understanding—but of *responsiveness,* of voices answering one another in conformity with a harmony that is *already* achieved. Nor can it be said that everyone is singing to God, as if he were a spectator and separate from the song; he *is* the song, its content and its source; they are all "Singing thir . . . Creator," not singing *about* their creator, but singing—breathing, uttering, and therefore ceaselessly replicating—him.

The point is even more precisely made in "At a Solemn Music" when Milton celebrates "the fair music that all creatures made / To their great Lord, whose love their motion sway'd."[3] In the first half of line 22, the preposition "to" suggests a distinction between the singers and the audience-object of their song; but in the second half, the song itself is revealed to have been impelled ("sway'd") by its putative recipient: their Lord breathes into them the love that they then return ("what could they else") to him. The result is "perfect Diapason"—harmony—that lasts so long as God's creatures remain "In first obedience and their state of good."[4] The key word here is "first"; the motion required is a motion that involves no departure from a position—of obedience and submission, of ceaseless praise—originally assumed; a standing still even though, to the untutored eye, there seems to be movement and variation. The model of this motion that is not movement is, appropriately enough, the "Mystical dance" of the Heavens, described in lines that provide still another gloss on "Celestial Song":

> Mystical dance, which yonder starry Sphere
> Of Planets and of fixt in all her Wheels
> Resembles nearest, mazes intricate,
> Eccentric, intervolv'd, yet regular
> Then most, when most irregular they seem:
> And in thir motions harmony Divine
> So smooths her charming tones, that God's own ear
> Listens delighted. (PL, V, 620–627)

It is this harmony that Adam and Eve join earlier in book V, when they offer their morning prayer: the style of the prayer is described as "various" (146), but the variety is only a surface phenomenon, for in whatever style they pray the desire that moves them is the desire "to praise / Thir Maker, in fit strains" (147–148); moreover, by the same logic, *any* strain is fit so long as praise is its content. The hymn proceeds (if that is the right word) by celebrating God's "glorious works" (153), but the work of the hymn is prevented by the work it celebrates, since all of these already, before the prayer is uttered and independently of its various motions, "declare / Thy goodness . . . and Power Divine" (158–159). The performance thus is rigorously self-reflexive: Adam and Eve sing God's praise by praising works that already praise him; in such a song, there can be no beginning, middle, or end, because it is at every point and at every instant the same. The motion to which the song urges God's creatures is the motion they "naturally" mime: "join all ye Creatures to extol / Him first, him last, him midst, and without end" (164–165). In a strict sense, then, there is nothing the prayer can do but testify to the prevenient power that is the cause of everything, including its own utterance. As Herbert puts it, "But who hath praise enough? nay who hath any?"[5] God is not only the object of all praise, but the producer of the praise he receives.

The moral is the one I have already drawn: in a celestial song, no one can be said to be doing the singing; rather, everyone is sung by an informing presence whose precedence is endlessly and involuntarily declared. Everyone is in the position of Wisdom and her sister Urania, playing in ways made possible by him before whom they play. This insight is proclaimed again and again in Milton's work, but even when it is unambiguously embraced, it bears a double aspect: if one regards the goal of the Christian life as the reabsorption of all discordant voices into the single voice of a universal choir ("O may we soon again renew that Song, / And keep in tune with Heav'n"),[6] the exchanging of one's individual (and therefore separate) identity for a corporate identity is a prospect viewed with unspeakable (a word not casually chosen) joy; but if one values, as one can hardly help doing, the sound of one's own utterances, even if what the utterances sound is a lament for a lost unity with the divine, the prospect of recovering that unity will be experienced as a threat. Promise and threat are thus indissoluble, intertwined with each other, and are experienced as such by all creatures, poets not excepted. Typically, Milton will present himself as someone who wishes nothing more than to serve ("I conceav'd my selfe to be now not as mine own person but as a member incorporate into that truth whereof I was perswaded") while he tends to displace the *anxiety* of service—the anxiety of the loss of agency and personal efficacy—onto others or onto highly fictionalized versions of himself.[7] The invocation to book VII is a particularly compressed instance of this double move by which Milton creates—or perhaps performs; just how much he is aware of the complexities of this moment is an open question—a drama that fully explores the tensions and ambiguities of his conflicted position.

Forlorn

The conflict is figured in gender terms. As we have already seen, the gender of Milton's muse is rendered obscure when the firm identification of Urania is ostentatiously withdrawn. The obfuscation is not casual, for when Milton says, "The meaning, not the Name I call" (VII, 5), he avoids what would in effect be a heresy, identifying the source of his inspiration as female. In a universe where, as it is so often said in the poem, God is "All in All," gender (e.g., III, 341), rather than being a constitutive and basic fact, is an anomaly, or at best an illusion (again, this is what "universe" means). Gender marks difference, variety, a plurality of perspectives, but in a God-centered universe difference and variety are accidental and temporary conditions, for finally all creatures play in the presence of the Almighty. Gender difference is like the vagaries of the starry spheres as they move in mystical dance; it is more apparent than real, allowed to emerge only so that the unifying power of a monistic deity can be repeatedly reaffirmed—as it is, for example, when the apparently independent efforts of both the good and the rebel angels are countered by the irresistible force of God's chariot, or when the priority of Urania and Wisdom is revealed to be secondary in relation to a precedent Almighty before whom they play.

By first naming Urania and then participating in her demotion, Milton, in the person of his epic voice, marks himself as a creature of the Father; but the drama of gender is not ended, and in the body of the invocation the speaker-poet displays a fear of the female that is unmistakably a form of castration anxiety:

> Up led by thee
> Into the Heav'n of Heav'ns I have presum'd
> An Earthly Guest, and drawn Empyreal Air,
> Thy temp'ring; with like safety guided down

> Return me to my Native Element:
> Lest from this flying Steed unrein'd, (as once
> *Bellerophon,* though from a lower Clime)
> Dismounted, on th' *Aleian* Field I fall
> Erroneous there to wander and forlorn. (*PL,* VII, 12–20)

Nominally, this is the language of courtesy, as when one apologizes for having presumed above one's class; but as is often the case, courtesy is a mask for darker feelings, and here it masks an accusation: "You've led me on." "Up led by thee" assigns the agency to Urania; the presumption, if there is any, is hers, and the poet is the innocent object of her urgings. Moreover, those urgings, as he recalls them, are as sexual as they are social. There are two scenes imagined here: in one, a reluctant guest (how reminiscent this is of Herbert's *Love III*) draws back from the invitation of a superior; in another (slightly submerged), a young man flees the advances of a powerful woman. This second drama is not foregrounded; instead, Milton displaces its anxieties into its apparent opposite—the scene of abandonment, with its attendant fear of being cut loose, of being unsupported, alone, "forlorn." But in choosing Bellerophon as the vehicle of this preferred fear, Milton (inadvertently?) alludes to everything he would push away; for as the poem's early editors remind us, Bellerophon's story begins with the unwelcome importunings of an aggressive female: "*Bellerophon* was a beautiful and valiant youth, son of Glaucus; who refusing the amorous applications of Antea wife of Praeteus king of Argos, was by her false suggestions like those of Joseph's mistress to her husband, sent into Lycia with letters desiring his destruction."

A young man of talent avoids the amorous nets of a designing woman who, in response to having been scorned, contrives to have her husband destroy him. As it turns out, however, the stratagem fails when Bellerophon "came off conqueror" in the "several enterprises full of hazard" to which he was put. It is then that he attempts "vaingloriously to mount up to Heaven on the winged horse Pegasus" and incurs the wrath of still another king, Jupiter, who sends a fly to sting the horse and throw the rider. In some versions of the story Bellerophon is blinded by his fall and, "Forsook by Heav'n forsaking human kind, / Wide o'er the Aleian field he chose to stray, / A long, forlorn, uncomfortable way."[8]

The relevance of Bellerophon's story to Milton's poetic ambitions and to his recent political fortunes (when he had reason to fear a restored king's vengeance) is obvious and obviously intended (especially given the fact of a shared blindness), but Milton just as obviously intends to restrict the scope of the allusion, since he invokes it in order to insist not on the similarities but on the differences between them. Let Bellerophon's fate not be mine, he asks, even as he describes himself in terms that make the two careers indistinguishable: "fall'n on evil days, / On evil days . . . fall'n, and evil tongues; / In darkness, and with dangers compast round" (*PL,* VII, 25–27). This act of misrecognition would itself be extraordinary even if it were not one in a lengthening series. To be sure, Urania is at first recognized without hesitation, but her identity is then blurred in a gesture of apparent scrupulosity ("The meaning, not the Name I call" [5]) that allows the issue of her gender, and with it the threat of female aggression, to remain unconfronted. Urania is then *re*imagined in a benign form as the gracious patroness, while her role as pursuer and seducer is hidden in an ambiguous phrase ("Up led by thee" [12]). She is then further hidden, indeed suppressed, when Milton alludes to Bellerophon's troubles but fails to recall their origin in the "amorous applications" of Antea. The poet may be, as he says, "with dangers compast round" (27), but a great deal of his (perhaps unconscious) energy is here devoted to *not* seeing the danger before his very eyes. Of course his eyes (as he notes) are darkened, but that disability is yet one more emblem of the *psy-chological* wound the poet is experiencing even as he denies it; for as Freud observes in "The 'Uncanny,'" "anxiety connected with the eyes and with going blind is often . . . a substitute for the dread of castration"—that is, the dread of being rendered power-less, of losing agency, of being unmanned.[9] This dread is at once the source of the energy in this passage and that which the pas-sage wants desperately to push away. Milton simply cannot bear to acknowledge that the force to which he prays—by any name and in whatever gender form—is the force whose disabling threat he fears, and he defends against that threat not only by recon-ceiving it in a succession of benign shapes, but by displacing it onto the condition he in fact desires: the condition of being adrift and alone, unsupported by—and therefore independent of—any higher power.

It is not that he lies when he says that he wishes not to be "for-lorn"; it is just that forlornness comes in two versions, each with its liabilities and attractions. To be forlorn is to be lost—that is, "to not be found" *(OED);* and one way of being lost, of not being pointable to, is to be known only as the effect and instrument of a superior agency, to be the singer of a "celestial" song in the sense defined above, a song that is not your own but is, as it were, community property, which is therefore also the status of the singer. The alternative mode of forlornness is precisely to be sep-arate from this corporate ensemble, to be unlocatable in relation to its normative center, to be divergent from its circular, centripe-tal paths, to be "Erroneous," to "wander." One who is in this con-dition is indeed lost, fallen, cut off, extraneous, on the outer edges; but he is also, and by the same analysis, found—not as an entity centered by primordial being but as an entity *decentered,* off to the side, separate, standing out from the crowd, distinct, unique.

In the surface rhetoric of this passage, losing oneself in the "Heav'n of Heav'ns" is the preferred form of loss, but in the lines that point the contrast, the instability of the opposition and the ease with which the positive and negative poles can be reversed become apparent:

> Half yet remains unsung, but narrower bound
> Within the visible Diurnal Sphere;
> Standing on Earth, not rapt above the Pole,
> More safe I Sing with mortal voice, unchang'd (PL, VII, 21–24)

The division of the poem mirrors the division of the universe into heavenly and sublunar regions, and each phrase extends and deepens the opposition between the narrow and the vast, between the visible and the inaccessible, between the temporal and the eternal. In the context of these oppositions, Milton finds himself, as he has already said, in his "Native Element"—that is, "on Earth" (and therefore bound to another female figure), where he is engaged in an enterprise less glorious than the one he has attempted in the first six books. But this narrowing is his salvation, not in theological terms but in the terms of his *personal* ambitions. A "narrower bound" is a bound which is limited and therefore one which can be extended in ways that mark an accomplishment. Someone who is situated narrowly rather than situated universally (that is, not situated) can proceed from one point to another and claim credit for his progress; his actions are measured out by time; they are "Diurnal," of a day, and of a day that differs from the day before and from the day that may follow; he lives in a world of risk and therefore in a world of possibility, and thus he can be said (as Milton says here of himself) to be standing—that is, to be visibly erect and erectly visible, distinguishable from others and from other potential versions of himself, both greater and lesser.

Rapt

In short, he is not "rapt," a word that in naming the condition he has escaped surfaces the sexual fears attending its prospect. To be "rapt" is to be taken out of oneself, to be carried away by force, to be ravished, to be raped; and this last is what Milton fears would happen were he to remain in Urania's grasp and therefore be incapable of standing on his own, of rising up to his full, autonomous height. No wonder he regards himself as "More safe" in the diurnal confines of earth; his very identity would be at risk were the rapture of Urania's embrace to be prolonged (as the Celestial song is, by definition, prolonged throughout eternity). Indeed, were he to be incorporated into that song, *he* would no longer be singing; and he could not say, as he says here, "*I sing*," an announcement in marked contrast to the more deferential yielding of agency in the invocation to book I: "Sing, Heav'nly Muse" (I, 6).

The remainder of line 24—"with mortal voice, unchang'd"— is at once tautological and explanatory of the bolder claim he now utters, the claim to *be* uttering. A mortal voice is, literally, the voice of someone who can die—that is, someone whose actions are necessary because he is distant from a goal (union with the divine) whose achievement will render those actions beside the point, since he would already be at the point to which they would bring him. A mortal voice is a voice that has somewhere to go, something to do, something to say; and while it is impelled forward by the hope of its eventual silencing (in the deep harmony of universal song), a mortal voice also has a stake in the deferral of that happy (?) consummation; for so long as it is still "on the road," so to speak, it can enjoy successes and failures, it can be noted and marked: it can leave a *mark*. A mortal voice, in short, is a voice that can have a *career*—and, as we know, no poet is more obsessed with the shape of career, with the hopes and anxieties of vocation and achievement, than Milton. In almost everything he writes, the urgency of the present occasion—be it theological, political, domestic, educational—is tied implicitly and often explicitly to the distance he has traveled or hopes to travel on the roadway of his ambitions; even when he meditates on celestial harmonies and eschatological visions, he issues reports on his own situation in relation to the quotidian pressures of historical contingency. Remember me, he says (following the example of Virgil); I'm the fellow who interrupted his studies to write the tracts against prelacy, the one who answered Hartlib's call for a treatise on education, and here I am again, still standing up for what I think is right, though my political enemies have triumphed and I have "fall'n on evil days, / . . . In darkness, and with dangers compast round, / And solitude" (VII, 25, 27–28).

This has the surface sound of a complaint, but it is also unmistakably a boast and the welcoming of an isolation ("And solitude") that allows the poet to present himself as the type of a beleaguered hero, a backlit figure in a highly theatricalized landscape. Thus, when he says, in the very same line, "yet not alone," the assertion must be heard in at least two tonal registers—as an expression of self-comfort ("someone up there likes me") and as a reemergence of the fear the passage has alternately surfaced and repressed, the fear that he will not be allowed to be alone, will not be allowed to *be*, will be engulfed in the embrace of an omnivorous woman who at this very moment seems to be sliding back into his bed: "yet not alone, while thou / Visit'st my slumbers Nightly" (28–29). Once again he puts a brave show on it, and yields the precedence to Urania in two famous lines: "still govern thou my Song, / *Urania*, and fit audience find, though few" (30–31). But despite the linking conjunction, the two lines fall apart. If Urania truly—that is, strongly—governs his song, then the

294

question of audience *is* moot because it will be assured; Urania's song is cosmic and therefore leaves no room for an audience—for a gap between producer and receiver—since every possible auditor is already a participant. Although Milton appears to be asking for guidance, he is really asking for a space in which to operate: "Give me just a few people who need to be moved somewhere, who are not already on a guided track; don't give me so much help that my efforts are overwhelmed and superfluous." Of course he does not explicitly push Urania away, out of his bed; instead he resorts to the strategy (of which he is perhaps unaware) he has employed before: he transfers his hostility to a substitute and insists on a distinction between that substitute and Urania, a distinction which simply cannot be maintained.

This time the proxy nemesis is the "rout" of Thracian women who first drowned out the voice of Orpheus and then dismembered him:

> But drive far off the barbarous dissonance
> Of *Bacchus* and his Revellers, the Race
> Of that wild Rout that tore the *Thracian* Bard
> In *Rhodope,* where Woods and Rocks had Ears
> To rapture, till the savage clamor drown'd
> Both Harp and Voice; nor could the Muse defend
> Her Son. (VII, 32–38)

Alastair Fowler is perhaps understating the case when he observes (in a note to his 1968 edition) that the "myth of [Orpheus'] dismemberment by Thracian women during the orgies of Bacchus seems to have focused some of [Milton's] deepest fears."[10] In this invocation, the focus is dispersed among other surrogate figures, for Bellerophon, in addition to sharing with Orpheus and Milton the characteristics of valor, abstemiousness, and isolation, also does battle with an Amazonian horde and comes off victorious. The question becomes: Will Milton join Bellerophon in his success, or will he become the heir to the fate of Orpheus? That fate brings to dramatic life the anxiety which is the content of this passage, the anxiety of being drowned out, of having your voice taken from you, of losing the contest for precedence and thereby losing yourself.

In these lines the contest is fought in the arena of a single word, "rapture." The word of course harks back to "rapt" in "rapt above the Pole," but this time it belongs, at least for a moment, to the mortal singer, whose voice famously has the power to control, to dominate, to shape the world, and even, as Milton reminds us in *Il Penseroso*, to constrain Gods: "bid the soul of *Orpheus* sing / Such notes as, warbled to the string, / Drew Iron tears down *Pluto's* cheek, / And made Hell grant what Love did seek."[11] It is just such notes—such expressions of "rapture"—that at first prevent the "crazed women of the Cicones" (*M*, XI, l. 3) from exercising their counter-rapture (the noun can mean either the act of forcibly carrying away or the state of being so carried). The sexual nature of their assault is unmistakable in Ovid's narration: the women are furious with Orpheus for having withheld himself from them and turned instead to young boys. (In book I he is said to have introduced homosexual practices to Thrace.) They are the proverbial women scorned, and so proclaim themselves when one of them cries, "See, see, here is the man who scorns us ("hic est nostri contemptor" [7]); and even as she says this, she hurls "her spear straight at the tuneful mouth of Apollo's bard" (8). Explication seems superfluous: as a penalty for having refused to play the man, Orpheus will be placed in the role of a woman, the sign of his masculinity turned against him with the intention of penetrating him and making him rapt. But the spear refuses its goal, turned back, as are the stones that follow, "by the sweet sound of voice and lyre" (11). At this point the contest for the phallus (and the voice is also a phallus, an organ of extension and potency), for the position of power, for the right to have the *say*, is stalemated; but then "the drums, and the breast-beatings and howlings of the Bacchanals, drowned the lyre's sound; and then at last the stones were reddened with the blood of the bard whose voice they could not hear" (18–19). Silenced, without voice and without power, Orpheus is completely overwhelmed, made into nothing, and when the women proceed to dismember him, their castrating act seems an unnecessary repetition of what they have already done.

All of this is encapsulated in Milton's "till the savage clamor drown'd / Both Harp and Voice" (*PL*, VII, 36–37), but in an excess of bitterness he cannot forbear adding one more detail that points the antifeminist moral: "nor could the Muse defend / Her Son" (37–38). The message is clear: if women aren't attacking you, they're failing you. And yet, as if he were himself blind to the significance of what he has just written, he turns immediately around and prays to a woman: "So fail not thou, who thee implores: / For thou art Heav'nly, shee an empty dream" (38–39). But is this, in fact, a prayer? It may have that form, but in the context of what precedes it—a parade of women who seduce or abandon—it sounds quite differently, as either a dare or a taunt. "How will you perform, Urania? Will you rob me of my voice by snatching me up to the Heaven of Heavens, or will you stand by while others of your sex drown me out by even harsher means?" The true intention (perhaps unknown to the intender) of the so-called prayer is to put Urania on the defensive, asked either to answer for her immanent failure or to renounce her efforts to appropriate him, to rapt him above the pole. Read this way, the lines are subversive of their surface function: to distinguish between Urania and the other female figures—Antea, the Amazon horde, the Thracian women—who suffuse this passage with so much threat. Milton may think (or want us to think) that in turn-ing to Urania he provides himself with a bulwark against that threat, but everything in these lines works to make her its very emblem and therefore a figure who must be at once pushed away and mastered.[12]

In short, the real content of the invocation is the struggle be-tween its speaker and its object, and the struggle continues when the invocation is formally over and the poet says, at the beginning of a new verse paragraph, "Say Goddess" (40). Once again, a ges-ture of apparent deference is in fact a move in a very serious game, for what Milton does here is recognize the Goddess from the podium, grant her a turn at saying, give her leave to speak, to play in *his* presence; it is he who says who has the say, and thus it is he who says even when she is doing the saying. What she is bid say is what Adam and Raphael said to each other after the angel's account of the War in Heaven. That is, Milton yields the floor of saying so that (by his permission) someone else can say what two other agents say in the course of a long conversational day. More-over, as embedded sayers, Adam and Raphael proceed to act out again the saying contest that introduces, and sets the stage for, their acts of speech. Adam invites—nay, implores—his superior to speak, and does so in precisely the terms employed by Mil-ton in the first line of the invocation: "Deign to descend now lower, and relate" (84). He then endows Raphael's voice with the Orpheus-like power to control nature: "the great Light of Day yet wants to run / Much of his Race though steep, suspense in Heav'n / Held by thy voice, thy potent voice" (98–100). "Held by thy voice" is like "rapt above the Pole" (23)—it declares the strong, indeed preemptive, precedence of one person over the other; but the question of whose voice is the most potent is not that simple, since it is Adam's voice (again imitating the epic in-voker) which constrains Raphael to speak, a strategy that Adam will later acknowledge to be part of still another strategy ("How subtly to detain thee I devise" [VIII, 207]).

There seems to be no end, no bottom, to this jockeying for verbal power, but in fact there is a bottom and it is located precisely where one would not expect to find it, deep within the structure of recessed sayings, in a saying reported by the sayer Raphael at the behest of the sayer Adam, both of whom are said by Urania ("Say Goddess") at the bidding of the archsayer (or so he would be) Milton. The saying Raphael reports is that of the "Omnific Word": "Silence, ye troubl'd waves, and thou Deep, peace, / Said then th' Omnific Word, your discord end" (VII, 216–217). "Omnific" means all-powerful, all-creating; it is the word that checkmates because it is the origin of all others, including the words that relate its story here in book VII. The moment the omnific word emerges in the text, it renders beside the point the verbal maneuverings of the poem's other agents—of Raphael, Adam, Urania, Milton—all of whom are now seen to be playing in his almighty (verbal) presence and by his dispensation. And this the omnific word does from what is apparently a position of (textual) subordination—the object of a relating of a relating of a relating. Indeed, one might suspect that in placing the omnific word so deeply within his structure, Milton hopes to contain it, to avoid the implications of "omnific"—the implication that *he* is at every moment being spoken—even as the adjective is bestowed; and if this is Milton's intention (however unselfconsciously deployed), it is one that has already worked itself out in my exegetical labors, for in analyzing this invocation I seem to have fallen in with its subtlest strategy: I duly noted the early appearance of "th' Almighty Father" (11), and then promptly forgot about him, put him out of my mind, transferred my attention to the succession of threatening women paraded in the lines that follow, and in so doing I have reinforced (by extending) a deeper defense against an even more primary threat, the threat of castration by the father.

For when one begins to look more closely at the passage, there are at least as many menacing or impotent fathers as there are aggressive women and ineffectual mothers. It is, after all, Praeteus who sends Bellerophon to what he hopes will be his destruction; and it is Jupiter who causes him to fall lest he become a rival in the heavens, the same Jupiter who would have been swallowed by *his* father had not his mother wrapped a stone in swaddling clothes, and the same Jupiter who is the father of Urania, Wisdom, and Calliope (the mother of Orpheus), and if the Muse could not defend her son, neither can the grandfather—nor could Apollo, Orpheus' father in many versions of the legend, Apollo, the *God* of poetry who appears only after the damage has been done to perform the belated rescue of a head already described as lifeless ("exanimis" [*M*, XI, 53]). Ovid makes the point (which Milton is surely remembering at some level) with a single word, *tandem*: "Phoebus *at last* appeared" (58). Where was he when the frenzied women drowned the bard's voice? Was he himself wary of encountering that castrating rout, or was he perhaps less than completely miserable to find that a singer of rival power had been silenced? I am not suggesting that we are meant to lean very heavily on these lines of inquiry or follow out to the end the associations they call up; I wish only to note that those associations weigh on the passage and freight it with vague forebodings of aggression and betrayal which always point back to a figure of male authority—that is, to the figure of God. The fact that it is female figures who are foregrounded in these lines only attests to the depth and extent of Milton's anxieties; better to shift everything onto the traditional repository of male fears rather than confront the truth acknowledged by Orpheus when he says "all things yield to the sway of Jove" ("cedunt Iovis omnia regno" [*M*, X, 148]).

Gladly Mixing

It is a truth Milton was continually proclaiming, yet one he could never fully accept; and his conflicted relationship with the ideal of submission is acted out in the careers of even his most exemplary heroes. The Lady of *Comus* has her moment of doubt and disequilibrium before she recovers the equanimity of perfect faith; both the speaker of *Lycidas* and the Samson of *Samson Agonistes* are inveterate murmurers who respond with bitterness to a world they never made and find impossible to understand; and even the Christ of *Paradise Regained* recalls moments when the desire to perform "victorious deeds" and "heroic acts" flamed in his heart.[13] It is only when Milton creates a character more or less out of whole cloth that he can even imagine what it would be like not to feel the stirrings he describes as "that last infirmity of Noble mind."[14] That character is Abdiel, the zealous loyalist, whose finest moment is not seen by anyone, including himself. It is a moment that follows upon something more visibly heroic, his rising to affirm his fidelity to the Father even in the midst of the Satanic host. Now he is on the way back to his friends, but the surprise that awaits him when he arrives is anticipated in the syntax of book VI's opening lines:

> All night the dreadless Angel unpursu'd
> Through Heav'n's wide Champaign held his way, till Morn,
> Wak't by the circling Hours, with rosy hand
> Unbarr'd the gates of Light. (*PL*, VI, 1–4)

"Unpursu'd" is an early clue as to what will soon happen—or, rather, not happen: Abdiel's flight is without the temporal pressure, at least in one direction, that usually gives such actions point. The significant shift, however, occurs at the end of the second line. When we first read it, "till Morn" seems an adverbial phrase modifying "held his way" and therefore a gloss on *Abdiel's* action; but line 3 reveals that in the fuller syntax "till Morn" is the object of the participle "Wak't" (the morn is waked) and then the subject of "Unbarr'd." What this means is that in the course of these lines the agency is taken away from Abdiel and given to the Morn, who now has the forward initiative. It is *her* way, not his, and moreover it is a way that will proceed independently of anything Abdiel does or doesn't do. The hours circle—that is, they don't go in a straight line but describe motions that return always to the same appointed place.

The effect of this image is to further undercut the urgency and point of Abdiel's linear flight; and that effect is itself redoubled when that flight is interrupted by a leisurely explanation of the subordinate and indeed decorative role of time in the realm of the heavens:

> There is a Cave
> Within the Mount of God, fast by his Throne,
> Where light and darkness in perpetual round
> Lodge and dislodge by turns, which makes through Heav'n
> Grateful vicissitude, like Day and Night. (4–8)

That is, for the sake of variety (here a purely aesthetic category) there is a light show in heaven that *simulates* day and night, that simulates the "Diurnal Sphere" in which the passing of time is attended by crisis, choice, and unpredictable consequences. In Heaven, time's passing is devoid of such risks because everything is always and already centered on the central and informing value of the universe; so that when in line 12 Raphael tells us that "now went forth the Morn," we are meant to understand that "now" merely marks a turn-taking and not a moment of poised urgency; and if we miss the point, the verse quickly reminds us of it: "Such as in highest Heav'n" (13). "Shot through with orient Beams" (15) further dissipates the already attenuated energy of Abdiel's flight, and for all intents and purposes Abdiel disappears from the passage, reemerging only as the *object* of the effect he had hoped to cause:

> when all the Plain
> Cover'd with thick embattl'd Squadrons bright,
> Chariots and flaming Arms, and fiery Steeds
> Reflecting blaze on blaze, first met his view. (15–18)

The "first" in line 18 is very precise: the view *precedes* his "taking it in." It is before him in two senses of the word: it is in front of him, and it was there before he saw it. In relation to it, he is superfluous; it doesn't need him, and the extent of his inefficacy is given a slow deliberate gloss: "War he perceiv'd, war in procinct, and found / Already known what he for news had thought / To have reported" (19–21). That is, Abdiel had thought that there was something he could *do*, something he could *say*, words that only he could produce, words that would make a difference because they would *be* different, not already spoken in the eternal present; but that thought, and the vision of self and identity of which it is an extension, are countermanded by a reality that has no place for them—the reality of the "Omnific Word."

At this moment Abdiel is exactly in the position the epic narrator occupies in the opening of book VII, confronted by the suffocating omnipresence of the deity he serves. What distinguishes the two is their reaction, or, rather, the fact that Abdiel doesn't have a reaction. The hinge between what he has just "met"—the castrating sight of his undeniable impotence—and what he now does is the word "gladly": "Already known what he for news had thought / To have reported: gladly then he mixt" (20–21). The extraordinary thing about "gladly" is that it participates in both actions (because it participates in two syntactic structures) and thereby acknowledges no difference between them: Abdiel would have been glad to report and he just as gladly mixes—that is, loses himself in a host already composed without his reportorial aid. I don't mean that he says to himself, "Well, that was a disappointment (not to have reported), but I can still enjoy the fellowship of my peers"; he doesn't say *anything* to himself. The two possible modes of action which for us would be seen as active and passive respectively are for him absolutely continuous, of a piece, alternative forms of service. He can take no credit for not feeling aggrieved at having his great moment snatched from him, because it never occurs to him to be aggrieved, and therefore he deserves credit precisely in the measure he would not think to claim it. As far as he is concerned, he just does what he does, or is what he is, and as he is named, the servant of God.

Thus, when God says to him, "Servant of God, well done" (29), he is really saying, "Good job at being Abdiel, Abdiel." Being Abdiel is being just one thing, all the time, being what Christ declares himself to be—"Mee hung'ring . . . to do my father's will"[15]—and what Milton sometimes claims to be: "I conceav'd my selfe to be now not as mine own person." But even here, the language betrays him: he *conceives* himself to have a corporate identity, but the act of conceiving, of thinking about himself in that way, is performed at a distance from what it contemplates; and so he fails of his claim and of his goal. But is it his goal? Does not a part of him want to fail, want to fall and wander erroneous and desolate on the plain, so that he can make his way, make his mark, make his career, speak with a mortal voice, a voice that sounds only because it is far from home, from *patria,* in exile, but a voice that sounds a note the exile loves as he loves himself?

PART III

The
Counter-Paradigm

CHAPTER NINE

The Temptation to Action

Disproportioned Sin

Love of self is the temptation underlying all others in a universe where true agency belongs only to deity, and the only act available to creatures is the (self-diminishing) act of acknowledging dependence on another. The temptation of self-love comes in many, in innumerable, forms, and in this and the following four chapters, I explore the forms Milton endlessly elaborates and caresses.

In the fourth book of *Paradise Regained*, after seeing Christ reject wealth, honor, arms, art, kingdom, empire, glory, fame, the active life, and the life of contemplation, Satan asks with an exasperation that has been shared by many readers, "What dost thou in this World?"[1] In book XII of *Paradise Lost*, Adam, in response to the "good news" of the incarnation, exclaims, "Needs must the Serpent now his capital bruise / Expect with mortal pain: say where and when / Thir fight, what stroke shall bruise the Victor's heel."[2] He is rewarded, as is so often the case in Milton's poetry, with a rebuke: "To whom thus *Michael*. Dream not of their fight, / As of a Duel" (386–387). Michael speaks from experience. Earlier he had dreamed of just such a duel in which *he* would be in the position Adam projects for Christ, the deliverer of a stroke that would once and for all ("one stroke . . . / That might determine and not need repeat") "end / Intestine War in Heav'n, the Arch-foe subdu'd / . . . Captive dragg'd in Chains" (VI, 258–260). The stroke falls, but it does not end intestine war; it merely provides the Arch-foe with an occasion for demonstrating one of the advantages of being incorporeal: he simply heals, like a self-sealing automobile tire. As different as they and their situations are, Satan, Adam, and Michael are alike in the relationship between what they desire and what they find. What they desire is that someone do something, that something happen; but in Milton's poetry that desire is invariably disappointed, either because the action is withheld, or because it occurs but is not decisive in the way that had been anticipated, or because it occurs and is decisively disastrous.

It is something of all three in the case of "At a Solemn Music," a poem that has been accurately, if unsympathetically, described by Russell Fraser: "All but the last four lines . . . are comprised in a single imperative sentence. The result is a stirring panorama, resonant, but static. Nothing happens."[3] This is not quite right. The sentence is a petition embedded in an apostrophe rather than an imperative; it is a request for action, that something be done, but curiously we never find out what that something is, even though it seems always on the point of being identified. The pattern is established in the first two lines, which are made up of four phrases in apposition to one another: "Blest pair of *Sirens*, pledges of Heav'n's joy, / Sphere-born harmonious Sisters, Voice and Verse."[4] One reads these lines by taking a breath and holding it, in anticipation of the petition that will follow, an anticipation that seems answered by the imperative "Wed" in "Wed your divine sounds, and mixt power employ" (3). But the force of the imperative is diminished when the action it names is one the blest sirens are already performing. The wedding of sounds defines their mode of being; therefore it is not something you can ask them to do, and the superfluousness of the request is confirmed by the adjective "mixt," a synonym for "wed." The request then amounts to no more than saying, "Blest pair of *Sirens,* be what you are," and we remain waiting for the specification of an event that will follow upon or be the consequence of the sirens' singing. Just such a specification seems imminent at the end of line 3, where the expectation is of a "so that" clause—i.e., employ your mixed power so that something will be effected. For a moment, that something appears to be the Orpheus-like action of making live dead things—"Dead things with inbreath'd sense" (4); but the last three words of the line ("able to pierce") reveal that this is not something the blest sirens will do—in the future, in the next moment—but something they already do; the relationship between the two lines is not one of an antecedent to its (requested) consequence, but one of a state to its modifier. Power is not exercised in line 4, but more fully characterized. Rather than moving forward to an event, to something that happens next, the verse simply marches in place.[5]

This is in fact what the poem continues to do and forces us to do, even while it encourages us to anticipate and desire a sequence and a plot. It does this by never quite completing what Fraser calls the panorama, although there are many points at which it seems to be complete. The first is at line 6—"That undisturbed Song of pure concent." One might think that the song is now fully characterized and that we can go on to something new, but lines 7–8 continue or expand the characterization by adding to it the song's audience: "Aye sung before the sapphire-color'd throne / To him that sits thereon." Again we seem to have reached a natural point of closure, but the next lines expand the scene further by introducing those who accompany the song: "With Saintly shout and solemn Jubilee, / Where the bright Seraphim in burning row / Their loud uplifted Angel-trumpets blow" (9–11). "Blow," like the other verbs that appear in the poem, is capable of indicating a punctual discrete act, but here it indicates an ongoing or durative activity; the trumpets are always blowing (just as the song is always sounding), and moreover they do not blow alone, as we discover in the next lines: "And the Cherubic host in thousand choirs / Touch their immortal Harps of golden wires" (12–13). "And" here tells us overtly what we have been told so many times before: we're not done yet; there's still more to fill in before we can proceed to what happens next. The connectives in this passage are all felt as "ands," even when the word is "where" or "with," as it is in line 14: "With those just Spirits that wear victorious Palms." These spirits take their place, a place we must make for them, alongside the blest pair of sirens, the sapphire-colored throne, him who sits thereon, the bright seraphim in burning row, and the cherubic host in thousand choirs. Line 15—"Hymns devout and holy Psalms"—sets the seal on the nonsubordinating, appositional mode of the poem by simply hanging there, unconnected to anything, until the following line connects it with everything: "Singing everlastingly" (16). This present participle belongs to no one of the available agents in the passage, but to all of them—sirens, saints, seraphim, host, spirits. And just as the line does not distinguish persons, neither does it distinguish times: not only is everyone doing the same thing; they are doing it all the time—"everlastingly"—and therefore at no one time that stands out from any other.[6]

These first sixteen lines enact a paradox: the poem refuses to stop or take a breath, and because it refuses to stop, it stands still. Or, to be more precise, *we* stand still—moving, it is true, from line to line, but finding that every line, rather than marking a succession, stands in apposition to all the lines preceding it: forward movement is retarded, even though the reader is always moving forward. As a result, a tremendous pressure is built up for a genuine—that is, cleanly sequential—next step; and it seems that such a step will be taken when line 17 begins with the causal construction we had expected in line 4: "That we on Earth with undiscording voice / May rightly answer that melodious noise; / As once we did" (17–19). Yet again, however, we are disappointed, and in two respects: (1) rather than bringing us forward into narration, the oft-anticipated step takes us back, and (2) it takes us back not to a punctual but to an iterative action, an answering that would be performed not once but continually. The poem is still standing still, refusing to finish with the panorama it is characterizing, and holding out instead the possibility that we may join it, "As once we did." What we want, however, is to move *away* from it to something discrete and finite, to an event, and in lines 19–21 we are finally given what we want: "As once we did, till disproportion'd sin / Jarr'd against nature's chime, and with harsh din / Broke the fair music that all creatures made . . . " "Till" is a real temporal conjunction; it separates states from one another. "Jarr'd" and "Broke," emphatically placed at the beginning of their lines, mark the moment of separation. The only punctual verbs in the poem, they report a decisive and climactic act; in a word, they narrate. What they narrate, however, is a disaster. Even as these lines satisfy our desires, they also label them by making their fulfillment coincide with the appearance in the poem of the Fall. Indeed, in reading the poem we are made to reenact the Fall by being made to feel impatient with the state from which it is a fatal departure. Like Eve, we tire of the endless celebration of "nature's chime" and wish to leave it behind for a narrated event; "disproportion'd sin" not only characterizes that event when it occurs, but names our repetition of it in the act of reading. The contrast between us and those creatures who remain part of nature's chime is immediately reinforced by the verb "stood": "Broke the fair music that all creatures made / To their great Lord, whose love their motion sway'd / In perfect Diapason, whilst they stood . . ." (21–23). "Stood" is important for what it does mean; it means not "suddenly stood" or "stood apart," but "stood firm." The difference is that in one sense the word indicates an overt, assertive action, and in the other a refraining from action; when men stood in their "state of good" (24), they declined to move. This point is one that Milton will make repeatedly in his poetry and prose: the impulse to action, to change, to sequence is always sinful because it has its source in a desire to be separate, to break away from the corporate existence of those who live and move in God.

The poem ends by expressing the hope that we may someday enjoy that corporate existence again:

> O may we soon again renew that Song,
> And keep in tune with Heav'n, till God ere long
> To his celestial consort us unite,
> To live with him, and sing in endless morn of light. (25–28)

This singing, when and if we join it, will be like the standing from which we broke away: as a member of a universal choir, the individual singer will be indistinguishable from his fellows. Disproportioned sin is disproportioned because it can be picked out; indeed, it issues from the desire to be picked out; what jars is what makes an individual claim on the hearer's attention; "din" is anything that does not make up a part in this harmony. Properly understood, then, the wish that we be united with God's celestial "consort" (at once a musical term and a reference to the mystical marriage) is a wish that we not be heard, that we utter sounds in such a way as to remain silent. The man who wants to sing alone is like the man who wants to stand alone, raised by his own merit to some bad eminence.

Not Yet

In the fourth stanza of the *Nativity Ode*, Milton himself is such a man when he expresses the desire to be first among those who offer praise to the infant Jesus:

> See how from far upon the Eastern road
> The Star-led Wizards haste with odors sweet:
> O run, prevent them with thy humble ode,
> And lay it lowly at his blessed feet;
> Have thou the honor first, thy Lord to greet,
>   And join thy voice unto the Angel Choir,
> From out his secret Altar toucht with hallow'd fire.[7]

The urgency of these lines is unmistakable and self-aggrandizing, despite the gesture toward self-abasement in "lowly" and "humble." Like so many other characters in his poetry, Milton wishes to perform an act that is at once decisive and distinguishing; he wants to be preeminent. But even as that wish is expressed, it is countered by the language of the last two lines and especially by the word "toucht," which identifies the power that is *already* inspiring him and is responsible for the words he is now uttering, as well as for the words he may lay at his Lord's feet. The movement of the stanza traces out the basic pattern of the poem: from the expectation of an imminent and necessary action to the introduction of a perspective in which the action is either unnecessary or has already occurred. It is a pattern that appears in the very first stanza, which opens with the flourish of trumpets: "This is the Month, and this the happy morn / Wherein the Son of Heav'n's eternal King, / Of wedded Maid . . . " (1–3). The verse seems to situate us in a historical present so that we are looking forward to an event, the birth of Christ; but in the next clause—"and Virgin Mother born"—the past participle tells us that the event is already in the past: rather than a movement forward, the clause refers back in apposition to "Son of Heav'n's

313

eternal King." The syntax then turns to report the already-born Son's action, but that too is an action already performed—"Our great redemption from above *did* bring" (4; emphasis added)—and the sense of dramatic urgency is dissipated. It is further dissipated when the next line takes away the immediacy of the event by reducing it to a report: "For so the holy sages once did sing." For a moment, in line 6, the urgency of the opening verses is reinstated in the anticipation of future act—"That he our deadly forfeit should release"—but in the alexandrine that closes every stanza of the poem, that act is characterized as ongoing, continual, and already in force: "And with his Father work us a perpetual peace."

In stanza II, expectation is once again given free reign when the sense is suspended for the first four lines and we are left waiting for a verb:

> That glorious Form, that Light unsufferable,
> And that far-beaming blaze of Majesty,
> Wherewith he wont at Heav'n's high-Council Table,
> To sit the midst of Trinal Unity . . . (8–11)

This is a deliberate evocation of power, and one feels that it is preliminary to the performing of a spectacular act; but when that act is finally reported, it is a withdrawal from the spectacular, and from action itself insofar as it is conceived to be assertive and immediately consequential: "He laid aside." Of course this is an expression of a familiar Christian paradox—"the weakness of God is stronger than men"—but it is also a deliberate backing away from the dramatic pressures exerted by the preceding lines. In the third and fourth stanzas, these pressures are exerted by Milton himself as he looks forward to the race his poem will run. To the expectation of an event *in* the poem, he adds the expectation of the event that *is* the poem, the expectation that it will be the centerpiece of an act of homage ("Have thou the honor first"). In

other poems, Milton stands aloof from his readers and characters, involving them in temptations that he himself avoids; but
here he is both tempter and tempted, at once encouraging and
acting out the desire for a spectacular conclusion, a single stroke.

In the hymn proper, he is joined by nature (stanzas I–III), un-
named warriors and kings (IV), the stars (VI), the sun (VII),
Truth, Justice (XV), and a host of others, all of whom are waiting
for something to happen and all of whom are disappointed in the
now familiar ways. Nature, trying to "hide her guilty front with
innocent Snow" (39), anticipates an immediate judgment, and the
verse encourages us to anticipate it too: "Confounded, that her
Maker's eyes / Should look so near upon her foul deformities"
(43–44). The "But" which begins the next stanza—"But he her
fears to cease"—not only ceases her fears; it also signals yet another withholding of action. Action seems to be imminent again
when "meek-ey'd Peace" is sent and is said to "strike"; but what
she strikes is a "universal Peace." "Strikes" is a verb that has built
into it the notion of surface contact; but here contact is never
made, because the verb's object is the very abstraction which in-
terdicts it. The following stanza presents a succession of happen-
ings, but in order to tell us that they will *not* occur. "No War, or
Battle's sound / Was heard the World around"; "The Trumpet
spake *not* to the armed throng" (53–54, 58; emphasis added).
True, line 56 reports that the "hooked Chariot stood," but we
must read the last word as one that signals not motion but the
stilling of motion ("stood still"). This is certainly how the kings
read it, as they sit "*still* with an awful eye, / As if they surely
knew their sovran Lord was by" (59–60; emphasis added). At every turn action is literally being stopped, but with such a dramatic air that the stopping seems a prelude to an even greater
action. That is why the "But" which opens stanza V—"But peace-
ful was the night"—is so revealing. It refers to nothing in the
text, but to the expectation that we share with the kings of our

"sovran Lord's" imminent arrival. In other words, "But" means "not yet—the great event you've been waiting for will be delayed." Indeed, "not yet" is what the poem continually says to us and to its characters, refusing to present events that have been heralded, or presenting them in ways that dissipate the potential for drama they seemed for a moment to contain.

The effect is double and paradoxical. Every withholding of climax merely increases the pressure for one. Even as anticipations are disappointed, they are raised again as we read of the stars "fixt" (70) and waiting for their Lord to "bid them go" (76), and of the sun looking forward to that moment when the "new-enlight'n'd world" will no longer need its "inferior flame" (81–82), and of nature thinking that "her part was done / And that her reign had here its last fulfilling" (105–106). When stanza XI begins with the words "At last," the formula is at least as answerable to our needs as it is to the needs of the characters. At last, the poem is going to begin; at last, the long-awaited moment is upon us; at last, something will happen.

What happens is what has happened so many times before. To be sure, there is, for once, a gratifying amount of detail: "a Globe of circular light" (110), helmed Cherubim" (112), and "sworded Seraphim / Are seen in glittering ranks with wings display'd, / Harping in loud and solemn choir" (113–115). What they harp, however, is described in the very next line as "unexpressive"— that is, incapable of expression, unutterable, and therefore in some sense unheard. With this one word, the physical and sensuous impact of the scene is diminished. It is further diminished in the following stanza, which pretends to describe the music but in fact only succeeds in distancing it from the moment of which it was to be the dramatic centerpiece. At first that moment is given just the prominence that would certify it as the location of a genuine (that is, discrete) event: "Such Music (as 'tis said) / Before was never made" (117–118). But the uniqueness of the event is compromised even in its presentation by the parenthesis, and it is further compromised by an exception:

> But when of old the sons of morning sung,
> While the Creator Great
> His constellations set,
> And the well-balanc't world on hinges hung,
> And cast the dark foundations deep,
> And bid the welt'ring waves their oozy channel keep. (119–124)

It is not simply that the music has in fact been made before, but that it is a music (of the spheres) that is always being made, even though man, since the Fall, has been incapable of hearing it. The progress (or antiprogress) of the stanza is from the present promise of "Before was never made" to the past punctuality of "sung" to the aspectual ambiguity of "hung," poised as it is between an action being done and one already done, to the continual nonterminal present of "keep." "Keep" is a primary instance of the kind of action the poem celebrates, an action that seems to be no action at all. It is a *holding* action in which power is not expended but husbanded, not exercised in one violent moment of release but exercised perpetually. It is what the spangled host do in line 21: "And all the spangled host keep watch in squadrons bright." Keeping watch, although it seems to an observer to be effortless, is the most arduous of activities because it requires continual attention; it is also the least immediately satisfying because it gives nothing back to those who perform it except the obligation to keep on. It is thus the perfect emblem of the posture to whose virtue the poem would educate us, even as we are provoked and tempted with the vocabulary of urgency, with "now" and "at last."

One might think that a pattern so often repeated would lose its capacity to involve us, that we would cease after a time to expect what has so often been announced and so often withdrawn;

but the desire underlying our expectations is sufficiently strong to survive all its disappointments, and in the stanzas that follow this one that desire is rekindled and labeled. It is a millenarian desire, a wish for an apocalypse, for an act so decisively climactic that no other act will ever be required—for a definitive resolution, and a resolution that will be all the more satisfactory because, while it is for us, it will take place outside us:

> Time will run back, and fetch the age of gold,
> And speckl'd vanity
> Will sicken soon and die,
>   And leprous sin will melt from earthly mold,
> And Hell itself will pass away,
> And leave her dolorous mansions to the peering day.
>
> Yea, Truth, and Justice then
> Will down return to men,
>   Th'enamel'd *Arras* of the Rainbow wearing,
> And Mercy set between,
> Thron'd in Celestial sheen,
>   With radiant feet the tissued clouds down steering,
> And Heav'n as at some festival,
> Will open wide the Gates of her high Palace Hall. (135–148)

This is the most inviting presentation of that for which we have been longing, and it is met immediately with the poem's most overt and crushing rebuke: "But wisest Fate says no, / This must not yet be so" (149–150). "Not yet" is what the poem has been saying all along, and here it says it openly, leaving everyone—poet, reader, characters—in the posture in which they have been so often placed by the verse, waiting for something to happen.

This last statement must be qualified, for not everyone is in a posture of expectation. Alone among the figures who populate the poem's landscape, the shepherds in stanza VIII are oblivious to the import of the moment. They wait for nothing, because they are aware of nothing; and they are characterized in a way that supports David Daiches' contention that "there is a deliberate demoting of the shepherds here."[8] They *sit* "simply chatting in a rustic row," ignorant of the fact that "the mighty *Pan* / Was kindly come to live with them below" (87, 89–90). The note of condescension is unmistakable: "Perhaps their loves, or else their sheep, / Was all that did their silly thoughts so busy keep" (91–92). Fowler and Carey tell us that we must take "silly" to mean "unlearned" rather than "foolish," even though the latter sense was fully established "by the last quarter of the sixteenth century"; but the editors are plainly resisting a meaning which, while it may be inconvenient to their interpretation, is clearly, and by their own evidence, there. The line and the stanza encourage us to patronize the shepherds by contrasting their behavior with the behavior of those more self-consciously active than they. They are out of step: while everyone else is on his or her toes, looking up in various poses of anticipation, they are simply sitting around and doing nothing.

In Order Serviceable

But this critique of their inactivity makes sense only from the point of view that has so often been rebuked when the poem says to the narrative desires of both characters and readers, "Not yet." If keeping watch and keeping in tune are the essence of true—as opposed to dramatically visible—action, the posture of the shepherds, unimpressive though it may be to the observer's eye, is finally the preferred one. In their concern with the ordinary round of their daily responsibilities, they may seem out of step with their more anxious brothers, but they are in perfect harmony with the rhythms of a universe whose foundations are "deep" (123) and eternally established. Like the music whose "chime" no human ear can hear, they move in "melodious time"

(128, 129)—in time that does not mark forward progress, but measures out spaces of equal duration in which questions of meaning and significance are not urgently raised because they have already been settled. If one can speak of a "plot" in a poem that resolutely refuses to move forward, the plot of this poem involves a reversal of values by which the shepherds are no longer scorned, but honored. The climax of this plot coincides with the entrance, so often heralded, of the hero, who, when we finally meet him, turns out to be the least active figure in the landscape. Indeed, no sooner has he appeared than he lays his head on a pillow and falls asleep.

And yet this inactivity, rather than once again blocking the exercise of power, somehow releases it; for as stanza XXV declares, "Our Babe, to show his Godhead true, / Can in his swaddling bands control the damned crew" (227–228). "Control" is a very strong verb, especially in this poem, and its assertiveness is in direct contrast to the babe's posture. How can there be an exertion of power without any exertion? The question is posed with even more force in stanza XXVI, where the recumbent infant is compared to the sun, pillowing his chin upon an "Orient wave." The image is a controversial one, if only because, as the *Variorum* editors remark, "*pillows* . . . seems more suggestive of the sun's going to bed than of his rising";[9] that is, as an active verb, it is curiously passive. Moreover, while it is transitive (and the first recorded use in English), the action taken affects only the agent: he doesn't overtly do anything to anyone; he doesn't do anything; he merely rests. It is all the more surprising, then, when this least dramatic of gestures has such dramatic consequences: "The flocking shadows pale / *Troop* to th'infernal jail" (232–233; emphasis added). The relationship between the sun's pillowing and the trooping shadows exactly mirrors the relationship between the "dreaded Infant's hand" (222) and the fleeing, shrinking, sighing pagan deities. In both cases, there is no contact: while the effect occurs, it is communicated by long distance; the agent does not stir himself, but simply shows himself.

This moment in the *Nativity Ode* establishes a pattern that will appear in almost everything that Milton writes. When the confrontation between good and evil occurs, it takes the form not of a conflict but of a contrast. The point is made explicitly in *An Apology against a Pamphlet*, when Milton praises the Parliament in these terms: "With such a majesty had their wisdome begirt it selfe, that wheras others had levied warre to subdue a nation . . . , they sitting here . . . could so many miles extend the force of their single words as to overawe the dissolute stoutnesse of an armed power."[10] On one side, great physical exertion and a martial pose; and on the other, a sedentary body whose only action is to express itself. That, however, is sufficient; for what defeats the armed force is not greater arms but its own recognition of the superior status of that which it would oppose. It is, as Milton precisely says, "overawe[d]," a word that perfectly describes what happens here to the pagan deities. They do not yield in battle; they literally fade away, testifying to the appearance in the world of something to which they must either be allied or submit. That is why the babe's victory is so easy, and so unspectacular; it is won not by struggling with external circumstances, but by ordering them, by serving as a center or point of reference in relation to which everything else falls obediently into its proper place. The pagan deities troop to their infernal jail not because of something the babe does (in the sense so often called for in this poem), but because of something he *is*.

This unexercised exercise of power makes in a dramatically undramatic way the point the poem has been making negatively by refusing to yield us the satisfaction of a climactic gesture: the true form of action is not an event but a mode of being, and it is a mode one displays not at one moment (highlighted by the pressures of the world) but at all moments, which are thus equally and indifferently its manifestations. Elsewhere I have called this a "politics of being," a politics that begins not with the desire for a certain outcome—although the desire for a certain outcome may be its local vehicle—but with a desire always to be in tune with Heaven.[11] No moment, then, is inherently more significant than any other, because every moment offers the opportunity either to persist in or to betray the principles of one's moral being. Action, in short, is interior—a disposition of mind and soul which, once achieved, is simply maintained in a variety of postures no one of which is more than its momentary form. The mistake would be to take one of those forms as the essential expression of action—to assume, for example, that an individual is acting only if he is somehow distinguished from his fellows, either by altering the face of the world, or by winning a race, or by writing an ode and presenting it *first;* for this would be to assume that action was intermittent, something one rouses oneself to on special occasions, something apart from, rather than constitutive of, living. It is just this assumption that we hold (or that holds us) while reading this poem. The eagerness both to observe an event and to participate in one places us exactly in the position Adam occupies when he asks, "say where and when / Thir fight, what stroke shall bruise the Victor's heel" (*PL,* XII, 384–385). We dream, as he does, of a local duel, desiring a single crisis-laden encounter. Both the *Nativity Ode* and "At a Solemn Music" first encourage that desire and then educate us to its significance: in one case, by fulfilling it at precisely the moment when it will be recognized as evil; in the other, by refusing to fulfill it at all but then accomplishing its end by means that redefine the very idea of action. That redefinition begins when we are introduced to the shepherds and is completed in these final stanzas, where virtue acts merely by showing itself and falling asleep.

It could be objected that such a view of action removes the possibility of drama. Exactly the reverse is true; rather than diminishing and devaluing drama, Milton's notion of action heightens drama by distributing it evenly over every minute of a man's life. The progress in these poems is only initially from the expectation of drama to its disappointment; for while one kind of drama is consistently denied us (except in those cases where it occurs disastrously), it is replaced finally by perpetual drama, by the continuing and never-ending obligation to be true to the best one knows, to keep in tune with it, to be ready to serve it, whatever that may mean, even if it means withholding action (in the gross sense) and doing nothing. ("They also serve who only stand and wait.")

That is what everyone is doing as the *Nativity Ode* ends: serving by doing nothing. "And all about the Courtly Stable, / Bright-harnass'd Angels sit in order serviceable." The last word of the poem says everything; the angels are "serviceable"—that is, able to perform services which they are not now performing. This ability is what underlies and gives value to any action they may take or decline to take; its source is a commitment, an inward allegiance, a choice of loyalties that, once made, can find expression in any number of postures, including the posture of sitting either in a rustic row or all about a courtly stable. It is thus an ability that need not be overtly exercised, because it is always being exercised as an orientation of the soul. It is precisely, then, a "harnass'd" ability, a power that in its readiness for action is the essence of action, at least as the poem has redefined it.

This redefinition of action as interior follows directly from the doctrine of Christian liberty as Milton expounds it in his *De Doctrina Christiana:* "Christian liberty is that whereby we are loosed as it were by enfranchisement, through Christ our deliverer, from the bondage of sin, and consequently from the rule of the law and man."[12] It is a doctrine, in other words, that frees man from the obligation to perform specific acts or to refrain from performing others; and Milton takes it so seriously that he is led, in the

second book of his treatise, to reject even the decalogue insofar as compliance with its commandments would involve going
against the prompting of faith. This does not mean, however,
that man is freed to do anything he likes. Christian liberty has
been granted us so that "being made sons instead of servants,
and perfect men instead of children, we may serve God in love
through the guidance of the spirit of truth"—that is, so that we
serve not because of some external compulsion, but because of
the prompting within us of the spirit with which we have become allied: "Moses imposed the letter, or external law . . .
whereas Christ writes the inward of God by his Spirit on the
hearts of believers, and leads them as willing followers" (1012).
Willing followers are those who are in a sense following themselves; for since they have internalized the law of God, their every motion, even when they are sitting or at rest, breathes it out.
As men of faith, they can only produce faithful works, and, indeed, as Milton insists, "faith . . . is the form of good works,"[13] a
category that has no fixed members but includes whatever issues
"from a sincere heart unbidden."[14] The regenerate man is unconcerned with particular performances, since his every moment is a
faithful performance so long as he remains regenerate—that is,
serviceable. This is why temptation in Milton's poetry often involves the substitution of a single punctual action for the continual action of keeping in tune, and the poet himself seems to yield
to that temptation when he expresses such high hopes for his
song. ("Have thou the honor first" [*Nativity Ode*, 26]); but it
is a temptation he resists when he is able to report the failure
of those hopes without any sense of personal disappointment:
"Time is our tedious Song should here have ending" (239).

The song is finally as anticlimactic as the event it so often
promises but never manages to narrate. He is not the first his
Lord to greet; indeed, he does not even get to greet him, for "the
Virgin blest, / Hath laid her Babe to rest" (237–238). And yet this

failure, insofar as it is accepted, is the mark of success, because it is a failure to stand apart, to be separate, to sing alone. By labeling his song "tedious" (which means belated as well as wearisome) and willingly giving it up, the poet joins the singers of another song, the singers of the fair music that all creatures make to their great Lord, whose love their motions sways. Here in the final stanza those motions are imperceptible and the music unheard, but to the inner ear and eye those absences merely signify how far we have moved from the unworthy expectations with which we began—expectations of drama, crisis, climax, plot, agency, and change. It is Milton's strategy in his poetry to detach us from those expectations and return us to a moment when nothing and everything is happening, to work us, after the example of Christ, a perpetual peace.

CHAPTER TEN

The Temptation of Speech

Let Us Wait

The sleeping babe at the center of the *Nativity Ode* grows up to be the young Jesus of *Paradise Regained,* and in that much later poem he is essentially the same figure, engaging in no action that the world would recognize as such, yet performing acts that are, as the verse says, "above heroic." These acts, not surprisingly, are also interior, without display or drama, so much so that it might be even more true to say of this poem what Fraser says of "At a Solemn Music": "Nothing happens." Again this is not wholly accurate. Satan is conspicuously busy most of the time, but his busyness is the busyness of a stage manager. He is constantly setting up scenes and arranging what he hopes will be confrontations, but his activity serves only to accentuate the anticlimactic nature of what happens when the scenes are played out and the confrontations actually occur. That is, the pattern of temptation-rejection which constitutes the whole of the poem's plot is itself patterned in such a way as to defuse the dramatic thrust it potentially embodies. Again and again Satan cranks up a huge amount of machinery, which in turn generates an enormous pressure of anticipation (What will the Son do? How will he get out of this one? What would I have done in his place?) only to be met, as we are met too, by an evasive and—in terms of the expectations the verse has encouraged—inadequate response: "No, thank you"; "I'd rather not"; "With my hunger what hast thou to do?"; "Think not but that I know these things; or think I know them not."

This stepping back from a situation, *after* the pressures it exerts have been acknowledged, is characteristic not only of the Son but of the unambiguously human characters who hang around the edges of the central drama in *Paradise Regained*. At the beginning of book II, we come upon the apostles (speaking chorus-like with one voice) and Mary, as they struggle to come to terms with the disconcerting fact of the Son's disappearance, and in the course of their soliloquies they display the pattern of inaction that is writ larger in the more extended temptation scenes. This is a pattern based on the disappointment of expectation, and it unfolds in two stages: (1) the establishment of a set of circumstances and the attendant felt need for an "appropriate" response, and (2) the subsequent withholding of that response. In this case the circumstances are established in the context of a formal complaint:

> Alas, from what high hope to what relapse
> Unlook'd for are we fall'n! Our eyes beheld
> Messiah certainly now come, so long
> Expected of our Fathers; we have heard
> His words, his wisdom full of grace and truth;
> Now, now, for sure, deliverance is at hand,

The Kingdom shall to *Israel* be restor'd:
Thus we rejoic'd, but soon our joy is turn'd
Into perplexity and new amaze:
For whither is he gone, what accident
Hath rapt him from us? will he now retire
After appearance, and again prolong
Our expectation? God of *Israel*,
Send thy Messiah forth, the time is come;
Behold the Kings of th'Earth how they oppress
Thy chosen, to what height thir pow'r unjust
They have exalted, and behind them cast
All fear of thee; arise and vindicate
Thy Glory, free thy people from thir yoke!
But let us wait.[1] (emphasis added)

In this passage the disappointment of expectation occurs on two levels: it is what the apostles are reacting to, and it is what we react to in the reaction of the apostles. They have been encouraged by the baptism of Jesus to believe that the deliverance of their nation "so long / Expected" is at hand; and just when the fulfillment of the scriptural promise seems imminent, it is apparently withdrawn. Understandably they react with perplexity and impatience, but, less understandably, that impatience leads neither to anger nor to disillusionment but to a renewal of patience—"But let us wait." To the extent that we find their resignation surprising (perplexing), it presents us with the same problem that the disappearance of Jesus presents to them. It is not on its face sufficient to the occasion; and our experience of its insufficiency is very much like our experience of the Son's conduct in the temptation scenes.

Significantly, the desire of the apostles for a dramatic and imminent redress of their many grievances (a desire we come to share) is the basis of the appeals and arguments with which Satan attempts to provoke the Son to action: "Thy years are ripe, and over-ripe" (III, 31); "Zeal and Duty are not slow, / But on Occasion's forelock watchful wait" (172–173); "each act is rightliest done, / Not when it must, but when it may be best" (IV, 475–476). In short, "the time is come," and if you seize it not, the deliverance of Israel will not be effected and the kings of the earth will continue to oppress God's people: "*Judaea* now and all the promis'd land / Reduc't a Province under Roman yoke" (III, 157–158); "Zeal of thy Father's house, Duty to free / Thy Country from her Heathen servitude" (175–176); "Might'st thou expel this monster from his Throne / Now made a sty, and in his place ascending / A victor people free from servile yoke" (IV, 100–102). In every instance, Jesus stubbornly reaffirms the resolution the apostles make here in book II—to do nothing at all:

> But let us wait. (49)

> I shall first
> Be tried in humble state . . .
> Suffering, abstaining, quietly expecting. (III, 188–189, 192)

> My time I told thee . . .
> . . . is not yet come.
> To his due time and providence I leave them. (396–397, 440)

Waiting is the only action (or nonaction) the characters in *Paradise Regained* ever take, and this includes Mary, whose moving expression of a mother's anxieties is preliminary to a similar declaration of passivity:

> what avails me now that honor high
> To have conceiv'd of God, or that salute,
> Hail highly favor'd, among women blest!
> While I to sorrows am no less advanc't,
> And fears as eminent, above the lot

Of other women, by the birth I bore,

. . . . .

But where delays he now? some great intent
Conceals him: when twelve years he scarce had seen,
I lost him, but so found, as well I saw
He could not lose himself; but went about
His Father's business; what he meant I mus'd,
Since understand; much more his absence now
Thus long to some great purpose he obscures.
But I to wait with patience am inur'd. (II, 66–71, 95–102; emphasis added)

Again, by omitting any transition between the anguished voicing of genuine needs and the unexpectedly sudden gesture of resignation, the poet calls attention to the perversity (in human terms) of his characters' nonresponse. For in neither soliloquy is Milton concerned to portray a mind whose processes correspond to our idea of a "normal" psychology; in both cases the conclusion—"But let us wait," "But I to wait with patience am inur'd"—is felt to be wholly discontinuous with the strong sense of urgency communicated by the lines that precede it. The result is a reading experience that can fairly be characterized as frustrating.

And, indeed, frustration is characteristic of much of our experience of *Paradise Regained.* Again and again the verse creates in us a need for resolution, in the form of some action or event, and again and again (as in "At a Solemn Music") it declines to fulfill the need it has itself created. When the apostles search for the absent Christ, the roll call of places they visit exerts a pressure for his discovery, not only in Judea but in the verse: "in *Jericho* / The City of Palms, *Aenon,* and *Salem* Old, / *Machaerus* and each Town or City wall'd / On this side the broad lake *Genezaret,* / Or in *Peraea*" (20–24); but the search and the forward movement of the poetry end alike in an anticlimax and in the disappointment of the expectations of both the apostles and the reader: "but return'd in vain" (24). In the account of his early life, the Son re-calls, and re-creates in his language, the attraction he felt, and now makes us feel, for decisive action:

> yet this not all
> To which my Spirit aspir'd; victorious deeds
> Flam'd in my heart, heroic acts; one while
> To rescue *Israel* from the *Roman* yoke,
> Then to subdue and quell o'er all the earth
> Brute violence and proud Tyrannic pow'r,
> Till truth were freed, and equity restor'd. (I, 214–220)

The rhetoric is martial, but Jesus declines its urgings (even though they are his own) and refuses to deliver the response he himself has called for: "Yet held it more humane, more heavenly, first / By winning words to conquer willing hearts, / And make persuasion do the work of fear" (221–223). The point is of course an orthodox one, but in the context established so forcefully by the verse—"To rescue *Israel* from the *Roman* yoke," "to sub-due . . . / Brute violence and proud Tyrannic pow'r"—it seems less than what is required, and we are left with the disappoint-ment of an issue unresolved, and a confrontation avoided.

These are small moments, and one would hesitate to make much of the pattern they embody were it not also the pattern of the temptation scenes, which are constructed in such a way as to make us feel the pressures of the issues they involve. The first temptation draws us in immediately, and Arnold Stein's com-ments are very much to the point: "After the long introduction, which has prepared us for a long contest, the sudden brush, abrupt and possibly final, catches the reader unprepared; in the immediate heightening of his sense of the dangerous excitement potential in the contest, he is, by the most physical of dramatic means, made to identify himself with the protagonist."[2] The question I would ask is, "Which protagonist?" for Satan's trap is baited in such a way as to make it impossible for the reader to dismiss its appeal as easily as Jesus seems to:

> But if thou be the Son of God, Command
> That out of these hard stones be made thee bread;
> So shalt thou save thyself and us relieve
> With Food, whereof we wretched seldom taste. (*PR*, I, 342–345)

"So shalt thou save thyself and us relieve." The subtlety of this suggestion, at least insofar as it works upon the reader, is to be located in its tail-like second half, "and us relieve." This is the first appearance in the poem of what Stein finely calls "the bait of charity" (91). The "us" in question are of course the men of the desert, born, as Satan says, to "much misery and hardship" (*PR*, I, 341); and the reality of their suffering is not diminished simply because the tempter is discerned to be other than he "seem'st" (348). That is to say, while Satan surely lies when he represents himself as one of the "wretched," this does not mean that there are none who live under the conditions he describes. All of the temptations in *Paradise Regained* are real, in the sense that they are posed with reference to real problems, and all of them, as Stein's summary statement indicates, are baited with charity: "The stones turned to bread would provide food for self and the 'wretched'; the acceptance of the banquet would relieve nature and her 'gentle Ministers' of their troubled shame over the hunger of the lord of nature; the affectation of 'private life' was depriving 'All Earth her wonder at thy acts'; the acceptance of Parthia would deliver the ten tribes, as their fathers were delivered from the land of Egypt" (91).[3] But if the concerns to which Satan's arguments speak are acknowledged and validated by the moral reader, they are either ignored or scorned by the responses of the Son:

> He ended, and the Son of God replied.
> Think'st thou such force in Bread? is it not written
> (For I discern thee other than thou seem'st)
> Man lives not by Bread only, but each Word
> Proceeding from the mouth of God, who fed
> Our Fathers here with Manna? In the Mount
> *Moses* was forty days, nor eat nor drank,
> And forty days *Eliah* without food
> Wander'd this barren waste; the same I now:
> Why dost thou then suggest to me distrust? (*PR*, I, 346–355)

Rather than deal with the issues Satan's challenge raises, Jesus seizes on what is almost a literary quibble to make his very special point. He takes "save thyself" in its spiritual significance and proceeds as if hunger were not a reality but a metaphor. As a result, the dialogue becomes a vehicle of *non*communication; we hear two voices supposedly addressing each other, but they issue from wholly different points of reference. The temptation is proffered in the context of a perceived human need, but the response is made in terms of the way in which Satan's request—"Turn these stones into bread"—reflects on the Son's relationship to God. "Why dost thou then suggest to me distrust" is the line that pinpoints *his* concern. "If I were to do as you ask, it would imply that God cannot sustain his servants without natural means. The examples of Moses and Elijah—who trusted—suggest otherwise, and it is in their tradition that I would enroll myself." On one level, of course, this is a perfect and orthodox response; but on another level (of which we cannot but be aware) it is profoundly unsatisfactory, if only because the immediate problem (and this continues to be true in every instance) is left behind, not even dismissed but simply unattended to—except perhaps by the reader, who in later scenes is himself one of those whom Jesus declines to help.

333

The parallel to the soliloquies of Mary and the apostles is, I trust, obvious. There is the same felt disparity between the presentation of the problem and the egregious passivity of the (non)response. Just at that moment when we expect an issue to be met head on, the speaker wraps himself in a piety and says, in effect, "Let God worry about it." Later it will be: let God worry about the Roman populace groaning under the yoke of an aged and sybaritic emperor; let God bring about the deliverance of the ten lost tribes; let God's word do the work some would assign to human eloquence.

Me Hungering to Do My Father's Will

This, of course, is a critique from a Satanic point of view, but it is the Satanic point of view that we share, at least during the early stages of the poem. That is to say, the poem's basic pattern—of pressure in the direction of action followed by a deliberate refusal to act—is as exasperating for us as it is for Satan. The difference, finally, is what is made of that exasperation. Satan is trapped by it, unable to deviate from his planned course of action even after it has repeatedly proved unsuccessful. Modern clinicians would call his behavior compulsive. Milton's diagnosis takes the form of a series of powerful and related images:

> But as a man who had been matchless held
> In cunning, overreach't where least he thought,
> To salve his credit, and for very spite
> Still will be tempting him who foils him still,
> And never cease, though to his shame the more;
> Or as a swarm of flies in vintage time,
> About the wine-press where sweet must is pour'd,
> Beat off, returns as oft with humming sound;
> Or surging waves against a solid rock,
> Though all to shivers dash't, th'assault renew,

> Vain batt'ry, and in froth or bubbles end;
> So Satan, whom repulse upon repulse
> Met ever, and to shameful silence brought,
> Yet gives not o'er though desperate of success,
> And his vain importunity pursues. (*PR*, IV, 10–24)

No amount of "bad success" will provoke Satan to reconsider his strategy and the assumptions behind it. He learns nothing from experience and is thus a perfect example of one who is "'morally' so indisposed toward truth that nothing would suffice to make [him] see,"[4] a mind so complacent in its own limitations as to be unteachable, even by the searchingly irenic method of dialectic.

As readers, however, we are in a different position, and the problem the Son's conduct poses for us is correspondingly different. Satan wants to know who Jesus is and is frustrated by his inability to force him out into the open. We know from the first who Jesus is, and if we are frustrated, it is because evasiveness and passivity are not part of what we know. Satan's interest in the Son's statements is limited to the indication they give of the success or failure of his strategy, while the reader's interest is a function of a predisposition to regard the Son as an exemplary figure. What is a challenge for one is a puzzle for the other. What does this mean? Why is the Savior responding in this curious way? In what sense are we to imitate *these* (non)actions?[5] Thus, while Satan's question "What dost thou in this World?" (*PR*, IV, 372) is rhetorical in the sense that he neither expects nor desires an answer, we readers, whose stake in the whole matter is very much greater, ask the question seriously: "What dost thou in this World?"

The answer of course is right there on the surface, where important answers usually are, and it is given innumerable times, although Satan never understands it and the reader's understanding is something he must work for. Not surprisingly, the Son himself provides the most precisely direct explanation of what he is doing: "Mee hung'ring more to do my Father's will" (II, 259). Every time the Son declines the opportunity to redress a wrong or meet a need, he refuses to claim for himself an efficacy apart from God. No matter what form Satan's temptations take, their thrust is always to get Jesus to substitute his will for God's, to respond to his own sense of crisis, to rely only on remedies which are at hand and in his own control. The temptation, then, whatever issues Satan attempts to attach to it, is preeminently a temptation to self-assertion—"save thyself" (I, 344); "if at great things thou wouldst arrive" (II, 426); "These Godlike Virtues wherefore dost thou hide?" (III, 21); "Aim therefore at no less than all the world" (IV, 105); "So let extend thy mind o'er all the world" (IV, 223)— and in relation to it, not doing anything is the most positive of actions. That is, doing the Father's will requires the relinquishing of one's own, the most difficult of all acts, although its visible manifestations are necessarily unimpressive. "What dost thou in this World?" I do my Father's will, and therefore *I* do nothing.

Obviously, the choice of a hero whose main business is the immolation of his own will presents certain difficulties (which are actually difficulties in the nature of the audience). All of the strengths, poetic and dramatic, are on the other side. Milton is as aware of this as anyone, but his strategy is not, as one might expect, to minimize the attractiveness of self-assertion or (somehow) to make passivity dramatically appealing. Rather, he chooses to regard our natural affinity for language and actions that are concrete and immediately satisfying as a symptom of a radical defect, which, if it is to be extirpated, must first be acknowledged. Accordingly, he deliberately provokes what will, in the context of a reader's predisposed sympathies, be recognized as the *wrong* response or at least a response that is problematic, and therefore a response we will feel obliged to think about. That is to say, the reader who is discomforted by the Son's behavior will be moved to ask a question—"What can this mean?"—and to the extent that he becomes able to answer the question, the source of his discomfort will be removed.

This suggests a pattern of (possible) progress in our career as readers—from impatience to understanding to approval—which constitutes a subplot in the poem's action. The main plot works itself out in terms of the Son's response to Satan; the reader's plot, in terms of a response to the Son's response to Satan. The Son declines to act on the basis of the motives Satan nominates, caring only to do his Father's will; but these are motives which are at least superficially appealing, and it is disconcerting when they are not only scorned but dismissed, as if the issues of hunger and poverty and tyranny were fictions. It is not that we want the Son to do what Satan asks, but that we want him to do *something,* even if it is only to explain himself more fully. What he does, however, is move on, leaving us to do the explaining (it is the task the poem sets us) and to come to terms with the inappropriateness of his response. If we succeed—and the critical history of the poem indicates that success is by no means assured—it is because our idea of what is "appropriate," and therefore *our* response to him, has changed.

This change of response, if it occurs, is an action parallel to the action the Son performs in the narrative: the subordination of the self. In the act of understanding the poem, or trying to, we become less self-centered; for to the extent that understanding involves approval of what the Son does, it involves also discarding the values in which the dignity of the self inheres—wealth, power, fame, charity, statesmanship, language, literature, philosophy, mind—and substituting for them the single and all-inclusive value of obedience to God. In terms of the choice the poem poses for us, a choice of responses, obedience to God is a function of our relationship to its hero. A successful reading of the poem will ultimately be marked by a *re*valuing of the Son's passivity, which implies of course a *de*valuing of assertive action and self-expression. The experience of the poem is, for the reader as well as for the Son, a denying of the claims of the individual will—each stage of it imposes a further restriction on the operation of that will—and, for both, the end of that experience is nothing less than the putting away of the self.

Talk

It is not surprising, then, that the pattern of action in the poem—the progressive narrowing (to nothing) of the area in which the self is allowed to operate—should be paralleled by a pattern of language in the course of which the individual voice is more and more circumscribed until in the end it falls silent. Speech no less than action (it *is* an action) is the potential vehicle of pride; the more one approaches the state of perfect obedience, the less distinctive and identifiable one's accents will be.

It is a commonplace of criticism to observe that *Paradise Regained* is a contest not only of wills but of styles.[6] Satan's language, especially when it becomes the vehicle of temptation, is full, luxuriant, rhythmically satisfying and rhetorically dazzling, while the Son's replies display a rather narrow range, from terseness ("What hast thou to do with my hunger?") to obfuscation ("Think not but that I know these things or think I know them not") to what is one of the worst lines in English poetry: "Mee worse than wet thou find'st not." These styles reflect the stances and attitudes of the two speakers: on the one hand, an imagination in love with its own fanciful creations; on the other, in Louis Martz's words, "a mind engaged in an immense effort at self-control . . . poised, tense, alert, watching any tendency toward elaboration, luxury, self-indulgence."[7] "Self-indulgence" is exactly right, for the Son's language, in its restraint and anonymity, is further evidence of his determination to give the least possible scope to the self. It is the verbal equivalent of standing and waiting, of doing nothing, and the judgment it makes on more personal styles is perfectly predictable:

> Remove their swelling Epithets thick laid
> As varnish on a Harlot's cheek, the rest,
> Thin sown with aught of profit or delight,
> Will be found unworthy. (PR, IV, 343–346)

This famously disturbing statement has caused Milton's admirers much embarrassment. Even Martz feels obliged to account for a judgment "so much more drastic and more violent than that made by the rest of the poem." The "whole poem," he explains, "qualifies and moderates this fierce renunciation."[8] I would say, rather, that the whole poem prepares us for this renunciation, which is as inevitable as it is sweeping. The increasingly marked contrast between the two styles coincides with the reader's increasing awareness of what it is that the Son is refusing to do: declare his independence of God. As a result, language becomes identified not only with the false values (wealth, power, earthly kingship) that are the basis of Satan's appeal but also with the overruling temptation they always represent—the temptation to value (and therefore to assert) the self.

It is for this reason that the drama of the temptation scenes is counterpointed by a sustained attack on "talk." The first epithet the Son applies to Satan suggests that the fiend's substance is largely verbal: "compos'd of lies" (I, 407). Lying, the Son continues, is "thy sustenance, thy food" (429), a food Satan offers to "the Nations" (432) in the form of verbal "Delusions" (443). When the Kingdom of Heaven is established, Satan will fall silent ("they shall find thee mute" [459]), and mankind will be nourished not by words but by the living Word which dwells in "pious Hearts":

> God hath now sent his living Oracle
> Into the World to teach his final will,
> And sends his Spirit of Truth henceforth to dwell
> In pious Hearts, an inward Oracle
> To all truth requisite for men to know. (I, 460–464)

There is in these lines an implied equation (later to be made explicit) between illumination and silence, an equation that quite probably has its source in Augustine: "For God speaks with a man not by means of some bodily creature making sound in bodily ears . . . Rather he speaks by the truth itself, if one is worthy of listening with the mind instead of with the body."[9] The man whose heart is the dwelling place of God's truth will find bodily sounds superfluous and distracting. This distinction between an inner and an outer word is one that Satan never understands, although in his volubility he continues to reinforce it. The ways of Truth, he complains, are "Hard . . . and rough to walk" (PR, I, 478) but they are "Smooth on the tongue." I may be unable to follow them, he says, but "permit me / To hear thee . . . / And talk at least" (483–485). Satan talks and talks and talks, and at every opportunity the Son displays his scorn for the productions of the tongue. You say that my years are overripe and I have not yet had my share of glory? "What is glory but the blaze of fame, / The people's praise . . . / And what delight to be by such extoll'd, / To live upon thir tongues and be thir talk" (III, 47–48, 54–55). For one who would live upon the Manna of the Word, there could be nothing more truly inglorious. Even celebrated heroes like Scipio gain a reward that is "but verbal" (104).

All the while, Satan's honeyed speeches grow longer and longer, until, in the description of Rome, "the rich, sensuous coloring and high rhetoric of the world" is carried "to its absolute and appropriate limit."[10] Characteristically the Son remains "unmov'd," and responds with a parody of the Satanic style:

> thou should'st add to tell
> Thir sumptuous gluttonies, and gorgeous feasts
> On *Citron* tables or *Atlantic* stone,
> (For I have also heard, perhaps have read)
> Their wines of *Setia, Cales,* and *Falerne,*
> *Chios* and *Crete,* and how they quaff in Gold,
> Crystals and Murrhine cups emboss'd with Gems
> And studs of Pearl, to me should'st tell who thirst
> And hunger still. (IV, 113–121)

So secure is the Son that he offers Satan a literary critique and even suggests additions that would make his tempter's presentation more effective. He also demonstrates how easy it would be for him to contend with Satan on his own rhetorical terms, were they not so contemptible. The anticipatory judgment of "sumptuous gluttonies" falls as much on the language as on the content of the succeeding six lines. By this point, the Son is less angry than bored; it is, he complains, "But tedious waste of time to sit and hear / So many hollow compliments and lies, / Outlandish flatteries . . . *talk*" (123–125, emphasis added). When Satan obliges with a more direct statement of his terms —"The Kingdoms of the world to thee I give; / . . . if thou wilt fall down" (163–166)—his offer, *and* his "talk," are rejected with "disdain": "I never lik'd thy talk, thy offers less, / Now both abhor, since thou hast dar'd to utter / Th'abominable terms" (171–173). Satan's "talk" and the kingdoms over which he claims to rule are allied in their inferiority to an inner word and an inward kingdom. For a moment, the fiend himself seems to acknowledge this—"let pass, as they are transitory, / The Kingdoms of this world" (209–210)—and in their place he offers, of all things, the ability to talk. The substance of the temptation has been the kingdoms of the world, the vehicle a language reflecting the values of those kingdoms. Having rejected the substance, the Son is now offered the vehicle:

as thy Empire must extend,
So let extend thy mind o'er all the world,
In knowledge, all things in it comprehend.
All knowledge is not couch't in *Moses'* Law,
The *Pentateuch* or what the Prophets wrote;
The *Gentiles* also know, and write, and teach
To admiration, led by Nature's light;
And with the *Gentiles* much thou must converse,
Ruling them by persuasion as thou mean'st,
Without thir learning how wilt thou with them,
Or they with thee hold conversation meet? (IV, 222–232)

It is in these lines that the true status of language in relation to the central issue of the poem is revealed. It is not merely that talk is valueless, but that Satan's invitation to value talk is an invitation to value the self. This is clearly what is meant when the Son is urged to "let extend thy mind o'er all the world." Satan is here an apostle of the creative imagination, of the poet as maker and self-acknowledged legislator of the world. The "thick laid varnish" of secular literature is the overlay of man's brain (what Herbert calls his "sparkling notions") on the clarity of God's word. Its superfluousness is the superfluousness of the individual mind to the validation of truth, and when the Son rejects the arts of language he does what he has been doing all along: he refuses to play God.[11]

The dismissal of pagan learning, then, is not a gesture discontinuous with what we have seen previously; rather, it follows inevitably from the hero's attempt to find a mode of action which embodies the least recognition of the self, and to the extent that we have come to understand his other attempts in this direction, we will understand this one too. For if the experience of the poem effects a change in our response to Christ's actions, it effects a corresponding change in our response to his language.

The reversal of values, away from the self and toward God, is also an aesthetic reversal. Selflessness and stylelessness are one.

Also It Is Written

To this point, our investigation of *Paradise Regained* has yielded a description of its movement which accords perfectly with the outline put forward earlier in this chapter: it is a poem concerned to work out the relationship between man and God, and it proceeds on two levels. On the narrative level, there is a progressive narrowing of the area in which the self is preeminent or even active; and on the verbal level, there is a corresponding diminishing, first of the complexity of language, and then of its volubility; and the two diminishings put pressure on us as readers to reverse our initial response to the stances of the protagonists. It remains only to point out that these patterns complete themselves at the poem's climactic moment, when inaction is raised to the level of disappearance and terseness of speech finds it apex in silence. I refer of course to the moment when Satan places the Son on the pinnacle, expecting him either to fall down and so prove himself no adversary or to cast himself down and so tempt God's providence. He does neither. He does nothing. *He* disappears: "To whom thus Jesus. Also it is written, / Tempt not the Lord thy God; he said and stood" (IV, 560–561). Line 561 is, as Barbara Lewalski observes, "notably ambiguous."[12] Does Jesus here say (as he has said before), "If I were to do as you suggest I would be tempting God's providence," or does he say, "You ought not to tempt your God, who I am"? This ambiguity has been resolved by A. S. P. Woodhouse, who declares for both meanings: "This is Christ's supreme act of obedience and trust, and it is also the long-awaited demonstration of divinity. The poem's two themes are finally and securely united; and 'Tempt not the Lord thy God'

carries a double meaning, for, in addition to its immediate application, it is Christ's first claim to participate in the Godhead. In
an instant, and by the same event, Satan receives his answer and
Christ achieves full knowledge of himself."[13] To this interpretation Arnold Stein long ago, in *Heroic Knowledge,* opposed a vigorous and compelling dissent:

> What has happened? Surely not that Christ is directly replying to
> Satan's challenge by finally declaring himself, by saying: thou
> shalt not tempt *me,* the Lord thy God! That would be to violate
> the whole discipline, so perfectly sustained, of Christ's moral
> and intellectual example: the witness of whence he is by the
> seeking of glory not for himself but for Him who sent him, the
> hungering to do the Father's will. (128)

> To see this as Christ's "claim" . . . is to abandon much of the
> force of the disciplined demonstration—as well as to abandon
> Milton's own passionate religious and moral belief, and his own
> disciplined unwillingness to pry into God's maintained myster-
> ies. (224–225)

Stein's objection can be met and yet sustained if we specify the
nature of the "claim" being made. The assertion that the figure
on the pinnacle is the Lord God is anything but prideful, for
Christ's "claim" to that identity rests on his demonstrated willingness to lose his own. He is God to the extent that *he,* as a consciousness distinguishable from God, is no more. The "supreme
act of obedience" is also the supreme act of resignation, a letting
go of the self so final that no trace of it remains. "Tempt not the
Lord thy God; he said." Who said? The Son, of course, since the
sounds issue from his mouth, but the words are not his ("Also it is
written") except in the sense that he has identified himself with
their speaker. It is not that he appropriates the words, but that
they, and their source, appropriate him. This is what Augustine
means when he declares that "the word of God is not another's

to those who obey it."[14] The man who wraps himself in the Scriptures, as Christ does here, becomes an adjunct of them and ceases to have an independent existence. This is not an extra-literary point, but one made by the reading experience itself, when we are unable to separate out the responsibility for this line. The voice we hear is not the voice we have come to know, but the impersonal voice suggested by the "it" in "it is written." Christ does nothing less here than find a way to assert selfless-ness. It is a linguistic miracle in which language, the primary sign of personality, becomes the means by which personality is extin-guished. The Son performs the impossible feat of saying silence and makes himself disappear.

In his place is a new and stronger self, the amalgam I-thou to whose presence the force of the ambiguity bears witness. The only response we can give to these lines is, as Stein remarks, a "gasp," in recognition of the tremendous power that has been re-leased by the Son's voluntary laying down of his identity. What is demonstrated here is not divinity, but the reward which awaits anyone (including the reader) who subordinates his will to that of the Father. Every man can be God if he answers Satan's ques-tion—"Who are you?"—as Christ does: "I am what the Father will make of me." To say "I am nothing" is to be (with God) ev-erything.[15] George Herbert spoke of this strength through weak-ness, gain through loss, power through inaction, as "imping my wing on thine,"[16] and in another poem ("The Holdfast") he draws the moral: "All things are more ours by their being his." In Para-dise Regained, that truth is dramatically validated by what happens to the Son when he succeeds (exactly the wrong word) in empty-ing himself of all but his hunger to do his Father's will. Every-thing he has renounced in his own name is restored to him ten-fold. The angels whose presence he refused to command in the wilderness now bring to him the fruit of life in place of the deadly fruit he had rejected: the victory he had scorned when the means and the time were specified by Satan is now his in the moment of Satan's defeat ("But Satan smitten with amazement fell" [*PR*, IV, 562]), and his earlier prophecy—"Who advance his glory, not thir own, / Them he himself to glory will advance"—is spectacularly fulfilled, as his triumph is celebrated not by the tongues of a miscellaneous rabble but by "Angelic Choirs" and "Heavenly Anthems." Even language and the arts of literature are returned to him (and to the reader) in the form of the magnificent Antaeus simile, pagan still, but now newly washed and baptized in the name of the Lord. Yet of all the things restored to the Son, the most important is surely the opportunity, so many times offered and so many times refused, to save. Whatever dismay the reader may at times have felt at the Son's evasiveness and passivity is now more than redeemed by the intensely personal reassurance tendered him in the poem's quietly powerful closing: "Now enter, and begin to save mankind" (IV, 635).

In other words, "Now begin to act." Action, which has before been the vehicle of temptation, is now not only allowed but enjoined. This is no paradox, but a final recognition of the distinction to which the Son has been faithful in the course of his trials, a distinction that is finely drawn by Northrop Frye: "The Christian must learn to will to relax the will, to perform real acts in God's time and not pseudo acts in his own."[17] In order to perform real acts—that is, acts in accordance with the will of God—one must first refrain from performing pseudo acts, acts which reflect and assert the will of the individual; so that the prerequisite for real action is the disposition to withhold action even in the face of situations which seem to call for it. It is this disposition that has informed the Son's behavior and presented so much of a puzzle to Satan and, for a time, to the reader:

> Suffering, abstaining, quietly expecting
> Without distrust or doubt, that he may know

> What I can suffer, how obey? who best
> Can suffer, best can do; best reign, who first
> Well hath obey'd. (*PR*, III, 192–196)

This ordering of obligations is mirrored perfectly in the form of the narrative and in the relationship between its events and the response of the reader. The Son suffers and obeys, and the subordination of his will to the will of the Father is reflected in his passivity. That passivity, in turn, acts as a constraint on the response of the reader, who would like to be able to applaud some decisive action. When the Son's triumph over himself is complete, his active powers (no longer his) are released; and this releases and authorizes the response of the reader. Moreover, the action we now applaud, the multiple defeats of Satan (past, present, future), includes or makes possible all the actions which we would have liked the Son to perform when they were urged by Satan—the feeding of the hungry, the restoration of David's throne, the quelling of tyrannical power, and the freeing of the people from their (inner) yoke. In short, action and response are purified together; one has its proper direction (provided by God) and the other its proper object (the doing of God's will), and what was disallowed to both hero and reader when the circumstances and the conditions were nominated by Satan (in the name of the self) is now authorized and approved when the circumstances and the conditions are nominated by God. What the poem asks that we give up it returns in exactly the measure of our compliance with its request.

Yet even here, when the frustration large and small of the verse and the narrative are swept away in a prolonged moment of action and response, it is a moment of anticipation and a response to events that do not occur within the confines of the poem. *Paradise Regained* remains true to its own self-imposed limitations, which are the limitations it has imposed on its hero and its readers, and ends with another of the withdrawals from drama and speech that have been the basis of its dialectic:

> Thus they the Son of God our Savior meek
> Sung Victor, and from Heavenly Feast refresht
> Brought on his way with joy; hee unobserv'd
> Home to his Mother's house private return'd. (IV, 636–639)[18]

CHAPTER ELEVEN

The Temptation of Plot

Dream Not of Their Fight

If the withdrawal from drama is a pervasive feature of Milton's work, it is a feature both readers and characters resist, and that resistance has its source in a profound misreading of the human situation and its relation to the possibility and agency of redemption. Nowhere is this clearer than in a moment I have earlier noted, when an excited Adam asks the archangel Michael a question. After a succession of mistakes and misreadings, Adam thinks that he finally discerns the shape of God's providential plan, and now understands what oft his steadiest thoughts have sought in vain: the meaning of the prophecy by which the woman's seed will bruise the head of the serpent. That seed, he now learns from Michael, will be the Son of God incarnate; and in response to this "good news" he ventures, as he has before, to predict the future: "Needs must the Serpent now his capital

349

bruise / Expect with mortal pain: say where and when / Thir fight, what stroke shall bruise the Victor's heel."[1]

Michael's reply is, as his replies so often are, a rebuke:

> To whom thus *Michael*. Dream not of thir fight,
> As of a Duel, or the local wounds
> Of head or heel: not therefore joins the Son
> Manhood to Godhead, with more strength to foil
> Thy enemy; nor so is overcome
> *Satan*, whose fall from Heav'n, a deadlier bruise,
> Disabl'd not to give thee thy death's wound:
> Which hee, who comes thy Saviour, shall recure,
> Not by destroying *Satan*, but his works
> In thee and in thy Seed. (PL, XII, 386–395)

These lines challenge, in both obvious and subtle ways, every one of the assumptions underlying Adam's question. When Michael says, "Dream not of thir fight," he means first of all that the fight is not exclusively theirs, and that Adam is wrong to assume the role of a spectator ("say where and when" is the demand of someone who is hoping for a front-row seat). He is also wrong to think of it as a fight: it is neither a duel—a single and dramatic encounter in which the winner takes all—nor local; that is, it is not limited in its effects to the infliction of this or that wound. It would make no sense for God to join with man merely to fight a battle he could have fought without moving one step from his heavenly throne. Indeed, God has already fought such a battle, and, as Michael points out, in no way has his victory (recorded in book VI) prevented Satan from giving Adam his "death's wound." Of course that wound was no more final than was Satan's fall from heaven. Adam is making precisely the same mistake he made earlier, in book X, when he expected Death to dispatch him in a single stroke (771ff.). Here he expects the father of Death to be dispatched in the same way; what he must learn is what he learned before, when he realized that death may "be not one stroke, as I suppos'd," "but a slow-pac't evil, / A long day's dying" (X, 809, 963–964).

What Michael tells him now is that redemptive history will be a long day's living, and that it is not to be thought of as a once-and-for-all encounter between mighty antagonists in relation to whom man is only an interested bystander. Insofar as there is a struggle, it is, first, a continuous one, and, second, one that, far from being external to man, claims him for its arena. This point is made forcefully in the space between lines 394 and 395 of book XII: "Not by destroying *Satan*, but his works / In thee." There is a double *correctio* here: salvation shall consist not of destroying Satan—who is less an independent force than a *choice* that is continually available to all men—but of destroying his works. Yet even this formulation must be revised, because as it stands in line 394 "his works" seem to be palpable and visible monuments to his power, a power that can be removed by an even greater power (for example, God's thunder). The delayed revelation of line 395, "In thee and in thy Seed," has the effect of emphasizing the interiority of the works—they manifest themselves in tendencies of human behavior—and thus of emphasizing the time (all of time) that will be required to extirpate them. That is why to "In thee" Michael adds "and in thy Seed." The contest between good and evil will be decided not just in a single combat, but in an interior purging; that purging will not be confined to the heart of one man, but must be effected in the heart of every man.

Adam, then, is wrong on three related counts. He is wrong (1) to conceive of the moral life as climaxing in a single decisive encounter; (2) to see himself in relation to that encounter as an outsider; and (3) to think of that encounter as an event in the world of circumstances rather than as a process that is continually occurring in the interior world of the spirit. He is entirely mistaken as to the nature of moral action, which he tends to identify with something that is measurable by the changes it effects in the external world. True moral action, however, is entirely internal, and always has the form specified by Michael in the very next lines: "nor can this be, / But by fulfilling that which thou didst want, / Obedience to the Law of God" (395–397). Again, Milton takes advantage of the line break to put the strongest possible stress on the important word: "obedience." This is the only rule of action Michael delivers, and it is followed immediately by a perfect and exemplary illustration: the Passion. As an act, the Passion is distinguished by the immobility of the actor. It would seem from one point of view—the point of view from which Adam calls for the heroics of a duel—that Christ doesn't *do* anything, but in fact he does everything. That is, he performs the only act that merits the name: he obeys, and it is "this God-like act" that, Michael declares, "Shall bruise the head of *Satan*" (427, 430). What is remarkable about this bruising is that it occurs without contact. That is, Satan's wound is inflicted at long distance, and is incurred not because of something that is *done* to him (in the crude physical sense expected by Adam) but because of something that is *shown* to him, a mode of being whose very presence in the world brings about his defeat. Christ does not force Satan to withdraw (as he does in book VI) but exerts a force on him by comporting himself in such a way as to frustrate all his wiles and stratagems.

The moment (which is here of course only anticipated) is characteristic of the "victories" enjoyed by Milton's heroes, who never clash with their great opposites, but repulse them merely by declaring and holding fast to a vision of the world in which Satanic power is an illusion. This is what the Lady in *Comus* does when she declares, "Thou canst not touch the freedom of my mind" (663), thereby denying the relevance of the (bodily) sphere over which the sorcerer has apparent power, and it is what Christ will do, again and again, in *Paradise Regained*. The declaration (whether in word or deed) is always received in the same way by the antihero, who reels as if struck by a blow, even though no blow has been landed. The pattern for this encounter (hardly an encounter at all) is set in the *Nativity Ode* when the fleeing of the pagan deities is attributed to the force of a recumbent babe, who exerts his control without moving from his cradle, and who, at the moment when his power is most felt, is in the act (if that is the word) of falling asleep (stanza XXVII).

The moral in all of these poems is the same moral Michael points to here: the true form of action is not something one *does* (a wound inflicted, a battle waged) but something one *is*. Or—to revisit the point as it was made in Chapter 9—for Milton, being *is* an action, which therefore is to be identified not with any particular gesture or set of gestures, but with an orientation or commitment of which any gesture can be an expression. What this means is that there is no possibility of locating the value of an action in its external form, in something that can be "formally, and profestly set down."[2] This in turn means that a list of virtuous actions—or, alternatively, of actions tending away from virtue—cannot be compiled, which in turn means that the idea of positive law, with its list of fixed external prohibitions, becomes untenable.

This removal of the law from external inspection follows from the doctrine of Christian liberty: "CHRISTIAN LIBERTY MEANS THAT CHRIST OUR LIBERATOR FREES US FROM THE SLAVERY OF SIN AND THUS FROM THE RULE OF THE LAW AND OF MEN, AS IF WE WERE EMANCIPATED SLAVES. HE DOES THIS SO THAT, BEING MADE SONS INSTEAD OF SERVANTS AND GROW UP MEN INSTEAD OF BOYS, WE MAY SERVE GOD IN CHARITY THROUGH THE GUIDANCE OF THE SPIRIT OF TRUTH."[3] The spirit of truth is the "internal law" that Christ "writes . . . on the hearts of believers," who are then led "as willing followers" (535). That is, the removal of one law, the external law of works, does not free man to do anything he likes (the antinomian conclusion which frightened so many in the seventeenth century), because it has been replaced by another law, which, insofar as it originates within, exerts even more compulsion than the precepts of the decalogue. Christian liberty, then, is a liberty that binds, and it binds one to a standard even stricter than the standard (of outwardly imposed constraints) from which we have been freed. "It is not a less perfect life that is required from Christians but, in fact, a more perfect life than was required of those who were under the law" (535). The greater perfection inheres in the scope of the new law, which extends not merely to a set of proscribed and prescribed actions but to every action man performs, since every action, if it is to be counted a virtuous one, must conform to the law written on our hearts. In the place of ten commandments, the believer has only one—do good—but the obligation to obey that command is continuous and uninterrupted.

This means that not only is there no list of virtuous and evil actions; there is also no moment at which the pressure to perform is greater (or lesser) than at any other; since service under the new law is a matter not of following directions but of *having* a direction (an orientation, a loyalty, an allegiance), one has it not at particular times and in response to extraordinary circumstances, but at all times and in response to any and all circumstances. Indeed, since every circumstance presents the possibility of either keeping to or straying from the way, there is finally no meaningful distinction to be made between them. The smallest incident (measured by a scale that Milton finally rejects) is as fraught with significance as the most dramatic encounter, because the issue—whether or not one will act so as to remain obedient to God—is always the same. Thus, when Michael says, "Dream not of thir fight, / As of a Duel," he not only disappoints a particular expectation; he disallows a powerful and compelling view of the moral life. In that view—which, for want of a better term, we can call "dramatic"—life is for the most part a succession of routine events punctuated now and then (and only for exceptional people) by moments of crucial choice. These moments arise when the pressure of circumstances confronts the individual with alternative courses of action, with ethical dilemmas, with fateful decisions, and it is the quality of his response to these dilemmas and decisions that determines the kind of person he will thereafter be. When this view of life informs a literary presentation, the result is a narrative that has the characteristics of a realistic novel: it is filled with characters who undergo crises which change them in ways so fundamental that they often seem to have new identities. They are, we like to say, tested in the crucible of experience, from which they emerge fully developed and mature, and, more often than not, both sadder and wiser.

In the perspective urged on Adam by Michael ("Dream not"), the key words in the previous paragraph—"dramatic," "crucial," "crisis," "climax," "change," "developing," "circumstances"—cease to have any positive value, although, as we shall see, they have a new value as a temptation (and it is a temptation to which Adam here falls). They do not have a positive value, because as notions they make sense—that is, make a difference—only if the great questions are yet to be determined, only if one is in the process of finding out what is important and what defines the sphere of one's obligations. In Michael's view, which is also Milton's, the great questions are already answered—the only important thing is to maintain one's allegiance to God, to obey—and one's obligation is simply to give that answer again and again, not at moments of crisis but at every moment.

Of course one could say (and I would agree) that rather than removing crisis, this makes crisis perpetual; but if crisis is perpetual, the very notion loses its cutting edge, since particular instances are now indistinguishable, a series of testimonies, in *superficially* different circumstances, to the same unchanging commitment. That is why crisis, climax, suspense, and so on are the vehicles of a temptation: they are implicated in a view of life in which commitment grows out of circumstances, a view in which the individual scrutinizes alternatives (of action and expression) offered to him by the world and chooses to ally himself with one or more of them. But for someone whose allegiance is inscribed in the fleshly tables of his heart, the choice has already been made, and the only alternative is the one presented indifferently by every moment and every situation: whether or not to remain true to that choice and to the value it represents.

Manlier Objects

This means that different situations do not present different challenges and that one cannot speak meaningfully of moments when more is at stake than at other moments or of choices that are more or less difficult and complicated. Indeed, to so speak would be to allow the world, in the form of the pressures exerted by its apparent facts, to define the sphere of one's obligations and to determine the value of particular actions; whereas in Milton's view, there is only one value—obedience to the will of God—and holding fast to it is the only action, an action in relation to which all others are equally valueless. It is finally a matter of how one regards time: in the ordinary (Milton would say "carnal") view, time is the *generator* of meaning, in the sense that issues crystallize and options emerge in the fullness of time; but in the view that structures Milton's prose and poetry, time is the *bearer* of a meaning that informs every point in it and is therefore constantly and repeatedly recognized by those who have the eyes (i.e., spiritual apprehension) to see it. It is in the context of the first view of time that notions like climax, crisis, change, suspense are powerful, because they all depend on the assumption that the shape of action will vary with the configurations that time happens to throw up; but if action is (or should be) unvarying, these same notions are part and parcel of a way of thinking that is mistaken and finally—because it substitutes an obligation to the world as it develops for an obligation to God as he always is—dangerous.

One can take it as a general rule, then, that if you find yourself thinking that one of two situations is the more pressuring or that this or that action will be the more decisive, or laboring to identify the absolutely critical choice in a succession of choices, you are focusing on the wrong things and misunderstanding the nature of the moral life. But these are precisely the things one focuses on in any narrative, whether it is the narrative of one's own life or the narrative of the lives of others. So that the final, and all-inclusive, conclusion to be drawn from Michael's rebuke ("Dream not of thir fight, / As of a Duel") is that it is wrong to conceive of life as a narrative—that is, as something with a plot, a sequence in which the order of events defines the possibilities of response and thereby determines the available modes of being.

That is why plot, in both Milton's prose and poetry, is always a temptation; it moves from events as they follow one another to a specification of their meaning, whereas the proper direction (in Miltonic terms) is the reverse—from a meaning always and already in place to the necessary and predetermined shape of each discrete event. That is, plot works against the obligation to which Northrop Frye directs us when he says that "the great events in *Paradise Lost* [and, I would add, in all of Milton's poetry] should be read . . . as a discontinuous series of crises, in each of which there is the opportunity to break the whole chain."[4] "Read" is exactly right, because it tells us that what is at stake is a way of reading, and reading not simply in a narrow sense but in the expanded sense Milton gives it in the *Areopagitica:* "what ever thing we hear or see, sitting, walking, travelling, or conversing may be fitly call'd our book."[5] Reading the book presented to us by life involves the same skills and dangers that attend the act of reading, narrowly conceived: the skill is to read within the assumption of a meaning that gives shape to events; the danger is to read in the opposite direction, from events in their sequence to the determination of meaning. It is the difference between looking to the world for guidance and looking at the world—or, better still, *looking* the world in an already guided way.

It is this distinction, with everything that hangs on it, that generates the strategy of temptation in Milton's poetry, a strategy that has only one object: to cause God's servants or would-be servants to exchange their single obligation, in relation to which value is already determined, for the manifold obligations which appear once one allows the determination of value to be made by empirical circumstances. This strategy is most brilliantly pursued by the Satan of *Paradise Regained,* who works it out in the second of the diabolic councils in the poem. It is a council Satan himself calls with the express purpose of devising a plan to deal with this newly risen enemy. He asks for suggestions and hears Belial advise "Set women in his eye" (*PR*, II, 153). Satan's response is at once amusing and instructive. He lectures Belial on the relationship of temptation to sensibility, characterizing him as so low-minded that he doesn't understand what might tempt a spirit less dissolute than he: "*Belial,* in much uneven scale thou weigh'st / All others by thyself" (173–174). In other words, Belial doesn't have the good taste required to be a skillful tempter. "Beauty stands / In th'admiration only of weak minds," Satan explains (220–221). By this he doesn't mean that strong minds do not admire; he means that what they admire is more substantial—in the sense of being a *better* vehicle of temptation—than beauty.

The most striking thing about this passage is the preponderance of words of measurement and scale: "worthier," "slightly viewed and slightly overpass'd," "wiser far," "more exalted,"

"Greatest things," "trivial toys," "manlier objects," "more show / Of worth, of honor, glory." These words and phrases trace out a poetics of temptation in which the world is populated with objects that are more or less seductive, depending on the moral status of one's intended victim. It follows, then, that in any given situation, and with respect to any particular man, some lures will always be more tempting than others, and the trick is simply to find the right one. It is from this perspective that Satan fashions his plan: he will arrange situations in which the Son is exposed to a variety of baits, and on the basis of his reaction he will work up to the bait that is most likely to be taken: "Therefore with manlier objects we must try / His constancy" (225–226).

The cornerstones of his strategy, then, are change and hierarchy: if something doesn't work, he will try something else; and what he will try will depend, to some extent, on the nature of previous failures. He has already, as he meets with his cohorts in book II, attempted the "something sudden" that he had proposed in book I (I refer of course to the first temptation, characterized by Arnold Stein as a "sudden brush, abrupt and possibly fatal")[6] and now he prepares to settle down to a longer contest in the course of which he will ascend the scale of "manlier objects." In what follows, he is ready to abandon any one of these objects as soon as it proves to be without appeal. "Of glory as thou wilt," he says in book III, "Worth or not worth the seeking, let it pass" (III, 150–151). He immediately bethinks him "of another Plea" (149). Each plea follows from what he thinks he has learned about his great antagonist ("thou . . . seem'st . . . / . . . addicted more / To contemplation and profound dispute" [IV, 212–214]) and when his last appeal is rejected, he simply pulls himself together and renews the assault from what he takes to be a different direction: "Another method I must now begin" (540).

For Satan, then, each change of scene brings with it a change of values, an upping of the stakes, a tightening of the screw. He strives always to keep the pressure on by presenting Christ with obligations that more closely resemble his own sense of duty and aspiration. In short, Satan labors to give the sequence a *plot;* and indeed his entire strategy follows from the assumption that he is a character in a plot, in a narrative where every change of scene brings new opportunities and new risks. What defeats him finally is the Son's inability or unwillingness (they amount to the same thing) to recognize the fact that there is a plot at all; for as Satan discovers, to his repeated frustration, the Son sees no difference at all between the various objects and actions offered to him in the course of four books. The series of adverbs and adjectives that introduce the Son's replies ("unalter'd," "temperately," "patiently," "calmly," "Unmov'd," "unmov'd," "with disdain," "sagely," "In brief") not only demonstrate the strength of his resolve, but indicate that the affirmation of that resolve is made in exactly the same way—that is, with equal ease—no matter what form the temptation takes. In no case is he unmoved or unaltered *after* a period in which alteration or movement seems possible; nor does his firmness require more of an exertion at one point than at any other. Where Satan's rhetoric continually suggests that he is ascending a scale of progressive lures, Christ's responses have the effect of leveling that scale by refusing to recognize it; and when he does, for a moment, recognize it, it is only to disallow the distinction on which it depends:

> Thou neither dost persuade me to seek wealth
> For Empire's sake, nor Empire to affect
> For glory's sake by all thy argument.
> For what is glory but the blaze of fame. (*PR*, III, 44–47)

In these lines, the Son simultaneously rehearses the order of temptations and empties it of any significance by insisting on the *equal* worthlessness of the putative goods (wealth, empire, glory) it presents. He does the same thing when he is "unmov'd" by the temptations of Rome:

> Nor doth this grandeur and majestic show
> Of luxury, though call'd magnificence,
> More than of arms before, allure mine eye,
> Much less my mind. (*PR*, IV, 110–113)

This brief passage is a compendium of both the content and the method of Christ's resistance. The words "grandeur" and "majestic" are in place long enough to be unmasked as "show"; and because of its position at the end of a line, "show" is the fulcrum of an ambiguity: Is it show of majesty or show of luxury? That is, is majesty being opposed to luxury as substance to shadow, or is what Satan has presented merely the show and not the substance of luxury (i.e., is there a true and praiseworthy luxury)? The ambiguity is not resolved but extended by the phrase "though call'd magnificence." Here it is the notion of magnificence that refuses to stay firmly in place. Is magnificence the true value of which luxury is the perversion, or is magnificence just the name with which the partisans of luxury attempt to legitimize their excesses? The question is raised only to be rendered moot by the words "More than of arms before" (112), which simply reduce everything Roman to the level of Parthian coarseness. However one might characterize what Christ has just been shown—as grandeur, majesty, show, or magnificence—it is ultimately of no more worth than the baits he has already rejected. It is not simply that the Son refuses Satan's offer, but that he sees nothing more in it than he did in the offer which Satan himself now labels inferior: "Thou justly mayst prefer," he says, "Before the *Parthian*" the "Civility" and "long Renown" of Rome (83–85); but the scale of perfection that provides Satan with the dramatic order of his presentation ("You're right to disdain that, but look at *this*") is explicitly dismissed by the Son, who sees no order but only repetition ("What you're showing me is just more of the same") and who therefore feels none of the pressure that drama brings with it.

In a final flourish, the Son dismisses still another of the scalar distinctions that are basic to Satan's strategy—the distinction between the eye and the mind. It is Satan's intention to dazzle the Son by setting, if not women, then something even more visually appealing in his eyes; the hope is that the Son will be moved to substitute what Raphael calls a "fair outside" (*PL*, VIII, 568) for the interior value to which he is pledged; but what the Son indicates when he says that the Roman vision does not even allure his eye is that there is no difference between what he sees and his judgment of it. He sees things (and actions) *immediately* in relation to their moral and spiritual status; his eye can be allured only by that which is good; and anything else will appear to him as unattractive from the very first. Satan's maneuverings assume a disparity between appearances (or surfaces) and reality; but in the eyes of the Son, surfaces are an extension of the value an object really has and therefore they do not conceal but reveal. As a result, he is never in danger of being "surprised" by "some fair appearing good" (*PL*, IX, 354), since what appears to him to be good will in fact be so. This unified perception also characterizes his hearing, so that an appeal designed to be plausible will immediately, and without reflection, be heard by him for what it is. That is why the advantage Satan thinks to gain from disguise quickly proves to be no advantage at all: as soon as the Son hears an impious suggestion, he knows (in general) the identity of the suggester, and he is himself so little impressed by this ability that he presents its results in a parenthesis: "(For I discern thee other than thou seem'st)" (*PR*, I, 348).

362

What confronts Satan, then, is someone who is not susceptible to deception, someone who is invulnerable to surprise, someone for whom everything is always the same and who therefore never feels the pressure of crisis (if crisis is defined as a moment set apart from all others in which the obligation to make a decisive choice is *uniquely* present). What confronts Satan, in short, is someone whose way of comporting himself has no relation to, and is unaffected by, the constituents of plot—deception, suspense, surprise, change, and crisis. It is no wonder, then, that he exclaims in exasperation, "What dost thou in this World?" for as far as he can see the possibilities of action in response to circumstances have been exhausted by the appeals he has already made:

> Since neither wealth, nor honor, arms nor arts,
> Kingdom nor Empire pleases thee, nor aught
> By me propos'd in life contemplative,
> Or active, tended on by glory, or fame,
> What dost thou in this World? (IV, 368–372)

In other words, "Since you refuse to act in the name of any one of these things, and since there are no other things in the name of which you might act, you finally are not acting at all." But in fact the Son *has* been acting precisely by refusing to act in the name of any of these things, for by doing so he refuses to make any one of them his God. That is, in each of the plots Satan constructs, one of these things has been put forward as the highest possible value; and therefore to resist the appeal to act in its name is to resist the temptation to substitute that value for the value of obedience to God. *Paradise Regained* is sometimes characterized as a poem of rejection, but in fact the Son never rejects anything because it is evil in and of itself but because, in the circumstances as Satan has arranged them, it is presented as crucial, uniquely compelling, and, in a word, necessary.

I Bid Not or Forbid

The terms of this rejection that is not a rejection are most explicitly stated in the Son's response to the claims made by Satan for Greek philosophy:

> These rules will render thee a King complete
> Within thyself, much more with Empire join'd.
>   To whom our Savior sagely thus replied.
> Think not but that I know these things; or think
> I know them not; not therefore am I short
> Of knowing what I ought: he who receives
> Light from above, from the fountain of light,
> No other doctrine needs, though granted true. (PR, IV, 283–290)

The Son goes on to say, "But these are false"; yet their falsity is, as it were, an extra-theoretical point, and is not the reason for their being rejected. They would be rejected, as the Son is careful to point out, even if they were true, because they have been offered as indispensable to his spiritual goal ("These rules will render thee a King complete / Within thyself") and therefore as a substitute for "Light from above." The metaphor of the fountain is quite precise here: if one is fed by the fountain, one has no need for the tributaries, although in circumstances where the confusion of the two is not an issue, one can drink from them or not, as expedience or charity may dictate. In short, this rejection is not a judgment, and indeed the Son goes to remarkable lengths in order to avoid, and even to evade, a judgment. First of all, he refuses to identify himself either as one who knows these things or as one who is ignorant of them (although he teases Satan and the reader with these alternate possibilities), and as a result the "therefore" in "not therefore am I short" follows from either of these conditions. That is, the knowledge he *is* claiming ("knowing what I ought") depends neither on his partaking of these things nor on his abstaining from them.

He therefore will neither affirm them as necessary nor condemn them as evil or forbidden, because to do either would be to make them the repository of value; whereas for the Son their value at any one moment inheres in their relationship to the obligation ("Mee hung'ring . . . to do my Father's will" [II, 259]) he has already identified as primary. Offered as an alternative to that obligation (you absolutely must avail yourself of these rules), they are evil because idolatrous (one is being asked to worship them); but offered in the absence of such claims, they may be embraced or not, as the occasion seems to dictate. To give them a fixed value, even a negative one, would be to make them the touchstone of moral judgment—embracing them or disdaining them would in and of itself make you either a good or a bad person—and, for the Son, the touchstone of moral judgment is always and unvaryingly the relationship of any alternative to his determination to serve. In short, "these things," and indeed all things, are neither good nor bad in themselves, but may at different times be one or the other depending on whether their use in particular circumstances advances or subverts God's glory.

The previous sentence is a textbook definition of the doctrine of "things indifferent," or *adiaphora,* a doctrine frequently invoked by Milton and one that holds the key to the structure (if that is the word) of *Paradise Regained.* Generally speaking, the doctrine of things indifferent comes in two versions, although they are not always precisely differentiated. The first and stronger version originates with the Stoics, who identify virtue with the self and believe that self to be sufficient. Consequently all things external to the self are lacking in intrinsic value or disvalue, and acquire value only in relation to an inner disposition or intention. Thus, the entire external world for the Stoics is a mass of *adiaphora,* which, depending on the circumstances, "could become either good or evil."[7] The second and more restricted version of the doctrine is theological, and depends on a distinction between that which Scripture explicitly commands or forbids and that concerning which it is silent. Francis Mason's definition is both typical and succinct: "Necessarie I call that which the eternall God hath in his word precisely and determinately commanded or forbidden, either expresly or by infallible consequence. Indifferent, which the Lord hath not so commanded nor forbidden, but is contained in the holy Scripture, rather potentially then actually, comprehended in generall directions, not precisely defined by particular determinations."[8] Mason goes on to assert that in the absence of an explicit command or prohibition a thing indifferent falls under the jurisdiction of the civil magistrates, "the Lords vicegerents upon earth, who according to the exigence of the state, may by their discretion command it to be done" (4). This is the conservative or Anglican position, which is countered by the Puritans' insistence that decisions concerning things indifferent should be left to the consciences of individual believers. Otherwise, they contend, the liberty that men enjoy under the New Dispensation is unlawfully infringed: "All such humaine lawes therefore, that . . . upon any penalties, binde men to those things that are confessed indifferent, which are such things as God hath left to the free libertie of man to doe or not to . . . doe: is a deprivying of men of that libertie that God hath graunted unto them, & therfore such a lawe is neither good nor indifferent."[9]

One sees immediately that the dispute over things indifferent is an aspect of the more general dispute over the authority of the ecclesiastical hierarchy in relation to the inner light of the individual. Nor is it difficult to anticipate the strategies each party pursues. The conservative right, citing over and over again 1 Corinthians 14:40, "Let all things be done honestly and by order," attempts to restrict the area in which the individual has competence, and Anglican apologists point regularly to the dire consequences of allowing every man to "doe what he list" (Mason, 9):

"He that denieth this [church authority over things indifferent], taketh away the Sunne out of the world, dissolveth universally the fabricke of government, overthroweth families, corporations, Churches, and kingdoms, and wrappeth all things in the dismall darknesse of Anarchie and confusion" (Mason, 13–14). To this fear of antinomian license the Puritan left opposes the doctrine of Christian liberty, which, in its extreme form, as represented by Milton, so expands the scope of individual conscience as to make even the commands and interdictions of the decalogue nonbinding and things indifferent. Indeed, the larger the claim made for the authority of the inner light, the larger the category of things indifferent, so that finally the left-wing definition is, like the Stoic definition, more philosophical than theological and tends toward the inclusion of everything. "There is nothing so good of it selfe, but it may be made Evill by accident, nothing so evill of it self but it may become good by accident. Nothing so good or Evil but it may become Indifferent by accident, nothing so Indifferent of it selfe but it may become Good or Evill by accident" (Bradshaw, 16–17).

By "accident" Bradshaw means "in a particular circumstance"; in his vision, therefore, good, evil, and indifferent are ever-present and ever-operative categories, but they are not attached to any stipulated list of actions and/or objects. What this means is that the expansion of Christian liberty is also the expansion of Christian responsibility; for if, on the one hand, no action or object is intrinsically good or evil, but, on the other hand, every action is either good or evil as it "doth either glorifie or dishonor God" in a particular circumstance, then the determination of the value of an object or action must be made again and again and one cannot look for help to the enjoinings and forbiddings of any fixed formula, even if that formula is the decalogue. The result is a moral life that is fraught with anxiety and danger, for in a world where every action, however small or large, is equally the potential vehi-

367

cle of good or evil, no action can be taken without risk; and, indeed, "a man may by takynge up a straw or a rush commit a Moral vice. For example if he shoulde use to doe it in the time of prayer" (Bradshaw, 20). Paradoxically, then, the strong version of the doctrine of things indifferent ends by declaring, as does Lord Brooke in *A Discourse Opening the Nature of Episcopacy,* that nothing is indifferent.[10] The indifference of things obtains only in their existence apart from circumstances; but since our involvement with things is always circumstantial, they are never, for us at any one time, indifferent.

This is precisely Milton's position as it is elaborated in several key passages in the *Areopagitica,* where he argues against identifying truth with any particular position or stance, for it is "not impossible that she may have more shapes than one" (328). This, as he points out, is precisely what is implied by the doctrine "of things indifferent, wherein Truth may be on this side, or on the other, without being unlike her self" (328). And this unwillingness to fix the shape of truth is tied explicitly to the principle of Christian liberty, by which right action is defined with reference not to things good and bad in themselves but to the spirit (of worship or idolatry) in which things indifferent are used: "What but a vain shadow else is the abolition of *those ordinances, that hand writing nayl'd to the crosse,* what great purchase is this Christian liberty which *Paul* so often boasts of. His doctrine is, that he who eats or eats not, regards a day, or regards it not, may doe either to the Lord" (328–329). In the *Areopagitica,* this Pauline principle is extended to the act of reading and books become things indifferent, neither good nor bad in themselves, but good *or* bad depending on whether they are well or ill used. It follows, as we saw in Chapter 5, that the licensing of books is a misconceived project because it locates the evil and the potential good in the wrong places—in the printed word rather than in the moral status of he who reads it; for "best books to a naughty mind are not unappliable to occasions of evil," and, conversely, "bad books . . . to a discreet and judicious Reader serve in many respects to discover, to confute, to forwarn, and to illustrate" (285).[11]

It is passages like this one which led me to conclude earlier that Milton's argument is not for or against the reading of books, but against making the reading or not reading of books (or the doing or not doing of anything else) the *proof* of either virtue or vice. As he says in another passage of the *Areopagitica*, "great care and wisdom is requir'd to the right managing of this point" (297). Care is required because the pitfalls are so many and so intimately related. On the one hand, one must be wary lest one embrace something (an object, an action, a person) as good in and of itself and therefore as necessary, for that would be to make it one's God. This is exactly what Adam does when he decides that Eve is everything to him, and he receives a precise rebuke: "Was shee thy God, that her thou didst obey / Before his voice" (*PL*, X, 145–146). On the other hand, one must be wary of declaring something (an object, an action, or a person) intrinsically evil, for that would be to shift the responsibility for evil from the intention or disposition of the agent to something external to and independent of him. This is what Dalila does, or tries to do, in a number of directions as she proves herself a virtuoso in the fine art of displacement ("The devil made me do it"). But on the third hand (that there is a third hand is what makes the "right managing" so difficult), one must not conclude that because things (and actions and persons) are neither good nor bad in themselves, it doesn't matter very much whether one rejects them or embraces them. It *always* matters; it's just that the way in which it matters is not fixed once and for all in a list of intrinsically good and bad things, but must be determined, and then determined again, in the innumerable situations that make up the moral life.

Being faithful, then, to the doctrine of things indifferent (in its strong or philosophical version) requires the withstanding of three temptations: (1) the temptation of idolatry—the temptation, that is, to label something (other than God) intrinsically good in and of itself; (2) the temptation to judgment (which is at once an evasion of responsibility and an arrogation of responsibility)—that is, the temptation to label something intrinsically evil; and (3) the temptation to relaxation—that is, the temptation to think that because things are neither good nor evil in themselves, they are neither good nor evil in practice. The relationship between these temptations is such that to withstand any one of them is to run the risk of courting another. In the very act of rejecting something as idolatrous, one may fall into the error of condemning it as inherently evil; and one may be so wary of the danger of either extreme, that no judgment at all will be hazarded and moral responsibility will therefore have been abdicated.

In *Paradise Regained* these are the errors that Christ is invited to make in every one of the temptations to which Satan exposes him. Thus, as we have seen, the temptation of Athens is not the temptation to accept the rules of Greek philosophy (and art and literature), but the temptation either to accept them (as necessary) or to reject them as absolutely forbidden, or to say that one's relationship to them doesn't matter; for in this case, when they are being offered as necessary, it matters very much, and they must be rejected, *for the time being.* The same formula (with slight variations) will do for all of the temptations. The banquet in book II is presented to Christ as something he must eat, or alternatively as something from which he must abstain either because, despite Satan's assertion to the contrary, it includes "Meats by the Law unclean" (II, 328) or because the meats may have been offered first to idols. Christ's response is striking for what it does not say—that is, for its evasiveness:

Said'st thou not that to all things I had right?
And who withholds my pow'r that right to use?
Shall I receive by gift what of my own,
When and where likes me best, I can command?
I can at will, doubt not, as soon as thou,
Command a Table in this Wilderness,
And call swift flights of Angels ministrant
Array'd in Glory on my cup to attend. (*PR*, II, 379–386)

These lines have sometimes been read as an admission (or realization) by Christ of his divinity, but they are nothing of the
sort. Indeed, they admit, or assert, nothing. Rather, everything
Christ says, he says in the context of Satan's assertions, which he
entertains as hypotheses—i.e., "Didn't you say (although I never
claimed it and am not claiming it now) that everything belonged
by right to me? And if what you say is true (although I am by no
means affirming it), then, by your own words, there is no need
for me to accept anything from you." In the second part of his reply, the evasive work performed by "Said'st thou not" is done by
"as soon as thou." That is, the boast Christ appears to make is no
boast at all because the power he seems to claim—the power to
command a table in the wilderness—he claims only insofar as it is
also Satan's: not "I can do this" but "I can do this as well as you
can." We, however, along with the two protagonists, know that
Satan's power is not his own—he himself makes the point at
book I, line 377—and therefore what looks like the assumption
(and presumption) of godhead is actually a refusal to claim it.
The statement Christ is making is finally as complex and intricate
as the doctrine (of things indifferent) he is affirming: "I don't
need you, since I can do it myself, just as well as you can; but
since you can't in fact do it yourself, neither can I; and the only
difference between us is that I know it, and glory in that knowledge."

It is a remarkable linguistic performance in which an assertion of radical dependence (on God, light from above, and so on) is at the same time an assertion of radical independence (of Satan and his gifts). Moreover, this is managed, and necessarily so, without saying anything about those gifts—that is, the food—at all. The whole point of Satan's stage setting had been to get Christ to pronounce on the food one way or the other. But he neither embraces it nor rejects it; instead he positions himself in such a way as to be making no judgment on it at all. That strategy is available to him because the food does not correspond to a pressing need (he feels hunger but fears no harm, since he feels it "Without this body's wasting" [II, 256]). In another situation, when the need was in fact pressing, his decision about the food—which is here to make no decision—might take another form; but here he can treat it as a thing indifferent, and reject it on grounds of convenience and expediency ("as I like / The giver" [321–322]).

Christ's performance here underlines a point that must be made with respect to each of the temptations: they are always more complicated than they at first seem, because the terms in which they are posed are not explicitly stated. As Satan presents it, a temptation inheres in the embracing of a thing or action, and therefore it would seem that the proper response would be simply to reject the thing or action in question. But as we have seen, this way of presenting the issue is as much of a trap as the proffered lure, because it makes externals rather than one's attitude toward them crucial. Christ therefore is always in the position of responding not to the overt but to the hidden terms of a temptation, and that is why his replies often seem oblique and beside the point. In fact they are reformulations of the point, in the course of which the true danger lurking in a Satanic appeal is exposed and thereby avoided.

In one exchange that danger is so well hidden that only Christ and a single literary critic seem to have noticed it.[12] As Satan prepares to leave the Son at the end of the first day, he makes what is apparently an almost casual request:

> Thy Father, who is holy, wise and pure,
> Suffers the Hypocrite or Atheous Priest
> To tread his Sacred Courts, and minister
> About his Altar, handling holy things,
> Praying or vowing, and vouchsaf'd his voice
> To *Balaam* Reprobate, a Prophet yet
> Inspir'd; disdain not such access to me.
>   To whom our Saviour with unalter'd brow.
> Thy coming hither, though I know thy scope,
> I bid not or forbid; do as thou find'st
> Permission from above; thou canst not more.
>   He added not . . . (I, 486–497)

It would seem that the Son is here being tempted to accept the example of Balaam as an argument for permitting Satan to stay; but the real temptation is to assume that the permission is his either to grant or deny. Balaam is brought in largely as a diversionary tactic designed to draw attention away from the presumption inherent in the alternative actions the situation would seem to demand. If the Son welcomes Satan he will seem to be accepting him, if only on a social level (one of the things the Son is never guilty of in this poem is civility), and if he sends him away he will seem to claim a prerogative that belongs only to God.

He does neither, and instead speaks in the precise and evasive language appropriate to the doctrine of things indifferent: "I bid not or forbid." It is not that he is indifferent to Satan's presence (he tells him more than once that he doesn't like him), but that he knows that a power greater than Satan's controls that presence: "do as thou find'st / Permission from above." In thus declaring the limits on Satan's freedom, he (characteristically) admits his own, and steps out of the trap that has been set for him, a trap in which Satan himself is the bait. Later, in book IV, Satan makes a quite different appeal, one that renders his presence far from indifferent, and Christ responds by saying what he declines to say here: "Get thee behind me" (IV, 193). The difference between this unequivocal rejection and the earlier refusal to reject is that in book IV Satan offers himself as an alternative object of worship—"On this condition, if thou wilt fall down, / And worship me as thy superior Lord" (166–167)—and therefore as an idol; and as an idol he must be personally repudiated, whereas as a mere presence in the world he can be left to higher dispensation.

Again we see how nice the discriminations are that must be made and how easy it is to blur them or override them. When the narrative voice comments at line 497 (book I) "He added not," he is paying tribute to the precision of Christ's performance; despite the opportunity to go too far in one direction or the other (by either embracing or judging Satan), the Son says just enough to establish his dependence, *and no more.* More would have almost certainly been self-assertion in some way or another, and Christ is in the business not of asserting the self but of giving it no scope—including linguistic scope—beyond that necessary to affirm his obedience. Indeed, to obey or not to obey is the only issue ever at stake in *Paradise Regained,* although Satan is always trying to divert the Son's attention to other issues, or, even more diabolically, to tempt him with a course of action that seems on its face to be the very manifestation of obedience.[13] That is, he urges the wrong thing but in a form that looks very much like the right one (it is a "false resemblance"), and in the first encounter that form is no less than charity. "But if thou be the Son of God, Command / That out of these hard stones be made thee bread; / So shalt thou save thyself and us relieve" (342–344).

Although critics have made much of the danger Christ would

court if he were to perform a trick in order to confirm his credentials or, even worse, in order to save himself (thus forgetting from whom salvation comes), little has been said about the brilliance of suggesting that Christ might be the agency of helping other people. While it is easy to see what is wrong with working a miracle at the devil's bidding, it is not so easy to see what is wrong with relieving the misery of others. The temptation to turn stones into bread is deliberately obvious and serves as a stalking horse for the real temptation, which is to do good works, or, more precisely, to identify the doing of good works not as Milton identifies them in the *Christian Doctrine*—as works informed by faith—but as works that answer to an empirically observable need. True works of faith may or may not redress social conditions, but when the redressing of social conditions is placed in the position of the highest obligation—as the action one *must* perform—then it becomes an action no less idolatrous than the action of falling down and worshiping a false God. Indeed, it *is* a false God, because it has been identified as the one indispensable thing to do and therefore as necessary to salvation. All of this is comprehended in Christ's cryptic reply: "Think'st thou such force in Bread?" (I, 347). The force that Satan attributes to bread resides only with God, who of course may, if he chooses, use bread as his vehicle. As always, the Son is careful not to err in either direction, by making too much or too little of a thing indifferent. "Think'st thou *such* force in bread" does not deny that there is *some* force in bread; and "Man lives not by Bread only" (349) silently insists (through the word "only") that bread is one of the things—although not the necessary and sufficient thing—man lives by. Again we see how great the care is that must go into the right managing of this point: if the Son had left out the word "only," he would have committed an error as fatal as the error he is explicitly tempted to commit—the error of making bread all.

Glory

The question "Think'st thou such force in _____" (you fill in the blank) identifies the danger and the way of avoiding it in every one of the scenes Satan constructs. Think'st thou such force in riches? In kingdoms? In arms? In manners? In civility? In literature? In philosophy? Satan continually offers these things as indispensable and necessary, and Christ continually rejects them *as they are offered,* while being very careful not to condemn them altogether and thus make them, rather than an interior disposition, the signs of evil. The pattern, as I have been arguing, is everywhere, but it is most fully on display in the temptation of glory that begins when Satan names glory as that which "sole excites to high attempts the flame / Of most erected Spirits, most temper'd pure / Ethereal, who all pleasures else despise, / All treasures and all gain esteem as dross, / and dignities and powers, all but the highest" (III, 26–30). Here in a brief compass are the two poles of danger in relation to which the doctrine of things indifferent is an uneasy—because always shifting—mean. Satan first offers glory as the most important thing (it "sole excites" and it is the "highest"); offers it, that is, as an object of worship. But then he also invites Jesus to make glory the object of judgment by providing him with the requisite vocabulary in the words "despise" and "dross." It is this second, and more subtle, invitation that the Son seems at first to accept when he asks, contemptuously, "For what is glory" (47), and answers that it is only the "talk" of those who characteristically admire what is not truly admirable: "Of whom to be disprais'd were no small praise" (56). This false, earthly glory is then contrasted with the glory of being marked with approbation "through Heaven" (62), and the example of Job is instanced as someone who was "Famous . . . in Heaven, on Earth less known" (68). There follows a catalogue of the actions that typically win earthly glory and renown—"what do these Worthies, / But rob and spoil, burn, slaughter, and enslave" (74–75)—actions whose just reward would be "Violent or shameful death" (87).

Had the Son stopped here, the conclusion would have been inescapable: anyone who achieves earthly glory, anyone who is famous, is necessarily the captive of false values and goals. But suddenly he turns on his own discourse and begins what will finally be the rehabilitation of glory, but with a difference: "But if there be in glory aught of good" (88). Glory, we are now told, can be good, if it attends actions that are not violent and self-seeking but, rather, actions of peace and wisdom. A new roll call of true heroes is then rehearsed, which includes Job (who may be more famous in heaven than on earth, but who is famous nevertheless), Socrates, and Scipio. The conclusion at this point would seem to be that glory is all right if it is sought for the right reasons. But that is exactly the conclusion the Son moves to forestall when he insists that if any of these men did what they did for the sake of glory, "The deed becomes unprais'd, the man at least" (103). That is, the good that results from the deed will stand—after all, "young *African*" did free "His wasted Country . . . from *Punic* rage" (101–102); but if he did it for fame, he will deserve no credit for it. Glory, then, is an unworthy goal no matter for what reason it is sought, and indeed it is acceptable only when it is not sought at all but simply befalls him who acts in a higher service. The model here is God, who, Jesus explains, does what he does "not for glory as prime end, / But to show forth his goodness" (123–124). It is true, of course, that as a consequence God does receive glory ("From them who could return him nothing else" [129]), but his possession of it is incidental to his action. Similarly, the man who advances God's glory, not his own, will sometimes receive glory as a kind of unlooked-for bonus ("Them he himself to glory will advance" [144]) which he will enjoy precisely because he did *not* value it as "prime end."

By the conclusion of this 150-line sequence, "glory" has been anatomized as the very epitome of a thing indifferent: embraced as the "highest" or "prime end," it becomes an idol, and as the embodiment of idolatry ("Thou shalt have no other Gods before me") it must be rejected; but in other circumstances, when it is something that happens to a man rather than something he actively seeks, glory can be accepted not as the reward of virtue but as its accidental by-product. Of course the very same thing can be said (and I have been saying it) about riches, arms, bread, literature, and so on—in fact about everything, since in the version of the doctrine embraced by Milton nothing is good or evil in and of itself, but everything is potentially the vehicle of good and evil, for everything can be used either in the service of God or as a means of departing from him.[14]

Not only does this place glory in the same category as bread, riches, arts, and so forth; it makes everything in this category (that is, everything) equal in the sense that no thing is potentially more a vehicle of idolatry than any other ("a man may by takynge up a straw or a rush commit a Moral vice" [Bradshaw, 20]). This means that the usual classifications of objects and actions, whereby some are inherently more noble than others, does not apply, and that it would be positively wrong, indeed sinful, to apply it.

In other words, one of the ways that the Son can go wrong in this poem is to take some things more seriously than others or to regard some decisions (for example, whether Satan should be allowed access) as relatively inconsequential. It is not simply that the Son sees every temptation (no matter what form it takes) as the same one, but that it would be fatal for him to do otherwise, because to do otherwise would be to assume that the choice between God and substitute loyalties (bread, riches, feeding the poor) is different insofar as the substitute loyalties are more or less good, and that therefore some temptations are more pressuring (because more plausible) than others. But any thing or action that is offered as an object of worship is by definition a vehicle of idolatry, and idolatry, like perfection, does not admit of degrees. It is no less idolatrous to nominate feeding the hungry as the prime end than it is to nominate riches or glory. No matter what position an object or action may have in some hierarchy of values, when it is put forward as an alternative to the value of worshiping God, it is of no value at all. It is this insight that Satan labors to subvert by setting up situations in which the Son should be more tempted than he was before (on the assumption, for example, that someone who rejects riches might not reject that which riches seek to gain—namely, kingdom and glory). But that is to assess things in relation to one another as they appear in an empirical field, whereas the Son is always assessing them in relation to the claims made for them as competing deities (or as competing epitomes of sin) and finding them (indeed he has already found them so before Satan begins) equally uncompelling.

The Temptation of Crisis

What I am saying then is not simply that the doctrine of things indifferent is to be found everywhere in *Paradise Regained,* but that *Paradise Regained* is a working out of the doctrine, and that because it is a working out of the doctrine, every moment in it is necessarily the same. (Everything is *always* at stake.) The consequences for what one can say about the poem are far-reaching and in large part take the form of what one cannot say. One cannot say, for example, that there is any significance to the order of temptations or to the fact that more lines are devoted to some than others. I do not mean that one could not find reasons for the differences in proportion: the Athens temptation may be more elaborate than the temptation of riches because Milton felt that his readers were more likely to be literary than material idolaters;

the glory temptation may take up a great deal of space because he wanted to include at least one full-dress example of a kind of analysis that was in other places left for the reader to perform. But these would not be reasons that are tied to the unfolding of a plot, to the gradual emergence of crisis, to a succession of choices, some of which are more important than others because they take the central figure further and further down a particular path until his destiny (for good or ill) is irreversible. In *Paradise Regained* one cannot say that this or that moment is crucial, because every moment is crucial (every moment offers an opportunity to be either faithful or idolatrous): one cannot say that *here* is where victory or defeat occurs, because the possibility of their occurrence is ever-present and ever-renewed; one cannot say that this decision makes all the difference, because it is a decision that will have to be made again in the very next moment; one cannot say "from this point it is all downhill," because the poem has neither steep inclines nor easy descents but is always pitched at the same level of tension that makes reading it so strenuous. Like the Son, *we* can never relax.

The fact remains, however, that these things which one cannot say about *Paradise Regained* are what critics are always saying, although they are not always saying them in the same way. To a great extent the history of *Paradise Regained* criticism is a history of attempts to establish just those kinds of distinctions (between one episode and another, between degrees of danger and risk, between the ease and difficulty of diverse temptations) that are subversive of the poem's lesson. Whether it is the triple temptation, or the three offices of Christ, or the neoplatonic tripartite soul, or the scale of ethical goods, or the responsibilities of the church, or the recovery by the hero of his divine knowledge, the models that have been proposed as providing the structure of the poem always have the effect of dividing it up, of foregrounding some moments at the expense of others, of identifying climaxes, resolutions, and dénouements, of declaring some scenes integral and others preliminary or ceremonial: the effect, in short, of giving the poem a plot.

The disagreement as to exactly what the plot is has led to differing characterizations of its shape, and to a host of questions and debates. Is the gluttony temptation an extension of the bread-into-stones temptation, or does it belong to another episode? If the first temptation is the temptation of distrust, what do you say about the temptation of the tower? Is the answer to this question to be found in Milton's following of Luke's sequence rather than Matthew's? Since the storm scene is not found in any of the biblical accounts, is it a temptation at all, or simply a "dramatic interlude"? In fact, how many temptations are there? Every number from three to nine has been given as an answer, and with each answer one or more of the temptations is divided into two, three, four, five, . . . parts. As Edward Tayler has observed, "The arithmetical gymnastics in this arena do not inspire confidence in our profession."[15]

There is an even poorer judgment to be made: the critics who are busy debating the kinds of schematizations and formal organizations that we should keep in mind when reading *Paradise Regained* are, in effect, doing the devil's work. It is Satan's effort in the poem to persuade Jesus to those differences and distinctions, hierarchies of values, and so on that will obscure the singleness of his obligation and get him to abandon what he knows to be the most important thing (obedience to God) for the thing (or action) that seems to be the most important in the light of some partial (i.e., empirical) perspective. It is Satan's effort, in short, to divert the Son's attention from his chosen allegiance ("Mee hung'ring . . . to do my Father's will" [*PR*, II, 259]) by urging on him the allegiances (to social reform, the arts, charitable works) that seem to be demanded by changing circumstances. That is why plot is so crucial to his strategy (a strategy in which he himself believes). Plot is always saying: the situation has changed and you must now rethink what it is that you have to do. The Son is always saying (even when he doesn't say it): the situation cannot have changed, because there is only one situation; and what you have to do is what you have always had to do—affirm your loyalty to God. Satan builds plots (like mousetraps) by presenting inessential differences as if they were constitutive, and the Son unbuilds them by seeing through those differences to the eternal choice (between God and idols) they really present. But what the Son unbuilds, the critics build up again, multiplying distinctions, insisting on progressions, labeling beginnings, middles, and ends, and in general acting as extensions of the Satanic effort.

They are, of course, encouraged in their activities by the poem, which after all does have four books, frequent changes of scene, varying styles, temporal signatures, announced shifts of topic, shorter and longer speeches—everything, in short, that would support the assumption that different things are at stake at different times. While it is true, as I have been asserting, that the poem is everywhere the same, it is not obviously so, and it is the task of readers to penetrate to that sameness amid so many signs of difference. It is a task made more difficult by the performance of the Son, who sees the signs of difference immediately for what they are (camouflage and distractions), and therefore does not need to go through the effort of setting them aside. As a result, he presents a difficult model—one who, as often as not, leaves out the steps that would enable us to follow him and therefore contributes to the possibility that we will misunderstand the nature of what he does.

This possibility is perhaps greatest in the tower or pinnacle scene, which has a critical literature of its own. The two points at issue are: (1) whether this is a part of the temptation proper or is a "climactic epilogue" to an action already complete, and (2) whether this confrontation is decisive in a way that its predecessors were not. Those who would detach the episode from the main body of the poem take their cue partly from the narrator, who says of Satan at the conclusion of the Athens temptation, "for all his darts were spent" (IV, 366), and partly from Satan himself when he announces, "Another method I must now begin" (540). To the extent that a reader takes Satan at his word (surely a questionable procedure), he will be prepared to find this scene unlike the others; but to the extent that he remains undistracted by this final stage direction (for so it is), he will be able to discern with Christ (who says at line 497 "desist, thou art discern'd") the same old trap, with its attendant and familiar dangers.

That trap takes the form (as it has before) of presenting the Son with two alternative courses of action, either of which would constitute presumption. He can "stand upright" (551) or he can cast himself down. The first would be an assertion of his divinity (an "I can command a table in the Wilderness" without the saving qualification of "as soon as thou"), and the second would be to make a trial of God by commanding him to a particular performance ("See, I am putting my trust in you; now save me!"). The strategy is once again to position the Son in such a way that anything he does will be to Satan's advantage; at the very least, Satan will finally know who his adversary is. If Christ stands upright, he is divine; if he falls, he is mere man; if he casts himself down, he will invite God to save him. And whether God or man, he will be violating the discipline of faith and obedience.

The Temptation of Scripture

If this were all, the temptation would be subtle enough; but Satan adds another turn to its screw by offering as a reason for casting himself down the testimony of Scripture:

> Cast thyself down; safely if Son of God:
> For it is written, He will give command

> Concerning thee to his Angels, in thir hands
> They shall up lift thee, lest at any time
> Thou chance to dash thy foot against a stone. (IV, 555–559)

The brilliance of this last move inheres in its apparent fidelity to Christ's own principle of action, as he has often invoked it. Man lives not by bread alone but by the word of God, he declares at the first encounter, and in every subsequent encounter the word of God is preferred to the various words spoken by the world. As recently as line 175, the Son has turned away a temptation with the formula "It is written," and when Satan appropriates the same formula here he seems to be inviting the Son to reaffirm an allegiance he himself has repeatedly proclaimed. This is not simply the temptation to presumption (although it is surely that), but the temptation of Scripture.

That is, in addition to the choice of standing or casting himself down, Satan gives Christ the choice of either embracing Scripture (and with it Satan's urgings) or rejecting it. Christ of course does neither; instead he adds it to the ever-growing and finally all-inclusive list of things indifferent. He does this simply by quoting it or counter-quoting it, thus giving felt life to an old proverb: the devil can also quote Scripture. What this means is that Scripture, like anything else, can be perverted to a bad use (the same point is made in the *Areopagitica*), and that therefore no verse of Scripture has an intrinsic value but receives its value— whether good or bad—from its appropriater. It is not the Scriptures but the Scriptures as they are filled with the spirit of God that are sacred; read in the absence of that spirit, by a (literally) unfaithful interpreter, they become dead letters. Satan presents the verses from Psalm 91 as if their meaning were fixed and beyond dispute. The Son's response rejects that meaning as Satan's (just as earlier he rejects the signs and portents of the storm: "not sent from God, but thee" [491]) and then, in order to show that it is the meaning and not Scripture he rejects, he attaches himself to another verse, one that identifies the impiety with which Satan has polluted a thing indifferent: "Tempt not the Lord thy God; he said and stood" (561). It is a brilliantly compressed moment that not only illustrates in the most rigorous way the doctrine of things indifferent (by extending it to include even Scripture), but also gives definitive form to the analogous doctrine of false resemblances:

> Who therefore seeks in these
> True wisdom, finds her not, or by delusion
> Far worse, her false resemblance only meets,
> An empty cloud. (318–321)

The distinction between true and false resemblances is a distinction not between different things (one of which is superficially like the other), but between different attitudes or intentional dispositions toward the *same* thing, which is therefore no longer the same. Thus, in this case, the Scriptures, when they are quoted by the devil or for diabolic purposes, are not true resemblances of themselves but are hollow forms, or, as the Son puts it, "empty clouds"—just as when bread is made into an idol, it does not nourish but wastes; and when poetry is detached from the praising of God, it is "As varnish on a Harlot's cheek" (344). Nowhere is Milton's relentless interiorization of value more dramatically on display than it is here, when his hero looks at the Bible itself and finds it no more intrinsically valuable than the things— bread, riches, kingdom, learning—he has earlier rejected in its name.[16]

It is by resisting the temptation to make an idol of the Scriptures that the Son can be said to stand: "Tempt not the Lord thy God; he said and stood" (561). That is, one way to read this line, and a way that will seem inevitable if one understands what the Son has done by answering Scripture with Scripture, is to read "and stood" as "and in doing (i.e., saying) that, stood firm, re-mained unaltered and unmoved." This reading has the advantage of deemphasizing the physical or punctual sense of stood, which, if allowed to be heard too strongly, presents this as a decisive and climactic gesture—i.e., he stood up in triumph, he stood revealed as God, and so on. But this is precisely what Satan (and some readers) want, and what the Son refuses to do: that is, treat this moment as something different, as one in which *more* is at stake, in which everything is settled—as, in fact, a fight, or a local duel.

Instead, the Son treats this moment as he has every other, not by making some definitive declaration or taking some action that would amount to the "single stroke" for which so many of Mil-ton's heroes and villains and readers long, but by being, as he has been so many times before, creatively evasive. He doesn't stand up, in a grand flourish of assertion, nor does he cast himself down, in an impetuous hazarding of all. He does the only thing that Satan could not imagine him doing: he does nothing, or, as Barbara Lewalski puts it in what remains the single best account of the moment: "he shows his divinity . . . by calmly maintaining the impossible position into which Satan has thrust him."[17] Just how impossible that posture is, one cannot finally say. Satan him-self is not sure of the matter: he only says, "to stand upright / Will ask thee skill" (PR, IV, 551–552). This suggests that there is a level of skill—short of miracle—which would suffice, but that Sa-tan does not expect the Son, or any other mere man, to have it. That he does have it, and that it is not a skill dependent on divine intervention (whether of the Son or the Father), is evidenced by the phrase "uneasy station" (584), which suggests not a revealed God standing gloriously at front and center stage, but a man who is doing the best that he can in a difficult situation to be true to the best that he knows.

The station is uneasy because it is precarious; that is, it re-quires balance. It is thus a perfect visual emblem of what has been required of the Son all along, a keeping to a path so straight and narrow that the deviation of a single step to the right or left would prove disastrous. What the Son does *not* do here—swerve in one direction or another—is the physical equivalent of what he does not *say* in book I: "he added not." In both cases the discipline of obedience is perfect, but it *is* a discipline, and one that must be exercised continually, rather than in a single and final moment after which all trial and struggle cease.

There is no final moment in *Paradise Regained*. In this last scene, which ends nothing, the Son does no more or less than he does before and will have to do again: he refuses to locate value in a thing indifferent, even though that thing is Scripture, and he refuses to reduce the moral life to a single climactic action in which everything is settled once and for all. Indeed, these two temptations—the temptation to either embrace or reject and the temptation to dream of a fight or a duel—are finally one and the same; for they are both invitations to externalize the moral life, either by making good and evil the property of things or by making the struggle between good and evil an event in the world of circumstances rather than a succession of events in the inner world of spiritual choice. By the same reasoning, they are both temptations that find their perfect expression in the dynamics of plot, which, by substituting the curve and arc of greater and lesser moments for the straight line of a moment endlessly repeated, relieves us of the obligation to be perpetually alert.

Vanquishing Temptation

It is of course always Milton's way to present his readers with the most compelling form of the temptation he would have them resist. And in *Paradise Regained* we are certainly invited to assume that this is the local duel of which Adam is to dream not. For this assumption we have no less an authority than the angels of heaven, who sing "Victory and Triumph to the Son of God / Now ent'ring his great duel" (I, 173–174). But then the qualification follows immediately—"his great duel, not of arms, / But to vanquish by wisdom hellish wiles" (174–175). And when the "vanquishing" finally does occur, it is like every other noncontest in Milton's poetry and prose. First of all, there is no contact; Satan falls not because he has been hit but because he has not been hit, because he has failed once again to draw from Christ that frontal assault, that deliberate single stroke, which would at least tell him where he is and with whom he is dealing ("For Son of God to me is yet in doubt" [IV, 501]). What amazes him is not a new revelation, but the ability of his antagonist (whoever he is) to evade the demand for a revelation without resorting to easy quietism (to do something at the same time that he declines to do anything). What amazes him is the Son's perfect balance despite an "uneasy situation," and, totally unbalanced himself (as he always has been), he falls.

But then he doesn't; that is, he doesn't fall in any sense that allows us to say, "Well, that's over," or even to point to that fall as opposed to any other. Rather, he falls and rises again and again, and for seventy-five lines. First he falls in a comparison with Antaeus, who in his own career mirrors the Satanic ability to rise again ("and oft foil'd still rose, / Receiving from his mother Earth new strength, / Fresh from his fall" [565–567]); then he falls in a comparison with the Sphinx (the answer to whose riddle is like the answer to Satan's question: man [572–576]), yet he falls not to the ground but into a seminar: "And to his crew, that sat consulting, brought / Joyless triumphals of his hop't success" (577–578). But this has happened before, and although we aren't told so, the diabolic consulting will no doubt produce new resolves and new plans. Meanwhile, Satan is no better or worse off than when Belial asked, in book II of *Paradise Lost*, "is this then worst, /

Thus sitting, thus consulting . . . ?" (163–164). The refrain "So Satan fell" at line 581 (*PR*, IV) already sounds much less climactic than the first report of his "fall" at line 562.

There are, however, other and severer falls in store for Satan, and they are rehearsed by the angelic choir at line 596ff. They recall Satan's first fall ("and down from Heav'n cast / With all his Army" [605–606]), and speak of this new fall as if it were an act of completion ("now thou hast . . . / . . . regain'd lost Paradise" [606–608]). But then they look forward to another fall that sounds just like the first ("thou shalt fall from Heav'n trod down" [620]), and this present fall is demoted to a preliminary status: "thou feel'st / Thy wound, yet not thy last and deadliest wound / By this repulse receiv'd, and hold'st in Hell / No triumph" (621–624). But he still holds something in hell and he will no doubt venture forth again, if only so that, again, the Son "Shall chase thee with the terror of his voice / From thy Demoniac holds" (627–628). When, at line 634, the Son receives the epithet "Queller of Satan," one can only read it as referring not to an action already performed and done with, but to an action that will have to be performed again and again. "Queller of Satan" is not a title you have by right after only one encounter, but a title that must be earned repeatedly.

The effect of what Joan Webber has called "these remarkable lines"[18] is to diminish the dramatic impact of any one of these falls by removing them from the story line of a plot into a timeless realm where they are eternally occurring. It is, as Webber goes on to say, a story "which is without beginning or end, and yet begins and ends at every point" (206). I can do no better than to reproduce her summary statement: "Both space and time are of infinite importance and of no importance at all. The Son is everywhere. He has warred, and has yet to war down Satan. Paradise is regained and Satan's power ended as if it had never been;

Satan still rules and is yet to be cast out. His snares are broken, but Jesus has not yet begun to save mankind. The Son is everyone and the battle is within" (207–208).

This is, of course, the lesson of Michael's rebuke—"Not by destroying *Satan,* but his works / In thee and in thy Seed" (*PL,* XII, 394–395)—but it is a lesson that one can never learn too often. In the closing lines of the poem, Milton gives us an opportunity to learn it again as he instructs us for the last time how *not* to read his poem. The moment is, as it should be, at once small and large—its pressure barely perceptible, yet as great as anything we feel in the course of four books. It is, quite characteristically, a moment between lines: "now thou hast aveng'd / Supplanted *Adam,* and by vanquishing / Temptation, hast regain'd lost Paradise" (*PR,* IV, 606–608). There are several surprises here. First there is the slight surprise of hearing that it is Adam and not the Father who is "aveng'd"—a surprise that reminds us that this was done for our sake, and not as a matter of family honor. And then there is the complicated ambiguity of "Supplanted," which means both overthrown or pushed off balance, as Adam certainly was by Satan, and superseded or ousted, as Adam is now by Christ, who, as Herbert never tires of reminding us, in saving us disables us to perform in any way that he has not already made possible. But the biggest (although in presentation very small) surprise is the one that awaits us in line 608, when we discover that the object of "vanquishing" is not Satan, as the military language and the scene just past would seem to dictate, but temptation. "Temptation" is not only the word we get; it correctly names our desire for the word we didn't get. That is, it is a temptation to expect something other than (the word) temptation; and insofar as we succumb to it, we prove again on our pulse the power and appeal of that dream to which Adam falls when he asks, "say where and when / Thir fight" (*PL,* XII, 384–385).

390

CHAPTER TWELVE

The Temptation of Understanding

Yet I Yielded

If plot is a temptation in Milton's work because it encourages the mislocation (in external forms) of obligation and value, it is also a temptation because as a form of cause/effect reasoning (in plot one thing follows from another) it encourages us to believe that events occurring under the aegis of Providence can be rationally understood. This is the temptation felt by everyone (including the reader) in *Samson Agonistes,* and its many versions are explored in this and the following chapter.

We can begin with a question. Had Samson remained as he is in the opening lines of *Samson Agonistes*—self-pitying and despairing—would he have pulled down the temple? The answer, perhaps surprising, to that question is yes; and if the Samson of Judges ("O God, that I may be at once avenged of the Philistines for my two eyes") is substituted for Milton's Samson, it could be argued that this is exactly what happens. I am not asserting the absolute independence of the play's two actions—Samson's regeneration and his pulling down of the temple; rather, I am admitting that I am unable to construct a formula which links them in a cause-and-effect relationship. And I believe that this is not a failure on my part but a true response to the experience Milton provides for his readers, an experience structured so as to leave unanswered the very questions it raises.

One such question is not asked by anyone in the play and so has gone mostly unnoticed by the commentators, although it intrudes itself into the reading experience on at least thirteen occasions. The question is: Why did Samson betray himself to Dalila? In *Paradise Lost* the corresponding question is: Why does Adam fall? And in both instances, for "Why," we may read "What is the explanation of," with everything that "explanation" implies. The first reference to the play's pre-plot is made by Samson at line 46:

> Whom have I to complain of but myself?
> Who this high gift of strength committed to me,
> In what part lodg'd, how easily bereft me,
> Under the Seal of silence could not keep,
> But weakly to a woman must reveal it,
> O'ercome with importunity and tears.[1]

Here the verse itself forces the questions the reader will continue to ask throughout the play. Only in line 50 is the "Who" of 47 identified as the subject (I, who) of "could not keep"; and as a result, words and phrases which are ultimately seen to be part of an absolute construction modifying "Who" shift in and out of the contexts created momentarily by the reader's efforts to make sense of the syntax. As line 47 is read, "Who" is likely to be taken either as a relative pronoun with an unclear referent (he who committed this gift of strength to me), or, less probably, as an interrogative (*Who* has committed this gift of strength to me?). Either reading points to God as the agent referred to, and however the lines are finally resolved, he remains implicated in the action whose explanation the reader is seeking. "In what part lodg'd" merely continues the ambiguity. Does the phrase qualify "strength" (lodged in whatever part whoever "who" is has lodged it?) or is it another interrogative (in what part is the strength lodged)? Or both? Or perhaps neither? If God is "Who," is he also the subject of "bereft"? (Is Samson once again accusing God?) If God is not "Who," who (the floating pronoun now mocks the reader) or what *is* the subject of "bereft"? If "bereft" is a participle and requires no subject, "how" (the question is there in the line) has the action of berefting been effected? By what agency? And why "easily"? It could be objected that these questions lose their urgency, indeed disappear, when the sense of the passage is finally unraveled: "I, Samson, who, this gift of strength having been committed to me, and along with it the secret of its maintenance (O how easily wrested from me despite my pledge of silence), could not keep it."[2] But they have been raised, and they have not been answered, certainly not by Samson: "weakly to a woman must reveal it, / O'ercome with importunity and tears." Here the reader is offered the relief of an "easy" syntax, but as an explanation of the "berefting" this is no more satisfactory than the epic voice's comment on Adam in book IX of *Paradise Lost:* "fondly overcome with Female charm." "Weakly" begs the question; "must" raises a new one (is it Fate?); and "O'ercome with importunity and tears" is a description, not an analysis, of the fact. Still, these two lines, because they are comprehensible and straightforward, *do* provide a resting place for the reader's mind (many readers rush immediately to them, only partly conscious of the difficulty of the passage) and allow him to move on, with Samson, to a consideration of the present situation.

But with the entrance of the Chorus, Samson is reminded of his shame, and he returns to dwell on the occasion of his sin:

> How could I once look up, or heave the head,
> Who like a foolish Pilot have shipwreck't
> My Vessel trusted to me from above,
> Gloriously rigg'd; and for a word, a tear,
> Fool, have divulg'd the secret gift of God
> To a deceitful Woman. (197–202)

Once more the fact itself is recalled ("have divulg'd the secret gift of God"), but we are given no explanation of it save for the self-contemptuous "Fool" and the glancing hit at Dalila. The force of these lines is felt not so much in the muted accusation of "deceitful Woman"—Dalila is not being cited as the cause—as in the phrase "for a word, a tear," and the sense of wonder conveyed at the ease of her victory. "How could I have violated my sacred pledge for such a creature?" Samson seems to ask. Thirty lines later, Dalila is found innocent of the main crime (betrayal of God) and Samson cries out once more against the *mystery* of his weakness: "She was not the prime cause, but I myself, / Who vanquisht with a peal of words (O weakness!) / Gave up my fort of silence to a Woman" (234–236).

In only 240 lines, Samson's fall has been alluded to no less than three times, yet our understanding of it has not been advanced at all. Of the explanations which might logically have occurred to the reader, the hero himself has rejected two (it was fate; it was my wife). At line 369, Manoa offers a third, and it too is rejected: "if he through frailty err." In this construction, "frailty" is abstracted from Samson and made to assume the burden of his guilt (this is Adam's ploy when he complains "thy terms too hard," "unable to perform"); but at this point Samson is jealous of his title to full blame ("Sole Author I, sole cause"), and he sup-

ports his claim with the most extended account of the event we
have yet heard:

> Sole Author I, sole cause: if aught seem vile,
> As vile hath been my folly, who have profan'd
> The mystery of God giv'n me under pledge
> Of vow, and have betray'd it to a woman,
> A *Canaanite*, my faithless enemy.
> This well I knew, nor was at all surpris'd,
> But warn'd by oft experience: did not she
> Of *Timna* first betray me, and reveal
> The secret wrested from me in her height
> Of Nuptial Love profest, carrying it straight
> To them who had corrupted her, my Spies,
> And Rivals? In this other was there found
> More Faith? who also in her prime of love,
> Spousal embraces, vitiated with Gold,
> Though offer'd only, by the scent conceiv'd
> Her spurious first-born; Treason against me?
> Thrice she assay'd with flattering prayers and sighs,
> And amorous reproaches to win from me
> My capital secret, in what part my strength
> Lay stor'd, in what part summ'd, that she might know:
> Thrice I deluded her, and turn'd to sport
> Her importunity, each time perceiving
> How openly, and with what impudence
> She purpos'd to betray me, and (which was worse
> Than undissembl'd hate) with what contempt
> She sought to make me Traitor to myself;
> Yet the fourth time, when must'ring all her wiles,
> With blandisht parleys, feminine assaults,
> Tongue batteries, she surceas'd not day nor night
> To storm me over-watch't, and wearied out.
> At times when men seek most repose and rest,
> I yielded, and unlock'd her all my heart,

Who with a grain of manhood well resolv'd
Might easily have shook off all her snares:
But foul effeminacy held me yok't
Her Bondslave. (376–411)

What is remarkable about this passage is the disparity between its direction and its conclusion. Everything seems to point *away from* Samson's yielding. He is not taken unawares; his experience with the woman of Timna has left him suspicious of all Philistines, and Dalila's approach is hardly subtle. The contest, as it is described, is almost ritualistic—the repetition of the "Thrice" formula serves to fix the combatants in their respective poses: "Thrice she assay'd," "Thrice I deluded her." At the worst, Samson seems to be winning a stalemate, and his awareness of her intent ("each time perceiving") and of the issue at stake ("to make me Traitor to myself") suggests that in a test of endurance, his will, informed by his greater dedication, will triumph. And then the forward movement of the lines is checked by the single word "Yet," the pivot on which the whole turns. "Yet" is the sum of the incredulity Samson has given voice to before (one thinks of Adam, "not deceiv'd"), and in its position it fairly shouts out the question, "Why?" Five lines separate "Yet" and "I yielded," as if Samson himself were unwilling to pronounce the damning words; in the interval he strives to soften the blow—and does, both for himself and for his audience(s), citing feminine wiles and wearying assaults. But the reader who accepts *these* as an answer to the question posed by "Yet" is met at once by a flat assertion of the hero's sufficiency: "Who with a grain of manhood well resolv'd / Might easily have shook off all her snares." "Easy" has been used before to characterize Dalila's victory; here it insists on the equal probability of a different outcome.

To experience these lines is to experience the mystery that lies at the heart of Samson's action. The precision with which the scene is set leads us to expect an equally precise analysis of the deed itself. Instead, we are offered the question-begging "Yet" and the feebleness of "overwatch't, and wearied out," an excuse so lame that Samson himself dismisses it in the very next line. In his final word (for the moment), Samson substitutes "foul effeminacy" for the "frailty" of Manoa's equivocation: "But foul effeminacy held me yok't"; and once more we end at the beginning, no wiser than before.

While the play moves on to other problems, Milton never allows us to forget this one. The inexplicability of what Samson has done is underlined by Manoa and suggested by his syntax:

> thou . . .
> Temptation found'st, or over-potent charms
> To violate the sacred trust of silence
> Deposited within thee; *which to have kept*
> *Tacit, was in thy power; true.* (426–430, emphasis added)

And Samson responds, predictably now, with a new orgy of self-recrimination:

> I
> God's counsel have not kept, his holy secret
> Presumptuously have publish'd, impiously,
> Weakly at least, and shamefully. (496–499)

To the Chorus' celebration of his Nazarite purity, he replies in the same vein: "What boots it at one gate to make defense, / And at another to let in the foe, / Effeminately vanquish't?" (560–562). However many times Manoa and the Chorus turn the conversation to other matters, Samson shows himself determined to indulge his preoccupation with the richly criminal past.

Dalila senses this, and plays to it, inviting him to embrace her in the name of their common weakness: "Nor shouldst thou have trusted that to woman's frailty: / Ere I to thee, thou to thyself was cruel. / Let weakness then with weakness come to parle" (783–785). "Weak" has been Samson's favorite term for his behavior; it constitutes his only explanation of what has happened to him; but hearing the word from Dalila, and along with it an echo of Manoa's personified "frailty," he is provoked to exclaim "All wickedness is weakness" (834). Here the reader may be moved to add, "Then all wickedness is a mystery, if we regard your own weakness as a model"; but Samson is not yet able to generalize from his own experience (it is a question, finally, as to whether he ever does so), and the only visible effect of his encounter with Dalila is a slight backing away from his insistence on reserving all the blame to himself: "unbosom'd all my secrets to thee, / Not out of levity, but overpow'r'd / By thy request, who could deny thee nothing" (879–881). While this is surely a moral advance, a movement upward from the inverted pride of "I, sole cause," it is hardly to be taken seriously as an answer to the question we have been asking. Overpowered? Yes, but *why*? Could deny her nothing? Obviously, but *why*?

The answer the Chorus gives involves the expansion of "could deny her nothing" into a generalized misogyny:

> Seeming at first all heavenly under virgin veil,
> Soft, modest, meek, demure,
> Once join'd, the contrary she proves, a thorn
> Intestine, far within defensive arms
> A cleaving mischief, in his way to virtue
> Adverse and turbulent, or by her charms
> Draws him awry enslav'd
> With dotage, and his sense deprav'd
> To folly and shameful deeds which ruin ends.
> What Pilot so expert but needs must wreck
> Embark'd with such a Steers-mate at the Helm? (1035–1045)

The Chorus is forever trying to categorize Samson, first as an example of the tragic fall-from-a-high-place (167), now as a major figure in its antifeminist mythology. If it can place him, it is no longer obliged to understand him. He becomes a particular instance of a general and implacable truth; the vexing problem of responsibility is referred back to the natural, fatal, familiar treachery of woman and finally to the God who made her.[3] The image of the shipwrecked pilot is Samson's, and by echoing him the Chorus hopes to gain his assent to its reading of his history. As readers, we are less sanguine; Samson has rejected the argument "from necessity" in several of its guises, and we now expect to hear still another declaration of his guilt, accompanied, perhaps, by an invocation to death. For the first time, however, the fallen champion declines the bait and remains silent, indicating by this omission a small advance in his struggle to escape the abyss of despair. From this point on, we hear no more of effeminate weakness and inexplicable yieldings. Harapha enters, and the focus of the drama shifts from the past to the present and to the challenge of new situations.

Our attention, of course, shifts correspondingly, but some part of our consciousness is left waiting (forever as it turns out) for an answer to the question we have been asking, with varying degrees of urgency, for more than one thousand lines: What happened to Samson? Were this the only unanswered question in the play, it would be difficult to justify my lingering on it; but it is only one of many, all of them interconnected. If Samson's yielding is an event apparently without cause, what of his marriage? Why did he marry Dalila? A mistake, replies the hero: whereas my first marriage, with the woman of Timna, was urged on me by "intimate impulse" (223)—that is to say, it was "of God" (222)—the second was prompted by my desire, which I reinterpreted as inspiration ("I thought it lawful from my former act" [231]). Samson has constructed a loose syllogism: I thought it was of God; it seems to have turned out badly; therefore, it was not of God. But the force of this argument may be diminished for us, since we know the end of the story. The promise that Samson "Should *Israel* from *Philistian* yoke deliver" (39) *will* be fulfilled when he is brought to the temple, and his deliverance to the temple follows upon this apparently disastrous marriage. Perhaps it, too, is of God. The Chorus seems to think so, for its assertion of the independence God enjoys from his own laws is supported by an allusion to his hero's choice of an unclean wife:

> For with his own Laws he can best dispense.
> He would not else who never wanted means,
> Nor in respect of th'enemy just cause
> To set his people free,
> Have prompted this Heroic *Nazarite*,
> Against his vow of strictest purity,
> To seek in marriage that fallacious Bride,
> Unclean, unchaste. (314–321)

Of course, one could argue that the "fallacious Bride" is possibly not Dalila but the woman of Timna; but my point—that the relationship between Samson's marriages and God's will is progressively less clear—is only strengthened by the ambiguity, if it is there. (Merritt Hughes, for one, assumes that it is Dalila who is referred to, and this seems likely in its context.)[4] Manoa muddies the waters still more when he implies that *neither* marriage is of God:

> I cannot praise thy marriage choices, Son,
> Rather approv'd them not; but thou didst plead
> Divine impulsion prompting how thou might'st
> Find some occasion to infest our Foes.
> I state not that. (420–424)

Ignoring the distinction Samson makes between them, Manoa assumes that the two "choices" are alike the issue of his son's wayward passion. On the claim of inspiration he will not pass judgment directly ("I state not that"), but one need not overread to hear the sneer in "plead / Divine impulsion."

Whom are we to believe? Samson, who uses hindsight (which we happen to know is shortsighted) to label one motion "of God," the other not? The Chorus, which sees both as manifestations of God's inscrutable will? Manoa, who sees only a double violation of tribal law? And if we decide the question by reasoning backward from the ending, we imitate Samson's presumption and rule out the possibility that from the vantage point of a further horizon our view of the event may prove to be partial. Samson's motivation in the matter of his marriages, it would seem, is no less a mystery than his subsequent weakness in the face of Dalila's assaults.

Equally mysterious is Dalila's motivation. Why does she betray Samson? In her own defense, she offers only contradictions: I did it for love (790); no—for the "public good," to which I subordinated my love (867–869); but, then, also for the fame posterity will confer on me (982). More likely for "*Philistian* gold" (831), growls Samson. Of course, we are less interested in Dalila's explanations for their own sake than for the sake of the response they draw from Samson and for the contribution they make (if any) to the revival of his spirits; still, one can't help wondering, and wonder is finally a large part of *our* response to the scene and to the entire play. The Chorus wonders, but then gives up the riddle for the comfortable generalizations of its misogynist creed:

> It is not virtue, wisdom, valor, wit,
> Strength, comeliness of shape, or amplest merit
> That woman's love can win or long inherit;

> But what it is, hard to say,
> Harder to hit,
> (Which way soever men refer it)
> Much like thy riddle, *Samson*, in one day
> Or seven, though one should musing sit. (1010–1017)

And why, continues the Chorus in the course of its musings, did the Timnian bride reject you, Samson, in favor of "Thy Paranymph, worthless to thee compar'd" (1020)? Why indeed? And why, for that matter, does Dalila come to the mill? To taunt? To further her original purpose, whatever it is? For the "public good"? The evidence, I think, tends to support the explanation offered by A. B. Chambers: Dalila suffers from "*malitia*" or "*pecandi studium* . . . a perverse love of causing harm."[5] In other words, hers is a motiveless malignity, and thus the perfect complement to Samson's causeless weakness.

Where Is the Middle?

If the questions I have raised could be answered, the universe of *Samson Agonistes* would be one in which the phenomena of experience open themselves up to the organizing power of discursive reasoning. That the opposite is true is what the reader comes to realize by joining with the characters in an attempt to account for the case of Samson. Either the lines of cause and effect which seem to obtain become blurred upon closer examination, or for one effect there are available an obfuscating number of causes. It is, to say the least, difficult to evaluate an action when the agent who initiates it cannot be identified with certainty.

Of course, an obvious solution to these problems is to refer them to God, the first and ultimate cause; but this has the effect of begging what is for the hero the central question of the play: In a world like this, what does one do? How does one act responsibly? How does one act at all? Looking at the evidence, Manoa decides that whatever man does, he will be mocked by the tendency of events to confound his expectations:

> O ever failing trust
> In mortal strength! and oh, what not in man
> Deceivable and vain! Nay, what thing good
> Pray'd for, but often proves our woe, our bane?
> I pray'd for Children, and thought barrenness
> In wedlock a reproach; I gain'd a Son,
> And such a Son as all Men hail'd me happy;
> Who would be now a Father in my stead?
> O wherefore did God grant me my request,
> And as a blessing with such pomp adorn'd?
> Why are his gifts desirable, to tempt
> Our earnest Prayers, then, giv'n with solemn hand
> As Graces, draw a Scorpion's tail behind?
> For this did th'Angel twice descend? for this
> Ordain'd thy nurture holy, as of a Plant? (348–362)

The movement of Manoa's thought also describes a syllogism: Thinking barrenness a reproach, I prayed for children; I gained a son and because of him I am unhappy; therefore, barrenness is a blessing and fatherhood is not; God grants our desires so that we may be ruined by them. The conclusion of a capricious God is arrived at by appealing to the law of the excluded middle: either children are a blessing or they are not. The alternative—the possibility that they may be both and that the complexity of the world may elude the formulations of logic—is not considered, for it would deprive Manoa of the right to his anger; better an irresponsible deity than one who is incomprehensible and hence unimpeachable. As it is, he can proceed to label the world "unfair" and advocate withdrawal from it, as he does when he urges Samson to live out his days quietly at home.

It would be a mistake, however, to draw too firm a conclusion from this speech, spoken as it is in the first flush of anguish. Manoa is not naturally impious; soon he will remind Samson that God is inclined to be merciful to those who approach him with humility (511). Nor is he by temperament a philosopher; except for this involuntary expression of pain and bewilderment, his attention is wholly occupied with practical matters. Still, however quickly he retreats from his questioning of God's ways, this complaint against the heavenly disposition of things has been registered; and the reader will have acknowledged its limited justness.

In contrast to Manoa, the Chorus is forever philosophizing, although it is hardly consistent—now an Augustinian upholder of God's inscrutability, now a reconciler of reason and faith in the tradition of Aquinas, at one moment echoing Boethius, at another adopting the rhetoric of Stoic quietism. There is, however, a kind of consistency in its concern to fit Samson into a larger scheme of things, and, significantly, it finally gives up trying. Initially the Chorus sees him as a "mirrour" of man's "fickle state," and in this classification, as John Huntley notes, there is more than a hint of "an unpredictable tyrant" who oversees "a world where Hebrews unjustly serve Philistines and champions are whimsically destroyed."[6] But in response to Samson's charge that strength and wisdom have been given to him in ill proportion, the Chorus turns pious defender of God's prerogative: "Tax not divine disposal" (210).

The confusion in the Chorus' thought (a confusion which the reader shares) is even more evident in lines 293–325. The Chorus begins by asserting "Just are the ways of God, / And justifiable to Men"; only fools will dispute this, it adds. And "Yet" (one senses it move here from the conventional platitude to the recalcitrant facts of experience) there are an unaccountable number of men who think God unjust and who find his edicts self-contradictory.

At this point, the tone changes from assertion to defense, perhaps because the details of Samson's history constitute something of an embarrassment. Come to think of it, wasn't he prompted by God to violate a law promulgated by God? Quickly a defense is constructed: in those cases where his ways are not justifiable, God has exercised his right to dispense with his own laws; and who are we to "confine th' interminable"? Now the embarrassment of God's possible involvement in Samson's marriages can be accommodated: "He would not else . . . / . . . Have prompted this Heroic *Nazarite*, / Against his vow of strictest purity" (315, 318–319). Still, the effort of excusing God has proved wearying for the choral intellect—how close the resemblance to those impious "Fool[s]" who are "by thir own perplexities involv'd" (304)!—and it is with relief that the Chorus concludes, "Down Reason then, at least vain reasonings down" (322).

The felt inequities of the human situation, however, usually manage to survive the attempts we make to explain them away, and later, as the Chorus experiences the full horror of Samson's anguish ("Hopeless are all my evils, all remediless" [648]), his cry of pain becomes the Chorus' as well.

> God of our Fathers, what is man!
> That thou towards him with hand so various,
> Or might I say contrarious,
> Temper'st thy providence through his short course . . .
> Nor only dost degrade them, or remit
> To life obscur'd, which were a fair dismission,
> But throw'st them lower than thou didst exalt them high . . .
> With sickness and disease thou bow'st them down,
> Painful diseases and deform'd,
> In crude old age;
> Though not disordinate, yet *causeless* suff'ring
> The punishment of dissolute days: in fine,

Just or unjust, alike seem miserable . . .
　　So deal not with this once thy glorious Champion . . .
　　What do I beg? how hast thou dealt already?
　　　(667–670, 687–689, 698–703, 705, 707; emphasis added)

The force of this speech is a reflection of the Chorus' new sincerity. No longer is it concerned to occupy a safe middle ground in the quarrel between Samson and God: no longer does it temper platitudinous consolation with hints of political betrayal ("Yet *Israel* still serves with all his Sons" [240]). No longer are the defense of the tribe and the maintenance of its traditions the Chorus' chief objectives. This is not a Hebrew complaint (except as it echoes Job, whose own credentials as a pious Jew have been challenged) but a *human* complaint, occasioned by the visible suffering of a fellow creature and uttered apart from any prior theorizing on the relationship of God and man.

Early commentators on *Samson Agonistes,* recalling Milton's models, assumed too easily that the Chorus speaks for the author. More recently we have perhaps erred in the opposite direction, by finding fault with the Chorus' every word. Surely the important point here is not the correctness of what it says, but the startling precision with which it articulates the misgivings we ourselves have felt, both as human beings and as readers. True, the Chorus does invert the question of the Psalmist—"What is man, that thou art mindful of him"—and so reverses the priorities of judgment; but in context, this involuntary impiety attests to the truth Milton is at pains to impress on us: limited though it may be, the human perspective is the only one we have. And from the vantage point of that perspective, the Chorus reports faithfully what it sees. More than that, it reports what we see. The reader who is ready to condemn the Chorus should first ask himself whether its observations differ from his own. Don't the just perish and the unjust prosper? Isn't there evidence in the world, our world, of "causeless suffering"? Haven't there been warriors who have labored long in God's service only to find themselves delivered, apparently by that same God, into the hands of the enemy? I could let Milton himself answer this last question.[7]

We are told by some that the doubts expressed by Manoa, the Chorus, and Samson concerning the intelligibility of the universe are to be attributed to their ignorance: if they knew, as we do, the end of the story, they would be less inclined to assert the unreasonableness of God's ways; for when the play is over and the divine plan has unfolded, everything is perfectly understood. But, in fact, do we truly understand anything, either in the course of the play, or when all its passions have been spent? Only by ignoring the inconsistency and the inadequacy of the explanations offered to us can we make sense of what happened *before* the play opens. And are we any more in control of the action which (apparently) takes place during the play—the recovery of Samson's faith? For a while, critics answered Dr. Johnson's charge in *Rambler* 139 (1751) that the play lacks a middle by substituting for the conventional "middle" the middle of an interior plot—Samson's regeneration—and in doing so they tended to assume a linear progression, more or less visible, from accusation of God to acceptance of responsibility to rejection of temptation to a reaffirmation of faith. But an examination of the text will not support this reading. Specifically, the movement from accusation of God to acceptance of responsibility is a movement downward, drawing Samson toward despair and involving him, more than any angry accusation, in the appointing of heavenly disposition. He begins by anticipating the reasoning his father will employ:

> Why was my breeding order'd and prescrib'd
> As of a person separate to God,
> Design'd for great exploits; if I must die
> Betray'd, Captiv'd, and both my Eyes put out . . .
> . . . Promise was that I

> Should *Israel* from *Philistian* yoke deliver;
> Ask for this great Deliverer now, and find him
> Eyeless in *Gaza*. (30–33, 38–41)

Here is still another syllogism: God has said that I will deliver Israel from the Philistian yoke; I am now the captive of the Philistines; therefore I will not deliver Israel from the Philistine yoke, and God has broken his promise. Almost immediately, Samson recoils from this concealed argument: "Yet stay, let me not rashly call in doubt / Divine Prediction; what if all foretold / Had been fulfill'd but through mine own default" (43–45). This is hardly an advance in humility, however, since God's power is still circumscribed if the fulfillment of his prophecy requires Samson's cooperation. A better question would be, "What if all foretold will yet be fulfilled, even though I cannot imagine how?" What Samson has done is to take upon himself the responsibility for the maintenance of the universe, in addition to the limited responsibility he has for his own action (significantly but uncomprehendingly, the Chorus compares him to Atlas, "Like whom the Gentiles feign to bear up Heav'n" [150]), and he will go on from here to encroach further on the prerogatives of the godhead by deciding that in his present condition God will not, indeed could not, make use of him:

> the strife
> With mee hath end; all the contést is now
> 'Twixt God and *Dagon*. (460–462)

> Now blind, disheart'n'd, sham'd, dishonor'd, quell'd,
> To what can I be useful. (563–564)

Hugging to himself the guilt he has so eagerly acknowledged, Samson comes finally, in his own words, to "faintings, swoonings of despair, / And sense of Heav'n's desertion" (631–632), and declares, "Nor am I in the list of them that hope" (647). God has cast me off, he laments, when, in actuality, it is he who has cast off God by committing himself to the reasoning of the despairing soul: "Now I have sinned; now I am damned; God will not overlook such sins." As D. C. Allen writes, "Despair, sprouting from sin and from a sense of unworthiness or from an unknowingness of mercy, is for corporeal man supreme disobedience to the will of God. If he continues in this state of spiritual sloth, the mind of man will turn to the death hunger, which may propel him, as Saul was propelled, into damnation as complete and eternal as that of the demons."[8]

What are we to conclude from these observations? Should Samson have continued to accuse God? Is he wrong to blame himself for violating his pledge? What questions like these serve to illustrate is the impossibility of determining exactly the connection (if any) between Samson's gesture at the point (or at any point) and the equilibrium he finally achieves. Accepting responsibility in this context (and in analogous contexts in which any of us may find himself) is both a movement upward and a movement downward; and the dissatisfaction my readers are probably feeling at this moment is not unlike the dissatisfaction Milton wants his readers to feel as their attempts to discover a logical pattern in Samson's spiritual history—attempts that the poem encourages—are frustrated. The pattern downward described in the preceding paragraph represents my own oversimplification of a progress that is hardly regular enough to be called a progression. As he moves toward a conviction that his "evils" are "remediless" (648), Samson also takes small steps in the opposite direction: he rejects the suggestion that he is to blame for Israel's servitude (241); he recognizes the true insubstantiality of physical strength (55); he rebukes Manoa's presumptuous quarreling with divine justice (373), although he goes on to assume presumptuously that divine justice could not possibly be reconciled to him (461); he is sufficiently aware of the moral dimension of his tragedy to prefer this kind of slavery to his "former servitude, ignoble, / Unmanly, ignominious, infamous" (416–417); but he is not yet aware enough to see how preferable both are to the bondage he is in the process of surrendering to. The qualifications I have attached to the last two sentences ("although" and "but") mirror the reader's experience of the first 710 lines: what looks to be an advance is revealed a few lines later to have been a step backward—although later still it may recover the status of an advance. As a result, while we have a sense of observing and participating in a continuing process, the mechanics of that process remain hidden from us.

Presumably, the give and take of Samson's conversations with his visitors is a large part of the process, but here, too, drawing lines of cause and effect is difficult. It is now a commonplace of criticism to cite as one of the chief ironies of the play the roles played by Samson's friends and enemies: his would-be consolers succeed only in reinforcing his despair, while the taunts of Harapha and Dalila rouse him from his lethargy and lead him once more to look to "the living God . . . Whose ear is ever open; and his eye / Gracious to re-admit the suppliant" (1140, 1172–1173). The evidence for this reading, of course, is Samson himself: he is at his lowest point in the speech of 606ff., invoking "death's benumbing Opium" as his "only cure" (630). Dalila appears soon after this, and Samson's spirits revive; the contorted syntax and irregular rhythms of his self-pitying laments give way to the straightforward vigor of anger and indignation. Harapha's challenges prod him to new heights of self-assertion, until at one point he speaks in the accents of a Tamburlaine:

> I only with an Oak'n staff will meet thee,
> And raise such outcries on thy clatter'd Iron,
> Which long shall not withhold me from thy head,
> That in a little time, while breath remains thee,
> Thou oft shall wish thyself at Gath to boast

> Again in safety what thou wouldst have done
> To *Samson*, but shalt never see *Gath* more. (1123–1129)

Within minutes of this he declares, "My trust is in the living God" (1140), and we begin to anticipate the glorious triumph of the foreknown climax.

But if this is one pattern in which the reader participates, there are others, equally insistent and even more visible. Consider, for example, Samson's reactions to the approaches of his visitors. When the sound of the Chorus' "many feet" reaches his ear, he wonders, "who are these? . . . / Perhaps my enemies who come to stare / At my affliction, and perhaps to insult, / Thir daily practice to afflict me more" (111, 110, 112–114). The tone here is nine parts self-pity (O what will this cruel world subject me to now?), and the focus of Samson's fear is entirely physical. The entrance of Manoa evokes a different response: "Ay me, another inward grief awak't, / With mention of that name" (330–331). Self-pity has been replaced by shame, a more honest emotion, if still a paralyzing one; and Samson's concern is now with his inner being. When Dalila appears, he is roused to anger: "My Wife, my Traitress, let her not come near me" (725); and the vigor of this—directed *outward*—strikes us as more healthy than the languor characteristic of his self-examinations. To the threat of Harapha, as it is discerned by the Chorus, he replies: "Or peace or not, alike to me he comes" (1074), indicating that whatever the world presents to him, he will not be disconcerted by it. This is full circle from the cheap sentiment of "my enemies who come to stare / At my affliction." And finally, the warning of the messenger—"Regard thyself, this will offend them highly" (1333)—elicits a firm distinction between his physical well-being and his inner integrity:

> Myself? my conscience and internal peace.
> Can they think me so broken, so debas'd

411

> With corporal servitude, that my mind ever
> Will condescend to such absurd commands? (1334–1337)

This progression has been noted by John Huntley, who imagines the corresponding changes in Samson's posture: "At the beginning, Samson is said to be lying. . . . He is properly imagined as propping his head to speak with the Chorus and perhaps supports himself by the elbow to speak with Manoa. . . . With Dalila . . . Samson is to be imagined speaking from a sitting position. He must be standing when he swings his fist and hurls his challenges at Harapha."[9] And Huntley proceeds to draw the reasonable conclusion: "Milton shadows Samson's spiritual development by symbolic changes in his posture. . . . Samson was prone, he raised himself, he sat, he stood, and now he walks off toward Gaza." Surely, this *is* how we are to imagine it, and any director who decides to stage the closet drama would be wise to consult Huntley's article; but whether or not these alterations are "symbolic of Samson's spiritual development" depends on which development the text is urging on you at any one moment. Is it the straight-line development suggested by this particular pattern? Is it the V-shaped development—really not a development at all—which emerges if we attend to the pattern of Samson's statements? Or is it the development within an individual confrontation, each of which has a life of its own, complete with advances and backslidings and surprises? All of these "developments" can be traced in the narrative, and together they give the reader a sense of orderly progress, even though, in logical terms, they do not mesh. That is to say, the continual availability of a number of structuring patterns allows us to feel that we understand what is happening or that what is happening is understandable; but because these patterns are independent of one another, we would be hard pressed to translate our feeling of understanding into a formula. In this respect, our experience is the experience of all individuals who move about in the world relying on the regular operation of laws which they would be unable to produce on demand.

Surely, one might object, there is a direct connection, say, between Samson's refusal of the living death Dalila offers—"the snare," "the fair enchanting cup"—and his escape from the living death he had been preparing for himself, the fair enchanted cup of despair. No doubt there is, but what is it? And is it any more direct than the connection between his rejection of Manoa's not dissimilar offer of a quiet life at home and the same escape? Samson does not help us to answer these questions; he is not an intellectual hero, and we never see him make the transference from the specific points of issue he debates with Harapha and Dalila to the larger and all-inclusive issue of the relationship of man and God. Obviously the transference is made (my use of the passive is deliberate), but all we see is the evidence of it in time: (1) Samson despairs; (2) he engages in a series of discussions with various persons; (3) he no longer despairs. Presumably the change from (1) to (3) has something to do with (2); we feel certain that it has; but we can only conjecture (with some confidence, perhaps) as to what that something is. The striking thing about the affirmation of faith which Harapha draws from Samson is its unexpectedness; it has not been prepared for, and it springs incongruously out of a military context when all our attention is centered on what appear to be the preliminaries to an actual combat.[10] The surprise we experience at this sudden shift in levels of discourse should alert us to the fact that what we see here is not the end of a linear and chartable progression or the conclusion to a chain of inferences, but an illumination—an illumination which surely has antecedents and therefore causes; but as to what they are, exactly—well, that is "hard to hit." What I am suggesting, as some of my readers will have realized, is that in terms of its central action—the recovery of Samson's faith—this is a play without a middle, or at least without a middle one can point to and analyze.

I With This Messenger Will Go Along

Most interpretations of *Samson Agonistes* imply that the play provides a formula for undoing the damage of an understandable—and hence remediable—failure; but if my description of its workings is at all accurate, the formula (if one exists) is unstatable, and the failure inexplicable. In the universe the characters inhabit—that is, in our universe—one becomes aware of two kinds of related uncertainties: an uncertainty as to the springs (or motivations) of human action, and an uncertainty as to the connection between events in the world of man and the will of God. In such a universe, obviously, it is difficult, first, to know what to do, and, second, to evaluate what has been done. The experience of both difficulties is forced on the reader when the Philistine officer summons Samson to the temple. What will he do? What would we have done in his place? As Samson first sees it, the issue is simple: "Thou knowst I am an *Ebrew*, therefore tell them, / Our Law forbids at thir Religious Rites / My presence; for that cause I cannot come" (1319–1321). As Samson employs it, the Law is an already programmed computer into which he feeds the components of any situation and from which he receives directions for action; as the concluding half-line indicates, the Law controls him by determining his choices; and it bears the responsibility for what he does. At this late date, however, we are likely to be skeptical of so mechanical a solution to a moral dilemma, especially if the dilemmas of interpretation which we ourselves have faced remain unresolved. It just isn't that easy, although everyone in the play wishes it were. After all, didn't the Law prohibit Samson's marriages? One wonders if Samson has learned anything in the last thirteen hundred lines.

In this crisis, the Chorus performs brilliantly, although its motive—a fear of disturbing the *status quo*—has nothing to do with the larger issue being debated. What the Chorus does is confuse that issue just when Samson has succeeded in defining (and evading) it. By challenging his interpretation of the Law, it immediately challenges the Law's status as an objective and adequate guide to action:

> *Chorus:* Consider, *Samson;* matters now are strain'd
> Up to the height, whether to hold or break;
> He's gone, and who knows how he may report
> Thy words by adding fuel to the flame? . . .
> *Samson:* Shall I abuse this Consecrated gift . . .
> Vaunting my strength in honor to thir *Dagon?* . . .
> *Chorus:* Yet with this strength thou serv'st the *Philistines* . . .
> *Samson:* Not in thir Idol-Worship, but by labor
> Honest . . .
> *Chorus:* Where the heart joins not, outward acts defile not.
> *Samson:* Where outward force constrains, the sentence holds;
> But who constrains me to the Temple of *Dagon*. (1348–1351,
> 1354, 1360, 1363, 1365–1366, 1368–1370)

The rhythms of this passage are hypnotic and support the open-endedness of the exchange; we feel that the discussion could go on forever and still be inconclusive, defining first outward acts, and then constraint, and then the conditions necessary to establish the existence of a state of constraint, and so on. As we swing back and forth between the Chorus and Samson, we are involved in a series of alternating assents to opposing points of view; we acknowledge the justness of one of the Chorus' arguments, only to find ourselves agreeing no less emphatically with an objection raised by Samson in the following line; and then we enter the cycle again. As a result, the clarity afforded by the Law at a distance is taken away, and in its place is substituted the debilitating clarity of an insight the play has been urging on us all along: no firm—that is, external—basis for action exists in this world.[11]

The fact that Samson himself clings obstinately to the point of law he had cited at line 1320 only sharpens our sense of dilemma; for we know that Samson will in fact go to the temple, yet we see that the urgings of the Chorus have only confirmed him in his determination not to go:

> Commands are no constraints. If I obey them,
> I do it freely; venturing to displease
> God for the fear of Man, and Man prefer,
> Set God behind: which in his jealousy
> Shall never, unrepented, find forgiveness. (1372–1376)

Samson returns in a circular motion to his original position and exhibits the same rigidity of mind that has already borne fruit in the excessive over-justness and self-critical rigor of his despairing speeches. (It is not for him to decide what God will allow or when he will forgive.) The impasse seems hopeless, and we might well anticipate the Chorus and say of ourselves: "How thou wilt here come off surmounts my reach" (1380).

Then, suddenly, without preparation or logic, Samson reverses direction: "*Yet* that he *may* dispense with me or thee / Present in Temples at Idolatrous Rites / For some important cause, *thou needst not doubt*" (1377–1379, emphasis added). The important word here is "Yet," because it signals a departure from the frames of reference—the Law and the possibility of interpreting it narrowly—within which the scene has been unfolding. (In some ways, this "Yet" is like the "Yet" Samson uses to introduce the strange fact of his yielding to Dalila.) In its context, the word is liberating; and to the extent that we too have been caught up in the give and take of the dialogue, we as readers are also liberated.

With Samson we move beyond the limits of choice dictated by the intersection of the situation and the Law, and accept the awful responsibility of freedom. For once exceptions to the rule are admitted, reliance on the rule becomes impossible, and every decision is again a discrete crisis requiring the individual's participation.

Samson decides to go to the temple, but not because the Law sanctions his going, or because the Law forbids it; his "may" admits both possibilities without insisting on either. His going is a gesture, signifying his refusal to be paralyzed by the inability of the Law (or of any other formulaic construct) to answer unambiguously every question put to it. He goes without knowing how he will come off and *because* he does not know how he will come off. In these lines and in his farewell speech, Samson takes extraordinary care not to appoint heavenly disposition in *any* direction. The conditional clause "If there be aught of presage in the mind" (1387) is a deliberate hedging, a recognition perhaps of his earlier presumption in rushing too quickly to conclusions about the divine will and his responsiveness to it. This *may* be one of the times God will not dispense with him at idolatrous rites. What need not be doubted is not Samson's interpretation of the situation (he pointedly offers none), but the power of God to do anything, through anyone, in any circumstances. And it is trust in that power rather than in the calculation of probabilities or knowledge of the Law which is the motive force behind Samson's "I with this Messenger will go along" (1384). At this moment he joins the worthies of Hebrews 11, who take provisional actions (going out not knowing whither they go) in the name of a certain faith.

Samson's decision, then, is as arbitrary and as inexplicable—in the terms we usually use to explain decisions, the terms underlying the questions this play refuses to answer—as his earlier failure. Yet in this instance the very arbitrariness of the decision—its independence of any rational or legalistic process—is its value, because as a nonreasonable act it manifests Samson's willingness to come to terms with the world as it is, rather than as he would like it to be. His despair had been the result of just the kind of reasoning that incapacitates Manoa and the Chorus; he had projected ultimate realities by rationalizing or logicizing on the evidence of things seen, and concluded from that evidence that all his evils were remediless. Now, by refusing to limit the possibilities open to God by the possibilities conceivable to man, he affirms his belief in a benevolence whose kind is *not* always known and the evidence of which is *not* always seen or understood.

Whether we as readers see this immediately, and confer on his action its proper value, is doubtful, partly because everything happens so quickly (between lines 1376 and 1377) and partly because we are occupied with a new problem, or with an old problem in a new form—the assigning of cause:

> Be of good courage, I begin to feel
> Some rousing motions in me which dispose
> To something extraordinary my thoughts.
> I with this Messenger will go along. (1381–1384)

Just what are these rousing motions? When does Samson begin to feel them? What part do they play (a) in Samson's breaking free of the Law's bondage and (b) in his decision to go to the temple? The rousing motions are usually taken to be the sign of God's intervention; and Samson so recognizes them when he offers an obviously ironic explanation of his change of mind: "Masters' commands come with a power resistless / To such as owe them absolute subjection" (1404–1405). As Joseph Summers writes, "We know that Samson does not owe 'absolute subjection' to any nation or person; he owes it only to God; and we see (or will come to see) that those 'rousing motions' have come as a command from that master."[12] Presumably we "will come to see" because at the end everything will turn out just as it was supposed to—that is, as God willed it; but while this is surely true on a higher level of generality (it could hardly be otherwise), the reader who remembers the history of Samson's "rousing motions" may be wary of labeling these new motions "of God." Samson himself is a conservative on the question. If there is aught of presage in the mind, he says—allowing for the possibility that there is not; and his parting words are a forest of qualifications:

> Happ'n what may, of me expect to hear
> Nothing dishonorable, impure, unworthy
> Our God, our Law, my Nation, or myself;
> The last of me or no I cannot warrant. (1423–1426)

The only prediction Samson will venture is that *something* will happen; whether this will involve the death he had despairingly invoked is uncertain. Line 1426 alone is a tour de force of noncommittalness, establishing consecutively the mutually exclusive alternatives—"The last of me or no" and dissociating the "I" from the influence that will determine them. Samson's only assertion concerns his resolution to be true to what he has termed his "conscience and internal peace"; this alone is in his control, if anything is. ("Our thoughts are ours, their ends none of our own.") Events and their final meaning belong to someone else. Of course Samson *hopes* that the thoughts stirring within him are prompted directly by God (rather than being merely permitted by him), but short of an angelic visitation—and he no longer expects this—he must rely, like all men, on his best lights.[13]

Nowhere is the blend of assertiveness and provisionality which characterizes Samson's new attitude more in evidence than in the gesture he makes in the temple:

> he his guide requested
>
> . . . . .
>
> As overtir'd to let him lean a while
> With both his arms on those two massy Pillars
> That to the arched roof gave main support.
> He unsuspicious led him; which when *Samson*
> Felt in his arms, with head a while inclin'd
> And eyes fast fixt he stood, as one who pray'd,
> Or some great matter in his mind revolv'd. (1630, 1632–1638)

Whether this is a prayer or a meditation, it serves to contrast the new Samson with what we know of the old, "a petty God" (529) who performed heroic deeds as a matter of course in the confidence that he was the Lord's chosen ("swoll'n with pride"). More than anything, this momentary withdrawal is a sign of the hero's abiding uncertainty: Is he doing the right thing? Is it God's will? Of course we can only conjecture as to what goes on in Samson's mind; the reader is left, as Arthur Barker says, "to decide, in terms of his response to the controlled mimetic movement, what is happening and is meant."[14] But influencing every reader's decision will be an awareness of the difference between this Samson and the Samson of Judges, who asks God to be his private avenger: "Strengthen me, I pray thee, only this once, O God, that I may be at once avenged of the Philistines for my two eyes."[15] Whatever Milton's Samson asks for, it is not vengeance—the inclined head would be incompatible with that—and in the context of "the controlled mimetic movement," it seems to be guidance or illumination; or perhaps he prays that the action he is about to take is answerable to the divine will. At any rate, he does take it, assertively and without hesitation, but by praying or pausing he acknowledges that even now his vision may be partial and his light "delusive."

To return to our questions: When does Samson begin to feel these rousing motions, whatever they are? We are first aware of them only *after* Samson has uttered his liberating "Yet." (Again I would call attention to the acceleration of pace felt here, in contrast to the drawn-out dialectic of previous scenes.) To all appearances, then—that is to say, as far as we know—this is the hero's victory, achieved by his own efforts with only the indirect (and inadvertent) cooperation of his interlocutors; but when the "rousing motions" are introduced three lines later, their influence is felt retroactively, and the independence not only of the hero's resolution ("I with this Messenger will go along"), but of the process by which he arrives at it, is called into question. The sharp outlines of the situation are suddenly—and irreparably—blurred, just as they are in *Paradise Lost,* book XI, when, after "following . . . the fallen couple's gropings toward redemption,"[16] we are informed by God that their contrition is the fruit of "My motions in him" (91). In both poems the result of the delayed revelation is not clarity but confusion: we are told one thing but have experienced another, and our final response is necessarily a conflation, however illogical, of both. Samson and Adam and Eve do it alone, but then they don't. (Of course, in *Samson Agonistes* the question is further complicated because we do not have an authoritative identification of the "motions.") In effect, then, the attitude with which Samson goes to the temple is re-created, in all its indefiniteness, in us as readers: we find ourselves unable to determine what part of the hero's decision is to be traced to his own hard-won intuition, and what part (if any) to the direct intervention of heavenly powers.

The difficulty of understanding, and therefore of evaluating, exactly what Samson does is only intensified by the curious treatment of the Philistines. Had Milton wished, he could have simplified our response to the destruction of the Philistine nobility to the point where it would have been indistinguishable from the choral response. The sympathy we feel for Samson is enough to prejudice us against Dalila and Harapha, who, when they appear, do little, surely, to win us over. If the messenger had discharged his duty imperiously—in the manner, say, of an S.S. officer caricature—and if Samson had gone at once to the temple and, without preamble, pulled it down, we would have been free to rejoice at his triumph without the embarrassment of any humanitarian reservations. But the messenger is not imperious or even hostile. On the contrary, he is solicitous. He urges Samson to obey the lords' command, lest he suffer even worse indignities; and when he warns, "Regard thyself, this will offend them highly" (1333), he tacitly dissociates himself from "them." He is "sorry" to see Samson's stubbornness (1346), but by using the word "stoutness" to describe it he indicates his respect for the man. And in the end, he is plainly relieved to hear of Samson's change of mind ("I praise thy resolution" [1410]), expressing the same hope which sustains Manoa and the Chorus: "By this compliance thou wilt win the Lords / To favor, and perhaps to set thee free" (1411–1412). When Samson meets this show of concern with a curt and prophetic "Perhaps thou shalt have cause to sorrow indeed" (1347), the irony, local and final, is at the expense of someone we know and like. This is not the Nazarite's finest moment.

Samson does in fact proceed immediately to the temple, but we do not see him for nearly two hundred lines, and then only in retrospect through the eyes of the Hebrew messenger. Meanwhile, we are left behind to be witnesses to the conception and nurture of Manoa's "windy joy" (1574), as he reports to the Chorus the results of his canvassing:

> *Manoa:* But that which mov'd my coming now, was chiefly
>   To give ye part with me what hope I have
>   With good success to work his liberty.
> *Chorus:* That hope would much rejoice us to partake
>   With thee; say reverend Sire, we thirst to hear.
> *Manoa:* I have attempted one by one the Lords
>   Either at home, or through the high street passing,

With supplication prone and Father's tears
To accept of ransom for my Son thir pris'ner.
Some much averse I found and wondrous harsh,
Contemptuous, proud, set on revenge and spite;
That part most reverenc'd *Dagon* and his Priests:
Others more moderate seeming, but thir aim
Private reward, for which both God and State
They easily would set to sale: a third
More generous far and civil, who confess'd
They had enough reveng'd, having reduc't
Thir foe to misery beneath thir fears,
The rest was magnanimity to remit,
If some convenient ransom were propos'd.
What noise or shout was that? it tore the Sky. (1452–1472)

The scene before our eyes unfolds in counterpoint to the scene we are imagining ("What noise or shout was that?"), and in the light of this double awareness, the figure of the bustling Manoa is invested with a terrible and poignant irony. (Those who have no difficulty in accepting the choral pronouncement—that all is best—should read this passage more closely.) But if Manoa's statistics trace out the form of an illusory hope, they are also, one presumes, accurate, and therefore unsettling; for they reveal the Philistine lords to be no worse, and indeed somewhat better, than any other cross-section of humanity; only a few of them are "set on revenge"; a few others are willing to be bought; the rest—that is, the majority—are "magnanimity to remit." In short, on the evidence—that is, on the visible and merely human evidence—they do not deserve the destruction that is about to be rained down on them ("What noise or shout was that?").

The last Philistine we hear anything of is the anonymous guide who "unsuspicious led him" to the pillars (1635). With the single characterizing word "unsuspicious," this nameless boy (for so he is in Judges) is made the receptacle for whatever compassion we feel for all those "good" Philistines who will perish in a few minutes. One need not be a worshiper of Dagon to demur when the Chorus exults, "O dearly bought revenge, yet glorious! / . . . with thy slaughter'd foes in number more / Than all thy life had slain before" (1660, 1667–1668; the Chorus appropriates the characteristics of the biblical Samson); and one must be something of a fanatic to agree with Manoa, who finds no cause for lamentation, only joy in the thought that "*Samson* hath quit himself / Like *Samson,* and heroicly hath finish'd / . . . Heroic, on his Enemies / Fully reveng'd . . . / With God not parted from him" (1709–1712, 1719).[17] Surely Samson does God's will (he could do no other), but whether or not the received interpretation of his action is the correct one is open to question—perhaps the Philistines are being rewarded rather than punished, as Faithful is rewarded by an apparently shameful death in *The Pilgrim's Progress;* in that case Samson would still be God's instrument, but not in the manner he or his friends suppose—and it is a question rendered even more perplexing by our inability to accept the slaughter of the Philistines with equanimity.

As the play draws to a close, we become aware of still another reversal of roles. It is the Chorus and Manoa who introduce and foster the notion of a deity whose ways cannot be comprehended; yet in the end they are busily comprehending them and him within the framework of their national vision (Ah, so that's what the Old Fellow was up to); in contrast, we the readers, who enter the play understanding everything because we foreknow everything, leave it understanding very little, least of all why two thousand people—many of them, to use the Chorus' own words, "not disordinate" or "dissolute" or "unjust" (701–703)—should die. By granting the Philistines the status of human beings, and insisting that we so acknowledge them, Milton again evidences his disinclination to allow us a comfortable perspective on Samson's action.

Does he allow us any perspective at all? Are we able to say anything about what Samson has done? Are there categories and formulas available within which we can evaluate and perhaps even explain? Without fear of contradiction, I think, we can say that God has willed or permitted (the distinction is unimportant) what the Chorus terms Samson's "glorious revenge"; but we do not know why (for what reason) this has been willed or permitted. That is, we do not know what the event means *sub specie aeternitatis;* and we cannot be sure (and there is some reason to doubt) that the meaning conferred on it by the Hebrew partisans—"hee . . . / . . . urg'd them on with mad desire / To call in haste for thir destroyer"—is God's meaning. Nor can we be certain of the connection (if there is one) between the drama we have been watching, the drama of Samson's "laboring mind," and the drama unfolding at the cosmic level. What we have in *Samson Agonistes* are two plots and two climaxes, an "outer" or "public" plot, with its dénouement in the temple scene, and an "inner" plot, which has run its course by line 1377, when Samson learns how to move about in a world where action is required but where explicit guidelines for action are unavailable. It is tempting, literally, to assume an intimate connection between these two plots, especially at those points where they coincide temporally; but to do so would be to mistake contiguity in time for causality—this has been the temptation all along for both the characters and the reader—and to fall into Samson's old error of appointing heavenly disposition by making his regeneration a *condition* of his fulfilling the prophecy. The fact that a regenerate Samson pulls down the temple is important—for Samson; but a despairing Samson likewise would have pulled down the temple, if God had willed it. There are many paths to the temple, and in terms of God's prophecy, although not in terms of Samson's salvation, one is as good as another. God is not limited by the moral status of the instruments he chooses to use. *As far as we know,* the intersection of God's plan—foretold by the angel—with Samson's victory over himself is accidental. This is not to say that God has nothing to do with the recovery of Samson's faith (heavenly dispositions should not be appointed in *any* direction, and that question is shrouded in considerable doubt), but merely to point out the danger of reading the universe fatalistically. Unless the crises of life are to some extent discontinuous (to what extent is a question Milton wisely does not answer)—unless in each of them "the important factor is not the consequences of previous actions, but the confrontation, across a vast apocalyptic gulf, with the source of deliverance"[18]—the idea of moral choice is a sham. The play, finally, asserts not that choice is illusory (although the reader himself has the choice of reaching that erroneous conclusion by failing to distinguish between the two plots), but that it is difficult.

In the end, the only value we can put on Samson's action is the value he gives it in context. Within the situation, it is an expression, however provisional, of his reading of the divine will; and insofar as it represents his desire to conform to that will, it is a virtuous action. *No other standard for evaluating it exists*—this is what the reader learns when his attempts to apply other standards are frustrated—and no other explanation of it can be maintained without distorting the experience of the play.

Only when we see this will we be capable of refuting Dalila's most unsettling argument:

> Fame if not double-fac't is double-mouth'd,
> And with contrary blast proclaims most deeds;
> On both his wings, one black, the other white,
> Bears greatest names in his wild aery flight.
> My name perhaps among the Circumcis'd
> In *Dan,* in *Judah,* and the bordering Tribes,
> To all posterity may stand defam'd,
> With malediction mention'd, and the blot

Of falsehood most unconjugal traduc't.
But in my country where I most desire,
In *Ekron, Gaza, Asdod,* and in *Gath*
I shall be nam'd among the famousest
Of Women, sung at solemn festivals,
Living and dead recorded, who to save
Her country from a fierce destroyer, chose
Above the faith of wedlock bands, my tomb
With odors visited and annual flowers.
Not less renown'd than Mount *Ephraim,*
Jael, who with inhospitable guile
Smote *Sisera* sleeping through the Temples nail'd. (971–990)

In other words: "What I did looks exactly like what was done by one of your revered heroines. Where is the difference between us?" And of course there is none, if we attend only to the appearances surrounding the two actions, and in the category "appearances" I include all the *external* justifications Dalila has recourse to—romantic love, love of country, priestly urgings, fame. By taking a series of stances (some of them contradictory) in relation to her act, Dalila betrays the quality of her moral life. She is prompted not by something within her, by her "conscience and internal peace" (1334), but by some abstract formula for behavior (like the Law) which is imposed from without and relieves her of the burden of making moral decisions. In a word, she is insincere. What Dalila does not see is that two persons may engage in superficially similar activities, yet still be distinguished on the basis of their respective intentions; in fact, no other basis for distinguishing between them is reliable. Fame is, as she says, double-faced, and therefore no true determiner of the value of a deed; results or effects are also double-faced, "with contrary blast proclaim[ing] most deeds" (972) according to the bias of the interpreter. Ultimate effects, which would provide a true standard of judgment, are known only to God; we can neither act by calculating them, nor evaluate actions as if we were cognizant of them. From the human vantage point, only intention is capable of being unambiguous (although we can never be sure that it is), and it defines the extent both of the individual's competence and of his responsibility, and therefore of what can be judged. As Milton puts it in *The Tenure of Kings and Magistrates*, "The vulgar judge . . . according to the event, and the lerned according to the purpose of them that do it."[19] Jael's superiority to Dalila is to be located in the extent to which her deed is a manifestation of her wish (intention) to serve God, rather than in the act itself, or in anything that can be said about it. And this is so partly because what can be said about it will be limited by the limitation of the observer, who sees only outsides. In another situation, Jael's determination to serve that same God might involve her in behavior which seems, on its face, incompatible with what she does in Judges; but the consistency which matters is internal. Similarly, Samson's act is praiseworthy because he intends it to be answerable to the divine will; whether it is or not, especially in the terms in which he conceives it, he cannot know, nor can we; and in relation to the problem of judging him as a moral being, whether it is or not does not matter. Milton brings us to this realization by making it impossible to justify Samson in conventional or external terms—that is, in the terms invoked (and therefore discredited) by Dalila; we are left only with the purity of his intentions, or perhaps only with the conviction that he wants his intentions to be pure.

The distinction between external and internal justifications is crucial to an understanding of what is happening in the last four hundred lines of the play. It is significant that Samson turns, in these lines, to irony as a mode of expression. His is a special kind of irony—an irony of humility which operates at his own expense, since it allows those around him to attribute to him motives he would consider base:

> knowing thir advantages too many,
> Because they shall not trail me through thir streets
> Like a wild Beast, I am content to go.
> Masters' commands come with a power resistless
> To such as owe them absolute subjection;
> And for a life who will not change his purpose? (1401–1406)

One reason for this speech is Samson's concern for his country-men; they see the situation in the context of their own special fears—"matters are now strained / Up to the height" (1348–1349) —and he generously decides to comfort them within that con-text. Another more essential reason, however, is his *unconcern* with the figure he cuts in the world of appearances; and this is re-flected, too, in the distance between his public personality—as-sertive and self-confident—and the radical uncertainty which possesses his inner being. The two plots I discern in the play cor-respond to the two levels on which the events taking place can be evaluated. Samson is indifferent to the judgment of those who find the meaning of his act in its visible effects, in the destruction of a "Hostile City" (1561); such observers do not penetrate be-neath the surface of the outer or public plot. The audience he seeks is of a different order altogether. "Fit though few," it in-cludes (in addition to God) those who interpret his performance in the light of an inner plot, the outlines of which are only imper-fectly shadowed forth in the evidence of things seen. In that plot, the dramatic and spectacular climax of the temple scene is an an-ticlimax, providing an easy and comfortable way out of the play for anyone who chooses to avail himself of it. Every reader has that choice.

All Is Best

Still another question remains. If it is impossible in reading *Samson Agonistes* to draw lines of cause and effect or to say anything definite about what happens, why do so many readers, including this one, find the play bearable and even invigorating? The formulation of an answer should begin with the admission that I have overstated my case. This is not a retraction, but a recognition of how much has been left unsaid. Along with all the uncertainties, the difficulty of distinguishing between inspiration and inclination, the softening of so many supposedly sharp focuses, there coexists a strongly felt sense of cosmic order and regularity. At every point, our inability to understand something is accompanied by a conviction that if we only knew enough—that is, if we only were gods—it could be understood. And while this may appear to be a contradiction, it is in fact Milton's triumph. For his purpose is not to deny the reality of a just and benevolent God, but to suggest that we cannot infer his benevolence or validate his justice from the known facts. He does this by presenting the experience of disorientation and confusion within a public and authoritative framework which is assumed to have significance; we begin by believing in the framework, and in the course of the play our belief is strengthened by our ability to predict events, even if we cannot understand them when they occur. In other words, our foreknowledge, which generates expectations so that the poem can disappoint them, is at the same time the proof of the stability called into question by those disappointments.

In the end, then, the statement "All is best" (1745) does have a meaning for us that is not wholly ironic, although this is not the uncomplicated and completely satisfactory meaning it has for the Chorus. All is certainly best from the vantage point God enjoys; but from the merely human vantage point, problems abound and the pain of experiencing them is very real. Somehow the play immerses us in that pain without shaking our faith in something which is ultimately—but for the moment unhelpfully—more real; we are made to feel simultaneously that God is always with us and that in moments of crisis we are, for all intents and purposes, alone. And so we learn, finally, that the choice is not between informed action and precipitate action, but between action taken on the basis of inadequate information—faith professing action—and paralysis. And if we are able to follow Samson, we learn to live with what we have learned.

CHAPTER THIRTEEN

The Temptation of Intelligibility

Justifiable to Men

The Chorus' understanding of its own pronouncement—"All is best"—is much simpler than my reading of it at the conclusion of the previous chapter. In giving voice to this benediction, the Chorus means to say only that the best of all possible things, the thing everyone in the play most desires, has finally happened: Samson is dead. Of course, I'm not being quite fair here. What the Chorus most wants is that things once more be as they were, and its moment of highest joy in the play involves the speculation that a revived Hebrew hero may "now be dealing dole among his foes / And over heaps of slaughter'd walk his way."[1] "That were a joy presumptuous to be thought" (1531), responds Manoa, indicating that he too wishes for nothing more than the return of the days when his son "walk'd about . . . / On hostile ground" "like a petty God" (530–531, 529). This is also what Harapha wants, for different reasons, when he says of Samson's change of fortune, I "wish it had not been, / Though for no friendly intent" (1077–1078); and it is what Dalila wants for more reasons than Samson can shake a stick at when she laments an event more "perverse . . . than I foresaw" (737) and attempts to mitigate if she cannot cancel the effects of her "rash but more unfortunate misdeed" (747). Everyone, in short, wants to turn back the clock—and this of course includes Samson, who is obsessed with the disparity between his present and past states: "Why was my breeding order'd and prescrib'd . . . / . . . if I must die / Betray'd, Captiv'd?" (30, 32–33); "Promise was that I / Should *Israel* from *Philistian* yoke deliver; / Ask for this great Deliverer now, and find him / Eyeless in *Gaza*" (38–41); "The base degree to which I now am fall'n" (414); "I was his nursling once and choice delight" (633).

The centrality of this concern with the relationship between the past and the present is established early in the play when Samson describes his "restless thoughts," which he says "present / Times past, what once I was, and what am now" (19, 21–22). Given that this line is composed almost entirely of temporal signatures, it is difficult not to read "present" (21) as a pun which telegraphs in advance the questions that follow: How do we present the present? How can we make sense of it? How can it be seen as congruent with the past? How has this happened? These and other questions soon to be heard are a response to what is perceived by everyone to be a gap, a break in the narrative continuity which would, if it were available, make intelligible the story of Samson's life. As it is now, however, the apparent contours (or noncontours) of that life constitute a problem, even a scandal, and if the scandal is to be removed, the problem must be solved, the break must be repaired, the gap must be closed. There must be something—shall we call it a middle?[2]—to occupy (and thereby obliterate or cover up) the space between what was and what is now.

The stakes in this effort—the effort of finding or devising a middle—are very high. To those who behold him or (and this is the more common case) avert their eyes from him, Samson's present condition constitutes an affront to their sense of the proper (or at least desirable) relationship between human actions and the will of God. When the members of the Chorus ask, "what is man! / That thou towards him with hand so various, / Or might I say contrarious, / Temper'st thy providence" (667–670), Samson is their chief exhibit; it is his history that "Unseemly falls in human eye" (690)—"Unseemly" because it is marked by disproportionate punishment ("causeless suffering") and a disregard at the time of present judgment of what has occurred in the past: "thou oft, / Amidst thir height of noon, / Changest thy count'nance and thy hand, with no regard / Of highest favors past / From thee on them, or them to thee of service" (682–686). God, it would seem, has a very short memory, and indeed, in the case of Samson, has forgotten or chosen to disown his previous dealings "with this once thy glorious Champion" (705). It is almost as if God were dealing with two different people, as if the Samson who was his "choice delight" (notice the pun in "choice") had nothing at all to do with the pitiable figure of the blind prisoner. He has, says Samson, "cast me off as never known" (641).

It is this twin discrepancy or discontinuity—between Samson's actions and his (apparent) fate, and between the "two" Samsons—that provokes the mental labors not only of Samson but of everyone in the play; and as we shall see, those labors are characterized by an extraordinary persistence and resourcefulness, as every tradition in Western literature and philosophy is ransacked for ways of rendering intelligible something that could not otherwise be borne. Samson, Manoa, and the Chorus will go to any length in their joint effort to piece together a story that can be read as a confirmation of the intelligibility (and therefore the predictability) of events in the world. What they cannot do is allow that story to remain fragmentary—that is, no story at all; what they cannot do (and here it is to Samson's advantage that he is blind) is look the once-mighty hero in the face.

This unwillingness to behold is illustrated repeatedly by the members of the Chorus, whose very first action is to deny what they have involuntarily seen: that "This, this is he" (115). Within fewer than ten lines of pronouncing this confident identification, they withdraw it by asking, "Or do my eyes misrepresent? Can this be hee?" (124). In the interim they have decided (this act is volitional) that what their eyes present to them is unacceptable—a change so total ("See how he lies at random, carelessly diffus'd" [118]) that the Chorus can deal with this only by declaring it "beyond report, thought, or belief" (117). This line is itself a report of the Chorus' intentions, to fashion for itself thoughts and beliefs more comfortable; and it begins the process by answering its own question—"Can this be hee"?—with a reminiscence which simply replaces the "hee" whose sight is so distressing with another, the "hee" of a happier past. What happens here is very much like what happens in *Paradise Lost* when Satan exclaims upon first spying Beelzebub, "If thou beest hee."[3] In both instances the question is the involuntary acknowledgment of a change which is then willfully displaced by a powerful verbal performance.[4] At first, "Can this be hee" is heard as a rhetorical question that calls attention to the change and therefore to the reality of Samson's present appearance: "Can this person with languished head unpropped and in slavish habit be the Samson I remember?" But in the twenty-five lines that follow, the remembered Samson is so powerfully evoked that the changed Samson literally fades from sight; by line 150, the past and the present have been integrated—made into a single story—by the simple expedient of making the present disappear. "Can this be hee" can now receive an affirmative answer ("Yes, this is the same Samson") because the impediments to recognition, the unhappy facts of lines 117–123, have been removed.

This is, however, only a stopgap measure. The members of the Chorus, literalists at heart, cannot indefinitely avert their gaze from the disturbing features of the present landscape, and at lines 151–152 they look directly again at Samson and ask, "Which shall I first bewail / Thy Bondage or lost Sight"?—questions that allow them immediately to intellectualize the hero's plight by finding that the alternative subjects for bewailing are one and the same ("Prison within Prison" [153]). But this is only a minor accomplishment compared to what they do next: turn Samson into an example of the wheel-of-Fortune principle, as elaborated in Chaucer's "Monk's Tale" and elsewhere:

> O mirror of our fickle state,
> Since man on earth unparallel'd!
> The rarer thy example stands,
> By how much from the top of wondrous glory,
> Strongest of mortal men,
> To lowest pitch of abject fortune thou art fall'n. (164–169)

What is wonderful about this from the perspective of the choral anxiety is that it allows the Chorus to look at Samson and to *not* look at him at the same time. The hinge of this "double motion" (the phrase is Herbert's) is the word "unparallel'd," a word whose claim is denied by the very rhetorical structure in which it functions: the structure of example. What *exempla* do (among other things) is define objects, persons, and events relationally so that they become intelligible as instances of larger and regular (and perhaps eternal) patterns. The one thing something identified (a word literally intended) as an example cannot be is "unparallel'd," since it is by an act of parallelism that it has been rendered knowable and familiar. The very moment at which the

Chorus declares Samson to be "unparallel'd" is the moment at which it succeeds in domesticating his "difference"—that which makes him a problem, a scandal, a broken story—into a parallelism. His example may be "rare," but it is an example nevertheless, and as an example it has been brought into the comfortable order of the comprehensible, even if the content of that comfort is the whimsical and unpredictable (but now predictable because generalized) turn of Fortune's wheel.

As it turns out, the Chorus is a virtuoso in this mode. When Samson resists the suggestion that he is responsible for Israel's servitude and reminds the Chorus of the tribal failure (in which it is certainly implicated) to act, his words serve only to remind it of "How *Succoth* and the Fort of *Penuel* / Thir great Deliverer contemn'd, / The matchless *Gideon*" (278–280). That is to say, the Chorus takes what could be easily heard as an accusation and as a challenge to received views and contrive to blunt its particular impact—its capacity to trouble and unsettle—by absorbing it into a tale already more than twice told. One can almost see the shrugging of the tribal shoulder: "Yes, that's the way it always is between champions and their people." The effect is to make the present into something that has already happened, an event at once predicted and rendered intellectually manageable by a formula ready and eager to account for it. This distancing of the present from itself is repeated and furthered when Gideon and Jephtha are instanced as alternative precedents for Samson's situation, and the process is complete when the failed hero ratifies his own rhetorical domestication by saying, "Of such examples add mee to the roll" (290). Adding him to the roll (and to the *role*) is of course what the Chorus has been doing all along; Samson does not so much reach a conclusion of his own as accept his place in a conclusion it has already drawn. (More about this later.)

This is impressive enough, but the supreme choral triumph

follows. After Samson declares himself willing to be added to the role of unappreciated deliverers, the Chorus seizes the occasion to discourse (somewhat irrelevantly) on God's ways, which, it says, are both just and "justifiable to Men" (294) even when they are contradictory; since God makes the laws, he has the right to disregard them when he chooses, "For with his own Laws he can best dispense" (314). On the face of it, one would not think that the Chorus would find this form of justification attractive, since while it preserves God's prerogative (by making him a voluntarist) it renders his ways incomprehensible, and comprehensibility is what the Chorus above all else desires. After all, if the need is for an account of Samson's career that makes it intelligible, it is hard to see how the need will be met by the assertion of a God who is at once unaccountable and unpredictable. But in a stunning move, the thesis that God's actions are not bound by the laws of reason is turned into a *reason* for, and an explanation of, one of his actions:

> He would not else who never wanted means,
> Nor in respect of th'enemy just cause
> To set his people free,
> Have prompted this Heroic *Nazarite*
> Against his vow of strictest purity,
> To seek in marriage that fallacious Bride. (315–320)

To say that God can dispense with his own laws would seem to remove his ways from inspection and make him "unreadable" by rational canons. But the Chorus simply "reads" him as having in this case dispensed with one of his laws; it recuperates rationality by deducing from the absence of any apparent reason the necessary reasonableness of what has occurred; it takes a doctrine of cosmic uncertainty and make of it certain knowledge.

As the play ends, the Chorus is still doing this, declaring God's

438

ways to be "unsearchable" (1746) and proceeding in the very same breath to search them:

> All is best, though we oft doubt,
> What th'unsearchable dispose
> Of highest wisdom brings about,
> And ever best found in the close.
> Oft he seems to hide his face,
> But unexpectedly returns
> And to his faithful Champion hath in place
> Bore witness gloriously. (1745–1752)

In these lines God's unsearchability is at once asserted and found to be only a temporary condition, a by-product of his narrative skill. Like any good storyteller, God doesn't give his point away at the beginning but withholds it, calculating the moment at which its revelation will produce the maximum impact. At this moment—the moment of the "close," the end, the wrap-up—everything becomes clear, unmistakable, immediately readable. Both God's intentions and Samson's status in relation to those intentions are fully known. The question of what Samson is and was (22) is definitively answered. He is what he always was, "faithful," and in his faith he has always been under the benign regard and protection of a God who only pretends "to hide his face." In the close, God's face is wonderfully open and public, and public too is the significance of his champion's life, a life that is no longer disjunctive but continuous, a life that in its continuity justifies not only the hero's actions (including everything from his marriages to his "self-slaughter"), but the coherence and intelligibility of the world in which those actions are performed.

Manoa is even more explicit about the satisfaction that attends the happy conclusion to a story that had seemed to be turning out badly:

> *Samson* hath quit himself
> Like *Samson,* and heroicly hath finish'd
> A life Heroic, on his Enemies . . .
> And which is best and happiest yet, all this
> With God not parted from him, as was fear'd,
> But favoring and assisting to the end. (1709–1711, 1718–1720)

That is to say, Samson has now shown himself to be the very same person we took him to be before his aspect seemed so drastically to change. There is no gap between what he was then and what he is now; his most recent (and conveniently last) action is just like his earlier actions and bears the same significance—evidence of a "life Heroic" and, "which is best," of a heroic life perfectly in tune with the will of a benevolently presiding deity who now emerges (as he will in the choral version of this speech) from behind the arras to reveal the good intentions that were always his even when we temporarily lost sight of them.

Of course this all holds good only if what is seen here is really "the end," Manoa's equivalent of the Chorus' "in the close" (1748); for only if there is no new turn to the story can we be sure that its significance is once and for all fixed. That is why Manoa's reference to "what may quiet us in a death so noble" (1724) is so revealing: the truly noble thing about Samson's death is that it quiets the doubts and anxieties so many have expressed so often, for it allows a summing up to be written without fear that it will be contradicted by any new movements on the part of an unpredictable hero. Before his death, Samson's very body was an emblem of meanings his friends and family could not bear to contemplate; now when that same body is forever quiet, speaks no more, they can adorn it with whatever meanings they desire, and that is precisely what Manoa now proposes:

> Let us go find the body where it lies
> Soak't in his enemies' blood, and from the stream

With lavers pure and cleansing herbs wash off
The clotted gore. I with what speed the while
(*Gaza* is not in plight to say us nay)
Will send for all my kindred, all my friends
To fetch him hence and solemnly attend
With silent obsequy and funeral train
Home to his Father's house: there will I build him
A Monument, and plant it round with shade
Of Laurel ever green, and branching Palm,
With all his Trophies hung, and Acts enroll'd
In copious Legend, or sweet Lyric Song,
Thither shall all the valiant youth resort,
And from his memory inflame thir breasts
To matchless valor, and adventures high:
The Virgins also shall on feastful days
Visit his Tomb with flowers, only bewailing
His lot unfortunate in nuptial choice,
From whence captivity and loss of eyes. (1725–1744)

In other words, let us erase from the body what time and history
have inscribed on it, and when it is once again a smooth blank
surface, let us inscribe on it those significances that support the
story we wish to tell ourselves. This is of course not a new notion, but merely an extension of the play-long effort by Manoa
and the Chorus to domesticate Samson by placing him in a tradition that makes his life intelligible. This time, however, they need
not fear that Samson will upset the intelligibility they make by
doing or saying something embarrassing (Gaza is not the only
one "not in plight to say us nay"); he is now their perfectly quiescent text (exactly what he has not wanted to be all along), and
not only can they fix him in exactly the posture that will be most
interpretively convenient—stuffed and mounted at the center of
a Samson theme park—but they can further stabilize him by surrounding him with signs and commentary: trophies, lyric songs,

and a continual recital of a legend in which his every act declares a comforting moral.

Moreover, they can finally position Samson in a way that establishes him in the proper gender relations. Even in its dormant state, his masculine valor will breed itself in the breasts of generations of young men; that is to say, he will realize that age-old male fantasy of procreation without women. Women will have their place, but it will be one marked by distance. They won't touch him, but only bewail "His lot unfortunate in nuptial choice," where "only" means both that is all they will regret, and that is all they will be able to do. In this misogynistic vision—the last of many in the play—all misfortune flows from defilement by women. Although Samson is now restored to God's favor, presumably even the temporary interruption of his relationship with God (the ultimate form of male bonding) could have been avoided had he only managed to withhold himself—a self figured in the text as "the secret gift of God" (201)—from the pollution of the female. The threat to his stability has always been the movement and fluidity that would follow upon contact with women. Whether the reference is backward to Spenser's Red Cross Knight, "Pourd out in loosnesse on the grassy grownd,"[5] or forward to Stanley Kubrick's General Buck Turgidson, obsessed with the loss of his bodily fluids, the state of masculine firmness (physical and/or hermeneutical) is always imaged as it is imaged here, as a walled-in (monumental) fortress that refuses the dissolving touch of female power.

Give Us Eye Witness

We shall return to the relationship between Samson and the threat of femininity, but for the moment I want to keep the focus on the efforts of everyone in the play, including Samson, to wrest intelligibility from a history that seems continually to upset it.

The goal is a world in which everything is securely in its place, plainly marked, clear and distinct in its outlines, and bearing a familiar and comfortable meaning. The appearance of something (apparently) unassimilable is the occasion first of anxiety and then of a determined attempt to contain the offending phenomenon, a sequence that finds an almost comic manifestation in the choral effort to make out the shape of an approaching Dalila:

> But who is this, what thing of Sea or Land?
> Female of sex it seems,
> That so bedeckt, ornate, and gay,
> Comes this way sailing
> Like a stately Ship
> Of *Tarsus,* bound for th' isles
> Of *Javan* or *Gadire*
> With all her bravery on, and tackle trim,
> Sails fill'd and streamers waving,
> Courted by all the winds that hold them play,
> An Amber scent of odorous perfume
> Her harbinger, a damsel train behind;
> Some rich *Phillistian* Matron she may seem,
> And now at nearer view, no other certain
> Than *Dalila* thy wife. (710–724)

The choral procedure is a parody of the Ramist logic of which Milton was a proponent. (It is entirely typical of Milton to indicate a reevaluation of a former position or method by assigning it to a suspect character.) That logic works by descending from general categories to ever more specific ones, until finally the item in question is uniquely identified. One begins, as the Chorus does, by interrogating the as-yet-unknown with terms drawn from the largest distinctions. Is it a fish or a mammal? Is it male or female? The first question is kept (at least rhetorically) in doubt by the continuation of the ship simile; the second question is preliminarily settled ("Female . . . it *seems*") pending a closer inspection. As the passage unfolds, Ramism joins with empiricism to produce the full choral epistemology: all one has to do is look closely enough, *zero-in* in the manner of a zoom lens, and the ambiguous object will come into focus and cease to present a problem. This is precisely what happens in nicely calibrated stages, as first the Chorus narrows it down to someone who is rich (as opposed to poor), Philistine (as opposed to Hebrew), and married (as opposed to virginal), before announcing triumphantly, "And now at *nearer* view, no other *certain* / Than *Dalila* thy wife."

But no sooner has the Chorus arrived at this comfortable destination than Samson (who speaks on the beat of their short line) upsets their apparent progress by challenging the categories on which it depends. He says simply, "My Wife, my Traitress" (725), and thereby reinstitutes the entire set of problems the Chorus has just labored to remove. Wife and traitress conjoined constitute a scandal; one who is the latter cannot truly be the former, yet by all apparent and "certain" marks (the marks the Chorus relies on) Dalila is a wife. (Behind Samson's exclamation are all the arguments of the divorce tracts, arguments that will surface again at line 885ff.) The Chorus does not respond immediately to this new challenge and for a while is a spectator, as we are, of the exchange between Samson and his wife/traitress. It would seem, however, that the Chorus has been thinking, for as soon as Dalila leaves, it pronounces on her in terms that make a virtue (at least epistemologically) of the categorical confusion she instantiates: she is a wife *and* traitress because that's what women are like; either because God "lavish't" (1026) more on their outward than their inward constitution, or because their nature is to be entirely self-centered, they are the very essence of inconstancy, "Of constancy no root infixt" (1032). It is another bravura performance, as once again the Chorus manages to take difference and disorder and integrate them into a seamless and continuous story.

The Chorus' greatest challenge is of course the event for

which all readers and interpreters have been waiting, the pulling down of the temple. It occurs offstage (the first in a series of distancings) and is reported by the Hebrew messenger who is an eyewitness to the play's great event. He is, however, a curious eyewitness, for we meet him running away from a scene whose sight has been too much for him to bear: "Oh whither shall I run, or which way fly / The sight of this so horrid spectacle / Which erst my eyes beheld and yet *behold*" (1541–1543; emphasis added). What follows is an almost comic contest between Manoa, who wishes to be told *immediately* what has happened, and the messenger, who is reluctant to be the bearer of bad news. Don't worry about a preface, Manoa urges, just say, for "we long to know" (1554). I'm out of breath and my sense is "distract," the messenger replies. Just tell "the sum," says Manoa (1557), leave the rest for later. Okay, all Gaza's "Sons are fall'n," blurts the messenger (1558), drawing from Manoa what we might call, if it were not for the anachronism, a Yiddish response: "sad"—but to Israelites "not saddest"—news, the destruction of a "Hostile City" (1560–1561). Who did it? "Samson," the messenger answers. Perfect, says Manoa, thinking that this is the happy end of the story. Not quite, says the messenger; there's more, and it isn't good. "Suspense in news is torture, speak them out," demands Manoa (1569), and the messenger has no choice but to yield the naked fact: "in brief, *Samson* is dead" (1570). Manoa receives this fact not as a definitive comment but as the occasion for an elaboration which may yet save the story. "By whom fell he, / What glorious hand gave *Samson* his death's wound?" he asks, hoping of course that some Philistine Hector has slain his son in a battle that will redound forever to his glory (1580–1581). When the messenger replies, "By his own hands" (1584), Manoa is left with a problem more grievous than the problem of death; for it would seem that by committing "Self-violence" (1584) Samson has ended "at variance with himself" (1585)—that is, in exactly the

445

condition everyone bewails in the opening lines. All, however, is not necessarily lost; the meaning of any fact, Manoa knows, can be turned in a positive direction if it is surrounded by the properly reassuring circumstances. He girds himself for one more heroic effort of interpretation. Tell us, he says, *everything*. Leave *nothing* out. "Give us if thou canst, / Eye-witness of what first or last was done, / Relation more particular and distinct" (1593–1595). In other words, tell us the precise facts and nothing but the facts, order them in a sequence of inevitable cause and effect, and do not leave any blurred edges or imprecise characterizations.

The messenger responds in the spirit of the request, and as he does he underscores the assumption behind it: that the true meaning of things can be derived from the configurations they present to the eye. This is also the assumption that informs the Philistines, who are said to have called Samson forth so that he could "show" the people (give them eyewitness evidence of) his strength—provide them, as the officer says, with "proof." (One wonders if Milton here recalls Othello's demand for proof that is ocular.) Just before he begins his relation "more particular," the messenger enrolls himself in the list of those for whom the spectacular (in several senses) is the way to knowledge. "I sorrow'd at his captive state, but minded / Not to be absent at that spectacle" (1603–1604). (In this revelation of a "sorrow" that is easily overswayed by a voyeuristic curiosity, the messenger marks himself as a candidate for future membership in the Chorus.) What follows is an excruciatingly detailed account of his day and of the theater in which he finds himself soon after sunrise. We are given its dimensions, the relation of the pillars to the ceiling, the respective seating positions and arrangements of the nobility and the "throng" (1609), a description of the security measures designed to contain Samson, an account of the feats he was asked to perform, a report of the patience with which he did the Philistine bidding, and, finally, the calling of an intermission. "At length for intermission sake they led him / Between the pillars" (1629–1630).

And then a curious thing happens—in the narration, that is. As tension mounts for the knowledgeable reader (and who is not a knowledgeable reader of this story?), the focus, rather than sharpening, blurs, in part because the messenger reveals, almost casually, that some of his information at this crucial juncture is secondhand: "he his guide requested / (For so from such as nearer stood we heard) / As overtir'd to let him lean a while / With both his arms on those two massy Pillars" (1630–1633). What happens next is that we don't know what happens next. For just at the point where the "particular and distinct" relation of the messenger should be delivering a final revelation—the payoff of the "nearer view" he has been offering at Manoa's request—a large gap opens up in the narration in the form of a moment of silence: "with head a while inclin'd, / And eyes fast fixt he stood, as one who pray'd, / Or some great matter in his mind revolv'd" (1636–1638). Again the description of the physical posture is precise, down to the inclined angle of the head, but the precision runs out when one asks what exactly is going on.

It is not simply that Samson "goes interior"—all of Milton's heroes and heroines do this; but usually they do it in circumstances that allow us to be certain in a general way of the significance of the moment. (When the Lady in *Comus* declines to explain "the sage / And serious doctrine of Virginity," we can easily fill in for ourselves what she fails to provide.)[6] Here, however, the moment is presented as radically indeterminate. "As one who pray'd" says neither that he is nor that he is not praying; he may be speculating on the shape of Hebrew history or wondering whether Dalila will be a casualty of the "feat" he is about to perform. There is at this moment an inverse relationship between information and revelation. The more we are told, the less we know, because there is a hole at the center that has the effect of distributing its absence over the field of facts designed to fill it.

Of course, Samson emerges from his silence to speak; but for reasons we shall discuss later, what he then says is not of very much interpretive help; and it is on the point of interpretive help that *Samson Agonistes* departs from any of the models Milton might have known. In all of the sources and analogues, this moment is the hinge of the action, and it is virtually saturated with interpretive direction. First of all, Samson is always quite explicit about what he is going to do, why he is going to do it, and what relationship it has to what he has done previously. He is going to pull down the temple; he is going to do it at God's direction; and he is being empowered to do it because by repenting he has been restored to God's favor. The sequence is quite standard. We see it, for example, in Marcus Andreas Wunstius' *Samson: A Sacred Tragedy*. Samson confesses his sins—"with conscience as my witness, I confess / That I myself, myself alone am cause / Of this unspeakable calamity"—and specifies as his chief sin the turning away from God's service to self-indulgence and shameful display: "having known fair winds of happiness, / I laid aside my reverence for God; / Puffed up in spirit, blind, devoid of sense."[7] He then calls on God to renew his strength, not so that he can gain mere personal revenge, but so that he may once again be the instrument of God's will and vindicate God's glory in the face of his enemies:

> O God, high ruler of the angel hosts,
> While in my wretchedness I call upon Thee
> With my last words, grant favour to my prayer:
> Punish through me the sinful mockeries
> Heaped on Thy godhead by this impious crew!
> Breathe back my former strength in these limbs;

448

> So may the glad, exulting celebrations,
> Prepared to scorn Thy deity and honour
> An evil idol, end in sad lamenting. (Kirkconnell, 46)

Theodorus Rhodius, in his *Samson* (1600), is more concise but to the same end:

> I grant my penalties befit my deeds,
> And yet vain worshippers, hatefull to Thee,
> Should not rejoice to see Thy servant's ruin.
> But what strange strength now floods into my veins?
> I go—and shall gain glory by my death! (Kirkconnell, 63)

In some versions this moral is drawn before the event. Hieronymus Zieglerus places it in a prologue to his *Samson: A New Tragedy* (1547).

> The temple's dread collapse
> Is a most certain witness that to foes
> God is a peril and no trifling one.
> Therefore let saints now living greatly hope
> That victory may be given them from heaven. (5)

In other plays, the commentary follows the event and is clearly intended to allay interpretive anxieties. In Wunstius' *Samson: A Sacred Tragedy*, Samson's mother is tormented by the fear that her son may have forfeited his salvation by committing suicide. A priest reassures both her and the audience on this point and on many others.

> in your son's demise, he did not lack
> Divine approval, for men testify
> That ere his death, he lifted prayers to heaven
> And his petition suddenly was granted.
> For God Himself, in that last victory,
> Poured out on Samson's frame a power divine. (52)

449

In Rhodius' *Samson* the messenger reports the catastrophe, as he does in Milton's version, but he is within hearing distance of Samson's "soft" prayer and is eyewitness to its immediate effects: "I saw his strength return / And pour into his body like a tide" (64). An even more authoritative commentator appears in Joost van den Vondel's *Samson, or Holy Revenge* (1600). He is "the angel Fadaël, who foretold / To Samson's parents his miraculous birth" (140), and now returns to wrap up the end of the story:

> Now has the steadfast hero carried out
> God's vengeance, through his zeal for God's own cause.
> Let not his death distress you; for his spirit,
> Freed from the body's blindness and all care,
> Is now at last in peace in the cool shade. (141)

And lest the audience miss the typological point, Fadaël drives it home:

> clearly understand
> That the example of his death and life
> Fortells a Saviour, of God's spirit born,
> Who shall be persecuted, as was he,
> And dying, deal a fatal blow to death. (141)

Now, as you will have noticed, in these plays almost everything said by Samson, his mother, the angel, various priests, and his boy guide (who always escapes, and in one version is converted on the spot) is said also by Manoa and the Chorus in the extraordinary combination of blood lust and interpretive lust that takes up the last one hundred lines of *Samson Agonistes*. The difference is that they pronounce on the event at several removes, and in the absence of any witness or revelation that would lend them authority, their words produce more problems than they resolve. Indeed, in order to make their interpretation cohere, they must invent details that are uncorroborated by anyone else. The messenger says nothing, for example, about the Philistines' being "drunk with Wine, / And fat regorg'd of Bulls and Goats," nor does he characterize them as being in "a spirit of frenzy" (*Samson Agonistes*, 1670–1671, 1675); these details are projections by the Chorus of what must be the case if its reading of the relationship between the catastrophe and God's will is to be seamless. Of course in the sources and analogues the Chorus' reading *is* seamless, because it is supported by what everyone says and does, and especially by what Samson says just before he acts. In *Samson Agonistes*, however, Samson says nothing, but merely stands a while with "eyes fast fixt" (1637); and when he finally does speak, it is not to God but to the Philistines and in terms that speak to none of the issues that are so straightforwardly resolved by the Samsons in other plays, and indeed by the Samson of the Book of Judges. Even at this late moment, his actions display the same discontinuity that so distresses his countrymen in the early scenes; he does one thing (decides to go to the temple) and then he does something else (tears it down), but between the two actions there is once again a gap and once again Manoa and the Chorus try frantically to fill it in.

The fact that they fill it in with sentiments and conclusions which, in other versions of the story, are at once confirmed by and confirming of a clear and unambiguous moral points to a key Miltonic strategy: everything that serves in the sources and analogues to produce interpretive certainty is also to be found in *Samson Agonistes*, but it is found in the wrong place—that is, in a place where it multiplies rather than reduces interpretive crisis. Nowhere is this more obviously the case than in the matter of the return of Samson's strength. In every one of the analogues (and also in the Cecil B. DeMille version starring Victor Mature), that return is dramatic and instantaneous, and, more important, it functions as a visible demonstration of what everyone is at the moment asserting: that a properly repentant Samson has now regained God's favor and is acting directly as His Servant. It is as if a button had been pushed: Samson prays, his strength returns, and in one version horrified spectators see Samson's hair growing before their eyes as he begins to shake the pillars. In *Samson Agonistes,* however, the return of Samson's strength is handled in a manner at once casual and precise. It is casual because it is mentioned parenthetically throughout, as a matter of no particular importance, and it is precise because of the care Milton takes to de-authorize it as an interpretive aid. At times it is not even clear what is being said. When Samson refers in passing to these "redundant locks / Robustious to no purpose clust'ring down, / Vain monument of strength" (568–570), does he mean that his hair has grown but he remains weak? Or is he once again strong but to no real purpose? The ambiguity is retained, even played with, in Manoa's expression of a hope that God has not entirely abandoned Samson: "Why else this strength / Miraculous yet remaining in those locks?" (586–587). Although the question is not directly raised in the encounters with Dalila and Harapha, we are allowed to assume that the strength has in fact returned. Why else would Samson threaten to tear them both to pieces (this in his supposedly regenerate phase) and refer, as he does when taunting the Philistine giant, to "this strength, diffus'd / No less through all my sinews, joints and bones, / Than thine" (1141–1143)? And when Samson debates with the Chorus the wisdom of obeying the Philistine summons to the temple, it is clear that he is once again strong: "Shall I abuse this Consecrated gift / Of strength, again returning with my hair" (1354–1355)? This might seem to suggest that the strength has been returning on this very day; but when the Chorus replies, "Yet with this strength thou serv'st the *Philistines*" (1363), it is clear that Samson has been strong for as long as he has been laboring in the mills. This clarity, however, clarifies nothing. True, we know "for a fact" that Samson has regained his strength, but what we don't know is when;

and because we don't know when, it is impossible to link the return of strength to any of the issues it so dramatically resolves in the other versions.

One of those issues is the issue of inspiration, or, as Samson puts it, of "rousing motions" (1382). In van den Vondel's *Samson, or Holy Revenge*, the idea of pulling down the temple is obviously heaven-sent: "By night," the hero says, "the Spirit / Hath shown a means to free myself from bonds. / Be of good cheer" (90). The parallel moment in *Samson Agonistes* is when Samson says to the Chorus, "Be of good courage, I begin to feel / Some rousing motions in me which dispose / To something extraordinary my thoughts" (1381–1383). As I observed in the preceding chapter, however, there is no identification of the source of these motions: the relation between them and his decision to go to the temple and whatever it is that he does at the temple remains obscure, if only because that decision has already been made and therefore seems to be antecedent to the rousing motion one might want to cite as its cause. The obscurity is deepened if we turn for illumination to previous moments in the play, for what we find is that the status of Samson's inward promptings has already been a topic of discussion in a way that is decidedly unhelpful. The discussion focuses on Samson's marriages and on the question of which, if any of them, has been inspired by God. Unfortunately, for those who desire interpretive clarity, there are, as I pointed out earlier, three answers to this question. Samson assumes that while his first marriage was inspired, his second was a mistake, prompted not by God but by a carnal affection which he misinterpreted as godly urging. Manoa thinks that both marriages were mistakes and serve only to illustrate what everyone already should have known, the folly of becoming involved with non-Jewish girls. The Chorus, ever ready to protect God's honor, regards both marriages as God-inspired and declares that in the case of Samson, God—for his own good reasons, doubtless—has "dispensed" with the usual requirements of purity. The result is that not only is the status of either or both of the marriages blurred, but blurred too is the status of what Samson refers to as the "intimate impulse" (223) of inspiration. It follows, then, that when he later reports on the "rousing motions" he begins to feel, there is no way to be confident that those motions correspond to some communication that is occurring between him and God.

The effects of the patterns I have been noting all go in a single direction. Each of them—the substitution of a moment of silence for a forthright declaration, the separation of interpretive pronouncement from the evidence that would validate it, the refusal to make dramatic and unifying use of the return of Samson's strength, the making indeterminate of the status of rousing motions—looks forward to the climactic act of the play and conspires to render it mysterious. Of course it is that act which in every other version is the dramatic and interpretive centerpiece; and by surrounding it with circumstances that obscure rather than clarify its significance, Milton departs from the tradition he inherits in ways that can only be deliberate. Moreover it is a tradition he himself invokes by nourishing the expectations that attend it. Samson, in his very first speech, laments his inability to perform the "great act" (1389) promised by the angel who foretold his birth; and as the play unfolds, the phrase "great act" and others like it ("worthiest deed," "huge exploits," "act heroic," "great work," "valiant acts") appear no less than twenty-five times. As the "climax" draws near, Samson returns to his first lament and speculates that perhaps, after all, "This day will be remarkable in my life / By some great act" (1388–1389). As he leaves for the temple, the Chorus recalls the angel's prophecy and the "wond'rous actions" (1440) Samson has already performed. Manoa then enters to observe that God would not have permitted Samson's "strength again to grow," "were not his purpose / To use him further yet in some great service" (1496, 1499–1500).

The Chorus' first response to the Hebrew messenger's extended narration is to assume that what has just happened is the fulfillment of the prophecy—"Living or dying thou hast fulfill'd / The work for which thou wast foretold" (1661–1662)—a conclusion that introduces the interpretive frenzy that continues until the end of the play. Like everyone else who dramatizes the story, Milton takes advantage of the fact that the audience knows in advance what will happen and is waiting for it; but unlike everyone else, he delivers the anticipated (and longed-for) event shorn of the links and firm connections that would enable it to satisfy the desire its repeated invocation has produced: the desire for a single action so dazzling in its clarity and force that the moral structure of the universe comes clearly into view and the relationship between God's will and events unfolding in history is fully known in a way that can serve as a blueprint for future action.

Loving Bondage

It is a desire Samson himself feels, but in an inverted form. Where the Chorus desires a reintegration of the Samson that was and the Samson that *is* in a single coherent story, Samson finds his coherence—his escape from discontinuity—in the harshness of his present fate; for by accepting that fate as his just desert, he fashions a narrative as closed as any fashioned by his father or his friends. It is a narrative of bondage, and although bondage is what he continually complains of, it turns out to be a protection against a freedom—a world of fluid contingency—he fears as much as anyone.

Within five lines of the play's opening, he describes himself as being "bound" to a life of servile toil that is "Daily in the common Prison . . . enjoin'd me, / Where I a Prisoner chain'd, scarce freely draw / The air imprison'd also, close and damp" (5–8). Here prison is piled upon prison in a way that makes the verse as suffocating as the experience it describes. In the lines that follow, Samson repeatedly characterizes himself as a "bondslave" (38) and complains bitterly that he is "In power of others, never in my own" (78), a state which is to him a living death: "Myself my Sepulcher, a moving Grave, / Buried" (102–103). These words are echoed and amplified by the Chorus, which says of the blind Samson: "Prison within Prison . . . / Thou art become (O worst imprisonment!) / The Dungeon of thyself" (153, 155–156). Later the talk turns to the servile state of the entire Hebrew people ("Yet *Israel* still serves with all his Sons" [240]), and Samson responds with a scathing indictment of men who "love Bondage more than Liberty, / Bondage with ease than strenuous liberty" (270–271). It is exactly the choice he recalls himself making when he yielded to Dalila: "Who with a grain of manhood well resolv'd / Might easily have shook off all her snares: / But foul effeminacy held me yok't / Her Bondslave" (408–411). It is a bondage he refuses to reenter when Dalila offers (as Manoa has offered before) to take him home, out of "this loathsome prisonhouse" (922) and into a life of "domestic ease" (917). "No, no," he cries, I will not "live uxorious to thy will" (i.e., in power of others, never in my own) "In perfect thralldom . . . / This Gaol I count the house of Liberty / To thine whose doors my feet shall never enter" (928, 945–946, 949–950).

But even as Samson bewails his prisoner state, he hugs it to him and participates in the fashioning of new chains with which to restrict his freedom. We have already seen him complying with the choral effort to enroll him in some list of examples ("of such examples add mee to the roll"). As an example of some general truth (heroes are always deserted by their fearful countrymen), Samson is not responsible for what has happened to him; that's just the way things are—and what can anyone do? The answer of course is nothing. The inaction and passivity of which Samson complains are given a kind of sanction by this easy moralizing, itself a variation of the "domestic ease" he correctly sees as a prison when it is offered to him by Dalila. Here he accepts it eagerly, unaware, it would seem, that by doing so he imposes just the limits on his movements that he is all the while lamenting. Those limits are even more severely imposed by another of Samson's mental actions (the relocation of labor from the political/social world to the world of the mind is a leitmotif in the play)—his assumption that whatever the future may bring, and however God may order his will with respect to the Hebrews, *his* life is over, his deeds, both glorious and ruinous, have written their final chapter: "This only hope relieves me, that the strife / With mee hath end; all the contést is now / 'Twixt God and *Dagon*" (460–462). The irony here is that his "only hope" is the relinquishing of hope ("faith is the substance of things hoped for"), the premature closing off of his own possibilities. To the externally imposed prisons of blindness and physical bondage, Samson adds the prison of a way of thinking that leaves him no room to maneuver, or rather (and in accordance with his own vocabulary) *relieves* him of the burden of further maneuvers, of acts that are performed (as he supposedly wants to perform them) freely.

He does it again in unmistakable terms shortly before the arrival of Dalila:

> Nor am I in the list of them that hope;
> Hopeless are all my evils, all remediless;
> This one prayer yet remains, might I be heard,
> No long petition, speedy death,
> The close of all my miseries, and the balm. (647–651)

The only list he will not enroll himself in is the list that imagines future possibilities, and when he rejects hope it is no surprise that he embraces death—that condition in which risk and possibility are finally escaped; nor is it a surprise when he imagines death as the close of a narrative, of a story whose moral can definitively be drawn, even if it is a bitter one. I began this chapter by saying that everyone in the play wants Samson to be dead, because alive he is a perpetual affront to the supposed intelligibility of the universe. Samson wants it too, and indeed he has been in training for it since his very first words.

The extent to which he wants it, and in it the perfection of the imprisonment he pretends to abhor, becomes clear when he answers the Philistine summons: "Thou knowst I am an *Ebrew*, therefore tell them, / Our Law forbids at thir Religious Rites, / My presence; for that cause I cannot come" (1319–1321). In saying this, Samson obviously upholds tribal law in a way one would expect the Chorus to approve (that it does not is an irony to which we will turn in a while); but less obviously and more crucially, he *uses* the law as a way of avoiding the burden of freedom. The language says it all: "I am an *Ebrew*, therefore . . . " The fact of his national identification determines in advance what he can and cannot do. He is written by Hebrew Law no less than the Philistines are by theirs, and if he is to be consistent he should himself be the object of the scorn he expresses when he remarks that they allow him a day of rest "unwillingly" (14) and only because "Thir Superstition" (15) demands it. The strong implication is that they cannot think for themselves, that they are in another's power, not their own, that they prefer the ease of programmatic devotion to a ritual formula to strenuous liberty—all accusations that apply equally to Samson at this moment. In the long list of prisons that hem Samson in—his blindness, the mill, the choral proverbs and *exempla,* his passion for Dalila, his father's smothering care—none is more straitening than the prison whose security he invokes and embraces when he declares, "for that cause I cannot come" (1321).

It is an answer the Officer refuses to accept, urging self-preservation as a reason for coming: "Regard thyself, this will offend them highly" (1333). Samson responds by shifting the terms of his refusal from "I cannot come" to "I will not come" (1332, 1342). The difference of course is that this refusal is made on behalf of himself, or, as he puts it, "my conscience and internal peace" (1334). This is a remarkable moment, not only in the play but in the long course of Milton's career, because what Samson says here in the name of an internal center of reference he refuses to abandon is what Milton's heroes always say at similar moments of pressure. It is what the Lady in *Comus* says when, threatened by the tempter with the prison of paralysis, she declares, "Fool . . . / Thou canst not touch the freedom of my mind" (662–663). It is what Abdiel is praised for when he says no in thunder to Satan: "Nor number, nor example with him wrought / To swerve from truth, or change his constant mind" (*PL*, V, 901–902). In the story Samson obsessively tells, constancy of mind is what he has been unable to maintain in the face of Dalila's entreaties. Repeatedly, he presents himself as a vessel unable to keep its contents from spilling, an enclosure of self violated by its own failure: "I myself . . . / Gave up my fort of silence to a Woman" (234, 236). It would seem entirely fitting then (at least according to one reading of the play) for Samson to signal his recovery of spirit and strength by once again claiming and demonstrating the inner constancy he had lost; but in an act of self-revision that is nothing less than breathtaking, Milton declines to make this moment the centerpiece of the action, and asks us to see that in citing his "internal peace" rather than the Law as a reason for refusing to move, Samson has merely exchanged one prison for another, one story already written for another no less closed to future possibilities.

What Milton does, simply, is allow this scene to continue in ways that finally undercut the theatrical satisfaction of Samson's standing up for his conscience and internal peace. In doing so, he completes a theory of personality that he had begun to construct in the *Areopagitica*. In the tracts and poems written before 1644, the designation "person" is reserved for those who are self-contained, possessed of and by an inner certainty that renders them forever the same, no matter what the changes in external circumstances ("He that has light within his own clear breast / May sit i'th' center, and enjoy bright day" [*Comus*, 381–382]). Such persons (exactly those celebrated by Ben Jonson in innumerable poems) are shown off by their opposites, changeable and shifting men, chameleon-like actors whose inner constitution varies from moment to moment and who, rather than being whole and unified, are "broken and disjoynted."[8] It follows that the obligation of persons so constituted is to hold themselves aloof and thereby avoid the pollution of alien contact. In *Areopagitica*, however, fixity of mind and judgment is stigmatized as the sign of spiritual sloth. Rather than being already complete, the true Christian self is imaged as "wayfaring"—that is, as always being on the way and never having arrived. To think that you have already arrived is to have mistaken a stage in the "making" of your knowledge for its perfection; it is to have failed precisely by assuming that you have succeeded: "he who thinks we are to pitch our tent here, and have attain'd the utmost prospect of reformation that the mortall glasse wherin we contemplate can shew us, till we come to *beatific* vision, that man, by this very opinion declares, that he is yet farre short of Truth."[9] The man who pitches his tent prematurely will believe that he has found (and become like) truth, but in fact he will have managed only to "settle falsehoods" (316). The alternative Milton urges in us is to embrace a life of "perpetual progression" (310), in which we successfully revise our received opinions and rest only in the certainty that there can be no rest. In the context of such a life, constancy of mind is what one wants to avoid, while change, discontinuity, and endless transformation are what one avidly courts. Insofar as there remains something like the "freedom" in whose name the Lady speaks, it is a freedom *from* whatever stage of illumination the mind has happened to achieve—freedom, that is, to *depart* from the mind's present configuration, as opposed to the false freedom (really bondage) of clinging to that present configuration and refusing to move beyond it.

Refusing to move beyond it is what Samson does when he declares "I will not come" and gives as his reason the integrity of "my mind" (1336). But whereas an earlier Milton would have applauded this resolution by allowing it to stand unchallenged except by appeals and arguments obviously specious, here he provides it with an immediate challenge in the response of the Chorus. The members of the Chorus intervene for less than exalted reasons: they fear that an obdurate Samson might occasion reprisals that would spill over onto them and they therefore urge him to go. Whatever their motives, however, their action has the effect of breaching the fortresses behind which Samson has immured himself. Samson's first fortress is the Law, and it is breached as soon as the Chorus disputes Samson's reading of it and demonstrates that, given certain background assumptions (about the nature of service, the relationship between outward and inner acts, the status of constraints), the Law can be read as authorizing the very act Samson sees it as forbidding. It doesn't matter finally which of the two readings is the more persuasive; what is important is that the Law, whenever it is invoked, is always and necessarily invoked in an interpretive form and that therefore the person who invokes it has *already* ventured beyond it. When Samson replies to the arguments of the Chorus by saying, "Commands are no constraints" (1372), he is referring to the commands of the Philistines; but the exchange itself shows (and Milton intends us to see) that the pronouncements refer equally to the constraints of the Law, which, because they are interpreted, bind the interpreter only in the sense that he is bound by his own constructions.

In other words, Samson is already free—a realization that is being forced on him by the choral intervention, and a realization that he pushes away even as it begins to dawn. "If I obey them, / I do it freely" (1372–1373), he declares, but then immediately, as if recoiling from the very word "freely," he proceeds to construct a new prison, this time calling it God: "I do it freely; venturing to displease / God for the fear of Man, and Man prefer, / Set God behind: which in his jealousy / Shall never, unrepented, find forgiveness" (1373–1376). What Samson does here is what he chided his father for doing earlier; he appoints "heavenly disposition" (373)—that is, he limits God's possible actions by the picture he *projects* of him. It is a form of idolatry in which, in place of God as he really (and inaccessibly) is, one puts the God of one's wishes and fears. The God of these lines is both; he is a God whose unforgiving nature Samson fears, but at the same time that very unforgiving nature is the object (and creation) of Samson's desire, since to have posited such a God is once again to have found a reason for not doing anything, for remaining in the place you are now in, for pitching your tents *here*. That is to say, at this moment God, or Samson's conjectured vision of a possible God, functions for him as an excuse, as a way of evading and in fact *denying* the freedom of mind he has so loudly proclaimed. I am saying not that Samson should project a different God, but that he should not project a God at all except as a being always in excess of one's conceivings. Paradoxically, Samson will be able to maintain his relationship with God only when he is able to see that relationship as one always on the move, as a relationship "anchored" by a conviction of its radical incompleteness. He must, in short, learn the full lesson of Christian strenuous liberty: that to be free of external constraints is to be in the condition that a younger Milton found horrible to contemplate, the condition of being forever immersed in "the perpetual stumble of conjecture . . . in this our dark voyage."[10]

Although we never see Samson arrive at that lesson, we see its effect in a single word, "Yet": "Yet that he may dispense with me or thee / Present in Temples at Idolatrous Rites / For some important cause, thou needst not doubt" (1377–1379). With "Yet" Samson simply abandons the assumption informing the exchange to this point—that he could rationally determine what God would have him do—and replaces it with the assumption that God can himself do anything he likes. The difference between this and earlier moments in which God's unfettered power is asserted can be seen in the word "dispense." When the Chorus declares at line 314 that "with his own Laws [God] can best dispense," it is at that very instant using the notion of dispensation to figure out exactly why God has done something (allow the Nazarite Samson to pollute himself with Philistian wives); but for Samson God's power to dispense means that one can *never* figure out exactly (without doubt) what God is doing or what he wants us to do, and that therefore whatever we do we must do it "freely," on our own, in the absence of any firm (unequivocal) evidence that it is what God wants. That Samson is not here merely reappointing heavenly disposition is made clear by the word "may." He isn't saying that God *has* dispensed or that he will or that he won't; he's saying only that one can never tell. The only thing you can be certain of—"needst not doubt"—is that you will never certainly know. It is at this point, when Samson has shaken himself free of the prisons to which he earlier clung—the prisons of the law, of the centered self, and of an unyieldingly jealous God—that the Chorus exclaims, "How thou wilt here come off surmounts my reach" (1380). The reach of the Chorus is bounded by its passion for intelligibility, for causal explanations that produce coherent and reassuring narratives in which the next step one takes follows clearly from an understanding of what God requires. In the absence of such a narrative, the Chorus simply doesn't know what to do.

What Samson does is say, "I with this Messenger will go

along" (1384). The significance of this final turn in the scene is precisely measured by his two previous declarations: "I cannot come," "I will not come." Different as they are, these resolutions, made in the name of the Law and the self, respectively, are alike in that they both proceed from stories fully told and fully determining. "I will go along," on the other hand, is spoken by someone who is not sure what story he is in and moves forward anyway, someone who is for the first time "venturing freely," hazarding action without any clear sense of what it means or of its exact relationship to God's ultimate design. The "will" here is the opposite of the "will" in "I will not come"; it stands not for the fixed position of a fully formed and independent self, but for a self "willing" to have its configurations transformed by a future it cannot read.

It is here that Milton provides his own explanation of something that had puzzled commentators for centuries: How can the swaggering and vengeful bully of the Book of Judges be accorded a place in the roll call of the heroes of faith as it appears in Hebrews 11?[11] Milton's answer is to shift the emphasis in the story from the so-called climactic act (which he renders radically mysterious) to the decision to move into the space in which that act becomes a possible one, a decision that is itself marked by a radical uncertainty. It is that uncertainty and the willingness to endure it that characterize the faith of the heroes in the Book of Hebrews, the most exemplary of whom is Abraham, regarded by Milton (as well as by Calvin and others) as the pure example of faith, "the best model of believing."[12] Abraham, the author of Hebrews tells us, "went out, not knowing where he went," or, in Milton's words, "Not knowing to what land, yet firm believes." Like Abraham, Samson goes out, or rather goes along, and he goes along to he knows not what and with a mind constant only in its willingness to encounter possibilities (of thought and action) it cannot anticipate. Going along is just that and no more—

a resolution to keep moving, to see what happens, take a chance, turn the next corner, walk the tightrope of experience and choice without a safety net. This is what it means to be free, to be in one's own power and not in the power of others; and while that freedom is glorious and liberating, it is also terrifying.[13]

Both the liberation and the terror are the content of Samson's last straightforward statement, his declaration to the Philistines that what he is about to do he will do "of my own accord" (1643). That is the only thing he says about it; he says not what it means, or how it relates to the will of God, or to the loss of his two eyes, or to the fate of his tribe—just that it is an action for which he has no final warrant except what he himself at the moment thinks best to do. It can be no accident that "of my own accord" is the exact opposite of what the Samsons of other dramatists say. What they all say is that what they do is done under the specific direction of God; and in contrast to their egregious humility, Samson's "of my own accord" might seem prideful and self-aggrandizing.[14] But in fact it is exactly the reverse, for it marks the moment when, unlike everyone else in the play and unlike himself only a short while ago, Samson refuses to claim knowledge of what God wants him to do; he declines to appoint heavenly disposition or to assume heavenly authorization for an action that he is about to perform on his own hook, hoping of course (faith is the substance of things hoped for) that it is the right action, but knowing only that it is the one that, for the moment, seems right to him.

Foul and Not So Foul Effeminacy

It is one of the play's many ironies that in the act of going along, of leaving the fortress of a (falsely) settled self for a world of process and transformation, Samson moves closer to the person from whom he has most wanted to distinguished himself. Although the encounter with Dalila touches on many matters, Samson's chief aim (as it is later in the scene with Harapha) is to distance himself from her, for he must be unlike Dalila in order to be like himself, a unified and wholly separate (that is, Nazarite-like) structure of conscience and internal peace. What disturbs him most about Dalila is her presentation of herself as a site occupied by the desires and inscriptions of *others*. She seems to be without inner resolve, the plaything of forces that vie for the right to inform her actions. Sometimes those forces are internal, reified figures of a faculty psychology like "conjugal affection," "fear," and "timorous doubt" by which she reports herself "led" (739–741); at other times they are external, "assaults" and "sieges" that "girt [her] round" (845–846). In a sequence of twenty-five quasi-allegorical lines, she reports the blandishments of princes, magistrates, priests by whom she is "Solicited, commanded, threat'n'd, urg'd, / Adjur'd" (852–853). In opposition to these on the internal battlefield of a pliable will, "Only my love of thee held long debate, / And combated in silence all these reasons / With hard contest" (863–865). Her decision is made for what Samson would think was the worst of reasons: she prefers the values and desires of others to her own: "at length that grounded maxim . . . / Of wisest men, that to the public good / Private respects must yield, with grave authority / Took full possession of me" (865, 867–869). Wholly in the power of others ("Took full possession of me") and not her own, she, as a separate being consecrate to herself and to an inner integrity, disappears under the covering weight of maxims, reasons, urgings, proverbs.

To all of this Samson reacts with accusations of "smooth hypocrisy" (872) and insincerity (874). This second charge is precise: insincerity is the absence of a relationship between what you say and do and what is inside you; it is a fracturing of character, which, if serious enough, raises the suspicion that finally there is *nothing* inside you, no stable commitment of a kind that "would have taught" Dalila "Far other reasonings, brought forth other deeds" (874–875). But even as Samson berates Dalila for failing to hold herself firm against external pressures, he inadvertently underlines the similarity between them, a similarity that emerges in the contrast he attempts to draw between her "pretended" (873) love and his true love, which he says "overpow'r'd" him and rendered him incapable of denying her anything (880–881). What he now accuses her of, allowing her will to be overwhelmed, is what he has himself done, and if we recall his earlier rehearsal (387–414) of his own surrender, the difference between them is less and less firm. Like her, he was "assaulted" day and night with pleas, "parleys," and "Tongue batteries" (403–404); like her he resisted for a time, and like her, "wearied out" (405), he finally yielded and became exactly what he now calls her, a "Traitor" to oneself (401). Or to put it more precisely, and as he puts it, at the moment of yielding he became a woman: "I yielded, and unlock'd her all my heart, / Who with a grain of manhood well resolv'd / Might easily have shook off all her snares: / But foul effeminacy held me yok't" (407–410). By "foul effeminacy" he means not the person of Dalila, but the feminine principle that has gained entrance into his heart and done its work of dissipating a "resolve" (or self-collection) that is precisely identified as "manhood." Throughout the play, this is Samson's most grievous affliction—the sense that the integrity of a closed and masculine interiority has been breached and profaned by the scattering and defacing touch of woman. The result of having thus "divulg'd the secret gift of God / To a deceitful Woman" (201–202) is, he is sure, to be "sung and proverb'd for a Fool" (203); and what is worse, as one so "proverb'd," he has been reduced to the condition of being a "scorn and gaze" (34).[15]

These self-accusations bear the marks of a rigorously worked-out logic in which "words," "weakness," and "woman" are lined up as equivalences. Weakness is the condition of displaying a womanish vulnerability to the power of words; it is the condition of having been written from the *outside*—"proverb'd"—of becoming a space of public inscription, a kind of billboard, successively and passively receiving the imprint of someone else's meaning. It is in this sense that Samson has become a "scorn and gaze." Having allowed himself to be emptied of God's secret writing ("Joy, I did lock thee up: but some bad man / Hath let thee out again"),[16] there is nothing in him that will resist the writings of others. Self-deprived of an inward integrity that would repel alien significances, he takes on the significances projected onto him by those who behold. He becomes quite literally a "gaze," an extension of whatever glance happens to fall on him, a continually mounted spectacle, a commodified object of appropriation, always in the power of others and never in his own.[17]

It is because he already sees himself as weak and womanish that he is so vulnerable to Dalila's contention that, after all, they are very much alike. True, she did "publish" (777)—put into general circulation—his secrets and thus deprive them of their potency, but what she did is what all women do ("a weakness / In me, but incident to all our sex" [773–774]), and, besides, it is what he had already done when he opened himself up to her: "To what I did thou show'd'st me first the way" (781). The reasoning is unmistakable: it is a "common female fault" (777) to spill one's insides; that is what you did; therefore you are, like me, a woman: "Let weakness then with weakness come to parle" (785). In response, Samson can only acknowledge that she is indeed his mirror image: "I to myself was false ere thou to me" (824); but in a furious act of self-laceration, he reviles the image and thinks that by reviling it he can restore himself to his previous "unpublished" and masculine state, "Impartial, self-severe, inexorable" (827). Unwilling to pardon himself (he will at least be firm in his condemnation of slackness), he offers her "Such pardon . . . as I give my folly," telling her to leave off her striving "to cover shame with shame" (825, 841). Later he invites her to follow him by stripping away all coverings, all "false pretexts" and "varnish'd colors" (901), so that she can be seen for what she really is, "Bare in thy guilt" (902).

But as it turns out, Dalila has no interest in doing without coverings. Indeed she welcomes them, embracing the very condition Samson continually bewails: the condition of being inscribed by the meanings of others. In her final speech, she anticipates a future in which she will live only as the matter of song and story. As far as she is concerned, it is just a question of whose colors she will bear, of which version of herself—constructed by others—will prevail, and in the end she puts her money on the Philistines. Perhaps in Hebrew legend she will be "With malediction mention'd" (978), but

> In Ekron, Gaza, Asdod, and in Gath
> I shall be nam'd among the famousest
> Of Women, sung at solemn festivals,
> Living and dead recorded, who to save
> Her country from a fierce destroyer, chose
> Above the faith of wedlock bands, my tomb
> With odors visited and annual flowers. (981–987)

So eager is she to be "proverb'd" that she assimilates herself to a narrative type (the woman who chooses patriotism before love) even before the story is written. She cannot conceive herself apart from some conventional category, and it really doesn't matter to her which category it is—the bearer of "common female faults" (777), the wife jealous of her husband's freedom (803–806), the savior of her country. The question of what she herself might be independently of these roles never occurs to her, and she looks forward with joy to the fate Samson cannot bear to contemplate: she will be wholly identified with "the public marks" (992) "Conferr'd upon" her (993). That is, she gives herself up to be whatever those who gaze upon her care to make of her; she puts herself into general circulation—becomes something published—and is, forever after, nothing more than an object of interpretive desire.

You will note that in the previous paragraph I have fallen in all too easily with Samson's perspective, reading the play as he reads it—as a devastating exposé of female changeability in relation to male firmness of mind. But that reading can hardly survive the (anti)climactic moment when Samson declares, "I with this Messenger will go along" (1384), for then he becomes indistinguishable from Dalila; he offers himself up to a future that will mark him in ways that he cannot know in advance; he moves forward into a story that, as far as he can tell, has yet to be written; he leaves the fortress (or is it the illusion?) of a centered, settled self and embarks upon a journey (going out not knowing whither he went) in the course of which the self will be endlessly revised by forces it cannot control. In short, he ceases to *be* a self—in the masculine sense of an entity already saturated with meaning—and becomes instead a text, a pliable feminized medium, something that acquires form only when it is read and which therefore can acquire as many forms as there are readers to interpret it or gazers to look upon it.

The passage from self to text has already occurred when, rather than turning his face away from observers as he has repeatedly done, Samson invites them to "behold": "I mean to show you of my strength, yet greater; / As with amaze shall strike all who behold" (1644–1645). The question is, what do "all who behold" (which includes Manoa, the Chorus, and us readers, as well as the Philistine nobility) see, and the answer is given in the ambiguities of Samson's vocabulary. What we all see is "show," a word that perfectly captures the high irony of the situation: as a verb, "show" means "to reveal"; but both in his language and in the act that follows, Samson reveals nothing and presents us only with a "show" of strength, a surface display, an exhibition, or, as the Hebrew messenger accurately terms it, a "spectacle" (1604). What remains hidden, what is not shown in this excess of show, is the relation of that spectacle to Samson's inner state (so important to the regenerationist reading of the play), or to God's will and design, twin obsessions of those in the play and its audience who would wrest intelligibility from the apparent wreckage of Samson's career. The act is characterized and then immediately performed ("This utter'd, straining all his nerves he bow'd" [1646]), but any hint of what it *means* (if it means anything) is precisely what Samson withholds from us when he withdraws into prayer or contemplation or whatever else he may or may not be doing in the moment that constitutes the play's final and most crucial gap.

Commentators have always recognized the nasty joke contained in these lines: the Philistines are about to be struck in ways that are more than ocular. But in fact the deeper irony returns us to the realm of the ocular and to everything that gazing and beholding have meant in the play. Everyone (including Samson) has been reluctant to look at him directly without the mediation of some signifying construct (proverbial wisdom, lists of maxims, exemplary tales, misogynistic mutterings, views of God's providence) in relation to which the events of his life can be seen to make sense. The one possibility no one has been willing to entertain (except for Samson in some moments of his despair) is that there is no sense to be seen (which is different from a flat declaration that there is ultimately, from the God's-eye point of view, no sense), and it is this possibility that Samson thrusts in our face when he says "behold" and shows us—nothing, a surface without depth, an emptiness, a lack just where a plenitude (of explanation, justification, and illumination) is most required. That is what finally strikes the audience and leaves its members, including us, "amazed"—that is, filled with panic, astonished, turned to

471

stone. One can hardly avoid the conclusion that with the words "behold," "strike," and "amaze," Milton is conflating the terrible visage Samson now presents with the face and look of Medusa—whose head, he reminds us in *Comus,* turned beholders into "congeal'd stone" (449), leaving them in a state of "blank awe" (452). In *Samson Agonistes,* the blank is the emptiness or lack at the heart of the story, the absence of an intelligibility that would allow us to master a narrative that disables us at what is supposed to be its climactic moment. We need no Lacan to tell us that to be deprived of mastery by the presentation of a lack—by the beholding of a Samson shorn of meaning—is to be castrated. The fear of castration is the fear that one's being is without ground, that identity is fluid, protean, unstable, in the power of others, never in one's own. It is a fear that finds its characteristic Western expression in the repeated presentation of woman—the defiling other—as changeable, fickle, without anything inside her (just as she is without anything on the outside of her). It is as just such a lack that Samson has characterized Dalila, and now, as he finally embraces strenuous liberty, he becomes himself that same feminine lack—a surface with no essence *in sight*—and thereby renders us incapable of performing the task we are assigned, the task of interpreting what he has done. As interpreters, we are never stronger than we are as the play opens; for then we know everything that will happen, and we know too what it will all mean; yet as foreknown events unfold, they are not clarified, but shrouded increasingly in mystery; until at the moment when we should be most in control—the moment when exactly what we foresaw comes to pass—we find ourselves bereft of interpretive resources, impotent before the very story whose meanings were once so firmly in our grasp.

The members of the Chorus, of course, feel no such incapacity. The moment in which Samson has surmounted their reach—slipped out of their proverbing nets, escaped their stories—has long since passed, and at the "close" they are busily incorporating it into a new narrative in which God bears "witness" to the fact and meaning of what has happened. But there has been no witness, God has not appeared, and what signs of his presence there are have been rendered ambiguous. In the regenerationist reading of the play (of which Manoa and the Chorus are the first proponents), God and Samson unite in the "great event" of whose meaning everyone is so confident. In the reading I have offered here and in the preceding chapter, God and Samson unite only in being inaccessible, objects alike of an interpretive activity that finds no corroboration in the visible world. When Samson leaves off assuming that he can decipher God's will and resolves instead to go along with whatever that will might turn out to be, he becomes as mysterious—as difficult to read—as the God whose disposition he refuses to appoint. There is simply nothing to be said about him, no "acquist" of wisdom with which we are "dismissed," despite the choral pronouncement to the contrary. The only wisdom to be carried away from the play is that there is no wisdom to be carried away, and that we are alone, like Samson, and like the children of Israel, of whom it is said in the last verse of Judges: "every man did that which was right in his own eyes."

PART IV

The Paradigm Reaffirmed
(Almost) without Apology

CHAPTER FOURTEEN

Gently Raised

Semblance Not Substance

It may have seemed that in stressing the indeterminacy and inde-
cipherability of *Samson Agonistes* I have moved far beyond the
"simple" picture of a Milton who rests confidently in his knowledge of the truth and in his ability easily to discern the one obligation that it would be death to slight. But I intend no retreat
from that picture, and if I complicate it I do so only to foreground a difficulty present in it from the beginning. Discerning
the one true obligation *is* easy; it is the obligation to do God's
will. The difficulty is to determine which of the many courses of
possible action is the appropriate location and fulfillment of that
obligation. Given the multiple paths available to us as fallen men
and women, how does one decide which of them to choose? Milton cannot give us an answer to that question—cannot give us a
formula or a set of criteria—because by interiorizing the landscape of choice, he has detached it from the realm of empirical

evidence and set us on a journey much like that of Abraham, who, in response to God's call, went out not knowing whither he went. The result is a life like Samson's, made up in equal parts of certainty ("My trust is in the living God" [1140]) and radical hazard ("I with this Messenger will go along" [1384]). At times in his prose and poetry Milton emphasizes the certainty; at other times he confronts us with the hazard; but in either mood, the basic imperative he urges is the same: refuse external guides and work from the inside out. The unpacking and exfoliation of this imperative has been the single aim of this book from the outset, and here, in the concluding section, I return to it yet again, beginning as I did in Chapter 1 with a single word.

More than sixty-five years ago, F. R. Leavis charged Milton with two crimes of which he has never been, and should not be, acquitted. The first charge is that his style does not sufficiently register the diversity and complexity of human life, especially in comparison with the styles of Donne and Shakespeare. The second charge is that he has an excess of character, by which Leavis means that he is "disastrously single-minded and simple minded, . . . reveal[ing] everywhere a dominating sense of righteousness and a complete incapacity to question or explore its significance and conditions."[1] (This is the same charge leveled more recently at Milton by some New Historicists and feminists.) The two charges fit together perfectly: it is because he is single-minded, and self-righteously so, that his style admits variety only in order to either banish or condemn it. The result is something akin to claustrophobia, and it is described by Leavis in terms that are justly famous: "In this Grand Style, the medium calls pervasively for a kind of attention, compels an attitude toward itself, that is incompatible with sharp, concrete realization; just as it would seem to be, in the mind of the poet, incompatible with an interest in sensuous particularity. He exhibits a feeling *for* words rather than a capacity for feeling *through* words" (21–22). That is, Milton's language does not direct us to a referent outside itself, but, rather, traps us within its own confines, demanding that we attend to the connections it is itself forging; the reality of the *medium* privileges itself over any reality that we might think prior to it. It is, in short, a jealous medium, saying: Thou shalt not accept any truths I do not offer you. The experience of reading such verse (or, more precisely, of being read *by* it) is, says Leavis, like combat, "a matter of resisting, of standing up against, the verse-movement . . . and in the end our resistance is worn down" (16). Leavis names this effect "tyrannical stylization" and says that it "forbids" (23), says no, again and again, in thunder. Milton, he concludes, "offers . . . for our worship mere brute assertive will" (28); that will, which finds expression in the style, has its origin first in the will of the poet ("I, John Milton, thus manipulate you") and second (that is, finally, ultimately) in the will of God ("I am the Lord thy God"). As J. B. Broadbent, another Cambridge Miltonist, put it, "Milton's learned vocabulary, with its demand for conscious construing and his distant perspectives, represents the authoritative unintelligibility of the parents' speech as heard by a child."[2]

It is not my intention to dispute this judgment; instead I would expand on it and turn it, perhaps, to Milton's advantage, and I will begin with a passage from *Paradise Lost* that illustrates much of what Leavis and Broadbent have to say. In book I, Satan stands before the host he has roused from its slumber on the fiery lake:

> he his wonted pride
> Soon recollecting, with high words, that bore
> Semblance of worth, not substance, gently rais'd
> Thir fainting courage.[3]

The key word here is "rais'd," a unit of sound that can bear several meanings; in this case the relevant homonyms point in opposite semantic directions: "rais'd," in the sense of elevated or honored, versus "razed"—that is, destroyed, made into nothing—which is itself closely allied to "ras'd," as in "erased" or wiped clear of marks. Milton is always alert to the possibilities of such puns, and this is in part what Leavis means when he speaks of the poet's feeling *for* words rather than *through* words. The self-consciousness of Milton's feeling for this word cannot be doubted; one need only recall "Satan exalted sat, by merit rais'd / To that bad eminence" (*PL,* II, 5–6), where the positive homonym is reinforced by "exalted" only to be undercut by "bad," which at the same time activates its negative opposite.

In both instances the wordplay is more than just that: it compels us to acts of cognitive reflection on crucial moral and philosophical issues; for what the two readings of "rais'd" alert us to is the equivocal nature of the action we are being asked to visualize. What Satan is doing, after all, is further encouraging his fellows in their rebellion against God; and in a universe in which identity depends on one's relation to godhead, to be alienated from deity is no longer to be, to be destroyed, to be razed. Once we see this (as I believe Milton intends us to), we see also that the adverb "gently" is precisely inappropriate, for gentleness and destruction are simply antithetical. Indeed, the point is even deeper: since gentleness is a positive virtue, and virtues cannot exist apart from the good of which they are the extension, an agent who has broken union with God (the source and very definition of the good) cannot possibly be acting virtuously, cannot be gentle (or courageous, or compassionate, or trustworthy, or anything else, for that matter). It becomes difficult to tell even what "gently" means here, or if it means anything; the one thing it cannot mean is gently; at the very most, the word refers to some surface features of Satan's physical behavior; he may be speaking in a low voice or extending his hands in a sympathetic or consoling gesture; but beneath that gesture, that surface, is nothing, a hollow core.

This, in fact, is just what the verse says about "gently" even before the word appears. "Semblance of worth, not substance" is a judgment that anticipates the judgment we will make on "gently" once we are moved to reflect on the adverb by the pun in "rais'd." The effect is a complicated and subtle one, and must be described carefully. As we first encounter it, the compound phrase "Semblance of worth, not substance" is read as referring to the "high words" Satan will soon utter; but we never hear them, and the energy of our anticipation is absorbed by "gently," which, as we finally come to understand it, is itself a "high" (lofty, honorific) word signifying nothing, a mere verbal semblance that is unattached to any substance. Here is a prime instance of what Leavis describes as the tendency of Milton's language to value itself (26); rather than directing us to the world of concrete experience, the words direct us to the experience of themselves, asking us to shuttle backward and forward between locations that have a merely textual existence: "Rais'd" is a comment on "gently," which is then seen to be glossed (proleptically) by "semblance of worth, not substance" (two words not sufficiently unalike), which is itself a retroactive gloss on "high words," which finds its true (and wholly textual) referent in "gently rais'd."

"Self-reflexive" is almost too weak a word for this sequence, or rather nonsequence; for one part of the effect is to retard forward movement, to prevent us from going in a straight line and therefore from following *a* line of story. Once the ambiguity of "rais'd" is registered, there are at least two stories occupying the same linguistic space, one in which a skilled and empathetic leader rallies his weary troops (in the manner of Shakespeare's Henry V) and another in which a malevolent force (indeed, *the* malevolent force) wreaks further havoc on those he has already led astray. Since one cannot decide between the stories except on the basis of evidence provided by one or the other of them, the reader's efforts to make narrative sense of what he or she is processing are frustrated. Moreover, this rupture of narrative continuity is intensified by the fact that in response to the demand of the verse the reader moves *backward*, stopped in his or her tracks by "rais'd" and then provoked to retrace steps that now point in different and multiple directions.

This feature of the verse's experience is answerable to the criticism of still another British Miltonist. In a well-known essay, Donald Davie complains that Milton's elaborate syntax "is employed characteristically to check narrative impetus."[4] Most narratives, Davie observes, are built on "the recognition, by poet and reader alike, that language and therefore the arts of language operate through and over spans of time, in terms of successive events, each new sentence a new small action with its own sometimes complicated plot" (74); but in Milton's poem, "the story, the narrative, is only a convenient skeleton; its function is to provoke interesting and important speculative questions" (76). This seems exactly right, and for reasons that Davie never quite tumbles to: the "speculative questions" the verse provokes are not questions of the kind Davie finds slighted, questions like "'What happened next?' or 'This happened—yes, to whom?'" (76); rather, they are questions that refer us to events that know no particular time and to issues that are relevant not to a moment of suspense but to *every* moment, questions like: "To what or to whom are you loyal?" "In what or whom do you believe?" "How do you decide what is right?" "How is the universe structured?"

It is not merely that such questions are larger and more inclusive than those raised in the course of a forward-leaning narrative that explores cause and effect on the micro-level of quotidian experience; it is also that these larger questions are obscured and overwhelmed if narrative considerations are allowed to occupy the foreground of attention. The fact that "Milton often deploys his 'plot,' the action of his story, in such a way as to frustrate our interest in it" (Davie, 83) points to a strategy by means of which the poet would alert us to the dangers of what I have called "plot-thinking," that form of thinking which refers issues to the configuration of some accidental convergence of opportunity, exigency, and crisis, rather than to the essential and abiding configurations of a world presided over by an eternal, omniscient, and benevolent deity. The question of whether Satan is gentle cannot, Milton would tell us, be settled by examining the empirical evidence—by looking, for example, at the present distress of his cohorts and assessing his efforts to comfort them; rather, we must look at Satan's underlying relationship to the value that founds and grounds the universe, and reason (if that is the word) from that relationship to the meaning of what he—or someone like him, someone who has "broken union"—does, no matter what the particular circumstances of his doing it.

In plot-thinking, one proceeds from the observable features of local contexts (who is doing what to whom, and for what apparent reasons) to the drawing of general conclusions; in antiplot or antinarrative thinking, one proceeds from general conclusions already assumed to the features of local contexts. In one kind of thinking, the visible and measurable world gives us our answers; in the other, answers antecedently derived and tenaciously adhered to give us the visible world. When Milton first provokes and then frustrates our narrative desires and expectations in the manner described by Davie, he is doing so in order to protect us from the limited perspectives that time urges on us in succession (perspectival limitation is, in fact, a definition of the temporal realm); and if this is in fact Milton's strategy, Leavis' strictures become less damaging. Although it remains true that the verse is preoccupied with valuing itself, it is at the same time *de*-valuing itself, for it is no less a temporal and corporeal medium than the mediums from which it would wean us. If the answers to the great questions of life do not reside in appearances thrown up by the shifting panorama of the visible world, neither do they reside (in the sense of being embedded) in the formal features of a poem, even of Milton's poem.

Where, then, do they reside? The answer is inevitable, given the strongly antinomian cast of Milton's thinking. They reside in us, in each reader who is asked to decide among the different scenarios projected by the multiple meanings of "rais'd." The decision is not made for us; for even though we are alerted to those meanings, nothing in the verse compels us to choose any one of them. It is certainly true that in a God-centered universe, a universe in which no value can exist apart from a commitment to deity, gentleness is a virtue Satan cannot claim; but the thesis of a universe so radically homogeneous is just that—a thesis, a proposition; its truth is not self-evident and universally compelling. Indeed, if it were, Satan himself would not have—could not have—thought himself into a state of rebellion. That state, of imagining a place not yet occupied by the "Omnific Word" (PL, VII, 217) is a possibility for anyone who (and I mean this literally) sets his or her mind to it. The crucial act is an act of the will, the act of a consciousness that must choose the story it is going to tell about itself, and, in telling, constitute the self so told. The reader who moves from the experience of "rais'd" to a rejection of the claim made in "gently" will be performing an act that not only structures (or rather unstructures) the narrative, but structures the mode of perception, the way of seeing, that will henceforth inform subsequent acts of reading; and the reader who grants even the slightest share of gentleness to Satan will have fashioned quite another narrative and quite another reading self. Again, nothing in the verse necessarily tips the balance; one can go as easily in one direction as the other.[5]

Telling the Difference

Both the ease and the extraordinary difficulty of which it is the flip side are on display in a single line, also from book I: "And Devils to adore for Deities" (373). The line precedes the roll call of the fallen angels and follows the narrator's account of their having been "blotted out and ras'd / By thir Rebellion, from the Books of Life" (362–363). Now their fame depends on those whom they "corrupted to forsake / God thir Creator" (368–369), those who were induced to worship devils rather than deities. The tone is one of incredulity: How could anyone be so stupid? How could anyone fail to tell the difference between devils and deities? But even as the line implies these questions, it answers them by blurring the difference it proclaims as obvious. The supposed great opposites are linked together by alliteration, assonance, and final consonant; and these two verbal mirror images themselves frame an internal duplication in the nearly identical sounds of "adore" and "for." The entire line breathes sameness at the same time that it insists on the perspicuousness of a distinction.

What then is the line saying? The question is itself another form of the question that provokes it: just as the line says both that devils and deities are easily distinguishable and that they are not, so does it provide no sure way of determining which of these assertions it is really making. That is, the line disclaims responsibility for delivering its own meaning and transfers it to what the reader does or does not bring to its experience. The lesson is the same one taught by "gently rais'd": the true significance of an action or an event or a text does not lie on its surface, waiting to be read off; rather, significance is conferred—read in—by the participant or observer, whose vision does not passively receive phenomena but gives them their shape. When

Abdiel says of Satan and his cohorts, "I see thy fall / Determin'd" (V, 878–879), he is not claiming a special insight into God's future plans; it is just that within the assumptions he holds (in fact they hold him) about the nature of God and of the universe that God informs, the fate of the rebels—cut off willfully from the world's only source of energy—is a forgone conclusion. Abdiel has no difficulty at all telling the difference between devils and deities, not because they wear these labels on their respective faces, but because by his lights—the light of the beliefs that structure his perception and therefore structure what there is to be "seen"— the labels literally apply themselves ("the things themselves conclude it").[6] On the other side, Satan is himself no less an extension of a set of beliefs, of assumptions that deliver to him a landscape complete with distinctions and basic categories. He too can tell the difference between devils and deities, but he tells it differently. He knows a tyrant when he sees one, and because he knows a tyrant, he knows that the struggle against tyranny will be an uphill one and that one must never give up trying ("courage never to submit or yield"; "And if one day, why not Eternal days?" [*PL*, VI, 424]). Telling the difference, then, is not an activity in which one simply recognizes from the position of an observer distinctions already in place, but an activity in which the distinctions one sees are constituted by one's ways of seeing, by what is inside one. "Telling the difference" should be understood in the strong sense of "telling," as stipulating the difference rather than merely noting it.

In that strong sense, telling the difference is for Milton the chief and only form of action. Whereas in plot-thinking action has as many forms as there are worldly circumstances (has therefore an infinite number of forms), in Milton's world circumstances are but the raw and ambiguous material offered up by time for configuring by an inward disposition. What is important on any occasion is not how things have turned out (as a historian might determine it), but whether or not one's inner loyalties have been maintained and strengthened. Success is measured not by the battles you have won or books you have written, but by the strength of your testimony, by the witness you give to what you believe. As we saw in Chapter 2, for Milton the moral life is an endless succession of occasions for giving witness, for testifying. That is why he declares in *Areopagitica* that what he is about to write "will be a certaine testimony, if not a Trophey";[7] whether or not the tract succeeds in its persuasive efforts and wins the day, it will already have succeeded as an outward manifestation of Milton's inner commitment. Later, in quite another mood, he attempts to dissuade his countrymen from choosing them a captain back to Egypt, and while he knows how little chance he has of success he nevertheless persists because he must say what is in his heart, even "though I were sure I should have spoken only to trees and stones, and had none to cry to, but with the Prophet, *O earth, earth, earth!* to tell the very soil it self what her perverse inhabitants are deaf to."[8] In the same period he proposes a reform in the financing of church ministers, and he does so with a similar lack of confidence in the empirical results of his efforts, "If I be not heard nor beleevd, the event will bear me witnes to have spoken truth; and I in the mean while have borne my witnes not out of season to the church and to my countrey."[9] The phrase "out of season" is a (Miltonic) joke: any season is the season for bearing witness to truth, even if the truth borne witness to is received as unseasonable by those to whom it is directed. In *The Reason of Church Government* Milton identifies with Jeremiah as one whose inner promptings will not allow him to keep silent, no matter how disagreeable or unhappy the event: "when God commands to take the trumpet and blow a dolorous or a jarring blast, it lies not in mans will what he shall say or what he shall conceal."[10] The man who resists the command will find himself reproached on the Day of Judgment for not having been among the "true servants that stood up in [the church's] defence" (805). In *Paradise Lost* God himself praises Abdiel, who "hast borne": "for the testimony of Truth hast borne / Universal reproach" (VI, 33–34), a stance later assumed by Noah when, in response to the "civil Broils" of his people, he "of thir doings great dislike declar'd, / And testifi'd against thir ways" (XI, 718, 720–721).

In each of these textual moments a voice testifies to its ownership by another, and the radical nature of the act is recognized even by Comus, in words we have several times revisited:

> Can any mortal mixture of Earth's mold
> Breathe such Divine enchanting ravishment?
> Sure something holy lodges in that breast,
> And with these raptures moves the vocal air
> To testify his hidd'n residence.[11]

Here the aesthetic of testimony is displayed in both its positive and negative aspects. The doctrine is positive in that it allies the testifier with deity ("something holy") against the pressures of mere temporal (plot-centered) appearances; it is negative in that the testifier is so subordinate to the something holy of which she is the residence that she, as a separate individual, scarcely exists. Of course these are not really two separate poles, but differing perspectives on the same condition—the condition of being an incorporate member of God's body; nevertheless the two perspectives are real and correspond to the different relationships you can have to the notion of an all-powerful God: you can affirm it joyfully, as the loyal angels do at a number of moments, or you can murmur at it, experiencing it not as a glorious promise but as an unbearable threat.

The one thing you cannot do is escape it, for there is nowhere to go. This limitation on a creature's maneuverability follows from "Milton's monism," and the key formulation is to be found in the seventh book of the *Christian Doctrine*. The subject is "Of the Creation," and Milton's purpose is to protect God from an account of creation in which either the matter of creation preexists Him (for then he would not be God, but would be secondary to the material he employs) or he creates matter out of nothing ("because it was necessary that something should have existed previously, so that it could be acted upon by his supremely powerful active efficacy").[12] "There remains only this solution," concludes Milton, "namely, that all things came from God." Moreover, although "there are . . . as everyone knows, four kinds of causes, efficient, material, formal and final. Since God is the first, absolute and sole cause of all things, he unquestionably contains and comprehends within himself all these causes" (307–308). That is, do not imagine that there is any place where God is not, any effect that has a cause other than him. The Latin word that is translated as "comprehend" is *complectatur*, which means "to encircle," "to surround," "to enclose"—all verbs that bring home the point: there is no way out, God is on all sides, you are inside him even when you think to contemplate him or oppose him ("Who can impair thee, mighty King?" [*PL*, VII, 608]). This is containment in the strongest possible sense— not an action directed at some recalcitrant other, but a prior action (of creation) so total and preempting that no other is ever allowed to exist.

This, after all, is what monism means: there is only one; variety is only a surface phenomenon beneath which there is a single unchanging substance; the many forms in which deity expresses itself reduce finally to one; in short, there is nothing that is *different*. To be sure, the world will display the appearance of difference, and that appearance will often be alluring, but in the end it will always be countered and dissolved by the revelation of absolute power, as it is in this sentence from the same chapter: "It is, I say, a demonstration of God's supreme power and goodness that he should not shut up this heterogeneous and substantial virtue within himself, but should disperse, propagate and extend it as far as, and in whatever way, he wills" (*Christian Doctrine*, 308). The heterogeneity exists only in the cul-de-sac of the sentence's middle, hemmed in on one side by God's power and on the other by his will. The effect is even stronger in the Latin, where the world translated as "heterogeneous" is *omnimodam*, which, while it means "of several kinds," has as its base *omni*—that is, "all" or "wholly"; the word itself at once proclaims and denies diversity. God's virtue is dispersed only so that it can be called back to its origin, so that it can more strongly testify to its containment.

This is in fact exactly the plan of creation, the production by God of creatures whose every movement will redound to his glory. The account in book VII of the creation of man makes just that point, and in a way that mimes the power it celebrates. Man, says Raphael, is to be "the Master work" (*PL,* 505), and while it seems for a moment that it will be man's work to be master ("endu'd / With Sanctity of Reason" he shall "Govern the rest" [507–508, 510]), the point of his mastery will be to acknowledge its source in the true Master: "But grateful to acknowledge whence his good / Descends" (512–513). "Directed in Devotion," he will take it as his chief business "to adore / And worship God Supreme who made him chief / Of all his works" (514–516). Technically the pronoun reference of "his" is ambiguous, but we understand it immediately as God's possessive which reaches backward to include the work (of being "chief") that man will supposedly be doing.

In the lines that follow, the prevenience of God, his prior occupation of all realms and states that might appear to indicate freedom and genuine difference, is insisted upon (one might say hammered home) again and again. Here, for example, is God's charge to mankind: "Be fruitful, multiply, and fill the Earth, / Subdue it" (531–532). At first the command to multiply suggests that God wishes the world to be diversely populated, but then the verb "Subdue" reveals that diversity will not really be tolerated. A few

lines later the pattern is repeated: first the promise of variety—
Adam is given "all sorts . . . all th' Earth yields, / Variety without
end" (541–542)—and then the qualification that (quite literally)
takes everything back: "but of the Tree / Which tasted works
knowledge of Good and Evil, / Thou may'st not" (542–544). The
variety is always and already reined in by an interdiction whose
pressure is always being felt, even when the unfallen pair is "on
holiday"; the freedom they supposedly enjoy is bounded by a reference point provided by another. In short, they enjoy it only by
leave; no matter how wide their choices seem, they live in a condition of constraint. They may be "Lords of the World" except
for "one restraint" (I, 32), but that restraint casts its shadow over
everything. The angelic chorus that greets the great Creator sings
the message, lest any reader miss it: anyone who would "from
thee withdraw" or seek "To lessen thee, against his purpose
serves / To manifest the more thy might" (VII, 612, 614–615).
The account of creation ends with one more rehearsal of man's
expansive yet straitened situation: "dwell / And worship him, and
in reward to rule / Over his Works, on Earth, in Sea, or Air, /
And multiply a Race of Worshippers" (627–630). As before, man's
rule is hedged in on either side by the power that permits and
that, by permitting, negates it; the price of rule is worship, the acknowledgment that the right of rule belongs to another. Line 630
says it all: multiplication (of difference) is allowed, even enjoined,
but only if its product is more of the same, an endless replication
of the image imprinted on every living thing, a succession of aco-
lytes to dance and sing before the throne of the Lord.

Difference and Writing

Paradise Lost is full of moments like these, moments that reassert
the power of omnipotence, moments that slam the door shut on
those differences that would, if they were allowed a genuine exis-

tence, threaten the homogeneity of a monistic universe. Such moments can be brutal, as when God's dreadful chariot simply rolls over the would-be rebels, or softly indirect, as when Raphael mildly explains that "one Almighty is, from whom / All things proceed, and up to him return" (V, 469–470). They can be extended, as in the War in Heaven or as in Eve's narration of the subordination of her own image to God's image in Adam, or they can be as brief as the realization that "gently" is not an adverb Satan can truly claim. The entire poem on every level—stylistic, thematic, narrative—is an act of vigilance in which any effort, large or small, to escape its totalizing sway is detected and then contained. Every movement outward from a still center must be blocked; every vehicle of that movement must be identified for what it is and then stigmatized as a form of idolatry.

And the forms of idolatry are innumerable; indeed they constitute almost everything that fills up the poem. Narrative and plot are vehicles of idolatry because they locate significance in some insight to be generated by time, rather than in the timeless, always present obligation to be aligned with the will of deity;[13] plot and narrative tell us that there is somewhere to go, whereas the true question (posed by every indifferent moment) is: What way shall one *be*? Drama is a vehicle of idolatry for similar reasons: it nominates moments of crisis (will she or won't she? what shall he do now?) and therefore presents a picture of the moral life in which crisis occurs only at special times rather than at every and all times. Like narrative and plot (which are its constituents), drama insists that some moments are different from others, whereas in Milton's vision all moments are the same. Sameness is threatened in a more general and pervasive way by any and all acts of representation; for representation—the imaging of something not present—is by definition a sign of distance from the real, and anyone who has recourse to it signifies his or her dependence on signifying, on secondhand knowledge, on the inauthentic.[14] In *Paradise Lost* the genealogy of representation is itself represented with geometric precision: its birth is the birth of Sin.

> a Goddess arm'd
> Out of thy head I sprung: amazement seiz'd
> All th' Host of Heav'n; back they recoil'd afraid
> At first, and call'd me *Sin,* and for a Sign
> Portentous held me; but familiar grown,
> I pleas'd, and with attractive graces won
> The most averse, thee chiefly, who full oft
> Thyself in me thy perfect image viewing
> Becam'st enamor'd, and such joy thou took'st
> With me in secret, that my womb conceiv'd
> A growing burden. (II, 757–767)

Sin is born of a being who has broken union—born, that is, out of a state of distance; she is a derivation of a derivation, a further removal from the center of reality; she is a sign rather than the thing itself, and the danger she represents is described precisely: those who look on her for a time ("familiar grown") will forget that she is secondary, something that came after, and will mistake the substitute for the genuine article. That is what Satan does when he takes joy in an image of an image and thereby produces (conceives) still more images ("A growing burden"); sign begets sign begets sign, all of which are forms of sin—that is, of idolatry. Nor is it an accident that Sin is a woman; for in the tradition Milton inherits and by and large accepts, woman is the chief vehicle of idolatry, the very essence (or nonessence) of difference, something created *after,* the first sign—the first, that is, not intimately related to the first—the primary form of temptation, of erroneous (wandering) worship, as the Son reminds Adam when he asks with devastating brevity: "Was shee thy God?" (X, 145).

Plot, narrative, drama, crisis, movement, change, representation, sign, woman—if the poem is continually on guard against the pull of these material and discursive forms, then it is continually on guard against itself, against the impiety of writing, of adding to or covering over a truth that is self-declaring and self-sufficient.[15] No wonder Davie concludes that *Paradise Lost* "never or hardly ever profits by what is a fact about it as about any poem— that it exists as a shape cut in time" (84); the poem's temporal existence, its desire to lean forward, is precisely what must be resisted, lest the monism of which it is intended to be the celebration be compromised. Resistance, however, especially resistance continually required, cannot but give life and energy to that which it pushes away. The very vigor with which the poem performs its task of vigilance tells us that there may be something to be vigilant against, that the eruption of difference may be an essential rather than an accidental phenomenon; it is, after all, at least curious that a discourse proclaiming the oneness of all life spends so much of its time fending off the challenges of supposedly illusory others. Everywhere one looks in the poem something or someone is trying to get away, set up a separate shop, escape to a private retreat, break out of a suffocating homogeneity.

One of those trying to break out, at least intermittently, is John Milton, whose relationship to the official morality of his own poem is at the very least ambiguous. The ambiguity surfaces now and then, but is always present when the ownership of the poem is itself an issue—whenever, that is, the poet is in dialogue with his muse. On those occasions (occurring famously in the invocations to books I, III, VII, and IX) the poet seems to be engaged in a paradoxical, even contradictory, effort to achieve humility, to lose the credit for his action, the action he is even now performing, the action of writing. He wants at once to leave his mark and have it erased; he wants at once to be raised ("with no middle flight . . . to soar / Above th' *Aonian* Mount" [I, 14–15]) and to be ras'd—that is, erased ("still govern thou my Song" [VII, 30]). This double and impossible position is perfectly reflected in the two halves of line 25, book I: "I may assert Eternal Providence." The line enacts the pattern we see so often: the momentary granting of agential independence, the "I" that stands alone and in relation to which "assert" is less a verb than a repetition (I assert I), is followed immediately by the assertion-dissolving assertion of "Eternal Providence." No sooner does a space open up for the emergence of individual initiative than it is closed, and closed by an authority that leaves no room for anything or anyone else. The single-mindedness of which Leavis accuses Milton turns back to claim the poet as its victim; the Milton for whom "everything is simply and absolutely so" is in danger of being silenced by that absoluteness; by offering "for our worship mere brute assertive will," he makes the (supposed) exercise of his own will an act of impiety. By celebrating the "Omnific Word" (VII, 217), he deprives his own words of a reason for being.

To put the matter as simply as possible: writing is itself an effect of difference, a sign of distance from that which, if truly known, would obviate the need for any addition, would make representation superfluous. One writes only if there is something that has not yet been said or someone to whom the good news has not yet been delivered; but in a *universe*, a homogeneous space in which all locations and all agents are occupied by the same informing spirit, there is only one thing to say—God is the creator and sustainer of all life—and everyone is already saying it simply by breathing out what God has breathed into his creatures. In such a world communication itself would be beside the point, since the circuit of knowledge would always and already be established and no one would be outside it; there would be no gap to be bridged, no secret to be revealed, no message to be completed. No one would speak in order either to perform or persuade another, because every other would already know what you know and be where you are. Sounds would be produced not because they meant something—meaning, after all, is always else-

495

where, something to which one's words point, something that emerges—but because they echoed the meaning already fully present, the meaning of *universal* presence.

Such sounds would issue not from anyone—from any isolated, free-standing agent—but from everybody, from the incorporate beings that lived in and through God's body; and they would constitute the tautological, circular sound of the world singing to itself, the sound of pure—that is, without purpose, design, or desire—testimony. This is the sound Milton does *not* describe in the closing lines of "At a Solemn Music": "O may we soon again renew that Song, / And keep in tune with Heav'n."[16] To keep in tune is to avoid being heard in a way that could be identified; it is only when one is out of tune that one is discordant and makes a "harsh din" (20), an unharmonious note, a note that stands out, a note that can be measured, a note that is noted. The ideal, then, is to be silent, to lose oneself in a chorus that has been "Singing everlastingly" (16) and whose song originates nowhere and everywhere.

The Politics of Testimony

But is this really what Milton wants? Is it what anyone can want, especially someone who conceives of himself (another phrase that should be taken literally) as a writer? What is it that Milton is doing when he puts pen to paper? He himself poses and considers that question endlessly in his prose and poetry, but it may be that he gives a deeper answer when the issue is displaced onto others. I am thinking of the participants in the War in Heaven, none of whom are writers in the narrow sense, but all of whom are engaged in an activity of which writing in the narrow sense is a mere token. That activity is inscribing, the making of marks, the institution of divisions and distinctions. The instrument is not the pen, but the sword; in the course of the battle, many a warrior on either side raises his sword with the expectation that with a single stroke (as is written of Michael) he might "end / Intestine War in Heav'n" (*PL,* VI, 258–259). The paradox is patent; the divisions of civil war—or, as Michael calls it, "hateful strife" (264)—are to be healed by another dividing gesture; the unity of heaven's undifferentiated surface will be restored by a stroke designed precisely to make a difference. Exactly the same thing is true of the stroke of the pen. Just as Michael and Abdiel (who lifts high "a noble stroke" [189]) and Satan hope to settle matters once and for all by a single blow, by "one stroke . . . / That might determine, and not need repeat" (317–318)—an act so efficacious that it is both the first and the last—so does Milton hope to resolve all doubts, set the affections in right tune, proclaim the first and last word, justify the ways of God to men.

But over both projects—the one military, the other discursive—hangs the reality acknowledged by Abdiel when he steps forward to challenge Satan:

> Proud, art thou met? thy hope was to have reacht
> The highth of thy aspiring unoppos'd,
> The Throne of God unguarded, and his side
> Abandon'd at the terror of thy Power
> Or potent tongue; fool, not to think how vain
> Against th' Omnipotent to rise in Arms;
> Who out of smallest things could without end
> Have rais'd incessant Armies to defeat
> Thy folly; or with solitary hand
> Reaching beyond all limit, at one blow
> Unaided could have finisht thee. (131–141)

These lines abound in ironies, some at the expense of their speaker. They begin by stigmatizing the stance of reaching, of aspiring, of standing up, of standing out—the stance of opposition to deity. Moreover, that opposition (at least as Satan conceives it) takes the form both of arms and tongues, a distinction without a difference. The uplifting of a sword and the extension of a tongue are alike gestures of independence and aggression, and both, according to the verse, are "vain." How can any one "Against th' Omnipotent . . . rise," since by definition the Omnipotent is Himself at once the cause and the location of all rising? If you rise against him, you are razed, and if you rise within him, wholly subordinate to his will and agency, you are also razed, as Abdiel is razed, when he rises to declare that he is one of those smallest things conscripted into an "incessant" army. Incessant armies perform incessant actions, actions without end, in two senses of the word. Action as it is conventionally understood is discrete and punctual; it alters circumstances, completes a project, brings something new into the world. But in the world of *Paradise Lost,* only one agent is capable of discrete action, of making a difference which, even as it is made, is reabsorbed into a new seamless unity. Only He can reach beyond all limit and not be engaged in a paradox, because "limit" is defined by where he has reached ("I am who fill / Infinitude" [VII, 168–169]). As soon as He has reached beyond, beyond is no longer, and since no one can reach beyond Him, "beyond" is not an operative category. In the same way, his hand is the only one that can be solitary—that is, efficacious with reference only to itself, "Unaided" because it is the aid and support of all other hands, a hand whose "one blow" need not be repeated because it is struck not in time but in eternity and therefore at all times. "At one blow," "at one word"— only God can do or speak so decisively that all other deeds and speeches are foredone and forewritten. The attempts of other agents to be thus decisive—to make everything right, to say all that need be said—is either unnecessary, as Abdiel acknowledges, or presumptuous, as Satan illustrates with his every word and gesture.

Nevertheless, one must act and live in time, and the question is how. One answer is given, at least in outline, in the description of the angelic warriors (a description that significantly applies to those on both sides): "each on himself reli'd, / As only in his arm the moment lay / Of victory" (VI, 238–240). Here is still another version of the ethic of testimony, with its union of assertion and humility: one acts positively, but within the knowledge that the effect (if there is any) belongs to another. The saving qualification is contained in "As"—as if the arm of each warrior held the balance of victory. But even as the formula is proffered, it reproduces the problem it supposedly resolves: "As" can either indicate the reservation that baptizes an otherwise presumptuous action ("not me, but my Master in me") or indicate a state of prideful delusion (each relies on himself, as if he could be the architect of victory). Which is it? This is the same question that was posed before by "gently rais'd" and by the devils that some adore for deities in the conviction (no more or less grounded than any other) that they *are* deities. And the answer is also the same: it is impossible to tell; no surface feature marks a difference that is supplied by an inner disposition that does not present itself for inspection and may even be opaque to the agent who lodges it. When the epic voice tells us that hypocrisy is an "evil that walks / Invisible, except to God alone" (III, 683–684), he includes in the group of those who cannot see it those who practice it. No one can plumb the depths of his own motives, know for certain that the gesture he proffers in the name of humility is not in fact (a fact only God would discern) a reemergence of pride.

Nor does it necessarily help to be aware of the danger. When, within a few lines of his stern lecture, Abdiel is said to lift "a noble stroke . . . high" (VI, 189), is that stroke free of the ambitions of which he has accused Satan? Is it "noble" in the sense of being delivered with no claim of individual efficacy whatsoever—nobly humble—or does "noble" (which is of course Raphael's word; his presence as narrator further complicates matters) make precisely that claim? Again, one cannot say; and indeed, the number of things about which one cannot say or about which one can say too much, too variously, is remarkable for a poem written in response to and in celebration of the absolute, the One. If it is Milton's conviction, as it surely is, that the world is everywhere informed by the same sustaining spirit, and if it is the case, as Leavis, Broadbent, Davie, and countless others argue it to be, that Milton relentlessly presses the totalizing claims of that spirit, why are so many moments in the poem marked by a radical openness and indeterminacy? Why at almost every juncture are important interpretive decisions at once demanded and rendered radically indeterminate?

One kind of answer to this question posits a conflict between the poet's republican politics and his "repressive" theology. Thus Herman Rapaport's account of "a mind committed to the republicanism of Rome and to ideals of freedom and liberty . . . but a mind also harboring a darker fascination with a dictatorial takeover, with what amounts to another absolutism much bleaker and more calculating than the foppery of Charles I."[17] But while Milton may indeed harbor a conflicted consciousness (and who, aside from God, does not), there may be a way of thinking about his project that accommodates and even reconciles its diverse impulses. The key is to recognize the relationship between his absolutism—his monism—and his epistemology, which is radically antinomian. That is to say, Milton's antiformalism, his refusal to identify truth with any of its local and temporary instantiations, his insistence on referring all decisions to the light of the individual conscience rather than to any external measure or prepackaged formula, precludes him from laying down the law even though he preaches the necessity of conforming to it. The law is simply to do the will of God, to align one's actions with His great design. The difficulty is in knowing, in particular circumstances,

500

exactly what that will is, a difficulty that would be obviated if the task of identifying God's will were given over to some author-ity—a church, a king, a book—which one might then consult. Milton, however, consistently inveighs against any such "implicit faith," any turning over "to another . . . the charge and care of . . . Religion,"[18] and insists that one respond to crisis by looking in-ward to the law written on the fleshly tables of the heart. The trouble, of course, is that not all hearts are similarly inscribed. By rendering value wholly interior, a matter not of specific actions urged or proscribed but of intentions holy or impious, Milton eliminates any basis for adjudicating the differences that will cer-tainly arise among diversely energized agents. The downside of the privileging of the inner light over any and all external com-pulsions is that one's convictions are supported (at least as far as one knows) by nothing firmer than themselves. In response to a challenge, one can only reassert what one believes; and in re-sponse to a doubt—a challenge from within—one can only hope that what one believes is answerable to a truth that withholds her full presence.

The resulting epistemological condition is eloquently de-scribed in *Areopagitica*: once "a perfect shape most glorious to look on," Truth now lies in "a thousand peeces" and her "sad friends" are left with the task of "gathering up limb by limb" the remnants of her body. The task, however, is endless—"We have not yet found them all . . . nor ever shall doe, till her Masters sec-ond comming"—and therefore we can only "continue seeking," "searching what we know not, by what we know, still closing up truth to truth as we find it (for all her body is *homogeneal* and proportionall)."[19] Here is a concise formulation of the vision that unites monism and the proliferation of difference: there is only one Truth and it is everywhere the same *("homogeneal")*, but its form is not available to us in our present state, and we must rely on whatever state of illumination we may have reached while at the same time resisting the temptation to identify that state with the fuller one we shall know at our master's second coming.

The politics that follows from this vision is one of tolerance and the welcoming of diversity, not because, as in some liberal traditions, tolerance and diversity are valued for their own sake, but because, given the dimness of our individual perceptions, one cannot be sure which of the paths we are urged to go down is the right one. No insight can be automatically dismissed, for "if it come to prohibiting there is not ought more likely to be prohibited than truth it self; whose first appearance to our eyes blear'd and dimn'd with prejudice and custom, is more unsightly and unplausible than many errors."[20] One must always be alert to the possibilities excluded by the limits of one's present understanding. No situation wears its meaning on its face, and thus every moment brings both the obligation to do the right thing and the risk that is attendant upon imperfect knowledge. The world, in short, is a place where the one thing needful (truth, God) is already known, yet access to it is always veiled. Action is enjoined, and one cannot hold back, but the grounds of action are always shifting and challengeable. From the vantage point of eternity all is settled and in place, but in the temporal crucible of human life one experiences only provisionality and the continual hazarding of being. Crisis awaits us at every juncture even though, in the last (which is also the first) analysis, crisis will always be recuperated by a God who effortlessly transubstantiates evil into "more good" (PL, VII, 616), taking back into himself what he had originally produced.

One can see, then, that the supposed contradiction between Milton's radical republicanism (the heart of his politics) and his equally radical absolutism (the heart of his theology) is a function of his having joined the ontology of monism—there is only one thing real—to an antinomian epistemology—the real is known only perspectivally, according to the various lights of individual knowers. Milton is at once postmodern in that he believes all determinations of truth to be local and revisable, and a hardcore objectivist in that he believes truth to be independent, stable, and unchanging. It is just that the objectivity and unchanging nature of truth is of no immediate help to those who must apprehend her through lenses that are limited and darkened, those who in the absence of direct access to her "glorious shape" must produce her in the approximated shapes of interpretive labor.

It is that labor which is enjoined on man by his epistemological condition (again *Areopagitica* is the relevant text), and its requirements and difficulties are anatomized in the first chapter of the second book of *The Christian Doctrine*. The chapter begins by declaring that "What chiefly constitutes the true worship of God is eagerness to do good works" (637) and then proceeds to a definition: *"Good works are those which we do when the Spirit of God works within us, through true faith, to God's glory."*[21] In place of the list of works we might have expected, we receive an account of them that places them behind a double screen. First, works are removed from the empirical world and given a residence in the Spirit—that is, in the attitude with which they are performed (this is a basic tenet of antinomianism). This is bad enough, since in order to determine whether or not a work is good one must look into the heart; but then it turns out that what one looks for is not the spirit of the agent, but the spirit working within him. Behind the observable work is an animating intention, and behind that intention is the animation of another. It is only when that other is present that a work is good and true, but the presence of that other leaves no palpable (formal, external) mark on its issue. One cannot tell good works from bad except by an exercise of faith that bears all the liabilities of its indeterminate object. Whether one is judging the actions of another or the actions performed by oneself, the same radical uncertainty obtains. "If I keep the Sabbath, in accordance with the ten commandments, when my faith prompts me to do otherwise, my precise compliance . . . will be counted as sin" (639).

But how does one know whether the impulse to set the written law aside stems from the prompting of faith or from some baser prompting? "How can one know, in the absence of required external laws, when one's decision to act is based on the direction of God's spirit dwelling in one's heart and when on personal desire?"[22] How can one know that when one writes "to justify the ways of God to men," that one wholeheartedly intends "justify" in a sense that yields all the glory to God (which would make the writing of the poem a work of "true faith," according to Milton's own definition) and does not reserve at least part of that glory ("that with no middle flight intends to soar") to oneself? The answer to all of these questions is that one cannot know and that the actions one performs must be hazarded without any external confirmation of their rightness. Not only does this mean that one cannot turn in moments of decision to a ready-made calculation of moral value like the Ten Commandments, but that one cannot infer with confidence from what was done yesterday to what should be done today. I rely once more on Northrop Frye's formulation: "At each crisis of life the important factor is not the consequences of previous actions, but the confrontation, across a vast apocalyptic gulf, with the source of deliverance."[23]

It isn't that previous actions don't matter (we shall see in our analysis of the morning quarrel in book IX how they are at least partly constitutive of present moments of choice), but that they are not determinative. In a crucial sense each situation is a fresh one, not because the obligation it presents is unique—the source of deliverance with which we would be joined is ever the same— but because the precise shape of that obligation is obscured, both by the shifting theater of a variegated world and by the darkened sight of men whose eyes are "blear'd" by desires they can never fully know. Frye's vocabulary helps us once again to understand the co-presence in Milton's universe of absolute certainty and a pervasive indeterminacy. The deity is omnipresent, but the "apocalyptic gulf" that divides us from him renders our attempts to apprehend him provisional and fraught with danger. Nor can that gulf be bridged, because the very efforts to bridge it are its consequences and therefore reconstitute it in the performing. There is nothing we can do but go on, in "continual seeking," in "perpetual progression," following a light we are never quite able to see and are prone to misidentify, like Abraham who in response to the call of God "went out, not knowing where he went" (Hebrews 11:8).

Freedom and Risk

I said earlier that representation—along with plot, narrative, movement, woman—is a vehicle of idolatry because it is by definition at a distance from God and therefore stands between men and their primary obligation. The implication was that representation should be shunned in favor of that which it obscures; but in the light of Milton's mature views, first fully emergent in the *Areopagitica,* any such implication must be withdrawn because representation—the interpretive conjecturing of what God is really like and what he really wants—is all we have, until our master's second coming. Although the prose and poetry are replete with exhortations to resist the appeal of secondary forms and embrace the one true way, it is amid secondary forms that Milton and his readers live, and the choice he and they face is not between the one and the many but among the many that assert, with a distressingly plural plausibility, the claim to be the One's authorized representative. This is, if anything is, the plot of Milton's work, and especially of *Paradise Lost*—verse after verse, line after line in which testimony takes the form of choosing between alternatives that are indifferently authorized.

Nowhere is the pattern more perspicuously on display than when Michael meets Satan and they exchange taunts. "Author of evil," Michael cries, and Satan replies, "The strife which thou call'st evil . . . wee style / The strife of Glory" (VI, 262, 289–290). That is to say, *who* is to say? In a world of free agents—agents not programmed by nature to reach certain conclusions—there are an infinite number of characterizations of any situation or issue. It is a question, finally, of what one believes; and belief, rather than being vulnerable to evidence, determines what will be recognized as evidence. We are always "styling"—constructing the details, small and large, of our lives, on the basis of assumptions that are their own and only support—and living as characters in the narratives we thus fashion. Satan and his cohorts style the strife of glory and live in a world where a tyrant unfairly armed with homemade thunderbolts seeks to restrict their freedom; they heroically struggle against overwhelming odds, exercising their ingenuity in efforts to match his arsenal (thus the invention of gunpowder) and managing at least to survive ("And if one day, why not Eternal days?" [424]). Michael and his friends style a different strife, not of glory but of obedience; in their world an all-powerful but inscrutable deity assigns them impossible tasks as a way of testing their loyalty, and they respond joyfully to conditions others might consider humiliating. It is not that Milton believes the choice between these stylings to be indifferent; it is just that choosing (deciding, affirming, testifying) is an action for which there are no guidelines and no guarantees; it is just that the choice can be made only on faith, and that no one who chooses is in a more secure position than anyone else—not Satan when he chooses to think himself impaired by the Son's exaltation, nor the Son when he chooses to believe that God "will not leave me in the loathsome grave" (III, 247), nor Adam when he concludes that he "came . . . here / Not of myself" but "by some great Maker" (VIII, 277–278), nor Satan again when he concludes (in direct opposition) that he was "self-begot, self-rais'd" (V, 860).

Here of course is another (and, indeed, climactic) instance of the pun with which this chapter began, and it encodes the same two scenarios: one in which the agent pulls himself up out of nowhere by his bootstraps (self-raised), and a second in which, by casting himself in the first, the agent destroys himself (self-razed). On its face (a face provided by Raphael), Satan's assertion is absurd: I am not a creature—something made by another—because I don't remember being created: "We know no time when we were not as now" (V, 859). But in fact this is an assertion no more absurd (without any grounds) than Adam's, for Adam is in the same position, knowing nothing before he was as he is now, constructing the reality of an inaccessible past, and proceeding on the basis of what he has constructed. "I can't remember my own origin, thus I must have spontaneously generated myself," or "I can't remember my own origin, thus I must have been made by a superior intelligence." The two stories are equally plausible and implausible—and who is to say which is the true one? Not Adam or Raphael, who in response to challenges can point only to signs that are a function of the story to which they are precommitted. Not the reader, who is himself already in a relation to some story and commitment when he arrives at moments like this one. Not even Milton, whose editorial interventions ("So spake th' Apostate . . . / Vaunting aloud, but rackt with deep despair" [I, 125–126], "fondly overcome with Female charm" [IX, 999]) have had the effect not of clarifying matters but of producing new interpretive disputes, disputes that began with the early commentary of Patrick Hume (1695) and continue in the writing of William Empson, A. J. A. Waldock, Catherine Belsey, and others. If the plot of the poem is one of testimony—

of moments in which various speakers either prove or betray themselves in words—it is a plot Milton does not preside over, but inhabits as one (and not a privileged one) of many styling voices. The burden of his song is interpretive freedom, the freedom of a will whose choices are unconstrained by a deity who will nevertheless pass judgment on them. Interpretive freedom is therefore at once a glory (because it accords the agent the dignity of self-determination) and a burden (because it subjects the agent to the dangers of self-determination). We must all raise ourselves by interpretive labor, at the risk of razing ourselves should those labors be performed in the wrong spirit and at the bidding of impulses rooted in self-love. Interpretive labor is what Milton narrates in the persons of his characters; interpretive labor is what he demands of his readers as they must make sense of the characters' making sense; and interpretive labor is what Milton performs with no more assurance than anyone else that he is on the side of the angels when he sets himself up as the architect of the conditions within which sense will be fatefully made.

The firmness of his architecture is such that it has earned him the hostility of readers like Leavis, whose judgment has been reaffirmed by Leo Damrosch: "Milton is the most imperial of writers, shaping every minute element of his mighty tale, guiding his readers at all points and perhaps even tyrannizing over them."[24] Although this is certainly accurate as a description of the verse's mechanics and perhaps of Milton's intentions, the effect thereby produced is almost the reverse. As many have observed, this is a poem one cannot read without being provoked to argue back. The first of God's speeches in book III is only the most egregious illustration of an experiential fact: the more totalizing the discourse—the more it attempts to fill every nook and cranny—the more energetically will those at whom it is directed struggle to escape it. Whether it is a part of Milton's design, or simply an effect of the interpretive freedom he celebrates, the structure that seems so monolithic and closed is at every point of its articulation productive of challenges in the name of everything it tries to exclude.

The tendency to exclusion accompanied by a claim to interpretive purity is especially pronounced in the early work. In the antiprelatical tracts and in the poetry of the 1645 volume, Milton delineates a universe in which an overriding truth embodied in a sacred text is embraced by one party and rejected by another in favor of its own carnal imaginations. In that universe, time is devalued as a medium of error and wandering; language is distrusted as an impious addition to the sufficiency of God's revealed word; and history—or, as Milton labels it, custom or tradition—is stigmatized as a collection of corrupted texts or as a veil that obscures a reality easily seen by those of a cleared and regenerate vision. As for those who don't see, they are such as cannot be taught and one simply leaves them to the judgment they will certainly face on the Day of Judgment.

This tidy, static, leakproof world is crafted and celebrated with a sometimes unholy zeal until 1643–1645, when, without explanation (at least Milton doesn't give one), everything changes. Fallibility of vision is predicated of everyone, not simply of the unregenerate. Consequently there is no one for whom the meaning of Scripture is perspicuous, and interpretation, rather than being forbidden as an unnecessary supplement to a self-declaring word, is enjoined. This in turn means that time and history are redeemed, since a skillful and laborious gathering is now required before the body of truth can be reassembled (if it ever can be). Choice is no longer a single moment of commitment which is clung to with all one's might; rather, choice must be made again and again in circumstances that demand ever new calculations and recalculations and bring ever new opportunities to go wrong, "to wander . . . forlorn" (PL, VII, 20). Contingency and difference, once denied and pushed away with a fear bordering on the pathological, are now acknowledged and embraced as the mediums of potential growth of "knowledge in the making." Women, previously stigmatized as the very incarnations of the secondary and idolatrous (or turned into men, as is the Lady in *Comus*), are now the bearers of regenerative and healing powers.

I do not mean to suggest that Milton simply woke up one morning to find his views wholly changed. Patriarchy and misogyny are hardly absent from *Paradise Lost* and *Samson Agonistes*, and *Paradise Regained* is in many ways a return to the flinty exclusiveness of *Comus* and the antiprelatical tracts. But the general point, I think, holds: the freedom that Milton once thought unproblematically grounded in a text notable for its "clearnesse"[25] is reconceived as a trial, as an interpretive crucible, as a field of opportunity whose rewards are inseparable from its risks. Risk is not an important component in the early prose and poetry, populated as they are by persons who are already and irrevocably on one side or another of a great dividing line; but risk is coincident with action when that line must itself be drawn by those who would position themselves in relation to it—those who want to feel that they know the difference between devils and deities and that, when they raise a hand or a pen, they do it gently.

"On Other Surety None"

Thinking Himself Impaired

One would think that risk would be less a feature of prelapsarian life than it is of ours, but as Milton sees them, the two conditions are more alike than not, and in his poetry the most dramatic presentations of risk as it relates to the burden of freedom center on the life decisions made by creatures not yet fallen. The first such decision is made by Satan, or rather by that angel of forgotten name who in the company of his fellows hears for the first time of the Son's exaltation. In terms of strict chronology (which is not always a helpful or even relevant perspective in this poem), this is the earliest moment in Milton's story (if we except the moment of the Creation) and one might expect it to be particularly revealing. Instead it is deeply mysterious, even as it offers us the (mental) action that sets everything else in motion:

> *Satan,* so call him now, his former name
> Is heard no more in Heav'n; he of the first

> If not the first Arch-Angel, great in Power,
> In favor and preeminence, yet fraught
> With envy against the Son of God, that day
> Honor'd by his great Father, and proclaim'd
> *Messiah* King anointed, could not bear
> Through pride that sight, and thought himself impair'd.
> Deep malice thence conceiving and disdain . . .[1]

The question, of course, is why? Why is Satan fraught with envy? The fact is introduced in a way that identifies it as anomalous: great in power and favor, *yet* fraught with envy. The answer, insofar as there is one, is to be found in the pointed ambiguity of "thought himself impair'd." On the one hand, this has the obvious meaning that in Satan's view he has been impaired—made less than he was—by the honoring of the Son; but it also bears the even more pertinent meaning that, in so thinking, he has impaired himself: i.e., he thought himself into a state of impairment by thinking himself impaired; he made himself less by his thoughts. That is to say—and the verse proceeds immediately to say it—the qualities that now constitute him (malice, disdain, envy) are qualities he conceives. (This moment is given its allegorical representation in book II when Sin springs full grown out of Satan's head, thus bringing to dramatic life the words of James 1:15: "When lust hath conceived, it bringeth forth sin.") It might seem that the lines provide a more external cause, first in "that sight" and ultimately in the God who has produced it. (This is the causal line that Empson traces.) But "that sight" is doubly mediated. First of all it is a sight, something seen, apprehended, not directly but from some perspective, and in this case from the perspective by which we ourselves approach it in the verse, "Through pride." "Through pride" also reaches backward to qualify "could not bear," another momentary route to an external explanation (there is something in the world that weighs

512

on Satan) that is immediately blocked: the inability to bear, as well as "that sight," is brought into being "Through pride."

What we are seeing here is the (self-)creation of an entirely new person, which is precisely what we have been told in advance of the event itself: *"Satan,* so call him now, his former name / Is heard no more in Heav'n." The one we now call Satan here calls himself into being. And not only himself. In order to think himself impaired, Satan must at the same time think others into the states of mind required by the one he now gives himself. He must conceive of a God who plays politics with his family, preferring one son to another; of a Son who is the undeserving beneficiary of that preference, of subordinates too craven to protest the obvious injustice (later to be called by him the "Minstrelsy of Heav'n" [VI, 168]), and of a world in which no one is honored except at another's expense.[2] All of this and more come along with Satan's thinking himself impaired, and once these shapes and interests have been thought—or, more literally, conceived, given birth to—they remain as the bottom-line categories of Satan's world. No evidence could dislodge them, because any evidence presented would be seen through the same lens ("Through pride," "envy," "malice," "disdain") that gave them (interpretive) being.

The point is made dramatically in the War in Heaven, when at God's command the uprooted hills retire "Each to his place." It is, to say the least, an impressive demonstration of godly power, but the rebellious host remain unimpressed:

> This saw his hapless Foes, but stood obdur'd,
> And to rebellious fight rallied thir Powers
> Insensate, hope conceiving from despair.
> In heav'nly Spirits could such perverseness dwell?
> But to convince the proud what Signs avail,
> Or Wonders move th'obdúrate to relent? (VI, 785–790)

The hapless foes see, but they do not see; specifically they do not see that they are hapless, because they see everything through the pride that constitutes their understanding both of themselves and of the adversary they now face. That understanding is not the product of independent and external facts; rather, it produces those facts in its own image, putting into the world a foe against whom they can hope to "prevail" (795). The verse is quite explicit about the process and about its direction from inner to outer: "hope conceiving from despair." That is, they conceive hope (and the possibility of prevailing) out of nothing; hope gives birth to itself, and in doing so transforms the landscape that would seem to preclude it:

> They hard'n'd more by what might most reclaim,
> Grieving to see his Glory, at the sight
> Took envy, and aspiring to his highth,
> Stood reimbattl'd fierce, by force or fraud
> Weening to prosper, and at length prevail
> Against God and *Messiah*. (791–796)

Again the verse is precise in relating (or rather dissociating) outer cause and inner conviction. The reality of "his glory"—that is, of God as source of all being and value—is not really perceived by the rebels, despite the appearance of the verb "see" in line 792; for by the lights that inform their perception, they are incapable of recognizing a power greater than their own. On the other side, Raphael, who in his narration proceeds by different lights, can only see what is lost on them, and his incredulity at their perverseness is registered in the enjambment of 792–793: "the sight" which should "reclaim" them (turn them from error) is instead made by them into the occasion of "envy." They "take" envy from themselves and project it outward onto "the sight," whose true shape (from Raphael's point of view) is consequently obscured. Envy and "reimbattl'd" fierceness may be an unimagin-

able response from the loyalist perspective, but it is the only response the rebels can imagine—that is, conceive—and in conceiving it they reconceive the configurations of its putative cause.

The answer, then, to the question, "To convince the proud
what Signs avail?" is: none. Already convinced, in the sense of being undergirded by a view of the world that declares in advance
all of its particulars, they either dismiss or make over the signs
that, seen differently, might move them in the direction of a different conviction. They stand "obdur'd"—that is, firmly fixed in a
position of belief from which they will not be dislodged, no matter what the signs. It is easy to see their behavior as Raphael does,
as the manifestation of a literally unbelievable obstinacy; but his
own view of the matter is epistemologically no different from
theirs. That is, his conclusions, no less than theirs, proceed from a
conviction (of God's primacy and goodness) that is invulnerable
to counter-evidence because it transubstantiates that evidence in
the very act of "receiving" it. What we are witness to in this moment is the clash of two structures of belief, of two *faiths*, neither
of which can claim support (except rhetorically) in the details of
a world each continually remakes. That is, the evidence they
might cite in confirmation of their faith is demanded by that
faith: for both, the direction of reasoning is from an antecedently
held picture of the way things are (with respect to the nature of
God and the possibilities in the world for action) to the shape a
situation *must* have, given that picture.

To say this is to say no more (or less) than what is implied by
the definition of faith in Hebrews 11, verse 1: "Faith is the substance of things hoped for, the evidence of things not seen." It is
through faith in what does not "appear" (verse 3) that one understands and gives shape to what does appear. It is faith in God's
goodness, despite appearances, that keeps the loyal angels loyal,
even when they are assigned tasks they cannot perform and required (as Raphael is) to do make-work when they would much

rather be doing something else (*PL*, VIII, 229–240). And it is faith in God's vulnerability, despite appearances, that sustains the embattled fierceness of the rebels even at this moment, when events seem to argue otherwise. The question "To convince the proud what Signs avail?" could be rewritten "To convince the godly what Signs avail?" and the answer would be the same: *no* signs will be sufficient.

In evidence, I offer the testimony of no less than the Son of God himself when he is assaulted in *Paradise Regained* by storms that Satan interprets as heavenly displeasure at Christ's failure to begin the work prophesied for him. What Satan urges "as a sure foregoing sign"[3] is dismissed by the Son, who says, "what they can do as signs / Betok'ning or ill-boding I contemn / As false portents, not sent from God, but thee" (*PR*, IV, 489–491). The reasoning here is not from the signs to a conclusion about God's purposes and ways, but from an already-in-place conviction of those ways to the meaning (or in this case nonmeaning) of the signs. Earlier in *Paradise Regained* the Son's performance is matched (within limits) by his followers, who must now come to terms with his disappearance:

> whither is he gone, what accident
> Hath rapt him from us? will he now retire
> After appearance, and again prolong
> Our expectation? God of *Israel*,
> Send thy Messiah forth. (II, 39–43)

What they want is a sign, but none appears, and it is despite this nonappearance that they reverse field and turn their doubt of "many days" (11–12) into its opposite: "he will not fail / Nor will withdraw him now, nor will recall, / Mock us with his blest sight, then snatch him hence" (54–56). In other words, he's not that kind of person, and given the kind of person he is (the evidence of which is not in appearances but in the faith they now exercise), it will surely fall out thus: "Soon we shall see our hope, our joy return" (57).

The narrative voice points the moral: "Thus they out of their plaints new hope resume" (58). That is, they conceive hope from ("out of") despair; they think themselves nonimpaired, although the visible landscape seems to provide signs of impairment ("what accident / Hath rapt him from us?"). In short, they perform exactly as Satan does in *Paradise Lost,* holding fast (obdurately) to convictions that are sustained by nothing but their own strength. The difference of course is that the convictions are different, and therefore give birth to different universes, ruled over by different deities whose qualities allow or demand different actions from agents in different relations to them. But in either case (or in any other that could be imagined) everything proceeds from the first conceiving act, that interior motion by means of which the (supposedly) external world is constituted in all its details. One might think that at some point these constitutive performances, these conceivings, will run up against some brute materiality, that an event *in* the world (as opposed to in the mind) will confirm one faith and disconfirm the other. Yet the obdurateness of the rebel host manages to survive even the experience of God's chariot and a nine-day fall into hell; having arrived, they pick themselves up and begin plotting in accordance with the same old convictions. And on the other side, no amount of contrary evidence suffices to shake the faith of those lone just men who pop up periodically in Michael's otherwise depressing chronicle; they all perform as Abdiel does, holding fast to what they *already* believe, "though Worlds / Judg'd [them] perverse" (*PL,* VI, 36–37).

Nor should one forget Milton himself, who, like others in his party, is left by the Restoration in exactly the position of those who see the promise of Christ's appearance (apparently) withdrawn: he must ask himself (in Christopher Hill's words), "How could the God who willed 1649 also will 1660?"[4] Milton answers (in *The Readie and Easie Way* and elsewhere) by supposing that 1660 is a judgment on the timidity of those "backsliders" who withdrew from the commitment made earlier to the true cause, and he casts himself as one who, despite all appearances, holds fast: "Thus much I should perhaps have said though I were sure I should have spoken only to trees and stones, and had none to cry to, but with the Prophet, *O earth, earth, earth!* to tell the very soil itself what her perverse inhabitants are deaf to."[5] Of course his opponents would have seen 1660 as a judgment on 1649; the regicides mistook their own base desires for God's will and now find that same God signifying his true design in the return of Charles. Each party has no trouble in "reading" events as confirmations of its respective faith, a faith that is sustained and extended by the very interpretive labors it calls into being.

Conceiving God

The point is that in Milton's universe interpretive labors of a world-constituting kind are performed by everyone, and that these labors begin by constituting or conceiving God, after which everything else follows.[6] In book VIII of *Paradise Lost*, Adam learns from Raphael exactly how it is done. The question of record is: Why are the heavens proportioned as they (apparently) are? Raphael answers not by supplying a precise astronomical account but by suggesting that if Adam grounds his perceptions in a firm of conception of God, everything else will fall into place: "for the Heav'n's wide Circuit, let it speak / The Maker's high magnificence" (100–101). Do not, that is, seek to read God's intentions by looking at the world; rather, look at the world through the lens of a godly intention (and character) already assumed. Raphael hastens to add that this is not a method for objective observation; it may be the case (in some ultimate perspective unavailable to man) that the heavens do not make a wide circuit at all:

> Not that I so affirm, though so it seem
> To thee who hast thy dwelling here on Earth.
> God to remove his ways from human sense,
> Plac'd Heav'n from Earth so far, that earthly sight,
> If it presume, might err in things too high,
> And no advantage gain. (*PL,* VIII, 117–122)

The way not to err (or presume) is to read whatever phenomena are disclosed to you by your perspective as further evidence of God's glory and goodness. If you do that, you can't go wrong, not because you will come upon the empirical truth, but because the truth is not empirical; rather, it is a reflection of the relation of any phenomenon (or person or action) to the deity. Raphael's lesson is also Augustine's in his *On Christian Doctrine.* Correctly interpreted, the Scriptures will always signify "the double love of God and of our neighbor."[7] Anyone who finds that lesson in the Scriptures, "even though he has not said what the author may be shown to have intended in that place, has not been deceived, nor is he lying in any way." That is, he is telling the truth at a level that underlies and overrides any of the more limited truths (about syntax, semantics, and so on) he may seem to be ignoring. When reading the text, the rule is the same as when reading the heavens: "Let it speak the maker's high magnificence."

Of course Satan has an equivalent, if different, rule that is no less powerful in its productive capacity. His rule is "Let it speak the maker's maliciousness (or weakness or envy)," and we see him teaching it to Eve in book IX.[8] (One way of thinking of the Fall is as a competition between two teachers of reading.) The text is what the unfallen couple has always read as the divine prohibition: "of the Fruit of this fair Tree amidst / The Garden . . . Ye shall not eat" (661–662). In their conversations prior to the fatal day, they had always considered this pronouncement within the assumption that it had been issued by a benevolent authority for reasons that were, no doubt, "good":

> needs must the Power
> That made us, and for us this ample World
> Be infinitely good . . .
> . . . . .
> . . . Then let us not think hard
> One easy prohibition . . .
> . . . . .
> But let us ever praise him, and extol
> His bounty, following our delightful task
> To prune these growing Plants, and tend these Flow'rs.
> (IV, 412–414, 432–433, 436–438)

Adam's vocabulary indicates that he knows (at some level) that the crucial matter is what they *think* of God's words—that is, of how they conceive them—which is finally, of course, a question of how they conceive *him:* if he is "infinitely good," then his intentions in imposing "one easy prohibition" must also be good. It all depends on what kind of person they think their God to be, and when Satan tempts Eve his chief strategy is to replace their conception of God with another: "Why then was this forbid? Why but to awe, / Why but to keep ye low and ignorant, / His worshippers" (IX, 703–705). When his words win "too easy entrance" (734) into Eve's heart, they issue in an entirely different picture of the deity: "what forbids he but to know, / Forbids us good, forbids us to be wise?" and the conclusion follows immediately: "Such prohibitions bind not" (758–760). What she really means is that such a *person*—one whose intention it could be to deny you wisdom—binds not; you have no obligation to him, no allegiance, no fidelity; and indeed the moment you think of him in this way, you have broken the link between you and a God who, in your world, no longer exists.

No matter what the issue then, every determination is at bottom a decision about how one conceives God, and this includes the determination of whether or not one can lawfully divorce. Milton's basic argument in the divorce tracts is that marriage was intended by God as a remedy for loneliness and not for the satisfaction of an animal desire. In the course of unfolding that argument, he considers Paul's pronouncement that "it is better to marry than to burn" and asks, "But what might this burning mean?"[9] It would seem to refer to the "motion of carnall lust"—but, no, says Milton, that cannot be, for "God does not principally take care for such cattell." That is, God (speaking through Paul) is not that kind of person; his concerns are higher, and therefore it could not be his intention in instituting marriage to provide for "the meer goad of a sensitive desire"; rather, by "burning" God *must* mean "that desire which [He] put into *Adam* in Paradise . . . that desire which [He] saw it was not good that man should be left alone to burn in; the desire and longing to put off an unkindly solitarines." The reasoning is circular, proceeding from an assumption of God's intention to a reading of his words as informed by that intention.[10] It is, however, the only reasoning the tract displays, and its principle is announced and embraced when Milton declares that "the way to get a sure undoubted knowledge of things, is to hold that for truth, which accords most with charity" (183); that is, assume that in any case God is always disposed toward charity, and then read his every word and action as a realization of that charitable disposition. (Again this looks back to Augustine, who tells us that "what is read should be subjected to diligent scrutiny until an interpretation contributing to the reign of charity is produced" [*On Christian Doctrine*, 93].)

Often this involves setting aside his words as they might be "vulgarly tak'n" (notice how closely this resembles what Satan does to the "single prohibition" in book IX) in order to arrive at a meaning that accords with one's image of God. In the divorce

tracts, the God Milton imagines (conceives) is unfailingly generous with respect to his creatures' weakness, and concerned always to promote their spiritual health. It follows, then, that he
could not possibly bind his creatures to impossible performances
or require that they continue in a relationship that cramps their
spirits: "He that lov'd not to see the disparity of severall cattel at
the plow, cannot be pleas'd with any vast unmeetness in marriage" (163). The direction of thought is always from a God who
has been preconceived in his inclinations to a rejection of any
meaning or intention that would ask us to think him otherwise
than we have preconceived him. Responding to the claim that the
permission to divorce granted under the Old Law has been withdrawn by the New, Milton replies with indignation: "Can we
conceave without vile thoughts that the majesty and holines of
God could endure so many ages to gratifie a stubborn people
in the practice of a foul polluting sin . . . ?" (172). The "vile
thoughts" that would accompany such a conception include principally the thought that a God who would damn for an action He
had permitted would himself be "vile" and "foul." It cannot be
"attributed to the justice of God and his known hatred of sin . . .
that his peculiar people should be let wallow in adulterous marriages almost two thousands yeares" (172). To think so would be
to cast "the reprooff . . . ev'n upon him who made the law" (173).
It is only if we take God's permission seriously that we vindicate his "misreputed honor . . . by suffering him to give his own
laws according to the conditions of mans nature best known
to him, without the unsufferable imputation of dispencing legally with many ages of ratify'd adultery" (189). What would be
"unsufferable" would be the imputation to God of such an action, for if he is a God who would either license sin or declare
sinful deeds he had earlier encouraged, there is no possibility of
understanding or following his will. In order to "save" him, we
must "conceave" of him in terms that enable us to worship him.

Once those terms are in place, the answers to questions will immediately be obvious. Does God's decree of predestination include reprobation as well as salvation? Were some foreordained to be sinners "before the foundations of the world were laid"?[11] This vexed problem poses no difficulties for Milton once he observes that "the aim of reprobation . . . is the destruction of unbelievers, a thing in itself repulsive and hateful" (*Christian Doctrine,* 173). One cannot conceive without vile thoughts a God who would decree something repulsive and hateful, and therefore "Clearly . . . God did not predestine reprobation . . . or make it his aim." The same reasoning disposes of the thesis that God has two wills—a revealed will, in relation to which he calls us universally to Grace, and a secret will, by which he predestines some of us to damnation. Surely this notion must be rejected, for "otherwise we should have to pretend that God was insincere, and said one thing but kept another hidden in his heart" (177). Even worse, we would think of God as one who would "order us to do right but decree that we shall do wrong. . . . Could anything be imagined more absurd than such a theory?" The word John Carey translates as "be imagined" is *cogitare,* which could also be rendered "be thought" or "pursued in the mind." Could anything more absurd than that this kind of God be thought? Rather, advises Milton, think into being another God, one who predestines to reprobation only those whom he foresees choosing reprobate ways. Only "imagine [*cogitate*] that you hear God voicing his predestination in these terms" and "you will dispose of countless controversies" (179). Indeed, you will do more than that; you will reorder and rearrange lives, change the basis on which people think of themselves and of the actions possible to them. No power on earth is greater than the power by which one conceives God in all his attributes and in that act conceives everything which must be the case given the (now) undoubted fact of such a God. "There is no doubt," says Milton in *Eikonoklastes,* that from "good desires rightly conceav'd in the heart, wholesom words will follow of themselves";[12] and with the addition of only a single letter, this formulation yields a statement that is not unfaithful to Milton's thinking about the constitutive power of thought: from "desires rightly conceav'd in the heart, wholesom *worlds* will follow."

It is not my intention to make Milton into a caricature of an idealist, someone who believes that "thinking makes it so" and that unhappy situations can be removed simply by declaring them otherwise. The fact that the visible world provides no firm (uninterpreted) basis for determining the shape of things (including the shape of God) does not leave us in a state of freedom as much as it leaves us in a state of almost unbearable responsibility. True, we are not constrained by independent evidence to a specific construction of the world, but this absence of (external) constraint is not the lifting but the imposing of a burden, the burden of hazarding (on the basis of insufficient information, without the support of the evidence of things seen) a construction which, once hazarded, will form the environment in which we thereafter live. That is, in the act of conceiving of God (an act made necessary by his removal of "his ways from human sense") we conceive, bring into being, put into place, a landscape in which actions are labeled "possible," "desirable," "mandatory," "unthinkable," and so on; and each time one of those actions is taken or avoided or not seen as a possibility, that landscape becomes ever firmer in its configurations and ever more resistant to a basic alteration. Our conceivings, even though they are grounded in nothing—in no brute empirical datum—produce grounds that one cannot simply wish away, if only because it is against their now-in-place background that wishes (or any other mental actions) could themselves be conceived. Our conceivings, in short, have consequences.

When Satan thinks himself impaired by the sight of the Son's exaltation, he also thinks himself necessarily into the posture of rebellion that leads to his subsequent actions: removing his legions to the North, marching against the loyalists, persisting in the face of any and all "evidence"; and, on the other side, when Abdiel "thinks" the same sight differently—declaring that, in anointing the Son, God is "far from thought / To make us less, bent rather to exalt / Our happy state under one Head" (*PL, V,* 828–830)—his subsequent actions (turning his back on the rebellious North, flying all night to God's camp, accepting without murmur that "what he for news had thought / To have reported" is "Already known" [VI, 20–21]) are equally determined. Gripped by a conviction that God is "good" and "provident" of his creatures' "dignity" (V, 826, 827–828), Abdiel is no more "free" to do otherwise than Satan—gripped by the opposite conviction—is free to return to the heavenly fold.[13]

The dynamics of a freedom that, once exercised, creates its own constraints are on display in Satan's soliloquy at the beginning of book IV. As he puts it to himself addressed as a third person, "[your] will / Chose freely what it now so justly rues" (*PL,* IV, 71–72) and, having chosen it, must now live with its choice; and since what has been chosen is rebellion and independence, the possibility of reversing the choice is one that he—as a being now *constituted* by rebellion and (false) independence—is incapable of contemplating: "But say I could repent and could obtain / By Act of Grace my former state; how soon / Would highth recall high thoughts, how soon unsay / What feign'd submission swore" (93–96). That is, having thought himself high ("self-rais'd," as he puts it at V, 860), he cannot rethink himself low; since submission is alien to an essence he has "freely" constituted, it is simply not available to him as an option; it will always be "feign'd," put on, not real, relative to the reality he has chosen to become. Having thought himself impaired, he has created a condition in which the state of *unimpairment* could be achieved only by a being wholly other than the being he now is.

The moral is clear and chastening: in a world where ways of thinking are constitutive of what can subsequently be thought about, you must be ever on guard against thinking yourself into consequences you will "justly rue." This is in fact the burden of Raphael's many warnings to the yet unfallen couple:

> That thou art happy, owe to God;
> That thou continu'st such, owe to thyself,
> That is, to thy obedience; therein stand.
> This was that caution giv'n thee; be advis'd.
> God made thee perfet, not immutable;
> And good he made thee, but to persevere
> He left it in thy power, ordain'd thy will
> By nature free, not over-rul'd by Fate
> . . . . .
>
> . . . for how
> Can hearts, not free, be tri'd whether they serve
> Willing or no, who will but what they must
> By Destiny, and can no other choose?
> Myself and all th' Angelic Host that stand
> In sight of God enthron'd, our happy state
> Hold, as you yours, while our obedience holds;
> On other surety none. (V, 520–527, 531–538)

> list'n not to his Temptations, warn
> Thy weaker; let it profit thee to have heard
> By terrible Example the reward
> Of disobedience; firm they might have stood,
> Yet fell; remember, and fear to transgress. (VI, 908–912)

> Be strong, live happy, and love, but first of all
> Him whom to love is to obey, and keep
> His great command; take heed lest Passion sway

Thy Judgment to do aught, which else free Will
Would not admit; thine and of all thy Sons
The weal or woe in thee is plac't; beware.

. . . . .

. . . to stand or fall
Free in thine own Arbitrement it lies. (VIII, 633–638; 640–641)

What Raphael emphasizes repeatedly is the relationship between freedom and the consequences of its exercise; it is at once the happiness of the unfallen couple, in that it gives them a dignity unavailable to creatures programmed for good, and it is the space within which that happiness can be either maintained or lost. They are created in a relation of loyalty to God, but it is within their power to default on that loyalty and to become differently constituted.[14] For them to continue "such" is to continue being the kinds of persons they now are; although Destiny has not made them, they can make their destiny—and not only theirs, for "thine and of all thy Sons / The weal or woe in thee is plac't." "Plac't" suggests the delicate balance of the situation: they are free to go in any direction they please, but the direction they go in will either extend or erode that freedom. Should they choose wrongly, there is no safety net to break their fall, no "nature of things" that will survive and contain their error; everything proceeds from their own strength (or weakness): "On other surety none."

The Labor of Self-Cultivation

Everything Raphael says is an expansion and reformulation of God's crucial and controversial characterization of the unfallen state: "Sufficient to have stood, though free to fall" (III, 99). That is, the possibility (or capability) of falling is what gives the act of standing meaning. (The two halves of the line exist in a relationship not of tension or antagonism but of interdependence.) Indeed, paradoxical though it may seem, the perfection Raphael attributes to Adam and Eve (and about which they will debate in book IX) has as its *content* their mutability ("God made thee perfet, not immutable"): the perfection that is theirs—the perfection of being free, as opposed to automatized, agents—requires that they be able to move away from God so that they have the possibility of moving ever closer to him in "tract of time" (V, 498). As commentators have increasingly come to realize, the Miltonic Eden is characterized by its dynamism. Whereas Milton's predecessors had often portrayed life before the Fall in negative and passive terms (a matter of not doing something in order to maintain a steady state), in Milton's Paradise actions are positive and creative, and what they create can be either good or bad. The possibility Raphael holds out of ascending to a perfection even higher than the one they now enjoy ("Your bodies may at last turn all to spirit") is inseparable from the opposite possibility: the descent performed by Satan when he thinks himself impaired and conceives malice, disdain, and envy. In a word, the Edenic situation is one of *growth;* the only thing Adam and Eve cannot do is stand still; every moment presents them with the opportunity of either affirming their loyalty and so becoming more like the God with whom they stand, or breaking their fealty and so taking on the aspect of the vices they have chosen. (Thus Michael in XI, 515–518: "Thir Maker's Image . . . then / Forsook them, when themselves they vilifi'd / To serve ungovern'd appetite, and took / His Image whom they served, a brutish vice.")

It is a question, then, of the direction in which growth (itself inevitable) will take them, and this means that their chief task, more important than the task of laboring in the garden (although, as we shall see, the two labors are finally the same), is the task of managing that growth, which is nothing less than the task of managing the production of themselves. The essential point was made long ago by Barbara Lewalski and J. M. Evans. "The poem's garden imagery," Lewalski explains, "identifies Adam and Eve not only as gardeners but also as part of the Garden."[15] "Much of the work Adam and Eve perform in Eden," she continues, "is an image of the work they should accomplish in the paradise within." In short, *they are their own chief crop.* "Adam and Eve, like the Garden, have natures capable of a prodigious growth of good things, but which require constant pruning to remove excessive or unsightly growth, constant direction of overreaching tendencies, constant propping of possible weaknesses, and also . . . further cultivation through art" (94). The pruning and propping and reforming of themselves will be effected not by tools but by thoughts, by acts of interpretation which must simultaneously be hazarded and vigilantly scrutinized: "Eden is an opportunity to grow in wisdom, virtue and perfection, and . . . Adam and Eve must take the initiative in interpreting what happens to them. . . . Normally . . . they respond to a new situation by one or two false starts or false guesses before they find or are led to the proper stance. But this human growth by trial and error, like the excessive growth of the Garden, is wholly without prejudice, so long as they prune and direct and reform what grows amiss" (100).[16] This last qualification perhaps deserves more emphasis than Lewalski chooses to give it; the dangers after all are at least as great as the opportunities for reward. In Evans' words, the "perfection of Adam and Eve no less than the perfection of the garden they inhabit is nothing if not conditional, for it requires their constant vigilance to preserve the balance of forces on which it depends."[17]

"Constant vigilance" well captures the experiential "feel" of Edenic life, a life filled with the tension and pressure of possibilities always on the verge of being realized or transformed. Nowhere are those tensions and pressure more on display than in the infamous "morning quarrel" or "separation" scene, an episode that at once foregrounds and enacts the double task of cultivation and conception. The foregrounding could not be more explicit:

> *Adam,* well may we labor still to dress
> This Garden, still to tend Plant, Herb and Flow'r,
> Our pleasant task enjoin'd, but still more hands
> Aid us, the work under our labor grows,
> Luxurious by restraint; what we by day
> Lop overgrown, or prune, or prop, or bind,
> One night or two with wanton growth derides
> Tending to wild. Thou therefore now advise
> Or hear what to my mind first thoughts present. (IX, 205–213)

Eve raises as a topic of conversation the problem of managing growth, and in doing so she extends the problem. The "first thoughts" she now presents are interpretive shoots, and it remains to be seen whether they will be propped and supported or pruned and lopped. The discussion of cultivation and its (apparent) discontents will itself be an instance of cultivation. In the process of deciding how to deal with a garden that is irrepressibly fecund, the unfallen pair interact with their own fecundity in ways that have consequences for the configurations of their own inner landscapes. In the course of answering the question of what it means to garden, they garden themselves—that is, they encourage and/or retard the growth of the thoughts by which their situation in all of its aspects is conceived.[18]

To be sure, this is not the usual way of regarding this scene, which more often than not provokes fits of moralizing and condemnation. John Peter Rumrich provides a typical example: "I . . . read the separation scene as being significant for our understanding of why the Fall occurs. In my view Eve represents . . . a regressive tendency within humankind. Similarly, if Adam were more secure or mature, less vulnerable to narcissistic injury, he, paradoxically, would have felt free to exercise his authority over

Eve more wisely. Neither is guilty of evil here, but both act immaturely, and that, in this context, means regressively. This sets the stage for the metamorphic catastrophe."[19]

It is easy to understand why critics respond in this fashion. An awareness of the Fall's imminence encourages a reading that infers backward from the foreknown event, and in the context of something so catastrophic one "naturally" wants to fix the blame. (Adam and Eve, as later readers or rereaders of the scene, will indulge this tendency in spades.) Once the blame is fixed, the next step is to generalize the episode by allegorizing it, by finding that Adam and Eve represent something—the female as opposed to the male principle, passion as opposed to reason; and of course inevitably there will be firm statements as to what the two *should* have done. Eve should have not wanted to work alone. Adam should have been firmer and less "domestic" (*PL,* IX, 318) in his "Matrimonial Love" (319). He should have exercised his authority. Behind these ex post facto admonitions is the assumption that had the two not separated, the Fall would not have occurred (an assumption Eve will forcefully question during the post mortem). It is within this assumption that people say things like "they should have acted more maturely," which means, I suppose, that they should have read ahead to the end of book IX and ordered their behavior accordingly. Rumrich and his fellows don't seem to realize that if Adam were "more secure" (that is, less precariously in place) or "less vulnerable to narcissistic injury" (that is, impervious to suggestions from his own consciousness), there would be nothing at stake in the conversation because it could only go one (right) way. The interest of the scene evaporates once one treats it as a piece of datum for decision science, for then one loses sight altogether of the *process* here being exemplified: the process by which free agents, "on other surety none," elaborate the very texture of their lives—elaborate themselves.

It would be better, then, to follow the lead of Mary Nyquist when she insists that the "separation scene dialogue" is "dramatic in mode."[20] By "dramatic" Nyquist means unmediated by a moral or logical perspective that is continually assigning (fixed) meanings to events as they occur; instead, the unfolding of the scene is marked by repeated surprises and unexpected turns (unexpected by both the characters and the reader, and insofar as it makes sense to say so, by the text itself), by what Marshall Grossman has termed "a strong element of the accidental and contingent."[21] That is to say, what we have here is not a (primarily) philosophical discussion of freedom and innocence, or an allegorical representation of the divisions in the human psyche, or a moral dilemma (how can Adam command Eve and respect her freedom?) badly resolved, but rather, as Evans puts it, "the paradigm of every squabble between husband and wife that has taken place since."[22]

It has been averred that the fact of such a squabble itself tells against the couple's innocence. Could such feelings and anxieties reside in unfallen breasts? The answer, of course, is in the argument I (and many others) have already made: the "raw material" of the Edenic character exists in potential, and can go either way (as Milton says in *Areopagitica*, the "matter" of sin and virtue "is the same"); feelings—roots, plants, buds—that might profoundly weaken the fabric of moral intelligence if left unchecked, can, if they are scrutinized and shaped, be the basis for an increased strength. If it is the business of Edenic existence to become ever more practiced, if Adam and Eve's task in Paradise is to grow in the exercise of obedience by discerning its imperatives in a number of situations, then their discussion here (even in its "dicey" turns) is not anomalous but paradigmatic, and paradigmatic not merely of every subsequent domestic quarrel but of Edenic life, conceived of as a succession of opportunities—as a whole. Indeed, one might go so far as to say that this scene is the most humanly significant one in the poem, for it displays and mimes all the resources and hazards that go to make up the experience of creatures who are forever elaborating the universe they inhabit.

It is this ceaseless and fecund elaboration that will be stressed in my analysis of the scene, although I should say immediately that the concerns focused on by other commentators will necessarily make their appearance here. While it is true, as I have said, that one misses the essence of the scene if one merely keeps score as the conversationalists take their turn, keeping score is also a part of what is going on—Adam and Eve do it twice—and therefore it is inevitably a part of one's response. For the record, and to get some matters out of the way in advance, here is my scorecard:

1. Eve is without fault when she presents her first thoughts; she is initiating exactly the kind of conversation she and Adam are supposed to have, one in which the features of their situation are at once discussed and (perhaps) reconceived.
2. Eve's understanding of the place of work in that situation is, however, flawed, and therefore
3. Adam is right to correct her.
4. Adam himself goes wrong (in ways that we shall examine) and finds himself at one point (296ff.) arguing for the importance of external appearances.
5. Adam recovers at line 342 and proceeds to say all the right things.
6. He stumbles again when he reasons himself into giving Eve permission, assuming incorrectly that he cannot simultaneously respect her free will and command her.[23]
7. None of this is fatal. The conditions that obtain as the scene ends are the same as when it began, in the essential respect:

Adam and Eve are still *in process,* working out the conditions
of their existence by thinking them through in contexts that
continue to proliferate—i.e., branch and grow.

Point 7 is of course controversial, and in time I will defend it;
for now, I assert it in order to insist (once again) that the scene be
allowed the contingency that attends its dramatic unfolding, a
contingency that disappears if it is always being understood in relation to an event of which it is supposedly a cause. In this connection it will be helpful to turn to Ronald Wardhaugh's study of
how conversation works.[24] Conversation, Wardhaugh explains, "is
generally . . . unrehearsed. It is essentially spontaneous, in that
you create its content and any structure it has in the course
of playing it out" (41). The tension in Wardhaugh's vocabulary
alerts us to his important point: the fact that conversations are
unrehearsed doesn't make them untheatrical; the roles one plays
may not be premeditated (although they can be, as in interviews
or proposals of marriage), but they are roles nevertheless. In a
conversation each participant "must present himself to the others. Each must at every moment decide who he is and what he is
doing, where he is and what he is saying, has said, is about to say,
or does not wish to say, and how all the foregoing is related to all
the other things done and said, and possibly to be done and
said. Each conversation, therefore, is a scene—or a succession of
scenes—constructed in the very playing by actors who create
their roles as they play them" (39–40). In short, Wardhaugh observes, conversation is a "kind of theatre" and "what is remarkable" about it "is its fundamental improvisational nature" (38).
That is, the participants are at every moment *making it up,* where
"it" stands not only for the particular thing now being said, but
for everything: "Each scene or episode is a new creation" (38).
We see, he concludes, "that a conversation is not simply *about*
something"; rather it "*is* something. It is a performance" (39).

One must be careful not to take this to mean that what happens in conversations is not real; for it is reality that conversations are the performance of; they are improvisational delineations of the world in which the improvisers will henceforth (at least for a time) be living.

Tending to Wild

This, then, is the perspective I wish to bring to the separation scene (although to call it that is already to focus too much on its result, as if that were the only thing at stake in its unfolding), and we can begin (this has been a long preamble to a tale) by rehearsing what has already been said: the topic is the cultivation of the garden, and the action is the cultivation of themselves by way of their discussion of cultivating the garden. Eve's first speech simultaneously describes the problem as she sees it and provides the vocabulary (of propping, pruning, and lopping) that will be descriptive of their efforts to deal with it. Not that this is all there is to be said about these lines. One wants to note the tension in "pleasant task enjoin'd" which signals in advance Eve's failure to understand that the task is a gift. She does understand something else, but not in a way that allows her, at this moment, to extend it to their situation: she understands that the more they do, the more there is to do ("the work under our labor grows, / Luxurious by restraint"[PL, IX, 208–209]). This is true not only of the work they do in the garden, but of the work they do in thinking about the garden and about everything else: the more thoughts they have in response to thoughts seeking resolution, the more problems they will have to resolve. There is no end to it, which is another way of making the point so many critics find so hard: that Milton's Eden is not static, is not securely what it is, and that in its *insecurity* lies its glory. This is exactly the point to which the conversation (itself much like a plant) will finally wind around;

and while we may feel when we reach it that we have traveled far from Eve's first gesture, that gesture already pushes us in the direction things will eventually take.

We must, however, resist the temptation to rush ahead. There are many turns and surprises to be experienced, and the first is Eve's proposal:

> Let us divide our labors, thou where choice
> Leads thee, or where most needs, whether to wind
> The Woodbine round this Arbor, or direct
> The clasping Ivy where to climb, while I
> In yonder Spring of Roses intermixt
> With Myrtle, find what to redress till Noon:
> For while so near each other thus all day
> Our task we choose, what wonder if so near
> Looks intervene and smiles, or object new
> Casual discourse draw on, which intermits
> Our days work brought to little, though begun
> Early, and th' hour of Supper comes unearn'd. (214–225)

Many have noted the ironies embedded in Eve's horticultural vocabulary. The woodbine, ivy, and myrtle are clinging plants that die when separated from their supports. They are also evergreen and therefore symbolic of everlasting life, fidelity, and undying affection. The myrtle is also the symbol of marriage. Roses in Paradise are without thorns and are a figure for innocence (the Virgin Mary, the second Eve, is often characterized as the rose without thorns—that is, without sin). In short, Eve's language says repeatedly "Don't separate" even as she employs it to argue for separation.

It is to these subterranean meanings that Adam will later respond when he urges Eve to "leave not the faithful side / That gave thee being, still shades thee and protects" (265–266), but his first response is to her assumption of a relationship between supper and work—and properly so, for in making that assumption she is in danger of misconceiving the structure of their lives. First of all, she thinks of the garden less as a paradise than as a place of threat, indeed as a place that *is* a threat, one they must continually stave off by hacking away at a growth that will otherwise overwhelm them. Moreover, she also thinks that unless they perform this close-to-impossible task they risk having their necessities withdrawn—a supper unearned is a supper someone may at any time refuse to provide—and behind that thought is the thought (or conception) of a God who would place them in that situation, a God who demands round-the-clock work from his creatures/employees and dispenses his rewards on the basis of a strict and mechanical accounting. And behind *that* thought is a conception of the work itself as something finishable, as a discrete task whose accomplishment will bring rest and a cessation of difficulty. (It is almost as if Eve had been reading about those other non-Miltonic Edens where nature manages itself with the aid, perhaps, of a built-in sprinkler system and of plants that effortlessly maintain their own states of manicured perfection.)

This is perhaps Eve's most grievous misconception, for it involves a failure to understand the demands of her situation even as she thinks about ways to satisfy them. The labor she is "enjoined" to is the labor of self-construction through the continual maintenance and refurbishing of the relationship that founds her being; and this is, by definition, a labor that can never be complete. Even were she to ascend "in tract of time" to angelic status, she would still be required at every moment to reaffirm her loyalty in the context of the new situations that experience throws up. Satan and Abdiel stand as the polar representatives of the choices that will always be before her, even when her body "may at last turn all to spirit" (V, 497). Given this understanding (which has slipped away from her), the suggestion to divide their labor makes no sense, for it is only in relation to *finite* tasks that the strategy could be successful; in the context of a labor that increases with every act intended to diminish it (here the homology with the garden as she describes it is precise), any division or parceling out is obviously self-defeating. Indeed, by thinking of her work as something that can be done once and for all, Eve undermines her ability to engage in her work—endless work—even as she is being called to it now. The error she courts is the error basic to every moment of temptation in Milton's prose and poetry, the error of externalizing the demands of the moral life by locating them in some measurable and discrete act, some "single stroke."

To his credit, Adam sees where the danger lies and moves immediately to address it:

> not so strictly hath our Lord impos'd
> Labor, as to debar us as we need
> Refreshment, whether food, or talk between,
>
> . . . . .
>
> For not to irksome toil, but to delight
> He made us, and delight to Reason join'd.
> These paths and Bowers doubt not but our joint hands
> Will keep from Wilderness with ease. (IX, 235–237, 242–245)

Adam responds to Eve's proposal by challenging (ever so gently, and with "mild answer" [226]) the assumptions that generate it. If you will only remember, he says indirectly, that God's dealings with his creatures are always marked by generosity, you will not conceive of our lives in the terms that underlie your "first thoughts" (213). What he is advising is that her first thoughts be of a God whose intentions are benign, and everything else will fall into place, including the place of work in that benign vision. When he calls on her to "doubt not," the admonition is precise and pointed: by imagining conditions in which they are threatened by nature and bound to a cycle of burdensome work, she implicitly indicts God's goodness and conceives of him exactly as Satan does, as a tyrant. An alternate conception may, at first, seem counterintuitive, especially given the fact, to which the epic voice testifies, that "thir work outgrew / The hands' dispatch of two" (202); but this is precisely what faith—and faith is the issue here—requires, an affirmation despite appearances. Adam's "with ease" may seem to fly in the face of the facts, but those facts themselves flow from a vision of things already assumed, and if that vision is changed, as Adam now urges, the facts will change too, and their work will be seen not as an irksome obligation, but as an opportunity to affirm their loyalty.[25] (Since the work is not needed by God, who could easily have instituted a Paradise that was self-maintaining, its only significance is, like the significance of the forbidden fruit, as a pledge of obedience.)

So far, so good. Up to this point, the conversation has gone much like the others between them, with Eve making an observation—as when she wonders why the stars continue to shine even when they two are asleep (IV, 657–658)—and Adam responding correctively—as when he reminds her they are not the only ones in the universe and that she should not "think, though men were none, / That Heav'n would want spectators" (IV, 675–676). But then things take a curious turn when out of the blue Adam says:

> But if much converse perhaps
> Thee satiate, to short absence I could yield.
> For solitude sometimes is best society,
> And short retirement urges sweet return.
> But other doubt possesses me, lest harm
> Befall thee sever'd from me; for thou know'st
> What hath been warn'd us, what malicious Foe
> Envying our happiness, and of his own
> Despairing, seeks to work us woe and shame. (IX, 247–255)

To say, as Nyquist does, that here "Adam introduces a new subject" (210) is to understate the case. What Adam does is say
something that has no relationship whatsoever to what preceded
it, and the question one asks is: Where did it come from? The answer (unsatisfying though it may be) is that it comes from nowhere, or rather that it comes from somewhere within Adam and
is projected out onto a landscape it immediately alters. The alteration is not small; for by imputing to Eve a motive "that nothing
in [her] remarks could have prompted,"[26] Adam produces—that
is, conceives—a picture or version of her that proceeds to take
over the conversation; and in the act of producing that version of
Eve, Adam also produces a new version of himself. If Eve now
becomes the kind of person who might grow weary of someone's company, Adam now becomes in his own self-conception (a
phrase literally intended) someone whom someone else might
grow weary of.

We recognize this moment and its psychology from our own
experience: Adam says, "Well, if you're tired of me . . . ," and Eve
is given the choice of either assuming the role he assigns her or
of adopting another. The role she adopts is precisely named in
line 271: "As one who loves, and some unkindness meets." The
"As" indicates both that she is striking a pose and that there are
other poses she might have struck. She might have responded,
"As one who deals gently with her lover's anxieties," or "As one
who for the sake of harmony lets something pass," or "As one
who is determined to put the best construction on things." To
some extent, her options are circumscribed by the situation instituted by Adam's "But if" (she has to say something, and no matter what she says—or even if she pointedly says nothing—it will
take on the significance the situation lends it), but she retains
some maneuverability nevertheless, and must bear responsibility for the direction she chooses to take. When she decides in
the direction of assuming (conceiving) "some unkindness," she

matches Adam's re-visionary gesture with one of her own; if he is going to imagine her as being incapable of sustaining a relationship ("if much converse . . . / Thee satiate"), she is going to imagine him as unkind—a particularly resonant word, since its literal meaning (not-kin) is a challenge to what has always been her understanding of the ties that bind them ("O thou for whom / and from whom I was formed").

It is this understanding that is even now being altered by their reciprocal thoughts. He thinks something about her, and she thinks something about him because he has thought something about her. I expected not to hear you say such things of me, she tells him, and wonders how he could harbor such thoughts, or rather misthoughts, of her: "Thoughts, which how found they harbor in thy breast, / *Adam*, misthought of her to thee so dear?" (288–289). In other words, I didn't think that you were the kind of person who would think that I was the kind of person implied by your thoughts. What is at stake is the conception each has of the other, and as they dispute (and impute) each other's thoughts, they generate ever new conceptions about which they can then dispute. Again the spiral is one that many of us will recognize: the aggrieved party asks, "What kind of person do you think I am?" and the other aggrieved party replies, "What kind of person do you think *I* am?"; and all the while they are making themselves into the kinds of persons they will be when the altercation ends; they are thinking themselves impaired.

Grossman remarks that at this point Adam and Eve have become "more interested in their effect upon one another than in the substance of their argument," and he faults them for a preoccupation with "a dramatically inflected sense of the self *staged* for the beloved other" (139). The criticism makes sense, however, only if the staging of the self in the theater of their relationship is a new action that can be contrasted negatively with an earlier and alternative state in which the self is not mediated but knows itself directly. But there is no such state. Adam and Eve have always known themselves relationally, as inferior to or superior to or equal to some other or others; and it follows, then, that their knowledge of the other is equally relational; self and other emerge together against the background (or stage setting) of differences already assumed. When Eve addresses Adam as "My Author and Disposer" (IV, 635) she sees before her not an unmediated Adam, but the Adam who is perspicuous for her given the sense she already has of their relationship. Nor has that sense always been in place; at one time she thought Adam (a construction that should be read literally) "less fair, / Less winning soft" than herself (IV, 478–479); and it is only after she has been persuaded to a new view of things in which "beauty is excell'd by manly grace / And wisdom, which alone is truly fair" (IV, 490–491) that she is able to think him superior, an act she cannot perform without thinking herself subservient. It is within this altered view of their respective identities and merits that she enters the present conversation, but this view—or stage setting or background understanding—is itself subject to alteration by the words she hears and the words she speaks. The choice the conversation (now becoming a quarrel) offers is never between authentic selves and staged selves, but between selves differently staged, differently composed of thoughts or conceivings in relation to which the world will be populated by different subjects for whom the field of action offers different possibilities.

The point is important because there is a tendency to view this scene as one in which a natural order is disrupted—in which, as Nyquist puts it, "a conversation . . . simply goes out of control" (209). To characterize the conversation in this way is to assume a stable center in relation to which one's interpretive activities could go astray; but if centers—points of reference, bottom lines, undoubted givens, grounds—are constituted by interpretive activities, if one's loyalties are not given but must be chosen, and, once chosen, maintained by nothing firmer than the firmness of faith ("On other surety none"), then control can never be lost, although at any moment it can always pass into another form. When Satan thinks himself impaired and conceives envy and disdain, his actions no longer flow from his faith in the benevolence and justice of God; they flow from a faith in something, and that something (the aspiration not to be a creature) centers his being (such as it is) no less than did the commitment from which he has slipped away. I am not saying that in Milton's world all commitments are equal or that there is nothing to choose between them; I'm saying only that all motions (physical and verbal) are informed by commitment, and going out of control is never an issue. What is an issue, continually, is the nature of the control at the behest of which agents act. In Augustinian terms, the question is: Whom do you love? What orientation drives your being, what unthinking (because already thought) sense of primary obligation impels you?

It is to this question that the Christ of *Paradise Regained* replies (even though no one has asked him) when he says, "Mee hung'ring more to do my Father's will" (II, 259), and it is the question Adam and Eve are answering at every moment of their lives. Rather than an instance of an exchange going out of control, the conversation is an illustration of how easy it is to come under the control of imperatives proffered not by any tempter but by the legitimate needs and desires all human beings feel. For a moment at least, Eve can think only of the imperative implied by a garden that grows luxurious by restraint: get this work done, no matter at what sacrifice. Adam corrects her, but even as he does so he is possessed by the fear of losing her affection, and in thrall to that fear he says things that are at bottom requests for reassurance ("You're not tired of me, are you?"). Eve, in her turn, misses the note of anxiety (hardly surprising, since she would have had no experience of a *vulnerable* Adam) and hears only a slight, which she then magnifies: You mean you think me incapable of fidelity unless you're there standing guard; you think that "my firm Faith and Love / Can . . . be shak'n or seduc't" (IX, 286–287). Adam is then in the position of having to back away from something he had not meant to say, and in his effort to make things right he says something even worse: Of course I don't doubt you—it's just that I don't want you to be in a position that might tempt a tempter, "For hee who tempts, though in vain, at least asperses / The tempted with dishonor foul, suppos'd / Not incorruptible of Faith" (296–298). The epic voice describes these words as "healing"—a derisive adjective, since what they are intended to heal or paper over is the breach opened up by his own sense of injured merit; and as is so often the case in such situations, the healing words only open the breach wider. What Adam urges here is a concern for appearances ("What will the neighbors think?"), and he flatly contradicts his earlier declaration that dishonor can come only from within: "Evil into the mind of God or Man / May come and go, so unapprov'd, and leave / No spot or blame behind" (V, 117–119). If Adam has forgotten or lost sight of this truth, Eve has not and she reminds him of it: if any foe "affronts us with his foul esteem / Of our integrity: his foul esteem / Sticks no dishonor on our Front, but turns / Foul on himself" (IX, 328–331).

This is an extraordinarily complicated moment, and one that should alert us to the inadequacy of any account of the scene that yields an easy moral. First of all, Eve is right; indeed, she seems to be recalling (anachronistically, except in the context of Milton's career) one of the central assertions in *Comus*: "Virtue may be assail'd, but never hurt, / . . . Yea even that which mischief meant most harm / Shall in the happy trial prove most glory. / But evil on itself shall back recoil." Unfortunately, however, she derives no benefit from being right, for at this juncture of the conversation her interest in the point is limited to its func-

tion in the thrust-and-parry pattern she and Adam are now enacting. That is, the substance of the insight, its implications for the
obligation they have to lead an obedient life, is subordinate at this
moment to the pleasure she must be feeling at having caught
Adam out, something she would not have thought possible when
she initiated the exchange. What happens here is typical of all domestic quarrels: even when one says something true, its truth
value is lost or obscured by the value it has in the quasi-military
maneuvers of the forensic battle; it becomes a debating point
rather than a point that refers beyond the debate to occasions of
life in relation to which it might prove useful. In this particular
quarrel, the overwhelming of substantive considerations by tactical ones is more than a generic feature of such encounters; it is a
replication in the *form* of the argument of the mistake now occurring in it. Eve says correctly that external assaults can bring
neither harm nor dishonor to a firmly settled will, but she forgets
the other side of this happy fact—that dishonor and harm can
have an internal location—and thereby overestimates the security
of their situation. That is, she makes external—merely tactical—
use of an insight which, if taken to heart, would alert her to the
danger within. She successfully counters Adam's thrust, but in
doing so sustains a (self-inflicted) wound to her understanding.

She of course has help. When the epic voice characterizes
Adam as "domestic" in his "care" (IX, 318), the rebuke is precise.
Like Eve, Adam has lost sight of what he should be caring about:
not the management of his domestic life, but the larger context
(of God's charge and their attendant obligations) in relation to
which domestic concerns acquire their significance. There is, to
be sure, a difference between the two: Eve wants to win, a desire
that is probably born the instant she realizes that winning is possible; Adam wants to heal ("To whom with healing words *Adam*
replied"), to repair the damage done by his having produced an
irrelevance rooted in anxiety. She scores points without being

able to apply the points to herself; he generates words designed to heal in one direction, with too little sense of the damage they might do in another. In their opposing and opposed ways, Adam and Eve combine to produce wanton growth, but neither can see it as wanton so long as its production seems justified, and indeed compelled, by the immediately felt challenges of the local ("domestic") context. Adam's overestimation of the harm that might attend the "attempt" of temptation "itself" (295) is not intended seriously; he merely says that on the way to his main concern, the defense of himself against the accusation that he has misjudged her: "misdeem not then, / If such affront I labor to avert" (301–302). That is, don't think of me as the kind of person who would think of you as the kind of person who is susceptible to temptation; I only want to spare you an unpleasant experience, and if it cannot be avoided, let me share it with you. The ploy fails, in part because Eve is herself no less involved in thinking about what thoughts are being thought about her, and she has no trouble at all thinking herself once again impaired: "but *Eve*, who thought / Less attribúted to her Faith sincere, / Thus her reply with accent sweet renew'd" (319–321). The "accent sweet" is the same with which she replied to Adam's initial response ("To whom the Virgin Majesty of *Eve*, / . . . With sweet austere composure" [270, 272]), and the repetition of "sweet" should alert us to a remarkable fact: no voice has been raised; even though the accusations and the recrimination have proliferated (again, like so many branches), the tone of the exchange remains what it was at the beginning, calm and mild, although one can perhaps imagine clenched teeth. Their composure has not been shaken; but in another sense of the word—settled condition of mind, a sense exemplified in the *OED* by this very line—their composure, their conception of themselves, has been unsettled many times, as each, in response to thoughts about thoughts the other is thought to be having, thinks himself or herself into ever new shapes of impairment, into jealousy, suspicion, injured merit, into every pose that can be struck by someone who says to someone else, "You just don't understand me."

Go

It is at this moment, when the plantlike life of the quarrel is tending to wild, that Adam performs an act no less spontaneous and unexpected (though in another direction) than the act of thinking that Eve might be tired of him. When Eve says (340–341) that Eden does not deserve the name if its state is precarious, Adam does not receive her words, as we by now might expect him to, in the context of his domestic anxieties. Instead, he detaches himself from that context and returns to the pedagogic posture he has so disastrously abandoned. He patiently explains in just what sense their situation is and is not precarious and in what direction the danger lies. Man, he declares, is "Secure from outward force; within himself / The danger lies, yet lies within his power: / Against his will he can receive no harm. / But God left free the Will" (348–351).

This reformulation of "Sufficient to have stood, though free to fall" is exactly right and to the point. The insecurity of Eden is its glory because it provides an arena of choice and testimony in which the free will can exercise itself for good or for ill. The question is: Why does Adam regain his cognitive and moral footing now, after so many false steps? There is no answer to this question, or rather the answer lies in the relationship of this very doctrine (of free will) to the unfolding of the conversation: while it is true that in the course of the quarrel Adam and Eve reconceive themselves in ways that have immediate consequences for what each then thinks to say, at any point it is possible for them to prune or lop the growth produced by their own unchecked thoughts—by thoughts that have tended, as they have here, to wild. Of course pruning requires a tool as well as an object-to-be-pruned. What is their tool? The answer is surprising but inevitable: the tool they employ, when they choose to employ it, is their thoughts. That is, thoughts are both the thing to be shaped and the instrument of shaping. Nor could it be otherwise in a world in which conceptions (thinkings about and therefore thinkings *into*) are grounded only in their own strength (faith) and not in some independently available standard or checkpoint in the empirical world. That is what "On other surety none" means: one's thoughts about the world are supported by other thoughts, which are in turn supported by other thoughts, and so on.

Not that there is no foundation to this structure of conceivings; it is just that the foundation is itself a conceiving, a first (mental) principle that stands on no other surety than the conviction (motion of the will) with which it is held and holds. For Satan, that conviction is of a God who could be petty and unfair—a conviction that generates, as we have seen, the entire world in which he (a newly conceived he) operates; for Adam, that conviction is precisely the opposite, and when he recalls himself to the task of self-gardening, he reaches for it immediately and wields it as his chief pruning tool: "O Woman, best are all things as the will / Of God ordain'd them" (343–344). That is, Adam begins (or begins again) by laying down the first constitutive thought one must employ in the construction of a world—the thought (again a matter entirely of faith, of willful assertion) of what kind of person God is; and then, with that thought in place, he can proceed to admit or lop other thoughts as they conform or do not conform to it. Growth is not stopped or even stunted; rather, it is managed in relation to a foundational growth that is itself rooted in soil no deeper than the soil it now provides.

It is important to note what this foundational growth, this thought that constitutes a world it then shapes and prunes, does *not* do: it does not tell Adam exactly what things are like, any more than Raphael ever tells him exactly what the heavens (apart from conceivings of them) are like. Rather, it tells him that whatever they are like, they are best because they have been put in place by a God who generates (because he is) the best. The reasoning goes: God is good, and therefore whatever seems to be distressing or puzzling must also be good, and it is our obligation to see things in ways that will assume—and, in assuming, bring into being for our viewing—that goodness. It is significant that as he recovers himself (a phrase I intend precisely: he recovers the self he had been losing in the quarrel), Adam returns to his best moment, the moment just before he unaccountably reconceives himself as the possible object of Eve's boredom. "Best are all things as the will / Of God ordain'd them" (343–344) is an expansion of "doubt not"; both are reminders of the central fact, which, if held to tenaciously as a support and prop, provides a perspective in relation to which all other facts acquire their proper—that is, God-oriented—shape. It is as if all the shapes, all the shoots, all the branches that had been allowed to flourish in the interim have suddenly been cut back, pruned, revealing once again an orderly and easily comprehended landscape.

Do not misunderstand me: the landscape thus revealed is not what remains *after* the undergrowth of thoughts and conceivings has been cleared away; for it, too, is the product of thinkings and conceivings, of the interpretive projection of deity, and, with deity, of the universe that follows from his having been projected in a certain way rather than in the other ways that are always possible. When Adam declares his firm (and constitutive) understanding of the structure of that universe, he is not doing something different from what he has been doing in the previous lines; he is doing the same thing—fashioning with his thoughts the world in which he chooses to live—but doing it in a direction from which he had for a time strayed and to which he returns with a stronger sense of it than he had at the beginning of the scene. I said earlier that the scene, rather than being anomalous with respect to other moments of Edenic life, is in fact just like them, albeit in a somewhat heightened form. It is a scene of opportunity, the opportunity to grow; and the realization of growth, should it occur, depends on the possibility of its opposite, the possibility that the occasion and materials for growth might be seized in ways that go wrong ("Sufficient to have grown, but free to wither or tend to wild"). In the end Adam does not go wrong, and the fact that for a time he seemed to be doing so makes the rightness he reachieves and reconceives a more positive fact than it would have been had an alternative outcome been impossible.

From this I draw the conclusion I already anticipated in my seventh point: the relationship of this episode to the Fall is entirely oblique; nothing follows from it in one direction or the other; the Fall is neither assured, nor rendered less likely; the matter is still poised, as it always has been, between the sufficiency to stand and the freedom (not all compromised by mistakes that stop short of the fatal one) to fall. This poise is nicely captured in the ambiguity, and indeed non sequitur, of Adam's concluding gesture. After articulating in the most full and precise manner possible the nature of their obligations and capacities, he says, "But if thou think, trial unsought may find / Us both securer than thus warn'd thou seem'st, / Go" (370–372). The first word of this unexpected (and in some ways incoherent) speech act should alert us to what is happening: the conversation is once again taking an unpredictable turn: Adam's success at negotiating the thickets of his own conceptually produced landscape does not insulate him against subsequent strikings out in directions tending to wild. Work in the garden, as I have already said, is endless; and just as no amount of it badly done leaves a situation that cannot be remedied (pruned), so no amount of it well done leaves a situation now free of hazard. Just what is hazarded or not hazarded here is a question I shall take up in a minute, but right now I want to emphasize the extent to which Adam's "But" does *not* follow from what precedes it; and since the "But" concludes the episode, insofar as the question of record has been whether Eve should separate from Adam and go, then *as* a conclusion it emerges *freely*, not in any sense determined by the moments leading up to it; moreover, if the conclusion of the episode is not determined by the episode, but floats free of it, then the episode is itself nondeterminative of that which is subsequent to *it*—that is, the Fall.

I am arguing, in short, for a reading of the episode in which it signifies its own causal irrelevance, and that reading is supported, I think, by the long-noted syntactic confusion of Adam's declaration: "But if thou think, trial unsought may find / Us both securer than thus warn'd thou seem'st, / Go." Almost any modern edition will gloss "securer" as "less heedfull" or "less on guard" or "too much relaxed." The reason is given by Richard Bentley: "*Securer* is a Word of ambiguous Meaning: it may signify *Safer;* or *Carelesser* . . . which Sense is here design'd."[27] Therefore, Bentley declares, the line should be amended to read *"May find Us both* LESS HEEDFUL, *than thus warn'd thou seem'st "* Bentley rejects "securer" as "safer" because it commits Adam to nonsense: "if you think you will be safer here than if you go out, then go out." But if that reading is nonsense, it is also more or less directed by the previous lines in which the word "secure" is used in exactly the sense Bentley wishes us to avoid. What this means is that the reader who settles upon "less on guard" as the proper interpretation of "securer" will do so after first assuming and then rejecting the interpretation "safer," just as Bentley does in the sequence of his note; and what *this* means is that the two readings will be consecutively present, and that therefore the climactic "Go" will be the consequent clause of two contradictory conditionals: if you think it will be safer, go; if you think it will be more dangerous, go. The point is one I have already made and is now made for me by the verse: resolutions in Eden are independent of what precedes them; the balance is always at midpoint, ready to tip over in whatever direction a free will happens to incline.

If this is so, the pressure usually put on this moment should be relaxed. It is not usually relaxed because commentators tend to follow (inadvisably, one would think) the lead of Adam and Eve, who at the end of book IX spend some time debating the wisdom and significance of this "Go." Eve asks, "why didst not thou the Head / Command me absolutely not to go . . . ? / . . . Hadst thou been firm and fixt in thy dissent, / Neither had I transgress'd, nor thou with mee" (1155–56, 1160–61). Adam replies, "what could I more? / I warn'd thee, I admonish'd thee . . . / . . . beyond this had been force, / And force upon free Will hath here no place" (1170–71, 1173–74). The intransigence of their respective positions prevents them (and insofar as we adopt their perspective, prevents us) from seeing the mistake they both make—the mistake of thinking that once Adam said "Go" the Fall is as good as done, and the unhappy choice is between disaster and the imposition of force. But as Dennis Danielson points out, had Adam said "Don't go" or even "I command you not to go," this would not have violated the freedom Eve could still have exercised simply by disobeying the command ("It is simply untrue that more than a mere warning would have forced Eve's obedience" [128]), just as she later freely disobeys the command of God. Danielson's argument should be extended further to the irrelevance of whatever Adam does or doesn't do at this juncture, for the sufficiency they have together each has alone and therefore the fact of their separation is not crucial. Had Eve stayed, either in response to Adam's "Don't go" or because she was satisfied with the points she had already won, they might possibly (and inexplicably) have decided to eat the apple in the very next instant. (Adam: "Well, what do you want to do now?" Eve: "I don't know; what do *you* want to do?" Adam: "I don't know; why don't we go and eat the apple?" Eve: OK.") On the other hand, had Adam said "Don't go" and had Eve (freely) decided to go anyway, she might possibly have rebuffed Satan's entreaties and told him, in effect, to get lost.

The fact that these alternative possibilities are not mentioned by either of them when they awaken to find "thir minds / How dark'n'd" (IX, 1053–54) should be seen not as an authoritative comment on the moment they now retroactively debate, but as one indication of what it means to have darkened minds. That is, the later moment should be read not as a gloss on the earlier, but as an illustration of the difference between them, which is the difference between prelapsarian and postlapsarian modes of being. It is as fallen creatures that they are unable to reason backward to the freedom of their action; this inability should not be projected back onto the period before they ordained it ("they themselves ordain'd their fall"), where it becomes the predetermined cause of its own effect. They are only *now* (at 1067ff.) not free, and at the mercy of the emotions that overwhelm them: "high Passions, Anger, Hate, / Mistrust, Suspicion, Discord, . . . shook sore / Thir inward State of Mind, calm Region once" (1123–25). Their "inward State of Mind" is no longer in their control; they cannot cultivate it, manage it, shape it. Instead, they are nothing more than the shapes imposed by forces that overtake them; they are now what they were not before: determined.

That is why book IX ends with these chilling lines: "Thus they in mutual accusation spent / The fruitless hours, but neither self-condemning, / And of thir vain contést appear'd no end" (1187–89). The contest has no end because the proliferation of its branches is unchecked by any central branch in relation to which momentary growths can be assessed and managed. That is what being fallen means: the tendency to wild is constitutive of a self that is unable to focus on, and therefore be fixed in relation to, a defining (of self and everything else) first principle. Once the assumption of a benevolent deity is removed by (or rather in) the act of disobeying him, the strength afforded the unfallen pair by that assumption is forfeit. The assumption can do work for them only so long as they willfully ("On other surety none") affirm it, and the penalty for disaffirming it includes the loss of the capacity to affirm it in the future—to have recourse to it, for example, in the effort to escape a vain contest. It is now, after the Fall, that such a contest has no end. Before, it could have ended as Adam (momentarily) ends it: by declaring, "Best are all things as the will / Of God ordain'd them." Now it will end only when God's "implanted Grace" (XI, 23) produces new "first fruits" (XI, 22)—as opposed to the "fruitless hours" of IX, 1188—and when Adam is once again capable of saying, as he says twice in the quarrel, "doubt not" (X, 1022).

Remembering Mercy

The action of doubting not—of remaining faithful—is what protects Adam and Eve from being overwhelmed by the fecundity of their own branching thoughts, although it is a protection that must be willfully invoked and therefore a protection that is within their power both to secure and to lose. Remaining faithful is not simply an act of ratification—of warranting one among several externally available accounts of the world; rather, the account (of a benevolent deity or of any other kind) and the world that follows from it will be the consequence of a positive exertion of the will, an exertion that is always possible but never automatic. It is an assertion that Eve is still able to make after the quarrel is over, as when, after acknowledging the apparent plausibility of the serpent's story and of the good effects of the forbidden fruit, she says, "But of this Tree we may not taste nor touch; / God so commanded" (IX, 651–652). Note the all-powerful "But"—the sign, here and elsewhere, of the capacity of the unfallen will *not* to be enmeshed in circumstances, even circumstances that issue from its own motions; a "But" that wins from the narrator a significant accolade: "thus *Eve* yet sinless" (659). It is when she is no longer sinless that Eve (like Adam) will not be able to say "But," will not be able to stop tending to wild, because having broken union (V, 612) she is nothing but wild, uncentered by the interpretive first principle she has pushed away. Indeed, the emblematic action that defines her new relationship to wild is the first action she performs after eating the apple: she worships a tree. Having abandoned the tool (the first, grounding, thought) with which she was once able to tame and cultivate her garden, she now surrenders wholly to it.

It is Adam, however, who provides the most dramatic illustration of what it means to disaffirm the first principle that centers being. He is speaking to Eve, preliminary to performing his part in the original sin, a performance to which he is already resolved before he speaks, either to her or to himself. It is significant that we never see Adam decide to fall, just as we never see Satan deciding but only the effects of his decision. It is quite different in the analogues, where Adam parades his indecision for many lines, saying things like "My spirit wavers in suspense"[28] and "I cannot tell now what I am to do."[29] Milton's Adam, in contrast, declares, "Certain my resolution is to Die" (*PL*, IX, 907), without ever allowing us to see the *ir*resolution that precedes his certainty. As a result, it becomes impossible to answer the most crucial question: When does Adam fall? Or, rather, we know when, but the knowledge doesn't help: Adam falls, or at least makes the fatal decision, somewhere in the middle of line 894:[30] "Speechless he stood and pale, till thus at length / First to himself he inward silence broke" (894–895). At some point in the interval before the "till" signals the beginning of what is already a set speech, Adam takes his stand, and what follows is the effect rather than the story of his resolution.

Predictably the effect is one of tending to wild, as Adam proliferates new accounts of their situation in the hope of finding one that can serve as a justification; and, again predictably, each account rests on a reconception of God, who appears alternately as someone who is a thrall to time ("But past who can recall, or done undo? / Not God Omnipotent" [IX, 926–927]), as someone who doesn't mean what he says (938ff.), as someone whose actions flow from an anticipation of what others will think of him (947ff.), and as someone whose primary concern is not to lose the labor he has expended in creation. It is after this characterization of the deity that Adam utters a half-line which is wonderfully ironic, at once on target and indicative of how far off the target his speculations now are: "Not well conceiv'd of God" (945). This is, of course, and has always been, precisely the issue: how to conceive of—interpretively establish—a conception of God in relation to which the facts and challenges of the world will be given a shape. On that conception everything depends ("On other surety none"), and the result of ill-conceiving God is here manifested at this moment, when Adam correctly identifies the primary requirement in the very act of failing to meet it. Rather than recovering a sense of God as, above all, a benevolent father (a sense he surrenders when he fails to attribute to God the quality of mercy and submits to what seems remediless), he conceives of God only in ways that will enable him to support his decision. Conceiving God becomes for him not so much a primary (i.e., first) obligation as it is a strategy in the service of faithless action.

The moment is made even more poignant by its similarity to the earlier moment when the Son also reasons from a conception of God, and reasons, at least superficially, in the same way Adam does—by assuming that God would not want to be conceived of in a certain way:

> wilt thou thyself
> Abolish thy Creation, and unmake,
> For him, what for thy glory thou has made?
> So should thy goodness and thy greatness both
> Be question'd and blasphem'd without defense. (III, 162–166)

The difference is that what the Son says springs from his conviction, announced at the beginning of his speech, that what characterizes God above all is his inclination to mercy; and it is from the assumption of this inclination—from this conceiving of God— that he comes to a conclusion about what God will, and indeed must, do. In effect the Son says to God, "I know you want to be merciful and would not wish to be thought of as one who would adhere only to the letter of the law, even a law that is your own." It is this accusation—that he is not merciful—that the Son imagines God pushing away. Adam, on the other hand, says nothing of God's mercy—it is precisely what he has forgotten—and imagines a God moved by shame and embarrassment, which, as he says, is "Not well conceiv'd of God" (IX, 945), but he says it in the context of a conceiving that is itself spectacularly not well.

It is not until line 1096 of the tenth book that Adam remembers mercy as a salient attribute of God, and significantly he does so just after the vain contest of the quarrel finally comes to an end. It is not Adam who ends it; in fact he seems determined to pick up where they left off when he rebuffs Eve's "Soft words" (865) by exclaiming, "But for thee / I had persisted happy, had not thy pride / And wand'ring vanity, when least was safe, / Rejected my forewarning" (873–876). And he continues, exactly as he had at the end of book IX, by generalizing Eve's behavior (as he sees it) to a prediction of the "infinite calamity" that women will bring "To Human life" (X, 907–908). Eve, however, declines the gambit; she refuses the role he has assigned her, the role she quite willingly played in the quarrel, the role of self-justifier, and instead she offers love—an offer that springs from nothing in the situation and certainly not from anything present in Adam. No less surprising than her gesture is the fact that it works. He responds, and, as he does, they reassume the positions characteristic of their unfallen state: she "seeking, / His counsel" (943–944), he offering it.

More important, in response to Eve's suggestion that they prevent future pain by performing death's office on themselves (1002), Adam returns to the way of thinking he had abandoned in the Fall: he reasons from, not toward, a conviction of God's nature: "doubt not but God / Hath wiselier arm'd his vengeful ire than so / To be forestall'd" (1022–24). Notice that Adam does not pretend to precise knowledge of God's capacities; he merely assumes that they exist and that they exceed man's predictive power: "I don't know what he'll do, but it will certainly not be limited by our sense of the possibilities." Moreover, Adam continues, whatever he does it will be consonant with the "mild / And gracious temper" (1046–47) he displayed while judging us. "Wee expected / Immediate dissolution" (1048–49), but that expectation proceeded from an incorrect conception of what God is like; if we will but remember (1046) his graciousness, and assume it as the basis of his future action, we will then know, with all the certainty that attends faith, that

> Undoubtedly he will relent and turn
> From his displeasure; in whose look serene,
> When angry most he seem'd and most severe,
> What else but favor, grace, and mercy shone? (1093–96)

The key word here is "seem'd": "He may have looked angry and severe, but we know, because we know what kind of person he is, that he really breathed grace and mercy." Rather than following from appearances, this "Undoubtedly" transforms appearances, and transforms them in the name of the attribute Adam failed to recall in his moment of trial: the attribute of mercy.

It is no coincidence that the word and the line return us to the conclusion of God's crucial speech in book III: "But Mercy first and last shall brightest shine" (134). It will shine, however, only if you believe in it—if by affirming God's nature, by conceiving well of him, you think yourself into a state of nonimpairment, and into a world everywhere informed by the grace that is answerable to your faith. Here in book III, God issues the challenge that all his creatures must meet: believe in me and in my mercy, for on that belief everything depends. When Adam and Eve, like Satan before them, fall, it is because they no longer believe—or, as God precisely says at the beginning of book X, man falls "believing lies / Against his Maker" (42–43). The opposite of believing lies is believing truths, with the emphasis on the positive act of believing rather than on the truths. That is, the truths in which you are asked to believe (the truth, for example, of God's mercy) do not present themselves for your approval; nor are they perspicuous in ways that serve mechanically to discredit alternatively proffered truths. Rather, the truths must be embraced *against* the available evidence, and that embrace is warranted only by its own self-sustaining strength. On other surety none.

Epilogue

The Temptation of History and Politics

I end with a report on a session held on my work at the 1993 meeting of the Modern Language Association. In that session I responded to papers delivered by three friendly but acute critics, Marshall Grossman, William Kolbrener, and Victoria Silver. I was moved by the occasion to reflect on the relationship between my work on Milton and my theoretical work, especially that part of it which constitutes a sustained critique of liberalism. My interlocutors were allied in their insistence that the two projects were really one. As they saw it, and I quickly agreed with them, whether the ostensible topic is Milton, Herbert, Skelton, stylistics, literary theory, legal theory, contract law, psychoanalysis, the philosophy of language, the history of institutions, free speech, affirmative action, interdisciplinary studies, historicism—the questions, the answers, and the obsessions are the same. The chief obsession is with the limits of understanding and the nature of consciousness; the chief thesis is that understanding is indeed limited, and that what limits it are the horizons—of experience, education, training—which set the boundaries of what can and cannot be done. In my story, agents are always and already situated, and efforts either to transcend that situation or understand its features down to the ground are always doomed to failure; and because they are doomed to failure, the situated agent is forever in the position of wanting to know more—of wanting to live not in the moment of quotidian urgency, but in the eternal moment of vision in the light of which temporal urgencies can be sorted out and assessed—and therefore in the position of being frustrated or disappointed, at least insofar as his desire to know and *be* more continues to be felt.

From this it follows, as Professor Kolbrener points out, that I set myself against liberal categories of thought and against liberalism in general; for it is the thesis—and dream—of liberalism that conclusions and actions can be justified "from scratch," that is, from a vantage point which is not already hostage to the presuppositions of some partisan agenda. It is the project of liberalism to step back from the beliefs and commitments (which it calls biases and prejudices) of particular, angled forms of life so that in the light of a perspective larger and more inclusive than any one of them, disinterested conclusions—conclusions that are faithful to the imperatives of Rationality—can be generated. It is my contention (and of course not mine alone) that no such stepping back is possible, and that for all intents and purposes we have no bases for action other than those that are immediately apparent to us. This is not so much a rejection of transcendence as a rejection of its unmediated availability, and it leaves me in an ambivalent but not paradoxical relationship to particularity and to history: the realm of the historical and the particular provides us with the light by which we see, but it cannot light the way to a realm beyond itself or even cast a light on its own foundations;

while the historical and the particular comprise the realm in which we live and move and have our being, we cannot help believing that there must be something else, and so we continue to seek it only to discover that whatever we find is one more version of the mortality we had hoped to transcend.

All of this is steadily seen by both Professor Silver and Professor Grossman, although they respond to it somewhat differently. In Professor Silver's account, I focus so obsessively on "the hopeless fact of our mortality" that my reader is "allowed no other relation except to death, no alteration of ideas except towards a kind of conceptual extinction," and she complains (ever so mildly) that "when every entry of experience or imagination we make is into one thought alone, we are bound to suffer a certain *ennui*. We might even stop reading." Professor Grossman also notes my invention of a reader who is "alternately deluded and frustrated," a reader perpetually in "search of himself" but who finds again and again that the "'truth' of the self is always elsewhere." This self, like the narrative flow in which it is immersed, can understand only "that the moment it desires and resists"—the moment when knowledge is complete and nonderivative—"does not occur."

This formulation helps us, I think, to see why "ennui" will not be the result of the self's repeated failure to discover either its origin or its full realization. First of all, the desire is self-renewing at the very moment of its disappointment. It is this self-renewing energy that drives the halting and circular narrative of Herbert's lyrics, in so many of which the speaker experiences a series of apparent triumphs ("Oh, my deare Saviour, Victorie!") only to find waiting for him the very condition—of distance, fallibility, incomprehension—he had thought to leave behind. "The Holdfast," with its desperately aggressive opening—"I threatened to observe the strict decree / Of my deare God with all my power and might"—is only the most obvious enactment of a drama in which every withdrawal from a prideful claim reconstitutes it on the other side of a gesture.

But if the desire for full and total knowledge, knowledge that knows no limitation of time or place, is thus frustrated, that frustration is itself welcomed, is itself *desired,* because by marking one more failure to transcend mortality, it reopens the space in which the pleasures of mortality—the pleasures of lament, lack, and utterance—can be enjoyed. In short, the desire—for absorption into a vision not bounded by time and death—and the resistance to it exist in a symbiotic relationship, each giving life and meaning to the other. No ennui here, no stopping of reading, but *endless* reading (and writing) made necessary and possible by an absence that, like the Fall—it *is* the Fall—can be experienced as fortunate.

What is fortunate about the Fall, about not being in the optimum place, is that there is somewhere for you to go and something for you to do—you can lament the fact that you haven't gotten there yet and may never get there at all. In the *Areopagitica,* the sad friends of Truth have the task of gathering up her scattered limbs, but, says Milton, "We have not found them all, nor shall ever do, till her Master's second coming." It sounds discouraging and even despairing, but in fact it is full of hope—hope that the task will never be accomplished and that therefore the efforts to accomplish it will never cease. Thus, what Professor Silver calls the "hopeless fact of our mortality" generates hope and gives time and history a reason for unfolding; and so much the better if that reason—we are not where we want to be—will never be removed.

It is the threat of that removal, the threat of having one's wishes and prayers actually fulfilled, that occasions the most anxious moments in Milton's poetry. Recall my discussion in Chapter 8 of the invocation to book VII of *Paradise Lost,* when the poet

at once petitions his muse and pushes her away in the fear that
were she to grant him his professed desire—to join with her in
celestial song and soar above the Olympian hill—his voice would
no longer sound, even in his own ears. That is why he takes comfort in the fact that he is now "Standing on Earth, not rapt above
the Pole," for it is on earth, composed of the dust to which he
must return, that he is "More safe" and can "Sing with mortal
voice" (23–24). More safe from what? From the success that is
also a dis-appearance, the success of being rapt, where "rapt"
means not only transported but taken out of oneself, carried
away by force, ravished and even raped in the sense of having
one's dignity violated in a way that makes one feel like nothing.

This is the dark side of the vision to which Milton continually
returns in his work, the vision of a heavenly choir in which singers are known not individually but as members of a corporate
ensemble—the body of Christ or the great chorus of angelic
praisers who sing a single note unceasingly and in unison, in
"perfect Diapason," in complete, nonindividuating harmony. In
relation to this vision, the sign of evil is to have an I-dentity, a separate existence, a voice that can be picked out in the crowd, a
voice that stands out, a *mortal* voice. A mortal voice is the voice
of a creature in exile; it is the voice of incompleteness, a voice
that in its every utterance declares its distance from a perfection
whose achievement (exactly the wrong word) would be its silencing. A mortal voice lives in time—what Donne calls a short parenthesis in eternity; and in that parenthesis, that digression created by the Satanic act of breaking union, a mortal voice can
have a story, a narrative, a plot; it can enjoy successes and failures;
it can be noted and marked; it can have a career, complete with
beginning and middle and end. It can say "*I* sing."

You cannot say "*I* sing" and mean it at the same time that you
are celebrating a monist universe, a universe where God is "All in
All"; or, to put the matter from the other direction, you cannot

celebrate a monist universe and mean it at the same time that you say "I sing." Milton notoriously tries to have it both ways, and as a result (and the entire history of Milton criticism is a testimony to this) the ways strain against each other, as the official morality of the poem—a morality pronounced and obviously endorsed by the poet—stigmatizes and resists the energies—also created by the poet and expressive of something within him—that would escape it. That is why Professor Silver's wonderful description of my textual readings is so apt a description of Milton's poem: "Picture Manhattan in gridlock: some sort of meaning is struggling to get out, to issue forth, even as all perceptible movement grinds to a halt." Picture a poem, a world, in which meaning is univocal and wholly contained in a master spirit that rolls through all things, and picture agents—men, women, angels—to whom freedom has been granted so that they can ceaselessly acknowledge their radical dependence.

Such a world and such agents can indeed be heterogeneous and "multiform"—two words Professor Kolbrener plucks from the *De Doctrina;* but the heterogeneity is only superficial, and if it is regarded, or regards itself, as more than that, as essential or constitutive, it becomes the vehicle of idolatry. If there is any section of *Paradise Lost* that appears to give heterogeneity—difference—its due, it is book VII, but the fecundity it displays in astonishing abundance is repeatedly reined in with a brutality that can only be intentional. "Be fruitful and multiply," says the creator to his creatures, "fill the earth"; and for a moment the expansiveness of the gesture fills the imagination, until the next two words of the divine instruction—characteristically withheld until the beginning of another line—tell the real story: "subdue it." That is, don't let anything get out of hand, out of my hand; and in the book's closing lines, the angels sing the same song: he who would "from thee withdraw" or seek to "lessen thee"—make you less than everything—"against his purpose serves / To manifest the more thy might" (612, 614–615). Against his purpose because the creature can have no purpose that is his own; there is only one purpose in a uni-verse and it is proclaimed with a vengeance in the command given at line 630: "multiply a Race of Worshippers." That is, proliferate difference, multiformedness, but only if every difference, every form, is more of the same.

Now if the plurality of forms—the face of difference—is only a surface phenomenon produced by eyes that fail to see the essential unity of all things, then the variety of events, that difference which emerges in and as time, is no less illusory; for given the radical homogeneity of a God-centered universe, the urgency of any one moment must be like—no, must be exactly the same as—the urgency of any other. It is gridlock once again, with the meaning that is struggling to get out the meaning of time as we are accustomed to think of it as post-Enlightenment liberals. Indeed, within the assumptions of liberalism time and meaning are mutually constitutive. Since what is significant is not known in advance, the choices we make and the actions we take, or fail to take, matter in the strongest sense: they create the world in which we will thereafter face other choices, in relation to which we will have to take other actions. But within the assumptions of Milton's theology, there is only one choice—to be or not to be allied with divinity—because there is only one meaning, and what might appear to be a succession of different situations is in fact the same situation wearing the thin disguise of temporal variation. There is vicissitude, to be sure, yet it is not linear and consequential but circular and finally cosmetic. There is quite literally nowhere to go and only one thing to do, and the essential truth about things will not be altered by either your success or your failure in doing it. It is this that puzzles the Satan of *Paradise Regained* when he asks Jesus, "What dost thou in this World?" and receives no answer, although the answer has been given before, in isolation from any particular person or circumstance: "Mee hung'ring more to do my Father's will" (II, 259). That is, "I am always doing, or trying to do and trying to be, the same thing."

As Professor Kolbrener sees, this reduction of the field of action to one action endlessly and repeatedly performed casts an odd light on politics, but it is not quite right to say, as he does, that I construct "a Milton for whom any particular actions—especially political interventions—are imagined to be fruitless"; nor is it the case, as Professor Silver asserts, that in my hands the seventeenth century becomes "a quietist's universe." It is just that the fruits grow not in the soil of human history, but, as the Attendant Spirit says in *Comus*, "in another Country," an *interior* country in whose abstract landscape one is given the opportunity over and over again to affirm or disaffirm one's loyalty.

That is the real form of action and the supreme form of politics, in which every moment brings the prospect of the greatest reward—"Well done, good and faithful servant"—and the greatest of dangers—"him . . . who me disobeys, breaks union, and that day . . . falls into utter darkness." It need hardly be said that Milton is continually performing political actions, and he certainly hopes that they will have the effects he desires; nevertheless, those effects are not what he aims at. He may or may not succeed in getting the licensing act repealed, but the discourse that attempts it "will be a certain testimony, if not a trophy." He may or may not succeed in removing the burden of prelacy from the church, but if he did not try, "what stories I should hear within myself, all my life after, of discourage and reproach." He may or may not succeed in removing the corruption of hirelings, but "if I be not heard or believed, the event will bear me witness to have spoken truth: and I in the meanwhile have borne my witness, not out of season, to the church and to my countrey." He may or may not succeed in preventing the Restoration—he knows that he will not—but "thus much I should perhaps have said though I were sure I should have spoken only to trees and stones, and had none to cry to, but with the Prophet, *O earth, earth, earth!* to tell the very soil itself what her perverse inhabitants are deaf to."

This is not quietism; it is faith, faith in an order whose springs are not always evident in the working of the visible world, an order whose stability and perdurability are radically independent of the patterns of cause and effect that seem so conclusive in the visible world. That is why history is not determinative in Milton's universe. What is important on any occasion is not how things have turned out (as a historian might assess it) but whether or not one's inner loyalties have been maintained and strengthened. Success—the fruit—is measured not by the battles you won or the poems you have written, but by the strength of your testimony, by the witness you give to what you believe. The perspective of history, of events as they unfold in linear time, is not a master code but still another temptation—the temptation of framing important issues in the context of accidental and fleeting configurations, the temptation of thinking that empirical evidence—eyewitness—can point one to a truth that always exceeds it.

It is this temptation that has overtaken Milton criticism in the form of the various historicisms noted by Professor Grossman, historicisms that, as he says, "rely on models of causality in situating a moment in which causality is . . . superseded." I said earlier that while historical knowledge is the only kind of knowledge we can have in this vale of tears, history cannot answer questions (How did it all start? What does it all mean? Where is it all going?) that assume a perspective either before it or after it. History cannot tell us what its own meanings *finally* mean. Indeed, historicism is antihistorical when it presents itself as a superior interpretive key. The great moments in life and in Milton's poetry simply do not yield their meaning to historical analysis; again as Grossman says, they "resist historicization, . . . remain excessive, uncaused yet decisive." Historical analysis is what the Chorus and

Manoa and, for a time, Samson try to provide so as to have both a perspective on the springs of past actions and a blueprint for future ones, but in the end the hero acts in a way that has nothing to do with the calculation of empirical likelihoods, and everything to do with his determination somehow to link up his will with the will of a God who has removed his ways from human sense. History is what the speaker of *Lycidas* tries to give to the event that refuses to be intelligible. History and historical analysis of various kinds are what Satan offers the Son, only to hear him reject their guidance in favor of an imperative (doing the Father's will) that is identified with no particular action but that can find its correlative in any action, including the actions of smiting Sisera through the temples, cutting off the head of a king, or refusing the request to feed some hungry people. History and historical analysis are what Adam and Eve succumb to in their different ways, she when the example of the snake's historical transformation is allowed to outweigh the divine prohibition (the fact that the example is a false one is irrelevant: as the epic voice says at the beginning of book X, they were to have obeyed, "whoever tempted"); he when the apparent unavailability of a prudent cause of action—he looks at the field of historical experience and it fails him, leaves him "remediless"—leads him to an action that he knows to be wrong. History is what Satan desires when he desires to break union and exchange an existence fully saturated with one master meaning for an existence in which meaning is waiting to be produced by agents who wrest it from contingency.

In each of these cases action takes a historical form in a material landscape, but the pressure to which the actor responds (or fails to respond) issues from an obligation that is outside or above history even when its expression is *in* history. That is why Kolbrener is on the mark when he says (in another place) that although Milton is continually elaborating a political program (especially in his prose tracts), he at the same time manifests "a

profound distrust of politics"[1]—that is, a distrust of politics offered either as an alternative to the desire to obey God's will or as
the necessary vehicle of the realization of that will. This means
not that Milton retires from politics or counsels others to do the
same, but that he participates in politics without believing in it either as the source of guidance or the determinant of his salvation; he commits himself to political goals as they emerge in moments of historical choice, but, as Kolbrener insists, he does not
regard those goals "as ends *in themselves*," because if he were to
do so he would be falling into "an idolatry of reason and the
state" (39). Milton is not indifferent to politics, but he is, finally,
indifferent to *"mere* politics" (39), to politics that seeks its end (in
both senses) in itself, a politics that regards itself or is regarded as
"self-begot, self-raised."

The point has been made with particular force and brilliance
by Thomas Luxon, who observes that for a Protestant of Milton's
temper, "whatever is 'historically real' has been disqualified from
being really (one force of the term 'spiritual') real."[2] The project
of typology, Luxon explains, insists at once on the historicity of
typological figures (Old Testament Jews, New Testament actors)
and on their status as figures that "mean or 'point to' something
'more real'" (42); and by so insisting, by refusing to allow any figure to possess its own meaning ("a poor thing but mine own"),
typology has the effect of "radically emptying out the category
of the historically real" (43). That is to say, the so-called historically real is real only if its claim to be complete and to have its
own meaning—its own reality—is seen through (a phrase that
should be taken literally) and recognized as a temptation. "Even
history's much vaunted concreteness, its definitiveness and alleged fullness, . . . do not save it from being rendered by the
'figural view of reality' as actually inactual, really unreal, and
definitively indefinite—fully unfulfilled and unfulfilling signs that,
unless grounded in a radically other reality, a reality one is both

forbidden and obliged to conceptualize, mean and are nothing at all" (52). This is exactly what I meant when I declared at the beginning of this book that everything that many readers find interesting in Milton's work—crises, conflicts, competing values, once-and-for-all dramatic moments—proceeds from error and is finally unreal. Error—deviation from the true path, departure from the saving center—*is* history, and its attractions are therefore as "natural" as they are fatal to entry into true life. What true life requires is "a new self, a self reborn outside of history, or more precisely, a self that is born by virtue of being parted from history, conceived and carried in the 'fleshly' womb of history's non-being, and, following the 'travail' . . . of worldly gestation, new-born into ahistorical reality" (54). It is not a requirement that anyone can fulfill; but what one can do (and the accents here are Augustine's) is continue to be carried within the vehicles of time, plot, history, politics, projects, objects, discourses, but in a way that uses them—figuralizes them—rather than enjoys them for their own sake.

This is what Milton does both *in* his poetry and prose and *with* his poetry and prose, which are themselves, after all, material forms of the kind that embody the ever-present danger of mistaking the historically real for the really real. The danger, Milton believes, must be engaged and even courted if it is to be (even temporarily) overcome; the forms that invite us to identify with their limitedness must be re-seen as signs of what they cannot contain. Nothing is to be rejected as a means; everything (except the really real) is to be rejected as an end. As Joan Bennett finely says, "When Milton's readers understand with his Christ that they are not at all of this world, then once again, as in Eden, . . . everything in the world is at the same time fully dispensable and fully available for their use."[3] But when do readers arrive at this understanding and thus enter into a healthy relationship with that which, if allowed an independent existence, would make them sick unto death? The answer is that nothing guarantees it, and that everything in the poetry provides the material and the occasion for going down another, disastrous, path. (If virtue and sin are the alternatives, "the matter of them both is the same.") The discipline is so severe that any one of us, including Milton and even the Son of God, is only half a beat away from relaxing it and so losing Paradise again.

INTRODUCTION

1. Sigmund Freud, *Beyond the Pleasure Principle,* ed. and trans. J. Strachey (New York, 1961), pp. 31–32.

2. *Paradise Lost,* book VII, lines 611–612, in *John Milton: Complete Poems and Major Prose,* ed. M. Y. Hughes (New York, 1957). Subsequent references to *Paradise Lost* will be given in the text and abbreviated *PL.*

3. *Comus,* line 596, ibid.

4. *Nativity Ode,* line 244, ibid.

5. "At a Solemn Music," lines 25–28, ibid.

6. *Paradise Regained,* book IV, line 320, ibid. Subsequent references will be given in the text and abbreviated *PR.*

7. Lucy Newlyn, *Paradise Lost and the Romantic Reader* (Oxford, 1993), p. 88.

8. David Mikics, *The Limits of Moralizing* (London, 1995) p. 55.

9. See on this point Kathleen Swaim, "Myself a True Poem," *Milton Studies,* 38 (2000). "The logocentric truth which Milton and his Protestant/Puritan culture celebrated was in fact essentially unstable, its fluidity always encouraging and rewarding the individual's growth, always looking toward an ultimate fulfillment—that moment in (or at the end of) time . . . when 'God shall be All in All' ([*PL*] 3.341)" (91). Individual growth has its fulfillment in absorption into Another, and as a result "the consciousness becomes divided, split between a projection of an unlimited deity in which it participates and a self-conscious realization of its own limitation, and therefore a realization that it should aspire to abandon a lesser self in favor of one that more fully partakes of the deity it expansively apprehends" (69).

10. William B. Hunter, *Visitation Unimplor'd: Milton and the Authorship of "De Doctrina Christiana"* (Pittsburgh, 1998).

11. Gordon Campbell, Thomas N. Corns, John K. Hale, David I. Holmes,

and Fiona J. Tweedie, "The Provenance of *De Doctrina Christiana*," *Milton Quarterly*, 31, no. 3 (1997): 67–117.

12. Stephen B. Dobranski and John P. Rumrich, eds., *Milton and Heresy* (Cambridge, 1998), p. 8.

13. Stephen Fallon, "Elect above the Rest: Theology and Self-Representation in Milton," ibid., p. 97.

1. HOW MILTON WORKS

1. *Comus,* lines 629–635, in *John Milton: Complete Poems and Major Prose,* ed. M. Y. Hughes (New York, 1957).

2. Wallace Stevens, "The Idea of Order at Key West," lines 42–43.

3. *Paradise Lost,* book II, lines 272–273, in *John Milton: Complete Poems and Major Prose.*

4. George Herbert, "Easter Wings," line 19.

5. *Paradise Regained,* book IV, lines 288–290, ibid.

6. *Lycidas,* line 91, ibid.

7. *Nativity Ode,* line 244, ibid.

8. For an authoritative account of the heroism of service, see Boyd Berry, *Process of Speech: Puritan Religious Writing and Paradise Lost* (Baltimore, 1976), pp. 170–190. As Berry observes, "The faithfull angels . . . constantly rejoice in their limited situation" (184).

9. See the discussion of the Reformation's conflating of saying, doing, believing, and seeing in Georgia Christopher, *Milton and the Science of the Saints* (Princeton, 1982): "To them, 'seeing' is verbal understanding, a grasping and taking to heart of a divine locution. Indeed, 'seeing' is believing some very definite divine words, for Luther maintained that in doctrine we see the face of God" (9); "Contemplation thus verbally defined became the hallmark of the active life" (10). Thomas Luxon, *Literal Figures: Puritan Allegory and the Reformation Crisis in Representation* (Chicago, 1995), p. 66, quotes a passage from Luther that seems particularly apt and to my point: "For heavenly things cannot be shown as present; they can only be proclaimed by the word. Therefore he [the Psalmist] does not say, 'I see, therefore I show it as a work,' but, 'I believe, and therefore I speak.' But those who boast of their own goods, and glory in something present—they do not have faith of those things, but sight. But we believe, and thus cannot show it by a work. That is why we only speak and bear witness. For faith is the reason why we cannot do other than to show our goods by the word, since faith rests in what does not appear, and such things cannot be taught, shown, and pointed to."

10. *An Apology against a Pamphlet*, in *Complete Prose Works of John Milton*, vol. 1, ed. D. M. Wolfe (New Haven, 1953), p. 890.

11. Ibid., p. 941.

12. Kenneth Gross is absolutely on target when he locates Satan's appeal not in his heroism but in his dramatization of the "myth of the self." Satan offers us a "persuasive illusion of what a self or a character might be." "It is not that I like Satan's voice, mind, or attitude better than those of other characters in the poem, but rather that Satan, at times, seems to be the only character *with* a voice, mind, and attitude." That is, Satan is the only character (at least before Adam and Eve fall) who is divided from the source of being and therefore in the grip of bottomless self-consciousness. This is his error and, as Gross says, his "lure." "Satan is an image of the mind in its dividedness from both itself and others, in its illusions of inwardness and power." Kenneth Gross, "Milton and the Romantic Satan," in M. Nyquist and M. W. Ferguson, eds., *Re-Membering Milton* (New York, 1987), p. 337.

13. John Reichert, *Milton's Wisdom: Nature and Scripture in Paradise Lost* (Ann Arbor, Mich., 1992), p. 158. James Shulman, in *The Pale Cast of Thought* (Newark, Delaware, 1998), similarly evades the logic and rigor of Milton's moral thought by romanticizing Adam's choice and making it an instance of a "complex morality at a complex moment" (132). Shulman sees Adam's valuing of "the created object"—that is, Eve—as a testimony "to the two impulses of the poem: toward doctrinal security and toward aesthetic appreciation" (141). But in Milton's view the second impulse is the impulse to idolatry—the detaching of the creature from the creator for the purpose of admiring it—and he unequivocally condemns it. Like Reichert, Shulman celebrates complexity, but at the price of losing all touch with the center and strength of Milton's vision.

14. Augustine, *On Christian Doctrine*, trans. D. W. Robertson (New York, 1958), p. 9.

15. I should acknowledge that this picture of Milton and his world is one that some critics reject and find repellent. See, for example, Lucy Newlyn, *Paradise Lost and the Romantic Reader* (Oxford, 1993), who complains that readings like mine "suggest . . . a Milton who subjugates fictive play to didactic tenor, manipulating intertextual reference so as to underline the powerful and abiding coherence of Puritan ideology" (71). That about gets it right.

16. On the centrality of the notion of secrecy to Milton's work, see Georgia Christopher, *Milton and the Science of the Saints* (Princeton, 1982), pp. 199–224. See also Sanford Budick, *The Dividing Muse* (New Haven, 1985), p. 124:

"The key terms of the poem are by and large kept inaccessible to definition. . . . Not only do *begin* and *end, act* and *wait,* and so forth, not have their usual meanings, but the poet repeatedly suggests that they remain withdrawn from referentiality as we know it."

17. *Christian Doctrine,* in *Complete Prose Works of John Milton,* vol. 6, ed. M. Kelley, trans. J. Carey (New Haven, 1973), p. 587.

18. *Tetrachordon,* in *Complete Prose Works of John Milton,* vol. 2, ed. E. Sirluck (New Haven, 1959), p. 637.

19. "Januarye," line 37, in *Edmund Spenser: The Shorter Poems,* ed. Richard A. McCabe (New York, 1999).

20. P. Sacks, *The English Elegy* (Baltimore, 1985), p. 98.

21. For a brilliant book-length discussion of the relationship between writing, violence, and the emergence/expression of the supposedly autonomous self, see Jonathan Goldberg, *Writing Matter: From the Hands of the English Renaissance* (Stanford, 1990). Goldberg argues persuasively that the discipline taught in Elizabethan handwriting manuals is the location of a struggle between the individual voice desiring to be itself and the forms that precede it. The struggle, then, is for mastery. A basic instruction in the manuals was "make a pen fitt for your hand," but as Goldberg points out, fitness for the hand is an ambiguous expression: "Which hand, the one that writes or the hand that is written, the handwriting? As the hand writing fits the handwriting, the violence against the quill necessary to make a pen fit for the hand displaces the violence that the pen wields, subjecting the hand to its demands" (82). "As the writing masters give instructions on how to turn the bird's feather into a tool of writing, their language continues to register the violence of the tool against the hand. It implicates, as I have suggested, the subordination of the writer's hand to his tool" (83). My argument in this chapter and Chapter 7 is that *Lycidas* is similarly a struggle between the first person voice's desire to be distinct and the appropriative force of the tradition in which he writes and which finally writes him.

22. As Joan Bennett observes, Satan in book IV "has come to the end of his own ability to interpret the phenomenon he is addressing; his own vast learning has left him ignorant. He cannot conceive the sense in which Christ will assume the throne of David" (*Reviving Liberty* [Cambridge, Mass., 1989], p. 197). Indeed, what Satan is ignorant of is the one truth (of God's preeminence and goodness) whose denial now constitutes him and limits his ability to conceive anything but error.

23. On Milton and kenosis, see Barbara Lewalski, *Milton's Brief Epic: The Genre, Meaning, and Art of Paradise Regained* (Providence, R.I., 1966), pp. 149–150.

24. *Samson Agonistes*, line 1382, in *John Milton: Complete Poems and Major Prose*.

25. *Areopagitica*, in *The Prose of John Milton*, ed. J. M. Patrick et al. (New York, 1967), p. 316.

26. On this point, see John Tanner, *Anxiety in Eden* (New York, 1992), p. 141: "The thought of God, inwardly grasped, undercuts every demonic evasion and denial."

27. William Kolbrener, *Milton's Warring Angels* (Cambridge, 1997), p. 152.

28. *Paradise Lost*, ed. Roy Flannagan (New York, 1993), p. 368, n. 146.

29. Linda Gregerson, *The Reformation of the Subject* (Cambridge, 1995), p. 227.

30. "Satan's ironic triumph over 'plain speech' leaves him ultimately subject to a power [decentered language] he had thought was his to command" (Gregerson, *The Reformation of the Subject*, p. 227, n. 27).

31. Cf. Kolbrener, *Milton's Warring Angels*, p. 156, n. 25: "The materiality of Satanic narrative, always asserting its own autonomy, . . . becomes a means for competing with God's 'Sentence.'" See also Stephen M. Fallon, *Milton among the Philosophers* (Ithaca, 1991), pp. 227–228: "Book 6 chronicles the devils' vain attempts to find ever-more powerful material weapons. . . . Having divorced interior from exterior, the devils recognize only a vitiated exterior. The 'cause' of the angels' might is 'hidden' from the devils because it is not a material cause accessible to empirical analysis: they refuse to see that true strength and wisdom cannot be sundered."

32. On the relationship between style, stylus, and the inscription of meaning, see Goldberg, *Writing Matters*, passim.

33. Cf. Fallon, *Milton among the Philosophers*, pp. 209–210: "In *Paradise Lost* evil, and thus downward ontological movement, is associated with leaking, excretion and purging. . . . Those who obey are sublimated and rarefied. Those who disobey are purged and excreted."

34. As has often been remarked, Milton pours himself into his characters, who are never distinct from him, even though different ones will have been endowed with different aspects of his personality. Annabel Patterson declares that every reader "runs up against the irreducible and insistent presence of Milton the author" (*John Milton* [London, 1992], p. 7). And Stephen Fallon notes that "if any author is in his or her texts, Milton is in his" ("The Spur of

Self-Concernment: Milton in His Divorce Tracts," *Milton Studies*, 38 [2000]: 120). Such statements do not contradict the postmodern dictum that the self is not a stable entity but is always being socially constructed; it's just that the self continually being constructed in Milton's life and works is always the same one.

2. MILTON'S AESTHETIC OF TESTIMONY

1. *An Apology against a Pamphlet*, in *Complete Prose Works of John Milton*, vol. 1, ed. D. M. Wolfe (New Haven, 1953), p. 922.

2. Cicero, *Rhetorica ad Herennium*, trans. H. Caplan (Cambridge, Mass., 1954), II, VI, 10, p. 175.

3. See Quintilian, *Institutio Oratoria*, trans. H. E. Butler (Cambridge, Mass., 1959–1963), vol. 1 (III, VII, 12–16), pp. 469, 471.

4. On this point, see also Cicero, *De Inventione*, trans. H. M. Hubbel (Cambridge, Mass., 1960), II, ix, p. 191.

5. *Rhetoric*, I, 9, 1367b, in *The Works of Aristotle*, ed. W. D. Ross (Oxford, 1946), vol. 11.

6. *The Reason of Church Government*, in *John Milton: Complete Poems and Major Prose*, ed. M. Y. Hughes (New York, 1957), p. 660.

7. George Puttenham, *The Arte of English Poesie* (London, 1589; facsimile reproduction, Kent State University Press, c. 1970), p. 195.

8. Augustine, *On Christian Doctrine*, trans. D. W. Robertson (New York, 1958).

9. *Nativity Ode*, stanza 27, line 244, in *John Milton: Complete Poems and Major Prose*.

10. Kathleen Swaim comments: "The transaction negotiates the question of which comes first, the truth or the 'I,' 'mine own person' or incorporate membership, . . . the owning or disowning of the self, with *own* here signaling both the verb of possession and a pronoun intensifier" ("Myself a True Poem," *Milton Studies*, 38 [2000]: 69). For a different view of the relation between reason and judgment in Milton's work, see Richard Strier, "Milton's Fetters," *Milton Studies*, 38 (2000): 169–197. Strier argues against a Milton who, like Luther, has "a conception of goodness as involving nonratiocinative spontaneity" (173). This is of course the Milton I describe in the pages of this book.

11. *Christian Doctrine*, in *Complete Prose Works of John Milton*, vol. 6, ed. M. Kelley, trans. J. Carey (New Haven, 1973), p. 471.

12. *The Reason of Church Government*, in *Complete Prose Works of John Milton*, vol. 1, p. 802.

13. *Areopagitica*, in *Complete Prose Works of John Milton*, vol. 2, ed. E. Sirluck (New Haven, 1959), p. 467.

14. *Of Reformation*, in *Complete Prose Works of John Milton*, vol. 1, ed. D. M. Wolfe (New Haven, 1953), p. 556.

15. *Reason of Church Government*, p. 803.

16. *The Readie and Easie Way*, in *Complete Prose Works of John Milton*, vol. 7, ed. R. W. Ayers (New Haven, 1980), p. 550.

17. *The Likeliest Means*, in *The Prose of John Milton*, ed. J. M. Patrick et al. (New York, 1967), p. 514.

18. *Christian Doctrine*, ibid., p. 638.

19. *Comus*, lines 1–3, 5–6, in *John Milton: Complete Poems and Major Prose*.

20. *Lycidas*, line 6, ibid.

21. *Complete Prose Works of John Milton*, vol. 1, p. 16.

22. *Reason of Church Government*, ibid., p. 822.

23. *Paradise Lost*, book V, lines 623–625, in *John Milton: Complete Poems and Major Prose*.

24. *Modest Confutation* (1642), p. 1.

25. For an excellent discussion of Milton's antinomianism, see Norman Burns, "Milton's Antinomianism and Samson's," *Milton Studies*, 33 (1997): 27–46.

26. J. K. Hale's "Milton and the Rationale of Insulting" (in S. B. Dobranski and J. P. Rumrich, eds., *Milton and Heresy* [Cambridge, 1998]), traces the Aristotellan and humaniot tradition of "Fffective insult" (163) and explains Milton's invective as examples of the "power and joy" humanists experienced when writing and reading exuberant, robust wit. While Hale is certainly right to find Milton's sources in this tradition, he misses the extent to which Milton *moralizes* it and turns the display of rhetorical virtuosity into an ethical testimony. Like the Modest Confuter, Hale praises Milton for a mere skill rather than for the vision that informs and justifies it.

27. *Tetrachordon*, in *Complete Prose Works of John Milton*, vol. 2, p. 637.

3. Problem Solving in Comus

1. B. A. Rajan, "*Comus*: The Inglorious Likeness," *University of Toronto Quarterly*, 37, no. 2 (1968): 121.

2. *Comus*, line 709, in *John Milton: Complete Poems and Major Prose*, ed. M. Y. Hughes (New York, 1957).

3. Especially in the light of the evidence uncovered by Barbara Breasted, "*Comus* and the Castlehaven Scandal," in *Milton Studies*, vol. 3, ed. J. D. Sim-

monds (Pittsburgh, 1971), pp. 201–224. For a detailed account of the scandal, see Cynthia Herrup, *A House in Gross Disorder* (New York, 1999).

4. Roger Wilkenfeld, "The Seat at the Center: An Interpretation of *Comus,*" *English Literary History,* 33 (1966): 174.

5. In this group I include, among others, R. M. Adams, *Ikon: John Milton and the Modern Critics* (Ithaca, 1955), pp. 1–34; M. Nicholson, *John Milton: A Reader's Guide to His Poetry* (New York, 1963), pp. 67–87; A. E. Dyson, "The Interpretation of *Comus,*" *Essays and Studies,* n.s., 8 (1955): 89–114.

6. Rosemond Tuve, "Image, Form and Theme in *A Mask,*" in Tuve, *Images and Themes in Five Poems by Milton* (Cambridge, Mass., 1957), p. 128.

7. See on this point A. S. P. Woodhouse and D. Bush, eds., *A Variorum Commentary on the Poems of John Milton,* vol. 2, part 3 (New York, 1972), pp. 932–938.

8. As William Madsen has observed ("The Idea of Nature in Milton's Poetry," in *Three Studies in the Renaissance* [New Haven, 1958]), this position is central to the Platonic-Augustinian tradition that finds a classic expression in Augustine's *On Christian Doctrine.* There "the important question is . . . Whom do you love? If, like Comus, you love yourself and your own pleasure, you are a member of the City of Babylon; if, like the Lady, you love God . . . you are a member of the Heavenly City of Jerusalem" (204). It is these two perspectives, these alternative loyalties, that are figured forth in the actions and statements of the characters, who do not merely hold different points of view but live in different universes.

9. Stephen Orgel, *The Jonsonian Masque* (Cambridge, Mass., 1965), p. 153.

4. UMBLEMISHED FORM

1. *Comus,* lines 1–4, in *John Milton: Complete Poems and Major Prose,* ed. M. Y. Hughes (New York, 1957).

2. *Paradise Lost,* book VIII, lines 624–625, 627, ibid.

3. K. G. Hamilton, "Structure of Milton's Prose," in R. Emma and J. Shawcross, eds., *Language and Style in Milton* (New York, 1967), p. 329.

4. Ovid, *Metamorphoses,* trans. F. J. Miller (Cambridge, 1960), vol. 1, p. 150, line 369.

5. George Sandys, *Ovid's Metamorphoses Englished, Mythologized and Represented in Figures,* ed. K. Hully and S. Vandersall (Lincoln, Neb., 1970), p. 136.

6. Ibid., p. 161.

7. Sigmund Freud, *On Narcissism,* in *Collected Papers,* vol. 4, ed. J. Riviere (London, 1925), p. 32.

8. Sandys, *Ovid's Metamorphoses,* p. 160.

9. J. M. Evans, in *The Miltonic Moment* (Lexington, Ky., 1998), describes as "mutually exclusive propositions" the assertions "that the Lady's gift is a strength, and that it is the Lady's own" (p. 64). In fact, these propositions are not at all mutually exclusive. The Lady's gift—of life-giving energy—*is* from God, but it is hers so long as she tends it and does not forsake it for other loyalties. The fact that her *integrity*—her unity of being—is to be found in her commitment to Another is not a paradox but a definition of what true identity is in a universe where God is God.

10. Ovid, *Metamorphoses,* vol. 3, line 405.

11. Virgil, *Eclogues; Georgics; Aeneid, Books I–VI,* trans. H. R. Fairclough (Cambridge, Mass., 1935), p. 264, line 328.

12. *Areopagitica,* in *The Prose of John Milton,* ed. J. M. Patrick et al. (New York, 1967), p. 325.

13. *An Apology against a Pamphlet,* in *Complete Prose Works of John Milton,* vol. 1, ed. D. M. Wolfe (New Haven, 1953), p. 892.

14. A. S. P. Woodhouse and D. Bush, eds., *A Variorum Commentary on the Poems of John Milton,* vol. 2, part 3 (New York, 1972), p. 967.

15. Ibid.

16. John Davies, "Orchestra," in *Silver Poets of the Sixteenth Century,* ed. G. Bullett (London), p. 336.

17. *Pleasure Reconciled to Virtue,* in Ben Jonson, *The Complete Masques,* ed. S. Orgel (New Haven, 1969), p. 273, lines 240–243.

5. Driving from the Letter

1. J. Illo, "The Misreading of Milton," in L. Baxandall, ed., *Radical Perspectives in the Arts* (Harmondsworth, 1972), pp. 180, 189.

2. Harold Laski, in H. Ould, ed., *Freedom of Expression: A Symposium Based on the Conference Called by the London Centre of the International P.E.N. to Commemorate the Tercentenary of the Publication of Milton's "Areopagitica"* (London, 1944; rpt. Port Washington, N.Y., 1970), p. 169.

3. J. Milton, *The Tract for Liberty of Publication,* ed. J. M. Patrick, in *The Prose of John Milton,* ed. J. M. Patrick et al. (New York, 1967), p. 271.

4. W. Kendall, "How to Read Milton's *Areopagitica,*" *Journal of Politics,* 22 (1960): 439–473.

5. E. Sirluck, "Introduction," in *Complete Prose Works of John Milton,* vol. 2, ed. E. Sirluck (New Haven, 1959).

6. Susan Woods, in W. B. Hunter Jr. et al., eds., *A Milton Encyclopedia*, vol. 1 (Cranbury, N.J.,1978), p. 74.

7. *An Apology against a Pamphlet*, in *Complete Prose Works of John Milton*, vol. 1, ed. D. M. Wolfe (New Haven, 1953), pp. 941, 949, 901, 890.

8. *The Doctrine and Discipline of Divorce*, in *The Prose of John Milton*, pp. 183, 184, 164, 162.

9. *Christian Doctrine*, in *Complete Prose Works of John Milton*, vol. 6, ed. M. Kelley, trans. J. Carey (New Haven, 1973), p. 639.

10. *Paradise Regained*, book IV, lines 322–327, in *John Milton: Complete Poems and Major Prose*, ed. M. Y. Hughes (New York, 1957).

11. *Comus*, lines 811–813, ibid.

12. *Of Education*, in *The Prose of John Milton*, p. 230.

13. For a related point, see C. Kendrick, *Milton: A Study in Ideology and Form* (New York, 1986), pp. 23–30.

14. This is a lesson that Milton teaches often. In *Paradise Lost* the "various laws" under which man lives always fail of their object—the removal of sin—but in that failure they perform the important and necessary function of leading us to conclude that "Some blood more precious must be paid for Man, / Just for unjust, that in such righteousness / To them by Faith imputed, they may find / Justification towards God" (book XII, lines 293–296, in *John Milton: Complete Poems and Major Prose*). And in the *Christian Doctrine* the New Testament itself is declared to be "uncertain and variable," transmitted to us by "a multitude of persons" whose errors cannot be correct in the absence of "an original copy in the author's handwriting" (*The Student's Milton*, ed. F. A. Patterson [New York, 1961], p. 1041). But it is precisely the intention of that author, says Milton, that his writings be imperfect and unreliable so that we will be led to seek beyond them for "a more certain guide." Thus, the Scripture is most authoritative when it de-authorizes itself and refers us away from its own form and "to the Spirit and the unwritten word" (1042).

15. *Tetrachordon*, in *Complete Prose Works of John Milton*, vol. 2, p. 637.

16. See on this point H. Limouze, "'The Surest Suppressing': Writer and Censor in Milton's *Areopagitica*," *Centennial Review*, 24, no. 1 (Winter 1980): 106–107.

17. On its first appearance in the tract as a topic, truth is "compar'd in Scripture to a streaming fountain" (310). Even as it is introduced, truth is twice removed, coming to us through the double mediation of writing (Scripture) and metaphor.

18. It is on the question of "inner constraints" that I part company with

Francis Barker's powerful reading of the *Areopagitica* in his book *The Tremulous Private Body: Essays on Subjection* (London, 1984). Barker takes issue, as I do, with the traditional characterization of Milton's tract as a major exhibit in the history of the achieving of "human freedom" (42); indeed, he believes that Milton is an (unwitting) participant in the formation of an "emergent pattern of domination" (47) which "founds itself on a separation of realms between the public arena of the state apparatus and another domain of civil life" (46). "Here," says Barker, "a new liberty is encoded, although it is but a negative one" since "the subject . . . may do as it pleases up to the point of transgression where its activity will be arrested by the agents of the apparatus who patrol the frontier between the two spaces." That is to say, the supposed freedom granted to the individual in this "modern settlement" is already compromised by a demarcation that excludes from his consideration (or meddling) the realm of public discourse. As a result, the operations of the individual—the very shape of his thought and actions—are precisely circumscribed by the powers from whose interference he is supposedly free. "The state succeeds in penetrating to the very heart of the subject, or more accurately, in pre-constituting the subject as one which is already internally disciplined, censored, and thus an effective support of the emergent pattern of domination" (47). By psychologizing difference and conflict—making them the timeless attributes of a timeless self—the new order succeeds in quarantining the very energies that might subvert it. In a supremely political act, a realm of the apolitical is created so that the agenda of the powers that be will be exempt from challenge by a domesticated and "free" self.

However accurate this may be as an account of a shift in the conceiving (and therefore the production) of the relationship between self and state—and I for one find it compelling—it will not do, I think, as an account of Milton or the *Areopagitica*. The separatist position with which Barker would saddle Milton belongs more properly to (for example) Roger Williams, who in *The Bloudy Tenet of Persecution* (1652) and other texts does in fact argue for a strict distinction between the realms of nature and grace and for the restriction of the magistrate's power to matters of civil peace. Milton, however, finds such a distinction unacceptable because it would mean that whole areas of one's everyday life would be exempt from the obligation to be ever doing the will of God, as dictated by the light of conscience. It is just such a separatist accommodation that Milton satirizes in the figure of the man who gives over his religion to some "factor" so that he can sit comfortably in his shop "trading all day" (312), free from the pressures of spiritual duty. This for Milton is a travesty of the doctrine of Christian Liberty, which, while it releases believers from the external constraints of "human judgments" and "civil decrees," puts them under the even severer constraints imposed by the injunction to obey the law of Love: "So far from a less degree of perfection being exacted from Christians, it is expected of them that they should be more perfect than those who were under the law. . . . The only difference is that Moses imposed the letter, or external law . . . whereas Christ writes the inward law of God by his Spirit on the heart of believers, and leads them as willing followers" (*Christian Doctrine,* in *The Student's Milton,* p. 1027). Thus led, they follow not at this or that moment but at *every* moment, with the result that their every action—in prayer, in the shop, at home, in public—is an expression of a perpetual and unrelenting commitment. Rather than being segregated from each other, the realms of the political and the private form an unbroken continuum united by the overriding obligation to be faithful to an unwritten but always-in-force law. The result, as Barker observes, is an extraordinary (because unrelenting) "inner discipline" (47); but far from being in the service of the state, it is a discipline that threatens to subvert the state (as it will in 1649) because in the event of a clash between what it demands and what the state would compel, the state will always be the loser.

Moreover, since it is a discipline that is never relaxed, it extends to every aspect of daily life. When Milton points out that the logic of licensing would finally mean the extension of control to styles of dress, dance, music, he does not, as Barker would have it, contemplate this prospect with "horror" (48); what horrifies him is the mistake of thinking that such control can be exercised from the outside, for what he himself envisions is the same control exercised from the inside by a censor whose strictness is an expression of the commitment that founds his being. Milton, in short, is much more revolutionary than Barker takes him to be: rather than encysting the self in a sanctuary of illusory privacy, he imagines the self as always open to the transforming actions to which its vision calls it, actions that will also transform the material reality in which it operates. If this seems unconvincing, just ask Charles I.

6. Wanting a Supplement

1. *Of Prelaticall Episcopacy,* in *Complete Prose Works of John Milton,* vol. 1, ed. D. M. Wolfe (New Haven, 1953), p. 625.

2. *The Reason of Church Government,* ibid., p. 757.

3. J. Derrida, *Of Grammatology,* trans. G. Spivak (Baltimore, 1976), p. 35.

4. J. Derrida, *Speech and Phenomena,* trans. D. Allison (Evanston, 1973), p. 87.

5. Derrida, *Of Grammatology,* p. 145.

6. Derrida, *Speech and Phenomena,* p. 87.

7. Ibid., p. 147.

8. Ibid., p. 159.

9. Derrida, *Of Grammatology,* p. 20.

10. J. Derrida, *Positions,* trans. A. Bass (Chicago, 1981), p. 6.

11. As Thomas Kranidas puts it, in the only other full discussion of the tract, "the battle is won in the first twenty lines." "Words, Words, Words, and the Word: Milton's *Of Prelaticall Episcopacy," Milton Studies,* vol. 16, ed. J. D. Simmons (Pittsburgh, 1982), p. 154.

12. *Comus,* book I, line 246, in *John Milton: Complete Poems and Major Prose,* ed. M. Y. Hughes (New York, 1957).

13. *An Apology against a Pamphlet,* in *Complete Prose Works of John Milton,* vol. 1, pp. 912–913.

14. D. Davie, "Syntax and Music in *Paradise Lost,"* in F. Kermode, ed., *The Living Milton* (London, 1960), p. 84.

15. K. G. Hamilton, "Structure of Milton's Prose," in R. Emma and J. Shawcross, eds., *Language and Style in Milton* (New York, 1967), p. 329.

16. Derrida, *Of Grammatology,* p. 106.

17. George Herbert, "The Flower," lines 19–20.

18. See the excellent discussion of this shift in Dayton Haskin, "Choosing the Better Part with Mary and with Ruth," in P. G. Stanwood, ed., *Of Poetry and Politics: New Essays on Milton and His World* (Binghamton, 1995), pp. 153–169.

19. *The Doctrine and Discipline of Divorce,* in *Complete Prose Works of John Milton,* vol. 2, ed. E. Sirluck (New Haven, 1959), p. 338.

20. Dayton Haskin sees the shift as one in which Milton no longer locates resistance to the plain truth in unregenerate hearts but finds it in the biblical text itself. See *Milton's Burden of Interpretation* (Philadelphia, 1994), p. 53. From this point on, Haskin asserts, "Milton came increasingly to write in ways that raised interpretive questions" (59). One consequence of this shift is Milton's inclusion of himself in the category of the fallible. In the earlier tracts, he dramatized himself as a man of unshakable virtue and constancy of judgment; but in the wake of his difficulties with Mary Powell, he develops a new understanding of the extent to which even the best of men can fall into error. For a

cogent discussion of the resulting tension between Milton's strong conviction of his own virtue and the equally strong conviction of this (potential) fallibility, see Stephen Fallon, "The Spur of Self-Concernment," *Milton Studies,* 38 (2000): esp. 225, 227, 229, 235, 237.

21. A. Barker, *Milton and the Puritan Dilemma* (Toronto, 1942), p. 71.

22. "Of Reformation," in *Complete Prose Works of John Milton,* vol. 1, pp. 568, 566.

23. In the divorce tracts the notion of "intention" acquires a new prominence in Milton's writing. Not only does it appear more frequently, but its appearances are more closely tied to interpretive issues.

24. In the *Christian Doctrine* Milton often begins a chain of reasoning by saying that we must "imagine nothing unworthy of God," and he often dismisses a position by descrying the image of God it implies. See *Complete Prose Works of John Milton,* vol. 6, ed. M. Kelley, trans. J. Carey (New Haven, 1973), pp. 160, 177.

25. *The Reason of Church Government,* p. 827.

26. *Areopagitica,* in *Complete Prose Works of John Milton,* vol. 2, p. 529.

27. *Doctrine and Discipline of Divorce,* in *Complete Prose Works of John Milton,* vol. 2, p. 260.

28. Ibid., p. 259.

29. Philo Judaeus, *On the Creation* (London, 1929), p. 227, cited in H. Bloch, "Medieval Misogyny," *Representations,* 20 (Fall 1987): 10.

30. Tertullian, "On the Apparel of Women," *The Ante-Nicene Fathers,* 4:20–21; cited in Bloch, "Medieval Misogyny," p. 13.

31. See on this point Victoria Kahn, "'The Duty to Love': Passion and Obligation in Early Modern Political Theory," *Representations,* 68 (Fall 1999): 94. "The marriage covenant for Milton is essentially a covenant between 'man and God' or even . . . a covenant between men."

32. M. Nyquist, "The Genesis of Gendered Subjectivity in the Divorce Tracts and in *Paradise Lost,*" in M. Nyquist and M. W. Ferguson, eds., *Remembering Milton* (New York, 1987), p. 106.

33. See J. G. Turner, *One Flesh: Paradisal Marriage and Sexual Relations in the Age of Milton* (Oxford, 1987), pp. 188–229. See also S. Fallon, "The Metaphysics of Milton's Divorce Tracts," in E. Loewenstein and J. G. Turner, eds., *Politics, Poetics, and Hermeneutics in Milton's Prose* (Cambridge, 1990), ch. 3.

34. D. Aers and B. Hodge, "'Rational Burning': Milton on Sex and Marriage," in *Milton Studies,* 13 (1979): 19.

7. LYCIDAS

1. G. W. Knight, *The Burning Oracle* (London, 1939), p. 70.

2. J. C. Ransom, "A Poem Nearly Anonymous," in C. A. Patrides, ed., *Milton's Lycidas: The Tradition and the Poem* (New York, 1961), p. 71. This essay was first published in *American Review*, 4 (1953).

3. *Lycidas,* line 165, in *John Milton: Complete Poems and Major Prose,* ed. M. Y. Hughes (New York, 1957).

4. William Madsen, *From Shadowy Types to Truth* (New Haven, 1968), p. 13.

5. Donald Friedman, "*Lycidas:* The Swain's Paideia," *Milton Studies,* 3 (1971): 33.

6. Stewart Baker, "Milton's Uncouth Swain," *Milton Studies,* 3 (1971): 35, 50.

7. Knight, *The Burning Oracle,* p. 70.

8. H. V. Ogden, "The Principles of Variety and Contrast in Seventeenth-Century Aesthetics, and Milton's Poetry," *Journal of the History of Ideas,* 10 (1949): 181.

9. J. H. Raleigh, "*Lycidas:* 'Yet Once More,'" *Prairie Schooner* (Winter 1968–1969): 317.

10. S. Elledge, ed., *Milton's Lycidas* (New York, 1966), p. 254.

11. *Comus,* line 4, in *John Milton: Complete Poems and Major Prose.*

12. *An Apology against a Pamphlet,* in *Complete Prose Works of John Milton,* vol. 1, ed. D. M. Wolfe (New Haven, 1953), p. 953.

13. *Of Education,* in *Complete Prose Works of John Milton,* vol. 2, ed. E. Sirluck (New Haven, 1959), p. 363.

14. *The Reason of Church Government,* in *Complete Prose Works of John Milton,* vol. 1, p. 807.

15. *An Apology against a Pamphlet,* in *Complete Prose Works of John Milton,* vol. 1, p. 871.

16. J. H. Hanford, *The Milton Handbook* (New York, 1954), p. 168.

17. A. S. P. Woodhouse and D. Bush, eds., *A Variorum Commentary on the Poems of John Milton* (New York, 1972), vol. 2, part 2, p. 647.

18. B. A. Rajan, "*Lycidas:* The Shattering of the Leaves," *Studies in Philology,* 64 (1967): 59.

19. Friedman, "*Lycidas:* The Swain's Paideia," p. 13.

20. Virgil, *Eclogue VI,* trans. Paul Alpers, in Alpers, *The Singer of the Eclogues* (Berkeley, 1979), p. 37.

21. Friedman, *"Lycidas:* The Swain's Paideia," p. 13.

22. M. C. Pecheux, "The Dread Voice in *Lycidas," Milton Studies,* 9 (1976): 238.

23. See *Paradise Lost,* book V, lines 803–807: "Thus far his bold discourse without control / Had audience, when among the Seraphim, / *Abdiel . . .* / Stood up." In *John Milton: Complete Poems and Major Prose.*

24. Quoted in Pecheux, "The Dread Voice in *Lycidas,"* p. 235.

25. *Nativity Ode,* lines 26, 243–244, in *John Milton: Complete Poems and Major Prose.*

26. M. H. Abrams, "Five Types of *Lycidas,"* in Patrides, ed., *Lycidas: The Tradition and the Poem,* p. 224.

27. Ibid., p. 229.

28. Friedman, *"Lycidas:* The Swain's Paideia," p. 19.

29. Marjorie Nicolson, *John Milton: A Reader's Guide to His Poetry* (New York, 1963), p. 110.

30. The phrase is Madsen's *(From Shadowy Types to Truth,* p. 13).

31. Thomas Rosenmeyer, *The Green Cabinet* (Berkeley, 1969), p. 53.

8. WITH MORTAL VOICE

1. *Paradise Lost,* book VII, lines 1–3, in *John Milton: Complete Poems and Major Prose,* ed. M. Y. Hughes (New York, 1957).

2. Ovid, *Metamorphoses,* ed. and trans. F. J. Miller (London, 1916), vol. 1, book 3, line 369; hereafter cited parenthetically in text by book and line for Latin and by page for English quotations, and abbreviated as *M.*

3. "At a Solemn Music," lines 21–22, in *John Milton: Complete Poems and Major Prose.*

4. Ibid., lines 23–24.

5. George Herbert, "Providence," line 141, in *George Herbert,* ed. L. Martz (New York, 1994), p. 104.

6. "At a Solemn Music," stanza I, lines 25–26.

7. *An Apology against a Pamphlet,* in *Complete Prose Works of John Milton,* ed. D. M. Wolfe, vol. 1 (New Haven, 1953), p. 871.

8. *Paradise Lost: A Poem, in Twelve Books,* ed. T. Newton, 2 vols., 7th ed. (London, 1770), vol. 2, pp. 6–7. The substance of the note was first given by Patrick Hume in 1695. For a full discussion of the Bellerophon allusion in all its complexity, see Stephen M. Fallon, "Intention and Its Limits in *Paradise Lost:* The Case of Bellerophon," in D. T. Benet and M. Lieb, eds., *Literary Milton,* (Pittsburgh, 1994), pp. 161–179.

9. Sigmund Freud, "The 'Uncanny,'" in Freud, *On Creativity and the Unconscious* (New York, 1958), p. 137.

10. *The Poems of John Milton,* ed. J. Carey and A. Fowler (New York, 1968), p. 777.

11. *Il Penseroso,* lines 105–108, in *John Milton: Complete Poems and Major Prose.*

12. Maureen Quilligan almost sees this when she observes of the Thracian women, "The danger is posed by a force that is, like the inspirational source, peculiarly female" ("The Gender of Milton's Muse," in H. Bloom, ed., *John Milton's Paradise Lost* [New York, 1987], p. 126). She does not, however, realize that the likeness extends to the danger posed, the danger of self-obliteration. Michael Lieb comes closer when he observes that "as much as Milton would like to believe that Urania is 'Heav'nlie' and Calliope . . . an 'empty dream,' his intense awareness of the sparagmatic fate of Orpheus and his own deep-seated fears . . . keep getting in the way" (*Milton and the Culture of Violence* [Ithaca, 1994], p. 68). Where Lieb locates the fear in the possibility of Urania's failing to protect the poet, I would argue that a successful Urania—a Urania who does protect and even envelop the poet—is what he fears, however unselfconsciously.

13. *Paradise Regained,* book I, lines 215, 216, in *John Milton: Complete Poems and Major Prose.*

14. *Lycidas,* line 71, in *John Milton: Complete Poems and Major Prose.*

15. *Paradise Regained,* book II, line 259

9. THE TEMPTATION TO ACTION

1. *Paradise Regained,* book IV, line 372, in *John Milton: Complete Poems and Major Prose,* ed. M. Y. Hughes (New York, 1957).

2. *Paradise Lost,* book XII, lines 383–385, ibid.

3. Russell Fraser, "On Milton's Poetry," *Yale Review,* 56 (1967): 189.

4. "At a Solemn Music," lines 1–2, in *John Milton: Complete Poems and Major Prose.*

5. This is the complaint of K. G. Hamilton in "Structure of Milton's Prose," in R. Emma and J. Shawcross, eds., *Language and Style in Milton* (New York, 1967), p. 329: "Milton, as a dialectician, is at times given to jumping up and down in one place."

6. Cf. E. M. W. Tillyard, *Milton* (London, 1930), p. 64.

7. *Nativity Ode,* stanza IV, lines 22–28, in *John Milton: Complete Poems and Major Prose.*

8. D. Daiches, "Some Aspects of Milton's Pastoral Imagery," in Daiches, *More Literary Essays* (Edinburgh, 1968), p. 103.

9. A. S. P. Woodhouse and Douglas Bush, eds., *A Variorum Commentary on the Poems of John Milton*, vol. 2, part 1 (New York, 1972), p. 106.

10. *Complete Prose Works of John Milton*, vol. 1, ed. D. M. Wolfe (New Haven, 1953), pp. 925–926.

11. Stanley Fish, *Surprised by Sin*, 2nd ed. (Cambridge, Mass., 1997), pp. li–lxv.

12. *John Milton: Complete Poems and Major Prose*, p. 1012.

13. *De Doctrina Christiana*, in *Complete Prose Works of John Milton*, vol. 6, ed. M. Kelley (New Haven, 1973), p. 639.

14. *An Apology against a Pamphlet*, in *Complete Prose Works of John Milton*, vol. 1, p. 941.

10. THE TEMPTATION OF SPEECH

1. *Paradise Regained*, book II, lines 30–49, in *John Milton: Complete Poems and Major Prose*, ed. M. Y. Hughes (New York, 1957).

2. Arnold Stein, *Heroic Knowledge: An Interpretation of "Paradise Regained" and "Samson Agonistes"* (Minneapolis, 1957), pp. 42–43.

3. One might add that there is a need also for the powerful eloquence which a knowledge of Greek and Latin rhetoric would presumably generate.

4. The words are Robert Cushman's in *Therapeia* (Chapel Hill, 1957), p. 216. Cushman is discussing Plato's belief that some minds are hopelessly indisposed toward revelation. The relevant text is the *Seventh Epistle* (344a): "Neither receptivity nor memory will ever produce knowledge in him who has no affinity with the object, since it does not germinate to start with in alien minds."

5. Readers will ask these questions in part because other, more natural questions have been precluded by the opening scenes (see especially I, 131–181), where we learn what will *not* happen. The Son will not fall to Satan's temptations—he will not even waver; and in the absence of narrative suspense, the center of the reader's interest is not the fact but the manner of the hero's victory.

6. See, e.g., L. Martz, *The Paradise Within* (New Haven, 1964), p. 183.

7. Ibid. See also Ken Simpson, "Lingering Voice, Telling Silences," in *Milton Studies*, 35 (1997): 191. "Whereas Satan's use of language reveals the silent voice of faithlessness, the creative presence, which is silent in itself but speaks

through the Word, emerges as language, is redeemed for the ministry of the Word."

8. Martz, *The Paradise Within,* p. 197.

9. Augustine, *City of God,* XI, 2.

10. Martz, *The Paradise Within,* pp. 186, 194.

11. Cf. Georgia Christopher, *Milton and the Science of the Saints* (Princeton, 1982), p. 209: "In speech, [Christ] enacts an immediate giving up of (claims for) the self and so prefigures future surrender of life."

12. Barbara Lewalski, *Milton's Brief Epic* (Providence, 1966), p. 316.

13. A. S. P. Woodhouse, "Theme and Pattern in *Paradise Regained,*" *University of Toronto Quarterly,* 25 (1955–1956): 181.

14. Augustine, *On Christian Doctrine,* trans. D. W. Robertson (New York, 1958), p. 167.

15. On this point see Thomas O. Sloane, *Donne, Milton and the End of Humanist Rhetoric* (Berkeley, 1985), pp. 265–266: "What does it mean to be the Son of God? It means, simply, that Jesus has placed his destiny solely in the hands of the Father whose will alone he will obey. . . . Satan has been thinking like a dualist, trying to distinguish Jesus' godhead from his manhood. But in Jesus' simple answer, two arguments come together in a statement whose ostensible ambiguity—I will obey God, I am God—means to the reader what it cannot mean to Satan: this obedience is at once manly and divine."

16. George Herbert, "Easter Wings," line 19.

17. Northrop Frye, "The Typology of *Paradise Regained,*" in A. Barker, ed., *Milton: Modern Essays in Criticism* (New York, 1965), pp. 440–441.

18. For readings similar to the one offered in this chapter, see Lawrence Hyman, "The Reader's Attitude in *Paradise Regained,*" *PMLA,* 85 (1970): 496–503. Mr. Hyman argues that "throughout the entire poem Christ progressively rejects those human values and human feelings that prevent him from realizing his divine nature" and that this action brings him into conflict with "the human values of the reader" (500). He believes, however, that the distance between the reader and Christ increases as the poem unfolds, whereas I believe that the effect of the poem is to bring them together as the reader strives to apprehend, and thereby match, the Son's performance. On this point see B. Rajan, *The Lofty Rhyme* (London, 1970), which emphasizes "the special kind of alertness" (122) required of the reader in *Paradise Regained:* "As the duel of the mind evolves in its stripped clarity we are meant to measure each movement of the combatants with an intentness not inferior to that of the writing itself.

... The act of reading thus becomes a specific foundation for growth in the reader's mind" (121–122). See also Jon Lawry, *The Shadow of Heaven* (Ithaca, 1968), on the relationship between the temptation of the Son and the analogous temptation of the reader: "The literary temptation for the audience, rather like theological temptation for the Son, is to fill a necessary vacuum by means of some decisive, traditional, fallen action. ... For both the Son and the audience, human error would allow the glamorous Satanic desire called impatience ... to best Christian patience in the desert 'Field'" (299–300). The radical interiority of the poem is remarked by Marshall Grossman in *The Story of All Things* (Durham, N.C., 1998), p. 263: "The Jesus of *Paradise Regained* is the highest of modernists. ... The change he effects—though it will transform the world—is presented as wholly interior and private—a transformation of the self that will empower and enable others to be similarly transformed."

11. THE TEMPTATION OF PLOT

1. *Paradise Lost,* book XII, lines 383–385, in *John Milton: Complete Poems and Major Prose,* ed. M. Y. Hughes (New York, 1957).

2. *The Reason of Church Government,* in *Complete Prose Works of John Milton,* vol. 1, ed. D. M. Wolfe (New Haven, 1953), p. 750.

3. *Christian Doctrine,* in *Complete Prose Works of John Milton,* vol. 6, ed. M. Kelley, trans. J. Carey (New Haven, 1973), p. 537.

4. Northrop Frye, *The Return of Eden* (Toronto, 1965), p. 102.

5. *Areopagitica,* in *The Prose of John Milton,* ed. J. M. Patrick (New York, 1968), p. 297.

6. Arnold Stein, *Heroic Knowledge: An Interpretation of "Paradise Regained" and "Samson Agonistes"* (Minneapolis, 1957), p. 42.

7. B. J. Verkamp, *The Indifferent Mean* (Detroit, 1977), p. 21.

8. F. Mason, *The Authoritie of the Church in Making Canons and Constitutions Concerning Things Indifferent* (1607), p. 4. S's and u's have been modernized.

9. W. Bradshaw, *A Treatise of the Nature and Use of Things Indifferent* (1605), pp. 25–26. S's and u's have been modernized.

10. See Lord Brooke, *A Discourse Opening the Nature of Episcopacy* (1642), pp. 26–27.

11. Of course, as Milton is quick to point out, the reading of books is not a matter regulated by the Scriptures: no "inspir'd author tells us that such, or such reading is unlawfull; yet certainly had God thought good to limit us herein, it had bin much more expedient to have told us" (*Areopagitica,* 286).

Therefore, reading is a thing indifferent even in the theological or legalistic understanding of the doctrine. Milton, however, is by no means limited to that understanding, and when he is pressed, as he is in the divorce tracts and the *Christian Doctrine,* he does not hesitate to declare that those things on which the Scriptures have pronounced—marrying, divorcing, keeping the Sabbath—are as indifferent (that is, conducing equally to good or evil) as anything else.

12. See B. J. Webber, *Wedges and Wings: The Patterning of "Paradise Regained"* (Carbondale, Ill., 1975), pp. 19–20.

13. Cf. B. Rajan, *Milton and the Imperial Vision* (Pittsburgh, 1999), pp. 309–310: "The rules of the meditative combat are remarkably simple. Satan has to make Christ an offer he cannot refuse. The Son, through his retreating refusals, has to demand from Satan an offer he is unable to make. The only offer Satan cannot make is that of a Kingdom constituted by creative dependence on a divine will to which Satan has been made alien."

14. Joan Bennett cites William Walwyn to the same point. Replying to those who criticized him for reading classical authors, Walwyn declares: "Whether I value these authors is not the question: the question is whether I value or reject them in the Lord's service." Quoted in Joan Bennett, *Reviving Liberty* (Cambridge, Mass., 1989), p. 193.

15. Edward Tayler, *Milton's Poetry: Its Development in Time* (Pittsburgh, 1979), p. 254.

16. See *Christian Doctrine,* book I, ch. 30, where Milton makes a distinction between Scripture which is simply external (i.e., the written word) and the internal Scripture which is written on our hearts by the Spirit: "Under the gospel we possess, as it were, a two-fold Scripture; one external, which is the written word, and the other internal, which is the Holy Spirit, written in the hearts of believers, according to the promise of God, and with the intent that it should by no means be neglected; as was shown above, chap. xxvii. on the gospel. Hence, although the external ground which we possess for our belief at the present day in the written word is highly important, and, in most instances at least, prior in point of reception, that which is internal, and the peculiar possession of each believer, is far superior to all, namely, the Spirit itself." In *The Student's Milton,* ed. F. A. Patterson (New York, 1961), p. 1041.

17. Barbara Lewalski, *Milton's Brief Epic: The Genre, Meaning, and Art of "Paradise Regained"* (Providence, 1966), p. 316.

18. See Joan Webber, *Milton and His Epic Tradition* (Seattle, 1979).

12. The Temptation of Understanding

1. *Samson Agonistes*, lines 46–51, in *John Milton: Complete Poems and Major Prose*, ed. M. Y. Hughes (New York, 1957).

2. There are other possibilities: "In what part lodg'd" can be read "In *whatever* part lodg'd" rather than as the secondary subject (along with "this high gift of strength") of "committed." No reading of these lines is completely—that is, narrowly—satisfactory.

3. See J. Huntley, "A Revaluation of the Chorus' Role in Milton's *Samson Agonistes*," *Modern Philology*, 64 (1966): 140–141.

4. *John Milton: Complete Poems and Major Prose*, p. 559.

5. A. B. Chambers, "Wisdom and Fortitude in *Samson Agonistes*," *PMLA*, 78 (1963): 318.

6. Huntley, "A Revaluation of the Chorus' Role in *Samson Agonistes*," p. 136.

7. To say that God acts without reference to reason is not to say that he is unreasonable. The first is a description, largely negative, of his ways; the other, a judgment in which reason is still assumed to be the standard of behavior. Of course, in a world ruled by either kind of God, the problem of acting responsibly is the same (on what basis does one calculate consequences?), but the subjects of a capricious God are less likely to come to terms with that world than are those who place their God above reason. In the course of *Samson Agonistes*, everyone has a turn at protecting the independence of the deity ("Tax not divine disposal," "Appoint not heavenly disposition"), but in context these statements constitute a warning against trying to outguess God (you never know what he's going to do) rather than a recognition of man's inability to reason about him at all. The distinction may seem slight, but it is all important, and we as readers must understand it if we are to understand what it is that Samson finally does.

8. D. C. Allen, *The Harmonious Vision* (Baltimore, 1954), pp. 76, 81.

9. Huntley, "A Revaluation of the Chorus' Role in *Samson Agonistes*," p. 142.

10. I should note here that the "rightness" of Samson's affirmation is felt almost immediately, even though it is unexpected. This double movement—surprise followed by an easy acceptance of what had at first seemed surprising—is characteristic of *Samson Agonistes* for reasons which will, I hope, become clear below.

11. As Thomas Sloane observes, back-and-forth argumentation is never the mode by which truth is apprehended in Milton. A Miltonic hero "practices . . . not controversy but the virtues of endurance and greater vision; those virtues

were acquired outside the poem, or before it begins." Sloane, *Donne, Milton and the End of Humanist Rhetoric* (Berkeley, 1985), p. 238.

12. Joseph Summers, "The Movements of the Drama," in Summers, ed., *The Lyric and Dramatic Milton* (New York, 1965), p. 172.

13. See on this point Dayton Haskin, *Milton's Burden of Interpretation* (Philadelphia, 1994), p. 179: "By having Samson himself make the claim that he feels 'rouzing motions' within him, Milton's poem reproduces and intensifies rather than eliminates an ambiguity about the relation of Samson's deliberative action to divine inspiration that is already present in Judges."

14. Arthur Barker, "Structural and Doctrinal Pattern in Milton's Later Poems," in A. Maclure and F. W. Watt, eds., *Essays in English Literature from the Renaissance to the Victorian Age, Presented to A. S. P. Woodhouse* (Toronto, 1964), p. 178.

15. Judges 16:28.

16. T. Greene, *The Descent from Heaven: A Study in Epic Continuity* (New Haven, 1963), p. 407.

17. For a contrary view that emphasizes a God of terror and dread, see Michael Lieb, "The God of Samson Agonistes," *Milton Studies*, 33 (1996): 3–25.

18. N. Frye, *The Return of Eden* (Toronto, 1965), p. 103.

19. *John Milton: Selected Prose*, ed. C. A. Patrides (Columbia, Mo., 1985), p. 269.

13. THE TEMPTATION OF INTELLIGIBILITY

1. *Samson Agonistes*, lines 1529–1530, in *John Milton: Complete Poems and Major Prose*, ed. M. Y. Hughes (New York, 1957).

2. In *The Rambler*, no. 139 (Tuesday, July 16, 1751), Samuel Johnson declared of *Samson Agonistes* that "it must be allowed to want a middle, since nothing passes between the first act and the last, that either hastens or delays the death of Samson" (R. E. Hone, ed., *John Milton's Samson Agonistes: The Poem and Materials for Analysis* [San Francisco, 1966], pp. 102–103). In the past forty years much critical energy has been expended in an effort to counter Johnson's strictures. For the middle he found wanting a number of commentators have substituted a psychological middle, the drama of Samson's spiritual regeneration, which, it is said, provides the lines of cause and effect that seem unavailable in the physical action. The regenerationist reading has achieved the status of orthodoxy and is well presented in two important books: A. Low, *The Blaze of Noon: A Reading of Samson Agonistes* (New York, 1974); and M. A. Radzinowicz, *Toward Samson Agonistes: The Growth of Milton's Mind* (Princeton,

1978). At the same time, a number of critics—Irene Samuel, John Shawcross, and Joseph Wittreich among them—have challenged the regenerationist reading from different directions.

3. *Paradise Lost,* book I, line 84, in *John Milton: Complete Poems and Major Prose.*

4. On this point, see J. Foley, "Sin, Not Time: Satan's First Speech in *Paradise Lost,*" *English Literary History,* 37, no. 1 (March 1970): 37–56.

5. Edmund Spenser, *The Faerie Queene,* book I, canto vii, stanza 7, line 2.

6. *Comus,* lines 786–787, in *John Milton: Complete Poems and Major Prose.*

7. Marcus Andreas Wunstius, *Samson: A Sacred Tragedy* [1600], in *That Invincible Samson: The Theme of Samson Agonistes in World Literature,* ed. W. Kirkconnell (Toronto, 1964), p. 39.

8. *Of Prelaticall Episcopacy,* in *Complete Prose Works of John Milton,* vol. 1, ed. D. M. Wolfe (New Haven, 1953), p. 639.

9. *The Tract for Liberty of Publication,* in *The Prose of John Milton,* ed. J. M. Patrick et al. (New York, 1967), p. 316.

10. *The Reason of Church Government,* in *John Milton: Complete Poems and Major Prose,* p. 643.

11. For full discussions of the difficulties Samson presented to exegetes and a history of the interpretive uses to which his story was put, see M. Krouse, *Milton's Samson and the Christian Tradition* (Princeton, 1949); and J. Wittreich, *Interpreting Samson Agonistes* (Princeton, 1986).

12. John Calvin, *Institutes of the Christian Religion,* trans. Ford Lewis Battles, 2 vols. (Philadelphia, 1960), vol. 1, p. 437 (book II, chapter X, section 1).

13. See on this point John Guillory, "Samson Agonistes in Its Historical Moment," in M. Nyquist and M. Ferguson, eds., *Re-Membering Milton* (New York, 1988), p. 165: "Milton has not defined freedom trivially as the alternative of obeying or disobeying the law, but rather located it in those hypothetical moments when the law is set aside." The result, as Guillory goes on to say in a wonderful phrase, is "the general antinomian wreckage" (166).

14. This is Wittreich's reading in *Interpreting Samson Agonistes.* He finds that the phrase "of his own accord" is used in the Scriptures "to imply a contrast between the false prophets who act of their own accord and the true prophets who act by divine commission" and concludes that it is "in precisely this way that the Messenger employs the same phrase in *Samson Agonistes*" (112). The point is a part of a book-length argument in which Wittreich contends that Samson is an antihero, a negative model for the reader and for the English people. Samson's actions, he declares, "instead of being executed against those

who defy God's laws, . . . are executed by one who is regularly defying those laws, the consequence of which, always, is that Samson and his people are moved into greater servitude, with Samson himself at the end of his story standing before his people as a prisoner, blind and in chains" (160). He supports his thesis by marshaling a number of sixteenth- and seventeenth-century allusions which suggest to him "that the Samson story, by the beginning of the seventeenth century, had acquired an overlay of political significance and further that it had become netted within a typological scheme, both secular and sacred, that exhibits a tarnished Samson—a Samson who, nurtured in blood, delights in vengeance and whose enterprise entails the wretched interchange of wrong for wrong" (244s). Rather than identifying Samson with Milton, as so many have done, Wittreich sees Milton, through the figure of Samson, weighing "past failures, his own and those of his nation, . . . differentiating his own historical consciousness from the more primitive one of Samson still too much in evidence among the English people" (283). Although I cannot follow Wittreich in his total debunking of Samson or in his regarding Samson as a foil for the more humane and exemplary Jesus of *Paradise Regained,* I find his book bracing and salutary, a much-needed counterweight to regenerationist pieties. I especially like his repeated demonstrations of contradictions in both the Samson legend and in Milton's treatment of it, and I agree with him when he declares that with respect to what "has always been the crucial question in interpreting the Samson story"—the question of the relationship between Samson's act and the divine will—"Milton is steadfast in his refusal to commit himself" (301). Moreover, he is surely right when he says that "the nonsequential, scrambled narrative embedded with *Samson Agonistes* subverts a consensus reading of the Samson story" (148). (For an early response, see P. J. Gallagher, "On Reading Joseph Wittreich," *Milton Quarterly,* 21, no. 3 [October 1987]: 108–113.) At the very least, Wittreich's argument adds to the already impressive evidence of a Samson who, from the first, has been "up for interpretive grabs," a problematic figure who, rather than representing some doctrine or truth, represents the difficulty (not to say folly) of extracting doctrine from the diverse and multidirectional materials of a decentered world—that is, of a world in which God has so removed his ways from human sight that we are left to our own interpretive conjectures. Milton finds in Samson a figure of deep hermeneutical trouble, and in his play troubles are not removed but multiplied.

15. On the topic of Samson and the feminine, see Michael Lieb, "A Thousand Foreskins," *Milton Studies,* 38 (2000): 211–214; Herman Rapaport, *Milton*

and the Postmodern (Lincoln, Neb., 1983), pp. 131–164; Jackie DiSalvo, "'Intestine Thorn': Samson's Struggle with the Woman Within," in Julia Walker, ed., *Milton and the Idea of Woman* (Urbana, Ill., 1988), pp. 211–229; and Marybeth Rose, "'Vigorous Most When Most Unactive Deemed': Gender and the Heroists of Endurance in Milton's *Samson Agonistes*," *Milton Studies*, 33 (1997): 83–109.

16. These are the first two lines of George Herbert's poem "A Bunch of Grapes."

17. I am here invoking in a general way the now extensive literature on the appropriative and commodifying "male gaze." See L. Mulvey, "Visual Pleasure and Narrative Cinema," *Screen*, 16 (Fall 1975): 6–18; E. A. Kaplan, *Women and Film: Both Sides of the Camera* (London, 1983); C. J. Clover, "Her Body, Himself: Gender in the Slasher Film," *Representations*, 20 (Fall 1987): 187–228; T. Modleski, *The Women Who Knew Too Much* (New York, 1988). These and other writers draw heavily on Lacan and on Freud's discussion of scopophilia in his *Three Essays on Sexuality* and elsewhere. The general thesis of these studies is succinctly stated by Mulvey: "In a world ordered by sexual imbalance, pleasure in looking has been split between active/male and passive/female. The determining male gaze projects its phantasy onto the female figure, which is styled accordingly. In their traditional exhibitionist role women are simultaneously looked at and displayed, with their appearance coded for strong visual and erotic impact, so that they can be said to connote 'to-be-looked-at-ness'" ("Visual Pleasure and Narrative Cinema," in G. Mast and M. Cohen, eds., *Film Theory and Criticism*, 3rd ed. [New York, 1985], pp. 808–809). This is of course Samson's condition when the play opens, and it is a condition he hates. Being the object of the gaze of others is for him the most insupportable form of the powerlessness he continually laments; and it is because he identifies that powerlessness and plasticity with the female that he so vehemently resists further feminization in his rejection of Dalila's appeal to their common weakness. In pushing her away (or in trying to), he pushes away that part of himself which has become a public display, an exhibit, a space of public consumption. Samson wants above all to recover the unity and integrity, the *self-possession*, that was lost when he allowed his "secret" to spill out. He wants to achieve a unity of being, or rather, in Lacan's terms, "the illusion of unity in which a human being is always looking forward to self mastery" ("Some Reflections on the Ego," *International Journal of Psycho-Analysis*, 34 [1953]: 15). Samson looks both forward and backward in search of that illusion, and it is only when self-mas-

tery is no longer what he seeks—when he decides to just "go along"—that the illusion no longer captivates him.

14. GENTLY RAISED

1. F. R. Leavis, "Milton's Verse," in C. A Patrides, ed., *Milton's Epic Poetry: Essays on "Paradise Lost" and "Paradise Regained"* (Harmondsworth, 1967), p. 28.

2. J. B. Broadbent, "Milton's 'Mortal Voice' and His 'Omnific Word,'" in C. A. Patrides, ed., *Approaches to "Paradise Lost"* (London, 1968), p. 115.

3. *Paradise Lost,* book I, lines 527–530, in *John Milton: Complete Poems and Major Prose,* ed. M. Y. Hughes (New York, 1957).

4. Donald Davie, "Syntax and Music in *Paradise Lost,*" in Frank Kermode, ed., *The Living Milton* (London, 1960), p. 83.

5. See on this point Regina Schwartz, "The Toad at Eve's Ear," in D. T. Benet and M. Lieb, eds., *Literary Milton* (Pittsburgh, 1994), p. 20: "Making reading an activity in which the reader is engaged in choosing identifications, [Milton] exposes his work to the danger that the reader may identify with the wrong character at the wrong juncture in his or her moral life."

6. *The Reason of Church Government,* in *Complete Prose Works of John Milton,* vol. 1, ed. D. M. Wolfe (New Haven, 1953), p. 850.

7. *The Prose of John Milton,* ed. J. M. Patrick et al., (New York, 1967), p. 266.

8. *The Readie and Easie Way,* 2nd ed., in *Complete Prose Works of John Milton,* vol. 7, ed. R. W. Ayers (New Haven, 1980), p. 550.

9. *The Likeliest Means to Remove Hirelings,* in *The Prose of John Milton,* p. 314.

10. *The Reason of Church Government,* in *Complete Prose Works of John Milton,* vol. 1, p. 803.

11. *Comus,* lines 244–248, in *John Milton: Complete Poems and Major Prose.*

12. *Christian Doctrine,* in *Complete Prose Works of John Milton,* vol. 6, ed. M. Kelley, trans. J. Carey (New Haven, 1973), p. 307.

13. Cf. William Kolbrener, *Milton's Warring Angels: A Study of Critical Engagements* (Cambridge, 1997), p. 144: "Providential history resists the temporalizing effects of narrative."

14. Cf. ibid., p. 145: "Representation in its very essence violates the promised unity—the monistic identity—of God with his creation."

15. As William Kolbrener observes, "All discourse, irreducibly material, elicits the *temptation* of idolatry" (ibid., p. 155).

16. "At a Solemn Music," lines 25–26, in *John Milton: Complete Poems and Major Prose.*

17. Herman Rapaport, *Milton and the Postmodern* (Lincoln, Neb., 1983), p. 176.

18. *Areopagitica,* in *The Prose of John Milton,* p. 310.

19. Ibid., pp. 316–318.

20. Ibid., p. 330.

21. *Christian Doctrine,* in *Complete Prose Works of John Milton,* vol. 6, p. 638.

22. J. Bennett, "Milton's Antinomianism," in W. Hunter Jr. et al. eds., *A Milton Encyclopedia,* vol. 9 (Cranbury, N.J., 1983), p. 14.

23. Northrop Frye, *The Return of Eden* (Toronto, 1965), p. 103.

24. Leo Damrosch, *God's Plot and Man's Stories* (Chicago, 1985), p. 120.

25. *The Reason of Church Government,* in *Complete Prose Works of John Milton,* vol. 1, p. 750.

15. "On Other Surety None"

1. *Paradise Lost,* book V, lines 658–665, in *John Milton: Complete Poems and Major Prose,* ed. M. Y. Hughes (New York, 1957).

2. Cf. A. H. A. Rushdy, *The Empty Garden: The Subject of Late Milton* (Pittsburgh, 1992), p. 195: "The way each character chooses to read the world governs the world that he comes to inhabit. Furthermore, that original choice not only constitutes the world he inhabits, but eventually the world he chooses to inhabit will govern his perception of it—will constitute him. . . . The ways of confronting the Other produce the self." Rushdy is commenting on *Paradise Regained,* but his account holds for all of Milton generally.

3. *Paradise Regained,* book IV, line 483, in *John Milton: Complete Poems and Major Prose.*

4. Christopher Hill, *The Experience of Defeat* (New York, 1984), p. 307.

5. *The Readie and Easie Way,* in *Complete Prose Works of John Milton,* vol. 7, ed. R. W. Ayers (New Haven, 1980), p. 550.

6. On this point see Georgia Christopher, *Milton and the Science of the Saints* (Princeton, 1982), p. 93: "Taking a position on God's character comes before a reading of his words. Luther likes to point out that faith reverses the Ciceronian dictum to pay attention to *what* is being said rather than *who* is speaking. Milton concurs: divine testimony 'gets all its force from the author.'"

7. Augustine, *On Christian Doctrine,* trans. D. W. Robertson (New York, 1958), p. 30.

8. Georgia Christopher observes that "Satan . . . offers a textbook case of how *not* to interpret Scripture. His is the ultimate heresy: hearing God's truth and believing it to be bad" (*Milton and the Science of the Saints,* p. 93).

9. *The Doctrine and Discipline of Divorce*, in *The Prose of John Milton*, ed. J. M. Patrick et al. (New York, 1967), p. 151.

10. See on this point Michael Lieb, "Reading God: Milton and the Anthropopathetic Tradition," *Milton Studies*, 25 (1989): 224. "Reading the Scriptures becomes for Milton an exercise in the discovery of God's intentions. . . . To read God is in effect a religious act: one must be careful to avoid the perils of misinterpretation." See also p. 222: "Reading God represents an act of creating God."

11. *Christian Doctrine*, in *Complete Prose Works of John Milton*, vol. 6, ed. M. Kelley, trans. J. Carey (New Haven, 1973), p. 168.

12. *Eikonoklastes*, in *Complete Prose Works*, vol. 3, ed. M. Y. Hughes (New Haven, 1962), p. 504.

13. Cf. John Stachniewski, *The Persecutory Imagination: English Puritanism and the Literature of Religious Despair* (Oxford, 1991), p. 337: "Satan . . . chose freely; but once he had chosen the die was cast. Paradoxically Milton gives choice such awesome significance that it turns itself into a form of determinism."

14. On this point see Marshall Grossman, *Authors to Themselves* (Cambridge, 1987), pp. 7–8: "It is this image of the self to be constructed that raises Adam above the beasts and endows him with the moral responsibility necessary to self-authorship. . . . [Adam and Eve] must author a life history conformable to that which God desires." See also p. 15: "The human individual is understood to author himself or herself over the course of a lifetime by accumulating judgments and choices and the experiences that follow from them."

15. Barbara Lewalski, "Innocence and Experience in Milton's Eden," in T. Kranidas, ed., *New Essays on Paradise Lost* (Berkeley, 1969), p. 93.

16. Cf. Dayton Haskin, *Milton's Burden of Interpretation* (Philadelphia, 1994), p. 237: "Adam and Eve are God's 'Masterwork' (VII, 505) above all in the sense that they are interpreters. As signs and sign makers, they are themselves dense with significance and possibility."

17. J. M. Evans, *Paradise Lost and the Genesis Tradition* (Oxford, 1968), p. 269.

18. See on this point Haskin, *Milton's Burden of Interpretation*, p. 223: "Adam and Eve are not only 'authors to themselves' but editors of their work—and God's work. The acts of lopping and pruning, propping up and binding together, are . . . analogous to activities . . . practiced with pleasure by mature writers."

19. John P. Rumrich, *Matter of Glory: A New Preface to "Paradise Lost"* (Pittsburgh, 1987), p. 196.

20. Mary Nyquist, "Reading the Fall: Discourse in Drama in *Paradise Lost*," *English Literary History*, 14 (1984): 206.

21. Marshall Grossman, *Authors to Themselves: Milton and the Revelation of History* (Cambridge, 1987), p. 137.

22. *Paradise Lost: Books IX–X*, ed. J. M. Evans (Cambridge, 1973), p. 20.

23. Here I follow the argument of D. Danielson, *Milton's Good God* (Cambridge, 1982), p. 127.

24. Ronald Wardhaugh, *How Conversation Works* (Oxford, 1985).

25. See on this point Donald Friedman, "The Lady in the Garden," *Milton Studies*, 35 (1997): 128. "The world of Adam and Eve before the Fall is a world of work. . . . Their 'sweet gardening labour' (IV, 328) is that which distinguishes them from other creatures and thus is the outward sign . . . of inherent human dignity."

26. J. Reichert, "A Case for Adam," *English Literary History*, 48, no. 1 (1981): 88.

27. *Milton's Paradise Lost: A New Edition*, ed. R. Bentley (London, 1732), p. 280.

28. *Adamus Exul*, in W. Kirkconnell, *The Celestial Cycle* (New York, 1967), p. 183.

29. *L'Adamo*, ibid., p. 255.

30. But see John Tanner, *Anxiety in Eden* (New York, 1992), p. 116: "One might . . . think that Adam sins the moment he 'resolves' to die with Eve. To take this position, however, one must either accept Adam's dubious claim that his fatal act is no longer free but inevitable, or concede that his professed willingness to sin is itself already a sin, whether or not he follows through with the deed."

Epilogue

1. William Kolbrener, *Milton's Warring Angels: A Study of Critical Engagements* (Cambridge, 1997), p. 35.

2. Thomas Luxon, *Literal Figures: Puritan Allegory and the Reformation Crisis in Representation* (Chicago, 1995), p. 41.

3. Joan Bennett, *Reviving Liberty* (Cambridge, Mass., 1989), p. 163.

The following chapters have appeared previously, in somewhat different form; thanks are due the publishers for permission to reprint. The introduction, Chapters 1, 2, 4, 14, and 15, and the epilogue appear here for the first time.

CHAPTER 3: From Earl Miner, ed., *Illustrious Evidence: Approaches to Literature of the Early Seventeenth Century* (Berkeley: University of California Press, 1975).

CHAPTER 5: From Mary Nyquist and Margaret W. Ferguson, eds., *Re-Membering Milton* (New York: Methuen, 1988).

CHAPTER 6: From David Loewenstein and James Grantham Turner, eds., *Politics, Poetics, and Hermeneutics in Milton's Prose* (Cambridge: Cambridge University Press, 1990). Reprinted with the permission of Cambridge University Press.

CHAPTER 7: From *Glyph*, 8 (1981): 1–18. Copyright © 1981 by Johns Hopkins University Press.

CHAPTER 8: From *English Literary History*, 62 (1995): 509–527. Copyright © 1995 by Johns Hopkins University Press.

CHAPTER 9: From *English Literary History*, 48, no. 3 (Fall 1981): 516–531. Copyright © 1981 by Johns Hopkins University Press.

CHAPTER 10: From Joseph Wittreich Jr., ed., *Calm of Mind: Tercentary Essays on "Paradise Regained" and "Samson Agonistes" in Honor of John S. Diekhoff* (Cleveland, Ohio: Press of Case Western Reserve University, 1971).

CHAPTER 11: From *Milton Studies*, vol. 17, Richard S. Ide and Joseph Wittreich Jr., eds., *Composite Orders: The Genres of Milton's Last Poems* (Pittsburgh: University of Pittsburgh Press, 1983). Reprinted by permission of the publisher.

INDEX

This book was set in Monotype Dante, designed
in 1954 by Giovanni Mardersteig, who was
influenced by fifteenth-century Italian types.
This particular typeface was chosen for its
Renaissance clarity and elegance.

Composition by Technologies 'N Typography,
Merrimac, Massachusetts. Printing and binding
by Maple-Vail Manufacturing Group
York, Pennsylvania.
Book design by Jill Breitbarth.